Geertje Tutschka

Law Firm Development

Geertje Tutschka

Law Firm Development

Establishing, Management, Leadership and Marketing

DE GRUYTER

Dr. Geertje Tutschka, MCC
Lawyer and Legal Coach with a Law Firm in Germany and Austria, Consultant and Trainer at CLP – Consulting for Legal Professionals (Munich/Salzburg)

Note:
All information in this work has been prepared to the best of our knowledge and belief, using all due care. Nevertheless, neither the publisher nor the author can accept liability for any errors.

ISBN 978-3-11-105782-8
e-ISBN (PDF) 978-3-11-105816-0
e-ISBN (EPUB) 978-3-11-105818-4

Library of Congress Control Number: 2023945891

Bibliographic information published by the Deutsche Nationalbibliothek
The Deutsche Nationalbibliothek lists this publication in the Deutsche Nationalbibliografie; detailed bibliographic data are available on the Internet at http://dnb.dnb.de.

Cover image: FatCamera/E+/Getty Images
Typesetting: jürgen ullrich typosatz, Nördlingen
Printing and binding: CPI books GmbH, Leck

www.degruyter.com

My husband,
because I love lawyers.

Preface

When my book "Law firm – establishing and management" (De Gruyter 2018) was welcomed and celebrated by the legal community, the publishing team at De Gruyter, and the many supporters and companions at German Lawyers Day 2018 in Mannheim on the 6th of July 2018 with a great champagne reception to celebrate the book launch, it was not the first book that tried to present this complex topic in a structured way. But it was the first book to achieve it in this comprehensive, holistic form with great practical relevance for Germany and Austria, without getting lost in theoretical discussions and claiming to be a textbook.

The legal profession as a bunch of strong individualists has managed to preserve a lot of individual freedom as a free profession in Germany in the last hundred years, the same goes for Austria – which is also reflected in their business, the law firms. Thus, there is no blueprint for a successful law firm; However, there are some important entrepreneurial aspects that every lawyer who wants to make their law firm profitable and their working life meaningful should know. Additionally, there are aspects that business consultants who are not lawyers may lack – because it is often difficult to convey to people from outside the industry that the legal sector and its business simply work differently.

The success story of the book had already begun at the German Lawyers Day 2018 with the meeting of industry experts who have had their say in the book, such as Markus Hartung, of Bucerius Law School at the time, who wrote the foreword, Sebastian von Glahn (TalentRocket), Johanna Busmann (BusmannTraining), Pia Löffler (Law Firm Marketing), Jochen Brandhoff (Legal Revolution), Martin Wohlrabe (Consilium), Katharina Miller (EWLA and European Commission), Dr. Arndt Eversberg (Roland Versicherung), and many more, to whom a heartfelt thank you is still due today.

The Beck publishing house interview series and entire webinar series at FFI publishing house as well as the Lawyers' Academy on the topic followed.

For young lawyers, two supplementary e-books have been prepared for MKG publishing house in cooperation with the Young Attorneys Forum of the German Bar Association on the topics of "Kanzleigründung – leicht gemacht" ("Founding a law firm – made easy") and "Die Kanzlei als erfolgreiches Unternehmen" ("The law firm as a successful company") with checklists and overviews. Interviews and reviews in all the major industry journals in Germany and Austria followed – but the most fun was undoubtedly the one with Dr. Dominik Herzog. The five-part series of articles in Haufe.Recht finally took up the essential content in condensed form in the fall of 2019.

At the law firm survey of the FFI publishing house in 2019, the Advotec action of Advoware at the German Lawyers' Day in Leipzig in 2019, the Legal Revolution in

https://doi.org/10.1515/9783111058160-202

Frankfurt in 2019 and in my lecture together with Prof. Dr. Kilian of the Soldan Foundation at the virtual German Lawyers' Day in 2020 as well as in 2021, with the DAV (German lawyers association) Austria on the topic of "Die Anwaltschaft in besonderer Verantwortung" ("The legal profession in special responsibility") and at least 2023 at the German Lawyers Day in Wiesbaden "ESG for Law Firms and Legal Careers" – there is hardly an event in the industry in recent years at which the book was not, is not and will not be present.

I am particularly proud that my work as an External Examiner at Middlesex University London, UK and KMU Academy Linz, Austria as well as this book, teaching material for the Master of Laws (LL.M.) degree program at Hagen Law School, Germany will shape future generations of the legal profession.When the book appeared in 2018, things like lockdown extensive digitalization efforts in the legal industry, short-term legal orders and succumbing to jurisdiction were not foreseeable – therefore it is all the more astonishing how relevant and pressing many chapters from 2018 were for many law firms in Germany and Austria in 2020/2021.
During this time, I was continuously available with CLP as a state-approved and funded consulting company for the legal industry: Above all, the Friday free crisis phone, the Clubhouse Talks as well as the Corona Special Webinar series from "Restructuring" to "Crisis Communication" to "Master Mind Law Firm" and the numerous interviews for podcasts, panels and magazines supported many colleagues in their fight for survival.

But I also continued to develop CLP:

At the world's largest hackathon, "We vs. Virus", organized by the Federal Government of Germany in the spring of 2020, the team of CLP supported the development of legal tech products in the fight against the virus as a mentor.

Today, we do not "only" work in an accessible way, but also with an office service that works on the integration of people with disabilities in the workplace. We our communication and dispatches are largely paperless and climate-neutral, since 2019 we have been using climate-neutral advertising materials, banning plastic containers of all kinds as well as food of animal origin in the offices, have also invested in our virtual learning platform for the CLP Academy for climate reasons and largely use certified organic hotels for our events and seminars. We actively support Lawyers4Future in terms of content, strategy and leadership, as well as the diversity initiatives PANDA Lab Law, Breaking Through, Women in Law Vienna, Legal Geek London, UN Women, ALICE, ADAN, NMKJ and, as mentors, AG women lawyers and the German Women Lawyers Association.

The second edition of the book has been supplemented not only with updates on the legal market and legal tech but also with the most important topics for the legal profession since the pandemic year: strategic positioning, leadership and future scenarios – the topics that have been driving and occupying our clients ever since.

Law firm development, therefore, remains an exciting topic with and after Covid-19: diversity and justice, climate and sustainability, social impact and historical responsibility are currently being redefined; along with our professional image.

This English version offers a holistic overview of the development of the legal market, the aspects of modern strategic law firm development and its international challenges, as well as specific insights into Germany and Austria.

The decision to translate this book into English for the international market, after many individual articles, was motivated on the one hand by the desire to open this conservative and nationalistic industry up to globalization, and on the other hand by the desire to familiarize law firms and lawyers worldwide with the German-speaking market, the European market and the international legal market. So today it is still going to be "bottom up" and I apologize for that.

When I presented my vision for the legal education of the future at "iur.reform" 2022 (see there or on YouTube), on the other hand, I advocated thinking of "builders of the future" an "international legal education" as a bachelor's education worldwide, who then learn "national legislative peculiarities" in a master's program, for example: in the future, therefore, it would be better to go "top down".

As the "Lawyer Whisperer" with over 15 k followers from the international legal industry today, I am a so-called micro influencer. I have not only been a lawyer in Germany and Austria for decades, I have also delivered over 2,500 coaching hours for lawyers in 10 years of my work at CLP and have been awarded Master Certified Coach (MCC) of the largest professional association for coaches worldwide, the International Coaching Federation (ICF), as well as Director of Training for the Legal Coaching Training Program of the CLP Academy, internationally accredited by the ICF, awarded the international Women of Law Award (UK).

Born and raised in the East German part of Germany, my motivation to study law was to understand the Unification Treaty of both German states in legal terms. In East Germany I was not allowed to study anything because of my activities – since then "asking the right questions" has become my trademark. My personal life experience of having lived in Detroit for several years in the midst of the automotive crisis has opened me up to the topics of globalization and cosmopolitanism, as has my intercultural education and international coaching training.

With my important contribution to change management in the joint work "Digitalization and Civil Procedure", published in 2023 in Germany, I was able to point out the necessary "counterpoint" that must be set against all digitalization, technologization and economic efficiency: for the people in this profession as the master builders of the future. At this point, I would like to thank my publisher for having the courage to accompany me in this vision. Thanks also to my eldest daughter Blanca Laurin Tutschka, who, as a cosmopolitan, has been instrumental in the translation into English and who will be holding her Master of International Business Administration the moment this book is published.

The legal market is just being conquered by AI, ESG, Legal Tech and digital natives …

And we, and you, are in the middle of it, with choices and creative opportunities. Not just for our vocation and profession, but for all of us together.

My vision is a legal industry whose DNA is justice and humanity. Timeless, reflective and forward-looking. Not only a reflection of society but also its role model. We can do law right – and really well.

What a chance!

Munich/Salzburg 2023 Dr. Geertje Tutschka, MCC

CLP – Because we love lawyers.
Consulting for Legal Professionals
www.consultingforlegals.com
www.Geertje-Tutschka.com

Overview

Table of Contents

Introduction

You are a lawyer, an owner of a law firm or a newcomer to the profession; you are an experienced colleague on the way to starting your own law firm – in any case, you are at the beginning; at the beginning of a big project: the successful establishment of your law firm, its management or development.

This book has the almost unrealistic claim to cover all law firm constellations: the single lawyer as well as the specialized boutique law firm, the medium-sized law firm as well as the large law firm. This undertaking may be unrealistic because law firms are as individual as the lawyers who run them and the business field in which they operate. As a result, not every chapter may be equally necessary or exciting for every reader. But there is more common ground among all the differences than is generally assumed.

It's like raising children: whether babies, toddlers or teenagers, some things never change and that includes their relationship with us parents. I can say this as a mother of three young adults and as a German lawyer who has been working for over twenty years in Germany, the USA and Austria in both her own and other law firms. For almost ten years now, I have been advising colleagues internationally on the subject of law firm development at CLP – Consulting for Legal Professionals, a consultancy specializing in the legal industry.

The fact is that bringing children and law firms into the world and accompanying them as they grow up undoubtedly requires nerves, commitment and perseverance. But the most important thing is to give them "roots and wings" and not just to get them through somehow.

Strategic law firm development should therefore take place consciously and proactively, purposefully and professionally. It should neither be growth and profit maximization at any price nor should it be reduced to a mere reaction to changes or even to "putting out fires in emergency mode".

Where and what do I want my firm to stand for in three, five or ten years?
Therefore, valuable questions are:
How much can I realize myself in the process?
Can I live and communicate the values that are important to me?
What does my firm do to make the world a better place?
Are the employees of my firm more than the sum of their competencies?
More valuable than the questions are the answers.

https://doi.org/10.1515/9783111058160-205

Why is this book needed?

It is not the first book dedicated to this topic. However, since its 1st edition in 2018, it is the first and still the only book that addresses the entire complexity of the topic of law firm development. In the meantime, numerous guidebooks and specialist books on founding or on management and even on marketing specifically for law firms have been released. There are also specialist books either from the perspective of managing partners of well-known law firms or specifically for young lawyers and individual lawyers. The special aim of this book is to look at these individual topics as a whole and from different perspectives.

Some will ask themselves perhaps, which raison d'être such an extensive hardcover book has in a time of digitization. Well, it is quite simple:

This book is a declaration of intent.

We have therefore taken special care with the cover design and the title so that it is not only decorative but also unambiguous. Whoever reads this book is up to something. There should be no doubt about that in their environment. I, therefore, recommend that you not only get a book for your desk (within sight of your boss, coworkers and assistance), but also one for your sofa corner (for friends and family) and one for your bedside table (for yourself and your significant other). With a hardcover book on this topic, you're making a clear statement: now you're getting serious. And it will be a weighty reminder to you every day.

Formalities:

For reasons of readability, I have used only one form – mostly the masculine – of the word. This is not to discredit the many strong female lawyers and successful female attorneys or to give the reader the impression that they do not have something to contribute to the subject – especially a top subject in the German speaking markets (because of the grammar specialties) and of course a subject of the legal industry. Quite the contrary. Please read the form used as you wish. I personally consider the choice of form only a "packaging question" that adds nothing in terms of content. I therefore also like to refrain from calling myself a female lawyer, since my qualification is not derived from my gender. For me personally, lawyer is perfectly sufficient as a professional title. Even if the gender discussion plays a role especially in languages like German.

When I have used the term paralegal in this book, I want it to be understood in a rather non-technical way: as a general, unspecified term for all employees who support the lawyer: from trainees to assistants, secretaries and typists to specially trained and qualified specialists.

As a lawyer admitted to the bar in Germany and Austria and, since 2020, President of the German Bar Association, Foreign Bar Association Austria, it was a particular concern of mine to write not only for the German legal market, but for the entire German-speaking market. If and to the extent that Austrian peculiarities need to be taken into account, they will be explicitly mentioned. As a law firm consultant, I would like to show that looking beyond borders can be useful.

A heartfelt thank you goes out to the numerous colleagues from small and large law firms, but also from my network of specialized service providers for the legal industry, who have not only enriched this book with their special expertise in marketing, acquisition, controlling, recruiting and much more, but have made it what it should be: a solid basic book on the subject of "strategic law firm development". In doing so, nothing is further from my mind than providing generally applicable construction manuals for law firms. Rather, I want to provide the reader who seriously wants to deal with this topic with an overview, structure and pragmatism in the complexity of the whole. Therefore, I refer in many places to special and supplementary literature. So, it is certainly worthwhile to have a look at the bibliography. Of course, special thanks also go to the dedicated team at De Gruyter, which, as always, has successfully accompanied this book project with professionalism and aplomb. "It takes a whole village to raise a child" – this also applies to the project of law firm development.

Is it even worthwhile to start a law firm today?

A very clear YES from me.
But you should enjoy change and new beginnings, have a sense of humour and be passionate. And be a good lawyer.

I love being a lawyer and an entrepreneur.
I love to accompany colleagues on their way.

A. The legal consulting market

Firm strategy meetings are usually driven by the idea of responding to negative developments in the short term:

A law firm has **grown** too fast and is suddenly confronted with the challenge that these small teams neither cooperate with each other in a resource-saving way nor want to go in the same direction.

Another law firm has obviously attracted the **"wrong" clients**, but a lot of them. The result: infrastructure and the necessary expertise are not (yet) available, existing know-how and resources remain unused.

The **third firm** sees itself as modern and **diversified.** The support program for young female lawyers is now paying off after a few years and the firm is proud of its first balanced gender ratio. But now precisely these future female partners are taking family leave, and even worse: they are not returning. With the departure of these future high potentials, the program is now not only judged to be a bad investment but there is actually a lack of the young talent that has been built up for the upcoming generational change at the management level. And time is running out.

These case studies will guide us through the book and will be discussed in detail in the respective chapters.

Tip:
Take the opportunity to apply what you have read in practice:
For each example, sketch out the problem and initial approaches to solving it in a few key words!

What do these case studies tell us?

On the one hand: the legal profession is as colourful as life itself. No two law firms are alike. No two lawyers are alike.

On the other hand, all these different law firms have one thing in common. They lack a concrete value-driven vision for the current situation and a strategy to implement it. Lawyers react to market movements, digitalization, and industry change. That certainly has to be the case. That's exactly how lawyers have learned to do it. And that's exactly how it works in the vast majority of cases: A problem occurs, then it's off to the lawyer.

But it is more important to act than to react. Knowing your market and your industry so well that you can change course early on and in a targeted manner, or even open up a new market and influence industry changes. To do so, however, you have to be willing to question yourself, your beliefs and your view of the world. And that is exactly what many lawyers find difficult. Because they are the ones who are paid to enforce their view of things.

https://doi.org/10.1515/9783111058160-001

! Developing the firm not as a lawyer but with the view of the business owner – that's what matters. In which market do we operate – and with which product? These are the central questions.

But let's start with the beginning:

Do you know your industry? What are the three most important factors affecting your industry at the moment, also known as "game changers"?

I. Numbers, data, facts

Why should you read this chapter?
You will learn WHO the “players” in the legal market are.

Overview
- Competitive pressure
- Gender- and generation shift
- Digitalization
- Conclusion

1. Provider
- Lawyers
  Lawyers (domestic and foreign) Notaries
  Mediators
  Students and trainees (D) / trainees (Ö)
  University teachers, professors, judges, in-house lawyers, administrative lawyers
- Legal competitors
- Non-lawyers
  Patent attorneys
  Chartered accountants
  Tax consultants
  Personnel consultants
  Management consultants
  Insolvency administrators, consumer protection, social services
  Other consultants
  Banks and insurances Legal portals
  “Legal corner” in media
- Legal Tech

2. Demand
- Consumer
- Commercial enterprises and institutions

167,000 lawyers are admitted to practice in Germany[1], working in 51,900 law firms. The number of lawyers admitted to the bar has thus tripled since 1990; since 2020, it has risen by 50 %. Whereas in 1950 there were approximately five thousand inhabi-

1 Current number: 167,092 according to BRAK statistics as of Jan. 1, 2021.

tants for every lawyer, today there are only about five hundred[2]. This puts German lawyers at the bottom of the European league table, also in terms of their average achievable income. Nevertheless, the industry generated a global turnover of 119.6 billion U. S. dollars in 2019, 7.4 billion U. S. dollars of which were generated in Germany alone.

In Austria, where there are 6,875 lawyers, the situation is different – especially if one uses the otherwise usual Germany comparison factor of "ten". On the one hand, this may be due to the much higher investment costs (training takes 3 years longer, which means that admission and practice costs are much higher); on the other hand, it may also be due to structural differences for in-house lawyers or for family breaks. And last but not least, there are certainly far fewer – and different – large law firms than in Germany[3].

Competitive pressure

Competition is fierce: many lawyers work eighty hours a week and more. Law firms are facing enormous costs or even on the brink of economic collapse.

These are all good arguments for the strategy of cooperation in our first case study with "growing pains".

There are two additional factors: On the one hand, globalization[4] now makes it easy to hire a German lawyer in Shanghai. On the other hand, the increasing equality of men and women does not stop at the legal sector. More qualified female lawyers for the same market and rising salaries for the previously poorly paid female lawyers are the result[5].

Gender- and Generation shift

This upheaval in the legal market is far from complete[6]. Strictly speaking, the industry is proving to be arch-conservative again, as the gender pay gap in the Ger-

2 see above

3 ÖRAK statistics as of 31.12.2021: half of them are registered with the RAK Vienna; otherwise, the majority are individual law firms.

4 In fact, it already started with the discontinuation of singular approval as well as the increasingly safe technical possibilities.

5 However, it should be noted that the 2-digit increase in the number of female colleagues has stagnated at 35 % in Germany since the turn of the millennium, according to BRAK statistics from 1.1.2021.

6 Prof. Dr. Harald Koch, "Anwältinnen im internationalen Vergleich", Anwaltsblatt 05/2017.

man legal industry is the largest in comparison to other industries[7], even though the first woman was admitted to the bar in Germany[8] almost a hundred years ago, namely in 1922[9]. And the share of female lawyers in decision-making positions and partnerships also brings up the rear compared to other industries[10], although today more women than ever are admitted to the bar[11].

A 2013 study by Prognos AG commissioned by the German Bar Association predicted "The future of the legal profession is female," which led many headline readers to infer this solely from the trend of the rapidly growing number of female law students. In fact, there will be more female lawyers than male lawyers in Germany in ten years' time if this trend continues.

But the study's predictions for the future were actually more differentiated: the futurologists predicted that the legal consulting market would increasingly demand so-called "typically female" qualities, irrespective of the gender proportions in the legal profession. Qualities such as diplomacy, negotiating skills, communication skills, empathy and a sense of social responsibility would take precedence over the formerly "typically male" success factors such as assertiveness, dominance, leadership and strength[12] and would be clearly preferred by clients in the future. This is similar to the overall socio-political trend toward "soft power"[13] and thus away from the previously dominant trend of "hard power" through military and economic strength. Soft power is based on cultural attraction and political role modeling[14]. These are all good arguments for the original strategy in our 3rd case study "gender and generational shift". And at the same time, it becomes clear once again that the failure of this strategy is precisely not because there are no good women lawyers in the industry, but because the industry cannot retain them.

---

7 Dr. Tutschka in "Female Leadership in der Legal Branche", p. 138 in djbZ 03/2017.

8 By the way, the first female lawyer in Austria was Marianne Beth, who was admitted to the bar in Vienna in 1929.

9 Maria Otto – the Maria – Otto – Prize of the German Lawyers Association is named after her and has been awarded since 2010.

10 Currently, only about 10–20 % of partners are female: e.g., at Clifford Chance the number was only 16 % in 2019, according to Dr. Kerstin Kopp, Business Insider, Dec. 23, 2020. Dr. Tutschka in "Female Leadership in der Legal Branche," p. 138 in djbZ 03/2017.

11 According to BRAK statistics of 1.1.2020: over 35 % in Germany; According to ÖRAK statistics of 31.12.2021: over 23 % in Austria.

12 Dr. Tutschka, "Jurist oder Juristin – (k)ein Unterschied", LTOfrom 16.12.2015.

13 Also relates to leadership, negotiation or communication.

14 US political researcher Joseph S. Nye describes this as "soft power" in his book "The Means to success in world politics" (2004).

Digitalization

And as if the ever-increasing competitive pressure and the fundamental transformation of the professional image from the grey-haired senior partner in the dark blue double-breasted suit with gold buttons and classic status symbols to the service-oriented client understanding at eye level were not enough, technical progress is now also making its way into the legal sector. For a long time, the legal industry was able to successfully fend off the inconvenient intruder with law and order, tradition and ignorance[15]. This can be seen in the successful prevention of the introduction of the "special electronic lawyer's mailbox" (beA), which could not be launched in Germany on January 1st 2016, nor on January 1st 2017, nor on January 1st 2018. But now digitalization has its foot in the door and can no longer be stopped. It is overtaking the legal industry with incredible force and speed, leaving no stone unturned.

This also shows that, despite all the prophecies of doom, the market for legal advice in Germany is still a very attractive one:

While the steadily increasing number of lawyers admitted to the bar is only a limited indication of the attractiveness of this market, because weak exam results that prevent employment in the judiciary, in companies or in public administration lead to a "flight to the legal profession"[16], the steady influx that the German legal advice market has been experiencing for some years due to renowned large English and American law firms is more informative.

The great interest that banks and insurers are developing in actively participating in the legal advice market also speaks for the attractiveness of this market.

The same applies to the emergence of new services for legal advice, such as the service "litigation financing" or "legal translation", or personnel intermediaries specializing in the legal sector, copywriters, PR specialists and communications professionals for sensitive public relations work, such as in cases that generate a high socio-political profile[17].

The automation of standard legal cases as a new legal product such as "geblitzt.de" or "Flight Right" or marketplaces for legal services such as "Anwalt.de" or "Legal Base" as well as Internet portals for legal information are also rapidly created. "Legal Tech" is the topic of the hour: Future congresses and legal tech trade fairs, fireside chats, specialist conferences and panel discussions, as well as the media, are al-

15 Some also claim that arrogance was involved.

16 However, this only applies to Germany; in Austria it is the other way round, since the separation of the lawyer training after the study with the trainee time of 5 years concludes with the lawyer examination and these lawyer candidates usually enjoyed a much more intensive training than other lawyers – and therefore are seen also gladly in other ranges we enterprises.

17 Such as consilium from Berlin or Susanne Kleiner from Munich.

most exclusively devoted to this topic, which is as much a source of anxiety as it is of business.

Technology companies and service providers are discovering the legal industry: whether hardware (such as the "lawyer's copier") or software (such as client programs), cloud and transfer solutions for industry-specific special data security, dictation programs, appointment calendars. It almost seems as if there is nothing left that does not exist. The keywords e-justice[18], beA[19], and "electronic file"[20] are among the most frequently used terms in the industry in recent years. In principle, this is not threatening. In fact, it simplifies many things and saves costs and time. However, the challenge here is that the structures and processes in the legal industry, which are poorly defined, must be changed as a result, because simply transferring paper processes from the "offline world" to online in an unimaginative and identical manner does not come close to exploiting the potential of digitization.

"A major challenge is to reflect the striving for ever greater efficiency in the processing of mandates on the production side, among other things through the use of software and experts who are not fully qualified lawyers; in parallel, it is becoming increasingly difficult and important to work out one's own differentiation with the defined target group in an ever tougher and more heterogeneous competitive environment.

Our full-service approach and intensive cultivation of client relationships ensures that we have a basic workload even in difficult economic times and helps us to react more quickly to special situations.

The biggest change in business consulting firms is the complete restructuring of the production chain: where previously only fully qualified lawyers provided advice, increasingly business lawyers, business economists and IT experts are also involved in various roles as well as software directly for the client."

Jörg Overbeck, Lawyer, COO Oppenhoff and Partner, Cologne

Few people are aware of this. In fact, even the conservative process is set next to the new process without further consideration. Duplications and systemic gaps are the fatal consequence, costs exploding and unimagined sources of danger increase the liability risk.

---

18 The term is used as a generic term for the use of IT in the judiciary and administration as part of the so-called e-government.

19 beA: Special electronic mailbox for lawyers (Germany-wide standardized communication system between law firms, courts and authorities, which meets the special security requirements of the industry and will hopefully no longer require special mention in the next edition); in Austria, electronic legal transactions (ERV) have already been common practice for decades, which means that the Austrian judiciary is probably now the world leader.

20 Industry experts predict that law firms will be "the last paper dinosaurs" in a world of paperless offices. Austria has already introduced electronic records for courts since 2020.

In our case study with the “wrong clients”, this is exactly what seems to have happened, and in the collapsing day-to-day business there is no time to deal with the inefficient structures. Instead, it means even more work, even more overtime, even less profit; more mistakes, more tantrums, more dissatisfied clients and resigned employees – a vicious circle.

Regardless of the risks and stumbling blocks, however, digitalization primarily offers opportunities and chances – not only for more efficient and faster work, but above all for innovation, i.e., new business areas and products. The industry must seize this opportunity. Here it is important not to miss the boat with its own clientele and the next generation of lawyers. But it is also important to be able to face the looming crises in the economy, democracy and climate. The fact that the legal sector had to fight for the designation “systemically important” in the pandemic crisis of 2020 shows how out of touch the “organ of the administration of justice” already is.

Conclusion

The legal industry is therefore currently being confronted with existential challenges and is being redefined in many areas:

1. Competitive pressure vs. globalization
2. Gender- and generation shift vs. change in job profile
3. Digitalization vs. economic and climate crisis

All factors intertwine and influence each other:

Competitive pressure has also increased thanks to the Internet and modern communication methods (digitization), which result in clients no longer only going to their local lawyer (globalization). Digitization, in turn, is raising the bar for the service aspect of legal services that clients expect. They no longer have to pay a high price for knowledge from their lawyer if it can be accessed on the Internet virtually around the clock and free of charge. This, in turn, is changing the traditional image of the lawyer, who must now also be available around the clock, but at the same time, thanks to the digitalization, can work more efficiently and from anywhere. His own demands for a fulfilling work life and a good work-life balance are increasing.

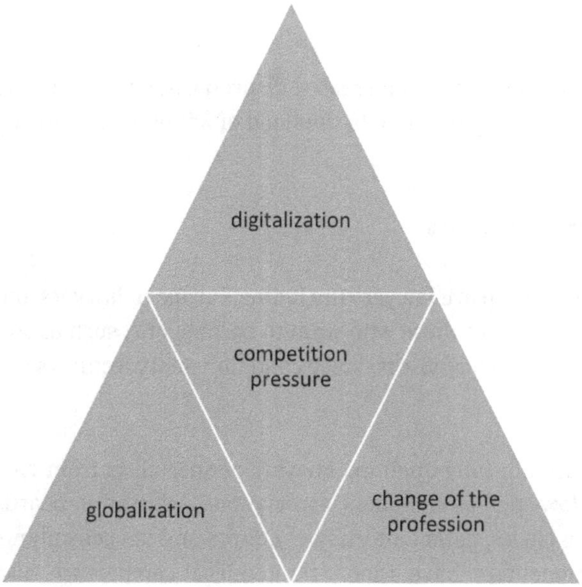

Challenges of the legal industry, © Dr. Geertje Tutschka

The complexity of the challenges from the outside is changing the industry from within. And this change makes it clear that the legal sector is also subject to the so-called "laws of the market", and more so than it realizes. The concept of "market laws" originates from the conservative economic theory of the 19th century and is not undisputed today, since the market is described in purely mathematical/physical terms and seems to be subject exclusively to pure constraints. State regulation or the assumption of responsibility is therefore not necessary. The human image of the so-called "homo economicus" is assumed, an unsympathetic and antisocial egomaniac[21]. Every market is determined by supply and demand and should regulate itself through the price (so-called market law).

A closer look at the providers and demanders in the legal market is therefore necessary.

Who is providing legal services today and who is asking for legal services?

21 Maja Göpel, "Unsere Welt neu denken", p. 62.

1. Provider

The fact is that the number of providers has increased disproportionately over the past ten years. However, this is only partly due to the flood of admissions in the legal profession.

There are three main groups to distinguish:

- Lawyers
  The numerically strongest group are lawyers (including European lawyers and mediators) and notaries as well as those who want to become one, such as students, trainees, assessors, or legal advisors, judges and university lecturers.

- Legal co-applicants
  In addition, those who are not fully qualified lawyers or specialists from narrowly defined areas of law such as chambers, associations, arbitration boards or, under certain circumstances, patent attorneys, auditors and tax consultants who, as professional competitors, have a more limited legal competence, also come into consideration.

- Non-lawyers
  In addition to legal tech, there is also an increasing number of non-professionals and providers without sufficient legal training (legal laypersons) from other sectors who are entering this market.

Lawyers: attorneys

Whether competition exists between lawyers depends on the areas in which they work and how they work. The specialist in road traffic accidents is not in competition with the colleague concentrating on public procurement law. The family law specialist is not in competition with the corporate law specialist. Much rather they can both complement each other in individual cases.

It is important for lawyers to look beyond the boundaries of their own practice area and to maintain contact with colleagues who work in other areas. In this way, new mandates can be won on the basis of recommendations from colleagues from areas in which they are not active.

Until a few years ago, it was true to say that the majority of small to medium-sized law firms operate locally, at best regionally, and that there is no competition between, for example, a law firm specializing in construction law in Munich and one in Berlin. These times are (unfortunately or thankfully) over. The abolition of the singular license pushed open a door that the legal market opened wide thanks to the simultaneously developing technologies and the Internet. Of course, today it does not matter at all where the lawyer has his office. It is true that some clients are still looking for personal contact and want to have a meeting in the office. However, the vast majority are eager, not just since the Covid_19 lock downs, to hold the necessary meetings with their lawyer during the day or after work from the comfort of their own home or office and to send the documents as a scan via email. Some can even get transparent access to your e-file this way. Thanks to smartphones, the lawyer can now be reached anywhere, anytime, and also has the "file" available everywhere – a curse and a blessing at the same time. Of course, the idea of working on files while lying on a sun lounger under palm trees instead of in a dreary high-rise office in rainy Essen is captivating – and at the same time, it's a nightmare if you're spending your long-awaited annual vacation week on that sun lounger. Nevertheless, many law firms already offer at least individual products and areas of law explicitly online, although here, too, it cannot be said conclusively that individual areas of law are better suited for this than others (such as "divorce online", for example, where experience has shown that it is always a matter of trusting, sensitive and process-accompanying support for the client, particularly in the case of divorce). Today, it can be said that there has been a shift from WHERE to HOW: online and digital are, above all, convenient and customer oriented. But holistic aspects, "full service" and "one stop" mentality play a role as well as the accompanying service by (legal) coaches, psychologists, project managers or agencies.

The "weight class" of a law firm does not per se play a role for what other law firms it competes with. The size of a law firm or the name recognition of a law firm are not synonymous with the quality of the legal service or the competence of the law firm in each individual case. It is true that clients generally compare law firms of the same size. However, an expert who has been in the media for years for a certain topic, has published, operates the social media accordingly and is present can compete with a large law firm even in front of a large client.

Lawyers from abroad can also be competitors. First and foremost, of course, the German lawyers who are located abroad. Especially in the out-of-court area, in consulting, but also in research, legal opinion and brief preparation, they are popular as cooperation partners for peak times[22]. However, European lawyers, i.e. lawyers who come from other European countries and have been admitted to practice in Germany, can also take over the tasks of domestic lawyers in many areas. Themati-

---

22 In the U.S., for example, fast-growing "giga-law firms" are recruiting thousands of lawyers worldwide as associates who work from home providing legal services in closely structured processes. This seems to be particularly attractive for female lawyers on family leave or with children in need of care. On the other hand, these "legal giants" are anything but social and career-enhancing as employers or cooperation partners.

cally, the legal advisors affiliated to the bar associations, who could be appointed according to former law, also belong to this group. However, this may also include "lawyers" from non-EU countries who cannot be admitted to the bar in Germany without further ado, but who nevertheless always find quite a decent client base of "compatriots".

Lawyers: notaries

The so-called "notaries-only" can also be competitors of lawyers. The competition of these notaries is limited to the extra-judicial area. The most important legal areas of competition with notaries are company law, real estate law, family law and inheritance law. In most cases, however, it is more likely to be a matter of a "joint" mandate, in which the lawyer selects the notary to be consulted for a notarization and monitors his work. Especially in the case of larger transactions in the fields of real estate law and corporate law, the draft contracts are prepared by the attorneys of the parties. The notarizing notary is usually limited to the notarization function.

Lawyers: mediators

The situation is similar for mediators who, as lawyers, have also completed special mediation training[23].

Mediators are "dispute mediators", i.e. they use special professional communication techniques to mediate the different points of view and guide the parties to find a joint solution. The aim is to avoid a court case and to settle the matter more sustainably and comprehensively on the basis of the parties' individual solution. Due to the impartiality, a mediator in these cases cannot act as a lawyer at the same time, before or after, but would then have to consult a colleague

Lawyers: students and trainees

Especially in the last decades, more and more students and trainees are looking for a connection to the practice at a very early stage, be it because they want to test themselves, finance their studies or prepare for a future job. Although these are neither professionally nor in their possibilities actually fully equal to a lawyer, they represent a not insignificant price competition, especially in metropolitan areas

23 Often non-lawyers are also mediators and try their hand as mediators in legal cases. This is different with legal coaches, who are always lawyers.

with many and large law faculties. Berlin lawyers, for example, never tire of complaining about such dumping prices.

But are they really true competitors? More likely future colleagues. For those lawyers who do not succeed in clearly distinguishing themselves from the trainees with their service portfolio should work on their law firm strategy. The major BRAO reform will tighten up the conflict of interest for trainees and academic staff in §§ 43ff BRAO from 2022.

Lawyers: university teachers, professors, judges, corporate lawyers

The same is likely to be true for judges and university professors as competitors of lawyers in the legal services market. In fact, the share of competition that lawyers face from these professional groups is relatively small. However the competition still exists. Aside from the opportunity to act as a criminal defence attorney, the domain of university faculty in the legal services field appears to be the preparation of expert opinions on complicated legal issues. Before embarking on major transactions or changing market strategies, the legal boundaries of which are not yet clear, it is not uncommon for companies to obtain expert opinions from renowned law teachers. These opinions are important for the company's project in two ways. On the one hand, companies appreciate the professional expertise, but on the other hand, they also appreciate the overwhelming effect such an expert opinion can have, at least occasionally, due to the particular fame of the expert.

Larger law firms in particular have developed a preference for including prominent university professors in the firm. The advantage for these law firms is not only the gain in professional competence, but also the increase in reputation and access to networks that these university lecturers can offer them.

Lawyers who work in companies or administration also offer legal advice occasionally or even regularly. However, this is not really likely to compete on the legal market. Rather, only activities as an expert, consultant or lecturer come into consideration, which in any case do not affect the legal advice market. The same applies to judges.

The Act on the Reorganization of the Law of Syndic Attorneys and on the Amendment of the Fiscal Court Code (Syndic Act) of December 21, 2015 in Germany has certainly brought more clarity in this regard. An evaluation of the Federal Government from 2020 therefore comes to the conclusion that the overall concept of a statutory regulation of the profession of in-house counsel has proven its worth[24].

24 BMJV from 21.10.2020.

Legal co-applicants

Legal services are also provided by chambers of commerce, industry associations, employers' associations and trade unions in varying degrees of intensity. The nature of the legal services ranges from information on legislative proposals that may be of interest to chamber members or companies belonging to the sector to legal representation before the labor courts by employers' associations and, to a greater extent, by a specially established legal protection company of the trade unions. The legal services provided by these associations appear to be free of charge from the perspective of the association members. In fact, however, the price for these services, insofar as it is not subsidized from other income of the associations, is hidden in the dues. No matter how professionally qualified an employee of these associations may be, there is one thing they are not: they are not independent. Associations pursue their own interests. That is legitimate. However, these do not have to be congruent with the interests of the association member. A client who is represented by an association will always have to ask himself whether the advice of his representative is solely in his, the client's, interests alone or whether, in individual cases, it may be in the association's contrary interests. Only with a lawyer the client can be sure that the lawyer is exclusively looking after the interests of the client and no other interests.

Non-lawyers: patent attorneys

The fields of activity of attorneys-at-law and patent attorneys essentially overlap in the areas of patent law, trademark law and – to a lesser extent – competition law. The training bases of the two professions are different. The professional strength of patent attorneys is usually more in the technical field; they are also almost always engineers. Although many patent attorneys have a high degree of specialization in the fields of law that concern them, they usually lack broad legal knowledge. Conversely, attorneys at law often have difficulty in acquiring the technical understanding that is indispensable for patent law. In patent law matters, therefore, only very few lawyers will succeed in seriously competing with patent attorneys. Lawyers who are interested in this special area of intellectual property protection and who usually also have the qualification of a specialist in intellectual property law should not so much fear competition from patent attorneys as seek cooperation with patent attorneys.

Non-lawyers: auditors

In addition to auditing tasks, auditors should primarily devote themselves to providing economic advice, but not legal advice to companies. This professional profile outlined by the German Auditors' Code has long since ceased to apply in practice. Far beyond providing economic advice to companies, auditors also act as legal advisors. In matters of corporate law, qualified auditors often succeed in taking a holistic view of economic, civil law and tax law aspects better than some lawyers. A large number of auditors also have legal training, and many are also admitted to the bar.

The "auditor's certificate", which actually only states that the accounts have been properly kept, is held in very high regard by the company subject to the audit. Generally, this status is also reflected in the esteem in which auditors are held. Although auditing and consulting do not actually go together, it often seems that the boundaries between the two areas are blurred. Auditors are well aware of the fact that they cannot provide legal services to companies consistently and in all the necessary areas with the required quality. This realization has resulted in a wave of mergers with law firms triggered by the large accounting firms in recent years. The synergy effects hoped for in connection with these mergers have, as far as the acceptance of the auditors is concerned, probably not been entirely to their satisfaction. Auditors occasionally complain that, although they obtain mandates for lawyers through recommendations, lawyers, on the other hand, only contribute to a small extent to the volume of mandates of the auditors. For lawyers interested in corporate law, cooperation with auditors or working in an auditing firm can be highly interesting. However, young lawyers should be aware of the fact that an auditing company always remains a company of auditors. Lawyers are usually regarded as outsiders.

Non-lawyers: tax consultants

In the field of tax law advice to companies and private individuals, tax advisors have almost completely replaced lawyers, with the exception of lawyers specializing in tax law. At first glance, this fact is all the more surprising, as many tax advisors have been trained in business administration, but not in law, and tax law is, in principle, nothing more than a part of special administrative law. The loss of this market segment is attributable to the legal profession itself. Some lawyers, in a completely misplaced arrogance, have taken leave of the supposed "calculator work" in tax law at an early stage. Tax law does not even belong to the basic subjects of legal education, although it is of the highest interest and importance for companies in a state that has one of the most complex and complicated tax systems in the world. Due to the lack of appropriate expertise, a large part of the legal profession is not even able to compete with tax advisors in the field of tax law.

It is not uncommon that partnership agreements, employment contracts and marriage contracts are drawn up by tax advisors. It is also not uncommon for such contracts to take sufficient account of tax issues, but due to a lack of corresponding know-how on the part of the tax advisor, they do not satisfy other issues of business law and, in particular, civil law. Not only in one's own interest, but also in the interest of the clients, it is recommended to cooperate as a law firm with a competent tax consulting firm at an early stage, since tax issues have to be considered not only in corporate law, labor law and family law, but today in almost every field of law.

Non-lawyers: personnel consultants

When HR consultants are consulted by an employee, they may also advise their client on the legal aspects of his or her new employment contract. One would think that managers with their first career successes would be used to working with a specialized lawyer on their own employment contract. In reality, however, this is often not the case. Especially renowned personnel consultants cooperate with lawyers specialized in employment law for such cases. By the way, the same also applies to personnel managers in companies, for example in the case of the very complex assignment of an employee abroad[25].

Non-lawyers: business consultants

The same applies to management consultants: Here, long-term cooperation established at an early stage between the management consultant and the corresponding specialized law firm pay off in any case. It is noteworthy that in Germany there is still a strict separation between corporate consulting and legal consulting, although overlaps are part of the daily business, especially in business consulting firms or in the area of M & A. In Austria, therefore, closer cooperation between lawyers and business consultants are quite common.

Non-lawyers: insolvency administration, social services, etc.

Pursuant to § 5 RDG[26] legal experts listed therein may be permitted to provide legal services to third parties in special areas. Subsequently, a distinction is made between legal services provided by registered persons – such as lawyers or expert companies and non-registered persons – such as lawyers or expert companies – and

25 See p. 5 "USA-Expat Quick Guide," by Tutschka, Kemper, Dittmeier.

26 Since July 1, 2008, the Legal Services Act (RDG; Gesetz über außergerichtliche Rechtsdienstleistungen) has governed the authority to provide out-of-court legal services. It thus replaced the Legal Advice Act (RBerG) that had been in force until then. Unlike the RBerG, the Legal Services Act does not regulate the provision of legal services in court; this is now governed by the respective procedural codes.

non-registered persons. The latter include, for example, employees of public authorities, insolvency administration, consumer protection or social services (§ 8 RDG).

Non-lawyers: other consultants

In particular, (insurance) consultants and debt collection companies offer legal services that would traditionally be assigned to lawyers. The better-known debt collection companies have a reputation among their customers for being cheaper and "less complicated" than lawyers. This may be true. However, no lawyer is prevented from working in this field as well. Well thought-out mandate processing standardized with the help of modern computer software should allow young law firms in particular to make competitive offers at attractive prices in this area as well – and indeed it is precisely these case scenarios that are the cause for further invention in the area of legal tech. For a law firm's success in this area, it will be crucial to convince the client that the firm can handle the collection cases smoothly and efficiently. Today, for example, the restructuring or insolvency consulting business is largely handled by business administration graduates, business administration graduates or business law graduates. In addition to these external consultants, colleagues, especially in the support of small and medium-sized companies, frequently encounter legal autodidacts who function internally as "quasi-lawyers". The entrepreneur and the employed managing director, both business economists, who, armed with the standard commentaries on the GmbH law, prepare themselves alone for a shareholders' meeting, are not so rare. In some exceptional cases, such autodidacts have actually acquired considerable knowledge. Far more frequent, however, are the cases in which autodidacts take for experience what they have been constantly doing wrong for many years. Autodidacts are usually "self-supporters". They advise themselves, but not others who might be considered as clients of a lawyer. A lawyer competes with these self-proclaimed "experts" only when it comes to providing legal services to the company that these self-taught people run.

They can also be pushed to top form every now and then among their colleagues, in a club or at a regulars' table. However, they are not real competitors. Legal advice by laypersons is prohibited by law.

Non-lawyers: banks and insurance companies

§ 5 RDG allows service providers from other sectors, who actually sell banking products or insurance policies or repair vehicles broken in an accident, to provide their customers with the associated legal advice. What they have in common is that although they cannot operate their businesses without core legal expertise, legal services for others have not been part of their core business to date. Banks and insurers act as legal advisors in many areas of law. What is unfortunate for their customers is that both groups of companies have considerable legal competence in their staff and legal departments, but these staff and legal departments are not available to the customer. The customer is dealing with sales staff who normally lack legal training. Advice on the structuring options for asset or company succession, but also assistance in preparing an application for a certificate of inheritance, is "provided" by banks[27], just as questions of building law or liability for material defects are often clarified by the architect.

Insurance companies impact the legal services market in a number of ways:

In the area of motor vehicle liability insurance and comprehensive insurance, there are recognizable tendencies on the part of insurers to squeeze lawyers out of the market completely. With elaborate campaigns, insurers advertise that in the event of a claim, policyholders leave the entire settlement to the insurer and the "subcontractors" it has engaged, such as workshops and experts who are contractually bound to the insurer. The lawyers' fees to be reimbursed by the losing side are to be saved by excluding the lawyers from representing the parties involved in a road traffic accident. From the insurers' point of view, the lawyers' fees are avoidable costs. It is suggested to the policyholder that he does not need the assistance of a lawyer because the insurance company will take care of the well-being of "its" policyholder. The fact that the insurance company is a business partner is cleverly concealed. If it is a matter of claims for insurance benefits, then the insurer is the opponent of the policyholder. This is because there is a clear conflict of interests: the policyholder wants to receive the highest possible insurance benefit, while the insurer wants to provide the lowest possible insurance benefit. A new model in this direction is the "obligatory" mediation offer to the insured: If the insured approaches the insurer with a cost protection request, he is first connected with a mediator who is to settle the case "quickly and unbureaucratically" for him. This mediator is contractually bound to the insurer with the aim of keeping the costs as low as possible and settling the case quickly. As a rule, the insured person does not receive detailed legal advice or information about what exactly mediation is and what it means for the legal claim. The insured person then only learns this from his or her lawyer to his or her complete surprise.

In the meantime, the large insurance companies have also tapped into the area of litigation financing, which is still relatively new in Germany. In order to encourage lawyers to bring clients to litigation financiers, lawyers are offered a sales commission typical of the insurance industry in the form of an additional fee, called "ProFi" or something similar. Furthermore, the model of "exclusive" lawyer pools is

27 Or by inheritance investigators.

also being expanded. These are lawyers who have qualified themselves in a certain way vis-à-vis the insurer in order to, for example, be listed as an ADAC lawyer and thus be recommended accordingly. The other side of the coin, however, is that these lawyers have contractually committed themselves to the insurer to certain cost reductions or a reduced fee.

From the perspective of lawyers, legal protection insurance offers both advantages and disadvantages. In smaller law firms and in individual practices – and thus with the numerical majority of lawyers – clients with legal protection insurance are regularly welcome. The disadvantage of the additional expense of correspondence with the legal protection insurer, which would have to be paid separately by the client, and possible debates about the amount of the subject matter and the accrual of fees is, in their view, more than offset by the high degree of certainty that a fee will be paid within an appropriate period of time. Another offer from insurers is the free legal advice service for insured persons, e.g. for associations, which is usually purchased from law firms with a low-threshold flat-rate offer by the insurers and can only actually cover the legal advice needs of the insured persons in very few cases.

Credit institutions still offer legal services primarily as a means of customer retention. Only in certain areas, such as foundations, do they openly offer their legal advice as a paid service. From the perspective of the bank customer, the legal service offered as an accessory appears to be easy to obtain, practical and, above all, inexpensive, because it is – supposedly – free of charge. Normally, the bank customer does not recognize the actual problem with this type of legal service. Because the bank is not, like the lawyer, an independent advisor and lobbyist. With legal services, which they use as a sales aid, banks also pursue their own interests in the sale of financial services.

In essence, banks offer legal services in the areas of inheritance law, foundation law, real estate law and corporate law.

In the area of inheritance law, the legal service provided by credit institutions is usually limited to providing generally understandable information brochures on the basic principles of statutory succession and the possibility of regulating succession by testamentary disposition. These information brochures often contain forms that bank customers can use to draw up the classic – but not always useful – "Berlin will". Templates for post-mortem powers of attorney can also be found there. The asset management departments of credit institutions (private banking) have increasingly opened up the foundation system and thus foundation law for themselves. The primary goal of credit institutions is to provide asset management services to foundations. This is accompanied by legal advice on the establishment of foundations. In the area of real estate law, the services provided by credit institutions go far beyond the granting of loans to finance the purchase price with the simultaneous granting of real estate liens as collateral. Almost all large credit institutions have subsidiaries that operate as sales companies, primarily in the area of private real estate. In addition to organizational services, such as arranging notary appointments, these real estate departments also advise their customers on the content of real estate purchase agreements. In addition, there is often a long-term cooperation with selected notaries. From the point of view of the customer, who has no idea that the seller of the property may also be one of the – important – customers of the same credit institution, the involvement of a lawyer seems unnecessary. Despite some approaches, the legal profession has not yet succeeded in convincing a broad public of the special advantages that the independence and, in particular, the partiality of a lawyer offers their clients. Investment banks regularly take a leading role in major corporate transactions. If they do not provide the legal advice themselves, they coordinate the activities of the lawyers called in. The "project managers" of corporate restructurings are often no longer the lawyers, but the investment banks.

The development is far from complete. However, it is also true that a specialized law firm with appropriate marketing can reach clients, but also insurers and credit institutions, and is gladly called in if fair and collegial cooperation is the basis.

Non-lawyers: legal portals

The interested party can obtain useful information on the Internet on various legal portals quite quickly and, above all, inexpensively or at a very low all-inclusive price. Only rarely, however, will it be possible to compile detailed knowledge with the help of the Internet or even to solve a legal problem completely. Objectively, the information that can be obtained via the Internet does not therefore make the use of a lawyer superfluous.

This is no different than when a sick person researches his or her symptoms on the Internet. The information will be of dubious quality; a visit to the doctor is indispensable if one is serious about recovery.

However, young companies in particular who want to save money (in the wrong place) occasionally fail to recognize this. Forms available on the Internet are used to cobble together general terms and conditions. Simple partnership agreements can also be found on the Internet. It is not always easy to convince a young entrepreneur that the form contracts he has found on the Internet do not meet the needs of his company and are at least in need of revision. However, in the event of a claim at the latest, it becomes clear that they will not be able to do so entirely without the support of a lawyer.

Non-lawyers: "Legal corner" in media

The same is true of the media: print media of almost all stripes now have a "legal corner" in one form or another. In business magazines, readers regularly find columns dealing with legal issues. In the major German daily newspapers, a few of which can afford to employ fully qualified lawyers as editors, there are always very interesting and in-depth articles on legal topics. Especially during the pandemic, the need for legal expert contributions was considerable. Lawyers should not regard contributions in print media on legal issues as "competition". Such contributions increase the public's interest in legal topics, raise awareness of the need to consult a lawyer, but are hardly ever suitable for solving a concrete legal problem and thus making the use of a lawyer superfluous.

Advice programs with legal content are still becoming increasingly popular on radio and TV. Some advice programs, such as ARD's Ratgeber Recht ("Law Guide"), have almost become icons of German television. Time and again, the editors of such advice programs try to help guests of the program who are plagued by a legal problem. However, this help does not always consist of providing legal advice and support in the judicial enforcement of their rights, but rather of exerting pressure by virtue of media power on the opponents, mostly institutions, which it has just become fashionable to condemn, irrespective of whether the person thus protected is actually entitled to the claim he or she asserts. Such self-appointed "citizen lawyers" sometimes have a relationship with the legal system that is not entirely free of tension. Except for the "outliers," in which editorial departments have tried to exercise their power of opinion in favour of mostly private claimants, such advice programs do not represent competition for lawyers. On the contrary, the advice programs, which deal predominantly with the problems of private individuals, help to clarify the need to consult a lawyer.

Another question, to be distinguished from the question of competition, is to what extent the Internet and media can and should be used by you as a lawyer in a targeted manner to implement your law firm strategy with the means of marketing and to bring your service portfolio to your clients.

Legal Tech

Legal tech as a collective term for all possible IT-based products for the legal sector is expected to play the most important role as a provider of legal services in the future. This does not refer to the legal portals described above, nor to software solutions for increasing efficiency in client processing. Rather, what is meant is, on the one hand, flat-rate offers for legal advice (such as Flight Right, Geblitzt.de, weniger-miete.de, online divorce, etc.) and, on the other hand, all IT equipped with so-called artificial intelligence and machine learning, which already work faster and more efficiently than any lawyer in the area of, for example, smart contracts, block-chain, etc[28].

According to a 2018 Future-Law survey, law firms lag behind in innovating such innovations at 68 %; in contrast, 96 % of legal service providers and 88 % of legal

departments are investing in this emerging "legal ecosystem" of technology specialists and lawyers[29].

Legal departments in Germany and Austria are probably relatively similarly well positioned, but Austrian lawyers are in many respects more open to technological change. This could be due to the fact that communication with the courts (ERV) has been electronic since 1999 and, with the "Legal Tech Hub Vienna," for the first time several large law firms worldwide joined forces in 2018 to jointly drive digitization forward[30].

Finally, we should refer to the provocative thesis of Richard Susskind in "The end of Lawyers", who ten years ago already predicted a fusion of legal and technological competence[31]

"The Davos Digital Forum, which I founded in 2018, is a think tank that covers far more traditional legal topics. I started with legal tech and the Swiss Legal Technology Conference, but very soon saw that the focus on legal topics is too small (for me). Law is always also involved, keyword "embedded law", but plays a subordinate role. In my view, this is the right positioning – to be actively involved in projects in order to move digitization forward together."

Petra Arends-Paltzer, Lawyer and Hackathon Mentor, Founder Davos Digital Forum, Switzerland

---

Back to our three case studies mentioned at the beginning:

All three firms offer solid legal advice by fully qualified lawyers and should therefore meet the demand. However, the reality is more differentiated:

The law firm with "growth problems" has seemingly done everything right as a provider, because cooperation and collaboration should pay off in the highly competitive market rather than grueling competitive battles. And yet, in the external perception of clients, the firm seems more like a school of small fish than a big fish.

But where's the flexibility and diversity, the swarm intelligence, when you're struggling through these growing pains and becoming an "immovable tanker"?

---

28 Wagner's recommendable book in "Legal Tech and Legal Robots" provides an exciting and up-to-date overview.

29 Future Law 2018 survey and "Future Fit Lawyer" study, Wolters Kluwer 2019.

30 Sophie Martinetz/Sarah Maringele in "Quick Guide Legal Tech," p. 83.; see also www.lthv.eu.

31 Richard Susskind in "The End of Lawyers", p. 270.

The firm with the "wrong clients" has apparently outdone itself and would now have to honestly ask itself whether it would like to change as a provider to suit its new clients or remain as it is and then say goodbye to these clients. Supply and demand seem to have been turned upside down here by a trigger. But what went wrong and what should the solution be?

Finally, the firm "without female partners" will have to ask itself anew what kind of firm it is today and wants to be in a few years and how this can be achieved. In doing so, they must be aware that they built up female partners primarily in response to a client need and not because they suddenly sorely missed female colleagues in their meetings or because the legislator forced them to do so. But what do you do when you, as a provider, have to admit that you will not be able to meet a relevant client's need?

Revisit your first set of solutions and answer the questions for each case study. i

---

Remember:
The providers of legal services were and are diverse. However, the new providers are characterized by efficiency, speed and cost-consciousness.

---

2. Demand

But as much as the legal industry is being shaken up and groaning under competitive pressure at the moment, the demand for legal services has never been greater.

In a society that bemoans its "flood of norms", which are becoming ever more complex and fast-paced, legal advice has become part of everyday life. The Covid_19 pandemic, which led to a massive restriction of fundamental rights and high economic losses with lock downs, and at the same time to many rules and regulations, has exacerbated this tendency.

But who actually asks for legal services?

Client groups can be differentiated according to their needs and the situation in which they use the services of a lawyer, in terms of the areas of law in which they require assistance and, last but not least, in terms of their price awareness. i

---

Consumer

The use of legal services by a consumer within the meaning of § 13 BGB is regularly characterized by an acute problem situation. Only rarely do consumers seek the advice of a lawyer for the purpose of risk prevention. With the exception of labor law, which is also of great importance to consumers, this group of clients primarily requires legal services related to private life situations, such as renting or leasing an apartment (tenancy law), concluding contracts for consumption purposes (law of obligations), starting a family and ending a marriage (family law), the formation of assets in the form of the acquisition of real estate (real estate law, property law, private building law and, in part, public building law), the passing on of assets to the next generation (inheritance law) and, last but not least, issues relating to cars (law of obligations, road traffic law, insurance law, administrative offences and criminal law). The list of these life situations and the associated areas of law does not claim to be exhaustive. However, it characterizes the areas in which consumers usually make use of legal services.

Most consumers are not used to dealing with lawyers (single shooters[32]). Consumers are usually only familiar with the circumstances and course of judicial proceedings from television series and feature films that are not exactly close to reality, and whose plots are often set in the Anglo-American legal sphere. This often leads to clichéd and inaccurate perceptions of the tasks and work of a lawyer. On the other hand, the situation is different with permanent clients who, for example, appear again and again with similar legal cases (as in the case of rentals) or with an entire portfolio of their private life (dismissal, divorce, neighbor disputes, criminal law, etc.).

In addition, consumers often choose lawyers based on recommendations from (satisfied) other clients in their circle of acquaintances (or the star rating on Google) or based on the appealing website, expert articles in the press or social media.

Consumers with legal protection insurance play a special role: They live in the belief, cleverly created and maintained by legal protection insurers, that "legal advice and representation in court costs me nothing because my legal protection insurer pays for everything." This assumption is only correct in some cases.
According to their standard terms and conditions, legal protection insurers usually only have to reimburse the fee calculated according to the tables of the RVG. Often, however, the inadequate rates in the remuneration schedule of the RVG do not allow for a cost-covering processing of a mandate. In addition, legal protection insurers (but also litigation financiers) not only recommend certain lawyers to their

32 Such as in the case of a dismissal or a traffic accident.

policyholders, but also send a form letter to the recommended lawyers in advance, informing the lawyer that "our policyholder intends to mandate the lawyer" at the statutory minimum conditions, in order to exclude a possible higher fee agreement between client and lawyer from the outset. Both of these factors, of course, have a massive impact on the legal advice market.

Business enterprises and institutions

In addition to consumers, companies and other institutions such as the public sector or non-profit corporations naturally also come to the market seeking legal advice. Medium-sized and larger companies are usually lawyer experienced. Young companies will soon be, because a company, regardless of the industry, cannot get by in the long run without competent legal advice. As a rule, companies are somewhat familiar with the way lawyers work. Their idea of the lawyer's service is less clichéd. Their expectations of the service are more concrete and specific than those of consumers.

Companies with their own legal department and thus with their own legal know-how are often an "easy" client from the lawyer's point of view, because the contact person on the client's side speaks the same (legal) language. On the other hand, companies with their own legal know-how may be more demanding and critical of the lawyer's service. In addition, companies are usually also very aware of their market power. This has an effect both on the negotiation of the fee and on the (increased) demands on the lawyer's service. For example, with larger clients in particular, it is now taken for granted that the law firms providing the services will adapt to the client's technical ecosystem and adapt their processes and IT to those of the legal department – not the other way around. It is also taken as a given that the law firm will observe the values and culture that apply within the company, as well as the diversity and compliance requirements. Traditional billing by "billable hours" (hourly rates based on the status of the clerk in the firm) is coming under increased criticism due to the tight budgets and a shift away from power and status. Therefore, experts believe it will soon become a thing of the past, making way for fixed rates[33]. More than ever, corporate managers are failing to show the same "brand loyalty" to their company's lawyers that they show to the manufacturer of their company car. The "beauty contests" that were still viewed with suspicion a few years ago, at least in Germany, in which several law firms are invited to compete for the award of a mandate, are now commonplace in the area of larger corporate mandates[34].

---

33 Dr. Tutschka, "The Future of the Legal Profession (Parts 1 and 2)," in CLP blog, Feb. 24, 2017.
34 Busmann, "Chefsache Mandantenakquisition", p. 39, DeGruyter 2016.

Despite the continuing increase in demand for qualified legal advice in an increasingly complex world, cost pressure and the growing diversity of providers are forcing clients in today's world to choose legal advice not only on the basis of trust and service, but also to make the issue of pricing a central factor. The "market laws" mentioned above are gaining in importance and threaten to push the legal market into arbitrariness.

Remember:
The market for legal services has thus become a demand-driven market.

This also means that clients are generally more willing to switch. No lawyer can be lulled into the deceptive certainty that his client of today will also be his client of tomorrow. Worse still, there is an increasing tendency to change lawyers during the course of an ongoing mandate.

At the same time, the legal market has lost its niche character and is being discovered by the large IT and Internet corporations[35].

What did you gain from the chapter?
The legal market, like other markets, is determined by supply and demand. Competitive pressure, gender- and generation shift, and digitalization are exerting massive pressure on pricing and costs. This means increased efficiency and lower costs for the legal market, but also attracts alternative providers and legal products from outside the industry.

This makes the market increasingly complex and diversified. However, it is important to understand and adapt to the fact that it is, above all, a changing market.

---

35 Kai Jacobs in Hartung, Bues, Halbleib in "Legal Tech – Die Digitalisierung des Rechtsmarktes," p. 189.

II. Legal Framework

Why should you read this chapter?
You will learn HOW the legal market is regulated and why it is not an ordinary market after all.

Overview
1. **Admission**
2. **Compensation**
3. **Regulations**

In some respects, as shown, the market for legal services is a market like any other. It is characterized by supply and demand and by the type of services being offered and demanded.

In many respects, however, the market for legal advice is not like any other. The influence of the legislator on this market is significantly different from that of other markets. Unlike in the case of other markets, for which the legislator essentially sets the framework in the form of competition law and antitrust law and increasingly also imposes requirements on equality and diversity, climate and environmental protection, and data protection, the legislator, as the holder of the monopoly on the granting of justice, exerts a massive and very specific influence on this market.

This begins with the state's monopoly on training and licensing, relates to compensation, marketing and competition, and ultimately concludes with specific requirements for insolvency, criminal law and the closure of a law firm.

The major BRAO reform is now a done deal: Effective August 1, 2022, the new Federal Lawyers' Act (BRAO) will come into force – as an overall system alongside the new Tax Advisors Act (StBerG) and the Patent Attorneys' Act (PatO). In addition, the prohibition of representing conflicting interests will be newly regulated.

1. Admission

Legislation is primarily concerned with admission to the market on the supplier side: Since July 1, 2008, the Legal Services Act (RDG) has regulated the authority to provide extra-judicial legal services in Germany and replaced the Legal Advice Act (RBerG) of 1935, which had been in force until then. Unlike the RBerG, the Legal Services Act does not regulate the provision of legal services in judicial proceedings; this is now governed by the respective procedural regulations.

For the supplier who wants to provide qualified services in the legal field, a solid legal education is indispensable. Despite all the justified criticism of the current system of legal education and its content, the law degree, enhanced by practical training following the degree, ensures high quality on the part of the supplier[1].

Pursuant to § 4 BRAO, only those who have either acquired the qualification to hold judicial office according to the German Judiciary Act or have fulfilled the integration requirements according to the Act on the Activities of European Lawyers in Germany (EURAG) or have passed the aptitude test according to Part 4 of the EURAG may be admitted to the bar. In the vast majority of cases, attorneys in Germany obtain admission to the bar by first acquiring the qualification to hold the office of a judge. This means that they successfully complete a law degree at a university with a First State Examination and, after the subsequent preparatory service, successfully pass the Second State Examination, § 5 DRiG. This hurdle is quite high. Traditionally, the "failure rates" for the first state examination are between forty and fifty percent, sometimes even higher. As is known, the rate of trainee lawyers who fail the Second State Examination is not particularly low either. So it is not all that easy to qualify for the judiciary. The qualification to become a judge is only one of many prerequisites for becoming a lawyer and is by no means an identical one.

In Austria, after successful completion of the JUS studies at the university with the Mag. iur., the future lawyer can expect an intensive five-year training as a trainee lawyer in a law firm – or as a candidate notary in a notary's office. This is concluded with the bar examination and registration in the list of lawyers according to § 1 of the Lawyers' Act.

Among lawyers in Austria "Konzipient" is still a common term for a trainee lawyer, in Switzerland "Substitut". While the trainee lawyer period in Germany, which lasts only a few months, is usually the quietest and is used to prepare for the 2nd state exam, the 5-year training of Austrian trainee lawyers is a back-breaking job. There are about 2,200 trainees out of 6,100 lawyers and they usually work 50–60 hours per week for these years at a small salary.

In addition, law can nowadays be completed with a bachelor's and master's degree, often in combination with business, which, however, does not qualify for admission to the bar. The LL.M. or doctorate after a university degree is a popular additional qualification for lawyers[2].

Legally, it is possible for the newly qualified legal assistant to apply for admission to the bar, set up an office and start practicing after taking out professional lia-

1 Branchenbericht der Sparkassen 2020, p. 19.

2 More about this in my essay on "Weiterbildung für Juristen" from 13.12.2020 on the CLP blog. Thus also the Master's program in "Legal Practice" at the FU Hagen, for which this book serves as study literature.

bility insurance. Generally speaking, this does not make sense from a business point of view, especially in Germany. The young lawyer must learn his profession. The best way for him to do so is to work intensively in a law firm during his legal traineeship. As a minimum, it is recommended to work as a salaried lawyer for at least one additional year. To me, this period still seems too short. For some "late starters", it takes three or four years to find out whether they are any good as a lawyer. Accordingly, it used to take about four years before a young lawyer was offered a partnership in a law firm. The increasingly difficult economic situation of lawyers has made the time until partnership significantly longer. The training period of a young lawyer, which can sometimes last several years, includes not only the provision of legal tools for practice, but also indispensable knowledge about the organization of the law firm and, last but not least, business management knowledge, which is completely left out of the classical legal training[3].

Last but not least, knowledge about the professional law of lawyers, fee law, liability issues, but also professional ethics are not entirely unimportant – areas of law that have so far been left out of legal training in Germany, at least to a large extent.

Professional law must be part of the basic training of every lawyer, regardless of whether he or she works in his or her own or another law firm. **i**

The Munich Bar Association welcomes every new colleague in the Bar District, whether they are new to the profession or an established partner, by sending them a current edition of the compilation of texts on the legal professional law[4]. This requirement has now been taken up with the major BRAO reform: Every lawyer must now complete at least 10 hours of training in professional law in his first year of admission (§ 43 f BRAO). § 43 para. 6 BRAO additionally imposes a general duty of continuing education on lawyers, but this is neither specified nor sanctionable. In 2017, a legal regulation with sanctioning of fines failed in the small BRAO reform in the German lower House of Parliament, so that Germany is now at the bottom of the league in terms of continuing legal education: Spain, Hungary and Austria, for example, have a sanctioned continuing education requirement; other countries have quality assurance systems through peer reviews. This has long since ceased to be about the specialist training that is customary in Germany, but rather about the acquisition of key competencies such as fact-finding or interviewing, law firm man-

3 Exemplary here is the Austrian lawyer training, which should also prepare the future lawyers in the trainee period for topics such as law firm organization, strategy and tactics in the mandate, rhetoric and professional law, etc.

4 Huff / Löwe (eds.), Textsammlung Anwaltliches Berufsrecht 2020.

agement, office organization and personnel management. After all, the EU Commission has been asking for some time now how Germany intends to justify its monopoly on lawyers by imposing extremely high hurdles on the entry to the profession, if there is no longer a mandatory further training requirement. More details on the admission requirements for law firms can be found in a subsequent chapter.

2. Compensation

In addition, the legislator regulates the market price. Regulation thus also affects the way in which legal services may be provided and at what price.

For example, the legislator imposes **minimum prices** in the area of forensic services. Only in out-of-court matters can the lawyer agree on fees that are lower than the "statutory" fees, § 4 (2) sentence 1 RVG, § 49 b (1) sentence 1 BRAO[5]. Although in the Federal Scale of Fees for Lawyers (Bundesgebührenordnung für Rechtsanwälte), which was superseded by the RVG, the agreed remuneration had been systematically regulated before the calculation of remuneration according to the tables of values of the schedule of fees, the table fee was consistently referred to as a "statutory fee", as it were as if the privately autonomously agreed fee was an "unlawful compensation". This applies even more to the RVG, which became effective on July 1, 2004, as it systematically regulated the agreement of a fee in § 4 RVG according to the calculation of the fee in accordance with the schedule of fees, § 2, (2), sentence 1 RVG. In § 22, (2), sentence 1 RVG, the legislator has even provided an **upper limit** for the attorney's compensation. The value in the respective matter may not regularly exceed EUR 30,000,000.00. Finally, the RVG provides a special form for **fee agreements** that deviate from the RVG in favor of the attorney. This is because a higher fee than the statutory fee is generally admissible and above all advisable if the statutory fees do not represent an appropriate or cost-covering compensation. According to § 49b (1) sentence 1 BRAO, fees lower than the statutory fees are only admissible in cases where this is permitted, for example in extra-judicial matters.

The written form is required for claims for higher compensation in money than the statutory compensation. This means that the written form stipulated in § 126 BGB is mandatory. However, in contrast to § 126 (2) BGB, the written form requirement only applies to the client's declaration, not to the entire agreement. Thus, it is

5 As of January 1, 2021, the attorney fees according to the RVG table as well as the expert and interpreter fees, compensation for jurors and witnesses as well as court fees have been increased linearly by 10 %, in social law matters by 20 %. This is a long overdue increase, the implementation of which is primarily due to the tireless efforts of the German Lawyers' Association.

a prerequisite that the client personally signs, i. e. by his signature or by means of his notarized hand sign, a separate (!) document from which the promise of the fee in a certain amount is evident. The written confirmation by the client is still required even if he has already agreed orally.

If the formal requirement is not met, the entire lawyer's contract is not invalid, but the lawyer may not demand a higher compensation than the statutory compensation for this case. The client therefore always owes at least the statutory compensation.

A cure of the violated formal requirement is possible e. g. by voluntary payment of the agreed fee. Fee agreements are only excluded for legal aid proceedings and for the lawyer obliged to provide advice aid pursuant to § 8 (2) BerHG.

From the point of view of the client, the lack of transparency of the compensation often creates the impression of "buying a pig in a poke". This is also due to the fact that the lawyer can naturally only provide vague information on costs in advance and that advance payment is rather unusual, with the exception of criminal law. The state fee schedule creates only apparent clarity. A non-legally trained inquirer will not be able to cope with the norms and the fee tables of the German Lawyers' Fees Act (Rechtsanwaltsvergütungsgesetz). In addition, the (subsequent) 34 | A. The Legal Advice Market discretion of the lawyer with regard to the scope and extent of the mandate is likely to be a special feature of the legal industry, which is rather unusual in other industries.

In the area of corporate consulting, the **billing** of an attorney's fees according to the **time spent** is probably still dominant[6], but this does not indicate how much the final service will cost. At the beginning of the mandate, the client usually does not yet know how much time will be required for the work. The lawyer faces a similar situation. It is true that the lawyer can rely on empirical values. Due to the interactivity of the lawyer's services, the client's influence on the time required to process the mandate is significant and difficult for the lawyer to estimate in advance. The possibility of compensation on a contingency basis was therefore desired by all parties[7]. With the Legal Tech Collection Service Provider Act (RDG), which is intended to enable the legal profession to compete fairly in the legal services market, the ban on

6 The usual hourly rates range from € 75.00–750.00, thus averaging € 350, depending on the area of law, qualification, ranking within the firm and location, with the vast majority of colleagues working at an hourly rate of between € 150 and € 250, according to the Branchenbericht (Industry Report) Sparkassen 2020,5; JUVE.de/ Rechtsmarkt/Stundenensätze et seq.

7 Hasso Suliak "Erfolgshonorare für Anwälte allseits erwünscht" in LTO of 28.11.2019.

contingency fees was also largely relaxed, in alongside the ban on litigation financing.

You can read about the details of the compensation systems and the level of compensation for lawyers in one of the subsequent chapters.

Finally, for the first time, free legal advice in familial, neighborly or similar close personal relationships is now permissible (§ 6 RDG). Anyone who provides legal advice free of charge outside of this close personal circle generally requires the guidance of a lawyer, but this has now also made student legal advice possible in Germany (legal clinics/law clinics[8]) in which law students provide legal advice free of charge to citizens seeking advice. This is certainly a long overdue step by the legislator, although in the end it is not without influence on the legal advice business and the expectations of the general public as to whether, when and how legal advice should be provided.

3. Regulations

And finally: A law firm is a **commercial enterprise.** Therefore, of course, almost all the rules that apply to other business enterprises also apply to lawyers in the same way, for example, the law against unfair competition.

However, special regulations under professional law, to which other providers of legal services are not subject, further restrict the economic development of lawyers. The gradual relaxation of the advertising right for lawyers (§ 43 b BRAO) is not a merit of the legislator, but a merit of the Federal Constitutional Court, whose Second Chamber of the First Senate does not tire of reprimanding the fundamental misunderstanding of the courts of instance with regard to the fundamental right of lawyers to freely exercise their profession.

The observance of these special rules is costly and can represent a competitive disadvantage compared to non-legal competitors[9]. However, lawyers should be able to present the special due diligence requirements imposed by the legislator on their work, their solid training and, in particular, their special duties of confidentiality and independence from the interests of third parties in the eyes of the public as the competitive advantages they actually are.

8 Branchenbericht der Sparkassen 2020, p. 18.

9 As well as the ban on third-party ownership: Branchenbericht der Sparkassen 2017, p. 17.

The rules of the game are determined by a whole series of professional laws and regulations:
- Federal Lawyers' Act (BRAO)
- Professional Code of Conduct (BORA)
- Specialist Lawyers' Code of Conduct (FAO)
- Lawyers' Fees Act (RVG) and Advisory Assistance Act (BerHG)
- Legal Services Act (RDG) with Introductory Act and Ordinance, Partnership Law (PartGG)
- Lawyers' Directory and Mail Order Ordinance (RAVPV),
- Electronic Legal Transactions Ordinance (ERVV)

The Austrian professional code of conduct is more or less parallel:
- Lawyers' Act (RAO)
- Disciplinary Statute
- Lawyers' Tariff Act (RATG), Compensation Guideline and General Fee Criteria (AHK)

In addition, at the European level:
- Professional Code of Conduct for Lawyers in the EU (CCBE)
- Law on the Activities of European Lawyers (EuRAG)

General regulations such as the German Criminal Code (StGB) or the Money Laundering Act (Geldwäschegesetz), the Service Provider Information Obligations Ordinance (DL-InfoV), the Mediation Act (Mediationsgesetz), the German Administrative Code (VwGO) and the Code of Criminal Procedure (OWiG) also play a role in the work of lawyers..

Particularly noteworthy is, for example, the obligation to take out professional liability insurance or pecuniary loss liability insurance (so-called admission policy or title coverage), whereby the minimum coverage amounts in Germany are €250,000 per insured event and in Austria €400,000 per insured event, as well as the obligation and the regulations on the formal establishment and set-up of a law firm and the special requirements on cooperation and advertising. This will be dealt with separately in the special chapters on marketing, for example.

Finally, there is some movement in the matter: Comprehensive new regulations will be made in the Federal Lawyers' Act (BRAO), the Tax Consultancy Act (StBerG) and the Patent Attorneys' Act (PAO) to reform the professional law of professional practice companies for lawyers and tax advisors. In it, the professional practice companies are to be offered a choice of all European companies, companies under German law and companies under the law of another EU and EEA member state, and even carriers of professional obligations themselves, admitted to the chambers and listed in the electronic directories. In addition, cooperation with other professional groups such as physicians and architects should be possible.

What did you get out of the chapter?
In this section you have learned about the state regulations and interventions in the legal services market in particular, their history and objectives, as well as other market restrictions.

III. The product of legal advice

Why should you read this chapter?
You will learn WHAT makes the product or service of "legal advice" and how it differs from Others.

Overview

1. **Representation of interests**
2. **Crisis intervention and Trust**
3. **Legal Coaching and Mediation**

A still widespread stereotype sees the lawyer as a rather ponderous legal expert who, after thoroughly subsuming the facts brought to him under the relevant norms, endeavors to provide the client with legally correct answers in a legal language that is at best comprehensible to experts. Ideally, he will also point out various possible courses of action, but will otherwise leave the client alone to a large extent with the decision as to how he should proceed in a meaningful manner.

Unfortunately, this cliché is not entirely unjustified. After all, even today, law firms are still far removed from a professional service mentality. Every lawyer should be conscious of being a service provider. Lawyers have to align their professional activities with the needs and wishes of their current and potential clients. They must always try to find out what their client's goal is and do their utmost to achieve this goal for their client. The meeting with "their" lawyer must not become an unpleasant experience for a client. Rather, the lawyer's cooperation with the client must be aimed not only at satisfying the client, but also at building a relationship based on trust.

The core product of legal services is described in § 3 (1) BRAO: The lawyer shall advise and represent his client. According to § 1 (3) BORA[1], the lawyer shall protect his client from loss of rights, accompany him in shaping the law, avoiding conflicts and settling disputes, protect him from wrong decisions by courts and authorities and safeguard him against unconstitutional interference and excess of state power. i

---

This naming of various tasks of the lawyer is not exhaustive. Both norms emphasize the "protective function" of the lawyer. A good lawyer, however, will not limit himself to reactive and purely defensive behavior, but will work actively – and if neces-

1 BORA – the professional code of conduct for lawyers in the version dated 1.1.2018.

sary, aggressively – to enforce the rights of his client. The formulation that the lawyer's task is to (only) "accompany" the client is inaccurate. A lawyer should not leave it at a mere accompaniment of the client. The client may expect support and assistance.

However, the reality in law firms has changed in recent years, especially when it comes to client relations: Service providers, service and client satisfaction are no longer foreign words. But the average client has now also altered his or her needs and expectations: Today, they no longer want (only) information. They get it from everywhere, sometimes more or less qualified and useful, but always on a 24/7 basis and free of charge. Access to qualified legal advice is no longer tied to the colleague around the corner but is also available 24/7 everywhere and often at very low cost. The sustainable development or acquisition of a client base is therefore of secondary importance for law firms (and can no longer be monetized when a law firm is transferred). In addition, the formerly feared switch of the client to a colleague for the next mandate is today absolutely common practice. What is feared and on the rise now, however, are changes of mandate during an ongoing mandate.

"What is the legal situation?" is a typical case question from university studies and exams. It is not uncommon for clients to ask this question as well. The assumption that the client only wants lexical information or even that the client demands the development of legal concepts and a scholastic solution of the "case" would be regularly wrong.

The client who asks about the legal situation really wants to know: "What should I do?". One should be warned against "rash consulting recommendations".

1. Representation of interests

The core of this legal advice and support is the representation of interests.

This begins with the lawyer correctly recording the client's situation, analyzing it from a legal point of view and evaluating it. An evaluation of the actual situation that may meet the requirements of an exam is not sufficient in practice.

In doing so, the lawyer should think through various scenarios of possible future trends and develop solution variants. The client should be fully informed of the results of the analysis and the evaluation as soon as possible. A wise lawyer will come up with different ways of solving the problem and describe them to his client. Special attention should be paid to incorrect preconceptions of the client about the legal context. The lawyer must correct these carefully but emphatically.

A lawyer's services also include choosing a mode of communication that is easy for the client to understand and being able to vary the language code at different levels according to the client's needs. Part of the lawyer's service is to "translate" statements of third parties, especially decisions of courts and authorities, for the client.

In legal proceedings, it is only natural that the lawyer assumes a leadership role. However, a good lawyer will not regard or treat his client as an "object of the proceedings" for a single moment but will involve the client in the conduct of the case. This applies in particular to the coordination of the litigation tactics with the client. After all, the lawyer is conducting the client's case, not his own.

An essential prerequisite for successful legal services is the lawyer's ability to perform. Performance in this context requires that the lawyer has the necessary legal expertise and the ability to use this expertise to the benefit of the client.

The client's satisfaction with the service is the ultimate goal of a lawyer's service efforts. This is by no means a purely altruistic goal. After all, a high degree of client satisfaction is an important factor in the success of a law firm. A satisfied client will (hopefully) recommend the firm to others. A dissatisfied client will not necessarily express his or her displeasure to his or her lawyer but will almost certainly do so among acquaintances.

How is client satisfaction achieved? Client satisfaction is the result of a comparison process. The client compares the service he expects with the service he perceives. Every client has expectations when using legal services. A client is dissatisfied if these expectations are not met. Conversely, however, the fulfillment of client expectations does not automatically lead to a high degree of client satisfaction. Rather, the client takes it for granted that his expectations will be met. Only when the client's expectations are exceeded feelings arise that can lead to long-term client loyalty.

Most clients can not judge the quality of legal services accurately due to their own lack of expertise in legal matters. They take the lawyer's legal expertise for granted. Whether a lawyer is "good", and whether one can be satisfied with their performance, is very often judged by clients on the basis of substitute indicators. These substitute indicators do not always have anything to do with objective legal qualifications. It is obvious that clients attach importance to academic titles and specialist attorney designations. It should also be evident that recommendations from satisfied clients help new clients to assess their lawyer. Only seemingly banal is the fact that the fulfillment of clichéd expectations also contributes significantly to client satisfaction. Clients who are entrepreneurs have more confidence in a lawyer wearing a dark suit than in a lawyer dressed in casual clothes.

2. Crisis intervention and trust

The work of a lawyer is no service like any other. It is characterized by a whole series of special features. One of these special features is that clients very often call on the services of a lawyer in an exceptional situation, in times of crisis. In many cases, companies need lawyers to prepare and implement important business decisions. Consumers in particular frequently call on the services of lawyers in emergency situations involving both economic and private matters. This requires the lawyer not only to have finely tuned senses for the emotional state of the person concerned, but also to be able to recognize an "issue behind the issue" in time. It also requires a certain degree of crisis and conflict management, which is primarily aimed at stabilizing the situation and building security and trust. Since crises are also changes within processes, a basic understanding of change management is essential for success in the matter and for the satisfaction of the client.

The special characteristic of the trust aspect of legal services is that it is immaterial, not "tangible". Important parts of the lawyer's service are not visible to the client. It is true that the client experiences his lawyer in conversation, in negotiations with third parties, and occasionally particularly intensively in the case of legal representation. As a rule, the client does not see an essential part of the lawyer's work, the research and the intellectual effort behind the preparation of a draft contract or a brief.

One of the greatest difficulties of legal service is therefore to make it visible and tangible for the client. Of course, a lawyer can send a client copies of the other party's letter with a so-called "red slip" of poor paper quality and the uncharitable note "for your attention". This kind of thing still happens often enough in reality. Indeed, many clients still put up with this. How positively does it affect the client however, if he or she receives a short statement summarizing the content of the letter sent from the other party along with a copy of the letter from the opposing party. Even if a thorough examination of the arguments of the opposing party is still necessary, the client can often be given an initial assessment and informed of the possible consequences of the arguments of the opposing party. Even if this is not possible, a lawyer can at least inform his client that and when the examination of the other side's arguments is pending. Furthermore, the lawyer should not only to introduce the client to his own argumentation and to discuss it with him beforehand, but also to have worked out a basic guideline for the mandate and the best strategy in cooperation with the client.

In addition, there is the high degree of **individuality in legal services**. Even in the case of recurring tasks, such as the drafting of the articles of association of a limited liability company, clauses that have been formulated once may be reusable for many cases. Nevertheless, the particularities of the client's interests, which are hardly ever absolutely identical in two cases, must always be taken into account. In mass proceedings, a certain degree of standardization may be achievable. As a rule, however, our own standard clauses and form books are a valuable and indispensable aid, but they do not solve the problem. And finally, the interaction with the client is of decisive importance. As a rule, the client's cooperation is necessary in the course of a mandate, since the client must repeatedly make decisions that the lawyer cannot relieve the client of. The client cannot simply let the lawyer's service pass over him, consume it. Rather, he is an important contributor to this service. Legal advice must therefore not only take into account the needs of the client, but also satisfy the demand of its target clientele. The firm must be able to offer legal advice on the problem areas and the areas of law that are typically demanded by the target clientele. This can lead to a law firm that is focused on family law, for example, also receiving more and more mandates on social security law or asylum law, because the target clientele brings this along. A law firm specializing in criminal law may unexpectedly find itself confronted with a large number of typical tax law mandates.

When it comes to **standard services**, such as litigation, answering legal questions, conducting negotiations for clients and drafting contracts, lawyers should always be aware that a large number of competitors offer exactly the same service. Their own conviction that the legal quality of their work is clearly different from that of their competitors is usually of little use. The difficulty with a quality policy conceived in this way is that, on the one hand, a whole series of competitors among the lawyers can at least deliver useful legal work and, on the other hand, that the client is regularly not in a position to judge the professional quality of the work, apart from obvious professional blunders such as missing a deadline or ignorance of current case law. It also goes without saying that every lawyer is covered by professional liability insurance for gross blunders, so that his certain "objective basic quality" of legal advice is guaranteed by the system that applies in Germany. The quality of the service product legal advice is therefore not to be measured here from the lawyer's point of view, but from the client's point of view. In principle, the client expects his lawyer to represent him in court if the worst comes to the worst. But does this alone make legal representation a product of legal advice? Legal representation only becomes a product when a law firm conducts legal proceedings for its clients not only in a legally correct manner, but in a special manner that differs from other lawyers. In order for litigation to appear to the client not as an interchangeable service, but as a special product of a particular law firm, it must be recognizably different for the client than the service of competitors. This can be achieved, for example, by providing additional services that are not necessary for the actual litigation: Clients who are inexperienced in court can be provided with an additional service in the form of a prior explanation of the course of the proceedings, possibly in the form of a flow chart. Structured pre- and post-trial discussions should actually be part of the standard repertoire of every law firm. Especially before a court hearing, it is necessary to foresee possible developments and to explain them to the client in order to protect him from surprises. In practice, the preliminary discussion often takes place in a short conversation lasting a few minutes in the court corridor, if possible within earshot of the opposing party. Emotional outbursts following a surprising oral hearing are not at all uncommon. Sufficient preparation and structured preparation for the hearing can avoid these scenarios by discussing possible developments and their consequences in advance. From the client's point of view, this can be a pleasant contrast to the services offered by other law firms. Especially in the part of his service visible to the client, a lawyer can do a lot for the "product design". This includes the uniform and appealing design of the documents presented by him, possibly having extensive documentation bound for the client or joint preparation with the client by means of overviews and graphical representations that make it easier for the client to understand the situation and possible developments.

Consulting mandate

In the classic consulting mandate, the lawyer inquires about the client's legal request in order to gather the necessary facts with the client. If these facts cannot support the legal claim, advice is given on possible alternative solutions. The client alone decides which solution to pursue and which is the best for him. This overwhelms many clients. And what is left behind is an unsatisfied client with a solution that is unsatisfactory for him.

For a long time, the knowledge monopoly of academic training protected legal service providers from having to deal with this dilemma. Today, digitalization is massively shaking the knowledge monopoly of the consulting industry and is having a serious impact on the consulting business. Thanks to the Internet, knowledge can be accessed anywhere and at any time, free of charge. Consultants need to rethink their approach and develop a new service culture in which the customer takes center stage once again. But the client has never gone to the office just for informative advice. They have always been interested in finding and implementing a solution. Today, however, in most client meetings, the information provided to the pre-informed client is reduced to a minimum, namely to the part that is not generally available: the information tailored to the client's individual situation.

Now, most lawyers understand the client's individual situation as a "factual situation". Objectivity and distance are basic principles in classic legal advice – and in the entire legal industry: the cataloging of the client file, the traditional meeting room (with the appointment and presence culture), the lawyer's and judge's robes, even the interior design of courtrooms and the rules of procedure were developed only for this purpose.

Starting from the factual situation, the legal request is defined (objectively as well as subjectively) and the lawyer begins with the appropriate assessment and information of the client.

Completely disregarded is usually,

- the emotional state of the client and the stage of the crisis situation or change process,
- which legal solution fits the client's value system and life goal,
- and how the relationship of trust required for the mandate can be established as quickly and sustainably as possible – the basis of every mandate.

A paradigm widely used in legal advice in this context is: "Legal advice is only professional and serious if the problem is approached and solved analytically and factually."

You don't want to "humanize" too much. After all, keeping an emotional distance from the client helps to keep a cool head. And indeed, the objectification of the conflict situation, in which the parties have in the vast majority of cases already discussed the matter thoroughly, is one of the core values of the legal profession.

Remember:
The objectified consulting mandate can in principle be replaced by technical solutions.

But does this also apply to the relationship with the client? How can the best legal solution be found for the client and individual advice be provided if the client is not perceived as a human being? The lawyer working in this manner today offers little more than a technology-based solution – and rightly fears that he will soon be replaced.

While the lawyer primarily provides his legal expertise and thus accompanies the client in disputes, negotiations or court proceedings, the legal coach offers a form of professional communication and process management, which provides the client with a protected framework for development and his own decisions. In both cases, the client remains the master of the proceedings and the lawyer/legal coach is solely committed to the client.

So, if pure advice, which used to be the core competence of lawyers, takes a back seat and instead competencies in crisis management, conflict resolution, empathy, communication and negotiation skills, strategic and systemic understanding now play an increasing role, then the lawyer will not be interchangeable.

This is nothing new. Other traditional consulting professions have also been developing in this direction in recent years. The consulting industry is becoming increasingly more approachable and human.

This distinguishes the consultant of tomorrow from algorithms and technical solutions; but also from other consultants. The consultant of tomorrow is not interchangeable.

However, not becoming interchangeable can also be achieved through a unique combination of different professional competencies, professional and life experience. So, if legal expertise meets communication and crisis competence, this coaching lawyer can pick up and understand his client much better in his current situation.

Sensitized in this way, the lawyer can grasp the client's crisis not only in legal terms but also in human terms, identify its stage and select the appropriate methods to lead the client out of it. These are not necessarily legal steps, but rather communication that addresses the client's need for security. The client feels understood and the lawyer can better classify and understand the client's information, but also adjust strategy and tactics as well as client management accordingly. This leads to a trusting and sustainable attorney-client relationship, and also to the right legal solution for the client. Business is stimulated. The lawyer can help on a human level and feels fulfilled and meaningful in his work[2].

Thus, an in-depth understanding of change and communication processes is essential for successful legal work. This guarantees not only satisfied clients, but also professional and thus efficient client management. Since this has not been taught in legal training to date, any more than business management know-how, it remains the task of the legal profession to provide postgraduate training in this area.

Today, clients come to the lawyer's office pre-informed – or do not even come in person – but they are still in a personal crisis situation and in a process of change (be it a dismissal by the employer, a penalty notice from the tax authorities, an impending insolvency). This makes them afraid and takes away the free-will of the visit (similar to a visit to the dentist). It's no wonder that lawyers don't necessarily have the best reputation, as they are regularly associated with all these negative situations and feelings.

According to the different models for crisis situations and changes, various stages are passed through, and always all of them, one after the other.

Without going into too much detail here: For the processing of the mandate, it makes a difference at which point in time the client comes to the office:

- of the "first shock" (e.g. he has just received the notice of dismissal)
- already in the crisis phase (e.g., he has already held talks)
- or acceptance (e.g., he has already reoriented himself).

2 *Dr. Geertje Tutschka* in: "Vom Jurist zum Legal Coach", in: TalentRocket from 15.8.2018.

In the first case, he is usually unable to provide all the relevant facts. The repression phase prevents him from doing so. The valley of deep crisis has not yet been reached. If the lawyer does not respond to this and does not provide more confidence-building measures rather than demanding facts, the crisis situation is quickly projected onto the lawyer, who is declared the "scapegoat". For the client, this can even mean that he remains in the crisis situation and moves in a "feedback loop" back to the event/shock. He remains trapped in the process with no chance of resolving the conflict. No legal solution will satisfy him.

If, on the other hand, the client only comes to the lawyer "after the milk has spilled" and he is already in the phase where he has come to terms with the sudden change, he will be able to support the lawyer much more easily and with more commitment in the preparation of the mandate. Uncontrolled emotional outbursts are not to be expected (anymore). For many colleagues, these clients are their favorites of all. They lean back and concentrate on their actual work, only to be surprised to find that the client is "gone" again at the first opportunity. The colleague has realized that at this point the client is no longer as open and grateful for an intensive client relationship as he or she was at the acute crisis point. At this point, the lawyer quickly becomes "interchangeable" and "arbitrary" if he does not invest very specifically, for example, with holistic services and actively in building up the client relationship. If a regular client is to be won, client loyalty must be sustained here.

All this can be learned and saves a lot of self-experimentation.

Communication and crisis trainings are therefore an ideal post graduate training for lawyers in any field of law. Unfortunately, these are routinely not integrated into professional training as "soft skills". Legal education focuses exclusively on specialist training: In the studies but also in the specialist attorney ships according to FAO: According to §§ 4 para. 2, 15 FAO, 15 hours must be completed annually online or offline to obtain the respective specialist attorney title, a maximum of 5 hours of which may be done in self-study. In the vast majority of cases, the compulsory further training to obtain the title of specialist lawyer alone consumes the annual time and financial budgets for further professional training. In Austria, since June 2021, there is a general obligation for continuing education according to § 10 para 6 RAO (however, there is no continuing education for specialized attorneys) of at least 36 hours within a period of 3 calendar years through participation in specialized continuing education events (worldwide, both in the form of a face-to-face event and in digital form); of which a maximum of 18 hours may be spent in self-study.

3. Legal Coaching and Mediation

Nowadays, clients no longer consult a lawyer just for his expertise. In most cases, they have already informed themselves on the Internet in numerous forums or legal portals. Expertise is available to anyone at any time and free of charge. Legal advice today has long since ceased to be the presentation of specialist knowledge, accompaniment and representation in court. And the craft of "consulting" was never on the timetable of future lawyers anyway. Fortunately, things are different for medical professionals: Or would you go to a surgeon who only has the theoretical knowledge, but never learned the craft? And that brings us to the topic: What is the "legal craft"? Subsumption, legal advice, litigation – all of these together or none of them?

Today, clients do not only come to the lawyer in crisis situations with the expectation that he will fix it for them. They come to the lawyer to have him apply and implement his "expertise" in order to change their lives. And not in any way, but according to their personal ideal[3]. The difficulty usually lies in the fact that the client himself does not know exactly what his ideal is[4].

Thus, the lawyer drills for motives with uncomfortable questions, provides feedback and recommendations to filter out this target and develop a promising strategy together. With respect for the client, a good lawyer will actually listen, take a step back, and not try to talk the client into their own or even just the standard solution – or immediately the one that will bring in the most. The goal is to find the right legal solution for the client's individual situation. He "coaches". And he usually does this without knowing exactly what and how he is doing what he is doing, but rather from his gut, so to speak. So perhaps it is time to recognize a new quality of consulting. One that, in contrast to "legal tech", emphasizes the human qualities of the lawyer – such as empathy and trust-building.

Meanwhile, there is a term for it: **Legal Coaching**[5]. But what is coaching in the first place?

- according to the common definition of the professional associations for coaches applicable in Germany[6]

---

3 It is assumed that this is done free of legal errors, and the fact that this is sometimes not the maximum of what could have been achieved is gladly accepted.

4 See p. 11 of the study "Dafür nehmen wir uns einen Anwalt – Erwartungshaltung von Unternehmen an modernen Anwälte im Konfliktmanagement," Bucerius Law School (CLP) in cooperation with Taylor Wessing.

5 Dr. Tutschka, "Legal Coaching – ein Hybrid" in NJW 30/2018.

6 Presented here only in excerpts. The complete position paper can be found at www.ro and table-coaching.eu.

"Coaching is aimed at individuals (or groups of individuals) and supports the person in shaping his or her personal development, social roles and cooperative relationships, as well as in coping with the demands of decision-making and action in working life. The coaching process is confidential, structured, method-guided and limited in time. The coaching goals and topics are determined by the client and agreed upon bindingly between coach and client at the beginning. Despite the goal orientation, the coaching process remains open-ended. Coaching is carried out by a coach whose (theoretical and practical) qualification is recognized by a professional association[7]. Clarification processes are initiated in the dialog between coach and client. By opening up new perspectives, room for maneuver is created, processes of change are stimulated and accompanied, and the ability to make decisions and take action is strengthened. Coaching is based on a service contract, in which the objectives and the framework conditions for the fulfillment of the contract are regulated. In contrast, the goal of expert consulting is to support the solution of a problem by simply providing special knowledge and communicating it to the consulting client. Coaching, on the other hand, is a form of reflective consulting in which the client's resources are accessed and the client is enabled to cope with tasks independently. Coaching therefore presupposes the willingness of the client to actively participate[8]."

- according to the internationally uniform quality standards for coaching[9] of the International Coaching Federation (ICF)[10].
  "Coaching is a collaborative and thought-provoking process that creatively supports people and organizations to enhance their personal and professional potential. The interaction with the coach guides the client to comprehensive clarity and active action. The coach encourages the client to discover themselves and their possibilities, accompanies them in developing their own solutions and strategies, and always recognizes the client's own responsibility. The ICF core competencies regulate the theoretical and practical requirements for the qualification of the coach, who acts according to the applicable ICF ethical standards."

7 In the absence of government regulation.

8 Excerpt from the position paper on the coaching profession of the Roundtable of Coaching Associations (RTC) for the German-speaking region from 2005.

9 Presented here only in excerpts. The complete definition, including core competencies and ethical standards, can be found at www.coachingfederation.orgor at www.coachfede-ration.de.

10 The ICF is the largest professional association of professional coaches worldwide and has been ensuring internationally uniform standards for over 25 years.

Although there are already legal regulations regarding the coaching profession and the practice of coaching in many countries – such as Austria and Switzerland – there is no such regulation in Germany. A current legislative initiative started in Germany in 2017 and for the first time defines the profession of coach and coaching according to the German-speaking professional associations (RTC)[11]. At the same time, it is simply a matter of time before the European Union comes up with a uniform regulation on the subject. At the moment, it has before it the so-called "Code of Conduct" of the most important professional associations for coaching, which speaks out against legal regulation and in favor of quality control by the professional associations[12].

For professional coaching today, therefore, good coaching training is essential, preferably one that is specifically tailored to lawyers and legal professionals[13] so that it can be immediately and easily integrated into legal counseling and everyday legal practice. For this application area, a basic training with the most important and effective methods and tools for the consulting industry is sufficient[14]. For business lawyers working in an international context, coaching training according to international quality standards (such as those of the ICF) is a good idea. Similar to the training as a specialist lawyer, the training alone does not already identify the lawyer as a certified specialist, but also certified relevant practical experience, which is ensured by the certificate of a professional association for coaches[15]. At its core, it is about communication skills and understanding how people "work," which helps lawyers better understand their clients. However, the knowledge and attitude of a coach also bring great added value in terms of self-development. The ability to practice self-reflection and humility in relation to the client's situation in turn benefits the understanding of the needs of the other person. Lawyers are then no longer just "technical idiots" who intervene insensitively in other people's lives but can take creative action here with a certain maturity. Knowing when coaching

11 Schwertfeger, p. 46 "Gesetzesinitiative will Coachingmarkt regulieren" in "Wirtschaft und Weiterbildung", 01/2018.

12 Dr. Tutschka in interview "Coaching day discussed regulation of coaching" Coaching-magazin 01/2018.

13 I offer such a training as a certified coach and trainer at the CLP Academy in German and English. It requires neither special previous knowledge nor a mediation training or a "general coaching training" and can be integrated and used in any legal counseling immediately after completion of the training.

14 Dr. Tutschka, "Coaching als Baustein der Weiterbildung", MyQ-Blog 09/2017.

15 Dr. Tutschka in interview, p. 55 "Coaching ist keine Beratung" in "IHK-Magazin für München und Oberbayern – Wirtschaft", 01/2018; Dr. Tutschka "Coaching vs. Beratung – eine Frage der Perspektive" Xing-Coaches Magazin 06/2017.

should not be used also requires a good understanding of the subject and its ethical parameters[16].

In contrast to mediation, the lawyer does not give up his partiality, i.e. he continues to represent the client's interests. Although a complete coaching process is also an option if the client is completely indecisive[17]. As a rule, however, the lawyer will only use special communication techniques (e.g. special questioning methods) selectively in the course of the mandate in order to support the client in finding his ideal solution, for which the lawyer can then create the legal basis.

Legal Coaching is understood as modern, qualified legal advice[18].

Remember:
Legal Coaching is a special intervention in the legal consulting mandate.

This is used in particular when the client seeks legal advice and legal assistance from a lawyer to protect and represent his interests but is still undecided as to which legal goal and result should be pursued.

However, legal coaching can also be applied in the corporate legal department, as a judge or prosecutor, or in administration and politics.

Legal Coaching is generally remunerated by means of a private-law agreement on remuneration, taking into account any special statutory rules (e.g. on lawyers' remuneration in accordance with the RVG). Similar to a specialist lawyer, a legal coach is considered specialized and can usually charge an increased hourly rate of at least €250.

The post graduate training for lawyers in legal coaching is based, like any other training in professional coaching, on the quality standards for coaching training, for example at least 100 training hours (80 % of which are in direct interaction with the trainee, meaning no pure distance learning according to the FernUSG) primarily on the coaching process by teaching various coaching tools and methods, the core competencies of a coach and the ethical guidelines.

On the one hand, the respective legal regulations and provisions for coaches, coaching trainings and the practice of coaching must be complied with and, on the

---

16 Dr. Tutschka, "Coaching ist das, was der juristischen Ausbildung fehlt" in Coachingmagazin 01/2019, Dr. Tutschka, "The new fish in the pond" Legal Business World 03/2019.

17 This requires a corresponding reorientation of the client's assignment after the lawyer has perceived this need and made it transparent.

18 Dr. Tutschka in interview, p. 54 "Es gab ganz entscheidende Entwicklungen" in "Wirtschaft und Weiterbildung" 07/2017.

other hand, the professional regulations for lawyers, such as the Lawyers' Act in Austria (RAO) or the Federal Lawyers' Act in Germany (BRAO).

Legal Coaching trainings with their combination of theory and practice are roughly comparable to the training to become a specialist lawyer (in Germany according to FAO) or to become a mediator according to the Mediation Act (MedG), are usually recorded as professional further training within the framework of the further training obligation and tax deductibility and cost similarly to these several thousand euros (currently > € 5,000). The training is completed with a training certificate, which should not be confused with the independent certification as a coach by a professional association. Ideally, the curriculum of the coaching training and the training provider including the training trainer are accredited by a professional association for coaches, which means that their quality standards have been checked.

Legal coaching as a special psychological intervention should not be practiced by legal coaching laypersons or by professions unrelated to coaching, such as mediators, supervisors, therapists or other similar professionals.

For the lawyer, this results in the further advantage that their extraordinary combined qualification also pays off financially and they also clearly stand out from coaches in other professions in terms of the value of their services.

The actual added value, however, results primarily from the lasting trust that is built up through client satisfaction: experience shows that this not only results in more follow-up mandates, but above all in more comprehensive mandates even in the initial assignment. This is the real advantage.

In addition to the monetary advantage and client satisfaction, two other points are mentioned by the graduates: Coaching training always leads to reflection on one's own values, communication patterns and leadership style, and thus to personal development.

Participants report that they now act with increased attentiveness and care – toward themselves, but also toward others. This benefits themselves and their personal environment, but especially their employees.

A well-functioning work-life balance and employee retention are therefore not entirely unwelcome "side effects"[19].

Mediation had a similar development when it was established in legal counseling a few years ago. There was a need for individual, autonomous dispute resolution beyond litigation and court decisions. Today, mediation is an integral part of the portfolio of legal consulting products, even though, strictly speaking, it could just as ea-

---

19 Dr. Tutschka "Legal Coaching: Jurisitsche Fachexpertise wirkungsvoll mit speziellen Kommunikationstechniken unterstützen" im Anwaltspiegel 07/2019.

sily have been assigned to court or arbitration proceedings – or at best to the "neutral" position of a notary public – and thus to the profession of judges rather than lawyers. Since September 2017, the certified mediator[20] according to the ZMediatAusbV exists (who, unfortunately, may also be a non-lawyer in legal disputes). Since 2016, there is also a Master of Law (LL.M.) for mediation in Germany, which is mainly used by young lawyers from commercial law firms. And in the meantime, even legal protection insurers support mediation in exceptional cases[21].

According to § 1 of the Mediation Act[22], mediation is a confidential and structured procedure in which parties voluntarily and independently seek an amicable settlement of their conflict with the help of one or more mediators. A mediator is an independent and neutral person without decision-making authority who guides the parties through the mediation process. And § 7a BORA specifies: The lawyer who calls himself a mediator has to fulfill the requirements according to § 5 para. 1 Mediation Act with regard to education and training, theoretical knowledge and practical experience.

Hardly anything has had such a lasting impact on the fundamentals of negotiation in recent years as mediation. And the number of lawyers training to become mediators continues to rise. Although the price of losing one's partiality as a lawyer in order to increase one's negotiation competence is high: the lawyer who accompanies the dispute entrusted to him as a mediator is liable as a lawyer but loses his attorney's credentials and can no longer bill as a lawyer. Especially in family law, the top application area of mediation, a new form of out-of-court settlement and mediation has therefore become established: negotiation and settlement with two lawyers trained in mediation, known as cooperative mediation.

In contrast to classical mediation

- no one in the process actually holds the mediator role,
- both parties are represented by lawyers and
- the lawyers are trained mediators who may even have been additionally trained as so-called conflict coaches (i.e. coaches who are only allowed to accompany in conflict situations)

Conversely, this also means that the mediators involved must be lawyers – a prerequisite that does not necessarily exist in classical mediation and therefore sometimes leads to intolerable results from a legal point of view, because legal laypersons bring about legal effects that they do not grasp[23].

---

20 For an overview, visitwww.zertifizierter-Mediator.de.

21 Matthias Irle, "Miteinander statt gegeneinander" in brandeins thema 05/2020.

22 Which was only introduced in 2012.

23 *Dr. Tutschka*, "Verhandlungsführung 4.0" in Soldan Insight Jan. 29, 2019.

But when exactly does pure legal advice, legal coaching or mediation make sense for the client?

Let me illustrate this with a simple example: If we consider the client to be a "traveler" who wants to get from A to B, then at the time when he decides to seek help, he finds himself in an unpleasant, usually from his point of view hopeless, often frightening situation. He does not know how to proceed alone, because he is at a fork in the road, because he has lost his way or because he is lost.

What does he need to move forward?

An overview board, a sign or directions? Great, then information from a book, newspaper articles, a consumer site or the Internet will suffice for him.

If he wants to ask an expert for directions and have them explained to him, legal advice is his choice[24].

If he wants this expert to accompany him along the way, to point out the advantages and disadvantages of each route to him at crossroads so that he can make better decisions, and even to stand by him in the event of danger or an attack, hiring a lawyer to handle the case is ideal.

If, however, he wants someone to take him by the hand, pick him up emotionally and sort him out so that he can think clearly for himself again, perhaps even help him with his luggage, take care of sufficient provisions and structure and facilitate his journey – and still know the right way – then Legal Coaching is his product, chauffeuring him to his destination as if he was in a carriage (= coach).

If, on the other hand, he or she is already in the midst of a dispute, a mediator can lay down rules and have a calming and mediating effect.

"Legal advice is becoming more and more complicated, and at the same time digitalization has simplified a lot of things – it just hasn't become more human. That's why we think this innovative approach to legal coaching is great and are pleased that the focus is finally being placed on the lawyer as a human being."

Anna Murk for Legal Layman[25]

---

24 In the North American and Canadian legal system, legal advice is very expensive and not affordable for many legal seekers. Legal Coaching therefore offers a way for legal professionals, as an alternative to legal advice, to enable legal seekers to navigate their own way through the process – adding to the pure legal information, litigation, tactics, any sources of stumbling blocks and the development of the client's strategy, all at a much lower cost than legal representation. With "The Legal Coaches Association" the first legal coaches in Canada have joined forces for this kind of legal assistance (Jo-Anne Stark, Mastering the Art of Legal Coaching, p. 13).

25 Anna Murk, "Der Mensch als Mittelpunkt einer juristischen Weiterbildung? Das gibts tatsächlich!" in Legal Layman 03/2021, a modern legal journal for non-lawyers.

Find out where and how legal coaches work around the world in CLP-Academy's interview series on "legal coaching".

Pure legal advice? That hasn't been happening for a long time. Today, lawyers are expected to be everything: strategists, managers, communication experts, super stars, actors, leaders, doers, psychologists and a good friend – and somehow even good lawyers. Isn't it about time to learn and practice the "craft", the HOW of legal advice in a professional and well-founded way?

The trend toward automation, standardization, and optimization is gaining momentum. However, professional relationship building and understanding cannot be technically optimized, nor can it be mapped by algorithms and legal tech. The personality of the lawyer, the human factor, will increasingly become the key function, as these two "special products" of legal advice show[26].

It's a people business[27] – applies more than ever before.

Trainings in comparison

What opportunities do I have to further my education as a fully licensed lawyer?

Even as a fully trained lawyer or attorney with professional experience, you should regularly invest in continuing your education: After all, your education (and degree certificate) is your most valuable asset, but it can quickly lose value if you don't deepen, update, or at least regularly refresh it.

In this context, the terms advanced training and continuing education are often used informally as synonyms for all kinds of lectures, discussion rounds, seminars, workshops, trainings and additional education. The providers are also diverse: in addition to academic providers such as the Distance Learning University of Hagen or the International University of Applied Sciences IU or the University and Business School St. Gallen (Switzerland), professional associations such as the **German Lawyers' Association (DAV)** and **lawyers' academies (DAA, AWAK)**, but also WoltersKluwer, Haufe, Beck and numerous individual institutes offer continuing education for lawyers. On central online platforms, such as at Fernstudiencheck.de, LTO or 1aAnwaltsseminare, the various continuing education courses are summarized, so that one can easily obtain an overview (albeit not a complete one) via the search engine.

26 Dr. Tutschka in "Der Anwalt als Konflikt- und Krisenmanager", in the CLP-Blog from dec. 3, 2017.
27 Gerber, p. 75 et seq.. "The E-Myth Attorney".

In the meantime, continuing legal education has reached the virtual world as well. It is important to distinguish between **synchronous** (live webinars with interaction) and **asynchronous online events** (exclusively with recorded instructional videos without interaction – so-called distance learning). Not insignificant in the context of further education at a university are the ECTS points awarded in each case, so-called European Credit Transfer System points, the European system for the transfer and accumulation of study achievements. One ECTS point stands for 25 real hours á 60 minutes of actual work for the student. The workload of an academic year for a full-time student is measured with 60 ECTS points.

What is the difference between subject seminars and other seminars?
In addition to subject-specific seminars on purely legal topics (the latest court decisions, changes in the law, special and peripheral topics), a growing number of other continuing education courses are also being offered specifically for lawyers. These include either **business and management topics** such as accounting, law firm software training and office organization or so-called **soft skills** such as voice and rhetoric, leadership skills or presentation techniques.

How is continuing or advanced education different from post graduate education?
After the general legal training, it is usually necessary to specialize and distinguish oneself from the colleagues for the client.

Similar to a medical specialist, a **specialized lawyer** can demonstrate in-depth knowledge as well as a high level of practical experience in their field and prove this with their specialist lawyer certificate. The numerous specialist attorney fields (approx. 25 in Germany) range from family law to traffic law and criminal law to tax law and can be acquired in different fields simultaneously. In the meantime, every third German legal professional can present at least one specialized attorney title[28]. In Aus-

28 and the number of specialist lawyers has increased from 11,080 (2000) to 57,065 (2020). In general, a maximum of two specialist attorney titles can be awarded: The awarding of the authority to use a third specialist attorney title is excluded by law (§ 43c I 3 BRAO) even if all requirements for awarding the title are met. § 43c I 3 BRAO, by limiting the authority to use a specialist attorney title to two fields of law, is a professional practice regulation that does not violate the fundamental right of freedom of profession, but is supported by reasonable considerations of the common good. AnwGH Celle, decision from 11.2. 2004 – AGH 24/03 (not legally binding) (reference: NJW 2004, 1113 et seq.). However, although the number of specialist attorney titles continues to rise, there is an increasing lack of young lawyers, especially in the oldest specialties, so that the numbers will decline in the medium term. In particular, the collection of legal cases and court proceedings is becoming increasingly difficult for the aspiring lawyers, since 1. court proceedings are steadily losing importance, 2. this regulation does not take into account the compatibility of work and family, and 3. it is

tria, there is no specialized attorney training. In contrast to non-specialized attorneys, specialized attorneys are obliged to regularly attend further training courses in their field of expertise or to update their specialized attorney title. The same applies to training as a mediator, conflict coach or legal coach. However, lawyers in Germany can also list so-called areas of practice ((having worked in this area for at least three years) or self-selected areas of specialization independently of specialist lawyer designations, but these areas are not then examined by an independent body[29].

Additional academic degrees such as the doctorate, i.e. the **PhD** (at the university), or the Master of Law (**LL.M.**) as a master's degree program also demonstrate in-depth (theoretical) knowledge in a specialized field with a certain scientific claim. Both degrees can also be obtained abroad by German or Austrian lawyers. As a rule, the title holders also achieve above-average exam results in general legal education. The titles are prefixed or suffixed to the name for a lifetime (in Austria, these are gender specific, e.g. Dr.in or Dr.a).

The most important differences to general and specialized further education are:
- The courses comprise at least 100 hours
- Training courses usually require interaction
- They conclude with an examination and a training certificate
- They cost several thousand euros
- They are regulated by law and controlled by a state body (exception: coaching)

Coaching is not regulated by law (neither nationally nor EU-wide nor internationally), but has been strictly monitored and regulated for decades by the professional associations for coaches with regard to training, quality, certification, and ethics. For more information, please refer to the Professional Code of Conduct, the Doctoral Code, and the Mediation Act as well as, for coaching, the Core Competencies and Ethics Guidelines of the International Coaching Federation (ICF).

Whether additional practical knowledge is required, the training can only be completed by (full) lawyers or they have to be renewed varies.

---

particularly difficult for lawyers in rural areas to collect such specialized cases, since the regulations for specialist lawyers are oriented to the conditions of the 1990s..

29 However, care must be taken here to avoid violating the advertising restrictions: The use of the designation "specialist for traffic law" may be used in practice brochures, Internet addresses and similar information media, but not on the letterhead, law firm sign or in advertisements. AnwGH Lower Saxony, decision from 27.10.2003 – AGH 4/03 (reference: NJW 2004, 1536 et seq.). The description "specialized in traffic law" or "expert in traffic law" without being a specialist lawyer is different. In addition, certified specializations such as "victim advocate of the White Ring", which the victim protection organization introduced only in 2021, are emerging alongside the certificate trainings for legal coach or mediator.

How do the courses to become a specialized lawyer differ from those to become a mediator, conflict coach, and legal coach?
While the training as a specialist lawyer conveys purely legal expertise, the training in mediation and coaching does not deal with legal topics, but primarily with topics from psychology and communication science (and can therefore usually also be completed by non-lawyers). In addition to teaching negotiation and negotiation techniques (negotiation and arbitration), these courses focus on the personality of the trainee in order to achieve reflection, personal maturity and self-management. The same applies to the training in supervision and mentoring.

In summary, this means:
- A specialized lawyer is always also a (general) lawyer.
- A mediator or coach does not have to have any academic or professional training and certainly no legal training – but usually has an academic education (often in psychology, communication, or social sciences).
- The exception is the legal coach: In this case, the same applies as with the specialized lawyer – a legal coach is always also a (full) lawyer.

What do the specialist lawyer title and the mediator or coach title have in common?
The courses usually comprise at least 100 hours (courses for specialist lawyers and mediation as much as 120 hours by law) and conclude with an examination and a training certificate, which also certifies practical experience.

The costs are staggered as follows:
- Specialist lawyer: from € 2,500
- Conflict coach: from € 3,200
- Legal coach/conflict coach: from € 6,500
- Mediator: from € 6,500

But which further training is actually beneficial for you as a lawyer?
According to the current evaluations of the Soldan Institute, an additional qualification such as the specialist lawyer title is beneficial for most lawyers:
- Specialist lawyers have higher hourly rates and annual revenues
- They feel they are "well versed" in their field and are more successful
- Clients today look for the specialist, i.e. the specialist lawyer

However, other factors such as the field of law, the location of the law firm, and even the number of professionals have a much greater impact on hourly rates and turnover. This still leaves points 2 and 3.

The hourly rate of a specialist lawyer is usually €150–300/hour; a legal mediator, conflict coach, or legal coach can charge this rate as well. Specialist lawyers are usually sought out BECAUSE of their specialization, while mediators are usually sought out by clients not because of mediation, but for other reasons. There are no surveys on legal coaches yet[30].

However, it must be considered that a mediator and conflict coach give up their partiality as a lawyer and thus their mandate relationship. They may no longer act as a lawyer in this matter or in subsequent matters and may only bill as a mediator/conflict coach. This is different for the specialist lawyer or legal coach, who can use his special knowledge in the client relationship and remains an attorney.

Realistically, it must also be said that the vast majority of legal mediators do not actually conduct any mediations in practice, as there is simply not much demand for them. The situation is different, however, when it comes to the practical application of specialist lawyer and coaching training courses, as these are always used on a selective basis.

Either way, all of these training courses are considered to be viable for the future:

Although the "business model" of specialist lawyer training is booming and almost 25 specializations have been created in the space of a few years, by no means have all areas of law been covered, such as climate law, data protection law, or the law of companies[31]. The mediation arguably has left its hype behind and disillusionment is setting in, especially in the legal profession. Mediation is of interest to only about 5 % of all professionals (2/3 of them are women!) and those trained in mediation use mediation in only about 5 % of their proceedings, which means that mediation accounts for only about 2.5 % of the law firm's revenues, although it is predominantly, to 58 %, billed on the basis of an hourly fee and not on the basis of a fixed price[32]. Nevertheless, alternative and sustainable dispute resolutions are still attractive and meet the latest trends.

Coaching is described as THE personnel development measure of the future and is represented as nearly inflationary with its universal applicability in economics and further training. Certainly, the market needs to be cleared of "wannabe coaches", but well-trained and highly qualified coaches are already pulling important strings in business and society, for example in the executive area, and can keep up with top lawyers in terms of salary.

---

30 Nicole Genitheim, STAR-Report 2018 in BRAK-Mitteilungen 5/2018, p. 221 et seq.

31 Sports law, included in the previous edition, was introduced as the 24th specialist lawyer in 2020.

32 Nicole Genitheim, STAR-Report 2018 in BRAK-Mitteilungen 5/2018, p. 222.

These are the three questions you should ask yourself before you decide to pursue education or training:

1. Does the training fit my personality, my client base, my business model?
2. Do I have a concrete goal for my personality/ career/ law firm and do I invest purposefully and regularly into the appropriate training and further education for me/my employees?
3. Do I regularly provide a sufficient and realistic training budget in terms of money and time?

... and now it's up to you to decide: Which continuing education is the right one for me?

"He who thinks he is something has ceased to become something." (Socrates)
"Learning is like rowing against the current; if you stop, you drift backwards." (Lao Tzu)
"Education is not the filling of barrels, but the kindling of flames." (Heraclitus)

What did you get out of this chapter?

You can understand "legal advice" as a special service with different facets, which is defined by law. You have understood that, depending on the client's situation, the needs of the client, and the skills of the lawyer, different formats such as legal coaching or mediation can be used.

IV. Pricing and added value

Why should you read this chapter?
You will learn at what price "legal advice" is purchased today.

Overview

1. **Added value**
2. **Regulated pricing**
3. **Fixed and flat rate**
4. **Conclusion**

The lawyer's fee, or more precisely its amount, is a sensitive issue. Many clients have only a very vague idea of the expected amount of the fee for legal services. Clients with legal protection insurance believe that they do not have to worry about the amount of the fee at all. Lawyers, too, approach the subject of fees with a strange shyness. In many cases, the matter of fees is ignored in the initial discussion with the client, and the client is not informed of the exact amount of the fee to be charged until it is too late.

One of the reasons for this surprising behavior of lawyers may be the fear of not receiving a mandate if the fee appears too high from the outset. In fact, the expectation of potential clients is "Now it's going to be expensive". However, if these potential clients are in their first meeting with you, they have consciously decided to invest a significant sum in professional legal advice because the matter is worth it to them. From a psychological point of view, therefore, the lawyer's reluctance and fear of scaring off the potential client is his own fear of receiving surprisingly high bills! The lawyer projects his own fear onto the client without asking him about his needs and responding to them.

Tip:
Try asking the client about their needs when it comes to transparency and payment of remuneration: How much clarification and payment options do they want? Is there a budget or an absolute upper limit? Is there tax leeway or special considerations on his side that need to be taken into account? What does success in this legal dispute or its settlement mean to him and what is it worth to him? Would anything else be important for the client and what would additional service be worth to him?

Concealing the expected cost of the legal service is not a solution. Sooner or later, the client will receive a fee invoice. If he is unpleasantly surprised by this fee calculation, then the anger is pre-programmed. And this completes the circle: the fear of a surprisingly high bill has come true like a self-fulfilling prophecy.

Remember:
Investments and payment flows must be planned and organized. Every unexpected bill is therefore a bill that is too high!

On the other hand, some lawyers do not discuss the fee issue with their clients because these lawyers themselves are not aware of what their service actually costs. An alarming number of lawyers give little thought to how the price of their service is to be determined, how high the costs of the mandate are, and what their own cost-covering hourly rate must be. The secretary's office or the accounting department writes the invoice or the partial invoice or asks for an advance whenever the lawyer initiates this within the office. There is a not-inconsiderable scope for design here. It is important to exploit this leeway on a mandate and client basis, taking into account the complexity of the mandate, the lawyer's own expertise, and reputation.

Remember:
When, what, and how to price is an essential part of the mandate and CHIEF RESPONSIBILITY. Pricing is one of the main parts of your preparatory work, along with the strategic preparation of the mandate.

Tip:
Once the client has submitted the client details – which only means that you have gained a rough insight into the subject matter – it is followed by the matching with
- your expertise (standard/special)
- your resources (time and workload)
- your mandate structure (A-client?)

The result of this matching is the basis of your pricing
The pricing is composed of the following parameters:
- Strategic concept proposal
- estimated time
- estimated costs (law firm services, your out-of-pocket expenses; not outside costs such as court costs)
- If applicable, mark up: special business, B-client/new customer, one-time mandate (single shoot)
- If applicable, markdown: standard business, A-client, follow-up business
- Expected adjustment of statutory fees (RVG)
- Value added tax (gross or net-due to Reverse Charge or small business regulation)

I recommend to give a short feedback to the client NOW with the aim to keep or reject the mandate. The feedback should include the proposal for the strategic concept combined with a cost estimate.

This proposal should always be discussed with the client. Once an agreement on the concept and cost estimate has been reached, the next step should be to communicate clearly regarding the payment modalities:

- Is there a legal protection insurance and does it cover the complete service?
- Is the settlement with the RSV to be carried out by the lawyer and if so – free of charge?
- Payment on account/ advance/ installment payment, separately related to expenses and remuneration
- Probability of recourse to the other party for the costs
- Invoice details (addressee, UID) and payment options
- Time horizon

Remember:
The cost estimate may be accompanied by a remuneration agreement, which is agreed upon when the order is placed.

---

1. Added Value

Added value is the goal of productive activity and transforms existing goods into goods with higher monetary value by creating goods with higher market value through the activities of the company and its employees and the invested costs[1].

1 B. A. Rutherford: Value Added as a Focus of Attention for Financial Reporting: Some Conceptual Problems. In: Accounting and Business Research. 7, 1977, p. 215.

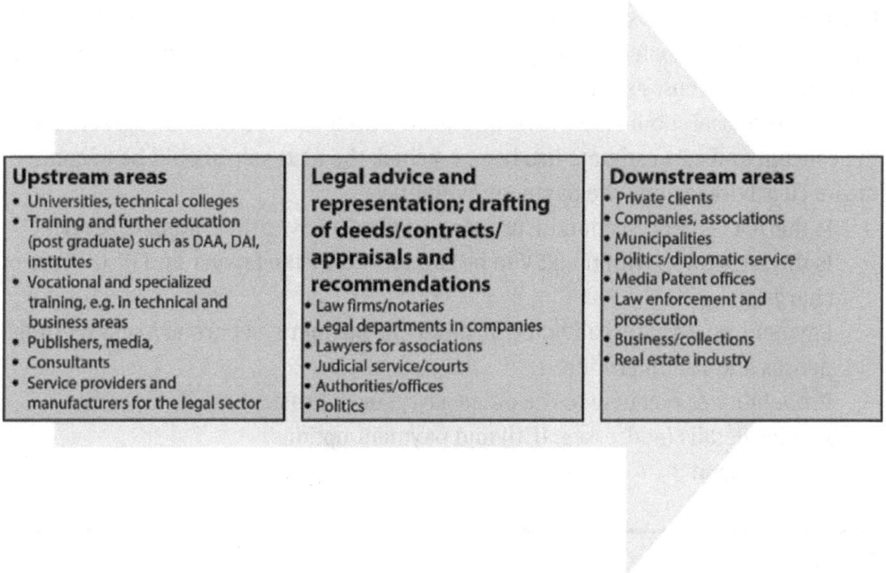

Value chain of the "legal advice" sector, © Dr. Geertje Tutschka

In short, added value is the amount by which output exceeds input[2].

The goal of economic activity should be to achieve the highest possible operational added value (profit). If the value of the input exceeds the output on a permanent basis, i.e. a negative added value (reactive power) is created, this poses a serious threat to the company's substance. However, due to the diverse use of the term in various economic fields in economic theory, it is to be applied primarily to the manufacturing industry and in principle does not apply to consulting services.

So how does one measure the "value" of legal services? By success, time invested, competence? To make it clear at the outset: From a business perspective, there is no objectively correct price for legal services.

Essentially, there are three methods for an attorney to determine how much to charge for their services.

One method is to conduct a **market comparison**. What price do other lawyers charge for their services? What price can be achieved on the market? The method of market comparison is problematic for lawyers because the required comparative data is hardly ever published. Colleagues will just tell a lawyer whether they usually charge according to the table rates specified by the legislator or according to their

2 According to the formula: Added value = total output – advance inputs.

time spent. A lawyer will only learn about details such as whether (higher) subject matter values are agreed with clients in order to take into account increased expenses, or what the exact hourly rates of a law firm are, on a case-by-case basis, and will also be able to fall back on the current average hourly rates regularly published by the Soldan Institute, without being able to go into his legal field, location, etc.

A second method of pricing is to base the amount of the attorney's fee on the **value of the service to the client**. A direct linking of the lawyer's fee to the result of the lawyer's service, a true contingency fee, is – still – prohibited by law, § 49b para. 2 p. 1 BRAO but will be largely possible with the major BRAO reform from mid-2022. Some may regret this. Clients often declare that they prefer a performance-based fee calculation. However, especially from the perspective of good lawyers, there are reservations about contingency fees. The legal service is an interactive service, which is provided in cooperation with the client. The client always has an influence on the success of his case through his own behavior. The lawyer stands in the second row, can prepare, advise and execute. The decision-making power, however, remains with the client. If lawyers were to agree on a purely contingency fee, they would be financially dependent not only on their own performance, but also on the skill and wisdom of their client. This is not an attractive prospect for lawyers in all cases. One solution to this problem may be to agree on an adequate basic fee with an additional success fee. Either way, it will be interesting to see how the new regulation will be received by the market, after having been anticipated for so long, and how case law will react to it. One thing is certain: the major BRAO reform has significantly increased the scope for design; however, this does not have to be used.

A third method calculates the price of the lawyer's service based on the **cost to a lawyer of providing the service**. The central question in this method is, "What is the cost of a lawyer's hour?" This question cannot be answered universally. This is because the cost structures of law firms vary widely.

In order to calculate the cost of a lawyer's hour, it is best to determine the fixed costs of a law firm for the period of one year. The fixed costs include the office rent, the associated advance payments for utilities, costs of office cleaning, premiums for insurance. The anticipated variable costs are to be added. Variable costs include items such as telephone charges, postage, the cost of office supplies, repairs to office equipment, a library budget (books and journals; refills), representation expenses, dues to professional associations, a marketing budget, and, this is usually the largest block of costs, making up almost fifty percent in law firms, the expense of staff salaries. A lawyer must first generate the sum of these costs in a year in order not to bring money with them, that is, to pay something for the pleasure of working in a law firm.

Since a lawyer also wants to earn something, the income that they would earn as an employee (fictitious or desired annual gross salary) must be added to the costs.

In addition, the self-employed lawyer must earn an appropriate return on the capital he has invested. If a self-employed lawyer earns the amount determined in this way within a year, then economically he is roughly in the same position as if he were working as an employee. He has not yet made any real profit.

To determine the price of a **lawyer's hour**, the sum of costs, return on investment, and desired salary must be divided by the number of billable hours to be performed by an attorney in a year. Care must be taken in determining this number of hours. If a lawyer takes a month-long vacation in a year and it is assumed that a month has an average of twenty working days, then a lawyer has 220 working days per year (11 months × 20 days). Since these 220 working days also include participation in training events and a few days of absence due to the flu (or Covid_19 quarantine), 220 working days per year will only be achieved if one or two public holidays or Saturdays are also used as working days.

It is a well-known fact that lawyers have a rather high amount of daily working time and, in particular, an excessively long "in-office time". However, the number of hours a lawyer spends in the office per day should not be equated with the number of billable hours. If one assumes that a lawyer spends an average of ten hours per working day in the office, this would result in 220 days × 10 hours = 2,200 hours per year.

However, a lawyer spends a considerable amount of their office time on client acquisition, checking deadlines, writing invoices, checking mail and e-mails, office management, administrative tasks, compulsory reading of legal journals and specialist magazines, or simply chatting with colleagues and staff. This time cannot be charged to the client. This time is not billable performance time. According to very optimistic assumptions, ten office hours should correspond to eight billable service hours. at least six billable hours per day may be expected from a lawyer. The number of billable hours per year in this case is 6 hours × 220 days[3] = 1,320 hours. Generally, one must assume that the hourly rate increases proportionally to the administrative effort – which for the time being only speaks for stability in income, but not for an increase in income over the years.

Warning to all lawyers: Now it's time to do the math.

So, what does a lawyer "earn"?

(The calculation example is based on a solo lawyer whose law firm does not have its own legal form.)

If the costs attributable to the lawyer amount to €10,000.00 per month (these consist for example of the running costs for office, IT and service providers such as

3 In the business world, 200 performance days per year are generally assumed.

cleaners and marketing agency as well as the personnel costs for non-lawyers or secretarial staff in addition to their personal costs such as social security contributions, registration and insurance costs) and thus € 120,000.00 per year, and if the lawyer wants to earn € 4,000.00[4], per month (at the beginning), thus € 48,000.00 annually, then he must earn a turnover of € 168,000.00, which means € 14,000 monthly. At this point it should be mentioned that the Statistical Reporting System for Lawyers (STAR) in its current report determined an average annual profit for the male colleague of € 104,000 with a turnover of € 195,000 and for the female colleague of € 65,000 with a turnover of € 142,000. Broken down by East and West, it is noticeable that in West Germany lawyers earn € 209,000 compared to € 152,000 of East German lawyers and West German female lawyers earn € 155,000 compared to € 121,000 of East German female colleagues. The STAR report also notes that, in addition to the firm's form and location, age and qualification through a specialist lawyer title have an impact (with a specialist lawyer title, € 207,000 is achievable instead of € 181,000; in a partnership, € 242,000 is achievable instead of € 158,000). At this point, one could state that female colleagues tend to be more economical and produce lower costs; however, the sad certainty is that decades after reunification, there is still a West-East divide and clear discrimination and unequal treatment of female lawyers. In this respect, the male West German colleague earns about 1.7 times, almost double, for the same work as his East German female colleague[5].

Remember:
the following numerical ratios can be assumed:
- The ratio of lawyer: ReFa is both personnel and financial up to the lawyer's income of € 5,000/ month 4 : 1 i.e. the ReFa costs approx. 0.25 % of the turnover.
- Under these circumstances, this calculation also applies to the lawyer: young lawyer ratio, but the salaried lawyer increases turnover; the ReFa reduces costs for mandates that can be standardized (but digitalization can usually do this better)
- Under these circumstances, sales are usually distributed as follows: 50 % owner, 25 % personnel, 25 % material costs (more on personnel costs in the next chapters)

So we see that our example cannot be about a female lawyer in any case, but rather about a male colleague in a single law firm without a specialist lawyer title and standardizable business in rural West German regions with a conservative staff ratio of

4 Note that this amount is not yet tax-adjusted and thus does not really end up as a "net" amount in the bank account – so it also only roughly competes with the gross annual salary of about € 100,000, the starting salary in large law firms.
5 BRAK's STAR Report 2020.

1:1.5 (i. e. e. g. one full-time ReFa and one part-time female lawyer, plus trainees if necessary), which causes him these relatively high costs. This means that he must earn an average fee per hour of at least (€ 168,000.00: 1,320 service hours) € 127.27 (excluding VAT) in order to achieve his goal. Therefore, from his turnover of € 168,000, he first pays his general bills, which are ideally tax-reducing, leaving him € 48,000 as profit. This amount he has to pay tax on, so that he has a monthly taxable income of € 4,000, i. e. a net income between € 2,000–3,000 per month. If the average is lower, then he earns correspondingly less. If the turnover per hour falls below € 90.91, then not even the costs of the law firm are covered. The lawyer not only earns nothing, he has to add money, he pays for the privilege of being a lawyer. In a modern, digitalized law firm with a staff ratio of 1:0.5, this turnover would mean that the founder of the law firm would pay 25 % in material costs and 25 % in personnel costs and would therefore go home with € 7,000 per month (i. e. approx. € 5,000). Not bad: that is almost double.

For our example lawyer, this means that he has to reduce his monthly costs from € 10,000 to € 8,400!

Tip: (for all number crunchers)

1. Also left out of the equation was the extent to which personnel, who usually account for a significant share of costs, also generate revenue themselves, although the rule of thumb is certainly that lawyers generate more than non-lawyers, and
2. what the monthly costs of € 10,000 are made up of, because different items have different tax implications, because, for example, social security contributions are not really deductible as office costs, and
3. whether additional assets/values have been created for the firm (legal tech solutions/patents, books/online seminars, possibly large mandates/long-term clients)

However, the determination of the average hourly turnover that a lawyer should achieve does not necessarily mean that they can only work profitably if they continuously agree on time fees. Corresponding turnover averages can also be achieved according to other fee models.

If we apply this example to a law firm founder, it is difficult to imagine that they can generate an average monthly turnover of € 14,000 right from the start. At least € 5,000 per month for the first 6–12 months seems very courageous. Then the share of costs should not be more than € 1.500–2000 per month (no staff, no office, no credit) to be able to live at least from € 3.000 per month (after adjustment).

What stands out in this calculation example?

Although the lawyer here apparently operates on the market with an average hourly rate (see above), he has to work 50 hours a week to earn € 2,500 (net) per month (not including Christmas and vacation bonuses)[6]. Illness-related absence, possible investments, e.g. in digitalization and further training, or simply the loss of long-standing employees and acquisitions are not included in this calculation and are usually added on top. Also not included is a possible redemption amount to his law firm predecessor or a significant repayment of a loan that may have been taken out when the law firm was founded. In addition, in this calculation, a maximum of 2 hours per day should be spent on day-to-day office management, and administrative tasks, such as personnel management, staff interviews, job interviews, contract management, account management and bookkeeping control, reacting to and repairing day-to-day office problems, partner meetings and strategic decisions, marketing, website, events, etc.. Another 2 hours on mandate work that is not billable because the mandate did not materialize, it is an existing client or the claim is not feasible.

Either way: even this time of 2 × 2 hours is more than scarce for all these tasks. And: After these 10 intensive hours a day, the lawyer comes home and has not taken care of their private things or personal needs until then.

What else stands out?

The young female law firm founder, who starts with just under a third of the turnover, does everything herself and has only 1/10 to 1/5 of the costs, but is likely to have significantly more idle time/leisure time, goes home with the same amount of money at the end. She has managed well if she has sold at least 12 attorney hours for about € 120 per week and with the remaining work comes to a maximum of 30 hours per week, whereby the secretarial work should only comprise 6 hours and the work on the law firm (e.g. for marketing and acquisition, because personnel work does not occur) should comprise at least 12 hours. If, on the other hand, she orients herself generously from the beginning on the cost structure of the experienced male colleague and also produces a third of his costs with approx. € 3,000 per month, she will probably have to stay in her nursery with her parents forever with € 1,000–2000 net monthly income. Only in this reduction our customers in the consulting practice notice, how unprofitable they actually work in their self-built hamster wheel. A look at the statistics underpins this: the average weekly working time in the legal profession in 2018 was 42.3 hours. Approximately 1/3 work more than 50 hours (here, men are disproportionately affected) and approximately 1/3 work less, i.e. part-time (here, women are disproportionately represented). In terms of annual leave, the

6 This may increase somewhat as sole alimony for a young family with a baby and toddler; nevertheless, in modest living conditions with a narrow annual vacation in some regions of Germany such as Munich, this is unlikely to be feasible.

self-employed fare the worst with 19.5 days, compared to 22 days for salaried attorneys and 26.8 days for syndicates[7].

Sounds like a back-breaking job? It is!

The fatal thing is that with this business model and this cost structure, the lawyer themself is their best horse in the stable. If this income is really only to be the initial income, there are three adjusting screws:

1. Increase their hourly rate to maximum market acceptance (approx. € 250/hour.)[8] through additional qualifications, which, however, the customer base usually only accepts in small homeopathic doses.
2. Increasing its stroke rate, i.e., increasing efficiency through smart processes, automation, standardization,
3. Cost reduction (e.g., reducing the ratio of lawyer to ReFa from 1:1.2 to 1:0.4 through digitization).

What does the practice look like?
to the 1st, the lawyer is reluctant to burden the relationship of trust with their client with a regular increase in their hourly rates or their clients (their market) do not allow for higher hourly rates.

to the 2nd. The increase in the number of strokes is usually achieved by a higher, often unhealthy and error-prone work tempo

To the 3rd, the cost reduction in ReFas is done through exploitation (more hours worked for less pay).

Is there an alternative?
What happens when you reduce your 50-hour week and bring in a colleague?
This is always a good idea if the colleague is at least equally strong in their client base and efficiency

- as a partner, because then, as a rule, the turnover doubles, but not the cost structure, which is now shared by two partners
- as an employee, because then the turnover is usually doubled, but the colleague earns less with their employee salary than is charged to the client.

7 Nicole Genitheim, STAR-Report 2018, BRAK-Mitteilung 5/2018.

8 No wonder that especially for female colleagues in family time who are faced with the choice: Founding a law firm (approx. € 120/hr.) vs. working as an associate in a global law factory (approx. € 250/hour) the choice falls on the latter, because either the working time can be reduced clearly to a half-day job for this money of scarcely € 2,000 net or they can contribute a relevant contribution to the family maintenance with € 4,000 net for 30 hours (with so-called home work mind you).

This basic principle of "economic success through growth" is therefore based on efficiency and exploitation. As a law firm owner, you have to understand this:

If the above example is cemented as a permanent state – as is the case in practice for many small law firms – this is the least economical model. Large law firms and their distribution systems have so far functioned according to this basic principle.

So, could this mean that the much-discussed work overload in large law firms is not so bad in comparison, or at least comparable? And do female lawyers perhaps earn more equally there, because it is not at all apparent to the client on the invoice from the large law firm whether a woman or a man performed the work? A look at the statistics helps here: Employed lawyers start with an annual salary of approx. € 100,000 gross in Germany (and € 122,000 in Austria) – so to compare with the courageous young lawyer who starts his own business in Germany, one would have to compare the net annual income with approx. € 50,000. Female lawyers start with (surprise: less!) € 98,000 and increase (surprise: increase by less!) to € 114,000 (so after 8 years they are about where their colleague is already after 4 years). Loss or reduction due to family breaks are of course not included. Nevertheless, this would obviously be the financially more favorable option for female lawyers, because on the one hand, family breaks are not easy even in self-employment, and on the other hand, this salary can hardly compensate for the toxic-masculine atmosphere in some large law firms. For example, it took almost 300 years for Freshfields Bruckhaus Deringer (founded in London in 1743) to appoint a woman to the top management position for the first time in 2021. The employee salary increases to about € 124,000 in Germany by the 8th year of employment; the partner salary increases to up to € 700,000 after about 10 years (with almost 10 times the cost and a higher tax rate in Austria). More about the remuneration systems in the next chapter[9].

What does this mean for our three case studies?

1. The "growing pains" of the law firm with its many autonomous small teams are an expression of the excessively high cost structure. From an organizational development point of view, this would-be large law firm is faced with the question of its raison d'être: if these teams do not make the leap into a cost-efficient, sensible overall structure to form a "large team", it will break up because it wears out its team members.
2. The realignment at the firm with the "wrong clients" cannot be postponed: the firm's management is therefore well advised to make the issue a top priority and either decide strategically against these clients or to cushion the realign-

---

9 brand.eins/thema 2021, Die Branche in Zahlen, p. 79.

ment not only with additional specialist staff but with additional resources for personnel, marketing and management.

3. And what should the firm do about the gender and generation shift from a business perspective? To refrain from such investments in the future? In fact, these are clear signs that this "system law firm" has passed its performance peak: From an organizational development perspective, any organization with its business model structures, processes, values and culture have a definite performance or life span if it is not renewed from within. Compensation and incentive systems have reached their maximum efficiency and exploitation and are no longer effective in the current employee market. Either new markets are developed or the "business model" of the compensation and incentive systems is changed.

   Or, in the end, is this not an economic issue at all?

2. Regulated Pricing (RVG)

The BRAGO, which still applied to mandates acquired before July 1, 2004, enjoyed astonishing popularity among many attorneys, which is also the case with today's RVG. The application of these rules is supported by their (apparent) simplicity, their commonality, the fact that legal protection insurers only reimburse lawyers' fees to their clients, the policyholders, in accordance with the tables created by the legislator and, last but not least, the fact that they allow lawyers to avoid fee negotiations with their clients by referring to the fact that lawyers' fees are regulated by law.

Both sets of rules assess the amount of the attorney's fee on the basis of the **value of a matter** in combination with activity fees that accrue depending on the attorney's activity. Both sets of rules provide for increases or decreases depending on the difficulty of a matter and the amount of work a lawyer is required to perform. One of the problems with these sets of rules is that an activity is regularly compensated only once. The second, third and possibly necessary fourth meeting with the opposing party or the second and third court date do not trigger a new fee. From a purely economic point of view, it is financially uninteresting, even harmful, for a lawyer to write a second letter or attend a second meeting in the same matter. The opposite is true in Austria, where every letter can be billed in principle – but here there is also a "contract preparation fee" from the Imperial and Royal period, which should protect against "waste of paper". The agreement of a minimum fee is associated with the risk for clients that minimum fees do not necessarily promote the lawyer's willingness to perform.

It seems strange to an entrepreneur to leave the calculation of the prices at which the entrepreneur offers his services to the legislator of all people. Many lawyers are far less sensitive in this regard. Is it because they do not consider themselves entrepreneurs?

The extent to which the fee calculation according to the fee tables presented by the legislator makes sense from an economic point of view or is possibly ruinous can be determined on the basis of **example cases**.

---

i

To some lawyers who have just set up their own practice, it may seem lucrative to take on the litigation of an average construction point case with an object value of EUR 20,000. Whether and, if so, to what extent such a mandate is actually profitable when billed according to the RVG can be determined by considering the values mentioned. As a reminder: The annual costs of a law firm should amount to EUR 120,000.00. The lawyer wants to achieve a personal income of EUR 48,000.00 per year. He wants to generate the required turnover of EUR 168,000.00 with 1,320 service hours.

Accordingly, he must achieve a turnover of EUR 127.27 per hour.

How much time will the attorney have to spend on the construction point matter and what fee will he be able to charge under the RVG?

The time commitment will consist of:

- Initial meeting with the client
- Review of the documents provided by the client and examination of the legal situation
- Dictation, drafting and revision of the draft for first pleading (statement of claim or statement of defense)
- Reviewing and examining the other party's first written submission and informing the client
- Further pleading for own client (replica or duplicate)
- Answering various inquiries from the client
- Preparation of the first negotiation date
- Attending the appointment (including travel to and from the appointment as well as waiting time in the hallway) and submitting the appointment report to the client
- Review of the evidence decision and preparation for the evidence meeting
- Collection of evidence and information of the client: brief on the assessment of evidence
- Evaluation of the other party's pleading for the purpose of gathering evidence and informing the client
- Review of the judgment and, if necessary, examination of the necessity and the prospects of success of an appeal (do not forget to file an application for correction of the facts within the time limit, § 320 ZPO).
- Cost determination procedure (even if this can largely be handled by non-legal staff)
  If the client does not work in a concentrated manner, it takes longer. Paradoxically, the better the colleague on the opposing party works, the less time is needed for this task. It is far more time-consuming to process a bad brief from the other side than a good one. In the course of the mandate, further consultations with the client, possibly only brief and conducted by telephone, will be necessary. This block of time can take on enormous proportions with unprofessional clients.
- Approx. 20.0 hours in total

According to the RVG, the lawyer can charge a procedural fee according to number 3100 of the table (with a rate of 1.3) and an appointment fee according to number 3104 of the the table (with a rate of 1.2) as well as the lump sum according to number 7002 of the table. This results in a total fee of € 1,635.00. If one divides this fee sum of € 1,635.00 by the time spent of 20 service hours, then one finds that the lawyer did not generate the targeted average hourly revenue of € 127.27, but only an average revenue of € 81.75 per hour with this mandate.

What does this result mean extrapolated? If the lawyer were able to bill all their service hours in a year at a fee of only € 81.75 per hour, then they would have to provide 2,055 service hours per year instead of 1,320 service hours in order to generate the targeted € 168,000.00. This means that the lawyer would have to provide 9.3 service hours per working day instead of 6 service hours per working day. If the lawyer remains at 1,320 service hours per year at an average hourly revenue of € 81.75, then they will have earned € 107,910.00 at the end of the year. Their costs amount to € 120.000,00. They have earned nothing. However, the lawyer must still generate the missing € 12,090.00 in order to at least cover the costs. If they cannot do this, they will sooner or later lose their admission to the bar, § 14 Para. II No. 7 BRAO.

Conclusion: The mandate with the "nice" dispute value of € 20,000.00 was not profitable. Further mandates of this kind will bring the lawyer to the begging pole, if they are not able to equalize these mandates and do not standardize and automate them. The "legal" fee is not the only permitted fee, but rather nothing more than a minimum remuneration.

A lawyer can counter this problem in several ways. First, he can try to drastically reduce his costs. The lower his costs, the lower the average hourly revenue he needs to generate in order to reach his profit target.

Another possibility is to reach an agreement with the client on a higher fee than the one resulting from the law. The agreement of a higher fee than the "legal" fee is permitted. However, in order to be able to propose an appropriate price to the client, the lawyer must calculate how much time he is likely to spend on the matter and how high the costs will be in order to achieve the fee that is necessary from the lawyer's point of view.

One "simple" way of abruptly increasing the lawyer's fee is to conclude a settlement. Clients who have experienced that the lawyer, who was so confident ten minutes earlier, vehemently pushes for the conclusion of a settlement in the conciliation hearing of a labor court case "on the urgent advice of the court" understandably cannot shake off the suspicion that the lawyer's sudden inclination to settle was perhaps also driven by his own interest in fees. Such mistrust is not a good basis for a trusting cooperation between lawyer and client.

3. Fixed and flat rate

From the client's point of view, fixed and lump-sum prices are a desirable proposition. The client knows from the outset what to expect[10]. They also make it easier to compare the prices offered by different law firms.

10 This is, for example, the business model of "Scheidungsmanager.ch" or "www.LegalBase.de".

This pricing is also interesting from the lawyer's point of view. The predictability of the expected fee is also convenient for him. However, the lawyer must go to the trouble of calculating beforehand exactly how high his effort in this matter is likely to be, in order not to work at a loss. This is not always easy. The need for explanation on the part of the corporate client with legal experience is significantly lower than that of the young start-up entrepreneur.

Agreeing on **fixed prices** for larger projects requires some experience on the part of the lawyer with regard to the scope that such projects can take on. From a business perspective, it is essential to include a buffer into the fixed price. If, for example, the lawyer assumes that the time required for a particular task will reach a total of about 50 hours and the turnover he is aiming for per hour is € 200.00, then agreeing on a fixed price of € 10,000.00 is risky for the lawyer. Any increase in expenses, which may be caused by the client or by business partners of the client, will nullify the calculation. The lawyer should include a safety cushion of at least 15 percent (additional) and agree on a fixed price of € 11,500.00 in the exemplary case.

If a lawyer prefers to bill according to the actual time spent or if the time spent is difficult to estimate in advance and the fixed price is nevertheless recommended, a so-called base amount can also be calculated as a fixed price, which is deposited with the currently calculated time spent with the condition that, if this time spent is exceeded, it is renegotiated or each additional hour is to be billed. By the way, renegotiations during an ongoing mandate are not at all unusual, since further details regarding the facts of the case can always arise afterwards, legally binding decisions are made, or the objectives or interests may simply have changed.

A special form of flat rate is the still extremely popular hourly fee. Like most other service providers, the lawyer is a vendor of time and effort. Therefore, billing based on the time spent seems to be the naturally correct billing method for a lawyer. Only if a lawyer can charge the client for every hour of his work in a particular matter he is protected against (his own) errors in the calculation of the time and effort to be expected for handling the matter. Some may use the indication of a particularly high hourly rate to maintain their own image. The possible objection that a time-based fee is unfair because it puts the qualified and fast-working lawyer at a disadvantage can easily be countered by the fact that hourly rates are to be assessed differently and the specialist can charge a much higher hourly rate than the lawyer who is still at the beginning of his career and still has to familiarize himself with the matter. There is a whole series of further objections to the agreement of a time-based fee at hourly rates: Clients fear that they will not be able to check the fee invoice sent to them, because they cannot check whether the amount of time claimed by the lawyer has actually been spent. Lawyers fear that clients, who are usually unable to assess the lawyer's actual workload, will complain that the lawyer is working too slowly. Remedy to a certain extent can be provided by billing as transparently as possible. Every lawyer keeps a time sheet on each day, either in paper form or with the help of an appropriate computer program. In the time sheet, the matter, the lawyer's activity and the time required for this activity are noted. A common practice was to take notes every quarter of an hour, so that every started quarter (or every completed quarter) of an hour is billed. However, in 2020, the Federal Court of Justice buried the 15-minute time-cycle clause, according to which, in the case of a time-based fee, fifteen minutes can be billed for each quarter of an hour or part thereof, in a form-based remuneration agreement (Federal Court of Justice, judgment of February 13, 2020 – IX ZR 140/19, AnwBl Online 2020, 604 as well as a parallel judgment of February 13, 2020 – IX ZR 141/19, see the discussion by Blattner, AnwBl 2020, 344). At least in the consumer mandate, the 15-minute time cycle clause is invalid, according to the BGH. It is true that a flat-rate time-period clause is effective as such. Lawyers do not have to record and charge for their services to the minute or even to the second. However, the Federal Court of Justice left open the question of what time cycle still appears to be acceptable – this applied both to the consumer mandate and, even more so, to mandates in the corporate sector. The Regional Court of Karlsruhe now clarified the situation somewhat in 2021: It considers a 5-minute time cycle to be acceptable in any case (Regional Court of Karlsruhe, judgment of January 19, 2021 – 6 O 213/18, AnwBl Online 2021, 740). In 2019, 6 minutes was still acceptable as 1/10-hour at the LG Freiburg (judgment of July 19, 2019 – 8 O 56/18) and OLG Munich (judgment of June 05, 2019 – 15 U 318/18 Rae; AnwBl Online 2019, 613 with further comment Schons). Blattner recommended the 6-minute time cycle after the BGH decision (AnwBl 2020, 344, 346). If the agreed time cycle is ineffective, the fee agreement remains effective nevertheless, in which case it must be billed to the minute. Even in the case of a time cycle, the recording should be done to the minute. Together with the fee calculation, the client is also sent a separate evaluation of the working time spent on the matter. However, the client's suspicion that the lawyer might have been able to work faster cannot be completely dispelled. Another concern of clients is that too many attorneys are "put on" their case in order to "stall for hours". In practice, something like this may happen. It is also relevant for this point that the legal service is to a particularly high degree a good of trust. The lawyer charging a time fee must earn and maintain this trust by always writing down the time correctly and fairly.

The absolute amount of a fee based on the time spent is difficult to estimate in advance. Larger companies that have a fixed budget for legal advice do not appreciate this, nor do private clients. If billing is to remain based on the time spent, lawyers can offer a cap. The cap is the maximum amount of the fee in a matter that will not be exceeded, regardless of the actual time spent by the lawyers. The offer of a cap requires a careful calculation of the expected time spent.

The amount of the time fee is not directly related to the economic benefit of the legal service for the client. From the client's point of view, this can be just as annoying as from the lawyer's point of view. Even cases of low economic value for the client can involve considerable professional problems that can only be handled with an expenditure of time that no longer bears any reasonable economic relation to the result. The lawyer should discuss with his client whether it would not make more economic sense to drop the matter. If, however, the client wants "the case to go through, no matter the cost", then the lawyer should ask exactly what monetary value the client attaches to the fulfillment of his affair interest. Conversely, there are cases in which an attorney can secure or create considerable economic value for the client with only a few hours of time. In such cases, a fair fee can only be achieved by agreeing on an unusually high hourly rate or by a combination of fee methods.

After all, it takes a certain amount of sales talent to convince a new client of the appropriateness of an hourly rate of €280.00 when the client declares that he has never paid more than €250.00 per hour. The lawyer can convince the client that he will receive a much higher benefit for the higher hourly rate than before. He can also point out that he works faster and that the absolute amount of the fee to be expected will be more favorable for the client despite the higher hourly rate. Especially self-employed professionals, in general, understand that law firms also have to cover their costs and therefore usually accept the argument of a solidly calculated hourly rate, if the service is right.

4. Conclusion

In a market dominated by demand, lawyers cannot always impose the billing mode they want. From the lawyer's point of view, it would also be unwise to stick strictly to a particular billing system. Lawyers must also be flexible in their billing behavior, geared to the needs of their target clientele.

It is very difficult to enforce fees other than those calculated according to the table rates of the RVG towards **clients with legal protection insurance.** Any necessary increases in the fee should be achieved by maintaining the billing method, for example by agreeing on an additional fee. In cases of existential importance for private clients, such as a dispute over termination of employment, the agreement of a time-based fee can be more easily communicated to the client with legal expenses insurance. Of course, the client is entitled to the insurance benefit.

For many colleagues, the mandate covered by legal protection insurance is a lucrative mandate. However, it is usually forgotten that the correspondence from the coverage request to the settlement is not part of the mandate, but an additional service for the client. The lawyer is usually not remunerated for this service, because he is supposedly on the safe side, not having to discuss and negotiate his fee in advance and not having to bear the risk of insolvency. This is a fallacy: as a rule, the legal protection insurance company will cut back on even the statutory minimum fee for business reasons, or at least get involved in lengthy discussions. Most colleagues will have relevant experience in this respect. From a business point of view, legal protection mandates are therefore far less attractive than they might seem.

By agreeing on **capping limits**, maximum amounts of a fee that cannot be precisely estimated in advance can be determined. Such caps are primarily in the interest of the client.

In the case of extensive projects that require intensive familiarization on the part of the lawyer, it can happen time and time again that a company abruptly terminates the project without any major economic benefit for the company having been achieved thus far. In order to take the heat out of the discussions about a lawyer's fee that is allegedly far too high for the client's little benefit – the client usually ignores the fact that it was he himself who aborted the project – a **minimum fee**, a basic amount to which the lawyer is entitled in any case, is agreed from the outset. The agreement of a base amount can be combined with the regulation that the hourly rates will continuously decrease from a certain number of service hours. In such agreements, the lawyer must ensure that his hourly fee does not slip below the cost recovery limit after a certain point in time.

Bait offers seem appealing, especially to younger lawyers, as a way to attract new clients. Initial work is done for a very low fee. For out-of-court work, the RVG allows fees to fall below the table rates. Lawyers do themselves no favors by agreeing to dumping rates. On the one hand, it will be extremely difficult to make it clear to the client after the end of the "bait and switch" phase that the lawyers actually have to charge a significantly higher fee. Second, excessive price competition has never benefited any industry. "Bargain hunters" are not loyal clients. This also applies to clients. Lawyers who value long-term client relationships should offer fair prices, not "cheap" ones.

In this case, exceptions confirm the rule. Colleagues who, for example, conduct large numbers of payment order proceedings for telecommunications companies can reduce their costs so significantly through streamlining effects that the handling of individual payment order proceedings can be offered at a much lower price than by a general law firm. To be fair, however, it must be said that the choice of law firm for the regular handling of payment order proceedings was not made on the basis of the price. After all, any law firm – whether small or large – will hopefully create systems and processes that allow for cost-effective, efficient processing in the face of a constant abundance of recurring standard services[11].

---

11 P. 14 "Effiziente Anwaltsorganisation", TeleLex.

Regular clients can (and should) be granted a **volume discount**. Strangely enough, only a few lawyers know which three clients generate their highest revenues per year, although most law firm software solutions can easily determine this with the appropriate settings. These three clients – depending on the size of the firm, this can also be five, ten or more top clients – are particularly valuable to a law firm and should therefore also receive special appreciation. This special appreciation can be expressed in increased service, for one thing. Secondly, "major clients" regularly expect a financial reward. There is nothing wrong with this. Lawyers just have to be careful not to become economically dependent on a few large clients.

In the case of larger mandates of high economic importance, especially in corporate transactions, fees are sometimes renegotiated. If the case is successful, the request for renegotiation comes from the lawyers. Once the matter has been concluded, the lawyer is entitled to a financial share in the success of his work. Legally, there is no claim to the success-dependent subsequent increase of the lawyer's fee. Nevertheless, there are unwritten customs in this area of legal services. Gentlemen's agreements sometimes bind more closely than notarized contracts.

Finally, a word on the payment modalities: The claim for remuneration, like any other claim, is due immediately in case of doubt, but this is hardly ever implemented in practice. At the very least, the lawyer should assert his legal claim to an appropriate advance payment[12]. In the case of a fee agreement on a fixed price or a time-based fee, an appropriate **advance payment provision** should be included in the agreement. With young lawyers a strange billing shyness is noticeable again and again. The sooner a lawyer gets used to not only doing his professional work well and quickly, but also billing promptly, the better. Most clients expect to receive a bill for their lawyer's services. However, they are annoyed when this invoice arrives "unexpectedly", for example, more than half a year after the matter has been concluded. If time-based fees have been agreed, lawyers usually bill their services on a monthly basis. Quarterly billing of time fees is also not uncommon. Those who work for larger companies must become accustomed to the fact that the company's internal audits and accounting processes can take up to three or four weeks before the lawyer's fee is paid. However, it should not take much longer. If it does, the lawyer must discuss the matter with his client.

Longer billing periods are risky for the lawyer. On the one hand, he must be concerned about the liquidity of his own firm. On the other hand, he should not bear the risk of the client's illiquidity for an excessively long period of time. Even

12 Even in relation to clients with legal expenses insurance, there is no reasonable reason to waive the lawyer's right to advance payments.

clients whose solvency was supposedly “as secure as that of the Bank of England” have gone bankrupt. If the insolvent client asks to be allowed to pay the fee claim in installments, hardly any lawyer will refuse this, since it saves him time and money to have the claim for remuneration titled and enforced.

We are used to paying immediately for most of the services we use. This is just as true for going to the movies as it is for using a hairdresser, a laundry or a car repair shop. There is no objective reason why it should be any different for a lawyer. If a private client has not paid his fee invoice after fourteen days, then something is wrong. Either he has not received the invoice at all (this is very rare), he does not agree with the invoice (this is more common) or he belongs to that group of people who like to use services but would prefer not to pay anything for them. A friendly payment reminder usually does the trick (and leads to the debtor’s default). I do not believe in second, third, “last” and “absolutely last” reminders. If the client does not pay after a reminder, then it is better for the lawyer to assert his own fee interests against the former client with the same intensity and consistency that he previously showed in handling the case.

However, opinions among colleagues differ widely on this point in particular. Some lawyers demonstrate a true angelic patience towards tardy clients and are also rewarded for it. The client keeps coming back. However, he also always pays very late.

In my coaching and training sessions on the topic of “money, compensation and value”, I can often make it clear to these colleagues relatively quickly that the way they deal with clients’ late payments reflects their own attitude to money. Here, there are often unconscious “paradigms” and “valuations” around the topic of “money” and “business” that need to be made aware of. Only then can a concrete decision be made as to whether one wants to hold on to them or whether they only block and say goodbye to them. In any case, it is worth not only to actively deal with one’s own hourly rates, but also to deal with one’s personal beliefs about money from time to time[13]. Because a tardy client may be annoying and costs additional time and money. But when this becomes a phenomenon, they only react to the “message sent out by the law firm”, that the invoice does not have to be paid immediately.

---

i Lastly a **Tip**:
There is no harm in offering the client an additional benefit in connection with the fee calculation, to which the client would not be legally entitled.

---

13 For example, “Money is not something to talk about”, “Money corrupts character”, “It is easier for a camel to go through the eye of a needle than for a rich man to go to heaven”.

Most attorneys conduct the correspondence with the legal protection insurer free of charge for clients with legal protection insurance. However, it should be made clear to the client that this service actually costs money and that this fee (which is not to be paid by the legal protection insurer) is a gift to the client for the additional service.

For medium-sized clients who do not have their own legal department, a lawyer can "sweeten" the fee invoice by, for instance, taking a look at the client's website and checking whether the client's homepage contains the information required under § 5 of the German Telemedia Act (TMG). This check does not cost much time and effort but can be valuable for the client. Some "experts" have specialized in issuing warnings for the absence of the information required by § 5 TMG. The client will be grateful for the (unbilled) tip, which is worth hard cash. However, the lawyer should let his client know the value of this free advice.

Finally, a sentence on the subject of follow-up business: very few lawyers have a conscious view of what can be generated from a mandate as possible follow-up business. A free tip can be a good start into a "chance mandate". However, it is better to invest in an open discussion with the client and ask him about his need for advice. This may be based on the mandate or the client's other circumstances. It does not always have to be a "legal problem". Making it clear to the client that, with good legal advice, important decisions can be made at an early stage is the best way to start a follow-up mandate.

What did you get out of the chapter?
You understand how the service "legal advice" can and must be priced.

V. An industry in transition: the law firm of the future

Why should you read this chapter?
You will learn about the most important "game changers" of the legal market, development trends and future scenarios.

Overview

1. **The digitization**
   - Legal regulation
   - Legal tech in the core area of legal activity
   - Legal tech with auxiliary function to legal activity
   - Legal innovation

2. **New job profile due to the gender and generational shift**
3. **Pandemics and economic crises**
4. **Future scenarios**

167,000 lawyers admitted to the bar in Germany, 500 inhabitants per lawyer. The number of lawyers has tripled since 1990. The lecture halls of the law faculties are overflowing:

What does the future hold for the legal industry?

In 2013, the German Bar Association commissioned the Prognos AG with the above study on the future of the German legal market. Prognos AG then presented its study on the future of the German legal profession, "The Legal Services Market 2030,"[1] with the following future scenarios at the annual German Lawyers' Day:

- The further increase in competitive pressure will intensify, especially in cities and metropolitan areas.
- This is associated with greater cost pressure, and the remuneration will continue to fall.
- Standardized knowledge and the provision of standardized legal solutions will increasingly be taken over by other providers and will diminish as a source of income for the legal profession.
- Another consequence of cost pressure will be that non-legal staff in law firms will be significantly reduced and their tasks will be increasingly handled by technical solutions.
- The lawyers' monopoly on knowledge will continue to shrink.

---

1 The study on the future of the German legal profession is available from the German Bar Association.

- At the same time, however, the personality of the lawyer will become of central and decisive importance in the competitive struggle. This will be supported by the increase in specializations and more diverse forms of law firms and mergers.
- Also, the further dismantling of judicial infrastructure will require that the importance of social institutions, but alternative actors, such as pro bono activities of the legal profession, alternative forms of financing, or even the involvement of mediators, psychologists, mediators, will be an exciting development opportunity for lawyers.

The fact is that the legal industry is at a turning point. The three major challenges mentioned at the beginning are clearly forecast in the study of the future and described in terms of their development trends:

1. The digitization

Digitalization is already a blessing and a curse for the industry. On the one hand, it opens up unimagined opportunities for communication and optimization. The acquisition and set-up costs of technical aids regularly pay for themselves more quickly than the training of new employees. Further staff reductions lead to cost savings and risk minimization.

– Legal regulation

This means that the legal profession will continue to move increasingly within legal grey areas when using technology and technical aids in the future. At the same time, however, there is no getting around the need to keep up to date with a certain basic understanding of technology in order to be able to assess legal risks. This technological change will greatly alter the work processes and the market situation for the legal profession[2]. Right now, the Bucerius Center on the Legal Profession is investigating whether legal tech has really made law firms rethink their business models and service offerings, revenue models, and organizational structures[3], having found in 2016, in collaboration with the Boston Consulting Group, in the study "How Legal Technology will Change the Business of Law," that legal tech could perform 30–50 % of the work of young lawyers.

2 Prognos, Der Rechtsdienstleistungsmarkt 2030 p. 138.
3 New Directions in Legal Services, ARK Group, Bucerius Law School (CLP).

After all, the major BRAO reform will make some things possible in this area from mid-2022: closer cooperation with other professions, especially engineers and technicians, will be possible. However, it will still not be possible to invest venture capital in law firms[4].

As of January 1, 2022, the special electronic lawyer's mailbox (beA), which was adopted in 2013 with the **law to promote electronic legal transactions** (the so-called eJustice Act), will be introduced on a mandatory basis for everyone. Like the special electronic notary's mailbox (beN), the special electronic public authority mailbox (beBPO) and the new electronic citizen and organization mailbox (eBO), the beA uses the **"OSCI Transport"** (Online Services Computer Interface) **protocol** which, with the introduction of EGVP, has formed the backbone of German judicial communication for many years. It guarantees the classic goals of integrity, authenticity, confidentiality and traceability in the transmission of messages by means of the so-called double envelope principle.

With the eJustice Act, the legal profession and public authorities are forced to make advance payments.

Worth mentioning are for example the **working group "Modernization of Civil Procedure"** commissioned by the Presidents of the Higher Regional Courts, the Court of Appeal, the Bavarian Supreme Court and the Federal Court of Justice, as well as the BMJV project "Tech4Germany" to facilitate a software solution for online access for citizens to enforce small claims and to increase the digitization of the courts, which is still in its infancy in part, or the citizen participation initiative "Rethinking Digital Administration" of the Bavarian State Ministry for Digital Affairs.

I have just had the privilege of contributing to the book "Die Digitalisierung des Zivilprozesses" (The Digitization of Civil Procedure) with the team of authors led by Prof. Riem from the University of Passau, which summarizes the most important findings from the transformation process.

With the so-called Digitalization Directive (EU Directive 2019/1151), EU member states must enable **online formation of corporations** by 08/2022. The German Bundestag passed a corresponding implementation law on June 10, 2021 ("DiRUG"). The law has already successfully passed the Bundesrat (upper house of parliament). Companies and founders will therefore be able to set up a limited liability company (GmbH) or the "Unternehmergesellschaft" (UG – with limited liability), which is popular with start-ups, from the **comfort of their office or home** from **August 1, 2022.**

---

4 More on this in the chapter on founding of the law firm.

Digitization also brings with it an internationalization of the German legal profession. Mandates are becoming increasingly international, which in turn places special demands on the legal profession[5].

The Prognos study goes on to say that the greatest potential ultimately lies in the optimization of law firm management and law firm marketing[6].
Law firm management in particular will benefit from the professionalization and digitalization of management tasks, as the resources of time, personnel and money can be used and controlled more efficiently through digitalization. It is estimated that about 22 % of the lawyer's work and up to 35 % of the assistant's work in the law firm can be automated in the future[7].

The constantly developing information and communication technologies offer numerous possibilities to meet the requirements of a flexible and transparent as well as customer-oriented legal service.

The digital file and the beA as well as the expansion of the IT infrastructure in law firms are mandatory prerequisites for this. Technological development in particular has been identified by Prognos AG as one of the central drivers for the development of the legal services market[8].

So, are innovation and LegalTech the enemies of the legal industry because they are disruptive?

Is Legal Tech eating the Legals?

LegalTech refers to technical providers that offer standardized solutions to problems. This includes, for example, providers such as Flight Right, Legal Base or Geblitzt.de[9], which offer flat-rate legal services at flat rates. Legal tech can be software solutions or intermediary platforms for legal services[10].

---

5 Heussen, p. 320, "Anwaltsunternehmen führen".

6 Prognos der Rechtsdienstleistungsmarkt 2030 page 176.

7 brand.eins/thema 2021, Die Branche in Zahlen, p. 79.

8 Prognos der Rechtsdienstleistungsmarkt 2030 page 180.

9 Caspar Tobias Schlenk, "Der Smartlaw Gründer startet das nächste Legal Start up" in Gründerszene of 4/3/2016.

10 A good overview is provided by Hartung, Bues, Halbleib, "Legal Tech – die Digitalisierung des Rechtsmarktes", 2017.

Remember:
Law firms are called upon to actively exploit the opportunities offered by legal tech, be it from a business perspective (efficiency, cost minimization, speed, risk management) or from a strategic perspective (recruitment, employer branding, customer and service orientation) or to open up new areas of business of their own.

In the following I would like to offer a brief overview of the current situation[11]:

In doing so, I am guided by Jens Wagner's "Kartographie der Legal Tech Landschaft" (Cartography of the Legal Tech Landscape), according to which legal tech can be divided into three basic categories or dimensions:
1. Legal tech in the core area of legal activity
2. Legal tech for the legally relevant framework
3. Legal tech with an auxiliary function for legal activity[12]

– Legal tech in the core area of legal activity

Software solutions
These include first and foremost document analysis and all data capture systems, as well as online legal databases and knowledge management systems for legal research, but ultimately also automated contract review and negotiation tools, legal generators and automated document creation. The latter, known as legal robots, are equipped not only with adaptive algorithms, but also with so-called artificial intelligence (AI).[13]

As an example of document generation, Legal Smart Documents, Law-lift, Team-Docs, Escriba, Consultimator, Goyaa, BlockAxs, Hotdocs, Legal OS. Legito, Prime Legal AI, Methodigy, Legalmatic, ScriptomatTemplafy, SMASH-DOCs, SMARTCONEXVertragsgenerator, top. legal and Janolaw can be named; for document analysis, DATEV, consilio, LEGARTIS. Codefy, Contract Analyzer, epiq, EVANA, inserve, juracus, Kira, KLDiscovery, Legility, NAIX and LeReTo are currently being launched.

11 While working on the first edition of this book, in 2017, the legal tech market was still quite manageable; many providers appeared as quickly as they disappeared. Therefore, I refrained from providing a detailed overview. That seems to be different now. The next (third) edition will show how many of the above offerings remain on the market.
12 Jens Wagner, Legal Tech und Legal Robots, p. 16.
13 Exciting insights offered by Jens Wagner, Legal Tech und Legal Robots, p. 56.

But also the so-called standardized legal services belong to this category, everything from FlightRight to wenigermiete, online-scheidung, right-now, Bryter, clarius.legal and legalzoom.com to rocketlawyer.com.

- **Legal tech for the legally relevant framework**

We are already familiar with these in the form of automated court and administrative procedures or even legal formal simplifications and requirements. The special electronic lawyer's mailbox (beA according to § 31 a BRAO) belongs in this category[14], as does the electronic file or the electronic integration portal (eIP) of the Bavarian judiciary[15] (keyword: eJustice and eGovernment).

New to the vast majority are the so-called Keyless Signature Infrastructure (KSI) Technology, Smart Contracts, Blockchain, Online Dispute Resolution, and Blockchain Arbitration.

- **Legal tech with an auxiliary function for legal activity**

Probably the most versatile area of legal technology are technical tools that are only marginally related to the actual provision of legal advice, but nevertheless shape the everyday life of law firms and have changed the law firm business in recent years. Most of these products were initially described as so-called "disruptive innovations", even though they had long been established in other industries.

---

14 The beA is now a mandatory reality since 1.1.2022 (Art. 26 VII ERV Act).

15 The electronic file is to become a mandatory reality in Germany by January 1, 2026 at the latest. Jens Wagner, Legal Tech und Legal Robots, p. 28. In Austria, this has been the case since 2021: the "Justiz 3.0" project was launched in 2013 and pilot operations of digital file management started at various courts as early as 2016. In 2019, around 700 judiciary employees were working with the digital judiciary workstation, where electronic files can be processed, assigned and viewed. The **ELAK (electronic file)** is a central concept of the Austrian eGovernment strategy, which since 2004 has enabled fully electronic file management, automated handling of business processes, archiving and seamless administrative cooperation between authorities (keyword: one-stop government). Today, the electronic file in the federal government (ELAK) is used as the central e-government system of the Austrian federal administration by the federal ministries, supreme organs, courts, outsourced legal entities and subordinate departments of the federal government. As a central element of business case processing, it is a crucial and integral part of the workplace of the future, which is already available 24 hours a day, regardless of time or location. In the future, the ELAK will be expanded as a knowledge platform and for the automation of processes with the use of artificial intelligence. 1.5 million files and 20 million documents are processed electronically with ELAK in Austria every year. Today, 12,000 users from the federal ministries work with ELAK, which functions electronically from incoming mail to processing – making ELAK a genuine European reference project.

i Disruptive innovation is a "destructive invention" that creates a product, technology, service or business model that does not have to adapt to the established "rules of the game" and "power relations" of the market or deliberately bypasses them. It usually begins in a small, inconspicuous niche of an industry and ultimately leads to the complete dissolution/destruction of existing business models, customer relationships, product lines and services, and may even lead to a reorganization of the market. The best examples of this are traditional gas stations in relation to e-cars or truck/bus drivers in relation to autonomous driving.

This includes general law firm software and tools as well as the virtual file, document management and workflow management, but also platforms for collaboration up to video telephony (such as Teams, Adobe, Slack, Skype, Zoom), legal spend management and eBilling, in other words everything that has to do with proper cost estimation and billing.

The so-called Legal Project Management (LPM), which basically works without technical tools, was specifically developed at the interface of definition and optimization of existing analog processes to digitalization, efficiency and evaluation.

The following are examples of law firm software: DATEV, RA-MICRO, STP-Kanzleisoftware, Renostar, AnNoText, Kleos, Advoware, Advolux, Kanzlei-Manager, LawFirm, Legalvisio, NOAH, rainmaker, ShakeSpeare. These differ on the one hand in the structure according to modules and functionalities and thus in the price structure, and on the other hand in their experience on the market. In addition to function and price, important parameters in the decision are, in particular, existing and functioning interfaces, but also the size of the law firm and a client structure that fit the software. More on this later.

Solutions for client communication currently include DATEV, 5FSoftware, Advobot, CODIAC, Iurio, MavonRA; for law firm tools, for example, DictNow, Anwalts-Gebühren.online, 4voice speech technologies, DictaNet, DragonLegal, LAS, jurmatix Legal Intelligence, LexSuperior, Philips SpeechLive, Veronym, vub Paperboy; for legal databases for research LEXinform, beck-online, Deutsches Anwalt Office Premium, ESV-Digital, LexisNexis, juris – Das Rechtsportal, Owlit, Otto Schmidt online, Wolters Kluwer Online. Also free and quite useful databases should be mentioned: Bundesanzeiger, nuzer.de, dejure.org, Gesetze im Internet, kommentar.de, Lexetius, omsels.info, openJur, Openlaws, Rechtsprechung im Internet, Urteile & Gesetze and Verwaltungsvorschriften im Internet.

This includes platforms for legal tech products as well as common legal platforms. These are collaboration platforms for working with the legal departments of large companies. In the case of large volumes of data or particularly sensitive, lengthy issues of relevance to criminal law, such as the "diesel scandal", but also in the case of M&A or regular patent applications, the company usually defines the platform, which presents the law firm with the challenge of not only adapting this platform to be compatible with its law firm IT, but also coordinating different platforms on a daily basis. A so-called Legal Mark-up Language or Common Legal Platform would significantly ease the burden on law firms.

This also includes so-called legal outsourcing and online recruiting. These are classic career portals such as Beck Stellenmarkt, azur JUVE, LTO Karriere, but also new ones such as Legal Careers, Karriere-Jura.de, Legalhead, TalentRocket, PERCONEX. In legal outsourcing, AdvoAssist, Axiom, Clarius.Legal, Digitorney, Lawyers on Demand, reThinkLegal, VARIO, Terminver-treter.com, clients&candidates, Xenion. Legal come into consideration.

Ultimately, however, this also includes all online marketing and online mediation platforms, such as 123recht.de, advocado, anwalt.de, anwalt24, anwaltssuche, Anwalt-Suchservice, Das Deutsche Anwaltsregister (DAWR), DASD Deutscher Anwaltssuchdienst, Deutsche Anwaltshotline, Deut-sche Anwaltsauskunft (for members of the German Lawyers Association), fachanwalt.de, fachanwaltssuche.de, JuraForum, jusmeum, ra-fachanwalt.de, rechts-anwalt.com. In addition, there are also the numerous lawyer networks, which usually also offer a presentation of their members in one form or another.

In the meantime, there are also legal tech consulting companies like Future-Law.at in Austria: LawApoynt, SFS, Unterschied & Macher, Advoservice, Advotisement and entire legal tech platforms like Reynen Court (including App-Store) or also the free offers of the ffi-Verlag like the Legal Tech Directory and Legal Tech Magazine as well as the Legal Tech Directory of Schweitzer Fachinformationen or one for Austria by Future-Law.at. Please note that not all tech solutions are country-independent.

Of course, these listings are not exhaustive and are constantly changing.

---

i

So-called legal tech directories[16] are published at regular intervals by a central body and provide a good, updated overview. The exhibitor directories for congress formats in the legal industry (such as for advotec of the Deutscher Anwaltstag, the virtual law firm expo of Wolters Kluwer or the Legal Revolution) are also helpful.

Moreover, professional associations such as the German Bar Association offer special rates for members in many places in the members' area for some of the solutions presented.

16 Legal Tech 2021: 150 Angebote für Kanzleien. Eine Marktübersicht, Fachinfo-Verzeichnis des ffi-Verlages.

A distinction must be made between these and the industry solutions developed by technical service providers for the legal sector. These are technical products that have been developed specifically for the law firm sector, for example, in the hardware sector the lawyer's copier from Konica Minolta or Rico, or in the software sector special law firm solutions for internal law firm processes. Admittedly, a lot is still in its infancy here and the legal industry is currently suffering from half-finished, half-baked products. However, the opportunity lies in supporting the technical service providers in developing a tailor-made, target group-optimized product that will accompany the legal industry into the future. With CLP, I have accompanied many hardware and software providers over the past few years in optimizing their products for the legal market and introducing them to this market in the long term.

The first steps have been taken with the beA. Law firm software that is capable of development, such as that introduced to the market years ago by RA Mikro, AdwoWare and STP, is available. The task is now to eliminate initial difficulties, close security gaps and create flexible interfaces in order to offer flexible solutions to the changing law firm market. It is no secret that more and more companies are discovering the legal target group as a new vertical market. Vertical markets, such as the education sector or the hospital sector, are increasingly becoming the focus of companies, and they are gearing both their products and their marketing strategies towards these vertical markets. Involving experts from these sectors at an early stage is of crucial importance: starting with the strategic orientation, during product development and later on when setting up the marketing concept. Companies such as RA Micro or STP rely on the employment of lawyers in product development or in the marketing department and in sales. Other companies tend to use external consultants and testing firms for their product innovations.

- **Legal Innovation**

Following examples from the tech scene and student initiatives, the first "hubs" developed, which are loose associations that brought together "professionals" from different sectors in the spirit of the new agility to rethink legal advice using methods such as Scrum[17], Kanban[18], Business Model Canvas[19] or Design Thinking[20].

What was really new?

The perspective was new:

Legal advice is consistently thought of from the so-called "user" perspective – but this can be the legal advisor as a user of a legal tech product such as highly specialized contract software just as much as the legal department of a company or the so-called end consumer.

Legal Design Thinking or Legal Project Management are methods for process control (on the one hand during development, on the other hand during optimization), which originally come from other industries and are specifically adapted to the life cycle of a mandate/file.

But the error culture was also new:

European and even more so German culture focuses on two aspects of development and growth:

1. Errors and their monitoring and repair
2. Weaknesses and their conversion into average values

This runs through our entire social system and is, of course, also inherent in legal education, the system of administering justice, and the legal industry. However, as a look at other cultures shows, it does not have to be this way. The innovation surge in Silicon Valley did not come about by chance on U. S. territory, and it is no coinci-

---

17 Scrum is a development method for products, but can also be used for project development. Originally developed for software engineering, it is now used in many different areas.

18 Kanban is a development method for production processes that is based on the consumption of materials at the supply point and at the point of consumption.

19 The Business Model Canvas is a type of "canvas" on which a business model or product idea is presented in nine sections ranging from its development to its distribution. It can be used as a sandbox for the business development of innovative ideas or as a strategic management template for existing products and services.

20 See explanation below.

dence that the start-up scenes in Germany and Austria have to overcome enormous hurdles in their search for investors.

The culture of error is deeply rooted in American culture in the "Pioneer" and "Pilgrim" stories, the "gold-digger" and soldier-of-fortune ancestors, the explorer and adventurer genes. "No risk – no fun" is certainly not a typical German motto and certainly not a maxim when it comes to law and order. And yet: In a world that is spinning faster than ever; in which today's invention is already yesterday's news, long-drawn-out conservative processes – which certainly make sense in the sense of risk management during calm periods – are not opportune. The Corona pandemic has illustrated this: Never has the development of different vaccines and going through the approval process been faster. Trial and error have replaced conservative risk management.

This is also the case in the innovation of Legal Technology:

It started cautiously with so-called "Retreats[21]", "Master Mind Groups[22]",

"Legal Design Jams[23]", and "Hackathons"[24].

The most impressive hackathon was certainly the German government's Wirvsvirus in March 2020[25]: Under the patronage of Chancellery Minister Helge Braun and the Minister of State for Digitalization together with co-organizers from the digital community (including Tech4Germany, Digitalrat, Prototype Fund), over 28,000 participants engaged in a 48-hour weekend marathon over the course of just a few days. In total, around 1,500 projects from almost 3,000 challenges were worked on in connection with the Corona pandemic. These include more than one hundred challenges from federal ministries or authorities such as the Federal Office for Civil Protection or the Federal Police. The rest of the proposals came from civil society, companies and clinics. Many of the projects were pure legal tech applica-

---

21 Retreats are actually spiritual relaxation time-outs, but today they have also gained acceptance as "general retreats from everyday life": So for the development of legal tech, time-outs outside of the office were created, in which undisturbed and "new" thinking could take place in a protected setting in small, selected teams.

22 Master Mind Groups are homogeneous groups that want to move forward together or solve a previously defined problem through regular mutual exchange.

23 Jams are essentially casual gatherings from the artist scene for improvisation, known for example among musicians as Jam Session or Poetry Slam for young authors/StandUp Performance. For the development of Legal Tech, this was called "creative time", e.g. for a midday meeting of one hour. Jams are mostly held in-house.

24 Hackathons are gigantic open (online) events (usually free of charge) with a specific task for the exchange and collaboration of numerous strangers with different origins, backgrounds and experience with the goal of achieving a first (interim) result for solving a problem within 24 or 48 hours of uninterrupted work.

25 www.bundesregierung.defrom 20.7.2020 andwww.wirvsvirus.org.

tions, and almost all of them needed legal support in one way or another, especially with regard to data protection and fundamental rights encroachment. I was there with CLP as a so-called mentor and accompanied various projects at the same time. Interesting and helpful initiatives emerged from some of them, for example on home schooling, food delivery and online stores of regional providers, but also contact tracing or optimal distribution of hospital beds. There was an almost continuous exchange via video, Slack and other platforms, several times a day we received central video live feeds, for example to Dorothee Bär and the organizers, and on Sunday evening we celebrated the first results. Afterwards, the so-called "Solution Enablers" continued and were accompanied in the search for investors, the production of the prototype, etc. The project was then presented to the public.

This was followed by student initiatives and think tanks[26] based on the U. S. model of ThinkLaw, such as Recode Law[27] or Legal Tech Lab Cologne or MLTech[28]. Later, hubs[29] and Meet-ups[30] sprouted up in almost all major German cities.

The Legal Tech Hub Vienna, an association of seven large Austrian law firms for the joint innovation of legal tech, was certainly one of the first and largest of its kind[31].

The Liquid Legal Institute is a similar association in Germany – on a democratic association basis – to jointly enable innovation. What is remarkable here is that the classic conservative business forms (GmbH, etc.) do not seem to offer the right framework for developing new business ideas and products, while at the same time sustainable and non-profit corporate forms such as the GmbH are probably not (yet) attractive for these associations[32].

---

26 A think tank is a so-called think tank of a self-contained group that conducts futures research by exploring, developing and evaluating political, social and economic concepts and strategies.

27 Recode Law is an initiative of students and law clerks that I supported, for example, at the annual Digital Justice Conference 2021.

28 Labs are associations for "field research" from different professions: For the development of legal tech similar to the jams so-called "creative and innovation areas".

29 An innovation hub uses the technical telecommunication term hub in the sense of network/ connection as a node where diverse ideas, actors and technologies converge and are creatively networked.

30 MeetUp is a non-binding, one-time networking meeting of an open group on a specific topic. "Legal Hackers" is a global movement of lawyers, policymakers, technologists, and academics researching and developing creative solutions to some of the most pressing problems at the intersection of law and technology. At local meetings, hackathons, and workshops, Legal Hackers identify problems and opportunities for how technology can improve and inform the practice of law, and how law, legal practice and policy can adapt to rapidly changing technology – for example, the "Munich Legal Hackers" since 2016.

31 *Martinetz/Maringele*, Quick Guide Legal Tech, p. 80.

32 I am currently working on a legal dissertation that addresses this issue.

Under Reinvent Law, university student groups then joined forces for the first time with law firms, legal departments and so-called Legal Tech Ventures[33] in order to bundle synergies. The Legal Tech University has recently become a partner. Universities are thus urgently trying to catch up with the legal tech movement. In the meantime, the first LL.M. in Legal Tech can be completed at the University of Regensburg[34].

“At EBS Law School, we are thinking about the future of legal education in a comprehensive and elaborate process,” says Prof. Dr. iur. Emanuel V. Towfigh, Dean of the Faculty. “An important part of this is how the law deals with digitalization. Legal tech, for example, already plays a significant role in law firms and companies today, while education is not dedicated to the topic. We want to counteract this with our new focus: Students should be made fit for the areas they will inevitably have to deal with in their professional lives.”[35]

Last but not least, eMagazine formats such as Rethinking Law, Legal Layman[36] or Legal Revolutionary should also be mentioned. The latter is the eMagazine of Legal Revolution, a multi-day congress format for the latest legal tech innovations.

Unfortunately, the German Bar Association (DAV) has not yet seen the need to dedicate a separate working group or other format to this. It would be conceivable, for example, to use certain collaboration platforms such as Slack or Teams. The newly established intervision platform in the closed member area of the DAV is probably not very suitable for this. The platform is running more poorly than it should under the AG Kanzleimanagement, which is not very visible. But that can still change.

So, the results of WoltersKluwer’s study “The Future Fit Lawyer” come as no surprise, according to which **only 68 % have currently taken their very first steps in the direction of legal tech** and **less than half, namely 49 %, are currently using exclusively new technologies.**

---

33 Legal tech ventures are investors in the broadest sense who support with know-how, capital and network.

34 The interview with the first professor and self-proclaimed Lawfluencer (Influencer in Law) Dr. Christina-Maria Leeb immediately before she became a professor can be found at /www.consulting forlegals.com/aktuelles/s/2/tag/interviews/

35 “Digitalkompetenz im Jurastudium” in: smartlegalmarket from 7.5.2019.

36 A format aimed at non-lawyers (i. e., users) and presented, for example, as mentioned earlier, the CLP Academy 2020 Legal Coaching Training – found at www.consultingforlegals.com/aktuelles/detail/news/der-mensch-als-mittelpunkt-einer-juristi schen-weiterbildung-das-gibts-tatsaechlich/.

- most likely to disagree was the partner team (55 %),
- second most often was the fear of costs (50 %) and
- as many as 31 % say that clients do not want this.

And yet, 66 % say they have been significantly more profitable in their use of technology, and 25 % have even developed their own internal legal tech products:
- 33 % have hired external IT specialists for this purpose
- 25 % have created innovation formats such as jams, hubs, labs for this purpose
- 22 % have collaborated with a startup

New positions have been created: Chief Operating Officers (COO) are responsible for optimizing processes, while “Innovation and Knowledge Directors,” “Legal Technology Specialists” and “Legal Operations Managers” drive digitization forward[37].

Remember:
As a result, however, law firms come in last when it comes to innovation in “legal technology”[38].

It is important to note here that none of these studies and surveys found a significant difference in the development or use of legal tech in any way among male or female lawyers. However, there were two factors that were shown to have a negative impact on the development and use of legal tech:
- The older the lawyer, the less he or she was involved with the topic of legal tech[39].
- The more homogeneous the decision-making group, the lower was the legal tech exposure[40].

The fact is: Today, 66 % consider legal tech to be the solution for efficiency and cost reduction. Another 19 % are using legal tech to improve their access to justice[41]. Yet in the early days of legal tech, only male voices could be heard on the topic: Only

37 *Ulrich Lüdke*, “Neue Kanzleimodelle” in: Unternehmervertraute from 30.12.2019.
38 The 68 % among lawyers contrasts with 96 % in legal departments, according to the study “The Future Fit Lawyer,” WoltersKluwer, 2019. This is also confirmed by the Future Law study “Die digitale Rechtsabteilung 2035,” 2019. However, it must be mentioned that legal tech here is mostly “office tech” after all, according to Pia Lorenz, “Closer to the business, but far from legal tech,” LTO, April 29, 2020.
39 This had a decisive effect particularly in the law firms where the decision-makers (partners) were of an older age.
40 And it didn’t matter at all whether it was an all-female/male partnership, homogeneous age structure, or ethnocultural affiliation.
41 brand.eins/thema 2021, Die Branche in Zahlen, p. 79.

male speakers, all-male panels, only publications by male colleagues. Just a few years ago, the Lawyers' Future Congress had planned an entire day on the topic – exclusively with men, since there were supposedly no female lawyers involved in legal tech, with the result that there was a boycott of participation among female colleagues. The initiative "Women in Legal Tech" therefore rightfully brought women on stage for the first time in 2018, and every year thereafter, and awarded them specifically for their engagement in legal tech.

It remains to be mentioned that the Austrian colleagues are well ahead of their German counterparts in this respect[42], presumably also because Austria has been using electronic communication in the judiciary and administration for decades[43].

Keeping track of new developments in this market and examining their potential for one's own law firm will become a key factor. Hopefully, the legal profession will see digitization as an opportunity and will not regard itself as a brake and doubter of digitization. The false start of the beA should be a lesson for the German legal profession in this respect[44].

Conclusion:

What do the possibilities of digitization mean for our case studies?

Tip:

First, try to pause and develop digital solution approaches for the three case studies:

1. Growing pains: are many small firms big law firms?
2. Wrong clients: Realignment and resource change?
3. Gender and Generation Shift: Turning Old into New?

What would it mean to establish a sensible and uniform IT infrastructure for the many small law firms scattered throughout Germany, and to redefine and standardize processes? If the whole thing is accompanied by a uniform virtual assistance and a resource-saving and solution-oriented virtual agile meeting structure for professional and law firm development topics?

42 At least, so the survey Future-Law, "Der Anwaltsberuf 2035", 2018.

43 If, for example, information from the population register is required, German lawyers have to be forwarded laboriously from one registration address to the next via a law firm software interface, by post or e-mail over a period of weeks, while Austrian lawyers simply provide up-to-date central information for the whole of Austria – online and in a matter of minutes.

44 It should only be mentioned in passing that Austrian colleagues have been using electronic legal transactions for decades without any problems – as, for that matter, have all municipalities and authorities; Pia Lorenz, "Ist das beA noch zu retten?", LTO, 28.12.2017.

What if a software solution tailored to the needs of the new mandates could cut the staffing ratio for the ReFas in half from 1:1 to 1:0.5 within a very short time? What if you could not only inspire young professionals with a state-of-the-art infrastructure and the possibility of working remotely, but also recruit them virtually anywhere?

What would happen if the needs of young female lawyers were taken into account when expanding the IT infrastructure? What if the next generation were left in charge of the most important clients and, thanks to digital solutions, could monitor client development at any time, while at the same time allowing unhindered access to partners at any time, who in turn focus on sustainable internal knowledge transfer? What if young female lawyers were integrated into agile development teams to help develop the next sustainable and ecologically sound legal tech solution?

What if?

2. New job profile due to the gender and generational shift

With increasing digitization, the possibilities of work-life balance as well as the demands of Generation Y and the compatibility of career and family will be better served. Nearly 50 % of law school graduates are already female, and more than 35 % of licensed attorneys are now female[45]. Even if they are still mainly working part-time or tend not to be in decision-making positions. Incidentally, with a quota of less than 5 % of female partners, the legal sector is at the bottom of the league, the same applies to the gender pay gap[46], in comparison with the German economy[47].

It is predicted that within the next ten years there will be a balanced ratio of women and men in the legal profession. In 2017 there were already more women than men, 52 % to 48 %, admitted to the bar[48]. This will lead to a fundamental change in values and a change in the professional image. The "gray-haired fox in a dark blue gold button double-breasted suit" is outdated. The same goes for the "shirt-sleeved darling Kreuzberg model". New role models are being defined. Companies are standing up for diversity and fairness and are now demanding this of their ser-

---

45 Dr. Tutschka, "Diversity in deutschen Kanzleien" in Edition F from 30.3.2016.

46 Dr. Koch, "Anwältinnen im internationalen Vergleich", NJW 05/2017; Dr. Tutschka, "The pink elephant in the room" in CLP – Blog from 24.5.2017.

47 Dr. Tutschka, "Female Leadership im Legal Sector", p. 137 in DjbZ 03/2017; "Justitia wir haben ein Problem" in JuraBlogs from 26.4.2016; "Männer und Frauen in juristischen Berufen" in Legal Tribune online from 16.11.2015.

48 Jessika Kallenbach, "Zukunft der Anwaltschaft ist weiblich" in Anwaltsblatt from 28.5. 2019.

vice providers as well, especially since heterogeneous teams have been proven to be more efficient[49]. Salary level and the prospect of partnership have long since ceased to be top priorities for the new generation of lawyers, but equality in career, power and money, as well as work-life balance and family time, and soon also issues such as "purpose", "social impact" and sustainability, will be.

New Work will also find its way into law firms: under the catchphrase New Law, attempts are already being made with the help of globalization and digitization to underpin legal services with worldwide "legal batteries". These worldwide recruited, mostly young lawyers are relieved of all administration, marketing and acquisition with a share of 70 % of their fee volume[50]. Thanks to legal tech, clients worldwide are served with smart forms. Artificial intelligence takes over the evaluation and day-to-day processing. For freelancers, the special cases remain. Paperless, remote, maximum freedom sound like New Work. Revenue sharing usually goes nowhere due to the lack of a large client base of one's own and the interchangeability of one's own performance. Nevertheless, this "Uberization of the legal market" is on the rise and is especially popular among young female lawyers in Germany and Austria on family leave, at least more popular than working in domestic large law firms in family-hostile and discriminatory structures. This is because, with the interchangeability of legal advice, they usually experience fair pay for the first time in their lives[51].

Despite all prophecies of doom: the legal profession is reinventing itself[52].

And how exactly does it do that?

Primarily with specialization and segmentation[53]:

The focus is placed on specialized areas, for example by acquiring further specialist lawyer titles, but also by specializing in selected client segments or by defining and profiling business areas. At the same time, regional focus is preferred to the opening of additional offices, and cooperation with other law firms, but also with other companies, such as management consultants and auditors, is sought instead. An increasing number of law firms are focusing on becoming so-called boutique law firms as part of their specialization. These are small law firm units that are highly specialized and have focused solely on one market segment[54]. Another model is that

49 Barbara Helten, "Tipps für den erfolgreichen Pitch" in lto from 25.5.2021.

50 I have already briefly mentioned these global "law factories" above in the pricing and turnover calculation.

51 Dr. Alix Frank-Thomasser, "Die Uber-Anwältin" in anwalt aktuell 06/20.

52 Dr. Tutschka, "Change is not in our DNA" in Huffington Post from 30.3.2016.

53 Richard Susskind, Tomorrow's Lawyers, p. 45.

54 Such as NEUWERK in Hamburg, Naber in "Partner vs. Associate" in the CLP blog of 6/17/2016.

small law firm units, such as the boutique law firm, can set themselves up as a so-called one-stop law firm through a supra-regional or supra-professional network. This means that mandates are provided with a holistic solution and flanking services can be provided by the network. The advantage of this is that the basis of trust of the mandate can be extended to other services and the client feels that he is being fully taken care of.

Ultimately, however, an initially regionally positioned but highly specialized law firm can also reorient itself by offering a niche product on a supra-regional basis, independent of opening hours or regional conditions, as a quasi-international "online law firm". These online law firms are significantly influenced by digitalization and are developing in areas of law that are also transnational and internationally oriented, such as data protection or IP law.

Specialization in the form of specialist lawyer titles is taken into account by the fact that more and new specialist lawyer titles are being established, such as specialist lawyer for business law in 2015 or specialist lawyer for migration law in 2016 and specialist lawyer for sports law in 2020.

It is also conceivable to split off certain special fields from larger areas of law, such as inheritance law from the FA for Family and Inheritance Law at the time and expatriate law from labor law in the future[55].

However, the future study also shows that the legal sector already has an oversupply of purely technical training and that there is an imbalance in relation to the training of so-called soft skills and personality factors.

This becomes clear from the fact that the increasing number of specialized attorneys can no longer automatically contribute to a profit, as was the case years ago, and that while market expectations demand specialization on the one hand, holistic solutions to problems are becoming increasingly relevant on the other[56].

Increasingly, therefore, the focus will not only be on pure legal applications and legal solutions, but more on a problem-solving and service-focused holistic offering. Fast response times, information transparency, a high degree of flexibility, a unique selling proposition and a trusting relationship with the client, as well as the inclusion of non-legal considerations from IT and technology, business, society and psychology will become decisive criteria.

Wolters Kluwer's 2019 "Future Ready Lawyer" study surveyed 700 young lawyers from the U. S. and 10 European countries (Germany was included; Austria and Switzerland were not) and found that

- coping with the increasing amount and complexity of information, and

---

55 Dr. Tutschka, Kuschel, Dittmeier p. 6 in "USA Expat Quick Guide".

56 Prognos der Rechtsdienstleistungsmarkt 2030 page 179.

- efficiency and productivity increase and
- understanding which technologies offer the highest added value in the legal market and respond to changing client interests will be crucial in the future.

Analytical tools and transformative technologies such as machine learning and artificial intelligence will be an integral part of legal services in the future.

Only one-third of law firms consider themselves prepared for this at the moment, because of a lack of technical understanding due to obsolescence and because no financial or organizational resources are available. Resistance from law firm management and fear of change are also cited. Only 68 % of law firms have invested in legal innovation to date compared to 98 % of legal service providers and 88 % of legal departments. However, as early as 2025, 75 % of lawyers will belong to the Millennial generation, who have grown up as so-called digital natives and use technology intuitively and naturally in their working and living environments. In addition, legal tech companies will invest massively in these new technologies and further expand their lead.

In the U. S., the battle for mandates will be decided primarily by who can best and most cost-effectively meet customer interests. In Europe, specialization and 24/7 service will be the decisive factors.

It is expected that this change will take place at increasing speed: smaller agile and flexible units will be able to adapt more quickly, so that a rethink is also underway with regard to the basic principle of "growth for economic success". Large law firms as we know them today will become a discontinued model: there will be a tendency for the size of law firms to decrease and for cooperations in the industry to increase[57].

Remember:
Future-proof companies are those that already
- invest in young, technology-savvy high potentials and a modern IT infrastructure,
- optimize their processes and expand their specialization positioning.
- The decisive factor will be whether the firm's management is willing to change and look ahead

Specialization and professional expertise, especially in the niche area, will therefore only be sustainable in combination with charisma and a trustworthy personality of the lawyer[58] as well as a corresponding corporate identity and a strong network[59].

57 Ulrich Lüdke, "Neue Kanzleimodelle" in Unternehmervertraute from 30.12.2019.
58 Dr. Geertje Tutschka, "Warum Gender Diversity in deutschen Kanzleien so wichtig ist" in Soldan Insight vom 25.2.2016.
59 Future Ready Lawyer, Wolters Kluwer 2019.

Client feedback and client satisfaction will become the decisive optimization tool for the legal profession. Already, in addition to purely professional training and rhetoric and performance training, personal development programs or additional skills such as intercultural communication, coaching techniques[60], mediation, business know-how, project design or marketing are being offered. This is supported by the trend that the legal profession has been growing since 2017 solely because the hitherto still relatively small subgroup of European lawyers under the EuRAG and lawyers from an ATS signatory state admitted under § 206 BRAO and the dually admitted syndicus lawyers are **growing significantly:** in fact, they have doubled from 10,642 to 20,243 between 2017 and 2020. They are characterized by multilingualism, intercultural understanding and an understanding of complex international economic interdependencies. In contrast, the profession of German-speaking practicing lawyers is shrinking due to aging (especially in the eastern German states and in the rural areas of western Germany), but also due to a graduation crisis. Despite continued high student numbers, only a fraction successfully completed their law studies and are available as junior lawyers. The forecast by Prof. Dr. Matthias Killian of the Soldan Foundation therefore assumes that the growth of the industry will come to a halt and even predicts a noticeable decline in the number of professionals by 2030. The forecast assumes a decline in currently established lawyers from 146,795 (with 165,901 lawyers in total for 2020) to as many as 119,942 in 2030. By comparison, in 2017 there were still 154,683 lawyers in private practice, which means about 10,000 fewer lawyers every 3 years[61].

Secondly, the focus will be on the “industrialization of legal processes. Increasing cost pressure will demand budgets that can be planned and calculated, measurability of legal services and increased use of legal technology. The growing demands of business on the legal market due to complexity, crisis and risk prevention and management will not only pass them on to in-house lawyers but also to external lawyers[62].

You are now at the beginning; at the beginning of the reorientation of your law firm, perhaps of a law firm foundation or even reorganization. In any case, at the beginning of an exciting process, at the beginning of a big task, at the beginning of a busy time. And it doesn’t matter whether you are just starting out in your professional life, want to reorient yourself after a family break and get a fresh start. Or

---

60 Dr. Geertje Tutschka, “Business Coaching für Anwälte” in NJW 24/2015.

61 Prof. Dr. Matthias Killian, “Niedergelassene Anwaltschaft schrumpft” in Anwaltsblatt vom 4.8.2020.

62 Inga Vogt “Das große Interview zur Zukunft der Rechtsabteilung” in ZUJ 01/2021, p. 44 et seq.; Georg Berger, “Die Industrialisierung des Rechts” in ZUJ 01/2021, p. 54 et seq.

you simply want to prove yourself as an entrepreneur, in other words as the owner of a law firm, at the peak of your career as a lawyer. You are in for a special time.

This book is intended to give you an initial overview of the next necessary steps, important questions and problem areas. Now it is up to you to roll up your sleeves and get started. One thing I can assure you: You are not alone! Welcome to the circle of law firm owners, dear colleague!

3. Pandemics and economic crises

Economic and business crises occur at regular intervals. Since 2020, we have learned that we must also expect pandemics and lockdowns that turn our working and living environments upside down for months or even years.

With the Ulrich Lüdke, "Neue Kanzleimodelle" in Unternehmervertraute lood of the century in 2021 and the EU Green Deal, it should have become clear to even the last climate crisis denier that things cannot go on like this in terms of sustainability, climate compatibility and species protection and that a courageous rethink is required.

What does this mean for the legal market? Hasn't it always benefited from crises in the past?

In fact, the industry is doing well. In view of the many special Corona regulations, the industry had an enormous need for advice, so that temporary court closures resulting in the delay of many proceedings were hardly noticeable economically, but rather welcome. According to expectations, the delays caused by the lockdown should have been resolved by 2022[63] – according to forecasts in mid-2021 before the partial lockdown at the turn of the year 2021/2022. After the significant slump in the industry in the fall of 2020 and the lean period in the spring of 2021, things are now looking up in the spring of 2022, according to anwalt.de (according to approximately 210 lawyers out of 4,300).[64]

Government subsidies and investment aid boosted the economy and also the legal consulting business. Other consulting sectors such as tax consultants, auditors and management consultants are also stable[65].

Nevertheless, a good third has suffered actual financial losses: in the Future Lawyer Study 2021, 40 % of lawyers said their business had declined; 51 % do not expect business to return to pre-pandemic levels before 2022. In addition, 61 % of orga-

---

63 This is the result of studies both for Germany (Future Ready Lawyer Study 2021) and for the USA (ABA Profile of the Legal Profession 2021).

64 According to the www.anwalt.deindex of February 2022.

65 *Alexander Sieben* "Gestärkt aus der Krise", in: Haufe, Taxulting from 16.4.2020.

nizations lowered their costs last year. There was hardly any demand for advice in criminal law, family law or traffic law – unlike in labor law and commercial law.

The situation in our case study 2 was an everyday occurrence for many law firms: the "wrong" clients were being attracted or existing clients were coming in with completely new, pandemic-related problems. Having to continually familiarize oneself with new special regulations caused confusion in any cost calculation, no matter how stable it was. In addition, there were considerable delays in client payments and many colleagues had to do more voluntary work. Enormously high investment costs due to the digitalization backlog as well as employee turnover due to poor crisis management and blatant management errors exacerbated the economic situation.

The aging of the industry was becoming noticeable: Colleagues on the verge of retirement were asking themselves whether they should still participate "in the final meters". At that time, there was no thought of handing over the firm, and certainly no thought of selling it. At the same time, however, health and family became more important to many. Lifetime was suddenly too precious to be spent in the office. And so, despite considerable financial losses, many colleagues retired early[66].

Health, family and lifetime also became a different priority for younger generations. However, home offices increased the workload immensely, especially for lawyers with small children or from socially disadvantaged backgrounds. For many, work and private life could no longer be separated. There was a lack of relaxation phases and clear closing time regulations for remote working, as the industry had successfully resisted this up to that point[67]. Burnouts and high stress levels were the result. This is extremely alarming, as the industry has also been struggling for years with increased addiction potential, rising suicide rates, more frequent depression and cases of sudden work-related death – still a taboo subject in this country.

However, nearly three in four attorneys (71 %) in large law firms also reported they were concerned that being in an office building during a workday would not be safe after 2020 for a variety of reasons, including inadequate ventilation and security in public spaces. Similar numbers of attorneys in law firms with 100 to 249 attorneys (68 %) and law firms with 50 to 99 attorneys (75 %) expressed the same concerns. Among solo attorneys, the figure is only 42 %, and among attorneys in firms with two to nine attorneys, 54 %.

66 ABA Profile of the Legal Profession 2021; Future Ready Lawyer Study 2021.

67 This is different in many German companies, which have years of experience with home offices and therefore no longer allow server access in the evenings, at night or on weekends, for example.

Vaccination prioritization has been very controversial, and in some cases rejected. However, vaccination refusers and corona deniers can also be found in law firms of all sizes.

As a result, more than a quarter of lawyers (29 %) in large law firms said they worry about raising health and safety concerns with their employer. Nearly half (47 %) said they fear being viewed as not committed to the firm if they do not return to work at the firm when asked. And 28 % said they feared being fired or put on leave if they did not return to the office when asked.

In addition, there was a deep division in society during this time with regard to political issues, which also extended across law firms:

Climate Change & Fridays4Future (Lawyers4Future), Black lives matter, MeToo & Gender Equality, LGBTQ+ & Diversity, and World Politics with Trump & Co.

Never before have the fronts been so controversial and hardened.

Can the legal industry therefore be described as crisis-resistant? Can we continue as before and focus on day-to-day business?

A very clear no.

As we have seen in the previous chapters, digitization is and will be one of the biggest drivers of change in the legal market. In just five years, the next generation of lawyers and clients will already make up the majority of client relationships, take the use and handling of technologies for granted, and integrate them quite naturally. To be prepared for this, technology companies are currently making huge investments.

The pandemic lockdowns should have convinced the last skeptic that large-scale representative paper offices are out of date and an unnecessary luxury that one must want to afford. In figures: Thus, even in the top 50 law firms in Germany, the ratio for home offices has leveled off from 5 % before Corona to 79 % in 2020/2021 to 42 % at the end of 2021: 33 % of the top 50 therefore want to reduce their office space[68].

Remember:
It won't work without digitization, smart technologies, effective processes and structures.

The real winners of the economic crisis, the lockdown, and the economic and climate crises are therefore the law firms,

- who have already invested in digitization before 2020

68 Die Branche in Zahlen in brand.eins/thema 2021, p. 78.

- and have modernized their processes
- and structures in line with the technology and have trained and inducted law firm employees accordingly.

After all, digitization doesn't end when the IT team has installed the new hardware and software and leaves the office again. The decisive factor is how well the new IT is integrated into daily work processes.

"Last year was the most comprehensive digital workshop ever. It made the whole community digital-savvy seven years early."

Jeroen Zweers[69]

Law firms that only began to think about digitization and its integration into the firm with the lockdown lost valuable time. If they also had to deal with lengthy discussions and decision-making rounds, it was almost impossible to catch up with the digitized law firms.

Smaller law firm teams were able to respond more quickly and flexibly – in decision-making and implementation. If, in addition, the teams were diverse – unafraid of new technologies and open to change – there was little "friction loss" and law firms were able to concentrate unhindered on efficient implementation.

Remember:

The need for digitization, which was intensified by the pandemic, turned out to be a game changer: the ability to develop became the decisive criterion for law firm success.

And these are the current top 5:

1. Digitalization as a basis for existence
2. Efficient processes and structures
3. Changeable law firm strategy and leadership
4. Tension area "law firm size"
5. Good employees and high potentials[70]

---

69 Future Ready Lawyer Study 2021.

70 This prompted me to give the topic of "Leadership and Human Resources Management" its own chapter in this current edition, alongside "Marketing and Acquisition".

Those who have had no time for the topic of law firm development and "have not earned any money for many years because of all the work they have done"[71], must now realize that they have focused on the wrong things and have slept through the dawn of a new era.

4. Future scenarios

What are future scenarios?

At all times, attempts have been made to predict the future.

From prognosticators, oracles and shamans to astrologers and fortune tellers, decision-makers have sought advice throughout the centuries. Sometimes using the knowledge of the past and the ancestors, sometimes with gut feeling and intuition.

Economics has tried it with numbers:

Forecasting and budget planning are classic forecasting methods based on a projection for a future period on the basis of data from a past period. Looking in the "rear view mirror" and "learning from past mistakes" are important.

Scenario thinking, in contrast, is essentially about identifying and analyzing situations that may occur in the future – regardless of the past. Think of scenario planning as creating multiple contingency plans for the same event, based on what are likely to be the most important risk factors (drivers).

The combination of these two models – **Scenario Planning** or **Scenario Forecasting** – is based on a comprehensive analysis of the actual situation.

1. the sector
2. the strategy of the firm
3. the forecasts

Identify the two most important "drivers" or even "game changers" for the future and thus develop a "scenario cross":

Forecasting and Scenario Thinking are the two topics that are currently

- causing a hype,
- scaring many people and
- seem to be circulating far too often in the (trade) media.

Future scenarios are thus developed by filtering out and evaluating trends: Those that are most likely to occur and those that are most important for the success of the company.

71 *Alexander Sieben* "Gestärkt aus der Krise", in: Haufe, Taxulting from 16.4.2020.

Remember:
While traditional strategic planning usually begins with agreement on a company's vision, scenario planning ends with the vision.

The Corona pandemic has given new momentum to future institutes and studies. What will change after Corona?

Using the methods described above, future institutes have defined human relationships and networking as the two most important drivers. The former could either succeed at the local level, which would give the Family Institute a new upswing, but would also rekindle the fear of everything "foreign" (nationalism). Or it could succeed globally, so that mankind could develop something like a new togetherness, a common plan[72]. A new, global sustainability paradigm would be developed. In this scenario, digitization will become the basis of existence. China with its dream of Chinese world domination: Local is then the new global[73]. Deloitte, on the other hand, sees the development of the German economy as the pivotal point: "The future of German companies will have an enormous influence on the German economy, society and politics"[74]. The decisive factor will then be whether German companies remain leaders in invention and development in the future or miss the boat and become mere production sites.

"In any case, the results of the analysis lead us to expect an economic structural change with consequences for an even more far-reaching cultural change. The exact direction is still very difficult to assess today, but only thoughtful and follow-up political action can avoid negative dynamics for individual protected goods in the Corona crisis. The political struggle to weigh up the protected goods will also be with us for a long time in the parallel climate crisis. Both crises are taking place on different time scales, but they must be dealt with today so that the transition from passive shock to active transformation can succeed."[75]

The fact is, therefore, that even without a pandemic, society has reached crucial points of change:

72 Zukunftsinstitut "White Paper 2021: Der Corona-Effekt – vier Zukunftszenarien".
73 Zukunftsideen für 2040, in: Laborpraxis Vogel.
74 *Marc R. Benioff*, Enterprises in Germany in 2030, Deloitte.
75 *Dr. Wolfgang Schade*, Überlegungen zu Szenarien der verkehrlichen und ökonomischen Folgen der Corona-Pandemie in Deutschland, in: Deutsche und Europäische Szenarien für 2013–2015 (M-Five).

Unrestrained growth toward a knowledge and prosperity society or away from the growth paradigm toward a sustainable and balancing society? Cultural change and the end of patriarchy, change of the 19th century working world[76].

Remember:
All of this has an influence on many aspects of the changes in the legal market, be it in the (re)evaluation of law and justice, the management and development of law firms as a business enterprise, or in the working environment of law firms.

So what are possible future scenarios for the industry?

According to the Future Ready Lawyer Study 2021, which was conducted in March 2021, exactly one year after the start of the pandemic, in ten European countries (including Germany) and the U. S., the biggest drivers in the legal market in the coming years will be:

1. Increasing importance of legal technology: 76 %
2. Changing customer/management expectations: 74 %
3. Focus on improved efficiency and productivity: 73 %
4. Ability to recruit and retain talent: 73 %
5. Managing increasing information volume and complexity: 72 %

This raises the following questions:

Will we be able to afford to forgo the majority of graduates and high potentials because we want to hold on to patriarchal structures that discriminate against, underpay, and repel anyone who is not white, male, and heterosexual?

Will they be able to afford to hold on to expensive, prestigious offices full of paper and long corridors with high energy costs, while advising clients around the world 24/7 with high energy costs?

Will we be able to afford to let those who neither understand nor use technology and who will retire from the firm in a few years make strategic decisions for the future of the firm?

According to these studies, the two most important "drivers" seem to be digitization and client satisfaction, which is more or less in line with the general studies on the future:

---

76 *Stefan Hradil*, Zukunftsszenarien für Deutschland, in: Bundeszentrale für politische Bildung (bpb) from 31.5.2012.

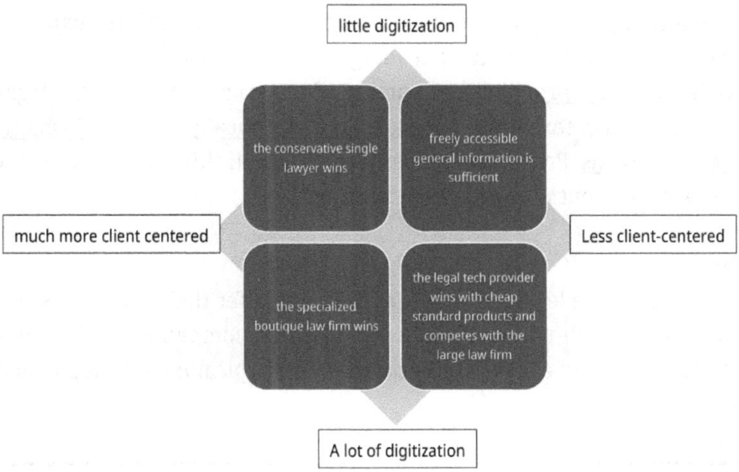

Future scenarios (c) Dr. Geertje Tutschka

Remember:
This makes it clear: with the two drivers of client orientation and digitalization, the medium-sized, modern and highly specialized boutique law firm will be the law firm of the future.

In my view, this prediction of the future suffers from the homogeneous determination of the starting position: legal technology is never an end in itself, but rather a means to an end. Efficient processes and the management of complexity are mandatory prerequisites – not additional drivers. In this respect, it would be important to know the composition of the information group of 700 lawyers from ten European countries and the USA: Of 699 white, heterosexual men over 55?

The fact is -law firms have two core target groups:
Clients and junior recruits

These are not really all that different, unless you try to squeeze the junior recruits into old-fashioned structures. Otherwise, the two groups complement each other quite well in terms of their needs, communication, skills, goals and language.

Clients:
The gap between the service requirements of the clients and the service portfolio of the firm is already widening, both with private clients and with business clients, because cost-saving, efficient, client-oriented and holistic solutions to increasingly complex problems with the highest degree of specialization are expected as a result

of the generational change and the growing demands of companies. These expectations are increasingly being disappointed, leading to a loss of trust[77].

Alternative legal service providers are entering the market faster than the legal profession is shrinking, increasing the pressure on economically weak, unfashionable and outdated law firms. Premature retirement and a definitive departure from law firm sales as a retirement provision are the result.

Junior recruits:

New Work will not spare the legal industry. Lawyers will offer their services remotely around the world, which will result in a loss of labor, competing foreign lawyers entering the market, and a loss of attractiveness for typical long-term partner structures.

"In science, for example, remote collaboration has provided breakthroughs for decades. Many companies work in cross-location teams on new products or services – often using time zones to speed up development. In fact, one could argue that concentrating activities on people who just happen to be in the same office is a constraint."

Sally Guyer[78]

---

92 % of management consultants assume that the proportion of remote work will remain high even after the pandemic. This assessment is closely related to the issue of sustainability: A management consultancy cannot, on the one hand, promote climate-protective measures to its clients and, on the other hand, give the impression that it is not sufficiently aware of issues like domestic flights.

The focus lies on CO2 emissions: After all, mobility is inherent in the project business of consulting, and travel to clients and project partners will inevitably be required in the future as well. In order to be more specific on this topic, the BDU has announced a "benchmarking exercise with regard to the CO2 footprint in consulting". For this purpose, mobility-related values for 2019 and 2020 are to be used. Thus, the effects of the Corona pandemic can be highlighted, as stated in the association's principles on sustainability. What is needed is a balance between direct customer contact on site and digital forms of communication – and this is where the new generation can play to its strengths:

Digital natives consider both forms of interaction as a whole, and the discrepancies between real and virtual encounters are perceived less strongly. The younger

77 *Harald Willenbrock* Hausrecht, in: brandeins thema 05/2020.
78 Future Ready Lawyer Study 2021.

generation thus has the opportunity to help shape a new form of customer contact culture in consulting companies[79] if they are allowed to.

Remember:
Reconciling customer proximity with new work and climate protection thus represents the update of people's business and calls for new approaches.

As the first generation to really grow up with technology, Generation Z "will be in a better position than any other generation to benefit from this growing demand for digital skills," according to a press release summarizing the study. Three characteristics of Generation Z are particularly advantageous for the future workplace: agility, creativity and curiosity. For the people's business of the consulting industry, these three skills are of central importance: young consultants who possess these qualities have a bright future ahead of them. Despite or even because of uncertain times[80].

Millennials (born between 1981 and 1995) are an optimistic generation who grew up during an economic boom and are considered spoiled by their parents. They will make up 75 % of the legal profession in the next five years, according to the Future Ready Lawyer Study 2021, along with people in their mid-forties today. But they are no longer game changers.

The members of Generation Z (born between 1996 and 2012) are already in the starting blocks, ready to take over: They are more pragmatic, having grown up during a recession. The pandemic caught them midway into adulthood in their early/mid-twenties, when they tried to use Fridays For Future to get their parents to rethink policies that would destroy their future livelihoods. The lockdowns hit them when exchanges, discovering so-called peer groups, and establishing new-ish partnerships and even dating were essential to their development but forbidden, banishing them back to their childhood bedrooms. Resilience is as firmly anchored in their DNA as a healthy scepticism about the status quo, but also a fear of the future. Members of Generation Z are more ethnically, sexually, politically and ethically diverse than any generation before, and they are well on their way to becoming the most educated generation – despite years of Home Study. They are reflective, mentally charged, and probably the most mature generation of adolescents we have ever encountered. What's more, they are the true "digital natives," with little or no

---

79 *André Boße* New Work, Nachhaltigkeit, Purpose – Consulting in der Post-Corona-Zeit, in: Karriereführer from 1.7.2021.

80 *André Boße* New Work, Nachhaltigkeit, Purpose – Consulting in der Post-Corona-Zeit, in: Karriereführer from 1.7.2021.

memory of the world before smartphones. They no longer see digitization as a threat to human relationships, but rather as an enhancement of togetherness: The expansion of technical possibilities for communicating with one another leads to an increase in quantity; offline togetherness is freed from mundane and boring sequences (e.g., finding appointments) and elevated to a new, more human quality. In this respect, a more human approach to legal advice is also expected[81].

These digital natives will complete their education and enter the workforce and economy in five years at the latest; in ten years, they will become decision-makers in the legal market.

Increasing social pressure, stronger political regulations, e.g. from the EU through measures such as the Green Deal or the EU taxonomy and, last but not least, a financial sector that is making sustainability a dealmaker in big steps, sustainability has developed into a core topic of economic success. More and more companies are realizing that if they want to survive on the market in the future, they have to deliver a good performance in the area of sustainability. Consultants fulfil the task of supporting their clients in analyzing the status quo, developing measures, developing parameters for effectiveness and, last but not least, anchoring sustainability in the corporate strategy. This broad panorama of sustainability consulting is particularly interesting for the next generation.

Human resources management will therefore play a key role: The right competencies in the right team composition will determine success. The highly competitive and now global market of future tech-savvy, internationally educated and cosmopolitan high potentials will be the arena of the legal market. This requires work and compensation models that appeal to these new generations; the old ones definitely do not[82]. Recruiting them is one thing, retaining them is another: Team building, firm culture and leadership are essential for this. 24 months of online onboarding in recruiting due to a Corona pandemic was doable – now it's about forming these new employees into a team and retaining them for the long term.

Complexity joins these two core target groups:

VUCA has been pushed through the organizational development world for years as a model for current complexity: VUCA is an acronym that was first used in 1987, following the leadership theories of Warren Bennis and Burt Nanus, to describe or reflect the volatility, uncertainty, complexity, and ambiguity of frameworks and situations[83], and does not stop at the legal market.

81 *Maurus Schreyvogel* Rechtsmarkt 2021, in: ZUJ 1/2021.

82 *Arne Storm* Alles was Recht ist, in: brandeins thema 5/2020; *Kristina Läsker* Das Ende der alten Welt, in: brandeins thema 5/2020.

83 VUCA: volatility, uncertainty, complexity and ambiguity.

Adaptation of the law will become necessary: Change is the New Normal – Organizations must therefore ensure, urgently, that their contracts and contract processes are fit for the purpose[84]. However, most business contracts to date have sought to create security and thus cement the status quo. They are intended to agree on fixed obligations and specify consequences for non-fulfilment and presuppose that nothing will change in the general situation. It's about risk sharing: liabilities, indemnities, performance obligations. Endless hours and large sums of money are invested in order to agree on conditions that ultimately prove to be irrelevant for dealing with pandemics and crises. Corona does not have to happen first; the BREXIT has also shown that legal structures do not last forever[85].

That was once! Today, contracts must be as complex and flexible as a clause library. One-dimensional solution thinking from A to B has had its day. Solutions take place simultaneously and centuries apart. Human rights reach far into the past and into the future. Today more than ever, data protection and ethics have to be considered by lawyers, especially in the context of new technologies and digitalization[86]. his is ensured by the EU Green Deal, but also by laws such as the new Supply Chain Act[87]. Humility in the face of ignorance is the new "omniscience" of the sciences. But a political responsibility is also increasingly discussed for lawyers. They have long since ceased to be seen merely as "craftsmen"[88].

It is about creating corporate values such as **brand value**, which is increasingly linked to sustainability. Looking at the human resources market, it is clear that an increasing number of young people are choosing an employer based on whether the job promises them "purpose". Companies that have not taken care of their sustainability issues are therefore no longer attracting talent, despite good salaries and the high attractiveness of the workplace.

And last but not least: Many companies have realized that their business model is not as well equipped against external shocks as they thought. Climate compatibility is one thing; with the latest court decisions, there are also human rights issues to consider[89].

---

84 *Hubertus Drinkuth* Der Nachhaltigkeitsberater im Interview, Karriereführer from 1.7.2021.

85 *Dr. Anke Nordemann-Schiffel* und *Dr. Julian Klagge* Brexit and Brands – Was Markeninhaber beachten müssen, in: Anwaltspiegel from 6.1.2021.

86 *Dr. Andrea Panzer-Heemeier* und *Tobias Neufeld* The next big thing im Rechtsmarkt: Nachhaltigkeit, in: Anwaltspiegel from 6.1.2021.

87 *Prof. Dr. Cordula Meckenstock* Rechtsmarkt 2021, in: ZUJ 01/2021.

88 *Ingo Müller* Furchtbare Juristen. Die unbewältigte Vergangenheit der deutschen Justiz; *Andreas Molitor* Die Wächter der Ordnung, in: brandeins thema, 05/2020.

89 *Hubertus Drinkuth* Der Nachhaltigkeitsberater im Interview, in: Karriereführer from 1.7.2021.

In addition to climate compatibility, there is also social compatibility. Socially responsible is the new wild card in any debate: e-justice and e-government are supposed to provide answers and facilitate access to the legal market. In addition to legal tech, formats such as legal coaching are trying to offer alternatives in the high-price markets of North America and Canada.

Whenever complexity is involved, the aim is to simplify – or to cushion possible consequences by taking precautions against risks. Forecasting and scenario design originate from precisely this endeavor: It is not primarily a matter of already knowing the future today, but of estimating possible negative consequences and protecting against them. But even forecasting and scenario planning did not predict the Corona pandemic of 2020/2021 – or did they? Haven't scientists always warned about this and were ignored because other possible future scenarios seemed more pleasant? It resembles the climate crisis a bit, doesn't it?

Either way, risk management is currently experiencing an enormous upswing – and not only among risk professionals, the insurers[90], – but is increasingly moving into the legal focus. It has always been immanent to legal issues, e.g., the distribution of risk in contract negotiations as described above. However, this topic has rarely had a place in strategy meetings: No wonder, since so far most of the reactions were to solve problems; precautions were never on the agenda.

Things have to change. The Corona lockdowns have shown how quickly and professionally hygiene concepts can be developed and implemented in law firms from scratch based on brand-new specifications. Experience with the implementation of data protection regulations from previous years and the establishment of data protection officers has shown that it can be done when it needs to be done. Data protection concepts and hygiene concepts are concepts for risk management. These must be expanded. At the same time, strategic planning should be added, which always includes a (crisis) plan B and, above all, builds up economic and human resources.

The winners will be those who take action now because they have learned from experience, not when it is already too late.

Conclusion:

The law firm of the future described above must therefore be modified as follows:

The medium-sized, modern and highly specialized boutique law firm that employs a high proportion of young, tech-savvy high potentials on the one hand and

90 *Prof. Dr. Bruno Mascello* Risikomanagement im Rechtsmarkt neu gedacht, in: Anwaltspiegel from 6.1.2021.

has a professional management team that manages risk on the other will be fit for the future.

5. Conclusion

What does this imply for our three case study law firms?

1. The numerous small law firms with the "growing pains" could, as suggested, heed the call of digitization, optimize their structures and processes, significantly reduce costs, and significantly increase the quality of life of their partners. Or -and with regard to these future scenarios, they actually have a choice -they consciously decide to remain cooperating small law firms (and to renounce the basic principle of "growing pains"). This does not per se rule out the proposed digital solution for increasing efficiency. However, it would be a clear change of strategy. The decision determines the future of the firm and must be made in a strategically well-considered manner in the partner group. In coordination with the values and goals and the vision of the firm's owners.
2. The firm with the "wrong clients" should elevate customer satisfaction to its core values and make this its internal guiding star. The successful reorientation can serve as a blueprint for future change processes. Customer satisfaction is one of the three criteria for the future.
3. The traditional large law firm would do well to reinvent itself: Instead of focusing on the needs of senior partners (financial security, continuity), who are planning to leave in the foreseeable future anyway, they should focus on the needs of their future partners, in line with Maslow's pyramid of needs (see below), which has been adapted to organizations: these would be the needs of an ideally diverse team of tech-savvy Millenials and Generation Z, who are multinational cosmopolitans. Gender Equality and New Work should be set professionally and financially to be able to compete with the international competition from "New Legal". The partners have a long way to go in terms of cultural change and diversity.

What did you get out of this chapter?
You have been able to take a look into the "crystal ball", into your professional future – so to speak. Whether and which of the things shown will actually come to pass is up to you, among others!

B. The law firm vision

What is law firm formation and management all about?

Every law firm, like every company, should have an "ideal version"[1] of itself. This is given to the law firm by the owner or by the team responsible for it. In principle, this ideal version should already be in place when the firm is founded and should not be based primarily on the market situation or the know-how of the employees. Rather, it should be based on the purpose for which the company, the law firm is founded or was founded in the past. Necessarily, the owner or the team should have a precise vision of where the journey should go and how they want to use the law firm for this purpose[2].

The process of developing such a law firm vision can be supported by a professional business coach who ideally understands something about the legal industry and law firm business. On the other hand, it is a different matter to seek advice from experts or consultants (in book form, seminar or consulting) or to bring an experienced colleague on board as a mentor. While the former where more oriented toward objective ideal versions, subjective experience plays a decisive role in the latter. A business coach, on the other hand, if he has been trained and certified as such[3], will orientate himself to the individual situation and together they will create a vision of the ideal law firm in less than a third of the time[4]. Decide for yourself whether this investment is worthwhile.

Of course, an ideal version of this kind can change, expand or reduce over the course of time. However, it should always be clear and stable, as if it were a "lighthouse" by which one aligns and orients oneself. Vague general phrases or a colorful bouquet of widely differing things are not suitable. Rather, this is an unmistakable sign that the company, the law firm is moving away from a clear ideal image of itself. It is then necessary to ask whether it still serves the original purpose or whether a new or reorganization is not due.

The idea of "providing legal advice in the German market" is therefore by no means sufficient for this purpose, even though the vast majority of law firms in Germany were probably founded for precisely this purpose[5]. Since the legal parameters

---

1 Some also call it "vision" or simply "goal," although the latter doesn't quite hit the mark.

2 Schieblon in "Kanzleimanagement in der Praxis", p. 24., Verlag Springer-Gabler.

3 Since there are many consultants on the market who merely call themselves coaches in a marketing-effective way, even though they do not actually provide coaching services or have been trained as coaches, I strongly recommend that you obtain the appropriate certification as a coach from a professional association (comparable to that of a specialist lawyer).

4 Dr. Tutschka, "Der Rechtsanwalt als Unternehmer", TeleLex, p. 17.

5 Claudia Bonacker, "Kanzleigründung und Kanzleistrategie" in Haufe from 20.1.2014.

https://doi.org/10.1515/9783111058160-002

for law firms should already be included in the objective, the whole thing must therefore be necessarily operated, for instance, with the intention of making a profit[6].

In this situation, however, another legal form may make sense, such as the establishment of an association or a foundation. The initiatives "Liquid Legal Institute" and "Lawyers 4 Future" (which I advise strategically) were faced with exactly such a decision – and ultimately opted for the legal form of a registered association[7].

6 Otherwise, your tax office may have the idea of classifying your law firm as a "hobby".

7 Kai Jakob, Dierk Schindler, Roger Strathausen, Liquid Legal: Towards a Common Legal Platform, p. 11.

I. Personality of the lawyer

Why should you read this chapter?
You will understand how to develop your individual law firm vision based on this general legal market inventory and the role your personality plays in it.

Overview

1. **Setting goals: SMART method**
2. **Status quo: what do clients want, what do they ask for?**
3. **Resource analysis (SWOT)**
4. **Restrictions, limitations, obligations**
5. **Lawyer vs. law firm owner**

In the beginning there is the idea, the desire for your own law firm. But then the needs of the clients, the market, the skills and personalities of the employees get in the way and the schedule of everyday business takes over.

Only about a quarter of newcomers to the profession start their professional career in self-employment with their own law firm. The vast majority want to gain professional experience first and start out as employees. After eight years, however, the ratio has almost reversed: almost two thirds of the professionals have become self-employed. This can be a promotion to partnership, but also leaving the original law firm and establishing or taking over a law firm.

The detailed knowledge of the legal market in general and in particular (for special fields, certain regions etc.) is crucial for success.

Most people start with a timeline for implementing the law firm formation project, focusing on when the ideal time to form a law firm is. Of course, it is always good to have a plan. However, if you are really serious about it, you should start with the development of a law firm vision:

On the one hand, this should include the business model, e.g. a special field, a particular service, as well as the positioning of this USP (Unique Selling Point) on the market. Ideally, the development of the unique selling proposition is preceded by a precise market analysis:

Is there really a demand for this solution? Where does the competition stand? Where, when and how does this offer work best?

On the other hand, it should also include what the firm stands for, what values are practiced there, and in what culture of togetherness the firm works: Should the firm contribute to the common good, stand for social or even socio-political commitment? Is the firm managed in a strictly hierarchical manner or do employees have a great amount of personal responsibility? Are feedback and suggestions for improvement welcome, and what about the culture of making mistakes?

Remember:
A firm should stand for certain values and be clear about the culture it lives in, and not only for reasons of professional ethics.

In the assumption that everyone else is like themselves, company owners repeatedly underestimate how important it is to not only have clarity about their own values and needs, but also to communicate them clearly. If the company is run by a management team, as is the case in the vast majority of law firms, clarity is lost at the latest when there has not been a sufficient agreement on a management style and a uniform set of values and employee culture. This is where writing helps.

Remember:
The advice that the lawyer repeatedly gives clients after an unsuccessful alleged agreement should definitely be followed in his own firm.

It is similar to the doctor Frankenstein, who, just because he can technically do so, joins body parts to a body and brings it to life. But is this thing therefore a human being? Certainly not: it lacks a soul, a heart, a moral compass. Frankenstein is an impressive plea for values, ethics and culture, and thus applies equally to companies and organizations, including law firms.

Of course, a special position is occupied by the so-called individual law firms, in which the lawyer is simultaneously the law firm in a personal union and which still make up approximately one third of the law firms. In this case, the law firm reflects the lawyer's personality and values.

The Business Model Canvas is an excellent tool for developing the business model. It can be used to work out in detail what is special about legal advice and the target clientele, the key contacts, acquisition and client communication, and much more.

But here, at the latest, a dilemma can arise: It's a people business.

When developing the business model according to the needs of the market and the corresponding values and culture, the question arises in the strategic implementation: Who are the right employees and colleagues for this? Am I the right person for this business model? What personalities does the client need? This can and should lead to an honest result, which in case of doubt can also mean deciding against an envisaged law firm division and instead including the perspective as well as the question of which employees and which know-how are actually available for the law firm foundation from the very beginning.

Remember:
A healthy self-assessment of one's strengths and weaknesses and an awareness of the firm owner's or partner's own values and life goals are important building blocks on the path to start-up.

Founding and running a business is always a profound self-experience and an opportunity for personal development. Founding a law firm therefore begins first and foremost with you.

The model of Spiral Dynamics (Beck/Cowan in: "Spiral Dynamics"), which was developed by the US psychology professor Clare Graves as early as the 1960s, provides an overview of human development in the form of a "universal map". To get acquainted with the complexity of Spiral Dynamics before founding a law firm helps to understand interrelationships:

- Why do start-ups need "anarchy" to be successful?
- Why do complex hierarchical structures keep large companies from going under, when they have been proven to be hostile to innovation and lead to homogeneous management teams?
- Why do buzzwords like "agility" and "new work" unsettle the older generation, which in turn views data security as "valuable"?

Therefore it depends decisively on your personality.

It's a people business[1].

This does not only apply to the clients and the satisfaction of their needs. This applies equally to the question of what you personally bring to the table.

Who are you? What defines you?

The participants in my workshops on this topic mainly think of their training as fully qualified lawyers, their titles and degrees.

But is it? Does even one client come to them as a lawyer because they have completed the 2nd state examination with xyz or because they have a doctorate?

The client comes because he has received a recommendation or because he found the appearance on the Internet appealing. During the first contact, he decides whether he likes the person. Whether he trusts.

Therefore, it is important to know who you are, what you stand for and which aspects of this are important to the client: Identity and identification.

1 Gerber, p. 9, "The E-Myth Attorney".

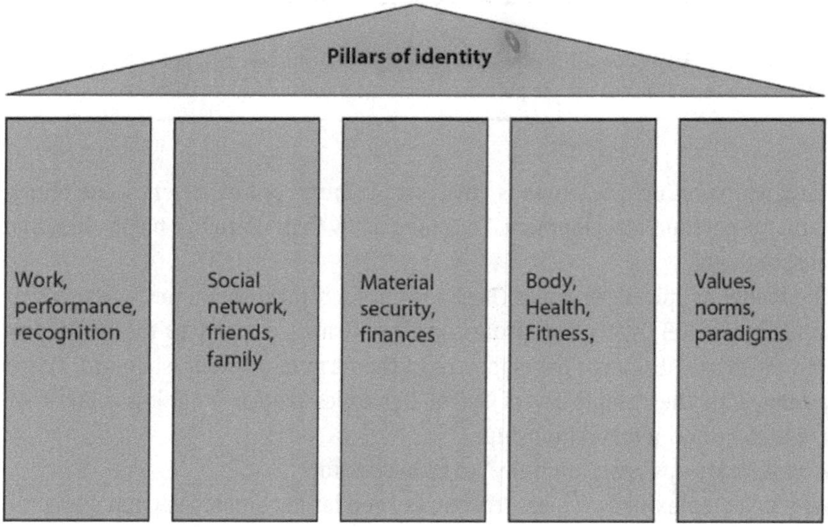

The five pillars of identity according to H. Petzold[2], © Dr. Geertje Tutschka

Identity is the uniqueness and distinctiveness of every human being. By identity (from Latin: unity of essence, equal, sameness) we understand our unique personality structure and the behaviors that we acquire or discard. Developing them is a lifelong process that takes place in interaction between human beings and their environment. The various aspects of the environment that influence the formation of identity are depicted by Petzold in the "five pillars of identity".

However, it is not yet primarily a question of which character traits you have: which leadership style you prefer, whether you are a team player, which learning type you are, how you deal with time and money, whether you are more the sales type, the buddy, the nerd, or the fastidious.

Of course, everyone has a certain image of themselves in their head. But very few people are aware of the individual aspects of this image and the relationship between them. Of course, this can only ever be a current snapshot[3].

Why is this important?

On the one hand, you yourself will only lead a fulfilled life and exude this if all aspects are in balance with each other. Your professional vision or law firm vision should therefore take this into account in order to be successfully implemented.

---

2 Hilarion Petzold was born in Germany in 1944 and is considered one of the leading figures in modern psychotherapy.

3 By the way, with the so-called wheel of life, the different aspects of the snapshot can be measured very nicely.

On the other hand, your colleagues and clients need information from these five aspects of your personality in order to get a "picture" of you. To see you as a person, to be able to do the sympathy check and, most importantly, to be able to build up a relationship with you and to trust you. Much of this information is given before the first contact (through articles, website, books, recommendations, office reception), some in the seconds before you greet the client (with appearance, body language, staging). The client will then take the few missing pieces of the puzzle from the conversation with you or fill them with "blueprints" from his drawers (i.e.: use preconceptions to fill the gaps). In order to be able to consciously control this process, it is important to know yourself and to emphasize the essential aspects for the client to the outside world.

Lawyers and law firms, however, tend to put the legal field, titles and degrees in the foreground and completely hide the person behind them. This not only makes them interchangeable, but also somehow pale, almost invisible and nebulous for the client, unapproachable, even intangible. This is the worst possible prerequisite for building a trusting relationship.

At this point, the objection is regularly raised in my seminars that, after all, one is selling one's expertise in a particular field of law and not oneself. I then silently point to the introductory sentence (the first sentence of this chapter).

Whatever you sell or think you sell, you will only sell it through your identity. You can only control what focus you want to put out there in each of the five identity areas. But be sure that gaps are filled with bias. If you want to position yourself as a criminal lawyer, you should have good reasons why you are a criminal lawyer and how that fits with your identity. If you are presenting yourself as a divorce lawyer, you need information from your own family context. Business lawyers like to think that they are in the clear in this respect, since their field of law has virtually no reference to the person and is therefore neutral. You can let the numbers speak for themselves. But here too, if you don't want to be interchangeable, you should think carefully about why M & A logically belongs to you. The client – in this case the contact person from the company – will not remember the perfect diagram, but he will remember Mr. Müller's story of how the subject of M & A found him.

So, start knitting not only your success story early on, but more importantly, your "personal story" that carries your area of law or your legal services product. **i**

Included in this, of course, is the question: **who do you want to be and where do you want to go?**

Everyone should answer this question for themselves in all honesty. A good starting point is usually the answer to the question: What made you get out of bed this morning? It can also help to ask "What do you want your obituary, your tombstone to say?" I prefer: What's the point?

The goal is to get a concrete idea of the ideal version of oneself, of one's life, in order to align oneself with it. After all, nothing is more frustrating than to realize in the end that you have lived someone else's ideal version.

I regularly offend many of my participants with this. They think that such considerations are a private matter and have nothing to do with their work and their law firm. After all, they are not an individual lawyer who is virtually identical with his law firm. But that is too short-sighted.

I admit that the answer to these questions is not easy to give. And it's certainly not something you'd want to discuss in a seminar with colleagues you don't know. And sometimes honesty also hurts at this point.

And yet: In the end, every law firm should be able to realize the personal life goals of each employee. And these people must be able to be experienced by the client.

If you have an ideal version of your life, of yourself, this is to be filled in with concrete goals[4]. Once the goal has been set, the next step is to ask: And how do I achieve my goal? That's where strategy comes into play. But what exactly is a strategy? According to its origin, strategy is a military term and means army command. Clausewitz understood strategy as the doctrine of the use of combat for the purpose of war. Less martially, strategy can be understood as a set of rules of conduct, of norms, all of which are designed to achieve a goal. All detailed decisions on the way to this goal have to be guided by this bundle of norms, the strategy[5].

How is a strategy developed? Strategy processes are often diffuse and tough.

In literature and economics there are many different models and methods.

I like to use this simplified structure for my clients to get started. It is a five-step process that enables everyone to grasp, work on and solve all the essential points for developing a successful strategy.

---

i

1. Goal
2. Status quo
3. Resources/potential
4. Constraints/limitations
5. Role, responsibility

---

4 R. Römermann, Lawyer Marketing Management, Rn. 639, assumes that law firm goals will last for a period of five to twenty years.

5 See also Hartung p. 12 in "Kanzleimanagement in der Praxis".

Essentially, this system works like a navigation device:

- First, the exact destination is entered,
- then the location is determined,
- the predefined software uses the information on speed limits, traffic jams, etc.
- Certain parameters determine whether highways are used, the direct route is chosen or similar.
- Finally, the optimal route is calculated, including kilometers and time.

The strategy method "5 steps to success" can give structure to the process, especially if it is an individual vision.

Remember:
The goal of the method is to reduce complexity.

It should be noted that this is a structured process of development; the result, its implementation and first steps are therefore not included.

The method at a glance

Goal:
SMART (Specific, Measurable, Attractive, Realistic, Timed)
START WITH WHY (Why, What, How)
KISS (Keep it simple, stupid)
also:
Vision, Mission & Purpose;
Mission Statement & Compliance/Rules of Conduct; Values & Culture

Status quo:
Inventory analysis
Analysis/anamnesis of the personality, the company as well as the environment (systemics)
Assessments, type analysis, personality profiles can be used here (HOGAN, MBTI, 360 Grad Feedback, StrengthsFinder, Enneagram)
PEST (Environment analysis for the structured determination of influencing factors)

- **P**olitical
- **E**conomic

- **S**ocial
- **T**echnological

The hard work consists in being able to substantiate the identified trends with sources rather than just deriving them from gut feeling. "No assertion without proof" is an essential prerequisite for making the environment analysis credible.

SWOT (includes status quo/target and resources/limitations as a matrix of 4).

After the analysis, the synthesis begins. From the environment analysis we know the opportunities and risks (vertical), from the company or personal analysis the strengths and weaknesses (horizontal). The goal in this step is to identify the five to seven main challenges[6].

- **S**trengths
- **W**eaknesses
- **O**pportunities
- **T**hreats

Role and responsibility:
The goal and inventory analysis are readjusted from the perspective of each role. Role and responsibility can include, for example, management responsibility/ caretaker, parenthood mother/father, external, private, honorary office and many more.

Resources:
Education, degrees, work experience
Personal life experience, talents, cultural background

Limitations:
legal obligations (e.g. welfare, profession, licenses, offices, permits)
personal commitments (e.g., wellbeing, resilience, health/illness, hobbies, language)

The method in application:
A start is made on working out the status quo and the target, and this is done gradually and in parallel.

Shortly before finalizing these two cornerstones, role and responsibility should be included to sharpen and specify the "angle" on the topic for both the goal and the status quo. Both will be readjusted.

6 More on this in a few pages on p. 139.

The resources and limitations can be worked out in parallel, selectively. It is important that these always relate to the goal and status quo (and role, if applicable), i.e. that they are relevant.

Once all five steps have been worked through, the process is usually in its final stage; the DREAM or vision has been completely worked out and the decision and the first steps towards its implementation are imminent.

Remember

The left hand (palm to the face) or the word DREAM can also be used as a "mnemonic" for the five steps. Each finger then stands for one of the 5 steps in the development of the strategy in terms of content and by hand signal.

D = Dream:	Target – "top" (thumbs up)
R = Resources:	Building Blocks of Success – "Be careful with it!" (Mom warns with her index finger)
E = Entrance:	Status quo – "It sucks" (extended middle finger)
A = Ambivalence:	Limitations – e.g. the wedding vows (the ring on the finger)
M = Mission:	Role – "Pinky Promise" (the "small obligations" of everyday life).

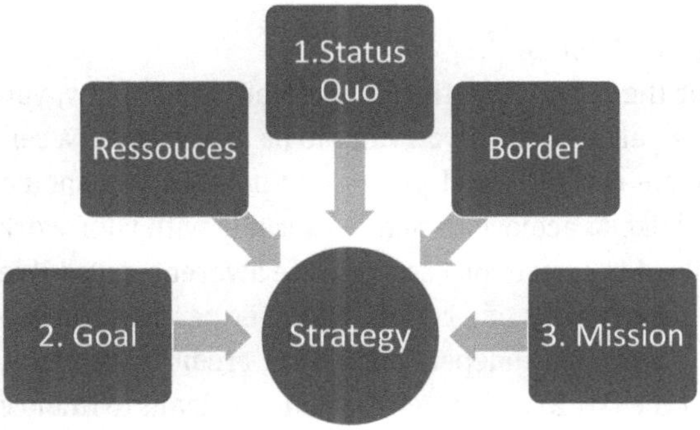

1. Setting goals

You can be creative in setting goals. However, general phrases such as "to be a good lawyer," to see yourself as an "advocate of justice," to be considered a "star lawyer" or simply wanting to become "rich and happy" do not describe goals as intended in this context.

SMART Method

For starters, every goal definition should be formulated in a simple, clear sentence and checked against these five parameters. I recommend that my law firms follow the SMART method commonly used in business management:

S = Specific
M= Measurable
A = Accepted
R = Reasonable
T = Time-bound

---

i *A "smart" goal of this kind can be, for example:*
I would like to have generated a total profit of €xxx with my law firm in the legal field xyz with two other partners and at least three employees at the end of the third year since its founding.

This corresponds to a SMART target definition[7].

If you want to be the best or the biggest law firm in a certain field of law, you should aim for the corresponding partnership. If you want to be an expert on a certain topic, for example, to promote certain social projects or policies, you should publish and lecture. If you would like to achieve something socially with your work as a lawyer, you should get involved in certain projects or raise awareness. Possible further economic goals are the achievement of a certain turnover per year, the exceeding of an income limit or simply the independence from credit institutions, which is achieved by the fact that the law firm does not take out any loans to finance its equipment and a possible expansion and grows from its own financial strength. Non-monetary or only partially monetary goals are also conceivable: e.g., to serve only very specific clients (consumers) or even to be particularly famous ("the best-known law firm in town").

7 Whether the target is appealing to you – i.e. whether it also touches you emotionally – is something you have to decide for yourself.

However, this goal can also coincide with law firm goals: for example, to achieve or maintain a certain size as a law firm. In law firm job offers, one often finds the wording that the firm is keen to have a manageable size in which everyone knows everyone else. Other firms attach less importance to this and would rather be a "law firm around the world"[8]. Another firm, judging by its smart firm motto, has set itself the goal of becoming consistently larger. The goal of a law firm can also be to gain a certain market share in a region. The market share can be related to a certain area of law, for example stock corporation law, to an industry (telecommunications companies) or to a certain type of client (medium-sized companies). A possible economic goal of a law firm is to specialize in one area of law, such as criminal law or labor law. A legitimate goal can also be the achievement of a certain reputation, an image ("the most family-friendly law firm in town"; "always there when you need them"; "the most capable negotiators far and wide"). Intra-firm goals can also be important. Some lawyers attach importance to a particularly pleasant working atmosphere in the office. Probably every lawyer strives to ensure that the employees feel comfortable in the office and enjoy working there.

All of these goals are not mutually exclusive, but they do not necessarily all have to be pursued in every law firm. Which goals a law firm wants to achieve is primarily a matter of taste or, better, the personal decision of the owner; but not only.

Supposed conflicting goals, that is, multiple goals that contradict each other, are almost always goals that were not SMART, meaning in particular that they were not realistic:

The goal of "specializing in social law" and the goal of "advising and representing exclusively small companies" do not go well together. Small companies do not have many social law problems. The prospective social law specialist will not be fully occupied with this clientele. The solution to the conflict of objectives may be to expand the target group of clients to include private individuals and social security funds.

The goal of "a small law firm with no more than four lawyers" does not fit with the ambitious goal of achieving "a fifty percent market share in traffic accident cases" in a large city. This cannot be achieved with only four lawyers.

The turnover target "processing turnover of each partner per year of at least EUR 400,000.00" can come into conflict with the firm's target "high degree of recognition through membership in associations". If a partner exaggerates the "unification", then he will hardly have enough time left to achieve his personal turnover target. It may also be necessary to adjust targets to the requirements of the market.

---

8 www.kleiner-law.de: "Kleiner wird größer".

---

i And last but not least: The legal profession is a strenuous and time-consuming profession. The time commitment Reports that salaried attorneys are required to work about 2,000 billable hours per year (plus time spent on administrative tasks, continuing education and acquisition) are by no means an old wives' tale. Partners, that is, law firm owners, sometimes work even more. However, such a high time commitment is not everyone's cup of tea, nor does it have to be. You will remember the general values from the economy on page 66: 200 performance days with approx. 6 performance hours per day (plus administrative tasks for at least 2 hours), i.e. a realistic 1,200 performance hours per year. Sooner or later, a lawyer will have to decide how much of his life he wants to devote to his profession.

Running a law firm is no less demanding. For many, being a lawyer and an entrepreneur at the same time can mean that private life often takes a back seat. This makes it all the more important to consider not only the goals for the law firm, but also those for one's legal career and private goals when setting goals:

A possible private goal that has a professional connection can be to never take files home to work on[9], or to never work longer than 10:00 pm. Thanks to digitization, Wi-Fi, and the widespread introduction of smartphones, laptops, and the like, accessibility and efficiency are basically available to everyone everywhere at all times. There no longer seems to be any natural limit: neither at night, nor at the weekend, during recreational leave, maternity leave or in the event of illness. In my experience, it takes more than just good time management to secure the important periods of rest and regeneration needed to satisfy basic human needs. First and foremost, it requires ego management as well as clear boundaries and assertiveness. Another private goal can be to take at least two three-week vacations per year, completely independent of other time commitments. Some lawyers are not prepared to devote their entire working energy to the legal profession. For example, there are colleagues who have also studied history and regularly publish highly regarded papers in historical circles. Their historical authoring takes up a considerable part of their working time. One must want it that way. There is nothing to be said against it.

Some people have the private goal of living in a certain region. The desire to do so may have family reasons or be motivated by a sense of home or by the high quality of life in a region. A very important and often neglected topic is partnership and family planning. This also includes a circle of friends, several generations of the family and a stable social network. On the one hand this belongs to the human basic needs and plays into the topic "recovery and Regeneration" itself. A lonely person gets sick faster, is exposed to an increased stress level and slips into burnout far more often. On the other hand, for many lawyers, conversations with friends and

9 Whether in paper form or digitally.

family are also a catalyst, psycho-hygiene, almost a supervision, to be able to deal with the human dramas of their clients in the long run. Ultimately, this is also a provision for retirement and an investment. Which is why I am seeing more and more lawyers who are consciously turning to professional support, be it to work through their professional issues and crises with a coach or supervisor[10], or to actually get to work on clearing up old imprints and paradigms with the help of a psychologist, in order to be able to develop their full professional potential and at the same time not to "wear out" partnerships and friendships that they have worked so hard to build up. But also a time-intensive sport such as horseback riding, mountain climbing or marathon or the acquisition of an animal, the learning of an instrument should not only be dismissed as a hobby, but can donate to the quality of life as well as generate energy and strength for the profession.

No one can dictate which goals a lawyer sets for himself or which strategic goals he develops for the firm. But not all goals are compatible with each other:

On the one hand, it can be difficult to agree on a single strategic direction and a uniform management strategy when there are several partners and a team of owners. In this case, it is helpful to call in experts who can provide professional support for partner negotiations in the form of team coaching, moderation or accompanying consulting, so that the energy-consuming debates can be mastered quickly and confidently. On the other hand, the systems implemented can run counter to the achievement of goals.

If the remuneration in a law firm is regulated by a lockstep system[11], then the new goal of a partner who has reached a remuneration level in this system that is commode for him, to exclusively work on mandates of legal history interest in the future, will perhaps lead to a cynical smirk for a moment, but after a short time to the (justified) anger of his colleagues. Despite all collegiality, the other lawyers will not put up with the fact that one of their colleagues seems to have set himself the goal of contributing less to the firm's success than all the others in the long run. In their origins, luring systems have something in common with the salary of civil servants. The longer a lawyer is with the firm, the more he earns. Therefore, modern lockstep systems also take into account the acquisition performance, the pure processing turnover, the share of administrative tasks for the law firm and other factors. Newer lockstep systems do not only know the way "upwards" to higher com-

10 Both are offered, for example, by CLP – Consulting for Legal Professionals specifically for lawyers by specially trained and educated lawyers.

11 A classic compensation system in large law firms, where the mandate profit distribution is awarded according to certain points; more on this in the chapter about Performance Systems and Compensation Management" in E. Law Firm Management and Personnel Management.

pensation rates. In recent years, there have also been downgrades, especially in international law firms.

An unskilful strategy can already contain the core for conflicts between colleagues. If the goal of a law firm is to motivate the lawyers it employs to achieve the highest possible acquisition performance, then it can regulate the remuneration of the lawyers according to the principle of "you eat what you kill"[12]. A lawyer handles only those cases that he has acquired himself. The amount of his remuneration depends on the amount of revenue he has acquired and earned himself. This system is not so unusual. Every individual lawyer works according to this principle and it is certainly also the system used by our case example No. 1 (the wannabe large law firm).

In a somewhat larger law firm, however, in which the attorneys specialize, this principle can lead to a situation in which newly acquired competition law mandates are no longer passed on to the competition law specialist, but are handled by the attorney who is actually responsible for employment law, who has now acquired the competition law mandate. The disadvantages for the law firm are manifold. The client is not "served" in the best possible way because it is not the specialist but the employment lawyer who handles his competition law case. At the next opportunity, the competition lawyer will consider not passing on the dismissal protection mandate that has fallen to him internally. Gradually, the lawyers in the firm are educated to form "individual firms within the firm". Our case study No. 2 (the law firm with the false mandates) probably also experienced a similar effect, with the difference that there was certainly no corresponding specialist in advance, but then one failed to purchase/train/build up such a specialist within a short period of time.

Remember:
The firm's goals must be formulated in writing. There is no way around this. The written fixation forces to concretize the goal. At the latest when reading through the wording, the phrases that are not suitable for the formulation of objectives will be noticed. Another question is whether all of the firm's goals must be published.

On the Internet, it is not uncommon to find visions and goal formulations of law firms under the somewhat pompous heading "Philosophy" on the homepages of law firms in the area of self-representation. As a rule, these formulations are all the more ambitious the further away from Europe the law firm is located[13].

In most cases, no clear distinction is made between values, visions and goals.

12 Busmann, "Chefsache Mandantenakquisition", p. 220.
13 Examples in Hartung in Schieblon "Kanzleimanagement in der Praxis", p. 27.

If you are clear and aware of your firm's values and vision, the whole world – and above all your clients – must of course know about it. It becomes more difficult if there is less clarity or even contradictions on this point. In this case, it is better to refrain from publication[14].

As a rule, goals do not belong on the homepage or in the firm's brochure, but they can be published under certain circumstances. In any case, they should be sufficiently known to all employees of the law firm. Goals that generate special benefits for your clients, on the other hand, can be published.

2. Status Quo

Position determination – Understanding the system of the law firm

Why determine where you stand when one thing is quite certain: things should not stay the way they are. When it comes to founding a law firm, you want to develop ideas and concepts, deal with products and services. Maybe you want to completely rethink the law firm and legal advice and become a legal tech entrepreneur. What sounds like "flow" inevitably ends in chaos if you don't follow some important basic rules – as Lewin's "3-phase model" shows.

In order to change and "rethink", one must first have an understanding of the service of legal advice and the construct of the law firm as an established system for providing this service. A look at the professional code of conduct as well as the accompanying regulations will help. As a "mini-organization", law firms are basically divided into two levels: Attorneys and non-attorneys with different levels of hierarchy. This system is manifested both by the established partnership rules and by legal regulations, which is why it is difficult to break it up.

But the players are much more important than these rules – because, as in soccer, it makes a difference whether you play on a Sunday afternoon on the village green or in the Champions League and how the team is put together. So determining where you stand also involves, above all, correctly assessing the competence, skills, expertise and potential of your colleagues and employees:

It's a people business.

Remember:
The composition of the law firm team is an essential and largely underestimated success factor.

14 read more about the firm's values, culture and ethics in the following chapter.

Now you can say: I'm just getting started. I have no idea who will be on my team. As the industry statistics show, two out of three lawyers do not start up on their own and as newcomers to the profession, but rather

1. are in partnership or at least office sharing together with colleagues
2. not newcomers to the profession, but already have at least five years of professional experience, which means that they have
3. leadership and team experience and
4. serve a substantial client base and are
5. positioned in the market.

Establishing a completely new law firm is therefore the exception rather than the rule.

The rule, in contrast, is the so-called spin-off and refoundation, which essentially has three causes:

1. entrepreneurial causes
2. professional causes
3. personal causes

Ideally, the entrepreneurial causes are based on business growth. This may mean that a change of legal form is now required for liability reasons due to client "heavyweights". But it can also mean that major clients make it necessary to open additional offices or to "incorporate" smaller local law firms, and that new partner structures have to be created.

The prime example of specialist spin-offs are the so-called boutique law firms – often founded by long-term partners from large law firms. These highly specialized small law firms consist of a few experts who have specialized not only in one field of law for a very specific target group, but often even in a single legal issue. The spin-off is the right way to go if this specialty is being crowded out by the "bread-and-butter business" of the large law firm. However, it is also interesting for the so-called complementary areas of law, which guarantee comprehensive advice to demanding clients and thus business and turnover for the firm's showcase areas of law, but which themselves hardly raise their department heads to partner level due to a lack of original turnover. Further examples that I have personally accompanied at CLP are e.g.

- the separation of attorney-at-law and patent attorney business
- the spin-off of legal tech products, management consulting or seminar and repetitor business from an existing law firm
- The outsourcing of a lawyer who acts as an external legal department for a major client (Catholic Church or umbrella organization as employer) and thus increasingly paralyzes the rest of the firm's business due to the conflict of interests.

Remember:
By far the largest number of law firm formations occur through the breakup or establishment of partnerships for personal reasons.

The personal causes for spin-offs and reorganizations come with life: people fall in love and argue, alpha animals, egomaniacs and top dogs have too little room to fight, and the clash of (values and culture) galaxies leads to Star Wars, because together you are not less alone. From my experience of several decades in the industry, personal causes are at the top of the list of causes for founding law firms. The revision, modernization and restructuring of the decades-old established partner appointment rules, and thus no less than the partnership agreement, is therefore critical to the survival of many law firms today in order to

- on the one hand, ensure the stability of the partnership and,
- on the other hand, motivate young lawyers to join the partnership in the first place.

One of many new approaches can be the use of modern recruiting tools for partner development. Why not analyze future partner personalities and mergers according to the Leadership Forecast Series of Hogan Assessments – as has long been common practice in large companies?[15]

The purchase or takeover of a law firm is strictly speaking not part of the establishment of a law firm.
Nevertheless, it should be mentioned for the sake of completeness: What was considered the "ideal entry into self-employment" not so long ago is simply obsolete today. Only in the few exceptional cases where the law firm is not identical with the (departing) law firm owner but has established its own brand with its own client base, may this still be successful today. As a rule, however, these (individual) law firms retire with the lawyer and do not ensure his retirement. This is due to the fact that the mandates are tailored to him and his person and are therefore not transferable, and most importantly because the client base is of the same age and is also retiring from business life. Therefore, the savings bank as an investment partner, just like other financial partners, generally applies reducing multiples for the sales value of a law firm[16].

15 For more on this topic, see E. Kanzleiführung und Personalmanagement.

16 see also the annual Branchenbericht (industry report) Sparkassen 2020, from the analysis of its financing customers.

The hot topic of legal tech brings a completely new and highly interesting aspect: It is obvious that law firms have to be innovative in order to develop products and services for the legal market. Many law firms have their prototypes in the drawer and their Alpha versions on the test track. But what is the next step? An idea has become a product and is now to be launched on the market.

Law firms should establish themselves in the legal tech business and not leave it to the non-lawyers: But is legal tech still law firm business?
It's about the very banal questions of every start-up: Where do I find investors, how do I build up marketing and sales? And the not so banal and specific question: Is this still a law firm business? Do I have the required license as a lawyer? Is the bar association or the trade office responsible? And when exactly should the "child" leave the house or better: when does it have to leave the house? Especially for the topics of investors, partnerships, sales and marketing, it is decisive, with all the regulations for legal advice, whether the product is brought to the market from a law firm or from a company.

The legal form in which the whole thing is then founded is decided by formalities, liability issues, common sense and personal preferences.
Established legal forms, from the civil law partnership to the office partnership and the limited liability company, should be taken into account, as should newer models: What is there to say against joining forces with other, not yet established colleagues within the framework of a cooperative, for example?

Kurt Lewin, social psychologist and founder of the so-called Berlin School around 1950, says: The path leads through chaos. Using the example of an ice block, he vividly demonstrates that the path from one solid aggregate state (ice block) to another (ice cube) must lead through completely unknown territory (thawing) and is thus hardly plannable. The fixed constants in his model are at best the actual and the final state.

What does the model for founding a law firm show? Chaos is part and parcel of the start-up project. You should allow it and get involved with it. According to Lewin, one thing is certain: chaos does not last forever and structures will be found.

But you should have done your homework and have your carefully evaluated site assessment not just in the drawer, but right on the drawing board for the design of your new firm.

The determination of the so-called status quo includes, on the one hand, the market analysis and, on the other hand, the realistic assessment of the current positioning and position in the market. The existing know-how and potential play a role as well as the legal framework, financial obligations, client base and structure.

Although lawyers are free to choose their goals, goal planning is of no use to them if their goals do not meet the needs of the market, that is, the needs of the clients. After a first phase of formulating goals that essentially correspond to the lawyer's wishes, the second step is to adapt the goals to the client's requirements[17].

But what do the clients want? What do they ask for?
It is no coincidence that I have given the legal market and its developments an extensive opening chapter. Even if most readers are hardly newcomers, in my experience lawyers tend to go through life with blinders on and do not even realize it[18]. Knowing only the legal market of one's region or area of law leads to one-dimensional decisions. A change of perspective can widen one's viewpoint considerably and promote an understanding of the interaction and complexity of the market. Knowing the entire market and its challenges is therefore a constant duty of every lawyer who is serious about his profession. It is at least as important to exchange views with others: with one's own colleagues in order to close gaps, with colleagues who are the complete opposite of oneself and with entrepreneurs from other industries. Only the diversity of perspectives can create the complexity that promises a touch of "objective reality".

Industrial and service companies usually answer such questions through a market analysis. Evaluation is the magic word. Be honest: When was the last time you conducted a client survey? And evaluated it. Lawyers predominantly lack the business management tools to conduct their own market analyses, even though the multitude of providers has never made it so easy[19]. Most law firms cannot afford professional market analyses by market research institutes. If one asks for data on the markets for lawyers, the crushing answer is: "The sales markets of law firms are in dense fog." It is possible to analyze, at least in part, the demand for legal services through some indicators. Some indicators are population density and business density in a region. Both indicators provide information about the number of potential demanders for legal services. With a little effort, the relevant figures can be researched by any lawyer for a particular region. The German Federal Bar (BRAK) provides annual basic data on the number of attorneys admitted to the bar.

Due to globalization, it is now possible for any law firm to offer its services worldwide – a factor that has only become established in recent years and of which the vast majority of law firms are not yet aware. Today, no shoe store in a medium-sized small town in Germany can live solely on its local business (its regular custo-

---

17 Dr. Tutschka, "Der Rechtsanwalt als Unternehmer", p. 38; Hartung in Schieblon, "Kanzleimanagement in der Praxis", p. 24.

18 And I'm not excluding myself from that.

19 Even if, admittedly, not all of them can be used for lawyers due to data protection reasons.

mers and walk-in customers)[20] – no matter how broadly positioned or specialized it is. So why do lawyers and law firm owners today still believe that their business is primarily local, or at best regional? My clients then like to put forward the argument of the "trusting client relationship". I then regularly reply that trust has nothing to do with eye contact, but with honesty and reliability coupled with solid craftsmanship and professionalism. Today, all of this can be mapped online and proven with facts and figures. Evaluation for online business is easier and better than at any retailer around the corner, whom I can only look in the face while shopping, without having twenty current customer testimonials immediately available.

Another argument that is often used is that the services provided by German lawyers are limited to the German legal market. Correct. However, the German legal market has never been only local or regional, and today it no longer takes place only within German borders. From my own experience as a German lawyer I know that German legal advice is not only urgently needed online today by many Germans living abroad but also by non-Germans who have German legal relations, for example in German border traffic with neighboring countries or economic/cultural/sports cooperation with Germany. Unfortunately, many law firm owners confuse their own reality of life with the reality and the actual opportunities[21].

It is true that the location of corporate headquarters can be important for law firms that focus on advising companies. After all, the "buyers" of legal services, legal departments and management, are regularly found at corporate headquarters. But just as some regions are overestimated, other regions are underestimated. Not everyone is familiar with the fact that the East Westphalia region is home to world market leaders. "Big business" takes place not only in Frankfurt am Main, but also around Bielefeld and Gütersloh (in the middle of nowhere).

Another indicator of the attractiveness of a region can be the concentration of law firms. However, this indicator should be treated with caution, as shown not only by the example of the new German states. Traditionally, many graduates stay in the cities where they studied, partly because these cities are very beautiful, partly because of convenience or family obligation[22].

A generally weak demand situation does not necessarily mean the decline of all law firms in this region. This has to do with the individual situation of individual lawyers. A colleague, for example, who is virtually "pelted" with new mandates by

20 And this has not just been the case since the pandemic with its various lockdowns and supply difficulties for certain subproducts.

21 Since it is rather unlikely for a German lawyer to be posted, expatriation law, for example, is an almost undiscovered area of law.

22 However, by the second year of online study, this aspect has become obsolete, at least for statistics.

a typical mandate intermediary, a legal protection insurer, does not mind that the demand for legal services in his region is declining overall. In the new German federal states, smaller law firms with favorable cost structures have benefited from the withdrawal of the large law firms.

Besides the analysis of the market, that of the competition and the competitors is crucial for success. Bar associations and the German Bar Association have fairly accurate data on the exact number of lawyers admitted to the bar and existing law firms in a region. Data on the density of lawyers in a region can also occasionally be found in business magazines. In my experience, the editors are happy to help with research on request. The number of non-lawyer competitors, in particular tax consultants, auditors and credit institutions, can also be determined with relatively little effort, insofar as they are relevant. The type of legal services offered by competitors and the areas of law in which they are active can be found out quickly. Competitors publicize and advertise their services through websites, law firm brochures, seminars and publications.

It is more difficult to determine the price that competitors charge for their services. Perhaps this is not (yet) important for most lawyers. The majority of individual attorneys and even smaller offices predominantly bill according to the tabular rates of the German RVG. Even if price pressure is clearly noticeable on the market for lawyers' services, there can be no talk (yet) of full-blown price competition. Pitching" and "paneling", the application of law firms for an an advertised mandate, in which price offers also play a considerable role, does not (yet) take place at most law firms[23].

For the market analysis, it is not only the current state that matters. (Possible) future developments must also be taken into account. For the first time, a generation that was able to build up its assets unencumbered by wars has begun to transfer its assets to the next generation. For the first time, fathers are also taking parental leave and implementing their entitlement to part-time work. Never before have so many start-ups been founded or online businesses transacted. Never before have so many assets been invested into Bitcoin. These social developments offer new consulting potential. The same applies to data protection, which cannot keep up quickly enough with digitization and new technologies. And I won't even bother with the words with P and C as further examples here.

---

23 Busmann in "Chefsache Mandantenakquisition", p. 39.

3. Resource Analysis (SWOT)

However, for the law firm vision and strategic orientation, not only the market analysis is necessary, but also the analysis of the own strengths and weaknesses, both of the lawyers and the law firm.

A realistic assessment of whether you as a lawyer meet the requirements of the market and can fulfill the demands of clients can and must be an important corrective in the strategic alignment. Weaknesses cannot and should not always be corrected. It is more promising to concentrate on your strengths[24].
A common method of analysis is the **"SWOT-Analysis"**[25].
S = Strengths
W = Weakness
O = Opportunities
T = Threats

This type of analysis records and evaluates the individual strengths, weaknesses, opportunities and threats of a lawyer and his law firm. It can cover the entire law firm and also only subareas or locations.

It is also possible to create them for individual clients. So-called "hard facts" (essentially everything that can be measured in concrete key figures) and soft facts (everything else: such as the quality of the client relationship, customer satisfaction, reputation) are measured, with a distinction being made in each case between internal and external factors[26].

Self-analysis requires a considerable amount of **self-criticism** on the part of a lawyer, because one's own shortcomings must also be revealed. This should not worry a lawyer too much. After all, the purpose of the analysis is to reduce any weaknesses that have been discovered. Which criteria are to be included in a SWOT analysis cannot be determined in a generally binding manner. This is because the criteria to be taken into account depend on the market conditions of the law firm to be analyzed, which are by no means uniform.

A lawyer must have the necessary specialist knowledge, the legal expertise, in order to be able to meet the requirements of a client. The idea that a lawyer can actually work in all areas of law with equally good quality is an illusion. Legal "omniscience" is not necessary at all if the law firm is reasonably oriented. A good basic legal education, combined with the willingness and self-discipline to constantly up-

24 Buckingham in "Entdecken Sie Ihre Stärken Jetzt", p. 223.
25 Hartung in Schieblon in "Kanzleimanagement in der Praxis", p. 28.
26 Hartung in Schieblon "Kanzleimanagement in der Praxis", p. 30.

date one's own knowledge and to expand it in the areas that are important for clients, is sufficient for a start.

Know-how does not only include legal expertise. A lawyer must also be able to solve organizational problems. This includes – quite simply – file management. The lawyer, whether employed or self-employed, must know and master the organization of a law firm. Structures and processes must run by themselves, make sense and support the client's interests. For practice purposes, every young lawyer should spend a few days registering incoming and outgoing mail and, in particular, noting down deadlines. It does no harm if the experienced office manager looks over his shoulder to be on the safe side.

The know-how of the lawyer entrepreneur also includes **business knowledge** and skills. Modern law firm software can clearly display the monthly income/expenses on the basis of existing data. The lawyer must evaluate this data himself. The entrepreneur lawyer must know his or her costs or the costs caused by his or her unit in order to be able to assess whether he or she is working profitably. Knowledge of marketing instruments and the ability to use them will be essential in the future.

It is then also generally assumed that **"fast, firm, friendly"** could be the short version of the requirement profile for every law firm.

Specifically, this means: **!**
- Accessibility of lawyers,
- speed of response and processing,
- reliability,
- comprehensibility of communication,
- friendliness,
- price of the legal service.

In addition, there are personal preferences, likes and dislikes. It is extremely unlikely that a lawyer will excel at tasks that are deeply repugnant to him. Those who devote themselves to criminal defence must be aware that they will not always be dealing with the best members of human society, and that they will often find themselves working in a jail. Some people are bothered by the hectic pace that can occur when dealing with injunction proceedings in the field of competition law. Self-analysis is not about assessing a lawyer's likes or dislikes. It is about finding out what kind of legal work he should concentrate on and what he should better avoid.

In order to meet, or better, exceed the expectations of clients, various material requirements must also be met: The office must be convenient for clients to reach. The location of an office and its furnishings say something – at least from the client's point of view – about the lawyer's self-image and the service to be expected. Today, however, with the pandemic and home office experience of recent years, this is just as true for a well-developed online meeting structure. From the client's point of view, the parking space in front of the front door, business hours on weekends or the lawyer's home visit may be more important than the furnishings of the office or the make of car of the law firm owner.

Not irrelevant is also the **technical equipment of the law firm**: Is communication with the firm easy and convenient for clients to use? Is the client processing and cost structure transparent, e.g. with my digital file? What other services does my lawyer provide for me? Do I feel understood and in good hands with my lawyer and his staff? All this can play a role today.

But even without using the SWOT analysis, it is important to address the issue of resources, potential and know-how of the firm, as well as to see the legal and actual constraints, limits and obligations.

The resources of the firm are first and foremost the employees, their expertise and competences (Man Power/Human Resources). In addition, there are specialists and employees with particular experience, special knowledge and know-how.

This can include colleagues, employees, trainees and apprentices, but also non-legal employees. The same applies to service providers such as the software provider, the cleaning company, the landlord of the office space, the website provider and the paper supplier. But also specialized services such as the tax advisor you trust or an extensive network of colleagues.

The firm's potential is primarily represented by its existing and future mandates.

But this can also include possible and existing cooperation partners, which can be companies depending on the respective field of expertise, car dealerships and insurers, but also courts that assign proceedings to you.

Potential analysis – What's under the hood?

You don't have to be Reinhold Messner to know that the success of first ascents on summit tours is decided by the WHO. The realistic assessment of the initial situation and an inspiring vision are important; but knowing yourself with your strengths and weaknesses is just as important.

This is where professional **personality assessments** such as

- the Hogan Assessment (probably the most internationally known assessment for executives),
- the 360 Grad Feedback,
- the Reiss Profil or
- the Profile Dynamics (a personality test that ties in with the above-mentioned Spiral Dynamics)

help, but smaller tests such as the **Strenghts Finder** also provide useful results.

It is also advisable to work with a **professional coach** who can help with various methods such as
- shadowing,
- mirroring,
- provocation or
- feedback.

to work out individual markers and paradigms.

Remember:
The successful establishment of a law firm is determined only to a small extent by education and experience. More important is the network of contacts; however, the personal and entrepreneurial skills of the law firm founder are decisive.

Personality is one aspect alongside education and experience. Personal resilience, flexibility and the willingness to leave one's comfort zone are further aspects. And of course, this process should not be limited to just one of several law firm owners, but should be extended to the entire partnership as well as the staff.

It's a people business

And because this is the case, existing and potential clients should also be included, as well as possible cooperation partners, such as networks and insurance companies, process financiers, ADAC, etc., who can contribute to the "bread-and-butter business" with so-called contract attorney status.

In addition to the potential inherent in one's own abilities or those of one's colleagues and employees – in other words, in the broadest sense, the "human resources" (HR) – there are often unused and unnoticed resources in finance and marketing.

Remember:
Instead of saving and reducing costs and investments, mandate optimization can often achieve significantly better and faster results with the help of legal tech and legal project management.

Financial resources can result on the one hand from savings: through strict cost and investment control (controlling), making law firm processes more effective and optimizing client service, e.g., through legal project management, but also through legal tech, that is, replacing expensive, inefficient human labor with less expensive software.

On the other hand, it is also about investments, financing and the exploitation of subsidies. In my experience, very few colleagues have dealt with the variety of possibilities, which is probably mainly due to the fact that founding a law firm today is no longer associated with buying a law firm for a large sum of money. However, this may also be due to the fact that many colleagues today still believe that it is better to keep the firm "small and fine, but mine" than to commit to success, i.e. constant growth, with a large mountain of debt.

Finally, the opportunities that arise from systematic (online) **marketing and sales** are still not well known and taken into account. It is true that marketing (in addition to acquisition) is a given for most people today (articles, flyers, advertisements, logo, etc.), as is the website.

Systematic online marketing, on the other hand, is still a foreign concept for many colleagues. On the one hand, there is a lack of technical understanding, and on the other hand, it is not clear to what extent professional law even permits it. Only a few brave ones give it a try, then master the market, find their way and more importantly: clients and business.

Finally, a word about the founder of the law firm himself: The importance of the resilience factor, in other words the measurement value that stands for personal resilience, was briefly mentioned above. Just like the strengths/weaknesses profile, this is supported to a considerable extent by the personal network of friends and family. It is best to start an adventure in good health and with reliable, trustworthy partners – especially in the private sphere. This means personal investment and advance performance. As mentioned before: It starts with you.

4. Restrictions, limitations, obligations

An open and honest assessment of all limitations and responsibilities should not be underestimated. These can arise from the law firm itself but also from the positioning or the personal circumstances of the firm owner. Considerations here include, for example, disabilities, caring responsibilities, parental obligations, but also loan repayments, competition clauses, personal dislikes, moral and ethical convictions, and so on. However, the analysis here should also explain which are unavoidable (such as legal aspects), which are only temporary and which are freely chosen. The general regulations of the legal market have already been discussed in detail in the introductory chapter.

5. Lawyer vs. law firm owner

Few law firm owners have ever looked at their firm from the perspective of what a complex set of requirements the firm must meet for employees, clients and themselves. And even fewer have thought about how different their own needs can be, depending on the role in which they are defined – whether as a lawyer or a partner. A third perspective opens up when one looks at this requirement profile as a manager with employee responsibility.

For example, as a lawyer, the acquisition of new law firm software can be quite desirable because it simplifies cumbersome processes. As a law firm owner, the question of ROI (return on investment) and strategic relevance naturally arises. As a manager, you will be aware of the concern of some employees that they will be replaced by inexpensive algorithms, and you will think about how these employees can now be deployed elsewhere in a meaningful way, and ideally even promoted, so that they do not take refuge in passive resistance when the newly acquired software is introduced.

As a law firm owner, role conflicts are a daily occurrence. Therefore, role clarity in the decisions to be made is the be-all and end-all.

How do I get role clarity?

1. No spontaneous decisions
2. Factual separation of roles (personnel, time, location)
3. Change of perspective
4. Set strategic priorities
5. Feedback loops in a protected framework

This can take place with a mentor or in a familiar circle. In the end, however, an experienced, neutral and professional coach offers the ideal support – and can be called upon at any time.

In any case, investing in one's own entrepreneurial skills should be at the top of every law firm founder's list of priorities, including personal development and not just education.

Because once again, the formation of a law firm begins and ends with you.

The question you should ask yourself, just like any other lawyer, is why do you want to start this law firm?

In order to practice the profession of a lawyer, it is certainly not necessary to establish a law firm. There are many possibilities to work for law firms as an employee (full-time or part-time) or, under certain circumstances, as a freelancer without being an entrepreneur, i.e. without being the owner of a law firm.

Perhaps we should take a closer look here at what exactly constitutes purely "lawyerly activity", in other words, where this ends and entrepreneurial activity begins.

The activity as a lawyer is file processing, legal research and factual information for the development of an optimal legal solution. It consists of contact with clients and appearances before courts and authorities (in written form through pleadings and in oral form during hearings). All in all, however, the work of a lawyer per se is little more than a fact-finding activity, a craft – if you will – with aspects of a client-oriented service. With a clear focus on communication, but also on cooperation and interaction with colleagues and non-legal staff, in administration or in the service area.

The diversity of legal work is like a colourful bouquet of skills:

Lawyer competences, © Dr. Geertje Tutschka

The success of this legal activity is determined on the one hand by the specialist knowledge, i. e. the legal know-how of the lawyer, which he has acquired during his studies and legal clerkship and during his professional activity. On the other hand, it is also determined by his life experience and his willingness to work in a client-oriented manner, as well as his ability to understand the real needs and goals of his client. Last but not least, his strategic and tactical skills in managing mandates and litigation are equally important, as is his understanding of business management and his practical approach.

Of course, the purely legal work does not require you to open or establish a law firm yourself. Nor does client contact and personnel management require it. In fact, the question of why you want to start a law firm is an independent and distinct question.

The product of legal advice can therefore be provided by any fully qualified lawyer. However, if you want to make money by selling and marketing said product, it is a matter of entrepreneurship.

Unfortunately, the term "law firm business" does not yet exist for everyone. For decades, the term "law firm" was not to be equated with the term "company". This was partly due to legal restrictions, but also to the profession's self-image as an organ of the administration of justice. Today, of course, it has long been recognized that a law firm should be run like a business. Founding a law firm is founding a company; managing a law firm is managing a company[27].

What is this important for?

On the one hand, of course, the wheel does not have to be reinvented here. Of course, one can fall back on many good and extremely good books and aids for management, leadership and marketing – while always keeping an eye on the special features of the legal industry and the legal regulations for the legal profession.

On the other hand, however, it is of decisive importance for your success that you strictly distinguish between your position as a legal clerk, i.e. lawyer, and that of the law firm owner[28]. And do so in every situation.

The firm requires that you, not as a lawyer, but rather as an entrepreneur, deal with issues of corporate development and management beyond purely legal activities. This includes, for example, personnel management, strategy and tactics, accounting and budgeting[29]. Keeping the two roles of attorney and law firm owner neatly separated and distinct will be your most important task[30].

The possible objection that a young lawyer who joins an existing law firm finds that the firm's objectives are already in place and therefore does not need to make any effort to define the objectives does not apply unconditionally. Even the young lawyer who joins a larger law firm must at least know the firm's objectives in order to be able to align his daily work with them. At best, the firm's goals should even coincide with his personal life goals and values as well as the ideal version of his "career". I therefore recommend that young attorneys should consider what a law firm stands for and what it wants to stand for in the run-up to the application process. The law firm vision should then be made a topic of discussion in the interview at the latest.

---

27 Dr. Tutschka, "Der Rechtsanwalt als Unternehmer", TeleLex, p. 15.

28 When starting out, make it a routine to ask yourself in which role you are making each decision in the office's daily routine. Then try to take the other position in each case. In my moderation of partner strategy meetings, I usually put the law firm (fictitiously) at the table of the partner round: change of perspective and AHAs follow immediately.

29 Dr. Tutschka, "Partner vs. Associate" in Kanzleijob.de from 17.6.2016.

30 Dr. Tutschka, "Kanzleigründung ist Unternehmensgründung" in Haufe from 17.12.2015.

So, whether you want to take on the position of law firm owner in addition to the role of attorney is something you should consider carefully.

Of the 165,000 lawyers admitted to the bar in Germany, around 80 % work more or less voluntarily in their own firm at least some of the time. Not all colleagues find it tempting to be their own boss, to have freedom of decision and responsibility, but also to bear the business risk of setting up a law firm. No wonder. The competitive pressure is getting tougher, the fight for clients is getting rougher and the number of insolvencies is increasing, as we have seen. Law firms today have to be one thing above all: profitable. The days when business and law firms were mutually exclusive are long gone.

Most law firm owners, however, still stumble into starting a business rather unprepared: young lawyers are still taught during their training that their dream job is found in legal work. Most of them have not heard of law firm management, business thinking and the creation of their personal law firm vision until they have completed their training. But it is precisely this law firm vision that determines the goals and strategy that will determine the economic success and future of the law firm from day one. Terms such as accounting, bookkeeping, marketing, personnel management, tax returns, as well as business know-how are only occasionally mentioned in legal training. Most law graduates only hear about business plans, unique selling propositions and target group definition when they are already working as lawyers or have founded a law firm. Thus, quite a few leave the management of the law firm to others, professionals who have learned the ropes. The lawyer himself wants to work legally, i.e. in terms of content[31]. Business necessities quickly become a nuisance.

In my work, I repeatedly encounter law firms in which these topics are stubbornly suppressed and faded out, or at least an attempt is made to outsource these topics to a specialist.

At the same time, the industry is flooded with consulting offers, seminars and manuals on law firm management. What is not recognized is that starting with law firm management would mean putting the cart before the horse. The law firm vision is the heart of law firm formation.

The fact is that the founding of a law firm, like any other business start-up, is determined by **three essential factors**:

31 Dr. Anja Hall, "Warum sollte man in der Großkanzlei nicht altwerden können?" in LTO from 29.6.2016.

1. The personality of the owner.
2. The business plan and strategy
3. The implementation of structures and systems.

One thing is certain: unlike in the business world, only a few lawyers draw up a business plan and develop a law firm strategy before starting their own practice.

In business, on the other hand, the implementation of structures and systems is often the sticking point at which companies fail when making the leap from a microenterprise to a small or medium-sized enterprise: after about 3 to 5 years or from a staff size of 5 employees. Only a few manage the change of the role of the company founder from general manager, girl for everything and all-rounder to company and personnel leader and strategic visionary. In the law firm business, however, it is almost impossible to withdraw more and more from the operational business and not work legally. This is where the law firm founder differs significantly from all other companies.

Successful founding and management of a law firm therefore always has to do with the extent to which the lawyer is able to perform his role as a lawyer and as the owner of the law firm side by side; in other words, to practice self-management. In my experience, however, there is another very serious difference between law firms and conventional companies: The complete underestimation of the role of the personality, the personal attitude and objectives of the firm owner. This may be arrogance in keeping with the firm's status. The historically induced confusion of titles and degrees with competence or the famous operational blindness[32].

But why is the personality of the owner so essential and decisive in the founding of a law firm?

First of all, the law firm business is a business that provides services by people for people. As we have seen, LegalTech, flat-rate providers of legal services and automated legal information cannot replace the human aspect of the lawyer, i.e. the personality of the lawyer, his charisma and life experience. This will be the decisive competitive advantage of every lawyer and every law firm founder, and it will play an increasingly important role in the future. Even more important, however, is that you will be able to measure the success of your law firm by whether you enjoy the entrepreneurial aspect: You are only good at what you like to do.

32 Dr. Tutschka, "Kanzleigründung ist Unternehmensgründung" in Haufe from 17.12.2015, Gerber, "E-Myth Attorney" p. 57.

But not everyone is a born entrepreneur. That's a good thing. And some things can certainly be learned or "bought" from specialists, such as marketing experts and tax consultants.

A good example here is the appearance of the Schnee-Gronauer law firm:

SCHNEE+GRONAUER UNTERNEHMER. ANWALT.

© Rechtsanwalt Schnee-Gronauer. Der Unternehmeranwalt
(Lawyer Schnee-Gronauer. The entrepreneur lawyer)

But you still have to manage the firm yourself. You should therefore have certain qualities such as visionary and strategic thinking, economic understanding[33], assertiveness and leadership qualities. Be honest with yourself here. A personality/ strengths test[34] or feedback from friends, colleagues or your coach can assist. As the owner of a law firm, you have an economic responsibility that you must live up to[35].

Setting up a law firm is setting up a business: sweaty, with lots of numbers and little legal work. You can hire specialists to support you. But the founder of the law firm and the decision-maker remains you or the group of partners. And you yourself also have the responsibility to bring your personality into the firm and to set the tone. Do not just accept it! Learn to love it! Nothing is as exciting as building up something of your own, watching it grow. And to leave nothing to chance. Your personal attitude and goals are the first step, the development of your personal or joint office strategy the second.

Only then are you really a founder of a law firm. Everything else is factual work.

Once you have answered the question why you want to establish this law firm and with whom, and why it is not enough to stay in the position of a lawyer, it is time for the implementation.

Finally, a few words on the distinction between the solo self-employed/ freelancer and the entrepreneur: In business, the timely and smooth transition from mere self-employment, which is more or less just the "commercial marketing" of one's own service, to a company is often decisive for the continued existence of the business. For it is only when the business also runs without its own service and person that it is really a company. In my experience, however, especially individual law firms or small law firms with up to 5 partners in the legal industry stay in this phase

33 "Commercial thinking" is what the BVerfG has called it (ruling of 12.12.2016, Ref. 1 BvR 2576/04).
34 A simple and effective test is Buckingham's "Strenghtsfinder" in "Entdecke Deine Stärken" (gallup).
35 Hartung in "Berufsbild des Anwalts" in LTO from 10.1.2018.

much longer, often even for the entire business period – and can get by in this way to some extent, because the law firm business is (so far) much less growth-driven due to state regulation.

This is currently changing: in the future, it will be even more important to determine the extent to which the so-called entrepreneurial gene is present – and lived – in law firm owners.

What did you get out of the chapter?
You have understood the role your personality plays in the development of the firm.

II. Firm and product DNA

Why should you read this chapter?
You understand the important role that values, ethics and culture play in law firm vision.

Overview
1. **Values, culture, ethics**
2. **Product and Fee Policy**
3. **The Firm Team**

Based on your law firm vision, the individual law firm DNA is to be developed:

What does your firm stand for? How does it implement this and with whom?

1. Values, culture, ethics

Developing your firm's values is an ongoing process. It starts with your values, those of your partners and employees.

What do you want to stand for? What do you want to advocate?

While most people are still relatively clear about their own values, very few think about the values of their firm. People like to save it for later, for when they have time for it. So never ever.

A decision with consequences. Because these values actually represent your work, your performance, and ultimately yourself. They should be clearly communicated and, more importantly, actually lived. Only then can they develop their full effect.

But what are corporate values?

They are readily defined as guiding principles in the company and form the moral compass that should influence all activities and decisions. The firm's culture and philosophy are built on these core values. They form the basis for the trust of their clients and the loyalty of their employees.

Therefore, always ask yourself what the most important values are for your law firm, what should distinguish your law firm from all the others. The elaboration

of these values can take place in a partnership process and should, by the way, also be repeated at regular intervals. In a relaxed, reflective atmosphere without time pressure and disturbance – if necessary under the moderation of an expert – one of the most important foundations for the establishment and development of your law firm can emerge.

Here you can see the result of such a process to identify the core values of a law firm.

Firm values, © Dr. Geertje Tutschka

In my trainings I like to use the drastic example of "Frankenstein" as already mentioned above: A scientist "builds" a "human being" with a lot of technical expertise and brings him to life without thinking about whether he has an identity, a soul, a conscience. He creates a sad monster.

With the appropriate know-how, you can bring many things "to life". Decisive for the success but also for one's own merit is, however, on the basis of which values did it come into existence? What was the motivation and what was the underlying human image? Does the product have a soul?

Once the firm's values are in place, it is important to build a corresponding culture upon them. This begins with client communication and the branding of the firm but must also be noticeable in events and meetings and in employee management. Transparency and reliability are created by rituals (such as the annual Christmas party), awards for special achievements, and written or unwritten rules for daily interaction. Feedback and control help to actually live these ground rules[1].

1 Heussen, "Anwaltsunternehmen führen", p. 305.

Important is:
- Values and culture must fit the people in the firm and
- values and culture must be lived by the people in the firm.

The German-Austrian management consultant Peter Drucker once summed it up like this: Culture eats strategy for breakfast. A nice example is the result at the Winheller law firm[2]:

"For us at Winheller, developing our firm's values and principles was as much a part of establishing the firm as the legal and business aspects. "If you get the culture right, everything else will take care of itself." Our core values are the basis of our daily work, the guideline for the expansion of our team and for new hires, and the compass of our strategic orientation and development. At the same time, we work on specifying and implementing them by putting them and our corporate culture to the test at regular intervals.

What's in it for us?

In business development, growth is easy once the foundation has been laid. We want to be well positioned in the market and arm ourselves against tough competition (large law firms, LegalTech). But we can only grow on a firm foundation. Our core values are this foundation.

Our core values are extremely helpful in recruiting: We don't hire anyone (anymore), no matter how great they are professionally and how much turnover they may bring with them, if they don't fit in with our company. We do very well with this. But it also took us a while to understand how important this is. Another valuable side effect of the Core Values: employees are much less likely to ask the boss for advice in difficult situations and can often make their own decisions."

Stefan Winheller
Attorney, LL.M. Tax (USA), specialist lawyer for tax law
Partner, Managing Director of WINHELLER Rechtsanwaltsgesellschaft mbH, Frankfurt a. M.

And where do ethics come into play?

There may be questions and decisions in the day-to-day work of a law firm that cannot be judged solely by law or by the firm's values. They lie in the gray area between right and wrong. This brings us to the topic of ethical behavior[3].

The German Bar Association (DAV) has been dealing with the topic of lawyer ethics for quite some time and in 2011 established the Anwaltliche Berufsethik (Professional Ethics of Lawyers) Committee, which is now called Anwaltsethik und Anwaltskultur (Lawyer Ethics and Lawyer Culture). The committee deals with the general issues of professional ethics. The guiding question[4] is whether there are ethical

---

2 which can also be read on the website atwww.winheller.com.

3 Dr. Streck, "DAV-Ratgeber für Junge Rechtsanwältinnen und Rechtsanwälte", p. 62.

4 The DAV is against the written fixation of professional ethical guidelines and supports an open, ongoing discussion. At the same time, it has taken the trouble to give itself a mission statement for the first time on its 150th birthday, which was developed in a process lasting several years at many

rules beyond the law or above the legal norms and, if so, whether there are norms for this in turn. If there are no norms for this, professional ethics asks what mechanism can be used to decide whether something is good or bad.

As a lawyer and attorney, you have developed a sound understanding of our legal system after years of study and practical training, and you understand international and political contexts. But your awareness of injustice, your sense of justice, was laid down much earlier: The foundations are already laid in the first three years of life, it is further developed with the development of language and complex thinking and by the first years of school, the development of your awareness of injustice, your sense of justice is largely complete, indeed you have already formed a certain understanding of the concepts of morality, law and order.

Thus, your sense of injustice and your sense of justice is on the one hand already genetically/biologically laid out as part of your individuality, but equally also the product of parental and "social" upbringing as well as your interaction with other people[5]. These experiences formed in early childhood shape our thinking and feeling our whole further life, because they are linked with emotions. Lessons in ethics and philosophy as well as the study of law and further education can at best further develop our sense of justice on the intellectual level.

So what do we, as seasoned lawyers, use today to judge our legal decisions about "good or bad", about "right or wrong"? You already guessed it: it is not primarily our legal education and professional experience.

A peculiarity for us in Germany, which has only now become a topic of discussion, is that our upbringing was more or less unconsciously influenced by the experiences of the post-war generations, an imprint that had been made far earlier by religions such as Christianity or certain forms of government, wars and treaties. Of course, the general moral concepts prevailing in Germany today, our idea of "law and order," even our legal system as a whole, are the product of the overcoming of National Socialism. However, the impact of the individual experiences in and after the world wars up to the most recent generation – i. e. up to the present day – is only just being researched. Traumatizing experiences of violence, loss of homeland and existential fears have been transferred unreflectively over decades as "life experi-

levels of the association under the guidance of experts and on the basis of professional ethics. This initiated an image change, which could be seen above all in the topics for the annual congress Anwaltstag: "Die Kanzlei als erfolgreiches Unternehmen" (2020) and "Die Anwaltschaft in besonderer Verantwortung" (2021). More about this in the blog at CLP on 11.06.2020 and in the news from 06/2021 as well as in a moment.

5 According to the philosopher of religion Martin Buber, "Der Mensch wird erst am DU zum ICH." (1923).

ences" and "convictions of morality, law and order" to the next generations and still guide us unconsciously today in our legal decisions[6].

That much has been done in this area in recent years is shown by the revision of the mission statement of the German Bar Association and the theme of the Lawyers' Day chosen for the 150th anniversary, "Die Anwaltschaft in besonderer Verantwortung: Leuchttürme der Anwaltschaft" ("The Bar in Special Responsibility: Beacons of the legal profession"), as well as the exhibition in the main office on the topic of the legal profession during the Nazi era and the new edition and further development of "Advokaten 1938" for the Austrian lawyers and the establishment of the "Maria Otto Prize" in 2010 – named after the first female lawyer in Germany in 1922 – to honor female lawyers. Finally, in the recent past, even the Beck publishing house set an example when, after years of struggle, it finally decided to rename the standard legal works for Germany (Schönfelder, Palandt and Maunz/Düring) after almost 100 years, instead of continuing to name them after Nazi jurists. Unfortunately, the courage was not enough to honor Jewish jurists or even female jurists by naming them instead[7].

---

i If you want to develop a deeper understanding of which paradigms, decision patterns and perspectives you have unconsciously internalized, you should actively deal with your very personal family war history or religious history[8]. In this context, too, it is important to write your own history, your "personal story".

But also highly topical issues such as the climate crisis and the supreme court decision on the protection of the rights of subsequent generations or the further development of species protection for wild animals and the animal welfare aspect for livestock are increasingly touching our professional ethics: even if it is when we as law firm owners discuss sustainable and climate-neutral work in the office[9]. In the end, however, it was the pandemic with the discussion about compulsory vaccination, the prioritization of our profession and triage that showed us how quickly and overheated ethical discussions can become. Or what do you think about the discussion of the exemplary function and special responsibility of the "institution of the administration of justice" on the subject of "vaccination"?

6 Ingo Müller, "Furchtbare Juristen. Die unbewältigte Vergangenheit der deutschen Justiz", p. 45.
7 Janwillem van de Loo, "Palandt umbenennen – das Ende der Geschichte?" in Anwaltsblatt from 28.7.2021 (Janwillem van de Loo had launched the "Palandt umbenennen" (rename Palandt) initiative with a website in 2016 and has been campaigning for it ever since.).
8 Bode, "Kriegsenkel: Die Erben der vergessenen Generation", p. 25 et seq.
9 I'll tell you about the decisions we made at CLP in this regard in the Author section at the end of the book.

2. Product and fee policy

Products have to be sold. This also applies to legal services.

However, generally only the legal product is advertised and neither the needs of the client are addressed nor the underlying values are mentioned. Sinek[10] gives a concise example in his classic "Start with Why":

You can, of course, promote the PC product like this:
"We make great PCs. They are user-friendly and look good. Do you want to buy one?"

Apple does it this way:
"We live to challenge the status quo. We believe in new thinking. Our products challenge the status quo: they're user-friendly and good-looking. We make PCs. Want to buy one?"

Apple advertising is not advertising, but a statement. This gives users the opportunity to identify with it. Such statements speak to us directly, go to the gut and to the heart. Everything else is advertising and wants to convince our head with information, statistics and arguments. This is exhausting and quickly becomes too much. It is therefore more elegant and far more convincing if you make the effort to hook your customers with your value-based statement.

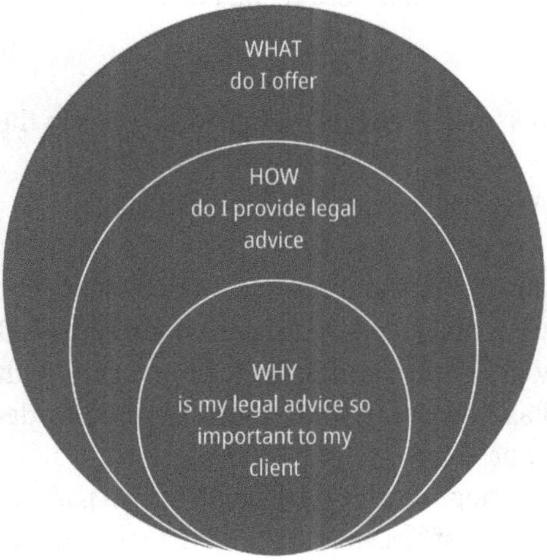

"Start with Why", © Dr. Geertje Tutschka

10 Sinek, "Start with why", p. 57.

Understanding legal advice as a service means not only responding to and satisfying the needs of the client, but also awakening new needs for legal services that the client did not have before. This does not mean the effect of "cross-selling", where a client who is satisfied with the work of the law firm in an employment law case also mandates the law firm in the future in corporate law matters. In this case, the client already had a need for corporate law advice, which he had previously satisfied with a competitor. What is meant is rather the generation of a need for advice that did not yet exist or at least was not yet perceived by the client. In addition to communication activities, this also requires the creation of new service products.

For a long time, inventing new products for the legal services market seemed difficult, if not impossible, at first glance. After all, a law firm is not an industrial enterprise where a new "commodity" could be developed. In fact, there were and still are a number of possibilities and opportunities to create new "lawyer products". Sometimes legislators and the media provide the impetus. Self-initiative and creativity are allowed. In particular, the buzzword **"legal tech"** is on everyone's lips in this context, a collective term for all possible, conceivable new product approaches, such as:
- Law firm software
- Cloud solutions
- Special security systems
- File archiving
- Standardized legal products such as "Flight Right" or "geblitzt.de"
- Legal advice at flat rates
- Lawyer platforms
- Highly complex hardware with many "special effects" designed to usher in the era of the "paperless law firm"
- Supplementary products for the beA (special electronic lawyer's mailbox)

The list is probably already outdated at this moment and can in no way be complete. New products and ideas are added daily. The interested reader can obtain very good summaries of the current status in any online format for the legal industry with minimal effort. Lawyers are in demand as consultants and experts for product development, test runs, marketing and product launch[11].

In addition, there is the need for consulting, which the legal industry in particular has in these difficult times. Seminars, workshops, authoring on the topics of the new challenges for colleagues, but also new event formats, conferences and trade

11 For example, I worked with CLP on the Europe-wide launch of the lawyer's copier.

fairs can be products. The same applies to the area of professional recruiting and personnel development for large law firms or the various mentoring programs in which experienced lawyers can try out new products[12]. In the meantime, experienced lawyers have also built up a second leg in the various areas of marketing and communication, e.g. when it comes to communicating sensitive issues or special lawyer marketing.

The following comparison shows the attractiveness of the legal sector as a target group:

Target group LEGAL	
contra	**pro**
• High competitive pressure	• Strong financial potential
• Strong market movement	• Long-term Relationship
• Traditional and conservative	• Development capability

Target group Legal, © Dr. Geertje Tutschka

"The service of commercial litigation financing has become firmly established in Germany and large parts of Europe since 1999. In contrast to the American model, the lawyer and the financier remain separate, i.e. the lawyer can concentrate solely on his work for the client. The litigation financier provides support where desired and – depending on the practice of the various companies – sometimes accompanies the proceedings to a greater or lesser extent. For the lawyer, this cooperation has several advantages: he can handle mandates that would otherwise fail due to the client's financial means. His fees are secured by the litigation financier, and finally, the latter contributes his specialist know-how. In addition to legal advice, the lawyer can offer the client an attractive solution, even as a "David" against a financially stronger "Goliath". The financier provides all the funds necessary for an optimal conduct of the proceedings and also assumes the risk of losing the case. As a rule, the financier's contingency fee ranges from 20 % to 40 % of the proceeds of a lawsuit. The company also finances mediation and arbitration proceedings. In Germany, there are three main providers: ROLAND ProzessFinanz AG from Cologne, Legial AG from Munich, and Foris AG from Bonn. Since the process financiers do not (may not) provide legal advice, a claim must first be assessed by the lawyer on the basis of the factual and legal situation. Only if the lawyer comes to the conclusion of predominant chances of success of a judicial enforcement, an inquiry is worthwhile itself."

Dr. Arndt Eversberg, attorney-at-law and member of the board of ROLAND ProzessFinanz AG, one of the most experienced litigation financiers in Europe.

12 Particularly for attorneys who are full-time employees in their own firms, it can be a welcome change to share their expertise with young colleagues in seminars and workshops or to present it to experienced colleagues and thus possibly also gain new cooperation partners.

This also includes making legal services or the bundling of new services easy for the client to understand. Hardly any potential client will voluntarily read legal journals. Generally understandable short presentations in daily newspapers or magazines may arouse the interest of individual potential clients. A new service product is not yet created with such an article. Presentation software and modern presentation technology make it possible to present even complicated legal contexts clearly and to show potential clients the benefits that the new service can bring them. It still seems to be unusual for lawyers to prepare service packages as computer-aided presentations for clients. However, the step from the indispensable Internet presence to the computer-supported presentation is actually not far. Large law firms, especially those that work intensively with auditing firms, maintain their own departments that professionally prepare such presentations and make them available to the firm's attorneys for acquisition purposes[13].

For small law firms, a neatly designed leaflet summarizing the components of a particular service offered by a firm will do. Such a leaflet can be distributed after a presentation to members of chambers of industry and commerce, trade associations and other interest groups, thus supporting the sale of the new "product".

A special fee policy can also help. Here, the focus should be less on the price itself and more on open and transparent billing, reliability and client comfort. Cooperation with a litigation financier, for example, is aimed at achieving this.

Ultimately, the distribution policy must also be geared to the product and the target clientele: **"How does the legal service reach the client?"** If you answer this question with a short "by mail", you are not completely wrong, but you have only understood one aspect of the distribution policy. Here, both the wishes and preferences of the target clientele in terms of material and personnel resources and the accessibility and availability of the lawyer should be taken into account.

Many law firms are currently working on their own products for their special field, for their clients or simply because they enjoy it. So, it remains exciting.

3. The firm team

The third pillar of the law firm are the people of your company. This includes the attorneys as well as the professional staff, the partners as well as the employees, but also special departments such as tax, insolvency, enforcement, IT, marketing and

---

13 This was the O-Ton in the 1st edition in 2018; in the meantime, Anna Murk and her team have launched the online magazine for non-lawyers "Legal Layman" described above, and young guns like Sue Reiter have specialized in "legal visualization".

accounting – even the cleaning team, the porter and other service providers of the law firm. They all represent your firm to the outside world and are the face of your firm[14].

So you should not only know and recognize your law firm vision and values, but also symbolize them. Finding – and keeping – the right employees is therefore one of the most important and at the same time most difficult tasks of every law firm owner[15]:

It's a people business.

What did you get out of the chapter?
You understood the important role that values, ethics and culture play in the law firm vision.

14 Busmann, "Chefsache Mandantenakquise", p. 17.
15 More about this in the next chapter.

III. Positioning and orientation

Why should you read this chapter?
You can align your law firm development with the law firm vision.

Overview
1. **What is your expertise**
2. **What differentiates your firm/product?**
3. **Target group**
4. **How do you serve your clients?**

You have already thought about why you want to establish your law firm. That is, why you would like to exercise the role of a law firm owner in addition to your legal activity, the purely legal activity. You have also thought about how you would like to implement this entrepreneurial activity and your law firm: whether as an individual law firm or in cooperation with colleagues or as a reorganization of an already existing law firm. You should now think about what distinguishes your law firm from other law firms.

The question of the current positioning on the market is particularly important in the case of reorganizations, splits or mergers of law firms in order not to lose resources and already existing client bases, service products or customer sources that could not be further used in one form or another; as start-up capital for the new law firm, so to speak.

But this question can also play a role in the establishment of a new company, namely when a lawyer becomes self-employed from an employment relationship[1]. But even a newcomer to the profession may have already built up a certain potential through internships, in the traineeship, on his previous professional career, from private relationships or from voluntary and leisure activities, which can now be quite useful to him. Even with established veterans, experience shows that these existing business sources are not always present and are used far less often than might be expected.

Positioning is primarily about identifying the market based on your ideal client and your area of law on the one hand and determining the market on the other hand[2].

1 And this is indeed what happens in the vast majority of new start-ups.
2 Trimborn von Landenberg, Erfolgreich starten als Rechtsanwalt, p. 25 et seq.

i

So, this is primarily about research activity.
You should find and get to know your competitors, your so-called competition in this field of law and for these ideal clients.
You should analyse exactly what your competitors offer and how much and how long they have been in the business? Accompanying economic analyses can also be important.
You should know the offers and products of your competitors, the corresponding marketing measures and how the market reacts to them.
Ideally, you have already gained experience as an employee of your competitors and therefore have a certain insider's view.

In the example of the music specialist mentioned below, it could therefore be a matter of determining what market growth and development the music market will take in the next 5 to 10 years (within Germany as well as worldwide).

Once you have sufficiently analysed the market and your competitors, it is time to position yourself, your area of law and your unique selling proposition in this market.

Again, this is about nothing more than the question: what differentiates you from your competitors, and why this represents added value for your clients?

From the particular problem of your clients, which you would like to solve, you develop your positioning, your target group definition and your special field of law. From this, in turn, the so-called branding will emerge[3].

1. What is your expertise

Why should you consider this?

In most cases, a law firm is dominated by one "face", one person. In traditional law firms, this can be the founder of the law firm, whose name the firm still bears and whose oil portrait hangs in the reception area. But it can also be one of the attorneys who has a particularly high public profile and appears in the daily press on a regular basis.

However, the face of the law firm can also be "the good soul of the house" for your clients: your long-standing employee who is known throughout the city. The point here is that you yourself strategically decide who should stand for you and your law firm.

3 See marketing in the chapter after next.

Your **unique selling proposition** (USP) will make it easier for you to attract the clients you actually want to work with. And thus to bring your special service, e.g. as an expert in a certain field of law, to the client.

As a lawyer, you may have already committed yourself to a particular area of law or have a very specific idea of how you would best advise your clients. You may also be in a better position than other colleagues to handle mandates in this area and to help them succeed because of your special life experience, such as experience abroad or experience in the legal department of a company, because you have built up know-how, a network and also expertise in this area.

Or you are still searching for your special unique selling point.

In principle, it must be said that the legal education alone is not usually suitable to provide you with your special unique selling point. It is true that it is possible to specialize in a certain area of law at an early stage during your studies due to the elective courses. During the legal clerkship, there is also the possibility to become particularly familiar with certain areas of law in the corresponding elective stations. On the other hand, there is usually a lack of suitable mentors, advisors or committed colleagues during the training period who, on the one hand, recognize your special abilities and strengths and, on the other hand, also offer a certain amount of assistance in choosing the area of law or are even prepared to lay the foundation stone for your specialization with you.

In my experience, lawyers typically use one of the following three paths to develop their specialty:

- In the first years of their careers, they try out various professions and various legal or other law activities in order to gain an insight and overview of the various areas, to acquire a certain amount of experience, and then, after 5 to 10 years of working life, to decide for themselves where their own strengths lie and how these can best be implemented in the further professional context.
- The alternative is to take the first opportunity that comes along and settle into it. This is supported by the fact that job satisfaction is typically determined to 80 % by a committed team, a motivating boss and adequate remuneration[4].
- The third possibility is to discover and develop one's own strengths and unique selling proposition with professional help from a mentor or a business coach. This person will certainly not be able to identify the unique selling proposition within the course of a single lesson or a one-day meeting. However, a coopera-

4 Jochen Mai, "Zufriedenheit im Beruf" in Karriere-Bibel from 1.5.2016.

tion in the form of a process over several months[5] is usually suitable to achieve clarity and target accuracy, which means an enormous time and cost saving compared to the other ways.

Since you have purchased this book and have taken the time to read it, I assume that you have already been thinking about founding a law firm for some time, and in this respect also about finding your unique selling point.

You realize that setting up a law firm today is fundamentally different from the way it used to be, when it was enough to hang an attractive sign on the wall of your house after passing your exams and wait for clients to walk in the door and bring you their legal mandates. Or that you enriched your hobby as an equestrian and hunter or your ambitions as a medical doctor or building contractor by extending your legal practice to this area, so that you could, so to speak, turn your hobby into a profession. This may still be true today in some areas, just think of the example of the music lover who recognizes the next hit of a newcomer band at the first note and later specializes in music contracts, copyrights and the rights of artists and musicians in general.

In fact, your special experiences, skills and personality traits are the key to your USP, your unique selling proposition. In terms of approach, this is hardly different from this traditional procedure. What is different, however, is the strategic-tactical approach: to find and define your USP in advance in order to finally develop the firm's positioning and strategy.

In order to find your personal USP, it is a good idea to gather all your special skills in a coaching process, e.g. on a flip chart. Writing by hand with a pen and using different colors is generally better suited to set creative processes in motion than just talking about it or typing into the keyboard of a computer[6]. Keep in mind: In the vast majority of cases it is a matter of finding a special combination of already existing areas of law, which at best correspond to one of your special personal abilities or a special personal life experience[7].

This can be, for example, that you have taken in a refugee child and now have special knowledge about the situation of refugees. But it can also be that you, as a dog owner, have special knowledge of certain hereditary diseases or certain behavioral problems of a certain breed or have experience in working with dog trainers. So, use all your personal experiences and characteristics to find your USP. In the end, it is precisely these combinations that develop not only unique selling points

5 a sustainable, promising process usually takes at least six or twelve months.

6 Even if you already know your unique selling proposition, your legal specialty, you should not skip this step.

7 Ben Schulz, "Artgerechte Bodenhaltung", p. 5.

but entire new areas of law, which at best make you an expert in this new field of law right from the start.

At the moment, the DAV has 24 specialist attorneyships. Approximately 2 new specialist attorneyships are added each year. However, you should not make the mistake of confusing a specialized attorney with your unique selling proposition. The unique selling proposition is primarily determined by your personality and not by your qualifications. At best, the qualification can support and document this personality and this special knowledge and skills[8]. These so-called cross competencies – which I will come to later on in the topic of marketing – are therefore your true capital: the specialist lawyer title is now a “standard building block” that should definitely be combined with a “special feature” – and by this I do not mean the combination of several specialist lawyer titles or specialist titles that only a few have! In the spring of 2022, specialist lawyers in labor law, family law, tax law, traffic law, and landlord-tenant law led the way and dominated the lawyer market with significant 20 % and 16 % and 6–8 %, respectively. So, these are the current standard building blocks in the lawyer business, without which you will not generate business in the future[9].

So, what differentiates your firm?
What problem do you want to solve for your clients?
What can you do better with your law firm than other providers?

2. What differentiates your firm/product

In addition to building your expertise, it is about placing this in the market of your target group with appropriate means: through your law firm.

In order to assert itself in the market, a law firm must define its own market, “position” itself in the market. This requires an independent profile. The firm must demonstrate the advantages for clients that set it apart from its competitors, a so-called USP (unique selling point), i. e. a unique selling proposition with regard to its products and services. These distinctive advantages do not always have to be the same for all groups of competitors.

One of the distinguishing features compared to non-lawyer competitors can be the special professional qualification of the lawyer. The price or the specialization

8 Ben Schulz, “Erfolg braucht Dein Gesicht”, p. 62.
9 statista from 25.01.2022.

of the service offered can also serve as a distinguishing feature compared to other lawyers, for example. In principle, however, the USP is decided by the two criteria "business field" and "target group".

In the legal industry, the business field is traditionally equated with the legal field. But it no longer has to be. "Flight Right" and "geblitzt.de" both work in the same field of business – namely, clients who are looking for a quick and easy solution to standardizable legal issues online. One, however, in transportation law and the other in traffic law.

"If you do everything, you do nothing right" – This truism also applies to the business areas in which a lawyer is active. The business areas of a lawyer can be defined and determined according to very different criteria. These criteria cannot be put in a generally valid order of priority. The decisive factor is that a law firm attempts to identify and choose the most appropriate business area from the bundle of possible activities on the market for legal services. In practice, lawyers use possible categories to classify the legal services market not singularly, but in combination with other categories.

It is possible for a law firm to focus on a specific product, for example, litigation in the field of administrative law, which is offered to all potential clients. It is also possible to focus on very specific clients, for example the professional group of physicians, to whom a comprehensive service is offered. This comprehensive support may then include not only advice and representation in the area of panel doctor law and medical professional law, but also in the areas of employment law, tenancy law (in relation to the practice premises) and possibly also road traffic law. It is obvious that such specializations are not yet concrete enough to create a sharply contoured profile of the law firm. In the first case, the law firm has not yet defined the target group to which it wants to offer its services (all customers). In the second case, there is a lack of focus on the specific needs of the target group.

Another criteria of market segmentation can be the decision for the price of the offered service. A law firm can decide to strive for price leadership (the most expensive law firm on the market) or cost leadership (cheaper than all others). However, considering only this criteria alone condemns a meaningful strategic orientation of the law firm to failure. This is because decisions on the range of products offered and on the target clients that can be addressed with such an orientation are missing.

Lawyers must therefore consider and decide which services they want to offer to which group of clients and at what price. It is possible to offer different products at different prices to two different groups of clients. For example, a law firm may decide to represent employees before the labor courts exclusively on the basis of the RVG scale fees. Entrepreneurs should be advised and represented in the area of competition law exclusively against agreement of a time-based fee. However, neither client groups nor product ranges can be combined arbitrarily. Law firms should therefore not take diversification too far. In order to create a clear profile of a law firm, the firm must not give the impression of being a "mixed legal store".

Based on their training, lawyers divide their professional world into areas of law. Almost all law firms have focal points in different areas of law. All too often, this focus is still random, much less planned. A law firm can achieve a clear strategic orientation, for example, by specializing exclusively in criminal law. There are also successful law firms that deal with nothing but labor law or administrative law. This is accompanied by the steadily increasing number of specialist lawyers. However, specialization in certain areas of law cannot be stringently maintained in practice. This is because a client's problem in a matter is not always limited to a specific area of law. Even standard matters such as road traffic accidents usually involve at least three areas of law, the law of damages under the German Civil Code (BGB), insurance law and criminal law or the law of administrative offenses. It is possible to place the handling of the civil law part and the criminal law part of this matter in the hands of two different specialists. From the client's point of view, however, this appears complicated and is not desired by him, at least in standard cases. After all, it is often not possible for clients to assign their problems to the "right" field of law. The lawyer who appears as a specialist in the law of contracts for work and services will not necessarily be identified as a "construction lawyer" by a layman.

The employment law specialist constantly advising a limited liability company will also want to represent the company in a legal dispute with the employed managing director. To do so, however, he must step out of "his" field of law. Strictly speaking, the employment contract law of the managing director does not belong to labor law. The managing director of a GmbH is not an employee. Essential norms regulating the rights and duties of a managing director are of a corporate law nature. The legal dispute between the GmbH and the managing director about the existence of the employment contract is also not settled before the labor courts, but before the ordinary courts.

A more promising approach is to focus on specific tasks or problem areas. A law firm can, for example, be geared to covering topics such as "profession and work", "all aspects of road traffic", "house construction and purchase" or "old-age provision with interfaces to asset consulting". Such areas of responsibility encompass several fields of law. The topic of "climate protection" is also becoming increasingly relevant for the legal profession. The lawyer's specialization is then based on typical economic contexts relevant to the client, not primarily on areas of law.

If a law firm wants to develop several fields of activity for itself, then these fields of activity must fit together. Lawyers who want to provide advice in the "high end area" of corporate law and at the same time represent interests in the area of residential tenancy law do not appear credible in the eyes of potential clients. Such a combination would be not productive. Inquirers will not trust such a law firm to be competent in either tenancy law or corporate law. Irrespective of this, client communication and marketing, as well as the firm's external appearance, are also likely to appear unprofessional.

3. Target group

One of the most important decisions in the strategic orientation of a law firm is therefore to define the target clientele that the firm wants to address with its services[10]. Every lawyer must answer the following questions for himself: **"Who do I want to work for? Who do I want to deal with professionally?"**

Once you have described your ideal client in this way, it is relatively easy to narrow down the associated area of law even further.

The next question should then be:

"What problem of these clients do I want to solve?"

So, your target group are exactly the clients
- who have a problem in a very special field of law
- for which you offer a solution
- who want your legal services
- who can afford your legal services

The type of clients to be served is the criteria for the division of business areas. A firm may focus on representing consumers, businesses or primarily the public sector. Further subdivisions will be necessary: What type of companies should be represented? Only companies in a certain industry? Only companies with a certain balance sheet total? Should consumers be represented in all legal matters or only in certain areas? In which sector should municipalities and public authorities be represented? In all areas of administrative law? Also in civil law cases?

Common distinctions of client groups into entrepreneurs and consumers have already been mentioned several times. However, depending on the personal preferences of a lawyer, criteria such as the level of education of clients, the level of in-

10 Dr. Tutschka, Der Rechtsanwalt als Unternehmer, TeleLex, p. 27.

come, membership of a social group, industry affiliation and regional references may also have to be taken into account for the definition of the target group.

In a market dominated by the demand side, such as the market for legal services, it is ideal from a marketing point of view to base the orientation on the needs of the target clients. On the other hand, the importance of the lawyer's preferences and talent for certain business areas or areas of law should not be neglected. Even if the demand for legal services in the area of white-collar criminal law may be great, a lawyer who does not want to have anything to do with criminal law and who possibly does not understand anything about it should not orient his target clientele exclusively on the criterion of the greatest demand.

For the determination of the target group of a law firm, a constant pendulum view between the needs of the desired target group on the one hand and the business field in which a lawyer wants to work on the other hand is required. Only if both areas are taken into account, a lawyer will be able to narrow down his target group sharply enough and promisingly.

Key points

Target group oriented marketing A, © Dr. Geertje Tutschka

The future are...

Target group oriented marketing B, © Dr. Geertje Tutschka

Lawyers must therefore consider and decide which services they want to offer to which group of clients and at what price. It is certainly possible to offer two different client groups different products at different prices. However, neither client groups nor product ranges can be combined arbitrarily.

And one final note:

Young lawyers who have just joined an existing firm often overlook the fact that their clients include not only the firm's clientele, but also the other lawyers in the firm and possibly, in particular, the senior partner whom they were hired to relieve. What are the needs of these "clients in their own office"? It will be a good strategic decision for a hired lawyer to also consider his own office as "his market", to whose needs he has to orient his activity.

4. How do you serve your clients

Your law firm vision should include, in as much detail as possible, all three key questions: **WHY, WHAT, HOW**[11].

We have already covered the first two points in detail and have also mentioned one or two other points in this regard,

- how a product/service can be tailored
- how your target clientele can be addressed
- how clever fee and price policies work
- how distribution policies can provide support
- how the firm's values determine the strategic direction

At this point, therefore, only this much in conclusion: The positioning and orientation of your law firm does not stop with your performance and expertise.

Your service must also be delivered to your target clients in a way,

- that the quality of your service is maintained,
- that this delivery is appropriate to your service
- that it is oriented towards the needs of your client and
- that your firm values are clearly recognizable here as well

i

Becoming aware of your own delivery process so that you can review it and correct it if necessary is an important first step.

And here, too, the aspect that the client must feel that his needs are being met and that the lawyer is perceived as a trustworthy partner plays a decisive role.

So, if you take away just one piece of information from this chapter, it's this:

---

11 Simon Simek, "Start with Why", p. 133.

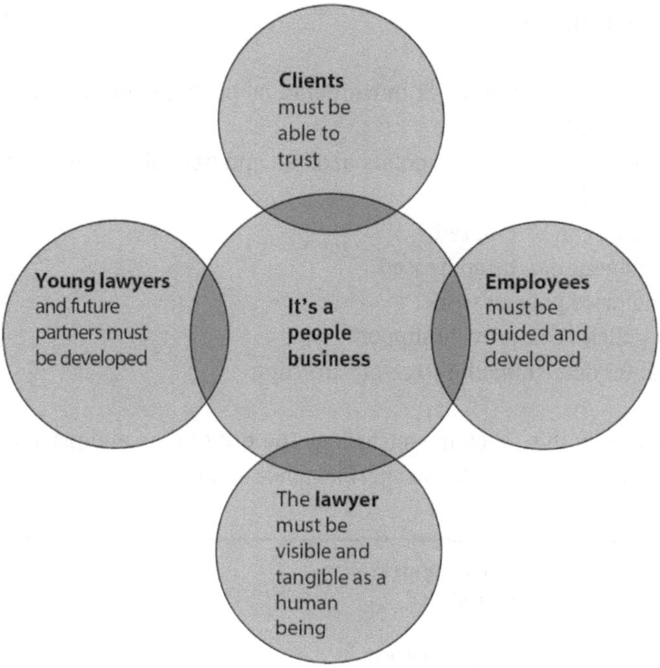

"It's a people business", © Dr. Geertje Tutschka

IV. Setting for the development of a law firm vision

Maybe you already have a concrete idea of what your law firm should look like and which areas of law it should cover, or maybe you only have a vague idea of it so far. In any case, you should now begin to refine this idea, to make it more concrete and to enrich it with as many details as possible until a tangible vision has emerged. This is not primarily about external factors such as market requirements, formal prerequisites for founding a law firm or qualifications. At this point it is more about an emotional/irrational presentation of your law firm. It is about values, about the firm's philosophy and culture. It is about the heart of your firm and your own positioning as a lawyer, an expert in your field.

Perhaps this was already the topic of one of your partner meetings. In my experience, however, this topic is only touched upon in passing at partner meetings in order to eventually answer the annoying questions of the marketing people who want to finally put a "law firm vision" on the website because there is a free space available for it. Most of the time, however, this topic also resonates as an underlying tone through the busy daily routine of the law firm and the strategy meetings.

It's high time to take a closer look at this range of topics. Perhaps you have already been collecting certain aspects and ideas for years. Now it's time to get out that box, open that special folder on your computer, take the post-it's off the pin board and spread them out on the table in front of you.

If you haven't done any of this yet, make time for it now. Depending on how far along your ideas and conceptions are, you should plan several hours for it: an afternoon, a weekend or regularly one to two hours of undisturbed time.

What does "undisturbed time" mean, I am asked again and again at this point in my seminars. Therefore, I would like to briefly discuss the "**perfect setting**" of such undisturbed vision work:

---

i

- a low-distraction room
- appropriate work equipment
- no screens, cell phones or technical devices
- sufficient water

You should ensure a distraction-free space in order to provide the appropriate framework for this important preliminary work. Experience has shown that objections such as: I have my best ideas in the shower/while jogging/sleeping/driving a car ... are often raised at this point. That may be and hopefully you collect these ideas as well. But in order to really get into a concrete working process, it is necessary to provide a protected space for this – without external influences[1].

So, is it enough to simply enter an "appointment with yourself" in your office calendar? In principle, yes, if you are not too distracted by other screens or work objects in the office.

However, take into account what type of learner you are.

If you are more of a visual type, remove pictures, books, technical supplies, art, project boards, and painted flip charts. Be sure to use colors, colorful post-its, if possible meaningful pictures and symbols for your vision work. Use a sheet of white paper at least A3 in size and liquid drawing pens.

If, on the other hand, you are more of an auditory learner, you should ensure complete silence or make arrangements so that you determine what sounds you hear.

Please refer to the following graphic for further details:

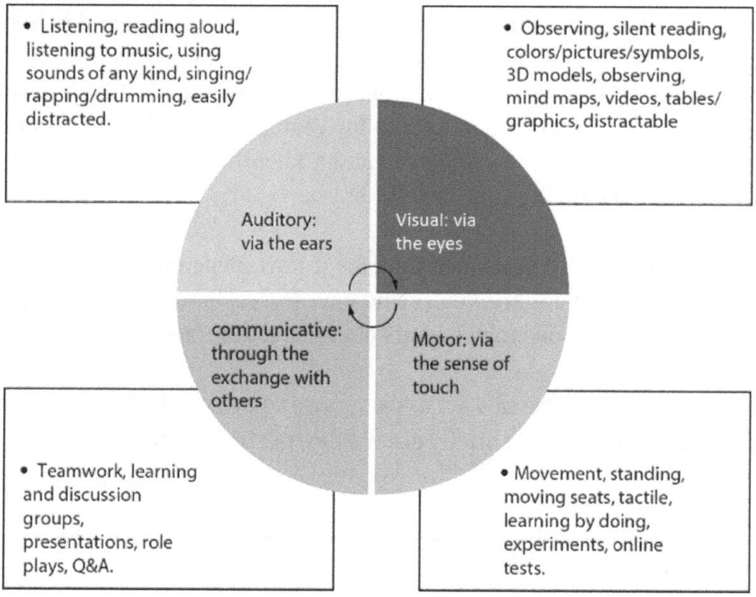

Scientists agree that handwriting promotes a more intensive thought process with more connections than mere typing or even dictation[2].

1 Nancy Kline, "Time to think", p. 131 et seq.

2 Prof. Ursula Bredel (Professor and expert for orthography didactics) in "Es ist gut fürs Gehirn mit der Hand zu schreiben", Die Welt, 15.1.2015.

In my experience, a large sheet of white paper, or even better, a flip chart, is especially suitable. It is important that the size exceeds the usual DIN A4 format in any case. The larger format gives room for creative ideas and different topics, opens mind and senses for new di-mensions. With different colored pencils you can thus collect your ideas and at the same time set priorities, establish relationships with each other, mark open questions. You can also work on it quite well with breaks, and also let it rest for several days.

Caution: During this phase, be sure to work alone first. Only after this process is complete, if necessary, consult friends, partners, colleagues and get their feedback. **!**

If you are a team player and need the input of colleagues or the exchange with them, or if you can only become really creative if you communicate, you should consult a professional coach who can support you in this phase of vision formation. A professional coach, who ideally has experience in the legal industry[3], will be able to accelerate and intensify this process[4].

Even if you want to establish a law firm together with colleagues or manage it as a team of partners, it is important that each person first develops his or her own individual law firm vision and only subsequently forms a unified law firm vision from these law firm visions.

If you cannot or do not want to consult a professional coach, there are several tools and methods you can use yourself to give structure to the development process and ensure that you do not forget anything[5]. However, it is important to choose the right option for you from the multitude of different possibilities.

Case studies:
In our three case studies, the question is whether the challenges these law firms are facing right now have to do with their law firm vision.

1. In the **"growing pains"** example, the many small teams not only work together inefficiently. They also steer in different directions just like many individual law firms. Obviously, this merger has always been viewed more from an operational perspective. However, all measures to harmonize processes will come to

---

3 Bärbel Schwertfeger (psychologist) in "Sie können alles erreichen", KarriereSpiegel from 6.12.2013.
4 Coaches specifically for the legal industry, for example, can be found at www.consultingforlegals.com.
5 Lars Lorber, "Menschenkenntnis – Der große Typentest", p. 79 et seq.; Marcus Buckingham, "Entdecken Sie Ihre Stärken jetzt!", p. 80.

nothing if one does not manage to establish a uniform management level on the one hand, and if this management level does not go through the vision process described above on the other hand. Determining the values and culture of the small firms with the personalities of the partners and building on this to agree on the values and culture of the large team, will be essential for future development.

2. In the example of the **"wrong clients"**, it should be asked whether the values and culture of the firm may need to be revised with regard to the new target group, but also in terms of new employees and possibly the increased use of technologies. This transformation process should definitely be taken as an opportunity to modernize the firm's vision and base the upcoming change process on it.
3. In the example of the **gender and generation shift**, the decision lies with the partners: if everything is to remain as it is, they will have to abandon the idea of being attractive to junior staff and clients. If they don't want to do that, they will have to change, not by introducing programs to promote women and families, but at the core: in values, culture and law firm vision. My recommendation here would be to involve selected junior staff in the process and to learn to listen to them. This is where the greatest potential lies.

What did you get out of the chapter?
You understand the importance of a law firm vision, how a law firm vision is developed, and how it is used in day-to-day law firm operations.

C. Law firm foundation

Let me start by giving you five good reasons not to start a law firm.

You don't have to start a law firm to practice law; but you do have to be a lawyer to start a law firm. Gone are the days when graduates could not find a job and were forced to start their own business. Statistics show that today, lawyers only trust themselves to start a law firm after careful consideration and several years of professional experience.

The number of new law firms has been stagnating for years and the number of admissions has been declining steadily since 2017, although the number of graduates from universities continues to increase slightly.

This may be due to the fact that large law firms in particular have a constant need for junior lawyers, but the legal advice market in Germany is largely saturated. It may also be due to the fact that the judiciary and administration are outdated and there is an increased need for young lawyers. Unimaginable a few years ago, the state is now proactively approaching both universities and the legal profession to recruit.

Also, more and more lawyers are flocking to alternative professions and industries that now offer quite attractive career paths for lawyers.

For the majority of lawyers, therefore, setting up a law firm is no more a desirable goal of their professional career than a partnership.

What are the arguments against it?

Reason 1: Legal limitations

The legal profession is a free profession. However, as an organ of the administration of justice, the lawyer must exercise his profession within certain limits prescribed by professional law. What gives the profession freedom and dignity on the one hand, limits it on the other – primarily from an entrepreneurial point of view. What is meant here are the regulations on inter-branch cooperation, marketing, training, remuneration and licensing, etc.

In times when law firms have to compete with the free economy for the limited market, these restrictions are increasingly becoming a burden for law firms, as legal tech providers, insurers and service providers in other industries are not subject to them by their very nature. In addition, thanks to digitization, expertise can now be accessed anywhere, at any time, and free of charge anyway, which is shaking the legal advice monopoly of the legal profession to its foundations and increasingly encouraging government, non-profit, and charitable institutions to expand their services in the direction of legal advice for the benefit of the general public.

https://doi.org/10.1515/9783111058160-003

Consequently, the legal regulations of the legal profession are no longer up to date. The major BRAO reform was therefore long overdue.

Reason 2: Entrepreneurial limit

It is no secret that especially in the area of small and medium-sized law firms a certain standstill has occurred and that many law firms do not achieve the turnover and profits required for successful, healthy growth.

Many law firms live "from hand to mouth" and are hardly profitable anymore.

The still problematic regulation on the "withdrawal of the license to practice law in the event of a loss of assets" discourages many law firm owners from filing for insolvency.

In many cases, the bureaucratic hurdles to closing down an uneconomical law firm before it becomes insolvent mean that it remains in existence, at least on paper, but is actually no longer in operation. From an entrepreneurial point of view, this is fatal, as a certain entrepreneurial risk is inevitably part of success – as is the right to a second chance. This is the only way to generate drive, innovation and development in the industry.

It is no coincidence that precise figures on law firm insolvencies and closures are still lacking, at least in the professional chambers, although they do exist. This is not doing any favors, as it makes it difficult to assess the entrepreneurial risk associated with founding a law firm, which makes it difficult for financial service providers and founders alike to make a realistic assessment and can turn founding a law firm into a "blind flight".

Thus, even in the second edition, the present book is alone far and wide with the topic about the closure of a law firm.

Reason 3: Competence limit

According to a recent survey by ffi Publishing,

- half of the owners of small and medium-sized law firms surveyed say they are "less well versed" in entrepreneurial topics and do not use any business development tools,
- one-third say they have at least "the most important business know-how" according to their own assessment; after all, just under one in four uses a business plan.
- However, every eighth person states that they do not know anything about being a law firm owner, and
- half of the respondents said they were at least interested in the topics of founding and developing a law firm, strategy and management, and positioning and

marketing, more so than in the "perennial favorite" of legal tech and digitization.

Remember
Starting a law firm has become more complex.
In addition, successful law firm management has become more complex, which every second participant confirms unreservedly and every fourth can confirm at least in part. Digitization has opened up unimagined opportunities, but it has also brought risks. New developments are taking place faster, making it almost impossible to keep up. Products are becoming short-lived and arbitrary.

Reason 4: Capacity limit

Surprisingly enough, according to the survey conducted by the ffi publishing house,
- one eighth state that they have not changed their way of working in the last 5–10 years and that this is working well,
- another quarter state that they are reacting to the increased demands and complexity with more "manpower" by working more themselves or with additional staff today than they did a few years ago,
- while the vast majority state that they are reacting with the conscious use of software and time management in order to become more effective.

None of the respondents has found the ideal solution so far. Finding good new employees to meet the requirements is causing great difficulties. In general, there is too much work for too little staff. This also makes growth almost impossible, as a law firm but also personally. As a firm owner, you are working at the edge of your breaking point.

Reason 5: Personal limit

Finally, personal boundaries must be mentioned. The topics of professional ethics, personal values, and personal imprinting also play a role here. Marketing, acquisition and sales are not everyone's cup of tea. Likewise, of course, health impairments or private obligations to relatives.

The crucial thing here, however, is: New values want to be lived. Work-life balance is no longer a buzzword. Life time has become more precious. Time for the family, for regeneration and health are more important than realizing not only professional but also entrepreneurial goals.

In the survey, one in two law firm owners said they had no time for the important things in life. There are still no meaningful studies on the health of professionals for the German and Austrian markets. The fact is, however, that the situation here is no different than in other countries: in the U. S., both the American Bar Association and the Institute for Well-being in Law have been trying to obtain reliable statistics for several years, with alarming results: the potential for addiction and depression is greatly increased, as is the suicide rate and the risk of sudden death at the desk.

In fact, the legal profession neither prepares one for founding a law firm nor for the associated entrepreneurial activity and management tasks. Strictly speaking, the practice of law actually hinders the establishment and management of a law firm – after all, the entrepreneurial tasks are regularly added after a long, intensive working day in the law firm.

You have to want to start a law firm. Or not – as these five reasons show.

Growing demands on the part of clients, increasing competitive and cost pressures, as well as advancing digitalization are placing particular demands on law firm leadership and management today. Nevertheless, legal training in the sense of a purely technical education has hardly changed. Entrepreneurial and business management topics are still not covered, although by far the largest proportion of lawyers still prefer the legal profession to a career in the civil service or in business. And as many as two-thirds of lawyers start their own business within the first eight years.

However, leadership issues, management tasks and entrepreneurial thinking are a natural part of everyday professional life for most of them much earlier, as legal work usually entails departmental responsibility with personnel and budget responsibility per se. No wonder, then, that according to a recent MkG survey from 08/2019, law firm development topics such as strategy, positioning and management are at the top of the wish list for further training among lawyers, but on the other hand are hardly offered for this sector or are not evaluated as further training (according to FAO).

In the 2018 MkG Special, “Erfolgreiche Kanzleigründung leicht gemacht” (“Successful Law Firm Formation Made Easy“), we put a special focus on how to go about starting a law firm as a young attorney.

In my years of experience in strategy work with lawyers, this preliminary work was still done very carefully in most law firms – but then disappeared into the drawer in day-to-day business. The long office days, especially in the early years, leave little time for creative and energetic revision of the original plans. Yet it is so important to stay on course or to make corrections in good time.

So the real challenge – as is so often the case – is to “stay on the ball” and make law firm development an ongoing topic.

But how does that work?

1. Asking the right question: What are you selling?
2. Business Model Canvas: Your Business Model Matrix with Future Potential
3. Controlling: The Hidden Champion

When Peter Drucker, a German-speaking top management coach from Vienna, developed his famous "fünf entscheidenden Fragen des Managements" (five crucial management questions) in the 1990s, he certainly did not have a law firm in mind: rather, he had turned from the social sector and work with hospitals to work with volunteers and NGOs – undoubtedly a very special sector.

Still, this question is dynamite – even for law firms: What are you selling?

When I asked the members of the Association of Insolvency Attorneys this question at their annual meeting, the first answers were generalities: Legal advice, representation of interests and service. But what is the debtor really looking for in an insolvency lawyer shortly before private insolvency? A colleague came forward after a break and said his clients were audibly taking a breath in and out in the office for the first time in a long time. Clients would regularly thank him for taking the stone off their chest and that they now had air to breathe again. Does he sell air? Lung therapy? Indeed, clients seek and find hope with him.

Knowing this means knowing your customers' needs, being able to offer the right products, and being able to tailor your marketing and sales language accordingly. In other words, attracting the right customers with the right service and the right product.

Financial and budget planning should definitely be used for less complex and especially timely law firm developments.

It is important not to "forget" your own salary. Also, the profit of the law firm should not be equated with one's own salary, at least not without further ado, because after all, investments are also to be made and reserves are to be formed with it. Another aspect is retirement provision: unlike in earlier times, law firms are no longer sold when they reach retirement age. Client relationships have become too short-lived and personalized; the structures and processes in most law firms still have too little significance and independent value. The purchase price therefore no longer secures the retirement of the law firm owner in addition to the pension entitlements and claims from the pension scheme of the lawyers. Retirement planning should therefore be included in the business planning of your law firm from the very beginning.

It is also advisable not to limit this planning to the financial perspective alone, but also to specifically plan for the time involved (as the equivalent of the time we all spend living).

Accurate **financial accounting** can be used to control the use and exhaustion of budgets – but it is not the sole yardstick.

It is also a prerequisite that **budgets** are planned and described in detail. Furthermore, the responsibilities and decision-making paths for spending the budgets must be precisely defined. It is advisable to introduce certain **upper limits** and to always work with a **dual control principle**. It should also be clear in advance what will happen if budgets are not used up or if **budgets** have to be **reallocated** because there is suddenly an unforeseen need for investment elsewhere. Risk and **insurance management** should not be missing either.

In many law firms, a certain need for improvement in the **definition of responsibilities and task profiles** as well as the description of **process flows and decision-making structures** is now apparent at the latest.

adapted, this can quickly lead to unrecognized time and money wasters in the client budget or – almost worse – frustrated employees who despair over every day disruptive factors. Law firm software can provide good support for the collection and review of the necessary data and processes for effective law firm management – ideally with work and time recording or client budget management (this will be discussed in more detail in the next chapter). However, such software cannot replace predefined responsibilities and processes.

And here's another tip that will have a significant impact on your law firm's success:
Budget planning should definitely include your entrepreneurial tasks. On the one hand, this means that the time used for these tasks should be financially compensated (so that it is not added on top as "unpaid work" after a hard day's work or simply left out). But it also means that the firm's turnover and profit must be continuously planned and controlled.

Finally, a word about your **personal resources in your dual function** as a law firm owner and lawyer: Sufficient regeneration and the preservation of your health as well as a fulfilling life must have top priority in order to be able to remain on the road to success in the long term. To neglect this or even to practice "overexploitation" is highly unprofessional – even if unfortunately our performance society presents the paradigm that only a painful effort can lead to success. Studies prove the opposite: A certain ease in everyday life is essential for success and absolutely necessary to allow and maintain creativity. Realize that you alone decide what you need and what is good for you[1].

The more careful your planning work was in advance, the easier it will be for you to implement it.

At the same time, you should not assume that you can clarify all contingencies in advance. So, do not be surprised, but formally expect that there will be resistance, imponderables and problems in the realization of your idea. Assume that the success of your law firm foundation will not be measured by the fact that you circumvented the problems or that there was a problem, but by the creative solutions you found for the realization of your heart's project despite these problems.

The establishment of your law firm is not limited from the outset to a certain number of wrong decisions and erroneous paths. **Here, too, the path is ultimately the goal.**
Nevertheless, you should not leave anything to chance.

As open as you are to the unexpected, you should stick to your plan and your original idea. Your law firm vision will be the lighthouse on your journey through uncharted waters, the summit cross on your mountain climb, the fixed star after you navigate your route in rough terrain.

Leaving nothing to chance means implementing your planning just as carefully.

The insights gained from your collection of ideas should be retained as guiding principles for further planning. Also and especially when it comes to the implementation of specialists such as tax consultants, business consultants, marketing experts and web designers up to the network of colleagues who are available to you with advice and support.

1 *Dr. Geertje Tutschka* a.o. "Die Anwaltskanzlei als erfolgreiches Unternehmen", MKG 2019.

I. Strategy

Why should you read this chapter?
You will learn how to translate your law firm vision into a concrete strategy.

Overview
1. **Founding concept**
2. **Business concept**
3. **Implementation of the law firm vision**

The first step for the realization of your law firm foundation is the preparation of your foundation concept together with your business concept, where one concerns more the general and special market and client structure and the other more the financial side.

The aim of this book is to provide you with an overview of the main issues related to the establishment of a law firm in order to prepare you for your discussion with the specialist such as the business consultant, tax advisor or start-up service. Every law firm foundation is as individual as a birth. It would be presumptuous to present a universal “recipe” here. It would be equally presumptuous to present myself here as a business economist, which I am not.

If you are like me, as a lawyer, in that fiscal number games play a rather subordinate role, which I like to leave to experts, this section is just right for you: You will be familiarized with the necessary basic knowledge and terms to talk through your concept with your expert at eye level.

For all others, I recommend the extensive and detailed literature on the business background of setting up a company.

1. Founding concept

The question of “how” you want to establish your law firm is more than a purely formal aspect. The answer to this question depends, among other things, on your law firm vision, but also on the professional situation from which you are founding and the available resources with which you intend to implement this law firm.

In other words, a key factor is the current situation and the options available to you. This means both the legal and tax aspects of a previously existing law firm unit. But also the expertise and competencies, office space and equipment, or network contacts and client opportunities that you currently have access to.

The following **models** can be considered for establishing a law firm:
- New and initial establishment (start up)
- Reorganization/spin off
- Merger/reorganization Acquisition/purchase of an existing law firm or joining one

Every law firm establishment is different and has its own choreography. The list is therefore by no means meant to be exhaustive. The fact is that, in contrast to earlier times, fewer law firms are founded today by newcomers to the profession, but rather in later years as a result of mergers, restructuring, spin-offs etc.[1].

A question to be distinguished from this is in which legal form you would like to establish the law firm. In practice, there are essentially four possible forms:
- the office partnership
- the civil law partnership
- partnership/association
- the lawyer-GmbH

With the major BRAO reform, additional legal forms and cooperations will be possible from August 2022. Thus, the GmbH and Co KG will come, which means that essentially all legal forms from Germany, the EU and the EU states and the EEA will be permissible. The professional practice company will also be liberalized and office communities will now allow cooperations with other liberal and commercial professions[2]. The family lawyer can then form an office community with the pediatrician or psychotherapist. So-called practice networks are also conceivable, as in the medical profession in rural areas, in order to combine logistics, IT technology, branch offices, quality assurance, professional exchange and junior staff training – e.g. in the form of a GmbH & Co. KG. This would even be possible across borders according to the European Economic Interest Grouping (EEIG), which facilitates cross-border cooperation of law firms in the EU. Finally, the double-storey professional practice companies according to § 59i (1) sentence 1 BRAO (new version) are now also possible, in which a partnership company holds all shares in a lawyer's GmbH. Worth mentioning at this point is also the recent BGH decision on the question of whether the right of the partners to issue instructions in § 37 GmbHG violates § 46 BRAO, which describes the activity as a lawyer as autonomous and independent,

---

1 DAV-Ratgeber für junge Rechtsanwälte und Rechtsanwältinnen, p. 219 et seq.; Prognos, Der Rechtsdienstleistungsmarkt, p. 21 etseq.

2 More in Dr. Nicolas Lührig, "Große BRAO Reform gilt ab 1.8.2022: Mehr Freiheit für die Anwaltschaft" in Anwaltsblatt from 14.7.2021.

which must be guaranteed contractually and factually. The BGH (judgment of 07.12.2020, AnwZ – Brfg 17/20) saw these requirements violated by the legal obligation to give instructions in the GmbH for the managing director of the lawyer. However, it should be emphasized that the BGH case law does not apply to managerial positions in all corporations. In a stock corporation, the management board acts without instructions and decides on the management of the company in its own interest (§ 76 AktG). The AG board's freedom from instructions could thus be reconciled with the independence required by § 46 BRAO. However, constructions are also conceivable in the GmbH which could guarantee the independence of the lawyer. If the GmbH managing director has the majority shareholding, the co-partners cannot, in principle, give him instructions. Similar results could be achieved with reservations of consent or voting agreements agreed under company law. The courts will still have to decide to what extent such contractual constructions can be reconciled with the BRAO.

Capital participation without the partners practicing the legal profession in the company will continue to be impossible, as will non-silent companies and partial loans. Law firms can gain access to outside capital by participating in non-lawyer companies (e.g. via a software company), but they cannot give others a share in the profits themselves, because investors are not allowed to have any influence on the legal activity and transparency is not guaranteed. And while in the commercial sector there are many funding opportunities for start-ups or even in times of crisis, these programs usually do not apply to the liberal profession. That means above all, each of the forms has characteristics, which should be considered for the optimal selection in its specific situation urgently. There are differences, for example, in registration requirements, legal personality and capitalization, liability of shareholders or partners, tax treatment or representation.

There is no patent recipe for the right legal form, but rather only an individual decision based on the current individual situation. Support from corporate law and tax experts is therefore urgently recommended in order to avoid difficulties, annoying formalities or, in the worst case, financial losses later on.

At this point, the book "Gründung, Erwerb und Veräußerung einer Rechtsanwaltskanzlei" (Foundation, Acquisition and Sale of a Law Firm) can be recommended. The team of authors includes Dennis Janz LL.M. and Dr. Thilo Schnelle LL.M. as proven experts in the field of tax law and criminal tax law with a business background, as well as criminal lawyer Dr. Arabella Pooth.

The development of legal tech products out of law firms confronts many with the challenge of spin-offs. The takeover of important market shares by pure legal tech companies as well as insurance companies is increasing the pressure on the industry enormously. For some years now, financiers have doubted the economic viability of transferring certain types of law firms, especially rural individual law firms, which are strongly owner-operated and have rarely embarked on the digitalization path.

Nevertheless, there is more movement than ever in the law firm market: takeovers, spin-offs, mergers and demergers, entries and exits, and the constant stream of young lawyers looking for a livelihood.

A book like this comes just in time, especially since comparable books on the subject are already more than 10 years old and therefore hardly useful as a professional guide.
The individual chapters (unfortunately) do not indicate which author wrote them with what expertise, although in some places the very different writing styles and the different tax, business or legal perspectives are noticeable.

Nevertheless, the team of authors has succeeded in presenting the complex subject matter in a structured manner. For the rather uninvolved tax reader, perhaps a bit too little basics and basic knowledge, but for the tax lawyer in any case a very helpful presentation.

It is also important to keep in mind that the book approaches the topic exclusively from a tax perspective and that the business and legal perspectives are only touched upon to the extent necessary for the tax presentation. Thus, the book can by no means be the only guidebook for founding or acquiring a law firm – but it does not want to be.

Individual chapters are exceptionally well done.

Chapter 4, "Gestaltungsmöglichkeiten bei der Wahl der Gesellschafterform" (Options for the Choice of the Form of Company), is characterized by its clarity. Chapter 1 "Bewertung von Anwaltskanzleien" (Evaluation of Law Firms), on the other hand, differentiates very nicely according to the respective criteria for the diversity of law firms.

The identification of problematic situations and pitfalls, cases of doubt that have not yet been decided, and scenarios for changes in case law create room for maneuver. In my opinion, the current topic of data protection and the special obligation to maintain confidentiality in the case of law firm transfers, particularly with regard to the special technical solutions in the law firms, the topic of brand value and evaluation of the (digital) "reach" based on the positioning of the law firm and the lawyers, the evaluation of the law firm's own product developments and references to foreign countries are somewhat neglected.

A very positive aspect is that many case studies and solutions are provided to enable the reader to gain a deeper understanding. The numerous checklists are also helpful, even if it is easy to forget, especially in the case of the latter, due to the general headings, that these should not be used as comprehensive checklists but only as tax checklists (e.g. for the sale of a law firm).

All in all, the team of authors has succeeded in producing a well-founded and comprehensive tax law reference book on the subject of law firm acquisition, which provides important impulses above all for the tax advisor accompanying the transfer of the law firm.
It can give the prospective law firm owner a good introduction to the tax-legal complexities of a law firm acquisition and prepare him or her for the conversation with the selling colleague or his or her tax advisor.

After reading this book, no fellow lawyer will ever again underestimate the tax structuring scope for his law firm. And with that, a lot has already been achieved![3]

Just a hint: The legal liability treatment should not play too big a role for the decision of the legal form, since the essential liability risk for lawyers can usually already be absorbed by the professional liability insurance.

! The development of a **foundation concept** is not only an important basis for you and your partners, but also serves as a basis for a so-called business start-up concept for financing applications[4]. Therefore, you should not only develop a foundation concept when starting a new firm, but also when joining an existing firm, when restructuring or when taking over a firm, or when revising an existing one.

Your foundation concept should not only deal with the legal market in general and your legal field in particular. It should soberly describe your law firm vision and corporate values, as well as your expertise, firm and product DNA, and the opportunities and risks of your establishment at that time in that particular location with that concept[5]. It thus lays the foundation for your future quality management and controlling.

It should include the areas of service, personnel and material resources, marketing and finance[6].

3 Dennis Janz u.a. "Gründung, Erwerb und Veräußerung einer Rechtsanwaltskanzlei".
4 For a detailed list, see for example Miecke in v. Landenberg, "Erfolgreich starten als Rechtsanwalt", p. 76, 104 et seq. However, a funding consultant can also work this out for you individually.
5 It is also likely to matter whether you are in a metropolitan area with a large number of lawyers, such as Munich with 22,150 lawyers, Frankfurt with 18,515, or Berlin with 14,025, or in a more "lawyer-less" area; Branchenbericht der Sparkassen 2020, p.8.
6 Individual examples can be found on the Internet, a general one can be found with Miecke in v. Landenberg, "Erfolgreich starten als Rechtsanwalt", p. 188 et seq.
6. Miecke in v. Landenberg, "Erfolgreich starten als Rechtsanwalt", p. 93.

A special topic is the **purchase of a law firm**, i.e. the purchase of an existing law firm or the complete takeover of such a law firm as a start-up or merger. While this was the most common way of founding a law firm until about 20 years ago, today it is probably one of the exceptions. The reason for this is the highly personal nature of the legal advice service. In very few cases have clients simply "transferred" to the successor. As we have seen above, there is a strong fluctuation anyway. And a client file says nothing about the turnover that can be generated with it, especially since, irrespective of the personal connection to the former lawyer, the clients usually have a similar age structure – in other words, they are also about to enter retirement age. Today, it is almost impossible to determine an economically realistic, objective value of a law firm. At best, a so-called personal practice value can be determined on the basis of a capitalized earnings value method[7], which, however, certainly also takes into account a certain sentimental value in the respective individual case. According to the German Federal Bar Association, the value of a law firm is determined by multiplying the adjusted turnover by a valuation factor, which is usually between 0.3[8] and 1.3[9].

In the vast majority of cases, the infrastructure sold along with the office is hardly of any value today, especially after the establishment of the home office in times of pandemics, since prestigious office equipment and the available technology are hardly of any value, unlike in the past[10].

In practice, **various models** of percentage profit sharing are offered for purchasing, but these must be examined carefully. It is true that the advantage of being able to start work immediately, virtually from day one, and of having access to existing infrastructure, reliable structures and processes should not be underestimated. However, individual dreams of having one's own office are certainly not feasible here for the time being, since it is especially important to take a step back and adapt at the beginning. By the way, special attention should be paid to the distribution of work and profits, as this is where the greatest potential for conflict lies. A comparison of the law firm vision and especially of the values and culture is particularly important in order not to participate financially in something that one does not support – regardless of the complementary nature of the legal fields.

---

7 Miecke in v.Landenberg, "Erfolgreich starten als Rechtsanwalt", p. 200 et seq.

8 The minimum factor of 0.3 is therefore already applied if the old lawyer is older than 60 years and it tends to 0 if, in addition, the law firm is managed in an uneconomical way, Branchenbericht der Sparkassen 2020, p. 20.

9 in contrast, the valuation factor for tax consultants is usually 2 due to the permanent mandates, Branchenbericht der Sparkassen 2020, p. 20.

10 Branchenbericht der Sparkassen 2020, p. 20.

An alternative can be the rather informal merger in an **office community**, where independent lawyers only take a share in the existing resources (rent, personnel, IT, etc.) in order to save costs and to achieve mutual business and flexibility in opening hours with additional competence and manpower. However, the contract should then not only regulate the pro-rata assumption of costs, but also the ownership of new investments. And although the lawyers in a joint office usually focus on complementary areas of law, a frequent point of discussion is the assignment of new mandates that are cross-territorial or cannot be explicitly assigned to any area. Here, too, agreement should be reached in advance.

However, small and medium-sized law firms will increasingly work together on a permanent or project-related basis. An example of this is the four female lawyers who have joined forces for a major mandate as "Event Lawyers" for approximately 4 years for the European Football Championship in Berlin 2024. The highly specialized boutiques (a specialist in sports law, in public procurement law, copyright and media law, an event specialist and a notary) were thus able to convince large law firms[11].

On the other hand, it is a new and complex question if it is a legal tech solution for which is to be founded.

Legal Tech Foundation

As we saw in the section on the legal advice market, legal tech is here to stay. The product range is as diverse as the providers. The additional digitization boost from the pandemic has led to major investments being made in this area. There is a lot of money to be made with legal tech – or so it seems – at the moment. Is it also a business model for lawyers? And how does it fit into a law firm?

When legal tech products and services are developed by lawyers, this usually happens "in passing": a problem in one's own law firm is solved intelligently with IT and it is recognized that there is potential for development. It does not matter which technology is used, whether it is a complex technology such as artificial intelligence (AI) or an already established technology. The decisive factors are customer benefits and effectively solving a problem. After all, technology is not an end in itself and is measured by the problems it solves.

So why not launch a product for other law firms that is separate from your own? After all, you yourself are highly satisfied with the technology. But is that enough?

11 Zander, in "Vier gewinnt" in Anwaltsblatt 3/2022, p. 138.

In business, this pilot would be used to start an extensive test phase. We would identify weaknesses, subject it to various stress tests, and survey target groups. One's own experience and one's own system are not the measure of all things.

Remember:
Assumptions need to be validated.

There are three possible scenarios for the development of a legal tech idea:
1. In-house: If the legal tech product is intended to support services within the law firm, a close connection to the firm makes sense.
2. Legal tech alongside the law firm: If the aim is to develop a business model that also works independently of the law firm, a separate spin-off would be preferable.
3. Legal tech instead of the law firm: Ultimately, a "reorganization" may also be an option if the law firm itself is no longer operated in the medium or long term, but the legal tech product should come into focus and the failure of the law firm also represents a thoroughly realistic future scenario. The question of closing/transferring and also insolvency of a law firm should be considered from the beginning, as this – unlike other companies – holds some formal "pitfalls".

In addition, there is the question of resources in the development phase of the legal tech product:

Resource lawyer

The time required for the development of such a product, for marketing and sales, but also for personnel work and operational tasks should not be underestimated. Especially if the spin-off is to lead to an own business, the usual mandate work will not be possible. Here, it should be considered whether to pursue part-time employment during the development of a legal tech business idea and whether to obtain additional support for marketing and sales.

Resource IT specialists

A decision must also be made about whether and how to work with IT developers. With a technology-based product, it is usually necessary to obtain additional technical expertise. On the one hand, a decision must be made as to whether this should be done by commissioning external developers, or whether developers should become part of the spin-off directly, either as employees or as partners. Here, too, the goal of the business idea is an important deciding factor.

In principle, it is advantageous to locate the core know-how within the company. This reduces potential dependence on external people. If the technical development is the core task of the business idea, e.g. because a new and complex technology is used, then this speaks in favor of integrating and involving these developers in the new company. If, however, the technical component is not at all in the foreground, then external development, for example by an agency or a freelancer, can make perfect sense, especially for cost reasons.

The cooperation between lawyer and developer is often new territory for both sides and can be a challenge. However, both professions are fundamentally similar in their working methods: Both have to work very precisely and logically.

Legal texts are also often compared to codes, as both are strictly logical. Nevertheless, working with people from other professional backgrounds always differs from working with "your own people" – especially in the area of communication. However, this does not have to be a disadvantage. On the contrary: interdisciplinary (agile) collaboration can be a very instructive and enriching experience. After all, a different background or area of expertise always brings with it different questions and perspectives on issues and their assessment.

In this context, the clarification of the management role and the rights to the product is not entirely unimportant.

Remember:
The selection of co-founders and developers should be thorough: Under certain circumstances, important technology decisions are pending that could be expensive to correct. The same applies to the right employees for marketing and sales.

Resource finances

If the offering represents a legal service, the prohibition on third-party ownership precludes direct financing by external investors, because a legal service must always be provided by a lawyer. If the offer does not represent a legal service, external financing is excluded if the legal tech product is to be developed and distributed within the law firm.

This makes a spin-off a highly attractive business development decision, namely whenever the development of the product will take some time due to complex technology or if it is to be brought to market very quickly with a high capital outlay.

However, it must also be clear that investors, as co-owners, are to be involved in all fundamental decisions and, in most cases, expect certain payment returns after a certain period of time. In return, they can often provide support through their experience or network and thus contribute a great deal of know-how in addition to pure capital. Of course, this only applies to professional investors who are purely economically motivated, meaning that they operate investments as a business model.

Special start-up services for such legal tech start-ups tend to provide support with the necessary infrastructure and formalities. Private investors from the family and circle of friends are usually pure "financiers" and exclusively personally motivated. On the other hand, it is a special case if the law firm itself invests in the legal tech company with services, e.g. by providing personnel, premises and equipment. Nevertheless, many founders prefer to "bootstrap" their company, i.e. to build it up without external capital.

In addition to professional law, questions of business and tax law must also be considered when deciding whether a spin-off should take place: As members of the liberal professions, lawyers are generally not subject to business tax. However, if you offer services as part of your legal tech offering that are not legal advice, this may trigger a trade tax liability. These questions should be examined in detail beforehand.

Today, large law firms have their own legal tech units in which solutions are developed for their own practices or for clients[12]:

Example: asgaro GmbH – Digital unit as an impulse generator for new processes
The asgaro GmbH emerged from a project work of the law firm lindenpartners. In addition to the two partners of the law firm, Thomas Asmus and Eric Romba, the company is also owned by Dr. Birte Gall, an economist and expert in digital transformation. asgaro advises clients on digital transformation and also develops its own legal tech products, the use of which does not require approval under the Legal Services Act, e.g. for handling inheritance law processes at banks.

One of the many arguments in favor of establishing an external unit was the fact that digital experts who are not lawyers cannot be involved as partners in a law partnership. In a separate unit, digital and legal expertise can thus be combined in a more balanced way to form a new discipline. Whether a digital project is ultimately taken up and realized by lindenpartners or asgaro depends above all on questions of professional law and proximity to legal advice. In this respect, the service profiles

---

12 *Dr. Sven von Alemann*, in: "Die Kanzlei als erfolgreiches Unternehmen", MKG 2019.

complement each other; at the same time, there is a natural separation in terms of external representation and commissioning. According to companies, the number of projects in which both legal knowledge and knowledge in the area of IT and digitization are required is increasing.

The conclusion: A digital unit can be an impulse generator for the rethinking of processes. In my experience so far, however, a law firm is already a unit whose structures form a good basis for working in an agile manner: Roles are regularly redefined and change hands as needed, ad-hoc project teams are formed and dissolved again; the teams work largely independently and the interdisciplinary grows gradually through new project managers, legal engineers, COOs and other team members.

Example: SKW Schwarz @ Tech GmbH – from a marketing vehicle to a subcontractor

SKW Schwarz @ Tech GmbH is a spin-off of the law firm SKW Schwarz. After Stefan Schicker, Managing Partner of SKW, had been actively shaping the German legal tech scene for several years through meetups and lectures, SKW Schwarz @ Tech was founded in 2018, primarily to support the firm's further technical development. SKW wants to focus on activities that are characterized by the interplay of manual and automated work. Here, a solid basic equipment of tools and automation is necessary. However, since business tax liability was also an issue here, SKW Schwarz @ Tech was spun off in 2018. In addition to organizing trainings and seminars, SKW Schwarz @ Tech 2018 also develops tools – internally for the firm as well as externally for clients. One successful event, for example, was the organization of an SKW-internal hackathon.

Example: nice.report – How efficiency-enhancing technology becomes a business model

nice.report was founded by experienced real estate lawyers from Berlin, who left a large law firm in 2015 in order to be able to offer advice on real estate transactions more innovatively and efficiently as 3A. Meanwhile, the shareholders of nice.report include the programmers who were decisive for the development. The impetus for the foundation of nice.report was the recognition of automation potential in the company's own legal advice. nice.report starts with the collaborative writing of due diligence reports by the lawyer on the one hand and the reading and evaluation by the manager on the other. The creation of the actual report becomes faster and better by creating a database of text modules for and by the user, which are suggested when writing the report. Thus, a better comparability is achieved and a more precise analysis can be made, which then opens up new possibilities for the reader to further process the report contents (e.g. overlapping analysis of several reports in the case of successive property purchases for a new real estate fund). This enables both lawyer and client to work more efficiently. nice.report's experience is that the concept can serve as a door opener for clients, who can see the effective processes the firm is working with. However, the nice.report team also found that a larger time budget is required to independently market and distribute the software[13].

2. Business concept

The business concept covers the entire financial side of your law firm business. In addition to the typical financial part of a classic business plan, the private financial needs of the lawyer(s) should also be taken into account. After all, as a lawyer you want to be able to live from it.

For the preparation of the business plan (financial part), you can consult experts (such as business and tax consultants) or use the many support offers from different providers and assistance from the Internet.

---

i

It is recommended to use special programs or software for this purpose[14]. Helpful tips and tools are also offered by the DAV's Law Firm Management Working Group, the general information portal for DAV members, and the FORUM of Young Lawyers. Also worth mentioning is the inexpensive "DAV Ratgeber für Junge Rechtsanwältinnen und Rechtsanwälte" ("DAV Guidebook for Young Lawyers") (€ 5), which consists of a collection of texts on various topics related to the legal profession and founding a law firm and is regularly updated. Numerous tips, checklists and software are available on the Internet, which are quite useful.

We also recommend courses offered by the Chamber of Industry and Commerce (IHK) and other providers and start-up centers, as well as the master's degree program "Lawyer and Legal Practice" (formerly "Anwaltsrecht") at the Distance-Learning University of Hagen[15] as well as the events of the Forum Junge Anwaltschaft of the German Bar Association (DAV), the German Lawyers Academy, the Soldan Institute or the German Lawyers Institute, among others.

I would also like to mention that women lawyers are particularly supported and promoted here, for example through "Frau und Arbeit" (Women and Work) and special support networks. In addition to

---

13 Ibid.

14 Corresponding business plan software is provided free of charge, for example, by chambers of commerce and industry, but also in some cases by chambers of lawyers.

15 You can find me there as a lecturer with my teaching scripts since 2015 or this book as recommended study literature since the 1st edition.

MentorMe and Panda Lab Law, the mentoring programs of the DAV Women Lawyers Working Group and the German Women Lawyers Association are particularly worthy of mention.

Less recommendable is the general start-up service provided by the employment office for founders from unemployment, IHK or similar. As a rule, these are not suitable for law firm start-ups, as they are primarily tailored to business start-ups and the BRAO (Federal Lawyers' Act) has very important special features in this respect. The well-known BAFA subsidies for business start-ups and management consulting are also rarely usable for law firms – at best for spin-offs with legal tech products. From our own experience, we at CLP – Consulting for Legal Professionals know how much our management consulting, which is specifically tailored to law firms, has to be standardized in order to obtain the BAFA license, so that the actual added value for our lawyers is almost lost. Nevertheless, we were able to support some law firms with it, especially during the Corona pandemic.

Remember:
Subsidies for freelancers and law firms are not available at the federal or state level, nor are they provided by bar associations, pension funds and the DAV professional association, as is common in other industries.

Costs include investment costs, operating costs and private living costs. This also includes your health insurance, professional liability insurance, business liability insurance, occupational disability insurance plus any insurance benefits for employees and trainees as well as pension provision with the pension scheme[16] or similar. For the planning of your revenues you make a forecast for the net sales and consider possible risks. In doing so, you also take into account losses and "lean periods" and consider how these can be bridged with replacement business.

Via § 4 para. 3 EStG, you as an individual lawyer can dispense with a balance sheet and merely prepare an income surplus statement[17]. You therefore have no obligation to keep accounts[18]. However, as a rule, a voucher accounting or a journal accounting will come into consideration in order to be able to keep the corresponding proofs[19]. Lawyer or client software is usually equipped with a corresponding system, ideally with an interface to the DATEV system of the tax consultant.

16 For a detailed list, see Miecke in Landenberg, "Erfolgreich starten als Rechtsanwalt," p. 208 et seq.

17 The more complicated determination of profits by means of a comparison of business assets is regularly not taken into consideration for newcomers to the profession, § 4 para. 1 EStG according to Philipp, "Die erfolgreiche Kanzleigründung", p. 134.

18 Miecke in Landenberg, "Erfolgreich starten als Rechtsanwalt", p. 221.

19 Philipp, "Die erfolgreiche Kanzleigründung", p. 135.

However, I also don't want to deprive you of the fact that the classic business plan is now controversial among experts. The start-up culture in particular is looking for modern, technology-supported methods that promote creativity and "think along". Agile teams and Scrum are the buzzwords of the day here. This may be of marginal interest for a classic law firm start-up.

However, there are two reasons why you should still look into it:

- this alternative can actually bring you back to your creativity if the "trauma of law school" or "the years in the hamster wheel of a big law firm" have completely buried it. But creativity is the key to your law firm's success.
- These models harbor technical affinity and potential for play. As we have seen, the legal market is currently experiencing unprecedented digitization. Not everything that seems possible here has been invented yet. These alternatives are an invitation to enter this playground[20].

The Business Model Canvas has become the tool of choice to visualize the business model and a startup idea and to test whether it also makes business sense. Many experts now believe that the Business Model Canvas can fully replace the outdated Business Plan[21]. It comprises nine elements: Target group, value proposition, communication and marketing channels, service, revenue portfolio and cost structure, key resources, activities and partnerships.

What is important to me at this point is simply to get you to think about what makes your law firm a business, a commercial business.

So you should define your economic goals, turnover and profit for the next month, the next half year, the next year, the next three, and the next five years in detail. And this is exactly where the problem lies: A business plan is always a "wish list to Santa Claus"; a dream, a vision. At best, it is a "declaration of intent" or a "projection", which, however, after only a few months no longer has anything to do with reality, a serious forecast or the actual development of your law firm business.

So the question is, why should you create a business plan or a business model at all? First of all, a business plan including the described start-up concept will be required by the lender (bank) in case of external financing.

20 Three founder books recommended here: Campus "Business Model Generation", "Business Model YOU", Ash Maurya "Scaling Lean".

21 Carolin Gattermann, "Drei Business Bücher, die jeder Gründer lesen sollte", Startplatz from 11.4.2017.

But even regardless of this, the answer is as simple as it is convincing: Because you need a plan, a goal[22].

Studies have shown that college students who already have a firm idea of their future salary at a certain point in time are 90 % more likely to actually earn that income than their college peers who only had a vague to no idea of what their income would be. Dealing with concrete numbers here means nothing more than translating your target groups, positioning and branding, which you defined precisely in the previous chapter, into numbers and business language. Whether you will actually achieve these expectations and calculations will depend on you – and on a multitude of other factors.

The perfect business plan usually lies somewhere between two parameters:

Between the most accurate market projection as the optimum and your dream result as the maximum. Whether your plan leans more to one side or the other is not a question of right or wrong, but a question of your type.

What is it the right way for your type? The business plan you create should first and foremost motivate you, give you confidence and self-assurance. But above all, you should be able to firmly believe in its realization. There is no happy medium. Only your own personal, individual way of creating your business plan and working with it.

Your financial part of the business plan includes three dimensions in a simplified way:

!

- Revenues
- Costs and investments
- Corresponding budgets and funding

With the revenues, it is primarily about the turnover, as only this is decisive for your calculation, i.e. the fee forecast[23]. These are, of course, primarily your net fee notes, but income from car rentals, consulting work, expert opinions and cooperation with partners should also be taken into account here. You can refer to the list of resources compiled above and map them in monetary terms, i.e. in figures.

When it comes to the costs that law firm founders face, you should distinguish between one-time costs and ongoing costs.

22 Dr. Geertje Tutschka, "Warum Ihr Kanzleibusinessplan jetzt zählt" in Huffington Post from 6.11.2015.

23 Miecke in v.Landenberg, "Erfolgreich starten als Rechtsanwalt", p. 202 et seq.

One-time costs include:
- Administrative fees: Admission fee, certifications
- Setup
- Hardware such as computer, fax, telephone system, etc.
- Law firm software incl. accounting program (if no subscription)

By far the greater part of the expenses are **running costs**, including:
- Rent and utilities
- Membership fees: Bar association, pension fund
- Insurance
- Personnel costs
- Telephone, Internet contract
- Marketing expenses
- Subscriptions: legal databases, journals, software, etc.
- Training expenses
- Credit redemption

Of course, this calculation or list also includes the associated costs, salaries, expenses and outlays as well as rent and employee salaries, but also the costs of your admission, so that in a second step it must be a matter of calculating the expected profit from the estimated income[24]. The costs of admission are bar association costs, professional liability insurance costs, memberships in pension insurance and health insurance. Beyond that it is also the basis for future investments, for marketing measures. You should present these positions here as substantiated as possible in the respective time periods.

Remember: **You are creating this business plan primarily for yourself!**

Even though in most cases the submission of the business plan is required for the application of a loan or for other governmental support, you should tailor this business plan exactly to your needs and prepare it in such a way that it is best usable for you in everyday life. If you are a numbers person, the business plan should show any figures that are important to you. Tables can also be helpful here. If you are a more visual type, chart overviews and bar charts can be helpful.

In addition, consideration must be given to whether acquisitions and investments need to be made, depreciation needs to be taken into account, or the use of share so-

24 Heussen, Anwaltsunternehmen führen, p. 262 et seq.

lutions or leasing models are alternative solutions. As mentioned, costs also include personnel costs as well as the costs of any service providers, such as the cleaning service, the IT service or the paper delivery service. As a rule of thumb, personnel costs account for 25–50 % of sales on average and marketing costs for around 10 %.

The cost of materials can be calculated very individually for the initial establishment, especially since leasing and share options as well as used basic equipment can be very price-conscious solutions at the beginning[25]. Classically-conservatively a material basic equipment of a single law office was calculated in former times generally with approx. € 100.000. Today an office service and a laptop with printer and cell phone may be sufficient in the first months and only trigger a material expenditure of € 2,500 in the first year.

As mentioned at the beginning, I have deliberately refrained from including forms and sample calculations. First, you can get these in much greater detail and more conveniently online today, so copying them out or even transcribing them is anything but timely for worksheets. Second, I don't want to give the impression that these are even approximate guidelines to meet. Of course, all you need to open your office is a telephone, a laptop, the Internet and an office sign. And of course, today you can work from anywhere – so you can work in your law office from Hawaii or from the playground in the city park. That is the beauty and also the difficulty of calculation. You alone decide what suits you at the moment. There is no right or wrong; no professional or unprofessional, as long as you plan your law firm as a for-profit business model.

From my experience, the most difficult item in this context is the "salary" that one assigns to oneself. This is too often wrongly equated with "profit". In fact, you should think about what you will do with the profit: invest in the firm or build security and reserves. Your personal circumstances also play a role here: do you already have maintenance obligations to your family, do you have to pay loans and credits (e.g. BaföG, car financing, etc.), do you have to support your parents or siblings with part of the money, or do you yourself have above-average expenses because of a hobby[26], that is important to you or a second degree or doctorate.

However, you should also take into account the part of your working time that you may have already committed to voluntary work or family activities. Your day also

---

25 Branchenbericht der Sparkassen 2020, p. 24.

26 Horses, skiing and golf are certainly the common ones here, but it can also be a diving or pilot's license.

only has 24 hours. And if you want to have time for your partner and child, this time is not available for the law firm. Not only family lawyers know that marriage and family is at least secondarily a financial matter and not only private pleasure. So be realistic in your planning. And check the prejudices and paradigms that may unconsciously influence your decisions. Of course, you can have fun and take time for yourself, or go skiing on a Monday if the weather is good and you like it. You alone decide – that is again the advantage of being self-employed, not only having to be busy "by yourself and all the time".

However, a necessary liquidity plan is often overlooked, i.e. the question of how to pay current costs or investments in relation to the timing of your income. It is important to keep in mind that clients do not always pay on time or that there may be defaults. "Driving on sight" also proves, it is worth when it comes to liquidity: you should be able to cover your running costs for at least 6 months, ideally 18 months, with the funds you have now, so that there are no unpleasant bottlenecks.

The salary of a lawyer usually increases with the years of work completed:
- Young lawyer: € 43,000
- up to 5 years: up to € 70,000
- up to 10 years: up to € 110,000
- longer: up to € 166,000

The size of the law firm is also an important factor influencing earnings as a lawyer. According to a survey by the Soldan Institute for Lawyer Management, lawyers in small law firms with up to ten employees earn between € 38,000 and € 55,000 gross annually. In law firms with up to 20 employees, the starting salary is up to € 75,000. In medium-sized law firms with approximately 20 to 100 employees, the gross annual salary can be up to € 100,000. Lawyers in large law firms – around 650 professionals in Germany – can expect up to € 155,000 in the first few years. A 2020 salary study by the Juve career portal shows that a starting salary of up to € 125,000 gross is possible in Germany's large law firms, but not the norm.

By contrast, entry-level employees in companies receive an average monthly gross salary of € 5,300 (as of June 2019). The larger the company, the higher the salary can be for young professionals. However, there are large differences in earnings depending on the industry. The top industries include the chemical and petroleum processing industry with an annual gross salary of up to € 108,100, mechanical and plant engineering – annual gross salary of up to € 106,300 and banks – annual gross salary of up to € 95,100. Associations, the public sector and the media industry bring up the rear. For lawyers in the public sector, the salary ranges from a good € 4,500 to just under € 8,000 gross per month, depending on grade and rank in the federal government. The media industry pays lawyers an average gross annual salary of € 61,700.

The income of judges and public prosecutors, on the other hand, is referred to as remuneration. The R pay scale is divided into pay grades R1 to R10 and R11 in tabular form. According to this order the remuneration is regulated uniformly for both occupational groups. Within the individual groups, the experience levels influence the amount of the pay and at the same time reflect the professional experience. Since the federalism reform in 2006, the federal states have been specifically responsible for the amount and regulations of the salary. This does not apply to federal judges, who are still paid in accordance with the Federal Salary Act (BBesG). In addition, the BBesG also applies if a federal state does not have its own state salary law. In general, the income for judges and public prosecutors increases with the classification in a higher grade and starts at about € 3,500 per month. It can rise to about € 12,000 per month for the general federal prosecutor at the Federal Supreme Court[27].

In the planning phase, not all information is available to a sufficient extent in most cases. Collect cost points again and again over several days, weeks and months or work with practice quotas. Many of these small hidden points are often overlooked, but in total they can throw even a well-calculated business plan off course. You can be creative when listing the intended investments, as long as they are within the appropriate budget. However, the main question at this point is which of the many possibilities should be prioritized and tackled first.

For the concrete financing strategy, the intended investments and costs are summarized in the so-called budget.

A **budget** includes three items:

1. Allocation to a specific topic
2. Amount of money to be made available to this topic
3. Time window in which the amount of money is to be available to the topic.

In addition, you should generally define what will be done with all your budgets in case the budget has to be exceeded, as well as what will be done with the unspent funds in case the budget is not exhausted.

In this case, a so-called emergency budget is a good idea, into which unused funds can be paid and unforeseen budget expansions can be taken.

For this emergency budget, too, you should think in advance about when such an emergency exists and who should ultimately decide on it.

27 gehaltsreporter.de: Gehalt Anwalt; Status: 01/2020.

In addition, after you have formed all budgets, you should compare them and check whether the importance of each topic in your law firm business is reflected by the amount of money allocated to the topic.

You should also compile budgets on different sets of issues and develop an overall budget from them.

Once you have determined and set up your budgets and fine-tuned the weights, the next step is to make sure how these budgets are financed.

In principle, three types of **financing** can be considered:

1. Equity
2. Profit
3. External financing

You should carefully calculate all three financing resources and set them up side by side to ensure that you have the necessary funds available for the budgets. As a general rule, it is recommended that financing primarily provide for the basic costs of your legal practice and that outside financing be kept to a minimum. However, a discussion with your tax advisor can clarify for your specific situation whether it does not pay off for you in the end to work with more outside capital than own capital.

A professional business plan is a prerequisite for obtaining grants or outside financing through bank loans. Possible subsidies that law firm founders can apply for are:

- Promotional loans from banks: Some banks, such as KfW, offer special start-up loans for start-ups and young companies.
- Start-up and growth financing (GuW) from the federal and state governments: The Federal Ministry for Economic Affairs and Energy (BMWi), for example, provides an overview of funding instruments.
- Start-up subsidy from the Federal Employment Agency: Anyone who is still entitled to unemployment benefits for at least 150 days and ends their unemployment with self-employment can receive this subsidy for a maximum of 15 months.
- Start-up allowance (ESG): Recipients of unemployment benefit II can receive start-up allowance for a maximum of 24 months under certain conditions.
- Subsidizing or assuming responsibility for business start-up consultations or seminars.

If your business concept is complete, please do not put it in a drawer, but create an overview, which you can pin in a clearly visible place at your workplace.

Develop a routine where you set aside a specific day of the week just for revising, adjusting and checking your business plan so that it is always adjusted to the current circumstances and state of your law firm business.

Only if you actually work with your business plan and make it the basis of your actions and decisions, the time spent on its preparation has really been worthwhile. Only with the help of your business plan will you be able to act entrepreneurially, strategically and according to plan as the owner of a law firm, to get through difficult times and to react to unforeseen events in a considered and confident manner.

3. Implementation of the law firm vision

You have now developed your law firm vision and an initial idea of what will differentiate your firm from other law firms and what value your law firm will add to your clients. You have also ensured that the necessary financial resources are available and have developed a financial strategy with your business plan. Based on this business plan, you must now implement your law firm vision in individual steps and develop a detailed law firm strategy.

Apart from the organizational aspects (which will be discussed in more detail in the following chapter), the first question is how you want to present your particular field of law within your firm, how you want to acquire your clients, how you want to design your service and how your values become a living team and leadership culture within the firm, but also generate external impact for the clients.

You can use a specific guiding principle for this, but also **define** individual important **values** that are particularly important to you. This will help you later on to keep your firm on course when it comes to circumnavigating imponderables and accepting detours. A symbol or mission statement can be a good guide here.

What is this important for at this point?

If your law firm is to become more than the "technical prerequisite" for your legal work, if it is to become an integral part of your employees' and clients' lives, this law firm must satisfy the needs of these people. As already explained in the previous chapter, these basic needs stem from the five most important areas of life: Your firm should therefore meet these needs at these five different levels of your "target group".

Maslow's pyramid of needs[28] shows that all human activity is motivated by the satisfaction of needs, with the lower four needs being the most important.

---

28 Abraham Maslow (born 1943) was a psychologist who studied human needs. His motivational theory "Maslow's pyramid of needs" is one of the best known and most significant of its kind.

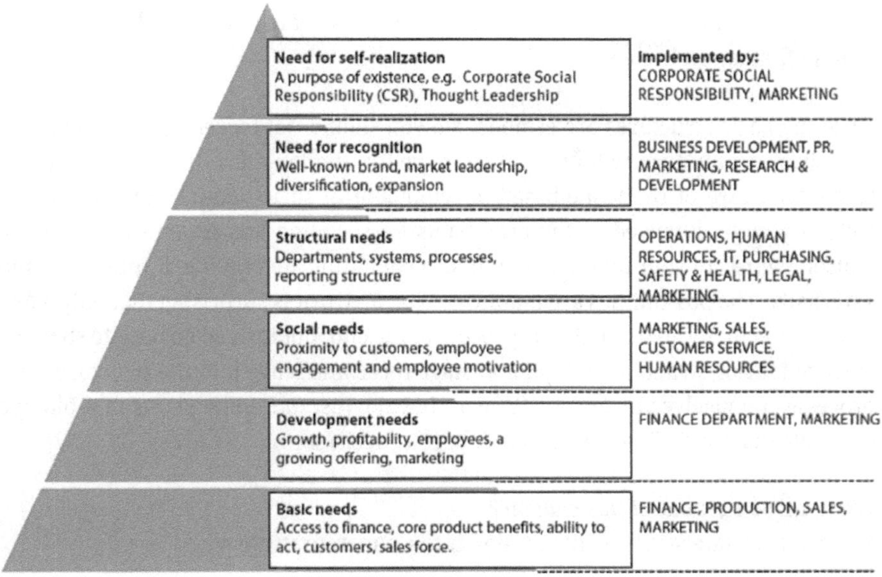

Maslow's pyramid of needs, © B2B international Marktforschungsinstitut

Whereby the lower four can be summarized as deficit needs and the upper category as needs of being or growth needs. Starting with the lowest category, the pyramid is built up according to psychological needs, needs for security, belonging, esteem and self-actualization. Development happens from the bottom to the top.

Today, it is generally accepted that companies – and thus law firms – also function according to this pattern. After all, you too founded your law firm to satisfy your clients' need for specific legal advice, a service or a solution to a problem.

The establishment of a law firm should therefore be just as "organic": You start with the implementation of the basics (furnishings, equipment, personnel, establishment of processes and structures). After that, it is first a matter of marketing issues, expanding the service, increasing the number of employees. After the first months you should deal with issues such as leadership and motivation of your employees (the probationary periods are now over), but also with sustainability and longevity of client relationships, since the first mandates are now completed and it is important to see these clients again in the future.

The office grows and additional facilities and systems or even adapted filing processes become necessary. The first filings are made. Some processes need to be optimized.

Now you need to pay more attention to your **external image** and think about your brand, branding and employer branding. You should decide whether you would rather train yourself in the long term and take care of the development of junior staff at an early stage.

Once the basic structures are established, you should not forget to enter the home stretch: Your law firm will only function well in the long term if you now successively take care of the value-based development of socio-political and social projects, if you get involved in the professional association and if you thus convey a "raison d'être" to your law firm – and also communicate and live it internally and externally. The possibilities are manifold. That is why it is surprising that only a few law firms actually go through this process to the end, but instead go back to step one at stage four or switch on autopilot at stage three and leave it to the structures and processes themselves to develop. Which they do. Just more like plants in a biotope or jungle than in an English garden. It is your decision.

What did you get out of this chapter?
You can translate your law firm vision into a concrete strategy.

II. Formalities

Why should you read this chapter?
You will learn the most important formalities.

The formal requirements for founding a law firm are not described in detail here, but only the essential information and the specialists you can contact. Each establishment of a law firm has its own specific characteristics.

Please be sure to take advantage of the extensive range of support and consulting services and seek individual advice to put together the right package for you.

The bar association responsible for you is primarily responsible for registering your law firm. The bar associations also have various information sheets and checklists on this, which I recommend you request. According to the BRAO, an **application** must first be **submitted to the responsible bar association**, which will examine the proof of qualification for the judiciary (the completion of the two state examinations) submitted at the same time as the application. **Proof of professional liability insurance** must also be submitted with this application, as this is a mandatory requirement for admission to the bar. Furthermore, proof of the "**establishment of a law firm**" must be submitted. This does not necessarily require office equipment. Not even a law firm sign is absolutely necessary. What is required, however, is a postal address within the jurisdiction of the bar association as well as contact data by telephone, fax or email (and in the future also the beA). In other words, accessibility of the law firm is to be ensured. As soon as the application for admission has been approved, there is an obligation to join the **Bar**. A corresponding regulation can be found in §§ 60ff. BRAO. The bar association is a corporation under public law and monitors compliance with professional law. It also acts as an advisory and arbitration body and provides information and training for members. The **chamber fee** amounts to approx. € 300,– per year.

Since this is generally independent of income, it must also be paid by newcomers to the profession and law firm founders. An exemption or reduction is generally not possible. In addition to admission to the bar and the conclusion of professional liability insurance[1], membership in a **pension scheme** (pension insurance) is also required upon admission to the bar. In most cases, the federal states have es-

---

1 The professional liability insurance must comply with the requirements of the BRAO, i.e. cover the specified amounts of coverage in Germany and abroad.

tablished **pension funds for lawyers**, which have voluntary or mandatory memberships. It is true that membership in a pension fund for lawyers is generally more positive than membership in the general pension insurance. Nevertheless, most professional colleagues would probably prefer a private insurance option. The pension insurance contributions are determined according to income. There is the possibility during long illness, maternity or also with no or small profit at the beginning of a law firm establishment to reduce the contributions to a minimum, i.e. to approx. €150,– per month. Just as there is a minimum contribution, there are also maximum contribution rates, which may then be relevant for you in the near future. For self-employed persons, the contribution is based on income, depending on the country. For comparison: In Bavaria, the maximum monthly contribution in 2021 is €1,320.60, the minimum rate is €165.10.

You, as a licensed attorney, enclose the registration form with the regionally responsible bar association:

- Curriculum vitae with current photograph
- officially certified copy of the second state examination if applicable
- proof of entitlement to hold an academic degree
- certificate of good conduct of document type N
- declaration that there is no reason for refusal according to § 7 BRAO, such as unworthiness p
- roof of professional liability insurance (§ 51 BRAO) or submission of a
- provisional confirmation of cover: the minimum insurance sum is €250,000 per insured event.
- Payment of the admission fee: The amount depends on the fee schedule of the respective bar association on average it is about €250.

Lastly, a word about setting up a **law firm abroad:**

The first step is always the registration in the home country, e.g. Germany.

First of all, a distinction must be made as to whether the law firm is established in another European country or in a so-called third country. In other European countries, every German lawyer can, in principle, establish himself as a so-called European lawyer. This does not mean that the lawyer is active in European law, but rather that the lawyer enjoys the European freedom of movement with regard to his professional practice. If the lawyer only settles abroad for a short period of time, it is possible to be exempted from the obligation to practice in Germany for one to two years upon application. It is then only necessary to provide a contact address and a contact person for official deliveries. If, on the other hand, the lawyer settles permanently abroad, this will fail in a third country in the vast majority of cases due to the lack of admissibility to the courts there. In the vast majority of cases, this will involve a posting to a larger law firm, so that this posting or expatriate status, and thus the underlying employment or posting contract, will also regulate the admission issues within the law firm. It is not possible to establish a law firm in a so-called third country. However, the German lawyer is of course free to pass the admission examination of the host country and then to establish himself there as a so-called domestic lawyer.

If a German lawyer settles in another European country as a so-called **European lawyer**, his further professional life will be determined by this double admission, i.e. he will always have to add the suffix of his home country (German lawyer, admission at the bar association xyz, Germany). He will therefore remain a member of the bar association in his home country and will also pay the corresponding bar association fees there. In addition, he will have to become a member of the bar association responsible in the host country and pay the relevant fees. Furthermore, he needs a professional liability insurance which covers the sums insured for the home country and the host country. Finally, a decision must be made as to which pension fund he is to be assigned to. In most cases, there are various options for assigning the German lawyer practicing abroad to the pension institution of the host country or to the pension institution in Germany upon application. Despite the European freedom of movement, the practice of the profession in other European countries is therefore determined by applications, paragraphs and official decision-makers, so that every lawyer should think carefully about whether it really makes economic sense to set up a law firm abroad, even if the unique selling point (German lawyer) is of course much easier to realize.

In addition to registration with the bar association, **registration with the tax office** is also required. The opening of the law firm must be reported to the competent tax office, which, if required, also issues a so-called clearance certificate[2] for the employment agency or the job center, if there are entitlements (keyword: bridging allowance when starting a business) after several years as an employed lawyer or bank. As a so-called free profession you will receive a corresponding tax number. I strongly recommend hiring a tax advisor who will advise you through all issues such as the advance VAT return, deductibility of office space within an apartment up to the proper preparation of a fee invoice.

Other **regulatory issues** may arise, for example, if you set up the office in a purely residential area or in a purely apartment building. Here, for example, questions must be clarified as to whether the commercial use of the premises is permissible or whether the premises must be rezoned accordingly. It must also be clarified whether sufficient sanitary facilities are available and the necessary fire doors and escape routes.

---

2 Miecke in v. Landenberg, "Erfolgreich starten als Rechtsanwalt", p. 232.

It would also have to be clarified whether the premises you are now using as a law office are actually intended to be rented out commercially by the landlord. In most cases, different regulations apply to commercial leases than to residential leases. The display of a law firm sign on the wall of the building may also require approval, as may the provision of parking spaces in front of the building.

The **obligation to maintain a law office** applies from the moment of admission, i.e. the lawyer must maintain a law office in the district of the bar association of which he is a member. For the proof of the establishment of an office it is sufficient to put up the office sign and to inform the chamber about the contact data of the office (address, telephone, fax, e-mail). This ensures that the lawyer can be reached. The obligation that the lawyer must also take up residence at the place of his admission to the bar (so-called residence obligation) no longer applies as of 1994. Working from home is compatible with the legal profession.

Not only since the pandemic has the question of law firm home office revived: you can also set up a law firm in your private apartment. However, you should ask your landlord for permission to put up an office sign. Otherwise, you may be subject to termination. However, since there is usually little public traffic that unreasonably affects other tenants, there is usually nothing to prevent you from obtaining permission.

The statutory minimum requirements for the furnishing of law offices also apply to law offices in private residences. Sanitary facilities, fire doors and escape routes must be available.

Finally, you should of course have health and accident insurance for your profession as a lawyer, as well as household contents and personal liability insurance. If you start immediately working with **employees**, you will need to register with the Employer's Liability Insurance Association, the Labor Office or the social insurance agency.

The following insurances are recommended: Professional liability insurance: This is a prerequisite for admission to the bar and therefore the first insurance that lawyers – and not only law firm founders – must take out. The BRAO reform as of August 1, 2022 obliges professional practice companies to take out independent professional liability insurance in the future.

Health and long-term care insurance: In principle, self-employed persons can either take out private health and long-term care insurance or remain voluntarily insured under the statutory health insurance scheme. The tariff should include the payment of daily sickness benefits in order to be covered in the event of a longer loss of earnings.

Occupational or disability insurance: Even if it is not mandatory, you should still take out this insurance. Running a law firm means a lot of responsibility and stress. Moreover, no one is immune to accidents or illness.

Voluntary unemployment insurance: As freelancers, lawyers have the option of taking out voluntary insurance. Prerequisite: Before taking up self-employment, they were in a compulsory insurance relationship (e.g. as an employee) for at least 12 months within the last 24 months.

Property insurance: If you have furnished your business premises at a high cost, property insurance is an option. Property damage in the office is insured with it.

Office liability insurance: If clients are injured in your office premises, this optional insurance protects you against claims.

Please remember to submit all required applications and registrations in due time, preferably before you start your activity, in order to avoid high administrative fines or even closure. Even if this part of setting up a law firm seems annoying to you and does anything but acquire future clients: Subsequent corrections, adjustments or subsequent notifications are not only expensive in the vast majority of cases, but all the more time-consuming.

What did you get out of this chapter?
You have learned the most important formalities.

III. Equipment

Why should you read this chapter?
You will learn what basic equipment is needed for the office.

Overview

1. **Infrastructure**
2. **Personnel and HR**
3. **Office equipment and IT**

Depending on the type of target clientele, the choice of office location can be of considerable importance. A law firm that caters to private individuals will place particular emphasis on easy accessibility of the office space, including by public transportation. If the law firm wants to serve "walk-in" clients, then the office space should be in a "walk-in" location in the city center. For a forensically oriented law firm, proximity to the court is an advantage. Proximity to the court is not primarily for the convenience of the attorneys, but to save time through short commutes in the interest of the client. In many cities, there are "lawyer neighborhoods," quarters or a few streets where law firms are clustered. The spatial proximity to competitors does not have to be a disadvantage. The law firm that sets up its office in such a neighborhood shows that it "belongs".

The choice of office location can create access barriers – which can be intentional. Office space in an office tower, in the immediate vicinity of the offices of large companies, indicates that this law firm is probably more interested in corporate clients than in a private clientele coming from low-income strata. Conversely, a general law firm should be wary of choosing an overly exclusive location because it may be a deterrent to the firm's target clientele.

The same applies to the interior design of the office rooms. Every target clientele will find bright and friendly rooms pleasant. The reception area and any waiting zones must be designed in an appealing manner. Exaggerations, regardless of whether the furnishings are "cheap" or "highly exclusive", are damaging. No client wants to have the impression that his lawyer is not prepared to invest in proper office furnishings, nor that his lawyer is indulging in excessive luxury (at the expense of the client).

1. Infrastructure

When establishing a law firm, you have the choice to start with the minimum equipment or with the optimal equipment, but then possibly financed.

Starting with the minimum set-up means providing a basic set-up of the office premises that allows all the technical requirements and furniture needed for the office operation and the workflows to be provided. The optimal furnishing, on the other hand, does not only represent the minimum requirements, but can already optimize structures and systems in these work processes and, if necessary, represent potential for expansion and development. In addition, it is naturally possible to make a thematic reference to the firm's branding when designing the optimal office furnishings, i.e. to incorporate the firm's special characteristics into the furnishings and fittings, such as being classically conservative or more modern and innovative.

Also, the law firm colors and logo can already be integrated into the optimal law firm interior.

The minimum requirements for the office equipment include first and foremost the requirements specified by the Bar Association for the accessibility of the office. This means that you should be reachable by telephone as well as by e-mail or beA. A landline or fax connection, on the other hand, is not necessarily required, as your PC can also handle this. However, in addition to a PC or laptop with a certain memory capacity, you should also have a good printer with copying and scanning functions. A good book calendar is also required. A desk, desk chair as well as office cabinets and storage space are a given. The same goes for basic office supplies. You should have the stamps personalized.

Likewise, a law firm sign should draw attention to the firm.

You should always decide on the optimal office setup if it is possible for you to start with a sufficient budget from the outset by working in partnership with others or in office sharing. One question that has not yet been conclusively clarified is under what conditions it is permissible to start a law firm in so-called co-working spaces. The issues of discretion and data protection must certainly be dealt with sensitively here.

Incidentally, a concept geared to the needs of young law firm founders is offered by Northcote in Vienna, which provides the infrastructure required for a law firm, along with office equipment, IT and personnel[1].

However, be sure to consult specialists to have your ideas for the office professionally implemented. Such specialists can be IT solution providers, but also interior designers, designers and even Feng Shui consultants. It's no coincidence that today the big hotel chains and fashion labels design their stores with designer fragrances, color specialists and branding experts.

---

1 See www.northcote.at.

Thus, when entering your office, the client should immediately be convinced of your competence and dynamism and be met in his needs. Do not underestimate the power of the first impression, even if in many law firms today the client entering through the door is of rather secondary importance and most mandates are handled online or by telephone, these office premises become the key factor in the next client meeting. And, of course, the future center of life for you and your employees. After all, you will spend the majority of your day in these premises: a pleasant, undisturbed and inspiring working atmosphere can definitely increase the quality of your work performance.

2. Personnel and Human Resources

Of course, you can run a law firm as a one-man office without any other employees, as a minimum personnel version. However, this is not recommended.

As a law firm owner, you already have the role of lawyer and the role of business owner combined in one person. In addition, you have to make decisions about marketing, sales and law firm development alone[2]. If you now also take over the telephone service, the paperwork and the file processing, it will become almost impossible for you to practice law. Therefore, you should think economically and ask yourself how you can find solutions that are adapted to your current situation.

It is not always necessary to start with a larger permanent staff right away. In the past, it was ideal if you were supported by a typist, a telephone operator, an assistant and someone who was experienced in financial and accounting matters, and if you also included a cleaner in your calculations from the outset, although this can also mean simply purchasing an appropriate service from a cleaning company, which does not count as personnel costs. Today, the rule of thumb is that for every full-time lawyer there is a lot of IT and a maximum of 0.5 assistants plus one trainee in the non-legal or legal field[3]. Personnel development in law firms is always marked by setbacks, and I don't mean that good female employees sometimes get pregnant or colleagues want to take parental leave or work part-time. There is a lack of both strategic involvement and professional HR managers. Induction and leadership are also problem areas in many law firms, which will be discussed in more detail in the next chapter. Only this much at this point: when founding a law firm, personnel is a risk and cost factor that should not be underestimated, and one is well advised to plan a new law firm with a modern 1:0.5 ratio of lawyers to

2 Michael Gerber, "The E-Myth Attorney", p. 9 et seq.
3 More at Andrea Fendt, "Der Rechtsanwalt als Ausbilder", 15 et seq.

"others" right from the start. The pandemic has led to a worsening of the situation for paralegal and notary staff: even higher workloads and worse working conditions. There was a large turnover of staff and a change of personnel, with the ReFas soon determining which jobs were attractive at all. Poorly paid and poorly digitized jobs could hardly be refilled. The same is true for attorney positions. The statistics show that a new position costs on average between € 5,000–7,000 (i. e., about two full months of personnel costs) and takes about 4 months from the time the position is advertised. This does not include the damage caused by the loss of know-how and clients, nor the investment required for new training and equipment[4].

We have already looked at income as a self-employed and salaried lawyer from many perspectives above. Starting a new law firm with a young colleague as an employee must not be a bad idea, since this way the topic of acquisition (increasing turnover) is ideally divided between two shoulders from the outset, leaving more time for law firm management and development. As a starting annual salary, you should certainly expect at least € 55,000 gross in this situation. In Austria, this is roughly comparable to an articled clerk who prepares for his bar exam during the 5 years in the firm (extended legal clerkship): With an average annual salary of at least € 45,000 gross (€ 3667/month).

But what kind of salary should one expect for **legal assistants**? According to the job portal www.Stellenanzeigen.de,ReFas in Munich can expect an average **salary** of € 29,725 gross for career starters to € 54,961 per year for "old hands". This means that the experienced professional receives about as much as the young lawyer in employment.

This means € 2,477 to € 4,580 gross/month under circumstances after social security contributions and wage tax not more than € 2,000 to € 4,000 net for the law firm employees (and thus at best not much less than the law firm owner).

Nothing else applies in Austria: Although there is no special training as a legal and notary secretary here (ReFa, ReNo or the equi-valent for patent law firms: PaFa). Nevertheless, according to the Labor Market Service (AMS) Austria Compass, a legal secretary (with a higher education degree) receives € 1,640 to € 1,830 gross. This is a lot and little at the same time: compared to other sectors of the economy, one can also earn € 1,440 gross with this field of work and competence profile, or a maximum of € 3,190 gross (approx. € 1,000–2,500 net) per month in large companies.

All in all: With social security contributions etc. as an employer, a cost factor of at least € 80,000 per year can be expected for a full-time employee.

The question is: Are there alternatives (beyond even greater digitization)? Today, flexible services are offered in a variety of ways: this can range from call cen-

4 brand.eins/thema 2021, Die Branche in Zahlen, p. 79.

ters to typing pools to work-time companies. Lawyers can also be booked as interim or so-called “Lawyer on Demand” with very good expertise from appropriately specialized staffing firms. A short internet search will provide you with the necessary contact data. This is not only cheaper in some respects than hiring a part-time or full-time employee from the outset for a longer period of time. Moreover, these services can always be booked flexibly if the law firm, with only one or two clients, suddenly finds itself confronted with an excessively large workload overnight. In this way, peak times can be absorbed without overworking and wearing out the existing staff.

In this context, it is also important to remember that all personnel must be trained, managed and developed, in other words, investments must be made in them. By investment, I mean first and foremost the allocation of time and the familiarization with the work tasks. Structures and systems have to be defined, work processes have to be established, responsibilities have to be regulated in order to allow several employees to work alongside and with each other. At the same time, control systems must be implied to ensure the proper fulfillment of the tasks at hand.

In addition, these employees must ultimately be formed into a team. This requires specific management measures, regular meetings, but also the introduction of reward systems, team events and routines. Experience has shown that it takes at least one year for a new employee to pay off. This is overlooked in most law firm start-ups and simply disregarded as a cost and time budget. However, it would be a mistake to forego this investment in the employee or to leave the employee to their own devices once they have been trained, only to lose them again soon after.

3. Office equipment and IT

Equipping a law firm with a telephone and (still) a fax machine[5] is a given. For all other technical office equipment, such as copiers, shredders and scanners, it is not always necessary to use the latest model. However, these devices must not be outdated either, so that efficient service is guaranteed.

When it comes to law firm software, you should choose a solution from a provider that can be easily expanded – and now also has the necessary compatibility with the beA. However, you do not necessarily need client software to get started. However, it can represent many helpful elements and create a certain order. The path to the electronic file, which is specified by the beA, is hereby taken. At the same time, accounting tasks can be performed cost-effectively and archiving costs can be kept

5 Attention: Only valid for Germany!

low. In many cases, a well-functioning law firm software can replace employees, mechanize and automate regular work processes, for example, in the registration of mandates, the information of clients in ongoing proceedings and in the cost reminder procedure.

Software

The market for law firm software is large and there are many providers on it – from well-known manufacturers such as advoware, AnNoText and RA-Micro to to new cloud software providers such as Actaport, Kleos and Legalvisio[6].

But what is important when choosing and how should you decide?

Almost every law firm software offers standard CRM functions such as file, address and participant management, the management of appointments, tasks, deadlines and resubmissions. When selecting law firm software, it is first important to determine the goal of the purchase for yourself.

Goal 1: (Completely) digitally map law firm processes

Many people are familiar with mountains of files that "pile up" on desks or in archives. This looks unsightly and can also become a data protection risk if there is no separate meeting room. When selecting software, it is therefore important to ensure that the office software has a well-structured file history and a document viewer with which documents can be displayed.

In particular, the combination of both simplifies digital work and makes it easier to dispense with paper files.

In addition, it should be possible to map office processes such as incoming and outgoing mail as digitally as possible and support all mail formats (e-mail, scans, beA and e-Post). This is because the processing of correspondence is often a central task in daily work.

Finally, you should also think about a digital archiving solution. Provided that the required guidelines for the tax office, chamber and DSGVO are adhered to, digital archiving is not only more cost-saving, but also more secure.

6 At CLP, we cooperate with several of these vendors, whether for product development, enhancement or marketing support – so you're sure to have seen us at some of them. However, we do not recommend any particular software and do not receive any commission, but use this insight and overview in our work.

Goal 2: Overview from an entrepreneurial and business perspective

If business aspects are important to you, you should make sure that your law firm software has integrated client and financial accounting. If you are active in the area of debt collection, it is also important to have receivables management that is as integrated as possible with prepared, automatic workflows. Some law firm software providers offer such functions for process automation for the area of debt collection, so that in the case of standardizable mandates, cover letters, resubmissions and important processes are completed for you directly when the file is created. This saves valuable time and makes you more competitive. Process automation also gives you the opportunity to implement standardized mandates as cost-effectively as possible in other specialist legal practices. When files are created, all important letters are generated and placed in the outbox for checking. This allows you to remain competitive, especially for these mandates, and to concentrate on the really exciting mandates.

Process automation and law firm controlling help you to establish a so-called Legal Project Management (LPM) in your law firm. This is when mandates are processed efficiently and standardized in the same high quality. With LPM, you focus on the entrepreneurial aspect and the needs of the client. This increases client satisfaction and ensures a good recommendation rate.

In order to be able to evaluate the growth of your law firm from an entrepreneurial point of view, it is advisable to rely on software right from the start that enables business management evaluations and law firm controlling with, if possible, integrated time and activity recording for all users of a law firm. In this way, you will always have an overview of the economic status of your law firm and will be able to recognize at an early stage which processes in the law firm are "time wasters" and have a negative impact on your profitability. Another factor: If you invest in marketing, a business evaluation is even more worthwhile. This allows you to regularly check how effective your marketing is, and which marketing channels are working. Law firm software that provides implemented or customizable fields in the file facilitates the evaluation. For example, the next time you send a Christmas greeting, you can consciously decide whether it would be better to send a hand-signed Christmas card by mail, a standardized e-mail, or whether it would be better to have a Christmas drink in the office or virtually.

Goal 3: Mobile vs. stationary work

The legal sector is also currently confronted with major changes in terms of working methods. Younger lawyers in particular are looking for a good work-life balance or are looking after clients over greater distances. Last but not least, the increased rents for law firm premises mean that the desire for mobile working is growing.

Here you should consider your current and medium-term needs. Do you have premises for your law firm or do you use coworking spaces where you rent workstations and premises by the day or by the hour?

If you work increasingly on the move, we recommend pure cloud software or software operated in a data center. The latter is currently offered by many established manufacturers. In both cases, the advantages are obvious: you have your data available at all times and can work practically from anywhere. In addition, you do not have to invest in cost-intensive law firm servers. This is not easy, especially at the beginning of a lawyer's career or the founding of a law firm.

But what are the differences between cloud software and data center based software? With cloud software, the data and documents in your law firm software are securely located in the cloud. However, in many cases you have to take care of the backup and data protection of the rest of your data yourself.

Tip

Do not forget about daily backups, protection of data stored on hard disks against theft via encryption and protection against viruses and Trojans[7].

!

With many providers who operate law firm software in the data center, this is taken care of for you, because they work completely on the data center server. This means that all data is backed up daily, and monitoring for virus protection, Windows updates and sometimes even updates to your law firm software are included in the monthly flat rate.

If you plan to do a lot of mobile work, you should check whether offline working is also possible or whether an Internet connection is available where you work.

If you are often on the road, it is advisable to invest in devices or software for mobile dictation. With the right tools, such as DNS Comfort and Dragon, dictations from the road can be transcribed by typists in the office or converted directly into written text using background speech recognition. This allows you to use the time you don't have for writing correspondence, for example in the car on the way from one appointment to the next. In addition to your own goals, which you are pursuing with the acquisition of the law firm software, there are other points that you should consider.

7 Excerpt from *Jeniffer Hülskötter* "Die Kanzlei als erfolgreiches Unternehmen", MKG 2019.

Goal 4: Compatibility with existing software and devices
You should ensure good compatibility with all other technical devices including software in the office, such as existing accounting solutions/tax advisor specifications, hardware such as PCs/printers/faxes/copiers, and the telecommunications system including mobile devices such as cell phones and tablets. In the end, this overall view should also include your law firm's data protection officer, whom you will need once you have ten or more employees who are allowed to access your client data.

Goal 5: Target group-oriented client communication
Depending on which clients are in your target group, there are differences in the way clients want to communicate with you. Private clients like to communicate via e-mail and messenger systems. Legal protection insurers, on the other hand, exchange information with lawyers via the drebis interface. In the future, the special electronic lawyer's mailbox (beA) will play an increasingly important role in the area of electronic legal communications. However, there are also options for digitally mapping conventional mail, e.g. via the E-POST service. To save time and money, it is also worth keeping your clients up to date at all times via a virtual file (e.g. onlineFile or WebFile). In this way, you can reduce inquiries about the status of the mandate, because all information and documents relating to the mandate are permanently available to the client.

It is therefore worthwhile, when selecting law firm software, to ensure that these interfaces to the above-mentioned services are available and that they are also integrated sensibly into the incoming and outgoing mail. This prevents media disruptions, which often cost time and lead to the old habit of resorting to paper files. If the communication interfaces are integrated into the software as effectively as possible, you will always have relevant information in one central location.

Independent of purely legal activities, good software can also support the entrepreneurial management of your law firm.
This is where the various aspects of personnel management come into play. From time recording, vacation and sick days to target agreements, talent development measures and further training, the potential of an employee can be precisely recorded and evaluated. Meaningful solutions for DSGVO-compliant document management, i.e. the storage of certificates, job evaluations, employment contracts or photos, are also conceivable.

The same applies to the digital support of building management: the recording, control and evaluation of costs for the office premises (rent, loans, investments, ongoing service costs, ancillary costs, parking costs, supply of office/ drinks/catering, etc.) are a central component of successful entrepreneurial office management.

Overall, the close-meshed control of your income and expenses, budget management and investments should also be software-based nowadays in order to have all the necessary data available in your controlling at any time and to be able to react with the right measures in good time if necessary.

Opting for software that offers only basic functions at the beginning seems reasonable at first. Many functions are not needed at the beginning and make the software too complex. However, when making your decision, remember that, for example, with the annual increase in the volume of files, integrated financial and client accounting eliminates many work steps and saves valuable time. Functions such as office controlling help to set up your office efficiently and economically. Should you then grow and hire new employees, a sophisticated rights management system is also important.

Tip:
To begin, take a look at the various law firm software programs. Create a criteria catalogue of what is particularly important to you when using the software and pay attention to the development potential of the application. Will the software still suit you in two to five years? Will it also support you if your annual file workload increases, you hire more employees or want to automate processes for cost-benefit reasons? Changing law firm software can be expensive. But if you realize that the software you have chosen does not fit your needs, don't be afraid to make the switch[8].

A word about the telephone:

Most law firms will still have a landline. However, this is becoming increasingly dispensable. Alternative providers are conquering the market. Most smartphones can provide all the essential tools for effective office communication. In addition to pure telephony, access to the email system can also be mapped.

In addition, the calendar and dictation function is also available, or research on the Internet is also possible. Even short notes and texts can be written, reminders can be automated processes can be defined. It is even possible to access the electronic file in the office from outside the office. With the appropriate software, it is also possible to give the client a concrete list of costs and fees for the current mandate at any time. All these functions make it inconceivable today for a lawyer to have ever worked without this means of communication[9].

8 Ibid.

9 Even if, with all the technical possibilities, there are only a few that actually meet the requirements for confidentiality and data security specified by professional law.

It is still true that a law firm's library cannot be good enough. Today, electronic storage media and the Internet allow research work to be done far more quickly and thoroughly than in the past. A law firm must take advantage of these opportunities. This also means that every workstation in a law firm must be equipped with a computer and Internet access.

Exchanging documents with clients is extremely difficult if the law firm uses only the ancient version of a common word processing program.

In the meantime, there are sufficient technical possibilities to give clients online access to the files kept for them. The client has the possibility to check the processing status of his case online at any time and to track and view all previous activities, including the documents created. Primarily companies, but also increasingly private clients, will gladly make use of such a service. A law firm should not wait for clients to request such a service but should offer it on its own initiative.

Communication via e-mail is a given. But other communication channels are also conceivable, be it dedicated, particularly secure communication channels or even, for less important messages, SMS, etc. But here, too, it is necessary to research exactly which of these providers have the necessary security standards[10].

---

10 As this market is developing rapidly, a printed book such as this cannot, of course, provide a list of providers that meet current security standards.

IV. Pay attention to your needs

Lastly, a word on resource conservation:

You should always and absolutely pay attention to

- the observance of recovery breaks
- sufficient sleep
- sufficient intake of water and
- healthy food and
- other bio breaks.
- sufficient exercise in daylight/sports
- health check up with the doctor and
- reducing alcohol, cigarettes, junk food (sugar and fat) does not hurt

Especially in the early days, many people put themselves under enormous pressure to succeed. Elated by the idea of the future law firm and its successes, endorphins and adrenaline can cover up basic needs and make them seem superfluous.

But remember: Your body and mind are your most valuable assets in your business. Like a high-performance machine, however, they need to be maintained and cared for in order to perform at their best[1]. Do not make the mistake of tapping into your resources at this stage, only to start the project of founding a law firm completely burnt out[2]. In my consulting practice as a coach and trainer for lawyers, I have seen some promising projects fail solely due to the burn-out of the owner.

Deal with yourself responsibly: just as good parents not only sacrifice themselves for the children, but also take care of their needs[3].

If you are really serious about starting a profitable law firm, about becoming a successful entrepreneur, then like "Rocky" you should get into your best physical shape before his big fight!

"The legal profession has always been my passion. By becoming self-employed, however, it feels even less like 'work', as I can organize my everyday life in exactly the way that suits me and my priorities. Of course, self-employment brings challenges, but also the maximum freedom."

Sarah Settele, self-employed lawyer in individual practice, Krumbach (www.Kanzlei-Settele.de)

---

1 Arianna Huffington, "Sleep Revolution", p. 8.

2 Ben Schulz, "Mit Vollgas in den Crash", p. 151.

3 Similar to the safety instructions of flight personnel in the event of oxygen loss, first put the oxygen mask on yourself and only then help people in need.

What did you get out of the chapter?
You have understood how your law firm vision can be turned into a law firm in a very concrete way.

V. Checklist for the foundation of your law firm

Founding concept:

- Law firm values and culture
- Law firm vision
- Law firm goal (short and long term)
- Positioning (branding, marketing and acquisition)
- Law firm Strategy

Founding formalities:

- two passed legal state examinations
- professional liability insurance in the basic legal version
- address for service in the district
- Application to the relevant bar association
- Health and pension insurance/professional association
- registration with the tax office
- Necessary official/licensing requirements for the law office premises

Business concept:

- Investment capital (start-up volume/grants/external financing)
- Revenue and profit
- Financing plan and budgeting
- Costs, expenses
- Investments

Management concept:

- Personnel concept
- Definition of processes, workflows and structures
- Concrete job descriptions and responsibilities
- Knowledge transfer
- Team building
- Personnel development through training, mentoring and coaching
- Sustainability and employee retention

Concept for infrastructure:

- Telephone system, answering machine
- Office account
- Law firm sign, stamp, letterhead definition
- PC system with client software and special connection to your communication system

- Copier with fax and scan function, printer
- Office furniture including security technology
- Office supplies and small equipment, deadline calendars and forms
- Lawyer's supplies (robe, lawyer's identity card, legal texts, commentaries)

D. Law firm management

Once you have founded your law firm and successfully placed it on the market for the first few months or perhaps even years, it is important to develop it continuously. Success means growth. Law firms that do not adapt flexibly to the market and react to it while constantly growing will not be able to sustain themselves in the long run.

So, don't be afraid to grow, but develop your firm consistently in the direction of growth. Assume from the outset that you will become larger, handle more and larger mandates.

---

i

In order not to lose track of this development, it is important to
- keep a fixed point on the horizon with your law firm vision.
- set interim goals and celebrate their achievement.

Otherwise, it can quickly feel like you're on a constant hamster wheel, never arriving. Your law firm vision helps you to stay on course. Of course, this is a course that can also be corrected and adjusted and should also be corrected and adjusted at regular intervals.

This makes it all the more important to define interim goals and celebrate their attainment. Only in retrospect do many people realize how far they have come and the development they have achieved. You yourself may only faintly remember the early days of founding your firm, your first employee or how the firm's sign was attached to the building. Imponderables and problems have long been forgotten. That makes it all the more important to remember them from time to time. Include colleagues and employees in this retrospective and use this opportunity to thank them. A law firm success is always also a team success!

But how exactly can you manage the growth of your law firm?

When developing your law firm, you should essentially proceed in the same way as when establishing it: The first step is to review your law firm vision and, if necessary, adjust it to include new aspects. Then it is a matter of developing a law firm strategy and defining intermediate goals. This should include market changes, emerging opportunities or new ideas. In the same way, however, defeats or successes achieved in the past should also be evaluated and included.

https://doi.org/10.1515/9783111058160-004

Finally, the structures and systems already established should be reviewed for efficiency and optimization possibilities. The aim here is to save time and money and to increase the quantity and quality of mandate processing[1].

So, make it a rule to establish strategy meetings at quarterly or half-yearly intervals to evaluate the course taken and correct it if necessary, and then once a year to define the strategy for the coming year.

Use so-called retreat days for this purpose. Retreat days are regularly used by law firm teams to retreat outside the office for two to three days, to talk to each other and, far away from the daily office routine, to exchange ideas about the values pursued by the law firm, to intensify personal contact and to strengthen the ability to work in a team. The law firm as a business is teamwork. If necessary, use experts to resolve conflicts, communication difficulties or moderation deficits that arise within the team and establish the retreat as a regular, fruitful necessity for your law firm.

1 Zach Davis, "Zeitmanagement für Rechtsanwälte", p. 34.

I. Structures, processes and systems

Why should you read this chapter?
Effective office management not only reduces costs but is also good for the office climate. Discover how it's done.

Overview

1. **Profitability, processes and systems**
2. **Project and crisis management**
- Legal Project Management (LPM)
- Legal Service Portfolio Management
- Legal Design Thinking
- Project Management
- Crisis management
- Integrated Dispute Management

3. **Business Development**
4. **Accounting, controlling, quality management and compliance**
5. **Knowledge building and development**

The adaptation of the law firm vision and strategy to the market or changed circumstances is accompanied by the adaptation of existing structures and systems or the implementation of new structures and systems. This is primarily a matter of defining responsibilities, levels of control and management, in order to clearly delineate the various areas from one another[1].

As described above, it can make sense to involve specialists and professionals from other fields, such as marketing, psychology or business administration, who can often take a fresh and commercially oriented look at the firm.

1. Profitability and office organization

As different as lawyers are, so are their work processes and office organization. Most of them have never thought about their own processes and structures. And many only realize that there is such a thing as office organization when they are

1 Efficient lawyer "Effiziente Anwaltsorganisation – Ablaufsicherheit durch optimierte Kanzleiprozesse" by TeleLex.

suddenly surprised by other processes in a different office.[2]. There are the lawyers who have “always done things this way” and resist any definition, review or even change. And there are the others who are happy to let themselves be surrounded by the structure of the assistants, as long as everything runs smoothly and is not a nuisance.

The profitability of a law firm depends to a large extent on

1. Revenue
   a) how many billable hours can be billed at
   b) what hourly rate.
   OR
   how high the statutory fees are according to RVG
   OR
   which flat rate remuneration has been agreed
   AND
2. which costs are opposed to this Revenues:

Depending on the area of law, the size of the law firm and the location, lawyers either charge mainly according to statutory fees or work with fee agreements. In the case of fee agreements, either the flat fee variant or the billable hourly rate variant is agreed. Lump-sum fees also include those mandates which can either be handled in a standardized manner for one client (e.g. in debt collection) or a longer-term assignment as a stand-by “external legal department” with a monthly flat fee.

The classic agreement based on hourly rates is mainly used in large commercial law firms to supply the costly substructure and is increasingly no longer accepted by the market.

As we have already seen in the opening chapter on the legal consulting market, the average annual revenues are as follows:

Business Lawyer Equity Partner	€ 250.000–500.000
Business Lawyer Partner	€ 180.000–280.000
Business Lawyer Counsel	€ 150.000–250.000
Partnership Lawyer	€ 242.000
Specialist lawyer	€ 207.000
Lawyer (west)	€ 209.000
Lawyer example front	€ 168.000
Female Lawyer (west)	€ 155.000
Lawyer (east)	€ 152.000

2 Heussen, “Anwaltsunternehmen führen”, p. 211.

Business Lawyer Associates	€ 80.000–140.000
Female Lawyer (east)	€ 121.000

Average hourly rates vary from € 130 to € 250 to € 390, which means they can be three times that amount without any change in the legal services provided. Top earners work in corporate law and compliance, followed by M&A and commercial and criminal tax law.

Of course, one assumes that in the high-priced sector investments have been made in professional training, expertise and experience. However, it is a fact that the cost share is also above average in this sector due to the corresponding personnel base as well as representative offices and equipment.

Overall, the remuneration for legal services has increased in recent years in terms of hourly rates (approx. € 200) and simultaneously decreased due to legal tech providers (approx. € 50), who offer standardized legal advice at low cost.

One reason for rising hourly rates is the number of specialist lawyers, which has increased dramatically in the last 10 years from 38,745 (2010) to 56,305 (2020) (one in four holds at least one title), with an increase in the number of specialist legal fields and multiple specialist lawyer titles (maximum of 3 possible). Another reason is rising costs for employees and investments in digitalization.

Effective office organization as a serious cost factor is only now being understood by most, when (mostly technical) service providers demand the definition of structures, responsibilities and processes in order to be able to optimally support the office workflow with software and hardware. In many law firms, it is even left to the provider to define and establish these processes – with only moderate success, of course.

With the introduction of quality management systems (QMS), however, not only can costs be reduced, but also a competitive advantage can be achieved. Recurring activities and processes – even beyond those already defined by the law firm software – can be bindingly defined and standardized to guarantee fast and uniformly high service[3].

However, the basis should be the respective business model and quality objectives on the one hand, and the needs and expectations of the respective clients on the other[4].

3 Branchenbericht der Sparkassen 2020, p. 17.

4 Kanzlei und Markt, 4/2016, p. 4.

In principle, according to § 50 BRAO, the obligation to keep a manual file applies. Traditionally, this is kept in paper form, sorted chronologically or commercially.

I would now like to claim that in times of electronic legal transactions and the digital file, the paper file is being superseded. In fact, virtually all files are now reproduced electronically. But only "also", because in fact there are now mostly two files: the paper file and the electronic file. To the delight of the paper manufacturers, who will soon have to fear the paperless office in every industry, except the legal industry. 97 % of lawyers still use copied or printed documents for their communication. Drawn documents are transmitted predominantly on the postal way, additionally also by fax, particularly since deadlines can still only be kept by sending printed documents. Contracts are always kept in several versions. In addition, e-mail communication is printed out for the file. So, the industry is still a long way from the paperless office or the digital law firm.

A special chapter on this path is the special electronic lawyer's mailbox (beA), which was introduced by the German Federal Bar Association (BRAK) in accordance with the Act to Promote Electronic Legal Transactions (Gesetz zur Förderung des elektronischen Rechtsverkehrs). Every lawyer and every law firm should be able to correspond with each other, with all courts and also with authorities in a particularly secure electronic communication procedure. This was to start already for the repeated time (which now finally took place starting from 1.1.2022 after the ERV extension law came into force). In Austria and other countries, this has already been the case for many years in legal transactions and in the judiciary and administration.

The advantages are obvious: the clearly defined and streamlined processes and structures in the digital office bring significant savings in processing time and the necessary personnel. There's no question about it: the digital law firm works cheaper and faster – and of course more reliably and securely. A clear competitive advantage.

However, a closer look at lawyers and law firms reveals that it is primarily a generational conflict: while young lawyers and new law firms tend to find it easy to introduce, implement and apply such processes, the older the age structure of partners and office staff, the more difficult it is for traditional, long-established law firms. This also gives them a competitive advantage in the fiercely contested market for "high potentials," of young legal talent: After all, dedicated office assistants and young lawyers of tomorrow do not want to spend their apprenticeship years with outdated processes and tools.

Original documents, deeds and contracts, certainly need to be kept in paper form. In fact, however, today everything can be scanned and digitally assigned and sorted (and the originals returned to the client). Even the archiving obligations (possibly up to 30 years) do not force a paper file. It is true that 60–70 % of all lawyers have already started to scan and electronically archive old files. However, the process is far from complete and will be one of the future topics of the industry. Various innovative technical archiving solutions are already being offered for the industry, but they are far from being comparable with professional ECM solutions[5] from other industries. Today, modern archiving systems are able to meet the legal requirements and save considerable additional storage costs. Incidentally, this is a cost and risk factor that only very few companies calculate as running costs.

The office processes revolve around the management
- the file (creation, keeping, storage, filing)
- the deadlines and dates
- accounting and execution and
- mail (incoming and outgoing)[6]

Deadline management is probably the most sensitive issue, as this is where the liability risks lie. It is advisable not only to assign a very experienced employee explicitly to the task of deadline management, but also to have a double deadline calendar (written and electronic) as well as a strict system of deadlines and dates (such as advance deadlines, emergency deadlines, resubmission deadlines, limitation periods, etc.).

Many of these processes, structures and systems are established by the assistants. The disadvantage of this is that the assistants often make themselves indispensable and chaos breaks out in their absence, or each assistant manages their own territory autonomously without communicating with others about interfaces and the handover of processes. It is therefore your task to determine, observe and control these responsibilities and the effectiveness of the processes and structures, and to correct them if necessary. Of course, you can enlist the help of an experienced office supervisor or office manager in this regard.

Perhaps professionally cost-conscious, auditors and tax consultants in particular ask why every lawyer actually has to have his own secretary. This question is not

5 Enterprise Content Management (ECM) is a set of methods, techniques and tools for capturing, managing, storing, preserving and delivering content and documents to support organizational processes in enterprises.

6 Geißinger, v. Landenberg, "Erfolgreich starten als Rechtsanwalt", p. 252.

unjustified. Only if a lawyer runs a mass department, he will fully utilize a typist alone. Language-aware dictation systems can replace pure typists to a considerable extent. The tasks of legal secretaries go far beyond typing from dictation. Except for some control functions, the entire office organization should be entrusted to the non-legal staff of a law firm.

Inquiries directed to the law firm, especially telephone inquiries, should be answered in a friendly, quick and competent manner. If there is a central telephone switchboard, then the corresponding employee must be trained in such a way that the caller is connected as quickly as possible to the contact person he or she wishes to speak to or to the person who can provide him or her with information. If the law firm serves foreign clients, then the receptionist must at least speak good English. Large law firms permanently employ their own interpreters and translators, a service that will probably be overtaken next by digitalization and ever-improving translation programs.

The impact that non-legal staff can have on outsiders cannot be underestimated. The client orientation of a law firm must not stop at the office staff. The external appearance of law firm employees is also important for the external image of a law firm. Neither casual leisure wear nor evening attire belong in an office, whereby the particularities of the client target group naturally also play a role here: a start-up will have different expectations than a bank.

---

i **Reachability and availability** of a lawyer are the be-all and end-all of lawyer distribution policy. The lawyer's service is an interactive service. With a few exceptions, it is the lawyer himself who conveys his service in direct contact with the client. Nothing annoys a client more than if he does not reach his lawyer or if the expected feedback from the lawyer does not materialize.

Lawyers should be available at least during normal office hours, i. e. Monday to Friday between 9:00 a.m. and 6:00 p.m., preferably until 8:00 p.m.. A solution can also be to ensure that the telephone switchboard is manned during the entire core working hours, possibly by using temporary staff or special central telephone services.

"I started in Vienna in 1988 as ONE WOMAN Show, initially in a small directing partnership together with a lawyer and directing partner, with whom I shared the costs of the first office premises. But after only one year, the space requirements of my office grew and so I moved into my first own office premises. I have now been working together with my professional partners in a law firm for over 20 years."

Lawyer Dr. Alix Frank, Partner of Alix Frank Rechtsanwälte GmbH in Vienna (www.alix-frank.co.at).

The permanent availability of lawyers may be desirable from the client's point of view. Practically, no lawyer can fully meet such a requirement. Anyone who has to draft a complicated contract or prepare a difficult brief needs contiguous blocks of a few hours of concentrated work that are not interrupted by telephone calls. It would be wrong, however, to have clients rejected by a secretary, possibly with the remark "Attorney XY has something important to do at the moment. Please call back later". The client feels set back and badly treated. Because from his point of view, his request is far more important than anything else the lawyer might have to do at the moment.

It is far better to inform the client in a friendly manner that unfortunately he cannot speak to the lawyer he wants at the moment, but that the lawyer will call him back at a certain time, if this is okay with the client. The promised call back time must be kept. If this is done reliably, clients will forgive the lawyer for not being able to reach them immediately on one or two occasions.

A lawyer should think carefully about what he uses a cell phone for. If he is in his office, he does not need it. If he is out of the office, not including travel time, then this usually has to do with a case that deserves his full attention. In addition, it is important to pay attention to who is listening in. Again and again, I experience how obviously "important" client meetings are held in the open-plan compartment of an ICE train without regard for fellow passengers, who are then force-fed the details of the mandate – the confidentiality requirement is completely overridden here.

Callers can leave a message at the office. If the call back system works and the client does not have to wait an unduly long time for an answer, he will not be annoyed if he cannot reach his lawyer at short notice. Conversely, clients appreciate it when a lawyer is not distracted by incoming telephone calls while talking to them.

Letters from the client, regardless of whether they are received by mail, fax or e-mail, must be answered within a specified period of time. It is not always possible to draft the expected answer immediately. Disturbances and inquiries of the client can be avoided by informing him when he will likely receive a detailed answer, which hardly costs any time.

Clients expect their lawyer to be at their disposal when it seems important from their point of view. As a service provider, a lawyer should refrain from measuring the necessity of a meeting with the client against "objective" criteria or from judging whether a further discussion with the client will advance the matter. The client's point of view is decisive. This view of the client often collides with the lawyer's time schedule and also affects the profitability of a mandate. The lawyer, who assesses his fee according to the remuneration law, cannot spend as much time as he likes on a mandate if he does not want to incur losses. In such cases, sensitivity is required. A friendly secretary who manages to arrange another appointment with the client that fits a little better into the lawyer's schedule is one of the plus points of a law firm.

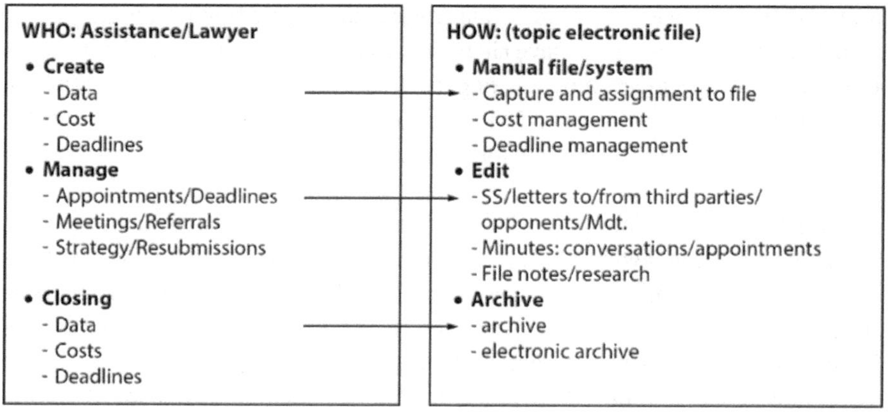

Workflow Client file, © Dr. Geertje Tutschka

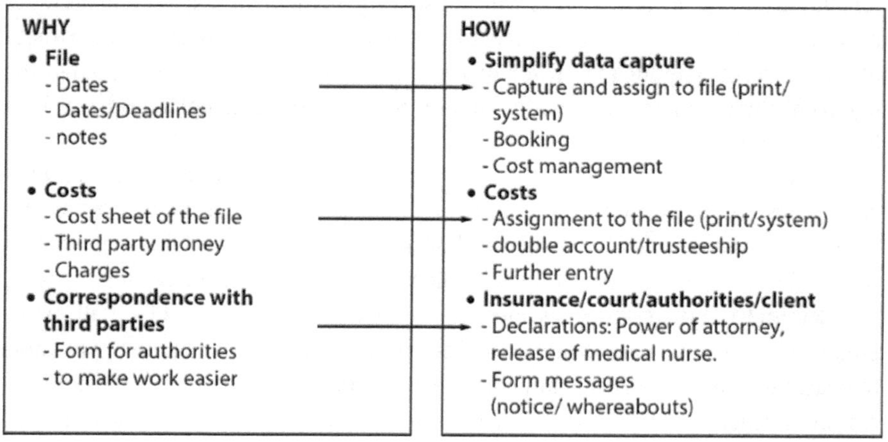

Workflow Templates/forms, © Dr. Geertje Tutschka

You found the most important forms and templates of the mothballed paper manual file at Soldan, e.g. the mandate entry sheet, the power of attorney, the long-distance call note, the note for forwarding a document, the deadline note, etc., I would like to recommend the detailed list of suitable law firm software from ffi-Verlag as well as the "Checkliste zu den Grundlagen des Mandatsmanagements" (checklist on the basics of mandate management) from Wolters Kluwer (both can be found in the bibliography), which is probably already out of date by the time you read this. Nevertheless, take advantage of the many opportunities to find out about current solutions and then decide how much paper filing your office still needs.

Accounting and billing:

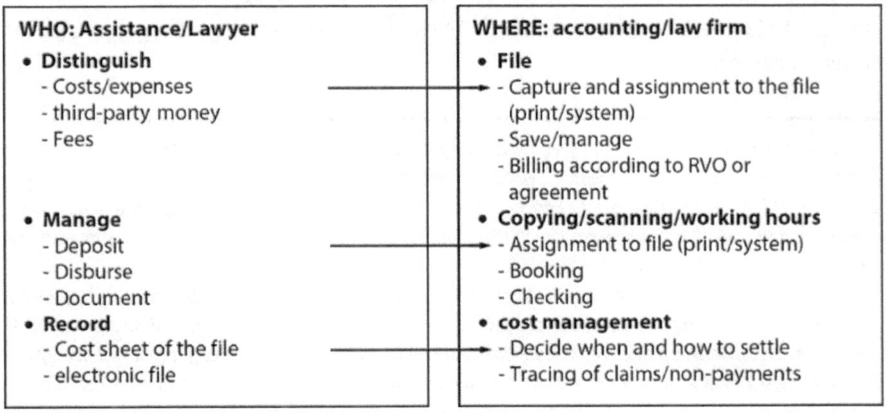

Workflow Cost management, © Dr. Geertje Tutschka

Information gathering and data management:

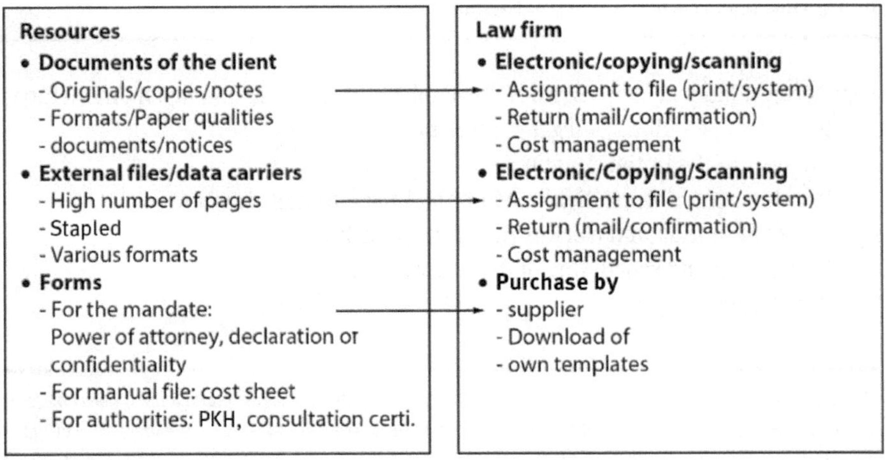

Workflow Data collection, © Dr. Geertje Tutschka

2. Crisis and project management

– Legal Project Management (LPM)

It is obvious that the digitization of law firm management in particular offers many points of reference to legal tech. Despite all the skepticism and reluctance, there are also many lawyers who have found their passion in rethinking the legal profession in technical terms[7].

"I have been fascinated by the topic of legal technology for quite some time and I am always discovering new facets. Particularly in combination with the work on traditional legal activities in the firm – in my case mainly in the area of IT law – I also really like the variety. Legal tech can be very practical, but it also makes it possible or even necessary to deal with numerous (legal) theoretical questions. I always like to describe this as switching from a frog's to a bird's eye view and back again.

In June 2019, I was accepted into the talent program 'Bayerns Frauen in Digitalberufen (BayFiD) (Bavaria's Women in Digital Professions)' as one of 50 women in Bavaria by the Bavarian State Ministry for Digital Affairs. My dissertation was published in September 2019 under the title 'Digitalisierung, Legal Technology und Innovation – Der maßgebliche Rechtsrahmen für und die Anforderungen an den Rechtsanwalt in der Informationstechnologiegesellschaft (Digitalization, Legal Technology and Innovation – The Authoritative Legal Framework for and Requirements of the Lawyer in the Information Technology Society)' by Duncker & Humblot Verlag. It deals primarily with the professional aspects of legal technology. I have also published widely on issues of IT, copyright, media and data protection law and given numerous lectures. Since the winter semester 2020/2021, I have been accompanying the newly created master's degree program Legal Tech (LL.M.) at the University of Regensburg as a lecturer."

Dr. Christina Maria Leeb, University of Passau[8]

Legal Project Management (LPM) is the application of project management methods and tools to the handling of legal matters by:
- Analysis of the initial situation
- Development of the individually optimal result/target situation
- Target definition and clarification of responsibilities
- Structuring and scheduling of the process steps
- Resource management

"In traditional legal education, the whole topic of project management and cost management does not come up. Of course, this is also reflected in the daily work of lawyers, whether in-house or in a law firm. But this is precisely where the opportunity lies for both sides to meet the growing demands: After all, the cost pressure on

---

7 *Andreas Hermanutz,* Kanzleiorganisation als essentieller Bereich der Digitalisierung, DStR 40/2020.
8 Read the full interview on the CLP blog.

law firms is growing, because very few in-house departments are still prepared to simply bill on the basis of hourly rates – which usually cannot really be calculated reliably in terms of the overall result – as they used to. But legal departments are also facing budget cuts and, like all other departments, have to show that they are making a contribution to the company's success on the basis of KPIs. This in an environment of increasingly complex projects and dwindling resources of competent lawyers on the labor market. Getting fit in the LPM can help everyone in this respect, not only to be able to continuously manage and control the costs and the often tight schedules of the projects, but also to have clear transparency about where one stands, where sub-projects are still stuck and how the use of (personnel) resources is distributed. As is the case everywhere, I believe transparency creates more trust between the parties involved and ensures a sense of fairness: the billing law firm no longer has to go through the hassle of demonstrating that it has deployed the processing staff in the best possible way and haggle over every hour, and the in-house manager can be sure at all times that he is getting good value for his budget through leaner processes, better integration with the external processors and the optimal use of resources, and that he can ensure that his goals are reliably achieved. This is also where the interface to the second major topic that is currently driving the legal world is to be found: Automation of processes through legal technology (LT), use of collaboration platforms, etc. LPM must use these tools wisely, whether in knowledge management, compliance incident handling, or transactional projects: If the law firm or in-house team uses LPM and LT wisely, it can (currently) generate an edge over competitors and free up time for lawyers to deal with the issues that still require a smart mind and no technology deployment. I know that many lawyers turn a blind eye to this in the hope that it will pass, but digital change does not stop at our profession and requires new skills. As a lawyer, using methods from the LPM and LT will probably seem completely normal in a few years. Anyone who doesn't recognize and adapt to this today runs the risk of missing the boat on the changing world of work."

Christina Sontheim-Leven, LL.M., Chief Legal and Compliance Officer, Postcon Deutschland B.V. & Co. KG[9]

"We use LPM, for example, for the organization of mass suits, in M&A projects, restructurings, award procedures or international IP management projects – all of these are tasks that benefit greatly from structured project management. But individual principles could also be applied to smaller projects, such as closely timed coordination of interim results with the client and other 'agile' approaches. With LPM, KPMG Law could more easily offer flat rates and calculate more attractive budgets. From a client perspective, this means increased professionalism at interesting prices. From the firm's perspective, it means a focus on core competencies: lawyers concentrate on their legal craft, quality increases. Even if every project is different and the method is still too young for a reliable statistical evaluation, I would estimate a double-digit percentage amount on average."

Philipp Glock, Site manager Leipzig and Co-Head Legal Process & Technology, KPMG Law Rechtsanwaltsgesellschaft mbH[10]

---

9 *Christin Sontheim-Leven*, LPM, Company lawyer 01/2020.
10 *Philipp Glock*, LPM, Company lawyer 01/2020.

– Legal service portfolio management

Portfolio management is a term used in IT (ITIL Service Portfolio Management), in finance (Investment Portfolio Management) or also in branding (Product Portfolio Management) to establish the optimal balance between investments and value contribution for the company: Legal services are not seen as separate projects, but as integral components of a uniform service portfolio.

It complements traditional legal project management by also enabling the status of legal services to be tracked throughout their lifecycle. In particular, Legal Service Portfolio Management enables the investment in specific legal services provided to the business to be tracked throughout their lifecycle and works with other service management processes to ensure that the appropriate returns are achieved[11].

"I started with Legal Tech and the Swiss Legal Technology Conference, but very soon saw that the focus on legal topics was too small (for me). S. I came across the topics of digitalization around Smart Cities as early as 2017/2018. This includes e.g. mobility, logistics, education + work, participation + communication, health, smart grids + energy. In my view, these are much broader and also more exciting topics than pure legal or legal tech.

Law is always involved, too – the keyword is "embedded law" – but it plays a subordinate role. In my view, this is the right positioning – to be actively involved in projects in order to move digitization forward together. The Davos Digital Forum, which I founded in 2018, is a think tank that covers far more traditional legal topics. The goal is to make the topics of digitalization, with a focus on smart cities/ smart villages, understandable for everyone using real 'hands-on' workshops. In other words, solutions to problems are demonstrated, providing suggestions for implementation. When you deal with topics that go beyond traditional jurisprudence, you broaden your background and suddenly see more light at the end of the tunnel. As a result, we only achieve new challenging goals when we work together with different people and professions."

Petra Arends-Paltzer, Davos, Switzerland[12]

– Legal design thinking

Originally developed in the 1960s by engineers as a method for creative product development, design thinking has also been used since the 1990s as a management method for solving various complex problems in business and society. Since the 2000s at the latest, Design Thinking has also been used for innovations in the service sector. There are now a large number of design thinking training programs; the most prominent of these include the d.school at Stanford University and, in Ger-

---

11 *Ignaz Füsgen*, Legal Service Portfolio Management, Legal Revolutionary from 24.2.2021.
12 Read the full interview on the CLP blog.

man-speaking countries, the Hasso Plattner Institute. Design Thinking thus has a very broad field of application and is used to develop innovations and improvements of all kinds. Legal Design refers to the application of two Design Thinking methods to legal issues such as the drafting of contracts or regulations. Design Thinking, also called Design Doing or simply Design, describes certain methods for the development of services or products.

This allows us to develop and train skills that most of us were neither born with nor taught in legal training and that are usually neglected in everyday legal work. These include a strong focus on the perspective of the users of legal services or work products, working in multidisciplinary teams, developing innovative and creative solutions, and dealing with not-yet-perfect solutions (or even failure) in an iterative work process.

"Legal Design is an innovation approach that uses frameworks and methods, especially from the field of design, to solve challenges with legal relevance in a holistic and user-centered way. With Legal Design, innovation processes in the legal field can be structured and targeted. This results in innovative digital as well as analog products, services, processes, systems and environments that are truly needed and willingly used. An important role here is to move quickly from planning to doing and trying out. At this point, many people limit themselves to the design thinking process. For me, however, legal design means using the whole range of suitable design approaches, such as human-centered design, behavioral design, business process modeling, and so on. The goal is to find out where and how these can best be applied in the legal field. My entry into the Design Thinking program at the Hasso Plattner Institute was in principle also a very practical introduction to the topic of legal design. The course is designed in such a way that you learn along the work on real projects right from the start. At the time, my team happened to have a Legal Design Challenge – even though the term 'legal design' didn't exist at the time: It was about improving Europe-wide cooperation between lawyers and NGOs in the area of asylum law.

But I didn't really realize what a crucial role design could play in the legal sector until I spent some time in my role as a design thinker at SAP. I had actually thought that my decision for legal design would be a decision against the legal industry. When the topic of legal tech suddenly became more and more important, I knew that user-centered software design would also play a major role there. That this would give me the opportunity to combine my skills in law, design and tech in a targeted way. In parallel, the Legal Design Lab was founded at Stanford and the first Legal Design Summit was convened in Helsinki. I was not the only one who had taken this path. With that, the thing finally had a name: Legal Design. Today, I use legal design primarily to develop new products and services, either for clients or together with clients and users. A classic example is the re-design of a legal document, such as an NDA or a guideline. The form, content, and presentation of documents are rethought, redesigned, tested, and further developed so that they are more accessible, better understood, and more effective. The use of legal design for the conception of software, apps or websites is also very common. I attach great importance to designing the innovation process individually for each customer instead of always reeling off the same program. I try to get my customers to work as user-centered as possible, even if the inhibition threshold seems to be particularly high among lawyers. It is also important not to leave clients alone – for example with a great concept for a new product – but to always think about the implementation. Our customers are mainly law firms and legal tech startups, and now and then also legal departments. What has surprised us is that we now also receive inquiries from companies outside the legal industry that are not getting anywhere with their law firms. They then want us to help them redesign the legal elements that their customers come into contact with, such as the process of signing a contract, so that they are as user-friendly as the rest of the user experience. The fact that I am a lawyer is important in that I can understand the particular challenges of the legal sector in general and our clients in particular in a completely different way than an innovation consultant without legal knowledge. My legal background also helps me to communicate with customers more at eye level. In the area of automation, my being a lawyer plays a role especially when it comes to ensuring that the legal logic that is to be mapped technically is stored correctly. With my co-founder Alisha Andert and my co-founder Joaquín Santuber, I have two very competent and interesting people at my side who bring a similarly complex skillset of legal, design and tech expertise. This is quite rare to find at the moment and I really enjoy working with the two of them. In addition, we have a top network of specialist lawyers, designers and developers, whom we call in as needed to realize projects. Working in interdisciplinary teams is a natural part of our work. In addition, there is a well-connected, global community of legal designers with whom we regularly exchange ideas."

Lina Krawietz, Legal Designer, Berlin[13]

- **Project management**

Of course, in law firms as in any other company, there are also projects on the topics of

- Business Development
  e.g. the development of a new target group, the Austrian market or the implementation of the DSGVO
- Marketing
  e.g. the revision of the website or the rewriting of client communication
- Human Resources Development
  e.g. the introduction of flexitime or the development of job descriptions

and other areas. Setting these up, taking responsibility for them, driving them forward, and finally completing and evaluating them properly is just as much a challenge in law firms as it is in any other company. In most cases, external service providers are called in, who have to be supported accordingly, require additional work and need a contact person. This does not always work optimally. This may be due to the fact that these projects do not have top priority.

In addition, law firm owners are certainly not very experienced in dealing with project management[14]. When is a project a project and when does it need to be managed?

13 Read the full interview on the CLP blog.

14 Foitzik, "Projektmanagement in Kanzleien", Kanzleimarketing.de from 21.2.2018.

- **Crisis management**

The distinctive feature is that legal services for problem solving are requested almost exclusively in crisis and conflict situations.

The client is usually in a "state of emergency" that threatens him "existentially". It makes no difference at all whether his private life is falling to pieces, his employment relationship as the basis of his livelihood has broken down, he is threatened with imprisonment or his company has slid into a financial fiasco. You don't go to a lawyer because you're doing well, but so that you can eventually do well again.

Biologically correct, humans generally react to these situations with "fight" or "flight". In any case, however, their rational and strategic thinking is limited. At the same time, at this moment they must visualize a solution to the conflict that is suitable for them, a way out of the crisis, a meaningful change in their situation: After all, you need a clear work order from them with the mandate. Any psychologist would declare this a "mission impossible". For you – for us – it is our daily bread.

First and foremost, special crisis management is required
- such as de-escalation,
- sensitive communication,
- building trust and security, but also
- guidance and instruction for mastering the crisis.

---

i

So, there are
1. special communication techniques required to reach the client at all. At the same time,
2. the basis for trusting cooperation must be created: a personal relationship between lawyer and client must develop. And
3. it is important to establish a goal/vision for the future ideal state and to accompany the client through this process of change with all its ups and downs.

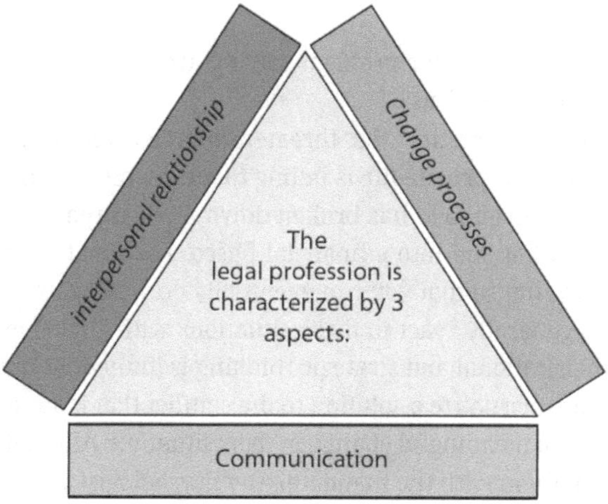

The different fields of activity of the lawyer, © Dr. Geertje Tutschka

Many of my lawyer colleagues expect to receive simple "instructions for use" for the "10 golden client questions" in our seminars, in order to be able to process every mandate efficiently and quickly from now on. No more seemingly endless client discussions about (apparent) trivialities. No more emotions and psycho-management in the office, but nice, clean, relevant facts. A dream for every lawyer.

Unfortunately, it doesn't work that way.

Nonetheless, day-to-day law firm operations can use a lot more efficiency and professionalism when dealing with clients in these types of crisis situations.

1. For effective communication, it is important to visualize its basic patterns

Communication is interaction

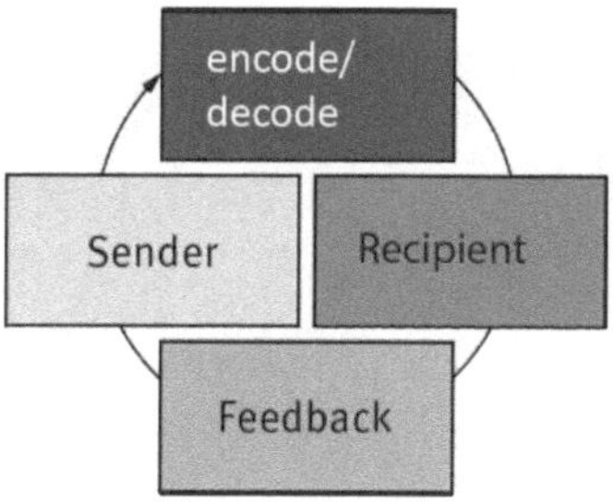

Communication, © Dr. Geertje Tutschka

A distinction must be made between
- "saying" and "meaning" for the **sender** and
- "hearing" and "understanding" for the **recipient.**

before the receiver in turn becomes the sender to respond (feedback).

This is all complex. However, it can be trained for professional use and consciously controlled with proven and scientifically studied techniques (such as mirroring, active listening, provocation, etc.).

2. Relationship building with the client usually happens through the initial meeting and the subsequent engagement of the lawyer. Every lawyer knows how sensitive this initial phase is for new clients. Here, professional client communication and accompanying marketing can support just as effectively as specially trained employees and defined processes.
3. Change processes also follow certain patterns and procedures, knowledge of which helps lawyers to classify the client's situation and current needs. This makes it possible to react appropriately and precisely to the situation. Surprising overreactions and excessive actions on the part of the client are avoided. The client feels met, trusted and satisfied.

According to Kurt Lewin, crises follow the pattern "Freeze-Unfreeze-Refreeze". He assumes that the normal state is characterized by stability and calm (like a solid block of ice: "freeze"). In contrast, the crisis is characterized by the dissolution of intact relationships, chaos and emotionality (just as the state of aggregation is changed during thawing: "unfreeze"). Before the situation stabilizes again (as in refreezing in a different form: "Refreeze").

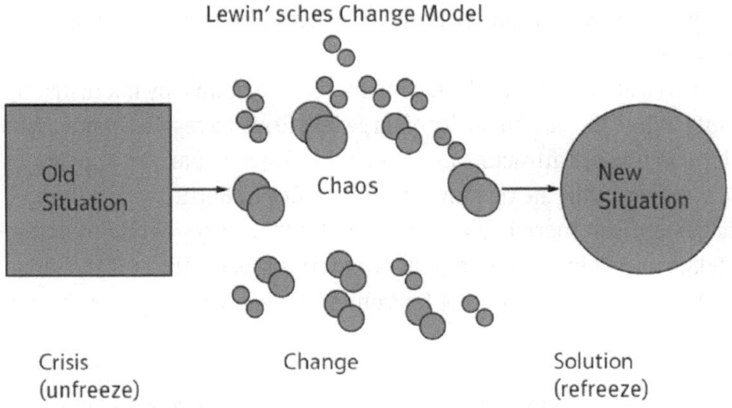

Change Model of Lewin, © Dr. Geertje Tutschka

Clients come to the lawyer in the phase of change, of chaos. The lawyer should "ward off", "repair", "shape" change and be a companion, confidant and sovereign partner. His mandate is not only determined by the field of law, but also by the individual situation of the client and in particular by where exactly in this process of change the client is at the moment. For us lawyers, this model is applicable both to the mandate period and to the individual proceedings (court or administrative proceedings), whereby the structures differ only minimally, just as they do in the various fields of law. In my many years of work with change processes, I have made the experience that a fourth small but significant section must be added: at the end of the chaos shortly before the problem is solved, there is always a "vacuum". Comparable to the "silent second" before an avalanche, a "holding of breath" takes place, energy is drawn off, as if the problem solution is staging its perfect appearance. What is this important for? If the client is already in this vacuum when he comes to the lawyer, he can only intervene in a securing way, but no longer in a formative way.

But how does crisis management work in the law firm?

Large law firms have made headlines in the pandemic like this:

Taylor Wessing is laying off nearly 100 academic staff with honors degrees in order to cut costs, even though last year it was publicly stated that their comparatively high pay was justified by the fact that these employees are an important pillar for attracting future high potentials.
To reduce costs, *Norton Rose Fullbright* is using its Flex program – as it did during the 2008 financial crisis – to motivate employees to work part-time and forego pay, even though the program was originally designed for staff development and a better work-life balance.

Freshfields freezes all salaries until 2021; others set an example by not distributing partner profits. While the vast majority of large law firms have at least put a hiring freeze in place, *Dentons* is attracting attention with five new partner appointees and *Graf von Westphalen* with the opening of a new office in Berlin.

Crisis management can therefore be carried out either way – while some are trying to consolidate purely in terms of numbers, others are using the crisis to set an example in the highly competitive market for young lawyers with employer branding.

Done. But also calculated? Whether these measures represent good crisis management by business standards will probably remain a secret of those involved, who hopefully included the now higher costs of the research work by the lawyers in their calculations, as well as the subsequent training costs for new staff. In any case, these measures – whether consciously or unconsciously – were a form of crisis communication, both externally and internally. And this is the supreme discipline of successful leadership. When security and stability decrease in every conceivable respect in a crisis situation, the teams usually pull together to master the situation together. In the Corona crisis, too, we have experienced various expressions of solidarity and perhaps feel more connected to our family and friends in some respects than we did at times when we could have met with them without hindrance. At the same time, there is a growing longing and need for leadership – leadership that leads responsibly and purposefully out of the crisis. Responsibility should be assumed above all for the people who entrust themselves to this leadership.

Recognized leadership assessments have examined certain personality types to determine how they react as leaders in the event of a crisis – i.e., under great stress – and how they assume this responsibility. *Hogan Assessment*, for example, uses both the function of self-assessment and the reputation we have built up towards others for this purpose. Surprisingly, it was found that not everyone primarily seeks closeness to others in crisis situations and certainly does not want to assume the necessary responsibility for others as a leader.

Instead, three critical behaviour patterns were identified:

The manager
1. Removes and/or isolates him/herself from the team,
2. seeks confrontation with individual team members, or
3. joins the team and forms bilateral alliances to control his/her own fears.

At the same time, these leaders often demonstrate strength of character in day-to-day business and are characterized by a broad following.

Especially in the first case, for example, these personalities often shine in everyday life as particularly conscientious and independent and are perceived as energetic communicators.

In crisis situations, on the other hand, their “jacket is closer than their pants” and they use their strengths primarily in their own interest and not in the interest of the team entrusted to them. Are you reminded of some of the crisis intervention and law firm management from above? Rightly so. Now such reduced information as the one mentioned above is certainly not the whole truth. Nor do such measures primarily reflect the crisis mode of individuals but were at best majority decisions necessarily supported by all.

And yet, as always in crisis situations, these measures and their communication represent a certain management culture. They may not necessarily be in line with the law firm vision and values presented on the firm's website, but they are all the more authentic. Crisis management and its sensitive communication is therefore the supreme discipline of successful law firm management, because it is here that the true values and entrepreneurial goals are expressed in an unadorned manner.

Ideally, the firm's values and the culture of the firm's management match those of its external image. This is relatively easy to feign in everyday business and even more so in economically stable times – in times of crisis such as these, distortions and frictions become obvious.

If the crisis interventions set and their communication do not match the external image and instead depict one of the three above-described critical leadership behaviors, the law firm will not only experience a massive loss of trust as an employer, but will also suffer severe damage in the trust-based legal consulting business.

How can this be prevented?

The importance of reflective crisis intervention and conscious crisis communication, even among law firm management, should have become clear to the vast majority of people. It is up to each individual to decide whether to set up an internal crisis team, call in professionals or at least start preparing a so-called emergency plan. In any case, the immediate aftermath of the crisis should be followed by a review of the firm's own leadership and a comparison with the firm's values.

And just as in business, crisis-proof and successful law firm management teams will have to be purposefully built and trained in the legal industry in the future. Personality tests, targeted team building, knowledge transfer and consciously applied development measures will play a greater role for the first time[15].

In fact, every change process, every "chaos" goes through seven individual process steps with regard to the client's personal state, his competence to make realistic decisions and personal development as well as changed perception and preferences:

---

15 *Dr. Tutschka,* Kanzleimanagement und Krisenkommunikation in Zeiten der Corona-Pandemie, Haufe.Recht from 29.4.2020.

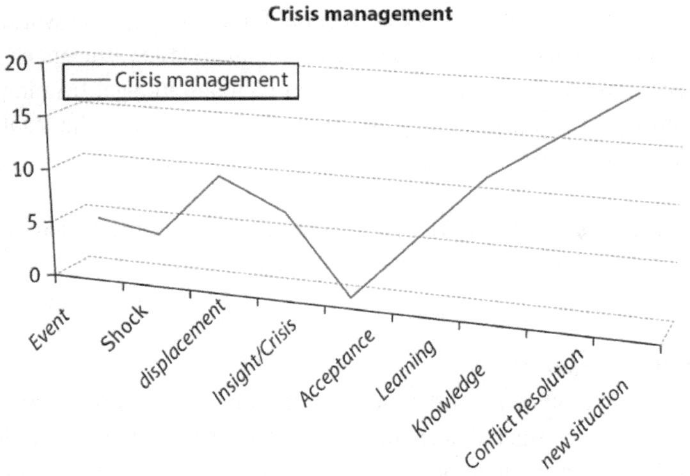

Crisis management according to Kostka/Mönch, © Dr. Geertje Tutschka

For the processing of the mandate, it makes a difference whether the client comes to the law firm at the time of the shock or already in the phase of crisis and acceptance. In the first case, he is usually not in a position to provide all the relevant facts. The displacement phase prevents him from doing so. The valley of deep crisis has not yet been reached. If the lawyer does not respond to this and provides more confidence-building measures here rather than demanding facts, the crisis situation is quickly projected onto the lawyer, who is declared the "scapegoat". For the client, however, this also means that he remains in the crisis situation and moves in a "feedback loop" back to the event/shock. He remains trapped in the process with no chance of resolving the conflict.

If, on the other hand, the client does not come to you until "the baby has dropped into the well" and he is already at the stage where he has come to terms with the sudden change, he will be able to support you as a lawyer much more easily and with greater commitment in the preparation of the mandate. Uncontrolled emotive outbursts are not to be expected (anymore). For many colleagues, these clients are the ones they like best. They lean back and concentrate on their actual work, only to be surprised to find that the client is "gone" again at the first opportunity. The colleague has failed to realize that at this point the client was no longer as open and grateful for an intensive client relationship as at the acute crisis point. Now the lawyer quickly becomes "interchangeable" and "arbitrary" if he does not specifically invest, for example, with holistic services and actively in building the client relationship. If they want their clients to become regulars and not just a flash in the pan, they need to build lasting client loyalty.

An in-depth understanding of such processes is essential for successful legal work. This guarantees not only satisfied clients, but also professional and thus efficient client management. However, since this has not yet been included in legal training any more than business management know-how, it remains the task of the legal profession to provide postgraduate training in this area[16].

It is therefore not surprising that, in addition to the law firm processes themselves, forms of mandate management are also being redeveloped:

- **Integrated Conflict Management**

In a further development of known conflict and arbitration processes, ADR processes, mediation and Smart Conflict Management, the conflict and its cause as well as the defined goal determine the method of conflict resolution in Integrated Dispute Management with the help of decision models, analytical tools, process risk analyses, Big Data-based forecasting tools and project management tools.

The advantages are obvious: it corresponds to the modern holistic approach to conflict resolution, is better suited to individual cases and creates the professional profile of the dispute manager, whose activities focus on strategy development and the coordination and monitoring of conflict management with the help of legal technology. The legal representation itself remains with the lawyers.

"Integrated Dispute Management is part of my career path and I will continually incorporate my experiences into this concept. But most of all, I hope it will be the impetus for a new discipline and, through the contributions of all who are passionate about it, create a new standard for dispute management and dispute resolution."

Dr. Johannes P. Willheim, JONES DAY, International Arbitration Attorney[17]

16 I recommend taking conflict and crisis management and communication courses specifically for the legal profession to optimize relevance and sustainability (such as those offered by me at CLP).
17 *Dietmar Dworschak*, Integrated Dispute Management, Anwalt aktuell 01/2021.

3. Business Development

Law firm development is still measured primarily in terms of revenue.

In Germany alone, the legal industry generates around 24.2 billion euros annually[18].

The total annual revenue of the 100 strongest business lawyers was US$114 billion in 2018 (10 billion higher than the total gross domestic product of Slovakia). In Germany, the total annual revenue of the 100 strongest law firms increased from 5.2 billion euros (2014) to 6.8 billion euros (2018)[19].

The 165,000 lawyers in Germany work in 62,000 law firms. Most of them are organized as civil law partnerships. The proportion of law firms with limited liability (Rechtsanwalts-GmbH) is stagnating; the proportion of partner firms with and without limited liability, on the other hand, has quadrupled. 65,000 lawyers, or one in three, are organized in the professional association of German lawyers (Deutscher Anwaltverein DAV). The Munich chamber still has the most members, followed by Frankfurt a.M. and Berlin. The total number of employees in the industry is 294,000. According to the Branchenbericht (industry Report) Sparkassen 2020, the credit default risk remains at a low level; the return on sales has increased significantly[20].

Rankings[21] measure the respective development of individual law firm revenues. It is worth taking a closer look:

At the top are the "Top 5" of the USA:

Kirkland Ellis	**4.155 Mill. dollars turnover**
Latham Watkins	3.768 Mill. dollars turnover
DLA Piper	3.112 Mill. dollars turnover
Baker McKenzie	2.920 Mill. dollars turnover
Dentons	2.900 Mill. dollars turnover

Top-Revenue Law Firms USA, October 2019, © Dr. Geertje Tutschka

18 Sam van Wijk, "Legal Tech – die Zukunft der Rechtsbranche" in politik-digital.de from 23.3.2017.
19 Wirtschaftskanzleien in Zahlen II, brandeins thema, p. 65.
20 Branchenbericht der Sparkassen 2020, p. 8.
21 Ranking as of October 2017.

Chicago-based Kirkland & Ellis has caught up in recent years and is the market leader with total revenues approaching $4.2 billion. It is also one of the world's leading companies in terms of revenue per lawyer employed – with each lawyer earning an average of USD 1.6 million last year. The core business of the legal giant is in the USA, where the company also employs the noticeably largest number of lawyers (i.e., 1,830 out of 2,598). In addition, the firm has offices only in China, Hong Kong, Germany, France and the United Kingdom. Kirkland & Ellis is currently representing Volkswagen and other carmakers in connection with the diesel scandal, as well as companies such as BP, Nike and Abbvie[22].
The so-called "Magic Circle", which designates the five major law firms based in London, includes Clifford Chance (8th), Allen & Overy (12th), Linklaters (13th), Freshfields Bruckhaus Deringer (16th) and Slaughter and May (72nd).

The Anglo-American-Chinese law firm Dentons is by far the world's largest law firm in terms of the number of lawyers it employs – but not in terms of total revenue. In terms of revenue, Dentons is only ranked fifth internationally. A relatively small law firm in terms of revenue, with a team of 8,862 lawyers, is the world's number two – the Chinese company Yingke.

1. Dentons: 10.977 lawyers (USA & China)
2. Yingke: 8.862 lawyers (China)
3. Baker McKenzie: 4.809 lawyers (USA)
4. DLA Piper: 3.894 lawyers (USA)
5. CMS (Germany)[23]

In comparison, the revenue figures of the large law firms in Germany (and Austria) are rather sobering. On the one hand, they reflect the respective ratio of the gross domestic product. On the other hand, however, they also reflect national regulations limiting the sector, the importance of legal advice for the respective economy, the revenue orientation of the law firms, and also the social understanding of the value of legal advice in general.

22 Christopher Wagner, "Die größten Anwaltskanzleien nach Umsatz" in Fachmagazin from 11.11.2020.

23 Ibid.

Freshfields Bruckhaus Deringer	**435,5 Mill. Euro Turnover (+2,6 % zum Vorjahr)**
CMS Hasche Sigle	343,6 Mill. Euro Turnover (+6,5 % compared to previous year)
Hengeler Mueller	271,7 Mill. Euro Turnover (+9,1 % compared to previous year)
Hogan Lovells	253,4 Mill. Euro Turnover (+15,6 % compared to previous year)
Noerr	231,5 Mill. Euro Turnover (+0,89 % compared to previous year)

Top-Revenue Law Firms Germany, October 2020, © Dr. Geertje Tutschka

Schönherr	**58,8 Mill. Euro Turnover (+3,0 % compared to previous year)**
Freshfields Bruckhaus Deringer	55,5 Mill. Euro Turnover
Wolf Theiss	55 Mill. Euro Turnover

Top-Revenue Law Firms Austria, October 2020, © Dr. Geertje Tutschka

It is worth noting that, for historical reasons, there is still a strict boundary demarcation between Germany and Austria in the European legal industry.

While the large law firms in Germany (especially those in Frankfurt) tend to be oriented towards the British, American and international markets, the large law firms in Austria (here in Vienna) tend to be oriented towards the Eastern European market. This leads to a situation where even in less large Austrian business law firms, work is traditionally done in English in order to do justice to the diversity of Eastern European languages. Also at many Eastern European universities, law is usually studied in English with a European connection. The overview also shows that in these different markets (Eastern Europe and Western Europe) large law firms can establish themselves to different degrees and that obviously very different competencies and strengths are required here.

In terms of productivity, measured by revenue per lawyer, Hengeler is the top ten law firm with the highest revenue, the only German firm to exceed the 900,000 euro mark. Among the British firms, Freshfields, with 854,000 euros per lawyer, leaves Clifford Chance, Linklaters and Allen & Overy well behind.

Specialized U. S. law firms with smaller German practices generate the most revenue per lawyer: Ten law firms with U. S. origins lead the ranking in terms of revenue per lawyer, with Hengeler in eleventh place and Freshfields in 14th. Sullivan & Cromwell holds first place with almost 1.2 million euros in revenue per lawyer. After all, 29 of the hundred law firms were unable to increase their UBT[24].

Economically speaking, Austrian business lawyers are doing extremely well, even if hourly rates like those in Germany are not achievable here due to the lack of large international law firms. Even during Corona, turnover increased by almost three percent. The total number of lawyers in the Austrian legal market increased by 2.4 percent last year – the strongest increase in more than a decade. Compared with Germany, however, the network of lawyers in Austria is still very thin. The country, which has a population of just under nine million, has just 6400 lawyers. By comparison, the 83 million citizens of the Federal Republic of Germany can consult more than 165,000 lawyers. In Germany, there is one lawyer for every 500 citizens; in Austria, the number is 1400.

One explanation for this is the country's lower economic strength. The Alpine Republic is home to far fewer corporations, especially those of international significance. This is still one of the main reasons why comparatively few foreign law firms, especially the highly profitable ones, have settled here. One exception is the "Magic Circle" law firm Freshfields Bruckhaus Deringer. Meanwhile, experts pinpoint another reason to the very conservative, male-dominated management ranks. Although half of the trainee lawyers are female, they do not make it in the legal market. The conservative structure is blamed for this: the admission costs are a multiple of those in Germany, and there is no provision for reductions during family time. Female partners are also not found in the largest law firms. They are more likely to be found in the medium-sized firms or to successfully set up their own law firm.

What is interesting at this point is how much the gap in sales figures is already widening among the top 5 in Germany.

24 Claudia Tödtmann, "Die umsatzstärksten Kanzleien in Deutschland" in blog.wiwi.de from 1.10.2020.

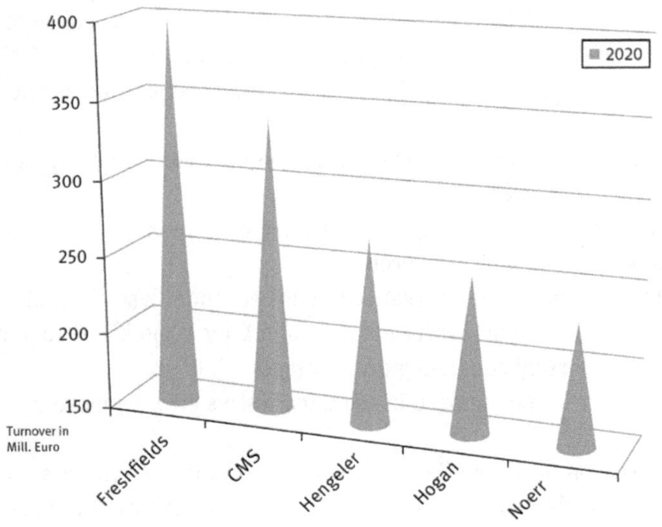

Comparison of the revenue strength of law firms Germany, October 2020, © Dr. Geertje Tutschka

However, it is no less exciting to see how different the respective growth in sales is. So, there may be some changes here in the coming years, even at national level.

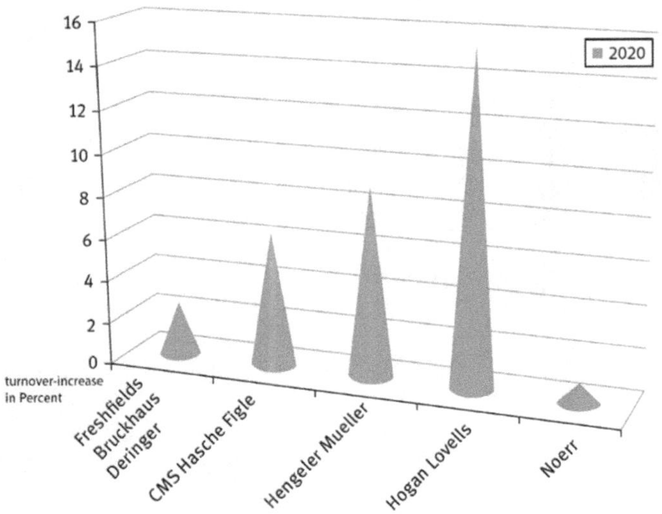

Comparison of revenue growth of law firms Germany, 2017, © Dr. Geertje Tutschka

The number of lawyers admitted to the German Bar declined for the first time in 2017 by 0.2 percent to 163,436.

However, German commercial law firms as a whole (not just the top 5) have recorded an average increase in turnover of 7 %[25]. Law firms without notaries' offices have generated approx. 3 % more turnover[26] per year, while notaries' offices have increased by only 2 %.

This may be due to the fact that both the top rate and the average hourly rate for legal advice are higher than ever before[27].

So the deal slump in the Corona spring of 2020 passed quickly in law firms: labor and insolvency law boomed thanks to Corona.

Only 22 of the 100 law firms therefore reduced their headcount last year. All of the top ten increased their headcount, with Heuking Kühn Lüer Wojtek and Taylor Wessing even increasing theirs by double-digit percentages.

In the aggregate of the top one hundred in sales, team sizes grew by more than six percent.

A multi-year comparison of the market as a whole, shows that an increase in the number of professionals first correlates with a – temporary – reduction in revenue per lawyer. In the long run, however, the figures show higher productivity in law firms with high turnover. The correlation between staff and productivity growth is significant[28].

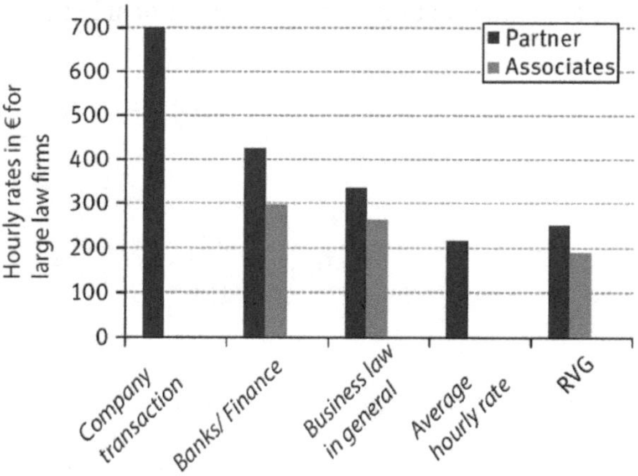

Ratio of hourly rates[29], © Dr. Geertje Tutschka

25 Branchenbericht der Sparkassen 2020, p. 2.

26 Branchenbericht der Sparkassen 2020, p. 2.

27 Statistical Yearbook of the Legal Profession 2017/2018 of the Soldan Institute.

28 Claudia Tödtmann, "Die umsatzstärksten Kanzleien in Deutschland" in blog.wiwi.de from 1.10.2020.

29 JUVE Rechtsmarkt 2016.

for comparison the RVG:
- Extrajudicial advice/expert opinion € 250 Initial
- consumer advice € 190.

On the other hand, the increasing number of specialist attorney admissions:

There are now 24 different specialist lawyer titles within the scope of § 43c BRAO in conjunction with the FAO, with specialist lawyers for labor, family and tax law being by far the most frequently used. With 53,600 specialist lawyer admissions for 42,900 specialist lawyers (one can hold up to three titles at the same time), every third lawyer now has such a specialization. And of these, more than 2/3 were able to increase their turnover after acquiring the title of specialist lawyer. The specialist lawyer for tax law increased his turnover the most with an average of 47 %[30].

However, the area of law also plays an important role:

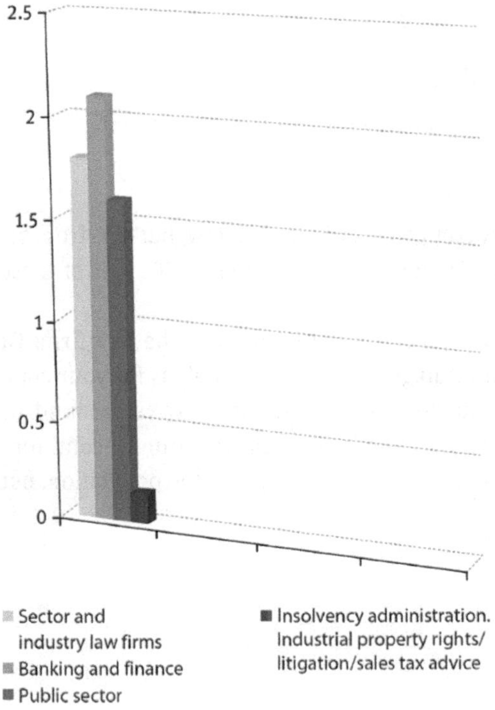

Ratio of sales by legal area[31], © Dr. Geertje Tutschka

30 Soldan Insight, 30.9.2014.
31 Branchenbericht der Sparkassen 2020, p. 21.

Sector and industry law firms thus generate the largest turnover, along with law firms for banking and finance, with turnover per lawyer of €456,000 and €715,000 per year, respectively.

However, if we look at the basic distribution of mandates among the various sectors, the overwhelming share of mandates comes from the low-revenue consumer sector:

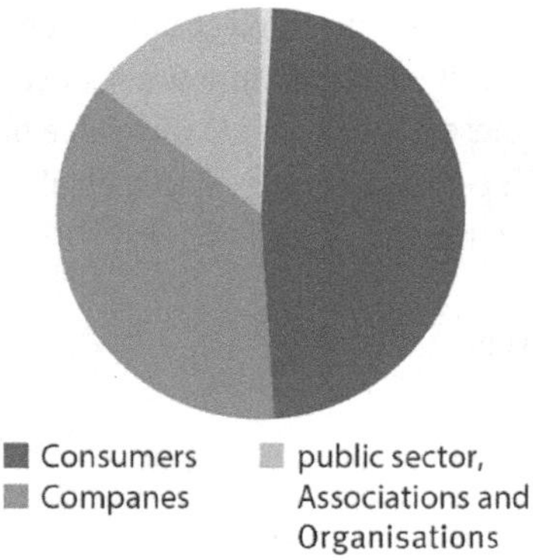

Mandate structure[32], © Dr. Geertje Tutschka

The consumer mandates come mainly from civil and criminal law, but also from social, administrative and tax law. It is also interesting to note that 50–70 % of these clients are regular clients[33].

Another aspect for business development is the location of the law firm. Of course, it makes a difference for your strategic orientation as well as for your competition and thus your marketing whether you are the only lawyer around or whether you have to compete with a large number of colleagues. Munich continues to have not only the largest density of lawyers in comparison to the population, but also the most lawyers overall.

32 Soldan Institut Insights, 1.6.2016.

33 Branchenbericht der Sparkassen 2020, p. 4.

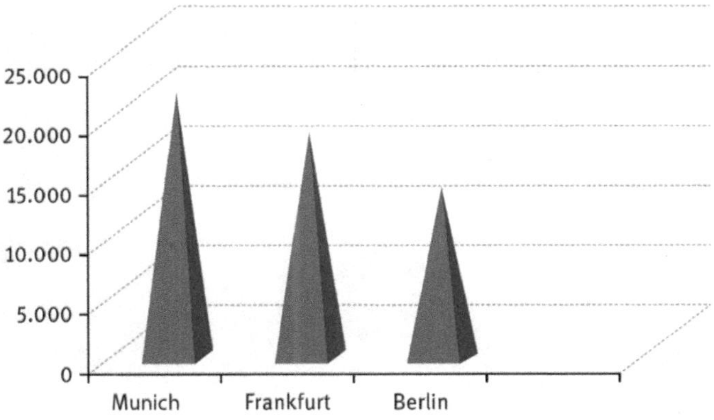

Lawyers by regions[34], © Dr. Geertje Tutschka

An interesting detail at this point might be that the whole of Austria has less than a quarter of the number of lawyers working in Munich. However, in a comparison of the top law firms in terms of revenue (see above), they generate only one eighth of the top German law firms and were thus only half as strong in terms of revenue.

This is particularly interesting because the proximity to the German legal system – even if the pitfall is in the details –, the local proximity but also the German mother tongue in combination with the possibilities of the professional freedom of movement of the European Union Austria could represent an exciting expansion of the German legal industry.

However, I would like to point out two peculiarities at this point:

The Austrian legal industry is (perceived) light years

- **ahead** in the introduction and everyday use of electronic legal transactions, which have been running smoothly between authorities, courts and lawyers for more than a decade.
- **behind** in gender equality, which is why the proportion of female lawyers is less than one-third despite balanced numbers of JUS majors[35] of the German one.

34 Branchenbericht der Sparkassen 2020, p. 8.
35 JUS is the faculty of law/legal studies at universities.

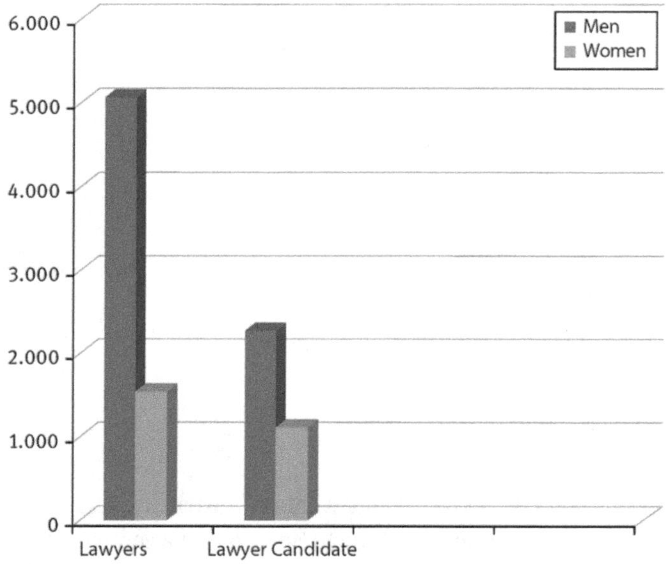

Lawyers in Austria 2020[36], © Dr. Geertje Tutschka

So regardless of your qualifications and location, your gender is now (unfortunately) also an aspect to be considered in business development.

The industry appears to be stable: The return on sales has been above 30 % since 2015 and thus ranks at a very high level compared to other industries. Specialty and boutique law firms in particular recorded very strong revenue growth and describe their earnings situation as very good[37]. Overall, the legal sector can be described as economically stable.

The probability of insolvency has declined and is well below the average for all sectors[38], with it being significantly lower in the west of Germany at 0.51 % than in the east at 0.86 %. For example, there were only two credit losses in Hamburg compared with ten in Brandenburg in 2016.

---

36 Statistics of ÖRAK as of 31.12.2020.

37 Branchenbericht der Sparkassen 2020, p. 11.

38 Branchenbericht der Sparkassen 2020, p. 2.

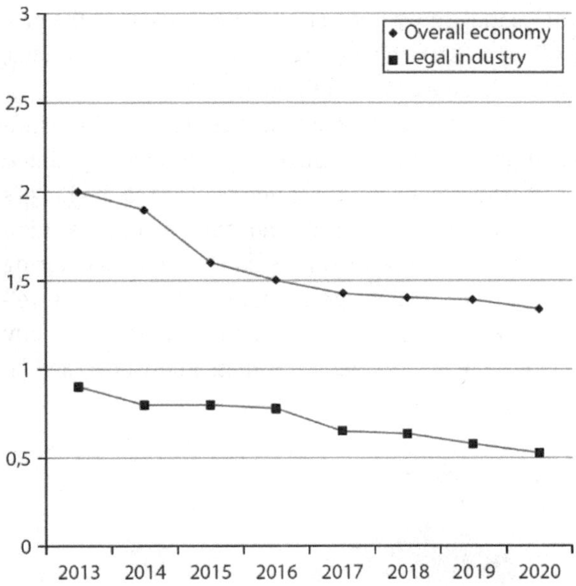

Creditreform – Risk – Indicator[39], © Dr. Geertje Tutschka

In total, there are just under 59,000 law firms and notary's offices in Germany.

- 2 % generate 40 % of the total turnover of the sector
- 3 % generate an annual turnover of € 250,000–2 million
- 70 % generate an annual turnover of up to € 250,000
- 25 % (approx. 15,000 individual law firms) only generate an average annual turnover of € 32,803[40].

In this context, it should be borne in mind that the imputed salary for the law firm owner can be assumed to be approx. 5 % and is thus in line with the average for the service sector[41]. At the same time, the starting salaries for salaried predicate lawyers in large law firms are around € 120,000. If you are a newcomer to the profession and are looking for the best possible entry-level constellation, you should definitely have tested your personal market value beforehand (at least on the basis of your exam results).

39 Creditreform 2020, ibid.

40 Branchenbericht der Sparkassen 2020, p. 8.

41 Branchenbericht der Sparkassen 2020, p. 12.

The following overview also shows that only a quarter of all newcomers to the profession actually start out as law firm owners. In addition to financial considerations, gaining experience in the "law firm business" may also play a role.

The much-discussed reform of the legal clerkship in this context has its justification: It can be informative and professionally orientating to become acquainted with all aspects of legal activities, from the public prosecutor's office to the judge's and lawyer's profession to the legal office. However, it is not sufficient preparation for founding a law firm, even if you work in law firms as much as possible during this time. This also applies to the five-year trainee program in Austria, which is followed by the bar exam: here, too, the five-year training with the lawyer covers only aspects related to the subject and the mandate and no business know-how, no leadership development, no marketing or the like.

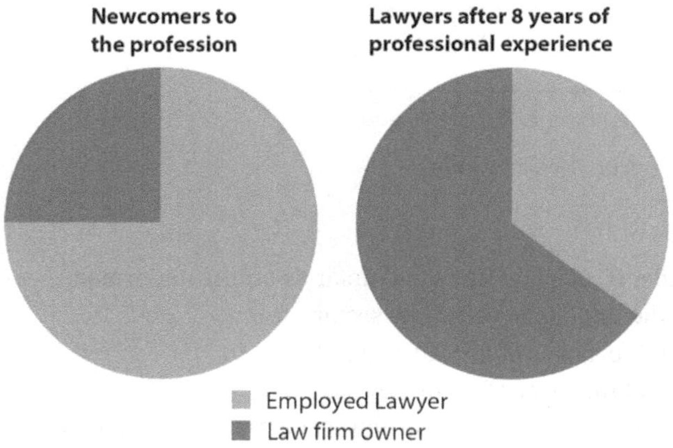

Relationship between salaried lawyers and founders of law firms[42], © Dr. Geertje Tutschka

Another important aspect of business development is the question of whether to start out as a single lawyer or as part of a partnership. As already mentioned above, the turnover of individual law firms is significantly lower, which is mainly due to a lack of specialization but also to inefficient law firm management. Resource sharing, mutual representation, but also the added value of diverse decision-making teams are the decisive plus points for the partner law firm.

42 Branchenbericht der Sparkassen 2020, p. 6.

Ratio of individual attorneys and Law firms with several partners

Ratio of individual lawyers and law firms with several partners[43], © Dr. Tutschka

But what is the forecast? Is specialization the "must have" for your business development? So is it worthwhile to acquire one of the prioritized specialist lawyer titles, such as specialist lawyer for labor law, in order to be one of the 2/3 lawyers who increase turnover?

A much more intensive look at the numbers is needed here:

While court proceedings are generally on the increase, they have decreased in the area of labor law, which can be attributed to the improved situation on the labor market. However, proceedings relating to Hartz IV have increased significantly[44]. The increase in court proceedings, on the other hand, is clearly reflected in family cases, which makes becoming a specialist lawyer for family law much more attractive.

With this starting position, it can be strategically much more effective from the point of view of business development to focus on less overcrowded areas, such as the recently established specialist lawyer for migration law, or on developing areas of law that do not yet have a specialist lawyer title at all, such as

- the rights of ownership and use on the Internet forced by the implementation of the new Data Protection Directive
- expatriate and assignment law, which has been a rather insignificant part of labor law up to now, will develop into an independent area of law due to the increasing globalization and growing importance of the assignment of employees

43 Branchenbericht der Sparkassen 2020,

44 Branchenbericht der Sparkassen Deutschland 2020, S. 9.

- the right of victims
- the law of associations and NGOs for the rapidly growing non-profit sector or
- specializing in investing in cryptocurrency (such as Bitcoin) as well as its tax treatment[45].

According to observers in the industry, however, the specialist attorneys' practices for traffic law, inheritance law and landlord and tenant law will also develop[46].

For business reasons, it can make sense to build up these new business areas with temporary support, for example with Lawyer on Demand, who have so far tended to be used for periods of downtime as interim. In addition to low personnel costs compared to permanent employment, the law firm retains sufficient flexibility to be able to react to market changes at short notice. Another aspect that should not be underestimated is the "helicopter view" of these high potentials, who usually bring relevant and comprehensive experience from a multitude of assignments in the business field and thus new ideas and a breath of fresh air into well-worn structures and thought patterns. Ultimately, the Lawyer on Demand scores with a large network and the potential to bring clients with them. Recruiters such as Xenion have already adapted to the special market situation of legals and explicitly place Lawyer on Demand with companies and law firms.

"In a time of transformation and digitalization in the legal workforce, the use of Lawyers on Demand offers flexible and tailored solutions for projects or to reinforce legal teams during downtime for both companies and law firms. Talented Lawyer on Demand can bring their relevant experience from various assignments and new perspectives from the outside. At the same time, as a Lawyer on Demand, a lawyer can build a balanced portfolio for the next step in their career as well as a strong, professional network."

Lawyer Elisabeth Gawrych, Lawyer on Demand, Wülfrath

However, business development can also consist of the formation of strategically favorable alliances. There is also discussion about whether the possibility of merging with other professions should be further softened in order to be able to guarantee holistic project work in the sense of agile teams. Only 31 % welcome the decision of the Federal Constitutional Court that lawyers can now join forces with pharmacists and doctors. According to the Soldan Institute, however, this inhibition threshold will disappear with the old generation of lawyers[47].

45 There is a huge demand for experts here right now for investor events and articles.
46 Anwaltsblatt online, 23.3.2016.
47 Soldan Insight, 4.2.2016.

Another question will be to what extent the admission of so-called Alternative Business Structures (ABS) in the German legal services market will at least partially abolish the lawyer monopoly and attract numerous new financially strong players into the market. Traditional financial investors such as insurance companies or banks could then acquire shares in law firms[48].

The further entry of auditing firms into the legal market, which recently increased the pressure on commercial law firms enormously, should not be feared, however: The new Abschlussprüfungsreformgesetz (Audit Reform Act) now ends long-standing client relationships after ten years[49].

Business Development bleibt einer der wichtigsten Bereiche für Kanzleien. Allerdings geht es dabei nicht nur um das Erschließen neue Geschäftsfelder. Sondern ebenso um die Optimierung der vorhandenen Mandantenstruktur. Was heißt das?

As in every company, there are also clients in law firms who generate a certain basic turnover for the law firm with large orders or a large number of the same orders. It is not only the car dealership or the expert who regularly cooperates with the law firm in traffic accident cases or the medium-sized company which uses the law firm with a framework agreement more or less as an external legal department. It is also about individual mandates, which generated an enormous increase in turnover or bring potential for follow-up mandates. These so-called A-clients can, for example, be door openers for guilds and professional associations, but also act as ambassadors at events[50].

However, very few law firms regularly evaluate their client structure in order to filter out these A-clients and make greater use of them.

In the economy the so-called Pareto principle[51] is already used for this purpose for a long time: According to this, 20 % of the clients usually bring in 80 % of the revenue. If one thus focuses on these 20 % with its strategic adjustment, its marketing and customer connection strategies, one obtains the greatest possible turnover increase.

---

48 Der Rechtsdienstleistungsmarkt 2030, p. 18, Deutscher Anwaltverein, Prognos.

49 JUVE online Nachrichten 11.7.2016.

50 Hamtschek "Prädikat Empfehlenswert – Die A-Mandanten als Türöffner" in Kanzleimarketing.de from 28.1.2018.

51 Vilfredo Pareto (1848–1923) lived in France, Italy and Switzerland. He developed his Pareto principle for increasing efficiency after he noticed as an economist for a bank that 80 % of the bank's turnover was generated by 20 % of its customers.

Pareto Principle

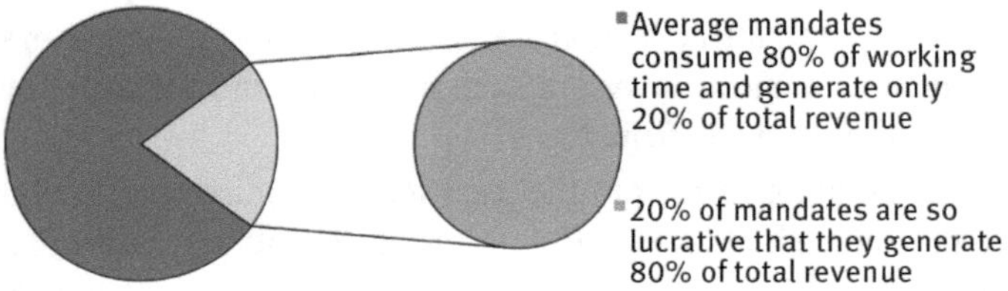

Ratio of sales and customers according to the Pareto principle, © Dr. Geertje Tutschka

Business development must therefore take place both externally and internally.

But it can also mean minimizing costs, bundling resources and standardizing quality. In the following, the importance of accounting and controlling, but also of quality management and compliance, will therefore be discussed once again.

4. Accounting, Controlling, QM and Compliance

The review of the lawyer's activities should be conducted from two perspectives.

On the one hand, quality control of legal services is indispensable. On the other hand, there should also be regular cost control:

Quality control is also an ongoing task in the law firm. Since lawyers market a service, the quality of their product must be checked according to various aspects.

Firstly, the **legal quality of the service** must be guaranteed. The legal advice must be correct. However, this is far from sufficient. The service must be provided in a timely manner. The best brief is worthless if it is not submitted on time. In addition, clients do not like to wait. They want their problem to be solved quickly. Advice is only useful to the client if he can understand it. Technical jargon does not serve the client. If the client cannot understand his lawyer's advice, then there is a risk that he will not follow his lawyer's advice simply because of the lack of understanding or misunderstanding. Ultimately, what matters is that the legal service helps the client achieve his or her goal. This may sound simplistic. But in fact, in practice, this is hardly ever the case in a discussion with the client. Why? Lawyers are simply not trained to do this. The purely technical university education leads to the accumulation of vast amounts of knowledge among students and later lawyers. A by-product of this training is the ability to procure and select according to relevance, as well as the ability to think abstractly. Since, due to the progress of digitalization and the Internet, any knowledge can now be accessed anytime and anywhere, legal education is more than obsolete. Thus, the former by-product is upgraded and represents the actual capital of the trained lawyers.

For later success in the profession, however, communication, presentation and performance skills are also required. This is not something that future lawyers bring with them without further ado. Many learn this laboriously in the course of their professional life. However, a profound education could support them enormously. Therefore, in recent years, **mediation training**, which includes a lot of negotiation skills, but also proper listening and questioning, has experienced a real boom, especially among fully trained lawyers who have already been in the profession for several years. Today even special Coaching training courses are offered only for lawyers, which are to help these to develop the crucial qualities in the lawyer occupation. It is absolutely incomprehensible why the state still declares professional training to be an absolute must for purely legal training but tolerates laypersons when it comes to communication skills. Or would you like to be operated on by a surgeon who has acquired medical knowledge in theory but has not learned to hold a scalpel?

And finally: An important, simple, but in practice often ignored control instrument is the critical reading of one's own written statements before they are signed. In larger law firms, **quality control of content** is usually established by submitting larger documents such as pleadings and draft contracts to a colleague for review and correction. The control of the external form and the comprehensibility of documents can also be assigned to non-lawyer employees of the law firm. If one's own employees cannot understand the text written by a lawyer, then in case of doubt the client will not be able to either. It is more difficult to check and evaluate the behavior of lawyers during negotiations, discussions or in the courtroom. A colleague from one's own law firm, who is not responsible for conducting the negotiations, can provide valuable advice. But investing in an external negotiation expert is also worthwhile. In good law firms, even the youngest lawyer has the right to propose changes, regardless of whether the draft comes from a young associate or the most senior partner. What matters is the quality of the work. Pride of authorship is written in small letters.

Quality certificates are available based on regular audits within the framework of **ISO or law firm-specific certificates.**

In a law firm, recurring activities, so-called processes, take place on a daily basis. For example, incoming mail and its further processing. These processes within the law firm can be standardized to ensure consistently high quality without neglecting the individual aspect of the case. The workflows are laid down in a special manual. These internal processes are regularly audited and certified by independent companies.

This ensures that, from firm to firm but also from region to region, the process remains independent of staff changes while maintaining the same quality.

A QM standard generally states which requirements the management of a company must meet in order to comply with a certain standard in the implementation of quality management. The standard can serve both as internal information for implementation within a company and as proof of certain standards to third parties.

According to APRAXA standards, QM has the following advantages for the client:

- Consistently high quality of the organizational processes
- Maximum efficiency through defined and clearly structured work processes
- Continuous development of the office processes
- Maximum possible minimization of sources of error
- More rapid processing of inquiries through optimized management of responsibilities
- Consistent quality standard in the event of staff changes or replacements
- Regular client surveys, thus continuous improvement of client satisfaction
- Systematic training and further education of all employees
- Certification according to DIN EN ISO 9001 for the area of law firm organization as a unique selling point
- Compliance with APRAXA quality requirements
- Certified law firms as well as law firms with a quality seal maintain a complaint management system and regularly survey their clients on their satisfaction. Independent service providers have determined a client satisfaction rate of over 95 %.
- More than 40 % of APRAXA lawyers from member firms are specialist lawyers in a particular field. This rate is already twice as high as the national average.
- Access to one of the largest German legal databases. This means that they always have access to the latest case law and specialist literature when working on cases.
- Connection to an IT system for electronic data exchange with legal protection insurance companies for rapid processing of coverage issues.

According to Hülskötter and Partners, QM offers the following advantages:

1. Clients increasingly use the Internet to find out about possible law firms that can represent them and almost inevitably come across the topic of quality management and certification of the same. When they then have the choice of whether to go for a law firm with or without a TÜV badge, in most cases the decision is made in favor of the law firm with the QM seal.
2. Especially the large insurance companies such as HUK or Allianz are increasingly pursuing a company policy of certified service providers. In other words, if listed law firms cannot demonstrate QM certification in accordance with DIN EN ISO 9001:2008, they will be left out when the insurance company awards new clients in the future.

Since in both cases a substantial economic damage is the consequence, the answer "Why quality management including certification?" seems to be a trivial matter. After all, the TÜV seal is being used more and more as a proven marketing tool.

An important criterion in the matter of quality management is the underlying manual, which precisely describes the principles of a law firm, which should guarantee the smooth processes[52].

When **controlling costs**, your business plan or business concept is the most important working basis. This business plan should be continuously adjusted, aligned and underpinned with new market experiences. It is also advisable to change to a quarterly review of the business plan or to a half-yearly planning. But regardless of this regular adjustment, you should take the time to continuously evaluate and implement the experiences of the past months. Have your accounting department and your tax advisor take a look at your cash position at certain intervals and prepare a prospective annual financial statement to check whether you are still on track. Take a close look at the figures for profit and loss, sales and expenses.

Examine monthly fluctuations and patterns and use your insight to align your billing and identify misinvestments and money guzzlers. Part ways now with unprofitable strategies, listless employees, and useless subscriptions and services. Do you need to adjust your accruals?

The verification can be done in four steps:
- Do I know all office expenses
- are all office expenses necessary
- can unused resources be converted into money if necessary
- can alternative providers save office expenses

---

52 Michael Hülskötter im advoblog fom 24.7.2018.

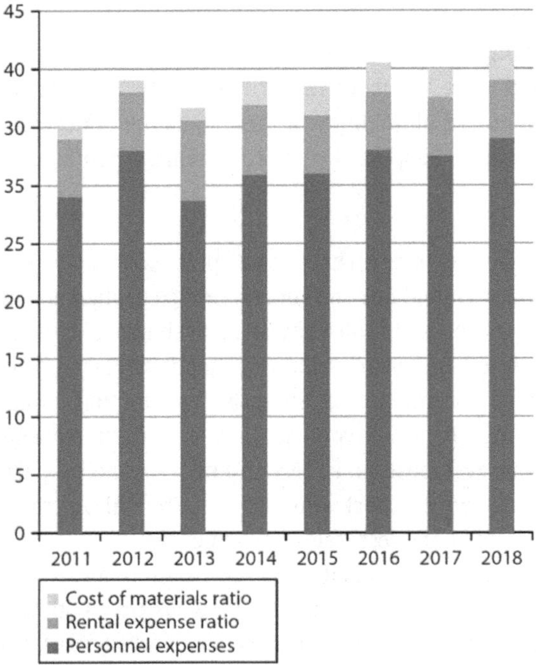

Costs in the office[53], © Dr. Geertje Tutschka

In general, personnel costs are by far the largest cost factor. Even staff savings and the introduction of legal technology do little to change this. The reason for this is the high cost of qualifications and the need for further training of employees and lawyers due to innovations in case law and legislation, but also the need for training in personnel and law firm management, as this is not taught in training, as well as technical training for the introduction of legal tech.

Of course, you have already created a precise cost table for your business concept. Now you need to check whether these costs are actually necessary to generate sales. In addition, a change of provider can lead to cost savings. Costs can also be reduced if premises are sublet (e.g. for seminars in the evening or at weekends), part-time employees work flexibly from home and do not need the writing desk, storage space, archives and materials are reduced[54]. In addition to the costs of office operations, you should also record your own employees' working hours. In order to track

53 Branchendienst der Sparkassen-Finanzgruppe, Status 01/2020.
54 Liker, "The Toyota Way to service excellence", p. 28 et seq.

down cost-intensive processes, you should document responsibilities, processes and working materials as well as the working time spent on specific activities[55]. This documentation can be used not only to streamline processes, but also to check what savings can be made, for example, by replacing these activities with technical aids. At the same time, this serves as the basis of the job description and "manual" for the induction of new employees.

Outsourcing measures, such as the outsourcing of certain routine and administrative tasks to external service providers (legal process outsourcing), are also an option for saving personnel costs.

However, the issue of **cash flow** also plays a role in the legal sector that should not be underestimated: remuneration for legal work is still mainly paid after the work has been completed and only after long periods of time. In addition, the loss of claims in the legal industry is higher than average. This may be due to hesitant and restrictive payments by (legal) insurance companies, but also to insolvencies. Strict cost control with cost-based fees and professional receivables management will be among the most important aspects in the future[56]. some cases, a significant reduction in the non-payment rate is also achieved with the commissioning of factoring service providers[57].

The Branchenbericht (Industry Report) Sparkassen 2020, attributes the reduction in the industry's overall cash flow rate to the significant increase in private withdrawals. At the same time, equity ratios have risen due to the retention of profits[58]. From a business perspective, there is no objection to private withdrawals and the retention of profits. If this is well considered and strategically prepared. In no case should this take place spontaneously "according to feeling" or because one defined the ratio for its lawyer salary (as a rule 5 % of the conversion) only as minimum. Instead, a conscious cash flow management should be pursued, e.g. by generating continuous sources of income beyond mandate terms (quarterly or monthly billing modes for framework agreements) or alternative sources of income (such as knowledge sales for trainings and seminars).

These decisions should not be made spontaneously or alone. Financial and tax managers belong on board, of course, as do owners and partners.

Should investments be made? Should payments be enforced this year or better postponed to next year? Have the budgets for further training and investments been exhausted? And have these investments already paid off or should they be

55 Namislo in Landenberg, "Erfolgreich starten als Rechtsanwalt", et seq. 517.

56 Branchenbericht der Sparkasse 2020, p. 13.

57 Ibid.

58 Ibid.

budgeted or invested differently for the coming year? The results should be discussed regularly in the team meeting so that changes can be jointly discussed. However, it is also important to inform all other employees adequately.

So, you should know where you stand at all times, especially in the last quarter. Maybe it was a strong year. In that case, it's important that you don't run out of steam so close to the finish line. Or maybe it was rather disappointing, because an important customer dropped out, your best employee was ill for a long time, or your partner broke up with you. Then don't give up. Develop an action plan together for the last few weeks. Only if your employees and colleagues know where they stand will they be able to commit themselves. It is important to think carefully about which actions will lead to maximum success at this time of year. In this context, you should also keep a critical eye on your client structure. On the one hand, it is important to check whether the strategic orientation and positioning has attracted the targeted clients so that the mandates fit your infrastructure. On the other hand, it is important to check whether these clients have achieved the turnover planned in the business concept and to what extent it makes sense to focus on some of the more lucrative clients and to part with other, less profitable clients[59].

Why controlling your law firm is a matter for the boss is explained by the entrepreneur attorney:

"In recent years, I have noticed an increase in the number of law firms in economic difficulties. In all the cases that I have had on the table as restructuring mandates or insolvency proceedings, one of the causes was that the lawyer did not have the right information at his disposal to be able to make decisions and steered the law firm, as it were, in a blind flight according to gut feeling. In addition to the "standards" – in particular, whether all invoices can be paid when due (liquidity), what profit the firm is making and how costs are developing – the lawyer entrepreneur needs answers to the questions of what the lawyer's time is worth and which mandates are "good". With the evaluations of most law firm programs, however, these questions can at best only be answered in rudimentary form. The first step, therefore, is to develop a reporting system tailored to your law firm that provides the information that is really needed to make the business decisions at hand. Ask yourself what specifically you need to know to run your law firm and don't rely on the information the programmer of your software thinks is useful. Unnecessary information is worthless! The limiting factor in law firms – despite all scalable business models – is still the working time of the lawyers. This must therefore be "controlled" particularly carefully and for each mandate – regardless of how it is billed. A suitable benchmark for comparing different mandates is the revenue per hour realized in the respective mandate. This is calculated as the quotient of the realized revenue minus the direct costs and the attorney time spent on the mandate. If this ratio is determined on an ongoing basis and for each mandate, a solid foundation is laid for positioning the law firm well. Even the most beautiful invoice (= billed turnover) is of no use if the fee does not end up in the account (= realized turnover). It cannot be emphasized enough how important it is to keep an eye on the collection of recei-

---

59 This can also include lucrative mandates with high travel costs.

vables, because fee losses have a disproportionate impact on profits: with an expense ratio of 50 %, a fee loss of 5 % leads to 10 % less profit. Controlling is a matter for the boss – take the topic seriously!"

Lawyer and graduate economist Dr. Andreas R. J. Schnee-Gronauer, Schüttorf.

But don't lose sight of your long-term goal as a law firm. It is easy to get lost in the day-to-day business and in the land of numbers. You can literally no longer see the forest due to the trees. Your long-term goal navigates you through detours and aberrations. Your annual result and your business plan are nothing more than another paving stone for the realization of your law firm idea. Therefore, evaluate deviations from the plan with a focus on the final result and do not leave your personal wishes and plans out of consideration.

Finally, a word about compliance and data protection. Data protection, a perfect imprint on all online profiles, as well as appropriate procedures for data and training for employees should have become routine by now. On the one hand, compliance should ensure adherence to the law, but also the implementation of the firm's values, standards and internal guidelines. The values internalized with your firm's vision should by now be lived as firm culture. This means that processes and responsibilities have been defined and standardized. However, this also means that certain routines and rituals are now part of it, as well as a certain tone of voice, a "welcome process" for new employees or even clothing guidelines, up to the specification of how the law firm answers the phone. This should also be written down and continuously updated, as it is here that your "firm DNA" becomes tangible and real for the first time. This is the basis for an effective and sustainable compliance, which encourages your colleagues and employees to implement these standards and routines in your law firm on a daily basis.

5. Knowledge building and development

In addition to personnel development and efficient office organization, the development and expansion of know-how is the third essential resource of the firm.

However, just as for personnel and law firm management, the lawyer and law firm owner is not paid for the acquisition and development of his know-how.

It is true that every lawyer has a "basic education" after his studies and legal clerkship. However, they have to acquire knowledge about their special field, communication and negotiation management, office organization and business development, personnel management and controlling "post graduate". What few people know is that they can apply for the "Quality through Training" certificate from the

German Federal Bar Association (BRAK) for this voluntary further training if certain content has been taught to a certain extent.

Interestingly, however, there is only a continuous training obligation of fifteen hours per year in accordance with § 15 FAO for holding a specialist title, five hours of which are also self-study. That is less than 20 minutes per week. Overall, the proportion of continuing legal education is actually an average of three hours for a 50-hour week[60].

Distribution of the lawyer's working time

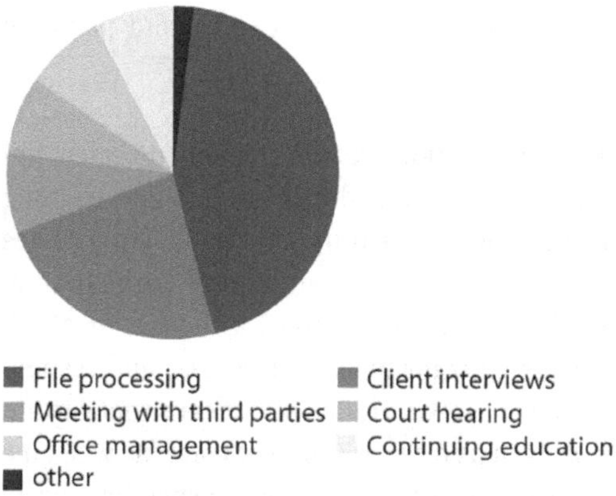

Average distribution of working time of a law firm owner[61], © Dr. Geertje Tutschka

Unfortunately, the study does not indicate how much of this is accounted for by purely professional training, how much by so-called "personal development" and how much by pure law firm management and business management. It is also not clear whether this includes self-study, coaching and mentoring.

The Federal Ministry of Justice, with the support of the German Federal Bar Association (BRAK[62]), ventured an initiative in the national implementation of the European Directive on the Recognition of Professional Qualifications to establish a general training obligation for the legal profession. The idea was to require a mandatory forty hours of training per year, including self-study. This was even to be sanctioned by a fine in addition to a reprimand. This would have meant an increase

60 Kilian, "Anteile der Arbeitszeit" p. 32, Anwaltsblatt 01/2018.

61 Study "Anwaltstätigkeit der Gegenwart" of Soldan Institute 2016. 1,593 lawyers participated in the study.

62 The BRAK operates the German Lawyers' Institute; the DAV the German Lawyers' Academy.

to at least forty-five minutes per week for all lawyers, but would still have been only a quarter of the actual training time (on average). The BRAK considered the obligation for young lawyers to undergo at least ten hours of further training in professional law within the first seven years to be particularly important, which would have been equivalent to an investment of around €150, since this has not been taught at all in legal training up to now[63].

"Continuing education is an elementary area of our profession. This is already laid down by law, in § 43a BRAO. Therefore, continuing education should also be given a status in the awareness of colleagues that ensures that we can maintain the quality of our profession. Many of our colleagues already comply with this legal obligation to continue their training – and this does not only apply to specialist lawyers under the Specialist Lawyers' Code. For the most part, colleagues know that high-quality legal advice is only possible if you take continuing education courses."

Dr. Ulrich Wessels, Vice President BRAK, President of the Hamm Bar Association, lawyer and notary in the law firm Dr. Koenig & Partner GbR in Münster, member of the Board and Treasurer of the German Lawyers' Institute[64]

Unfortunately still unsuccessful. Thus, there is still no general obligation for lawyers and legal professionals to undergo further training in Germany, and it is therefore still the sole responsibility of the professionals themselves, both as to WHETHER and HOW they do so. The exception is the professional law for newcomers to the profession. In Austria, this general duty of continuing education was introduced in the summer of 2021.

"Continuing education means a career advantage and market advantage also over non-lawyer competition! Continuing education makes our quality visible to the outside world and is a top advertising measure. Especially in times of digitalization and legal tech, it is not only the FAO training that secures the position in the market, but also and especially the examination of topics such as entrepreneurial law firm management, strategic management of the law firm and modern forms of client acquisition. Take advantage of your opportunities!"

Lawyer Anke Haug, Managing Director www.advoknowhaug.de, **Anwaltsseminare und Fortbildung GmbH, Renningen**

---

63 These include professional liability risks, restrictive competition regulations, but also the obligation to maintain confidentiality.

64 Pia Lorenz, "Am Wahlkampf gescheitert" in LTO from 4.4.2017.

One of the main tasks of professional human resources and talent management is to select the training and continuing education necessary for the successful orientation of the law firm. Many law firms have now set up in-house programs for these "standard training courses", which young lawyers can attend on a quarterly basis or in so-called summer academies. These programs focus, for example, on negotiation skills as well as pitch and presentation. In addition, certain training budgets are usually made available, which can be used for additional qualifications and degrees, for example.

Knowledge management and knowledge transfer in every law firm today includes not only the standard library (laws, commentaries, reference books) and subscriptions to the most important legal journals, but also a professional research program tailored to the special field of the law firm with access to online databases[65]. Also, the regular attendance of advanced training meetings, congresses and network meetings should be included. In which extent and to which area is alone in your decision. A comprehensive description can therefore not be given at this point.

Another question, however, is how to deal with **in-house knowledge**. This knowledge management includes office organization, templates and building blocks for special areas of the law firm, but also the experience of long-standing employees. According to Heussen, 75 % consider knowledge management important. However, only 5 % of the turnover is invested in it[66].

In his view, successful knowledge management requires:

- Implementation in values and strategy (budget)
- Determination of a responsible person
- Collection, processing, systematization, documentation of knowledge
- Fee regulation
- Quality management

Unfortunately, competition and time pressure still boycott this important resource in most law firms today[67].

For **our three case studies**, this means that it might be possible to optimize firm number one, because the uncooperative small teams can be expected to live their own processes. For case study two in particular, however, the strategic realignment for the new mandates must also include an adjustment of the processes. And what is the situation in case three? There is certainly too little information

---

65 Schwohnke in Landenberg, "Erfolgreich starten als Rechtsanwalt", p. 384.
66 Heussen, "Anwaltsunternehmen führen", p. 206.
67 Ibid.

available for this topic area. Therefore, I invite you to consider various hypothetical scenarios and their possible solutions for yourself.

What did you get out of the chapter?
You know the most important topics and levers in law firm management.

II. Time management

Why should you read this chapter?
You will learn the most important methods and tools for effective time management. Because time is money – and lifetime.

Overview

1. **Work-Life-Balance**
2. **Communication**
3. **File work and research**
4. **Efficient office processes**

Do you know this?

The long-awaited annual vacation is just around the corner. For weeks you have been working on clearing your desk of all important things and deadlines, postponing appointments, clearing away things that have been lying around during weekend and night shifts, and briefing the good-natured colleague who will be taking over as your vacation replacement.

And now this happens: the very project you have been working on for years is going to develop the "show down" at the very moment you are about to start your vacation. The all-important finale will take place in the ten days! During your vacation.

You have the choice: to skip your vacation; to declare your indispensability to your partner and family; or to go on vacation and let your colleagues take the credit: The laurels for the months of tough communication, political-tactical games and the many night shifts. You know what I'm talking about?! Good. Welcome to the club!

This means that you have reached a certain level on your career ladder. You can already guess what I'm about to tell you: You are one of the chosen, indispensable ones! Career level + status + pay grade + responsibility = indispensability.

So, what about vacation? Of course, you are legally entitled to it. The same applies to overtime capping and overtime pay. You can even be charged back for approved vacation days after a certain level of involvement in e-mail communication and telephone calls. We are lawyers. So much for theory. Does this help you? No.

Because your employer expects your indispensability at your cost price, of course. And if you are your own boss anyhow, the whole thing is on your account and your esponsibility anyway.

What does all this have to do with time management?

Could you have changed anything about that with good time management? Does it help you now in deciding for or against the vacation?

Time management is self-management. And it's always just about this one question:

WHAT IS IMPORTANT TO YOU AT THE MOMENT?
What has priority?

Is it important to you to finish the all-important finale of the project with a brilliant twist? Does the soothing pat on the back or the awesome bill take priority?

Or is it important to you to feel the warm white sand between your toes while you wait for the sunset? Can you think of nothing better than watching the two little ones at the water's edge protect their sandcastle from the waves? Is there nothing more important than counting the brown dots in the gray-blue eyes next to you?

What is important to YOU right now?
Your answer shows you the way. Without guilt. Without an annoyed "SOON".

---

i

The important thing here is that you answer this question honestly for yourself and communicate the answer honestly to your loved ones. Nothing is worse than lazy compromises, half-truths or feigned attention.

What is important is your attention. No matter what you decide: Your attention will turn to it and make it a unique moment.

The important thing is that you decide. Because without a decision, your attention will jump back and forth between all sorts of things; nothing will capture your attention long enough to be able to develop. The people around you will be frustrated at not getting an answer from you: Because of the diffuse signals you send out, they will be constantly attracted and repelled by you and will not know where you are with your attention at the moment.

What does this have to do with time management?

Time management is self-management. And constantly answering the question: What is my priority? To focus on it with your full attention.

Nothing else applies to your law practice and your law firm: without good time management, both are futile endeavors.

Perhaps you are at the beginning of your professional career as a lawyer. Maybe you are just starting your professional life. Or maybe you are just starting up again after a family break or simply after a career change from other legal professions: In any case, you are about to realize the project "I, the lawyer and law firm owner". A beautiful project. A demanding profession.

As you know, apart from you, almost 165,000[1] others thought the same in Germany alone. With the population continuing to decline, that's only about 500 people

---

1 Aktuelle Zahl: 165.551 BRAK-Statistik from 1.1.2020.

per lawyer[2] at the moment, one of the lowest ratios in Europe. And German clients are no more litigious than their European neighbors. German lawyers by no means earn more per mandate than their European colleagues. The competitive pressure is great. Many lawyers work eighty hours a week and more. Law firms are on the brink of economic collapse. So you would do well to deal with questions of time management in the law firm, in the legal profession.

You would think that good time management is just an "app" away.

Never before have there been so many guides and aids on this subject as there are today. Sophisticated planners and organizational systems in printed and digital form create order and predictability. Almost daily, new online services enter the market to help you complete your tasks and save you time. Appointment reminders, dictation and translation systems, floral services, round-the-clock childcare, flexible opening and working hours, cleaning and delivery services free up your time. Healthy fast food in concentrated or pureed form, personal trainers and fitness products guarantee health without wasting time. Digitization has revolutionized information procurement and communication: key positions in the legal profession, let's just think of research activities and legal dealings with courts and authorities, have never been easier. And never so complicated. While other industries primarily benefit from this, it is primarily a headache for lawyers.

After all, how can a profession whose practice depends on law use innovative technology for which the existing laws are not made and which it no longer fully understands itself in order to be able to guarantee data protection, for example? These are questions that have been on the minds of the legal profession long before the introduction of the beA.

Information can now be obtained around the clock, in almost infinite abundance, but usually from dubious sources. Automated legal information on the Internet additionally reduces law firm business models. Added to this is the constant (24/7) availability of each individual, the dissolution of traditional opening and rest times (day-night, week-weekend, office vacation), the mixing of professional and private life.

And last but not least, the challenge of realizing family and career in equal measure during the so-called "rush hour" of life, without having to ask oneself later, in one's late forties, whether one has not climbed the wrong career ladder at the expense of the family.

2 The number of lawyers admitted to the bar has tripled since 1990. In 1950, there were still 5,000 inhabitants for every lawyer.

Due to the long periods of training and the associated late start to a career, this today often coincides with the start of a family, which has also been postponed. The intensive period of caring for small children and the absence due to family time usually collides with the first permanent position in which one would like to prove oneself as a young lawyer or even with the double burden of a career plus a part-time doctorate or postgraduate studies in business administration. My career coaching sessions for young professionals focus almost exclusively on coping with this double and triple burden – usually combined with an initial intensive phase of questioning how much one has fulfilled the needs and expectations of one's parents or one's own with this profession and where exactly this path should lead. If, on the other hand, this double and triple burden did not take place during this phase because one focused completely on one's professional career and faded out one's private life, I then have these very candidates at the latest in their mid-forties, when they have reached a certain career level, with the question of meaning in career coaching.

There is no question about it: the profession of a lawyer and running a law firm are time-consuming and the daily work routine is dominated by meeting dates, deadlines, red deadlines and court dates. At the same time, our strength and our lifetime are limited. Accepting this limitation and managing our resources wisely is the beginning of good time management.

Remember the time of your First State Law Exam and the preparation for it. While some may have "gone off the grid," I'm sure some have managed to work "on the side" and/or take care of children and family. Some may also have managed to pursue their hobbies. During the traineeship, the "time pressure" increased because of the various tasks that had to be completed before the second state exam: exam preparation, study groups, exams and, in parallel, the training stations, perhaps a job, family or even a doctorate.

But each day has only twenty-four hours for everyone. Why do some people have "no time" and others do? It is not because of time itself, but because of the activities we develop: Those who "don't have time" are occupied with too many, too difficult or unimportant things, while others take care of the "right" things in a well-organized way.

If that doesn't convince you, then take a mental look at the people who, in your eyes, are successful both professionally and privately: Aren't they often the ones who not only "make a career" and spend all their time on this, but also read books, travel or play an instrument, meet friends and have time for their family at the same time?

As you can see from the scope of this section, I consider the importance of this topic to be immense. At the same time, it plays into many areas already discussed:

the right positioning of your firm, the right equipment, the right people can "save time" and, of course, the right structures, the right controlling.

But in my opinion, to really understand time management, you need the "Big Picture". S. I'll allow myself the luxury of going a little further here and not just contributing tips on how to increase efficiency and profitability.

In order to be able to really "manage" time, one must presuppose that there is such a thing as time. And that this something can be organized in some way, so that it is quantitatively better allocated. We presuppose that time is finite, can be wasted, and that it is good to have time.

Time. It accompanies us throughout our lives, determines all important and unimportant events, defines whether we are young or old, at what pace we move and what things we turn to. Time is money. You don't have time, you have to take it. And nothing is as old as yesterday's newspaper.

But the question is: Is time a paradox, which does not exist at all?

If the time does not exist, but is only an illusion, then in reality there is no course of events. This "course of events" would only be our subjectively erroneous perception. Hard to believe, if one often has too little time or stares anxiously at his aging process. The mathematician Hermann Weyl has described this in his book "Philosophy of Mathematics and Natural Science" already in 1927 as follows: "The scene of the reality is not a standing three-dimensional space in which the things are conceived in temporal development, but the four-dimensional world in which space and time are indissolubly intergrown. This objective world does not happen, but it is – par excellence; a four-dimensional continuum, but neither space nor time".

Time as a fourth dimension was already described in 1895 by the British writer Herbert George Wells – in his novel "The Time Machine". And even earlier, in 1884, the British mathematician Charles Howard Hinton speculated about a four-dimensional space-time, in which ordinary particles occur together as threads; an almost prophetic anticipation of the "world line", which plays a central role in the theory of relativity.

The four-dimensional reality is often called "block universe", because it does not develop, but is there as a whole and at once, as it were. If God existed and if he existed outside of time, as the church father Augustine believed, he could, so to speak, survey the world in its totality from beginning to end. The concept of the unchanging block universe goes back to the American psychologist and philosopher William James. In his essay "The Dilemma of Determinism" from 1884 he criticized the idea of determinism, which contradicted the idea of free will.

Ashtekar's colleague Carlo Rovelli, a physics professor at the University of Marseille, also believes that time is a mirage: "Even if I cannot prove it, I am convinced that time does not exist. I believe that there is a way to describe the functioning of nature without using the concepts of time and space. Space' and 'time' will remain meaningful only within certain approximations – just as the term 'water surface' loses its meaning when we look at the atoms of water in detail: If you look closely enough, there is no such thing as a water surface at all." It's much the same with time and space: "They're just macro-scale approximations – illusions that our consciousness has created in order to understand reality." The "flow" of time is an illusion within the framework of relativity theory. Everything is, in a sense, "fixed at once" in space-time.

How scientists define "time" is one thing. Another thing is how you feel "time", how you deal with it. This can be genetically and individually determined but also determined by education and society. In general, for example, it is assumed that men understand "time" as something rather (one-dimensional) linear, which is why our current social understanding of time is defined by the patriarchy for centuries as "history – present – future" virtually on a timeline. The female principle, on the other hand, understands "time" more as a (two-dimensional) wave or better (three-dimensional) spiral. The female understanding of time says, things repeat themselves (like the tides, the monthly cycle, the seasons, life cycles and karma), again and again but never identically. Similar to the study of law, where one starts with the general part of the BGB and semester after semester "further layers are applied" or better one moves from the general to the specific, the totality of the legal system (of the universe?) can only be grasped at the end (or only at the beginning)[3]. It is probably also striking that "punctuality" and "time value" obviously do not mean the same everywhere in the world. Five minutes of delay can already trigger a diplomatic crisis in Western Europe. In Eastern Europe, not even five days can do the same. Time is relative – in more ways than one.

But back to the essentials: What is it important for?

It is important that you become aware of your personal determination of "time", your very own understanding of this illusion. And not to assume it as "generally valid". Time and punctuality are completely value neutral. Only you (evaluate) it and that according to your subjective idea of it. If you have made yourself aware of your genetic disposition and your social imprint on the subject of "time", it is your individual personality characteristics that matter. Because, of course, we Western Europeans are not all punctual and we Germans are not always reliable.

3 As a synesthete, I have a completely different understanding of time anyway.

First, you should find out for yourself what "time type" you are.
People are different: While one plans everything down to the last detail and does it very thoroughly, the other plans next to nothing and always gets to the crucial point right away; one works slowly but steadily, the other often reacts spontaneously. The next is a "slob" who sits in front of a table full of files, constantly pushing a lot of unfinished business in front of him and thus "shuffling" from one task to the next; one regularly has enough time for private things, while the other never does. The four types described below can be identified by how each of us deals with given deadlines, how we discipline ourselves and others, how much energy we have for the fulfillment of individual tasks, but also by how we set our own goals and work towards achieving them.

The DISG personality model forms the basis:
DISG: Dominant – Initiative – Steady – Conscientious (Gewissenhaft)[4].

The different behavioral styles are derived from the fact that people tend to be more extroverted or introverted and more people-oriented or fact-oriented[5]. We all have very different strengths and weaknesses. Those who know, use and build on their strengths while being aware of their weaknesses can be most effective. So take your time and try to find out which type you are.

The **dominant type** is task-oriented and extroverted. Control and results are absolutely important to him. This type analyzes facts quickly, can distinguish between the essential and the unessential, does not lose sight of his goals and notices immediately if the concrete situation endangers the achievement of his goals. He evaluates activities in a result-oriented way. Dominant types want everything to be done as quickly as possible; that's why they don't like to put off work but prefer to do many things in parallel or on the side. They put pressure on others accordingly. Punctuality is important to them and they dominate conversations with others. If something is important to them, they interrupt others, but conversely do not want to be disturbed. However, the dominant type does not want to deal with boring work. He only does what absolutely has to be done. Because members of this type often start too many tasks next to each other, they often work in a disorganized manner and underestimate the time needed to complete the tasks. Disorder and hectic are often the result of this behavior. It helps dominant types to take their time, formulate their goals and set priorities. If they want to take on new tasks, they should plan their accomplishment and the time required in detail in advance. They should

4 Seiwert, Wenn Du es eilig hast, gehe langsam, p. 201 et seq.
5 Seiwert, Wenn Du es eilig hast, gehe langsam, p. 204 et seq.

also pay more attention to their peers and colleagues by not asking too much of them on the one hand and actively listening to them in conversation on the other.

The **initiative type** is people-oriented and extroverted. Motivating, convincing and influencing others is important to them. Initiative people act spontaneously, rarely analyze, are always open to new, interesting tasks and change priorities frequently. They are emotional and prefer talking to others rather than working. They attach more importance to relationships, plan optimistically and do not pay so much attention to time and deadlines. On theother hand, initiative people are often late because of this and have a poorly organized office. They always get caught up in too many tasks and like to be distracted. Routine work is avoided and only done when absolutely necessary. Members of this type organize themselves better when they are forced to do so (e.g. by the threat of loss of reputation). It helps initiative types to finish things consistently before they start something new. They should plan their tasks and set priorities. Furthermore, they should pay attention to punctuality and not allow themselves to be interrupted – especially not by unimportant things.

The **steady type**, on the other hand, behaves in a people-oriented and introverted manner. Stability and harmony, support of others and orderly relationships are important to him. The steady types work thoroughly, slowly, consistently and reliably. They weight their tasks, create and keep order, and are well organized; they work one thing at a time. Members of this type need time to think through their tasks calmly and bring their professional authority to bear. Like the dominant type, they are punctual. On the other hand, steady types find it difficult to say no. Because they do not want to strain their relationships, they avoid confrontations. They prefer to work on less urgent and less important tasks than on more demanding tasks with deadline pressure. Too many tasks at the same time overwhelm them. These people are reluctant to take on responsibility, but confirmation from others is very important to them. Steady types should have more self-confidence and also say no more often. They should be creative in their search for more efficient ways of working and try them out rather than always sticking to tried and tested procedures. It is also helpful if they consult and coordinate with others more often. Steady types should start the working day earlier to avoid time pressure and think more about the results than about the amount of work.

The **conscientious type** is task-oriented and introverted. Doing the right thing precisely and accurately while avoiding trouble is important to him. Conscientious types have a tidy desk where everything has its fixed place. They are always punctual and well-prepared and scrupulously observe regulations. To make sure that everything is done correctly, they prefer to ask questions often. Everything is planned and prepared in detail. On the other hand, the conscientious type tends to get bogged down in details. That's why it's difficult for them to make spontaneous decisions. He often spends too much time on planning and preparation, which he then lacks for the actual execution of the task. If a task does not fit into his concept, he rejects it. It helps the conscientious types to think critically about their planning times, not to analyze everything in detail and to focus on work results. Everything doesn't always have to be perfect. So they should also scale back their high expectations a bit. These types should be aware that mistakes happen; they cannot plan for every risk and every eventuality. Goals should be set realistically, and finally, conscientious people should be at least as attentive to their fellow human beings as they are to abstract rules and regulations.

In addition to these four different types of dealing with time and organization according to the DISG model, people can also be divided into **systematics and chaotics** according to McGee. As mentioned above, some people are well organized, while others live in chaos, i.e. disorganized. These people are therefore not less intelligent, sloppy, stupid or lazy, they simply handle their time differently, process information differently and motivate themselves differently[6].

Only if you know what type you are, you can identify the things you need to pay attention to in order to manage your time efficiently.

Systematics plan in advance, orient themselves strictly to the clock, think in a concentrated and focused manner, and pay attention to order. In addition, they do not orient themselves too much according to what others expect of them, but more according to their inner signals.

McGee-Cooper speaks of
- monochronic time managers,
- convergent thinkers, and
- intrinsically motivated people.

In contrast to the systematic people, chaots cannot be pressed into a clock scheme. They often want to do several things at once and are not predictable. They think in different directions and always have new ideas and also react to what others want from them.

McGee-Cooper speaks of
- polychronic time managers,
- divergent thinkers, and
- extrinsically motivated people.

6 McGee-Cooper, "Time Management for Unmanageable People", p. 25.

Another point that should not be underestimated is the question of what type of learner you are. After all, you are reading this chapter because you are dissatisfied with the current situation and want to change something (see above).

But your individual performance and life situation also play a significant role. Of course, it makes a difference whether you are young, old or pregnant; whether you couldn't sleep all night because of the baby or because of your back pain, you are an early riser or a night owl and how you eat.

Most people have a very high willingness to perform in the morning, a low in the early afternoon, another intermediate high later, and then the **performance curve** drops continuously from the early evening[7]. But there are also people who describe themselves as "night people" and prefer to work in the evening and at night. More quality, both in terms of the results of the work and in terms of quality of life, is achieved by those who take advantage of the phases of high motivation to perform.

So find out for yourself what your own performance curve looks like: One way is to take notes over a period of time about how you feel at what time of day. You will recognize a certain rhythm and should take this into account when planning your day. But you should also keep in mind the rhythm of the work week and the weekend. The break that the weekend brings allows us to emotionally process the work done during the week and to prepare for the next week. You can also boost your energy by adopting an appropriate **lifestyle**: a healthy diet consisting of more fresh fruits and vegetables and whole foods, less caffeine and more herbal teas, juices and plenty of water will have a noticeable effect right away. Don't worry, you're not supposed to completely change your life overnight, but try partially replacing one or two "bad" habits with a healthier alternative. When you feel the positive effect, it will be easy for you to cut back on other bad habits. Along with this, you should engage in physical activity and conscious breathing. Slow, deep inhaling and exhaling can significantly refresh your energy level[8].

Your workplace should also meet your needs. By that, I don't just mean that it is ergonomically designed for you and complies with the essential occupational safety recommendations. Above all, it should appeal to your creativity: because that is your most important resource in everyday work. It makes no difference whether you need

- an empty, tidy desk,
- a well-organized desk based on the Toyota principle, or
- lots of piles of files and "creative" chaos around you

---

7 Seiwert, "Das neue 1×1 Zeitmanagement", p. 50 et seq.

8 Seiwert, "Wenn Du es eilig hast, gehe langsam", p. 195 et seq.

It must be "your" desk, i.e. it must reflect your working style. A desk reflects your personality. Co-working spaces and law firms in which there are no defined work-stations, but rather everyone sits down in the morning with their box at one of the free communal tables, therefore award themselves individual potential development.

Time management is therefore not possible per se. We have no influence on how fast or how And that brings us to the topic: What is our sphere of action? Or better, what should be our sphere of action? What do we want to bring about? Be clear about what you want to bring about in your life and what is particularly important to you. It is your time. Your life. Decide consciously what you want to spend your time with.

Perhaps not everything can be done at once. Maybe some things also "have their time". With most things – and especially with the important ones – it's not a matter of when you do them, but that you do them. Please be aware of this when I give you tips for more efficiency in the following. It's about being able to focus on the really important things and not dilly-dallying with secondary matters.

1. Work – Life Balance

You should therefore start by working out your own personal goals – your "bucket list"[9], if you like – your core values and life vision, so that you can align your priorities with them. The same applies here as for your law firm.

At this point in my trainings, the objection often comes up: "What does that have to do with work-life balance?" And that brings us to the question: What is work-life balance?

Is it about how much life is still possible at the end of work? Is it about whether work is your life – and vice versa?

"If you live for what you do, you never have to work again."

Is that it? There is enough routine work, unloved sideshows, obligatory exercises, which one cannot get rid of, which cost life time and energy.

The aim of my explanations on the subject of "time management" is to give you simple and practicable tips on how to deal sensibly with your valuable time in order

9 The "bucket list" contains all the things you would like to achieve or experience in life.

to reduce stress at work on the one hand and to have time for the other "beautiful things in life" on the other.

You should help yourself to gain free, i.e. unscheduled, time. "Having time" should be the first goal of efficient time management! However, if you only strive to "use time" even more efficiently, without linking a goal to it, you will probably create more, accomplish more and earn more. Whether this makes you happier is questionable. I am convinced that we can achieve this if we manage to align our time management in such a way that we meet individual needs and rhythms at the same time.

Not all of you will implement every tip; we are all far too different as individuals for that, just as the tasks we want to master will be completely different. But I hope to be able to sensitize you to many, often seemingly trivial, issues.

Of course, I did not invent time management. For many years, this topic has become increasingly popular, and you can find very many good books by international authors on it. I see my task as giving you practical tips for your daily work as a lawyer or law firm owner. You will achieve your goals more easily, be more balanced and hopefully not lose the fun at work.

Doing the right thing first

Once you have found out which personality traits you have and which type you tend to belong to, the next step is to define your personal goals and priorities. It sounds so obvious and simple: **Define your goals!**

But put a blank piece of paper on the table in front of you, take ten minutes and write down what your professional and personal goals are.

---

i

Goals can arise from four main areas[10]:

1. life itself
   By life is meant life in the biological sense; this includes, of course, health, possibly children, or safeguarding the lives of others.
2. the wish of your parents
   By your parents' wish it is meant that they (usually unconsciously) associate a wish with their child which indirectly controls the child's life.
3. Your talents and weaknesses
   It is obvious that talents and weaknesses have a significant influence on the goals of every human being.

10 Küstenmacher/Seiwert, "Simplify your life", p. 287 et seq.

4. Your life dream
   And finally, everyone's life dream plays a role, the vision that we all may have had at one time and have probably long since lost sight of. Because: Without a vision or a mission statement in front of your eyes, it is very difficult to purposefully follow the path to it.

You will notice that this is not so easy: Of course we all want to be healthy, successful and happy, but what does that mean in concrete terms for each individual? What activities do we develop to achieve our goals?

Only if the goals are clearly, vividly and succinctly described, will it be possible to actively, but also subconsciously, direct one's own life towards achieving them. With a reactive attitude to life, you will not reach your goals if you passively submit to every situation in life with the attitude that you cannot influence the future anyway.

According to a long-term study conducted by Harvard University on the careers of graduates over a ten-year period, the following results on goal attainment emerged:

- 83 % had no objective for their career and now had an average income
- 14 % had a clear objective for their career, but did not put it in writing; They had on average three times the income of the first group,
- 3 % had a clear, written objective for their career; They made on average ten times as much as the group mentioned first[11]

Besides the vision you may have of your life, there will be some goals whose realization will extend over a period of several years, some goals can be achieved within a year, quite a few, of course, in shorter periods. If you do not lose sight of the "big" goals in your everyday life, you will automatically orient the other goals to your dream. So first define your goals in writing. You should formulate not only the professional, but also the private goals. Because you can only be successful as a person with all your roles and with all your responsibilities.

Once you have defined your goals, the next step is to set **priorities**.

As already mentioned, you have different roles in your private and professional life, in which you also have more or less responsibility (sole proprietor and owner of a law firm, doctoral student, specialist lawyer in training, speaker, partner, father, son, brother, neighbor, member of the parents' council, member of an association, etc.). You get into stress mostly when you have to fill too many roles at the

11 Seiwert, "Wenn Du es eilig hast, gehe langsam", p. 95.

same time. Especially if you let your job take over so much that your relationship, family, hobbies, health or cultural interests are neglected, your professional and private life can get out of balance.

What is the best way to deal with this situation? You will gain **more quality of life if you concentrate on the essentials**. Of course, some of your roles are predetermined, you cannot give them up (e.g. parents, relationship partner, main professional tasks, possibly a certain hobby). In most cases, there are many "secondary roles" that you can cut back on. Be aware of which roles you might be able to do without altogether. Maybe you don't want to be treasurer in your club for a long time and just don't dare to realize this wish? Other roles you can possibly reduce to fewer activities? Always orient yourself to your goals, which you have now formulated in concrete terms.

According to Zach, you should focus your time management on doing the "important but not urgent" things. This does not mean that you simply ignore the urgent things. According to Zach, urgent things will no longer exist when your time management is optimized[12].

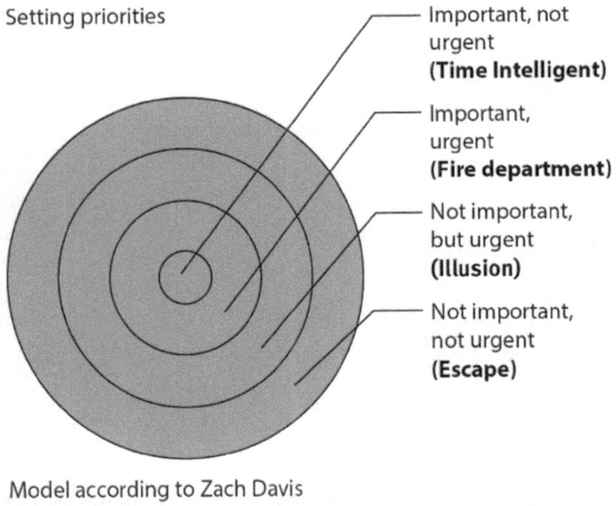

What to prioritize, © Dr. Geertje Tutschka

12 Zach, "Zeitmanagement für Rechtsanwälte", p. 13.

If you want to set priorities correctly, you should also pay attention to what you can do best, what you enjoy doing the most, and what you can achieve the greatest impact with in view of your life's dream[13]. Because then you are most likely to be able to make a decisive contribution to achieving a particular goal. But if you neglect your strengths in favor of your weaknesses, your performance will be average at best. Finally, you also need to be specific about priorities, which means you should consider which tasks you actually have in which of your roles. Only then can you set priorities.

The tasks to be accomplished are more or less important and more or less urgent, i.e. there are
- important and urgent,
- unimportant and urgent,
- important but not urgent, and
- unimportant and non-urgent tasks.

According to Eisenhower, these parameters can be depicted like this[14].

Setting priorities

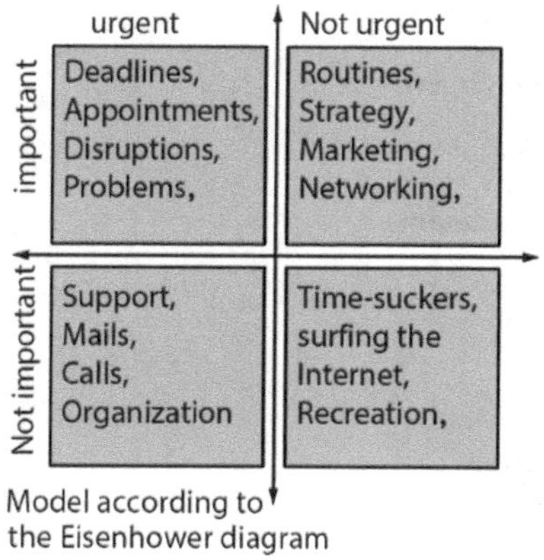

Setting priorities, © Dr. Geertje Tutschka

Figuring out the different priorities means that you have to deal with the individual tasks. If you don't do that, you will certainly deal with many things that are brought to you, even though you don't actually have to make them your tasks.

13 Seiwert, "Wenn Du es eilig hast, gehe langsam", p. 142 et seq.
14 Töpfer in Landenberg, "Erfolgreich starten als Rechtsanwalt", p. 288.

All planning

You can fit a lot into **one week**, even if you are fully occupied at work: In addition to work, you can also do private things, maintain friendships, pursue your hobbies and ideally also have a little time for yourself. That this is not an unrealistic ideal situation is shown by the fact that there are some people who manage to do this. And that is the goal of efficient time management!

However, if you start the week on Monday morning by going to work to get through all the tasks that are thrown at you by Friday evening, and you haven't planned for other things, you won't be "free" until Friday evening. However, after an exhausting work week, everyone is more or less exhausted on Friday evening, and on the weekend a number of other tasks that one did not get to during the week compress themselves. There is usually no time for oneself and sooner or later this leads to dissatisfaction and irritability. If, on the other hand, you draw up a weekly schedule and realistically plan the completion of professional tasks in addition to private ones, and also schedule your private life and time for yourself, you will feel good[15].

So take some time at the end of the week and write down everything that needs to be done in the coming week. A visit to the dentist and a friend's birthday party should also be on the list, as should time for your family or partner.

And this is where the time types developed above come into play again:

If you belong to the "systematics", you will create a clear and detailed weekly schedule and then organize the week accordingly.

If you are more of a "chaotic" person, don't force yourself to make a traditional weekly schedule: Write on small pieces of paper (one for each task) and then place them on the table in front of you. Think about how much time you need for which action and place the slips of paper on the table in front of you in the appropriate order.

The important thing is simply to create a **realistic weekly schedule**.

---

i

No matter what your weekly schedule looks like: You can cross off what you have already done. This always gives you a good feeling and you will keep track of the week. The most important planning principle is to put it in writing. A written plan unfolds (psychologically) a certain commitment: you work more goal-oriented, in addition, the written plan relieves you, because you do not have to remember everything, and in this way you automatically document what you have done and when. The weekly plan cannot and should not be very detailed. It is more about the arrangement of the week.

---

15 Töpfer in Landenberg, "Erfolgreich starten als Rechtsanwalt", p. 285.

But also **every single day** and especially every working day should be planned if you don't want to be determined by the tasks and concerns that are brought to you: First of all, note down the tasks to be accomplished. If you use one of the forms for this, as they are offered in the different time planners, you make the work and the handling of your daily plans[16] easier for yourself. Then it is important to realistically calculate the time required for the individual tasks, because experience shows that we often take on far too much, with the result that we are frustrated when we have not managed to do everything. Buffer times for completing unforeseen tasks should definitely be planned for. You will need to decide which tasks you want to accomplish on a given day, because you will almost never be able to complete everything on your to-do list in one day. So prioritize, cut back, and transfer tasks to others as well. Finally, you should regularly check whether you have completed the tasks according to your daily schedule.

Whether you opt for a weekly plan or a daily plan – or combine both – is up to you. In any case, you should always start the day with the morning routine, focus on the priorities of the day and structure the day in essential sections.

PLANNING		
Weekly-plan	**vs.**	**Daily-plan**
• 5 priorities per week		• 2 priorities per day
• More overview		• More focus
• More flexibility		• More controllable

My tip: Focus on the morning routine

Planning, © Dr. Geertje Tutschka

We cannot plan everything in advance. That's why it's important to plan **buffer times** in your everyday working life. Only then will you be able to deal with an unexpected deadline, for example, or to do a favor for a friend who asks you to, or to take your car to the workshop because it no longer runs. But even if nothing unexpected happens, you'll need buffer time, simply because we're not machines and can't always run our daily schedule exactly as we planned. It's a fallacy to think you don't have time for buffer time. With this argument, many colleagues plan their workdays completely and sooner or later "hit the skids". After all, it's not as if you do nothing in an hour that was scheduled as buffer time, that is, you waste the hour

16 Seiwert, "Das neue 1×1 Zeitmanagement", p. 38 et seq.

just because nothing unforeseen happened. Of course, you can and will use this hour to accomplish another important task. But you remain in the pleasant situation of being in control of your own time, you are not dominated by tasks. This is essential.

While buffer times are there to complete additional or unexpectedly time-intensive tasks for which there would otherwise be no time, i.e. which you could only complete by sacrificing your private time, you should also plan for **time-outs** in which you want to work in a concentrated and absolutely undisturbed manner. I'm sure you're all familiar with the "saw blade effect": if you are distracted from your work for even a moment, you need a disproportionate amount of start-up and familiarization time to continue working from the same place[17].

So if you know that a certain task requires your full concentration, plan a corresponding time-out in which you are not disturbed (not even by the telephone). When you eliminate the saw-blade effect this way, you not only gain time, but you also feel much better. And if you don't need a scheduled time-out for a difficult task, then use this "quiet hour" for other tasks or for yourself. Therefore, you can only win.

A simple way to create a daily plan, following the tips presented above, is the so-called **A-L-P-E-N method**. Each letter stands for a specific step:

- note down tasks,
- estimate the length of the task,
- reserve buffer times,
- make decisions,
- follow-up.

Fun and joy are decisive for self-motivation. Those who **start the day on a positive note** will accomplish the tasks at hand more easily and probably better than those who are annoyed or stressed. But how many of us set the alarm clock too late or sleep too long with the result that they have too little or no time for breakfast let alone for their family or partner, only to rush through rush hour traffic to the office where the first meeting has already begun. Therefore, make sure to start the day on a positive note. Take time to read the newspaper or have a good breakfast, go for a run or whatever else you feel like doing, and start the day with positive energy. A positive start not only has a positive effect on the fulfillment of your tasks, you also communicate with your environment: If you are in a good mood, you treat your employees accordingly, and this also has a positive effect on your work and the working atmosphere.

---

17 Seiwert, "Das neue 1×1 Zeitmanagement", p. 53.

No – not my construction site

The pressure in working life increases because of the fear for the job or the fear for contracts (mandates). But in private life, too, the double burden of work and family often means more tasks for the individual. However, those who allow themselves to be overburdened or overwhelmed by this will sooner or later become irritable, tense and dissatisfied, perhaps even ill.

Therefore, say "no."

- if it is not your responsibility
- if you have too many tasks to do.

If you know your goals and priorities and make daily plans, you can easily recognize when to say "no." This applies to private life as well as to work. A healthy self-confidence makes "no's" possible. When we say "yes" even though we mean "no," we allow ourselves to be manipulated along the lines of "You can do that easily!" Of course, a strong ego helps against this. A brusque "no" can put a strain on a business or private relationship. It is therefore important to sell a "no" in a relationship-oriented way, e.g. by asking for some time to think it over or by first acknowledging the other side's concerns. Of course, you can also say "no" confidently, although you should not give reasons for doing so in order to avoid further discussions.

Yes – but garbage

If, on the other hand, it falls within your area of responsibility but is worthless because it does not contribute to any of your priorities, use the wastebasket. This applies to mandates as well as to inquiries, offers and mailings.

Throw away paper when you know you don't need it. This applies to all kinds of documents that pile up on your desk or even in your inbox in no time. After all, sorting through such piles or picking something out from there takes a lot of time. Throw away uninteresting junk mail immediately (you can delegate some of this). But you should also throw away other documents (e.g. invitations that you cannot or do not want to accept or info letters on topics that do not interest you). In the age of the Internet, you can retrieve almost any information at any time anyway, so the inhibition threshold to throw something away should be lower. What you don't throw away should be stored or filed with a system.

Yes – small first

Similar to rescue missions, make "kids first" your mantra for mini-tasks. When is it a mini-task? When the time and energy involved is manageably small and there are not a lot of them going on at the same time.

You're probably familiar with this: you have to quickly get a birthday card, take the shirts to be ironed, pick up the bank statements, change a light bulb, call back an acquaintance, etc., etc. All of these things are, after all, quite quick to do – that's true. But if you want to do all of this in addition to your scheduled tasks, if you haven't scheduled this time, then you will quickly "hit the skids". In total, the time required adds up noticeably. Be aware of this and either consciously plan the completion of these mini-tasks into your daily schedule or delegate them. Perhaps you can also cancel one or the other action completely.

In any case, quickly checking off the smallest tasks clears your to-do list and diary, and provides a sense of achievement and motivation for larger tasks. So if you can do smaller tasks "right away", you should do it. You will gain time because you will only have to deal with the individual task once, at the time it is presented to you. Moreover, you do not have to plan the completion of this task for a later time. Of course, it is only possible to complete tasks "preferably right away" if appropriate buffer times are available. You should also not let the high benchmark prevent you from completing a task as soon as possible: "The performance should be "as good as necessary", not necessarily perfect.

Yes – but delegate

Delegating tasks is an efficient means of gaining time to complete other tasks that cannot be delegated, but also time for oneself. In doing so, a task can either be delegated permanently or limited to one-time cases. Of course, the person who delegates tasks always retains management responsibility as the "superior". If you delegate tasks, you should transfer the necessary competencies and the responsibility for action to the person concerned[18]. If all steps were specified down to the last detail, i.e. if the person to whom a task is to be delegated had no responsibility for action, his or her motivation would probably be diminished. Most people react positively to the transfer of responsibility. Of course, in your professional life, you need to select the right people, delineate areas of responsibility, delegate a task as early as possible, and encourage, advise, and provide the person in question with all the necessary information. If you delegate several tasks, you must coordinate them. And finally, of course, you must always check that everything is working in your favor. Only then does delegation make sense. A key benefit of delegation is that it allows you to leverage the knowledge and experience of the person performing a task for you.

18 Seiwert/Buschbell/Mandelkow, Zeitmanagement für Rechtsanwälte, p. 135 et seq.

If you do not just delegate undemanding tasks to others, but challenges, you will in doubt promote the independence, initiative and competence, but also the motivation and satisfaction of the person to whom a task is delegated. Therefore, you should also emphasize the appeal of the individual task when you delegate it to someone else. If the task is too large, you should delegate it with intermediate goals and regularly check that the other person is not overburdened. You should also delegate routine and preparatory work in particular for the purpose of relieving yourself. If the tasks are unpleasant or boring, talk about them with the person concerned and perhaps also delegate a more demanding task to show what you think the person is capable of. In this way, you can certainly boost motivation.

Yes – but plan and manage

It happens that things are not (yet) "ripe" to be implemented by you.

Either because it is a task that you have to accomplish as a team, or because certain service providers are involved (e.g. the web designer in the creation of the website). Then your task is not to do it quickly yourself, but rather to set up a project management with responsibilities, processes, timelines and control sequences.

A useful tool to grasp complex processes in their entirety in order to be able to develop structured project management is the creation of a so-called "mind map", on which the various aspects are collected and then placed in relation to each other. This can be developed by yourself but also by whole teams. Professional guidance and moderation can make the meeting productive, effective and time saving.

If, on the other hand, the initial aim is to slowly feel out where certain things should develop, "brainstorming" can be a good method for collecting the team's ideas and thoughts on the subject. However, this method should always be fully mapped in the two sequences "storming" and "norming".

Exposing time thieves

I'm sure you're all familiar with this situation: You've planned something and realistically scheduled the time required for it, and then things don't go as planned after all. The many small but insidious time thieves, who always take your attention for "just a moment", have struck again. The first step is to unmask the time thieves and then say goodbye to them effectively. Be honest: It is often our own fault if we do not complete a task in the time allotted. Everyone knows themselves best and can no doubt quickly list the things that often get in their own way. Again, it is best to write this down and think about strategies how you can best catch these inner time thieves. In the following, I will discuss typical time eaters and ways to control them:

Procrastination: the "inner couch potato"

There are countless life situations in which we have to overcome an inner resistance again and again in order to put into action what we actually want. Whether it's about brushing up on our foreign language skills, cleaning up the apartment, calling our parents again, eating healthier, drinking less, exercising more, or calling back a client, solving a (supposedly) difficult legal problem for a specific case, or continuing to work on an unpleasant file. There are diving examples from all areas of life. If you find out in which areas of life you let yourself be taken by surprise by your "inner couch potato", if you find out which nasty tricks your "inner couch potato" uses, then you can develop strategies to overcome your "inner couch potato"[19].

Our "inner couch potato" has three attack options:

– Preventing a decision to act
  Often we cannot decide to do something because we tell ourselves things like "I'll never do it!", "It's much too difficult!", "I don't have the time!", "I should do it once ..." or "Why should I of all people do it?" As you can see: If we do not take a decision seriously, then its implementation can fail[20].
– Disturbance of the decision itself
  If we only formulate our goal vaguely, e.g. "I'll do my tax return soon" or "I'll eat healthier", then we lack the concrete designation of what we want to do. However, a resolution can also be disturbed if we take on too much at once, i.e. something unrealistic, e.g. "Starting tomorrow, I will run 20 km every day".
– Preventing or impairing the execution
  Finally, we prevent or interfere with the execution of planned tasks by distraction, for example, by having to do something else before completing the planned task or by giving up with the motto "There's no point in doing anything anyway".

---

i

If you have your "inner couch potato" figured out, you will be able to keep him in check and he will not steal your valuable time.

– Therefore, define your goals clearly and unambiguously,
– start implementing the tasks concretely
– and stay disciplined in accomplishing them.

---

19 v. Münchhausen, "So zähmen Sie Ihren inneren Schweinehund", p. 32.
20 Töpfer in Landenberg, "Erfolgreich starten als Rechtsanwalt", p. 291.

Perfection: The high benchmark

Those who place very high or too high demands on themselves may not even start a job because either the time available is not sufficient to solve the task perfectly or because they lack the necessary self-confidence. In our society, perfectionism[21]: is what counts: everyone wants or is supposed to be faster, richer, better, more beautiful, more successful. But in reality, perfection is rare and fleeting. Not everyone who has very high expectations of themselves demands the same level of perfection from their fellow human beings. Therefore, lower your expectations a little and become active. Completing a task, even if perhaps not everything is done perfectly, is much better than having it in front of you for a long period of time.

The time thief on a visit; The external circumstances

In addition to the internal time thieves, we are also bothered by the many time eaters from the outside. The individual disturbance is often only of short duration, but over the course of the day, the lost time adds up:

- A caller who asks for "a quick information" and does not suspect or think that this will not only disturb you at work, but that the quick information may have to be worked out in a longer time (every law student knows this nuisance),
- spontaneous visits of acquaintances in the office,
- calls from friends,
- but also unnecessary calls from clients or
- the visit of a colleague who would just like to talk to you for a few moments,
- but also the e-mails, mails etc. arriving on your PC.

Everyone reacts differently to these external disturbances: some block everything out rigorously, others – e.g. initiative types – even like to be distracted from their work, and still others try to do everything at once.

Close the door: A few of the time thieves simply come to your study because the door is open. The disturber who comes to you in this way may not even feel that he is disturbing you. It is more difficult when you have to knock because the door is closed. As soon as you work with several people, you should make sure that you clearly communicate when you absolutely do not want to be disturbed and when you are open to which "disturbances".

21 Töpfer in Landenberg, "Erfolgreich starten als Rechtsanwalt", p. 292.

i

For example,
- with the door closed, you can say that you absolutely do not want to be disturbed ("time-outs"),
- with the door ajar, you can say that you may only be disturbed "in case of emergency" (of course, you then have to define what is meant by such emergencies),
- and with the door open, you can say that people may ask you if they can disturb you for a specific request.

Control

You have set goals, planned how to achieve them, made decisions, worked on the realization of your goals and organized yourself accordingly. Now you should definitely check whether you have actually achieved the goals you set. If necessary, you can take corrective measures and thus improve your self- and time management[22].

Whatever the tasks you want to accomplish, professional, social or family, you should regularly take the time to ask yourself
- if you are accomplishing the tasks necessary to achieve your goals or
- if you have lost sight of them, if you are tackling these tasks according to their weighting or
- if you have lost sight of the priorities you have set,
- if you have kept to your schedules,
- if you have the disruptive factors and time thieves under control,
- if you have stopped bad habits,
- if tasks delegated to others have been completed by the appropriate people in accordance to your interests, etc.

You should make **self-critical process checks** in writing. The compulsion to write something down forces you to deal with the individual issues in concrete terms. Only then can you also recognize at which points you can start with corrective measures. The results you achieve can only be classified as positive or negative against the background of your goals. You should therefore regularly check whether you have achieved the daily, weekly, monthly, annual as well as your longer-term goals. In the case of complex tasks, you should check whether you have achieved intermediate goals. Depending on the result of your goal control, you should draw the resulting consequences, in detail:
- First, check which goals you have achieved and which tasks you have to complete.

22 Seiwert/Buschbell/Mandelkow, "Zeitmanagement für Rechtsanwälte", p. 229 et seq.

- Then visualize which goals you have not achieved and, above all, what the reasons for this were.
- Now you can adapt your further plans to the current situation, in order to be able to realize the reaching of your goals.
- Make sure that you carry out these controls at an early stage so that you can initiate any corrective measures in good time.

In this way, you will soon be in a position to make schedules that are realistic to implement, and to work with the necessary discipline to complete your tasks. This is a prerequisite for good time management.

Basically, you can look at performance improvement or time management from two perspectives: from the perspective of efficiency with a focus on reducing "time thieves" or from the perspective of increasing effectiveness.

EFFICIENCY and EFFECTIVENESS

Efficiency: Reduction of	Effectiveness: Increase of
Time Traps	Profit
Idle	Status
Doublings	Hierarchy level

Efficiency vs. effectiveness, © Dr. Geertje Tutschka

While the latter is about good planning and implementation, the former is mainly about strict controlling. Time recording, for example, can of course be effective controlling on the one hand to assess the need for optimization.

If, on the other hand, you take the time to record your activities, it can show you whether you are really concentrating on the important things, your priorities[23].

EFFICIENCY vs. EFFECTIVENESS

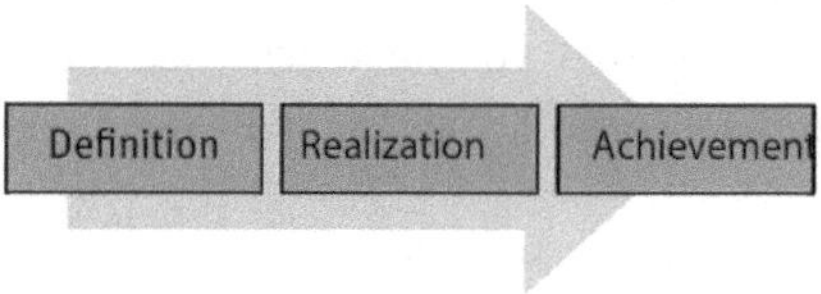

Effectiveness, © Dr. Geertje Tutschka

23 Heussen, "Anwaltsunternehmen führen", p. 69.

EFFICIENCY vs. EFFECTIVENESS

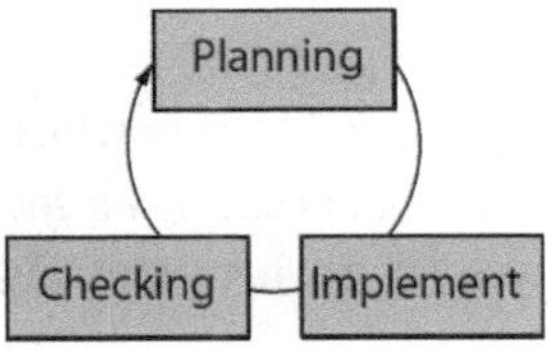

Efficiency, © Dr. Geertje Tutschka

Ideally, the two should go hand in hand so that effective measures pay off through efficient cost control, for example:

EFFICIENCY and EFFECTIVENESS

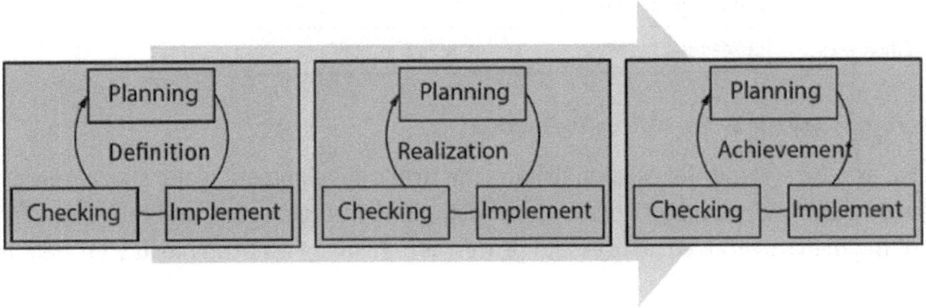

Efficiency vs. effectiveness, © Dr. Geertje Tutschka

The starting points

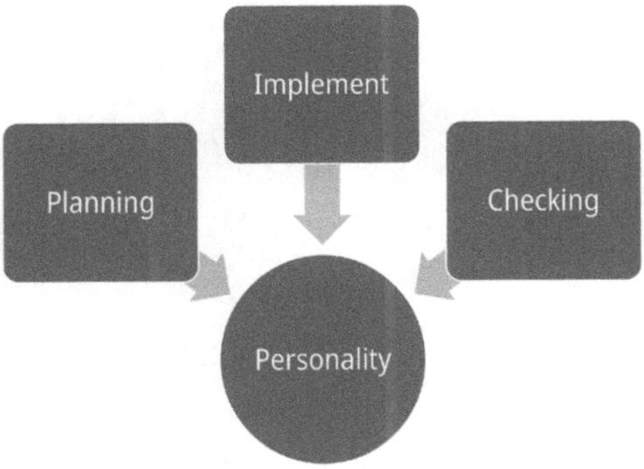

Starting point personality, © Dr. Geertje Tutschka

Many of the general efficiency models play into your role as a lawyer as well as your role as a law firm owner. In order to optimize your own workflows with good time management, it depends largely on your own personality, such as the time types mentioned above. On the other hand, when it comes to ideal time management in your law firm, your personality takes a back seat and other aspects play a bigger role.

It is important that you are very aware of the role and perspective from which you are deciding which measure to take when making a situational decision. As you can see in the following comparison, the respective objectives differ when assessing the question of which measure should be selected:

Your role determines your actions

	Lawyer	Firm owner
Focus	Career	Law firm
Money	Salary	Profit
Legal field	Lawyer specialization	Positioning in the market
Employees	Colleagues/Trainees	Employees/staff

Lawyer vs. law firm owner, © Dr. Geertje Tutschka

So, as a firm owner focused on driving the firm's development, your own career is less important than the firm's overall positioning in the market, and the efficiency of the firm's overall structures and processes is relevant – not so much your own.

EFFICIENCY and EFFECTIvENESS plus ROLE

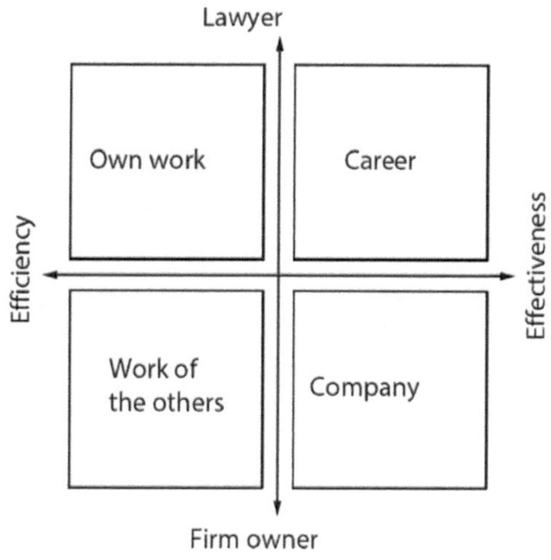

Efficiency and Effectiveness vs. Role, © Dr. Geertje Tutschka

The general efficiency models are always applicable and for everyone.

In the following, these will now be applied to concrete processes in the day-to-day work of lawyers. Some of them go into great detail and may be routine for some "old hands" anyway. In my experience, however, there is always something new for everyone – even if it is only to question one's own processes and procedures one more time. Lawyers in small to medium-sized law firms at the beginning of their careers will no doubt be able to get the most out of this.

2. Communication

As a lawyer, you know that the **telephone** is your most important means of communication, but you also know how much time is wasted on the phone. Yet the telephone is an essential interface between client and lawyer. On the one hand, it is a very important tool for immediate, rational communication and the exchange of information; on the other hand, it is a huge time eater. Lawyers often spend several hours a day on useless phone calls.

The most common phone sins are: 1

- When you want to call someone and you don't know the right number,
- when you make a call without having a specific goal,
- when you are ill-prepared for the conversation,
- when you make a call at an inopportune time,
- when you make a call without the documents necessary for the conversation,
- when you don't write down keywords before the call,
- when you don't explain your intention for the conversation,
- when you monologue instead of actively listening,
- when you don't take notes on the phone,
- when you don't make specific agreements with the person you are talking to.

At the same time, the telephone offers an incredible time advantage over all other communication options, because information is exchanged immediately. You can save costs (postage, paper, personnel costs) and avoid the accumulation of unnecessary paper. In addition, any questions can be clarified immediately, and the personal contact with the interlocutor (such as a judge or a colleague) often provides the basis for exchanging information that would probably not be exchanged in written form. Whether the telephone contributes to saving or wasting your time is up to you.

As soon as several people (secretarial staff and/or lawyers) answer the phone in a law firm, there is a risk that a client who calls several times about the same matter will receive different information from different people. It should therefore be clearly regulated who is the right contact person in which matters. Of course, depending on the structure of the law firm, a number of different variants are conceivable. If only one person is responsible for the telephone, then many problems do not arise in the first place. There is no risk of different people having or passing on information concerning the same mandate. It is also possible that one person takes incoming calls and then forwards them to the responsible secretary. In case of doubt, the secretary responsible for a lawyer can even provide information on the matter (e.g. whether a written pleading was received from the other side). In larger law firms, this form of office organization (the formation of teams consisting of attorney and office staff) is common and makes absolute sense. If the lawyer himself has to speak to the caller, then the office staff member responsible for him can, in case of doubt, better judge whether or when he has the opportunity to do so. In addition, an employee who has an overview of the attorney's mandates can direct specific questions to the caller and in this way make the attorney's work easier.

Keeping call lists is part of good office organization. All incoming calls are noted in writing on a list, stating the date, name of the caller, the matter, the caller's concern and where the caller stands. Such call lists document all calls. As an attorney, you can regularly track who has called. You can also see if a client tried to reach you several times and, if necessary, call him back even though he did not ask for it. That makes a good impression, of course. But you can also see whether a client has really tried to reach you several times (as he may reproachfully claim). Often, calls cannot be put through to you because you are out of the office or in a meeting, or because you do not want to be disturbed. In such cases, your office staff should properly "handle" the caller. Perhaps a question from the caller can be answered by your secretary. If the client needs/wants to talk to you, you should promise to call him back within a certain time window in the spirit of good service. In addition, you should ask what the caller is specifically interested in. As a lawyer, I need the client's name, I need to know when I can reach him at which number and what he wants from me (this is particularly important if several cases are being handled for this client).

If you have appropriate **call lists** kept, you can call callers back in a very targeted manner. Targeted and therefore efficient because you know the caller's request, so you can prepare accordingly. You can also call back in a targeted manner because you know when you can reach them and at which number.

Otherwise, you can quickly waste valuable time by repeatedly trying to reach someone in vain. It is not only the time wasted by dialing the number and waiting that is important, but you also have to prepare for the planned conversation before each call attempt, which takes a lot more time. In this way you can save a lot of time in relation to a full working day and you also avoid the unpleasant situation that your client "catches you cold" because you do not have his case in mind. However, be scrupulously careful that promises made to your clients are kept at all costs. Otherwise, you risk a loss of trust that would be difficult to repair.

Almost everyone has an **answering machine**. However, it is necessary to critically assess the advantages of this device. Only in a few cases will clients (and others) be content to leave a message on tape. Usually they will call again to discuss the matter, or, if it is a matter of making an appointment regarding a new matter, they will call another lawyer right away. But especially as a solo attorney who does not have a full-time staff, you should have an answering service so that incoming calls "reach" you even in times of your absence; it is especially about absences during normal business hours. The caller should be given the opportunity to leave messages on tape. In the announcement, you should say what information you are requesting from the caller (e.g., name and phone number) and within what time frame the tape will be played. If you allow callers to leave messages on tape, you may be able to take action on the specific matter before calling back. If there is no such possibility, it is questionable what the answering machine is supposed to do at all. One thing is certain: messages on tape have to be processed by someone. This costs time, of course, and – this is the disadvantage compared to direct contact during a call – any queries cannot be made. In law firms where the telephone is manned continuously during business hours – with the exception of the lunch break – an answering machine is not necessarily needed. In some law firms there is no answering machine or only one with an informative message without the possibility of recording, in many there is. In the end, it is a question of marketing how one decides.

You should carefully consider whether or to whom you disclose your **private number**, i.e. your cell phone number (e.g. generally on business cards or in individual cases). This bears the risk that you may be disturbed at any time. On the other hand, there may be situations in which it is extremely important to receive information as quickly as possible. Irrespective of this, some clients often wrongly expect you as a lawyer to be available all the time. We service providers have to distinguish ourselves every day anew among many competitors. Permanent availability is certainly one of the essential aspects of good marketing. My experience is that clients who have my private number are usually reluctant to use it. When I give this number to individual clients, it is always with the request that they only call me in "emergencies" or in specific situations. On the one hand, this shows my commitment to the specific mandate; on the other hand, I still have the option of rescheduling a call to my office hours if I see that the matter is not so urgent.

Meetings with clients often cost much more time than necessary. However, once a client is in your office, it is often difficult to find an end: Unless you have agreed on an hourly fee, clients tend to want to clarify one or two legal issues "by the side" more or less. In addition, they are regularly unable to distinguish between what is essential and what is not, with the result that they talk too much, which costs valuable time. Irrespective of the fact that you should of course steer the course of a meeting by skilfully conducting the conversation, you can certainly replace a number of meetings with **telephone appointments**[24]. As for a meeting, lawyer and client should be prepared and thus you can specifically work through the points to be clarified on the phone. Especially if a personal meeting with the client has already taken place, i.e. if lawyer and client already know each other, telephone appointments are a favorable alternative to meetings in the conventional sense.

Documentation is "half the battle" for the lawyer. This is not only due to liability aspects, but simply because of the correct processing of mandates: anyone who deals with thirty, forty or more files per day cannot remember what was agreed with whom in which matter. It is therefore absolutely essential to document what was the content of a telephone conversation. Often, you do not have the opportunity to initiate the next step of legal action immediately after a telephone call. In my experience, it is therefore a good idea to make a note at the end of each telephone memo under the heading "Whereabouts" as to whether and, if so, what is to be done next in this matter.

Meetings with clients often get out of hand if they are not conducted in a targeted manner (unless an hourly fee has been agreed). This is because the individual client typically has a "big" problem that occupies him massively. In addition, he is regularly unable to distinguish between what is important and what is not, so that if he is not guided or slowed down, he will talk about everything that he thinks is important. The problem that facts important for the lawyer are often incompletely communicated in the process is another problem. It is true that the client must feel picked up and understood. But that does not mean that the lawyer must always be available to the client. There are clients who, as a matter of principle, (would like to) arrange a meeting with their lawyer after receiving a letter in order to discuss further matters. If you allow this to happen, you will probably waste valuable time completely uneconomically. You should therefore always check the necessity of a meeting and, if necessary, refuse to arrange an appointment and instead arrange a telephone appointment. Of course, you should explain this to the client in a comprehensible manner. You will see that clients will accept this procedure if they know that it will not hinder the processing of their case. In addition, the time frame of the meeting should be determined in advance and the necessary information/documents should be made available to each discussion partner. In addition to the ap-

24 In the age of videoconferencing and video calls, the boundaries between telephone and meeting appointments are becoming blurred anyway. At most, the new data protection regulations impose certain restrictions here with regard to the security of the providers.

pointment, you should also precisely agree on the specific topic, the reason for the meeting. This may sound trivial, but any ambiguity costs time. Make sure – especially if several interlocutors are involved – that everyone is informed in writing of the time and place of the meeting. It is unfortunate if an interlocutor is missing because no one felt responsible for informing him or her of the appointment. Also, define the goal of the meeting. This allows the meeting to be focused and results oriented. Side issues are identified and eliminated.

Such goals must always be formulated in the abstract if the interests of the parties involved are different:
- Working out the points of agreement and disagreement in discussions with opposing colleagues or parties
- Working out the goals and motivations of the parties. If you know why someone wants or does not want something, you can better understand their goals and develop specific proposals for compromise. (Essential element of mediation.)

It sounds trivial. But always start meetings **on time and well prepared**. This is the only way to effectively implement your daily schedule. Irrespective of this, you will upset your discussion partners if they have to wait, and this, by extension, will put a strain on the meeting and the relationship with the discussion partner.
Prepare a **day agenda with time constraints**. Particularly in an ongoing matter concerning a complex issue, you as the negotiator can repeatedly work towards compliance with these specifications in terms of time and content. In addition, the meeting can be planned in terms of time and content and is therefore efficient. Of course, drafting an agenda takes time. However, this time is well invested. If there is no agenda, it is much more difficult to conduct the meeting.

You can also prepare a **list of questions**, which can be particularly useful for initial meetings. In addition, it is advisable to work with checklists for routine tasks. Checklists, like questionnaires, are an effective means of requesting essential information. Checklists can even be sent to the client for answering in advance, so that one can prepare for the planned meeting in an even more targeted manner.

Listen actively. If you **"actively listen"** to your conversation partner, you are following an important rule of communication, because the person speaking is being signaled that what he is saying is being heard and understood. If he does not have this impression, he will repeat the same thing over and over again. As lawyers, we can usually tell very quickly whether or not a set of issues is relevant to the case we are working on. However, these "stories" can be important for the client to grasp and classify the facts of the case. React accordingly: If you sit back disinterestedly, you will hear the same story again and again because the interlocutor, who wants to be understood after all, thinks he has not yet been able to make himself understood.

It is therefore a matter of mastering the balancing act between purposeful conversation and “active listening”. Signal to your counterpart that what he or she is saying has “reached” you, and then steer the conversation back in the right direction.

This is how you show interest:

- Remain turned towards your counterpart
- Nod in agreement
- Actively ask questions
- Make brief written notes even if the description is irrelevant
- Briefly summarize the content of the conversation
- Direct the conversation to essential content

---

i Your own summary of the result of the conversation is very important because it ensures that you have correctly understood what your counterpart has said. At the same time, you show them that and what you have understood. Any necessary corrections can be made immediately. Otherwise, there remains the risk of a misunderstanding, the discovery and correction of which during the course of the mandate is unpleasant, possibly even risky and, above all, time-consuming.

Unannounced visitors disrupt every schedule. Anyone who is working to full capacity should therefore generally not be caught off guard. Clear instructions for secretarial staff on how to deal with this situation are therefore important. However, there can of course also be exceptions here in the case of particular urgency

Finally, a word about (internal) meetings. In most law firms of a certain size, there are regular “discussion groups” (e.g. every Wednesday afternoon). However, these meetings are often unproductive and get bogged down in banalities. The really important decisions are left undecided or no agreement can be reached. The primary goal should be to establish an intelligent meeting structure that is tailored to the needs of the firm and that is both goal-oriented and resource-saving. I recommend NOT having to switch roles in meetings. Meetings should therefore be thematically separated and serve a specific purpose:

1. the professional and mandate-related exchange (lawyer role)
2. the daily routine or its management (management role)
3. the strategic development of the law firm (leadership role)

In addition, quarterly appointments for business development, personnel and projects should be scheduled, as well as a strategy weekend at least twice a year.

Additional meetings of the supporters and project teams as well as possible preparations, external input, training etc. are added.

Within meetings,
- clear rules should apply,
- a tight agenda with time specifications and
- a record of results and decisions should be maintained

Today, modern software solutions make creation easy and creative. It can also help to make something your own from the range of tools and methods for effective meetings. Specialist literature or individual training can provide an overview; an external coach is also happy to provide initial guidance in redesigning the meeting until routines have become established and a new meeting culture has been established.

3. File work and research

As a lawyer, you have a lot to do with paper; in particular, the contents of court hearings, meetings and telephone calls are documented. An obligation to keep hand files arises directly from the professional code of conduct for attorneys.

With the exception of very simple matters, different information from different sides comes together per client, including:
- Correspondence with the client,
- correspondence with the client's legal protection insurance,
- correspondence with the opponent, opposing counsel,
- correspondence with courts and authorities,
- correspondence with third parties (e.g. litigants, witnesses, experts).

Furthermore, important data concerning each individual client must be documented in the individual file, as well as incoming and outgoing payments. Efficient file work therefore means that you have to organize how you can easily and quickly find your way around the individual file. It is best to compare the different forms of organization and discuss them with colleagues to find out which form suits you best.

Important **data** must be noted not only electronically in the file itself, including:
- Name and address of the client/opponent/opposing counsel,
- if applicable, name of the company with indication of the representative body,
- telephone and fax number with indication of whether it is the private or the business number,
- e-mail addresses,
- information on the client's legal protection insurance (name, address, insurance number),
- indication of the responsible court together with file number.

Standard software for lawyers offers these possibilities as a matter of course. And most law firms are still light years away from a pure e-file.

In many cases, however, the good hand file sheet, which contains the essential core data, is still filed in the front of each file. This enables you, for example, to telephone the parties and other involved parties at any time without having to search out the telephone numbers beforehand. Of course, this electronically stored data must be maintained. As much as up-to-date core data is worth, it can take a lot of effort and time to determine the correct data if the stored data is no longer up to date.

A **work-friendly sorting of the files** can also contribute to efficient work. As already mentioned above, a wide variety of information comes together. You will need all this information in the course of processing the mandate, sometimes several times. Depending on the volume of documents relating to a mandate, file covers or folders can be considered. There are different types of file covers (e.g. double or single filing, filing from left to right or vice versa, different colors). Regardless of the fact that files of individual lawyers or concerning different fields of law can be identified by different colors, the file covers offer the possibility to file the master data sheet and the cost sheets separately, as well as client correspondence and correspondence.

It makes sense to file the master data sheet on top, after which the account sheets could be filed (since they are only one or a few pages that can easily be skimmed over when looking for other information from the file), then the correspondence with client and opponent and others can be filed.

For subdivision, colored dividers are suitable, which extend on the side beyond the DIN A4 pages, so that you can note the contents in the margin. With this system, more subdivisions are possible than with file covers, so that one can also file invoices separately and/or the correspondence with the legal protection insurance. In addition, important documents can be marked with colorful "post-its". If so many documents belong to a mandate that they alone fill one or more folders, then you can create a normal file with a file cover and leave the documents in the folder, whereby there should be a reference to the folder in the file. Only those who can quickly find their way around their files can work efficiently, make phone calls or argue soundly in front of a court or in meetings. Sorting files systematically is therefore essential for efficient work. If several lawyers work in one office, it may be that each has his own file management system. This is of course possible. The secretarial staff must adapt to this accordingly; especially if they each work for several attorneys, it is cumbersome to follow different systems. Errors are easier to make, and this can mean that a considerable amount of time is needed to find and correct them. It is obvious that it is more efficient overall if one system is used uniformly in an office.

File work can be greatly facilitated if essential information or thought processes are summarized in the form of **file notes**. As already mentioned, we sometimes process thirty or more files in one day. Moreover, a mandate can extend over several years. Anyone who has to leaf through the entire file and read important pleadings each time in order to recapitulate a complex matter will need incomparably more time than someone who has noted down the essentials in file notes. In addition, work is much more fun when you don't have the feeling that you are wasting your time on duplicate work. File notes also make it easier for a colleague to work when he or she has to substitute for the clerk due to illness or a scheduling conflict. In addition, you will be forced to distinguish between what is essential and what is not, and if you sketch out your argumentation for defending or substantiating a claim in key words, you will inevitably recognize early on where any weak points are. In the interest of our clients, we are usually expected to provide an early assessment of the opportunities and risks we see, just as we are regularly asked to provide information on the time frame of the individual mandate. The more accurately we make such forecasts (which is often simply impossible), the better the client feels advised and the better we can plan ourselves. Based on this fact, memos can be easily prepared.

Today, the spectrum of legal activities is so broad that it is impossible to handle every case. Specializations have been developing for years. Even the so-called general attorney often does not handle public or criminal law mandates. The fact that mandates are handled by lawyers who are well versed in the relevant area of law or who have chosen their focus of interest accordingly is definitely in the interest of the client. But efficient work and thus time management is also better possible when **specializations** are used by lawyers. Therefore, after an initial orientation phase, you should perhaps strive to develop a specialization. This can relate to areas of law, but also clients, e.g.:

- Specialized attorneyships (e.g. in labor, social, family, insolvency, administration, insurance or criminal law),
- focus of interests and/or activities,
- specialization in certain – also "exotic" – areas of law (e.g. ski law),
- specialization in client groups (e.g. employers, landlords, women).

Cooperation with specialized colleagues naturally makes a lot of sense within the same law firm, because the mandate in question remains in the law firm. In the case of a sole practitioner or a small law firm, it will often not be possible to handle all mandates "in-house". You could, however, agree with one or more external colleagues to recommend mandates of one area to them if, conversely, you are sent mandates "of your" specialty. If you are not forced to familiarize yourself legally with every new case, you can expand your actual specialization and position yourself better in the market – and on top of that you save time and minimize the risk inherent in half-knowledge. In addition, you can plan better in case of doubt, because you can calculate how much time you will probably need to deal with certain issues.

Secretarial staff can also specialize and use this to work more efficiently. One or the other employee may have **specialized knowledge** in the following areas:
- Telephone (through telephone training in acquisition and customer retention, one can also specialize in this area),
- dunning,
- foreclosure,
- guardianship matters,
- traffic accident matters,
- billing.

Make realistic **notes of deadlines and resubmissions**. Above we talked about making weekly and daily plans. In our profession, it is now mandatory to note down deadlines and resubmissions. This already results from the professional law as well as from reasons of quality assurance. Otherwise it would not be possible to process a large number of mandates in parallel. Today, every lawyer's software contains deadline and resubmission calendars, which you should definitely use. There are different deadlines to distinguish:
- Statutory time limits, e.g. statute of limitations, notice of material defects, time limit for filing an action for protection against dismissal in labor court proceedings, separation year in the case of divorce
- Court-imposed deadlines, including emergency deadlines, e.g. for filing a statement of defense, statement of defense, appeal, statement of position, payment of advances on court costs
- other deadlines e.g. deadlines set by the opponent for comment or payment

The appropriate actions must be taken at the latest by the time the deadline expires. In the case of filing a statement of defense or a statement of grounds for appeal, this may mean that several hours of work, including meetings, have to be spent. Of course, one then "hits the skids" if one only becomes aware of the expiration of such a deadline on the day of its expiration. Deadlines are typically set externally, so you must take this into account in your weekly and daily planning. Depending on the required action, each deadline should therefore be noted in the calendar in conjunction with a so-called **advance deadline** (of e.g. eight or ten days). This way you can plan realistically. If you have a list of deadlines relating to the next week printed out and presented to you every day, you will always have a good overview of all deadlines to be met. In addition, files should be resubmitted at certain times.

Such resubmissions are often noted in the following cases:

- State of affairs
- Opinion given
- Payment received from opponent
- Advance paid by client
- Invoice paid
- File suit
- Send draft letter to opponent to client to clarify details

Most attorneys use computers in their offices and have the current week's deadlines submitted to them on a daily basis. Regardless of this, you should make a note in your own calendar of those tasks (including deadline matters) that take a lot of time to complete. This way you can always plan specifically. If, for example, in one week you have to do three difficult briefs, prepare and host a child's birthday party and attend a court hearing to which five witnesses have been summoned, then only schedule the absolutely necessary resubmissions for that week and do not schedule any additional time-consuming tasks. In this way, you can avoid the coincidence of too many or time-consuming tasks to a certain extent. Deadlines should always be processed as early as possible. This way you can avoid unexpected questions from your clients, who usually get nervous at the latest in the week before the deadline, if the requested action has not yet taken place.

When you deal with a file, you should dispose or initiate something purposefully. Avoid just "pushing" the file by doing nothing but assigning a new resubmission.

If, for example, you have set the opponent a deadline for payment of your client's claim for compensation for work, then you should have the file resubmitted the day after the deadline expires in order to check whether payment has been made.

- If yes, then you must pay out the third-party money without delay (possibly after offsetting against your fee claim),
- if not, then you should discuss the further steps with your client
- (file a lawsuit or apply for an order to pay and ask for an advance payment).

It is best to do this immediately.

In the second alternative, for example, it would be inefficient to initially put the file away again in order to ask the client at a later time how to proceed. Each time you process a file, you should be clear about the next step and make a decision based on it. In this way, the processing of the file is driven forward. This is regularly in the interest of the client and at the same time goal-oriented and efficient. In addition, this benefits not only you, but also your secretarial staff.

ℹ At this point, let's talk about **efficient communication** again:
You often have to ask your clients questions (about the facts of the case, about further proceedings, about witnesses). The more vague you formulate such questions, the more likely it is that the clients will not give the complete answer. You will then have to ask again, which in case of doubt means that the file will have to be brought back to you, processed and tidied up again. Therefore, ask very specific questions, e.g. by asking for the first name and surname as well as the address of a witness or exact time and place details or exact product descriptions. Use simple and colloquial language – less in a legal context. You are your client's lawyer and are paid to "translate" complicated legal situations in a generally understandable, individually sensitive way with a clear proposal for a solution. If your client has to ask questions or does not understand the question, you have not done your job – and produced costs without added value for your law firm.

Many letters that lawyers are confronted with on a daily basis contain wording that is incomprehensible to the legal layperson and therefore give rise to further correspondence or communication:
- What does "order for the determination of costs" mean?
- What does the requirement to pay an advance (in connection with an order to take evidence) mean?
- What does "default judgment" mean?
- What does it mean when a judgment has been issued but is not yet final?
- What does "date for pronouncement of a decision" mean?
- What do specific legal statements mean (e.g. joint and several debt, retention of title, subsequent heir)?

If you send the copy of pleadings or resolutions to your client merely "for information", he will call you in case of doubt and ask for it. You can avoid this telephone call if you send a brief explanatory cover letter. I have therefore gotten into the habit of always providing clients with appropriate explanations. This saves you and your secretarial staff a lot of time every day, and clients also feel particularly well advised. Use standard letters and text modules when appropriate. This way you can save time. You save your employees time because they only have to make a few individual insertions in the text:
- Request for coverage from the client's legal protection insurance,
- notice of defense to the court (after an action has been filed against the client),
- explanation of the possibility of contesting a judgment,
- request for assessment of costs/compensation of costs.

The same applies to short instructions. You don't have to dictate everything. This has the advantage that the secretarial staff immediately know which brief instruction is involved in each individual case. For example, it helps to attach a corresponding written brief instruction to a stack of files rather than just dictating it, in order

to give employees a better basis for deciding when and who deals with it. In the following cases, you can work very well with brief instructions:
- Entering reminders in the calendar,
- sending a copy of a letter to the client,
- payment of third-party money,
- initiating a request to the Residents' Registration Office regarding the opponent,
- requesting an excerpt from the Commercial Register regarding the opponent,
- final filing,
- filing files in folders, combining or separating files.

In this context, it is important that the office staff are instructed exactly what to do in which case. But that is just a question of good delegation.

After the end of a mandate, the file must be **closed and archived**. This can be delegated well and even arranged by means of a short order. In this way, one can not only save time, but also space (filing cabinets are not cheap). The prerequisite is, of course, that the client's order has been fulfilled, that all bookings have been made (including payments) and that client documents (e.g. titles, original documents, receipts) have been returned. If you manage a mandate purposefully and with progress, you will automatically reach the point where the file must be closed. However, do not neglect to actually initiate the final filing. If you do not do this, you will be confronted with your file corpses at some later point in time. If you then can no longer remember the mandate, let alone its completion, you will inevitably have to go back and re-file. This work is absolutely unsatisfactory and robs valuable time. Here you should also keep in mind at what filing volume it is worthwhile to use an electronic filing system.

As lawyers, we are confronted with a vast amount of **literature**. In addition, there are the articles in the professional journals as well as the daily newspaper, long newsletters, magazines, and maybe even a normal book. Managers are said to spend about 30 % of their time reading; lawyers spend at least the same amount of time reading. So if you achieve an increase in your reading output, you can gain a corresponding amount of time for other things. Select reading material. If you are curious about all the incoming mail and then read through everything that spontaneously interests you, you will have to admit at the end of the day that much of it did not need to be read at all. You should therefore consciously decide what you read and what you do not read. What you have to read for professional reasons, you can certainly define well. What you should and want to read, you should read purposefully and result oriented. If you find that you don't need to read something at all, then don't bother with it any further.

You can cut out important passages from longer texts from a copy you have made and attach them directly to a file, for example[25]. You can also create a folder in which you file individual cut or copied texts sorted by topic.

Improve your reading method and speed.

Orientational reading

The reading material is grasped for the first time in order to estimate what awaits you as a reader. While "skimming", you should remember which information is important to you. If necessary, you can immediately make marks in the text or write out keywords. Pay attention to key words and concluding sentences. Newspaper articles, commentaries, and professional articles typically contain the important information at the beginning or at the end; you can specifically read these passages.

Studious reading

Means comprehensive and evaluative reading. Capture the content in short bullet points. Don't be afraid to edit texts you read by marking them. Important passages or key words can simply be marked with highlighters, but you can also use certain characters to emphasize different things (e.g. "!" for important, "?" for questionable, "P" for problem, "C" for copy, etc.). If you have found your own system for marking texts and remain faithful to it, you will be able to find your way quickly and easily in texts once edited, even after a long break.

Summarizing reading

Means synoptic compilation of the content as well as critical evaluation of what has been worked out. Read titles, subtitles and headings as well as content notes, prefaces and blurb texts. You can quickly "skim" passages with obviously less information content, but you should read important passages carefully and slowly.

to work out individual markers and paradigms.

---

i You can increase the reading speed with some practice as follows
- Reading syllable-by-syllable instead of letter-by-letter,
- avoiding internal talking along,
- focused instead of superficial reading,

---

25 Also use the photo function and the screenshot of your smartphone to quickly and easily assign something to the e-file.

- eye movements instead of head movements,
- reading in a comfortable, convenient position,
- eliminating distracting environmental factors (e.g., noise, inadequate lighting).

4. Efficient office processes

Many office processes can be standardized and thus made more efficient. Clear instructions to employees are a prerequisite for this. So is the creation of lists and systems.

Resubmission lists

Files are to be resubmitted for a wide variety of reasons. I have already explained this above. However, this does not mean that the lawyer himself has to see every file. Some resubmissions can be delegated directly to employees, so that they can then initiate the next step themselves, e.g. “Advance on costs paid, if necessary reminder and new resubmission”. With virtual resubmissions, it is not necessary to take the individual file in hand, because you can initiate the next step “from the head”, e.g. “Response from the client there? (If a statement from the client had been received to date, you would already know this as a lawyer. A short letter to the client as a reminder and a new resubmission can be ordered without the file).

The regular resubmissions should be assigned to a specific place in your workroom – which in any case is something to consider with regard to client confidentiality, and not just since the new data protection regulations. However, they should not lie on your desk. You should process these files completely every day. If you do not do this, you will generate a pile of files within a short period of time, and soon no one will know which files are in them. This can mean tedious file searching, but also has the consequence that the processing of the individual mandates does not take place progressively, which cannot be in your own interest, but also not in the interest of your clients.

Deadline lists

Deadline lists should be printed and updated daily for the week or next two weeks. So should the advance deadlines. Depending on the action required, you should have different advance deadlines noted. The completion of certain deadline matters can be delegated, e.g. in the case of a deadline for the payment of an advance on court costs for the commissioning of an expert: If the money has already been paid by the client, an employee from the secretary's office can also arrange for the timely payment to the court and then delete the deadline. In any case, deadlines must be deleted as soon as the requested action has taken place. Otherwise, there is a risk of irritation, which in turn can cost a lot of time. It is impossible to remember everything when there are so many files; if you fail to delete a deadline after it has been completed, you will have to pick up the file again to make sure that everything has been done.

File Management System

In many law firms, several hours (!) are wasted every week – sometimes even every day – searching for files because they are not in the defined places. This can be avoided if it is ensured that each file is always in "its" place (e.g. hanging files in alphabetical order in the filing cabinet, folders accordingly on the shelf).

In the following cases, files are inevitably not in "their" place:

- when the lawyer works with the file (the file is on the desk or at home),
- when the lawyer is on the way to an appointment (the file is in the lawyer's suitcase or in the car),
- when mail is assigned (the file is in the inbox),
- when the file is resubmitted (the file is in the resubmission box),
- when the lawyer has dictated something (the file is in the dictation box),
- when the lawyer has given a brief instruction (the file is in the brief instructions box).

Files should **only** be removed from "their" place in cases where it is not otherwise possible, i.e. if a file is not being worked with, it should definitely be returned to "its" place immediately. Many client programs already offer the possibility of initiating much essential file work without the paper file, and this from several workstations at the same time. Also, make use of the function of some client programs to track the location of the paper file in the office[26]. Avoid creating piles of files at the lawyers' or secretaries' offices.

Postal system

Filter your mail or have it filtered. Give specific instructions as to what should be sorted and presented for filing, scanned or processed immediately. Even the em-

26 Some attorneys still work with so-called missing sheets, noting where an individual file is when it is not in "its" place.

ployee responsible for incoming mail can throw away individual items of mail without first presenting them. Give corresponding instructions for advertising mail. Some people have these bundled in a separate folder. In this case, it is essential to define who will review and clear out this folder and at what intervals.

The **technical possibilities** also place new demands on the legal profession to adapt their work processes and their technical aids to the needs and working methods of their clients. With all the striving for modernity and contemporary legal advice, neither the legal framework conditions of one's own work should be overlooked, nor should the special relationship of trust between client and lawyer be disregarded.

The technical aids also require adjustments in the relationship to the clients and the possible circle of clients, e.g. in the terms and conditions of the mandate concerning the use of electronic communication as well as the manner and content of law firm websites. In the German Bar Association (DAV), the Information Technology Working Group deals with IT law issues and the Lawyers' Management Working Group with information on IT and telecommunication technology issues specific to law firms. Since 2006, there has been a specialized bar for information technology law (IT law), which is trained and experienced in questions of IT, software, Internet and telecommunications law, as well as the specific questions of copyright and trademark law, in particular domain law, data protection, criminal law, public procurement law, international and procedural law, each with a different focus.

Data protection and data security have not only been an issue since May 2018. The new version of the GDPR is accompanied by numerous tightening measures to protect consumers and data owners. The installation of a data protection officer is still prescribed from a certain number of persons in automated data processing and will be the norm in the modern law firm. It is therefore necessary to determine how many persons, regardless of whether they are full or part-time, employed or freelancers, or proprietors, are involved in the automated collection, processing and use of personal data. As previously mentioned, an external data protection officer can also be appointed without giving rise to concerns of a breach of the obligation of professional secrecy.

Data protection must be distinguished from data security. The former covers the protection of personal data in the sense of reducing data volumes. Data security means the protection of IT systems (hardware, software, infrastructure, networks, data) against the risk of loss, destruction or use, i.e., misuse by unauthorized persons. The processing, storage and communication of information must be designed in such a way that the confidentiality, availability and integrity of the information and systems are ensured to a sufficient degree, threats are identified and risks are minimized (IT risk management). The IT basic protection manual of the Federal Office for Information Security (BSI) can provide useful basic knowledge for this. In addition to concise basic information, the BSI offers the IT security guide and the IT basic protection catalogs for downloading on its website[27].

Software is always the target of hacker attacks looking for security holes. The latest updates close these security gaps. Antivirus programs (virus scanners/virus protection) detect, block and eliminate computer viruses, computer worms and Trojan horses. The obligation to update existing software is now recognized by the courts. A firewall is a system of software (packet filters, proxy servers) and hardware components (routers, hosts) that restricts access between different computer networks in order to implement a security concept. A firewall is used in a law firm at the interface between the local network and the Internet. Data backup must be performed manually or automatically on a regular basis, ideally on a daily basis. Finally, a system for backing up data should be installed and, for safety's sake, a check should be made to see whether the data has been backed up properly and whether the data can be restored in the event of an emergency.

The most important measures at a glance:
- Update software
- Install/configure anti-virus software
- Install/configure firewall
- Manage and restrict user rights
- Encrypt sensitive data
- Data backup
- Employee training
- Create emergency plan

The equipment of the law firm with **telecommunication solutions** can vary greatly from law firm to law firm. Nevertheless, the exact implementation is an important component in the time management for the law firm.

Standard should be:
- Fixed-line telephone system,
- answering machine,
- fax machine,
- mobile phone/smart phone,
- card reader,
- franking machine

27 www.bsi-bund.de.

The telephone system is a switching device that connects several terminal devices, e.g., telephones, fax, answering machines, both to each other and to the public telephone network. The switchboard is the main functional unit of the telephone system, whose input and output channels are switched by a control unit. The advantages of using a telephone system are, firstly, the free internal calls between the various terminals connected to the system. Secondly, the chargeable exchange connections (lines) are better utilized, since not every terminal requires its own subscriber line. The telephone system has its own additional functions for managing and processing telephone calls, such as call forwarding, toggling, call diverting, call lists, individual call and charge evaluations. In addition, there is often an answering point where calls are answered centrally and forwarded to the appropriate persons. A telecommunications system can also be used to define which calls can be made from individual extensions and to what extent extensions can be reached from outside. Switching between internal and external calls is usually performed via a one or multi-digit prefix, the traffic segregation digit. This is often the "0", which is also the usual traffic digit in Germany. Telephone systems are also available for small units. When deciding between desktop and cordless units, it is important to consider which functionalities are needed. A cordless unit certainly makes sense for the office if there are long distances. Today, however, a headset for the telephone service is common because it is practical and healthy for the posture, and it also keeps the hands free. By the way, the telephone service of the office can also be completely handled by service providers. These offer individualized telephone and secretarial services at a flat rate or basic price.

Despite the introduction of the PC workstation, the work of lawyers is also strongly characterized by **dictation** on the desks of professionals. Whether via good speech recognition programs or classically as a recording on a smart phone or separate device: a good dictation unit is just as effective a tool for optimal time management as high-quality devices for the transcription service (with headphones and pedal). After all, nothing is as time-consuming and tedious as poorly functioning technology or disruptive noise. Here, too, external secretarial and typing services can be put to good temporary use.

Document research for legal texts, decisions, legal literature in professional journals, commentaries and reference books as well as samples, application forms, register excerpts, pieces of evidence and publications about professional associations and conferences is mapped in a time-saving way today by using online or CD-Rom research options or knowledge management tools. The Internet also offers a good opportunity to search for legal information. There are portals that provide legal information, databases of court decisions, law firm websites with legal information, websites of the respective associations with online publications or conference documents, and much more. In a joint project with juris GmbH, the Federal Ministry of Justice makes almost all current federal law available free of charge on the Internet at www.gesetze-im-internet.de.The laws and legal ordinances can be downloaded from the Internet. The laws and ordinances can be accessed in their current version. They are continuously updated by the documentation office of the BMJ[28]. The portal of Saarland University offers a large selection of state and European legal norms[29]. The legal norms of the European Union can be found at http://europa.eu.int/eur-lex/en/.

What did you get out of the chapter?

You know the most important methods and tools for effective time management related to the workflows in law firms. Now you just have to apply them!

28 Please note: The legal texts available on the Internet are not the official versions. These can only be found in the Federal Law Gazette at www.bundesanzeiger.de,which is a subscription service for which a fee is charged.

29 Athttp://www.jura.uni-sb.de/.

E. Law firm governance and personnel management

Personnel development is one of the most important building blocks in law firm development: Your employees are your most important resource, your greatest potential, your figurehead with existing and future clients.

Due to the shortage of skilled workers, law firms continue to have problems finding suitable personnel. The increase in personnel costs in general is also an issue for many law firms. Law firm owners try to compensate for this by introducing law firm software that automates processes and procedures and makes them more effective and efficient, thus saving on staff. However, they usually compensate for this primarily by increasing their personal working hours.

Retaining employees in the firm, on the other hand, is not (yet) a problem for many when it comes to smaller and medium-sized law firms where, despite the enormous workload, there is usually a rather familiar and personal atmosphere. This compensates through the strong ties to the law firm and the high level of trust. In the entire legal industry, however, there has been a **trend toward changing law firms** and employers, especially in the last five to ten years – both among attorneys and law firm employees. Experts see the reason for this in the strong uncertainty in the industry caused by far-reaching changes, but also in the growing awareness of and demand for one's own quality of life and meaningful, fulfilling work.

When developing an existing law firm, law firm owners face two sets of issues:
1. Do I have the right people on board to achieve my strategic goals?
2. Can my employees develop in such a way that they will master future challenges, or do I need differently qualified and talented professionals?

In order to determine the exact need for competencies, strengths and qualifications, the so-called "SWOT analysis" can help. Here, the strengths (S for strengths), weaknesses (W for weaknesses), opportunities (O for opportunities) and risks (T for threats) are developed for each individual employee[1].

At the same time, the requirements of the market for the law firm are also included in the SWOT analysis: New Work, Work 4.0, agility, flat hierarchies – the labor market is currently facing a transformation that does not stop at the legal sector. Law firms will also have to think about whether new fields of work and responsibilities will be needed in the future in order to master these challenges. For

1 You may remember the tool from one of the previous chapters.

https://doi.org/10.1515/9783111058160-005

example, law firms of a certain size now not only have gender officers, but also so-called feel-good managers.

Possible issues in human resource management with SWOT analysis:
- Work organization and processes (keyword: agile leadership)
- Work locations and hours (keyword: work-life balance)
- Work content and tasks (keyword: new work)
- Work culture and leadership (keyword: employee responsibility)
- Work models and forms (keyword: new partner models)
- Work resources and tools (keyword: knowledge transfer)

Entrepreneurs who want to be perceived as responsible employers in the future must proactively address the two major issues of our time and take a stand: Diversity and climate change. This is not easy for many law firms, especially because the rather conservative industry has remained largely unaffected by all kinds of upheavals and reforms.

Nevertheless, avoiding these issues for as long as possible is perceived – both by employees and customers. Decide for yourself what you want to stand for. My recommendation: Even a polarizing stance is better than none. As a lawyer, you should always take a clear stand on sociopolitical issues – and at the same time be aware of your responsibility as a role model.

The battle for so-called high potentials – i. e. particularly talented and high-performing employees – has been raging for a long time. Today, employees are allowed to be more demanding. After all, they want to take on more responsibility themselves. Employer branding (i. e., marketing for recruiting new employees) is increasingly becoming the third important pillar of marketing, which until now has tended to revolve around new and existing mandates.

Above all, however, it should serve to attract and bring aboard the right employees; in other words, those who fit the corporate culture.

Finally, the key role of the supervisor, the manager, should be discussed at this point. As a lawyer and law firm owner or partner, you already have a dual role, which does not exactly make decisions easier. Even if, for example, the banal update of a law firm's software can certainly be a relief in the daily work from the lawyer's point of view, it can become a disaster from the entrepreneurial perspective, because it becomes apparent that this (time and financial) investment can at best be a short-term solution, but not a long-term one.

And this brings us to the heart of the matter: As a manager, the first thing you need to do is clarify your role. In which role function do you have to perform this task? Only if you have a clear picture of this can you exercise the associated rights and duties.

As a manager, you actually have a total of four levels to consider: In addition to your **personal role clarification**, the relevance for the **overall system of the law**

firm is always important. On the one hand, this is where your responsibility for the continued existence of the firm comes into play (and as you know, not all decisions for the firm are in your personal interest or in the interest of your employees). On the other hand, the **special task definitions of the employees and your own self-management** also come into play here.

Another, not entirely insignificant aspect is your own personality and socialization. Even today, leadership styles vary from strictly hierarchical to coaching styles. As a manager, you should at least have reflected for yourself whether you can be assigned to one or the other leadership style. Above all, however, you should also have reflected on whether this leadership style is good for your firm and your employees. It is no coincidence that awareness of one's own leadership is an essential component of strong leaders.

In addition to reflecting on one's own leadership style (which, by the way, can also be supported very well by tools such as 360-degree feedback or the Hogan Leadership Assessment), it is therefore especially important to also have a sense for the development status of one's own law firm: Where exactly is it located, for example, in the system of so-called Spiral Dynamics. What leadership style would the firm and its staff ideally need now?

A law firm lives from and through its employees: It's a people business. Constructively dealing with the requirements of your law firm and the potential of your employees while at the same time considering yourself as the greatest challenge in the further development of your law firm is certainly claim enough.

I. Leadership and leadership styles

You will learn how to recognize good law firm leadership and what you need for it.

Overview

1. **Partnerships and other forms of collaboration**
2. **Managing Partner and management team**
3. **Performance management and compensation systems**

Law firm development is personnel development[1]. The human factor is the essential resource of every law firm[2]: It's a people business. However, topics such as employer branding, talent and diversity management are only slowly finding their way into strategy meetings.

The way you work together, leadership styles, employee motivation and retention, but also team building and knowledge transfer are key factors on your way to becoming a successful law firm, no matter what size. But how can leadership and employee motivation succeed today? Who actually leads in a law firm?

As a lawyer, you are a legal administrator, the producer of the legal advice product. In this function, you manage legal staff and colleagues, perhaps even a team or a department, and, certainly, the assistants and technical staff, as well as trainees.

As a law firm owner, you manage the law firm. Managing a law firm is managing a company. From a business perspective, ideally the owner is not the same as the manager or director. Why? There may be conflicting interests.

From a certain size, law firms therefore afford "managing partners" who are responsible for both the daily and longer-term central management tasks and thus relieve the lawyers in their legal activities as well as the partners for the strategic work. This is an advantage not to be underestimated, which is added to the central, transparent and sustainable internal management of the law firm managed in this way.

So as an independent lawyer, you lead in more ways than one. How well do you do that and what is your actual leadership style?

1 According to JUVE, in the last 10 years a law firm needed an average of 50 % staff growth to maintain its position in the market, JUVE Handbuch 2017.

2 Dr. Kraus in Schieblon, "Kanzleimanagement in der Praxis", p. 52.

According to the **study** “Emotionale Führung am Arbeitsplatz” (**Emotional Leadership in the Workplace**) by the management consultancy Rochus Mummert[3] German employees give their bosses a devastating report card:

- **Recognition and praise? Non-existent**
  No reprimand is praise enough – this is apparently the attitude of bosses. Only one third of employees can look forward to words of praise and recognition from their managers. Positive reinforcement of desired behavior is now part of the standard repertoire of modern education in parenting and pedagogy, even in dog training. In personnel management, however, it has still not been adopted by the majority.

- **A sympathetic ear for problems? What for.**
  Only one-third of those surveyed have a boss who is always available to help with problems and in crisis situations. Otherwise, it seems that in stormy seas, the crew on board fights without the captain. No wonder, because only two out of ten bosses can apparently deal with criticism.

- **Employee discovery and development? No interest**
  Anyone who wants to develop in their job and perhaps move up within the company is dependent on their direct supervisor. However, four out of five employees do not feel supported by their boss in their career planning.

The results are sobering: only one-third consider their own boss to be professionally competent and suitable as a boss in terms of character. For this purpose, 1,000 employees from all sectors were surveyed. The results are therefore fairly representative and applicable to all professions, including the legal sector. According to this study, only bosses who prefer a more coaching style of leadership are apparently judged differently.

- more than half of the employees consider their coaching boss to be unreservedly professionally suitable and absolutely suitable in terms of character.
- and just as many also attest to their boss always being approachable in the event of problems.

3 The study “Emotionale Führung am Arbeitsplatz” (Emotional Leadership in the Workplace) was conducted by the HR consultancy Rochus Mummert and published on April 26, 2016. 1,000 employees in Germany were surveyed for the study.

"The most popular and qualified type of supervisor among employees is unfortunately underrepresented in German companies. Not even one in four employees works for a company where coaching is a top priority," says Hans Schlipat of Rochus Mummert. "Yet only an emphatic manager in the style of a coach has the potential to positively influence every employee and thus the success of the entire company in the long term. He acts authentically and also picks up the individual emotionally from where he is at the moment." However, a very important aspect of this is to use coaching to develop an understanding of the fact that the firm is a self-contained system in which certain things can develop a certain momentum[4] and which management style the respective employee needs. Not every employee can be managed equally well with one and the same management style[5].

But as a boss, does it always come down to being popular with employees? No, of course not. Leadership means making and implementing uncomfortable decisions. Always aiming for consensus may make you a good team player, but not a competent boss. There are situations that are better handled with one leadership style or the other.

However, you should be aware of your own preferred leadership style and not drive on "autopilot" following the motto: I've always done it this way.

How do you evaluate your leadership style[6]?

This can be done through anonymous **employee feedback**[7] or through special coaching such as "coaching on the job" or "shadow coaching". In this case, the coach accompanies the manager silently in the background for a while, as it were like a shadow, so that he or she can then give feedback from the position of an "objective observer". Problematic interactions with employees, team difficulties, communication deficits or even "operational blindness" can be uncovered in this way.

According to Rochus Mummert, for example, the vast majority of bosses lead in a "commanding" manner. How reasonable is it to look for the most talented and highly qualified employees in personnel recruiting, only to conservatively rely on blind obedience and degrade employees to dependent stooges. This is followed by a demanding style (16 %), a visionary style (15 %), a democratic style (13 %) and an emotion-oriented style (10 %).

4 König, "Einführung in das systemische Denken und Handeln", p. 195 et seq.; Lencioni, "Die 5 Dysfunktionen eines Teams", p. 157.

5 Blanchard, "Führungsstile, situatives Führen", p. 23.

6 Again, you can use your profile from the "Strengthsfinder" (gallup) or take one of the other more detailed tests, such as the Reiss Potential Test.

7 Such as through the method of "360 degree feedback".

A successful boss consciously employs a coaching style of leadership over and over again:
- because motivated employees achieve twice as much and are more creative
- because only in this way can the full potential of a well-functioning team be exploited
- because employees who stand behind him strengthen his own position in the company

By staying in conversation with his employees, asking them the right questions and actively listening:
- **Ask open-ended questions.** These are questions that cannot be answered with YES or NO, so-called W-questions e.g. "What can you do differently here to achieve a successful result?" Ask the question, "What else?".
  After each question, sit back and let your employee think and come up with the answer. In this game, if you move first, you lose! The simplest question is "And?" Also use techniques such as mirroring (repeating) the employee's statement.
- **Listen.** First and foremost, this means managing your own ego and attention, i.e., turning off e-mails and cell phones, scheduling enough undisturbed time, paying attention to your own energy curve and that of your coworker. But active listening also means listening for nuances ("the topic behind the topic"), interpreting facial expressions and body language (correctly). Or taking the intercultural context into account.

None of this is new. Properly applied, however, it is an art that, like everything else, is better learned with a well-founded and certified education.

Because nothing is more dangerous than half-knowledge and misunderstanding. It is no coincidence that investing in basic coaching training is now considered modern leadership training.

But no matter which leadership style you lean towards, as a boss you should ensure a **positive working atmosphere** by
- conveying that you enjoy your work
- having a positive basic attitude towards your employees
- being attentive and present[8]

8 As an example of many good books on leadership, here is my favorite book on the subject, which gets to the heart of the matter in a short, concise and entertaining way: Lundin, "Fish," p. 87.

People tend to be engaged and productive only when they are satisfied and feel seen. While pressure may be appropriate and helpful in a crisis situation in the short term, it creates resistance as a permanent pressure that unnecessarily drains energy and attention.

And finally: When was the last time you thanked your colleagues, employees and assistants who support you in your successes and have your back? I'm not talking about the monthly paycheck as "compensation," nor am I referring to the regular employee talk or the chat in the coffee kitchen. I mean the concrete and explicit recognition of another's performance as a valuable contribution to the firm's success. Sometimes a little attention is enough. Sometimes, however, it has to be a very clear THANK YOU. In the midst of everyday stress, don't forget to notice the people around you. And do not underestimate the potential that lies in this gesture:

When you say thank you, show your **appreciation**
- for the support you have received. And you will be supported even more.
- for the person. You consolidate loyalty, attachment and trust.

In large law firms, bonuses, special allowances and profit sharing are not uncommon. They are intended to spur employees on and provide a certain amount of compensation for the many unpaid overtime hours, night and weekend shifts. The prospect of a partnership can also motivate employees to perform at their best. The disadvantage: If these incentives are a regular part of the compensation system, employees expect them and see them as part of their compensation entitlement. The intended additional motivation does not apply. Instead, fear of loss arises, which tends to demotivate and frustrate. The result: service by the book. A real gesture of gratitude and motivation, on the other hand, are irregular and surprising rewards:
- This means that the random reward remains the exception to the rule and retains its "cherry on top" status.
- The reward has a retroactive effect: the boss/company expresses gratitude and appreciation for the success achieved.
- The Spot Award acts as a motivation booster in the future.

And at around ten percent of the annual salary, the investment in such **spot awards** remains manageable and at best calculable in the intended result. So should a portion of the profit earned be spontaneously transferred to the respective employee according to the watering can principle? No. A Spot Award handled in this way would undermine employee motivation and cause unrest in the team.

i

It is important to adhere to the following three basic principles for Spot Awards[9]:

1. *Transparency*
   The allocation of the award must always be accompanied by individual feedback and take into account a certain team fairness. With skillful communication, the allocation should be easily comprehensible for everyone involved.
2. *Proportionality*
   The budget of the award should be in the financial context of the regular remuneration and the profit achieved. Experts recommend an amount of 5–10 percent of the gross annual earnings.
3. *Connexity*
   Ultimately, the Spot Award should be factually and temporally related to the result achieved. A monetary amount is not recommended. To be the incentive described above, the award should show that the boss/company has put thought and effort into expressing its appreciation and motivating. This can be personalized non-cash prizes (engraved fountain pen, etc.) or certain status symbols within the office organization (certain parking space/office, special furnishings). These can also be special retreats, events and locations, which additionally strengthen the team spirit or are connected with premium further education.

A spot reward as an incentive, which rewards and motivates and at the same time strengthens the team, is therefore the ideal building block for companies such as law firms, whose greatest potential and greatest risk are their employees!

Leadership

First of all, leadership must be clearly separated from the terms leader and management:

Leadership: This is about being a beacon, taking responsibility. Visions, values and inspiration are important to motivate employees intrinsically.

Leader: Leader is more about the technical supervisor who generates performance based on the given hierarchy or with pressure.

Management: A good manager takes care of effective processes and efficient organization. He makes resources available for problem solving.

Good leadership needs

1. Self-reflection and relationship management
2. Fine communication technique and
3. understanding of employee needs.

9 Dr. Tutschka, "Spot Awards – der ideale Baustein für die Personalführung" from 20.6.2016 in CLP-Blog.

So, I want to start with some of the common communication tools:

Friedemann Schulz von Thun's **four-ear model** is also known as the four-sided model or communication / message square. The communication model states that every utterance of a person conveys four messages simultaneously:

1. Announcement
   What do they reveal about themselves?
2. Subject level
   What are they talking about?
3. Appeal
   What do they want from me?
4. Relationship level
   How do they relate to me?

Remember:
The 4-sided model shows where misunderstandings have arisen or may arise in the process.

The factual level still shows the same on both sides, but different interpretations and evaluations usually come into play as early as the self-revelation and relationship. Misunderstandings arise when the receiver perceives a piece of information from the sender differently.

Similarly, the **sender-receiver model,** one of the simplest and most technical communication models, by Claude E. Shannon and Warren Weaver. It states that in communication there is always a sender and a receiver.

The sender encodes its message into a signal (e.g., speech). The receiver picks up the signal (in this example with his ear) and decodes the content. During the transmission there can be disturbances, which cause misunderstandings[10].

Examples of disruptive factors:

- Interlocutors speak different languages – translation can change the original content
- Ambiguities
- Sarcasm that is not understood
- Unclear expressions
- Outside noises
- Lack of attention

10 The so-called Organon model also assumes similar communication patterns.

The classic **iceberg model** comes from Sigmund Freud. The renowned psychoanalyst was convinced that most of our communication takes place invisibly. Like an iceberg, 20 percent is visible (the so-called factual level) and 80 percent is hidden beneath the surface (the relationship level). This is what makes exchanges between peFreud's model has been adopted and rethought by various scientists – even outside the field of pure communication science. For example, the 80-to-20 split is known as the Pareto principle.

Paul Watzlawick expanded the previous models. He summarized them with Don D. Jackson and Janet H. Beavin to the five axioms.

Among other things, they describe interpersonal communication that takes place on a meta-level.

This includes the fact that people always communicate, even if they do not do so directly according to their own judgment. Therefore, according to Watzlawick, non-communication is impossible.

1. One cannot not communicate.
2. Every communication has a content aspect and a relationship aspect.
3. Communication is always cause and effect.
4. Human communication uses analog (nonverbal communication) and digital methods (verbal communication).
5. Communication is symmetrical (at eye level) or complementary (hierarchical).

Which leadership style is actually most effective is determined by the following criteria:

- System and role in the system
- Employee and
- manager

This is where the values and culture of the firm come into play on the one hand (see Spiral Dynamics: Which people does the system need?), and the role of the manager on the other. It makes a difference whether I am only a professional supervisor or whether I am a personnel developer or even a partner in charge. Of course, the personalities and values of employees and managers also play a role.

Employees can be selected specifically according to certain skills and competencies, but also according to types and characters, to ensure an ideal team composition.

It is important to understand that employees have needs in the sense of Maslow's pyramid of needs in order to be satisfied:

- They want meaningful and challenging tasks.
- They want to see and feel that they are part of the whole, but they also want to be seen as a person.

- They want to be respected and valued for their work.
- They want to share their wishes and ideas in order to make their contribution.
- They want to be able to rely on the word of their supervisor.

However, satisfied employees are not yet committed employees, and certainly not employees who are committed to the firm in the long term. But it is an important prerequisite.

You can recognize committed employees by their positive attitude; by the fact that they identify with the firm's values and see the big picture[11].

But how can I increase employee satisfaction and engagement?

Tasks, responsibility, meaning and well-functioning processes are one thing. Good employee discussions are the other:

The conversation choreography should have an arc of tension (like an essay). There is an introduction, a main part and a conclusion. Emotions and exchanges should clearly increase in the main part, have the appropriate space, and then be calmed down again in the conclusion. Ideally, conversations are ended in a positive partnership, with a clear awareness of what has been discussed and with what goal, and who is responsible for what next steps and by when.

The introduction can be started with small talk and a consolidation of the relationship level, e.g. by satisfying immediate needs (coffee, water, sunscreen, chair, etc.). Then the main part starts with the manager's thematic introduction and the goal of the conversation, followed by feedback (the manager's own perceptions are described in positive-negative-positive terms). The employee's view and the supervisor's expectations follow and are discussed if necessary. Context and overall objective, scope for negotiation are clarified and solutions are proposed. Goals and measures are jointly agreed, resources are made available, and the next steps and deadlines are clarified, ideally all of which are set down in writing. After a short summary and, if necessary, feedback for the superior, the meeting is concluded with small talk[12]. The whole thing should last 30–60 minutes and take place in regular fixed appointments in a protected setting.

11 Mitarbeiter Engagement verstehen, kununu.

12 This corresponds more or less to the structure of legal coaching conversations, which is why the perfecting and deep understanding of why and how this is implemented in practice in order to achieve optimal conversation success is at the heart of our legal coaching training for lawyers at the CLP Academy. In addition, we learn and train how to consciously shape the three parallel levels of conversation: relationship, subject level and environment/context.

The top 10 reasons why employees leave are[13]:

1. Leadership style inadequate
2. Team problems
3. Disunity of the leadership team
4. Overload (too much work and/or content overloaded)
5. Processes and workflows not defined, illogical, outdated, ineffective
6. IT and work equipment outdated
7. Security (financial/economic, but also free of sexual assault and aggression)
8. Meaning (sustainability, further development, commitment, valuable work)
9. Payment
10. Family reasons

The management style used plays a not insignificant role.

Leadership styles are differentiated according to how much decision-making authority the employee has:

- Authoritarian
- Patriarchal
- Bureaucratic
- Consultative
- Participative
- Delegative
- Democratic
- Relationship-oriented
- Cooperative
- Coaching

This is where the employee's decision-making authority increases.

But what does that look like in law firms?
Unfortunately, the data material is scanty. Nevertheless:
The management styles of small to medium-sized law firms are based on the existing structures. This means from classic conservative/authoritarian/ patriarchal to bureaucratic/consultative. With increasing size, a distinction must be made between the management styles of the respective superiors based on the law firm culture and the division of tasks between management and partners: The partners, and in particular the equity partners, are the fulcrum of the firm. They determine values, culture, vision, positioning and strategy. Even the most professional modern

13 *Sabine Olschner*, Jedem Partner sein eigenes Süppchen, LTO from 16.4.2021.

management team cannot really compete with them. Therefore, the work there tends to be consultative/participative. In only 6 % of law firms does management actually make authoritarian decisions[14]. Nevertheless, only 13 % are satisfied with the firm's management. Truly delegative, relationship-oriented or cooperative and coaching work is only done in individual cases within well-functioning business units. As you might have guessed, these are surprisingly staffed by much younger professionals.

On the other hand, we find something different in legal tech development:
The legal market is in a state of flux. With digitization, innovation has conquered the legal industry. However, this not only brings about innovations in the legal tech sector that simplify dull standard work, but also those that cause entire business areas of the legal profession to suddenly vanish into thin air. These innovations are often accompanied by the need to revise and redefine structures and processes in law firms. Many law firms have been catapulted from the paper file Stone Age into the here and now of the digital file, and not just since the special electronic lawyer's mailbox (beA). Today, the lawyer is directly and always accessible to everyone, at least by e-mail, and thus finally comes to the eye level of the client; but also often to the limits of his resilience.

Law firms are now eager to keep pace: Innovation hubs are being set up to create legal tech applications with ambitious young lawyers or bought-in IT nerds and to generate new business areas. Or at least to generate a certain marketing effect: for clients but also for employer branding. Innovation Awards show the diversity of the results.

The question must be posed: Does this accomplish anything?
It is certainly true that innovation is no longer just a freestyle activity for companies today, but a mandatory program if they want to remain fit for the future. It is also true that studying law is not a creative course at the Waldorf School. On the contrary, it has driven many an ambitious person out of being creative once and for all. So can innovation hubs and innovation awards inspire legal creativity?

According to Kohl-Boas, Head of HR Northwest, Central & Eastern Europe at Google, innovation requires more:

1. Culture of innovation and ownership
2. Information and infrastructure
3. Adapted decision-making processes and leadership

---

14 Marktstudie “Moderne Führungsstrukturen in Kanzleien” from Schön u.C.

Innovation hubs and legal tech working groups supported by law firm management can initiate a certain culture of innovation. However, many then lack a certain structure to be able to develop creativity. This can include techniques such as Scrum. But creativity can also be supported by many other tools. Through an appropriate working atmosphere, for example, but also through personal responsibility, information and a supporting infrastructure. This can mean that strategic decisions of the firm's management or certain turnover figures are communicated transparently to the development team or, for example, also internal client information.

However, the most underestimated factors are leadership and decision-making processes. Here, law firms simply fall back on the existing hierarchical structures for the innovation teams; however, it is obvious that innovation requires different structures than a strictly hierarchically managed law firm. Agility is required, the courage to take risks, but also a different culture of making mistakes. In my view, there is also a fourth component: cross competencies. This applies to both employees and managers. Cross competencies require a certain degree of professionalism, experience and know-how in one area, namely the legal field, on the one hand, and in a completely different field on the other.

This confirms that cross competencies, such as foreign language skills, are playing an increasingly important role in the legal sector. In large law firms in particular, business fluent English is a prerequisite in addition to the native language. In times of globalization, legal training in more than one country, or even complete legal training in two different legal systems, is also welcome. Increasingly, however, there is also a demand for lawyers working in the business world to complete additional academic training, e.g. medicine in addition to specializing in medical liability law or business administration. However, the cost-benefit analysis is unlikely to be very convincing here. Nevertheless, the demand is often made that lawyers should at least understand what they want to regulate. This is often countered by the argument that one has acquired sufficient basic knowledge and understanding in the relevant areas – medicine, IT, STEM or business studies – by constantly working on corresponding mandates. This may be true for in-house lawyers, who can access the expertise of relevant specialists or other departments in the company at any time and have thus always worked in so-called agile teams to a certain extent. However, this is not the case for most lawyers, who, even if they have been exclusively responsible for certain areas of law for a long time, do not have any specialist knowledge.

A sensible, resource-saving alternative can be the implementation of so-called agile teams. These are teams consisting of employees from different disciplines or professional groups, usually with flat hierarchies. In this way, competencies are bundled, problems are comprehensively processed and decision-making processes are simplified. In the meantime, this method, which was developed in the IT sector, is being applied across all industries in order to meet customer needs faster and better. The first forays into legal consulting have taken the form of mergers between various professional groups, such as lawyers with medical professionals in medical liability law, with experts in traffic accident law, with architects in construction liability law, or with tax consultants. Nevertheless, this development will continue, as there is simply a great need for cross competencies that cannot always be represented in one and the same person.

Such agile teams require special leadership, especially when they are part of a conservative corporate culture that is characterized by hierarchical structures and regimentation rather than innovation and personal responsibility. This is all the more true in a digital world that sometimes creates massive insecurity among employees – because IT can now replace people, "enslave" them in terms of processes, and control their data.

The basic needs of employees identified in a Google study from 2016 should therefore definitely become the focus of management. According to the study, employees long for:

- Security: More in the psychological sense than in the actual sense (emotional and communication management)
- Clarity: In structures, goals and tasks (reliable relationships)
- Significance: Of one's own work, of corporate values

Remember:
Agile leadership is able to combine different leadership styles according to the situation and to respond to the needs of the employees.

This requires first and foremost know-how, but also good self-management and, above all, ego management. The common assumption that the IT-savvy partner or ambitious young lawyer is also the most suitable team leader is therefore wrong[15].

However, one can learn to do this. To be able to do this as a lawyer, a coach can help. The coach works out strengths and weaknesses, analyzes potential and drives development. However, development can only take place in the lawyer himself, and inwardly.

A coaching training or a training in "agile leadership" will start much deeper and will generate more sustainable successes also externally: And this is ultimately what matters when the lawyer is assigned personnel responsibility or the development and leadership of such agile teams for the purpose of enabling innovation. He will develop

15 *Dr. Tutschka*, Agile Leadership in a digital World, Legal Revolutionary 07/2018.

an understanding of human relationship systems, needs, communication patterns and paradigms and will be enabled to better understand his client, but above all himself. In order to lead a team to creative excellence, one must first and foremost work on oneself. Self-reflection, ego management, mindfulness, change of perspective, setting and achieving goals characterize him. In his coaching training, he has therefore dealt with his own strengths and weaknesses, fears, triggers and beliefs. This is intensive and not easy and usually leads to a different self-image and relationship to oneself. However, this lawyer does not easily slip into a burn out or a deep life crisis. He has grown personally and matured. This will make him a reflected and introspective boss, for whom mutual respect is important, but also clarity, transparency and trust. He knows what he and his firm stand for and which employees fit his firm and the team. But he also knows the needs of his employees and therefore deals with personnel and team development. Structures and processes should support the individual responsibility of the employees and not hinder them. He can mediate in team conflicts. Difficult issues are not ignored, but approached sensitively. Employees are happy to come to the office and identify with their work, so that the entire team pulls together, which ensures a healthy working atmosphere.

The benefit of such training for lawyers with management responsibility is therefore obvious: it pays off for him personally because he himself is more satisfied.

- It pays off in his environment because his employees are happier.
- It pays off in his business because his clients are more satisfied.

And last but not least: Such additional training also represents valuable combinations of so-called cross competencies for lawyers. Combined with their individual professional and life experience, they become distinctive, not interchangeable. Agile. And that is the only way to the future of the consulting industry in the digital world[16].

But beware:
The use of coaching in leadership has long been dismissed.

On the one hand, it didn't fit the zeitgeist of leadership. On the other hand, there ethical concerns if the use of coaching in a leadership context is not made were sufficiently transparent and certain boundaries are observed. The use of coaching tools, a coaching mindset and the conversation choreography of a process are permissible if the responsibilities of the leadership relationship are preserved and are not changed in the sense of coaching.

---

16 *Dr. Geertje Tutschka*, Agile Leadership in a digital World, Legal Revolutionary from 31.7. 2018.

Remember:
Complete coaching processes in the leadership relationship are NOT permitted with or without clarification.

And last but not least: The American psychologist Daniel Goleman has developed the concept of Emotional Leadership, distinguishing between six different leadership styles in terms of emotions: visionary, coaching, emotion-oriented, democratic, demanding and commanding.

Whether the legal industry ever gets there remains to be seen.

However, because the freedom to shape one's personal management style depends crucially on one's own role, responsibility and duty in the law firm system, the management structures in the partnerships and the management values of the partner agreements are examined below.

1. Partnerships and other forms of cooperation

Anyone who cooperates with colleagues beyond an individual law firm is quickly faced with the question: What is the best way to do this?

In addition to the legal forms described above for (inter)regional cooperation or office sharing, there is also the possibility of partnership and joint practice.
Partner is who
- owns shares in the company ("part owner")
- receives a share of the profits (also shares the risk)
- has voting rights (and the right to information)

Of course, partnerships per se harbor considerable potential for conflict – just like any good marriage[17]. It is the task of the partnership agreement, but also of the partners' meetings, to manage, balance and resolve these conflicts.

Most partnerships, unfortunately, are still driven by the two thoughts
- that each lawyer desperately wants to achieve partner status and is willing to invest
- that each partner wants to remain a partner.

---

17 I myself am married to a lawyer and have run our law firm in partnership with him – so I know why this comparison is so fitting.

Therefore, they usually have a sophisticated system for what future partners have to "deliver" as an initial contribution on their way, which often takes several years. On the other hand, there is no incentive system for young lawyers who do not want to become partners. The initial contribution almost always consists of a combination of revenue generation and client potential, special talents are at best considered a bonus, the monetary measurement of this initial contribution is missing[18]. This pyramid system has only one rule: "Up or Out", i. e. either you climb the ladder step by step as a so-called associate to partner status or you leave the firm[19].

The retirement of a partner due to age is usually regulated in detail, although difficult scenarios can arise here as well, as reported by the DAV Committee on Lawyer Ethics and Lawyer Culture: Partnerships are not for eternity, or at least not for the duration of one's professional life – they are more likely to be partnerships for stages of life. Legal issues are usually regulated in detail in partnership agreements. But the ethics of partnership interaction tend to be neglected, especially the cultivation of respectful interaction and a culture of discussion. Most senior partners may not like the fact that they have to negotiate with newcomers nowadays, because they, as the so-called boomer generation, have often simply continued the existing contracts, which were based on growth and unconditional commitment to the firm. The next generations, on the other hand, are looking for their meaning in life outside of the professional realization as partners. Today, partnership contracts must therefore be flexible enough to withstand this and be supported by a culture of mutual respect and appreciation[20].

A partner change, on the other hand, is generally not envisaged. Nor are temporary absences or loss of performance due to family time[21]. Thus, it is not surprising that despite strong personnel growth in large law firms, still than 10 % appointed partners are female[22] and lawyers are the taillight in equal couple relationships[23].

In my career coaching sessions with young lawyers, I experience time and again how far removed this system is from the reality of life for the next generations. At the same time, the partners, as part of the law firm system, find it very difficult, if not impossible, to empathize with these new value models. Thus, the implemented career development programs pale into mere cosmetic measures. The necessity of a change in values for the law firm is negated. This is a system error that is already grating hard in the gears of law firms.

18 See the story by Mag. Kosa LLM. of Schönherr In CLP's blog of 2.5.2016.
19 Hartung in Schieblon, "Kanzleimanagement in der Praxis", p. 101 et seq.
20 Markus Hartung, "Auf ewig Dein" in Anwaltsblatt from 8.1.2021.
21 See the story by Dr. Schoenbohm of Linklaters on the CLP blog.
22 Dr. Byok, "Partnerinnen-Barometer 2015"; Heussen, "Anwaltsunternehmen führen", p. 123 et seq.
23 Dr. Tutschka, "Female Leadership im Legal Sector", p. 137, DjbZ 3/2017.

Partnership

The following are typical legal career levels on the path to becoming a partner:

- Entry-level: Associate/Senior Associate
- Advanced: Counsel
- Expert/Owner: Salary Partner/Senior Salary Partner, Managing Partner, Senior Partner, Equity Partner

The general profile of requirements and performance as well as an overview of competencies may vary from firm to firm. Deviations can be found in the partner title descriptions, in the compensation system and in the requirements for the business plan.

The following additional criteria are also decisive:

- Concrete selection criteria for external entry into each partner level (value alignment, targets, competencies)
- Concrete selection criteria for the onboarding and integration process and evaluation
- Concrete selection criteria for internal entry into the next partner level (client pool, revenue, BD strategy, business plan)
- Partner compensation system (lockstep, merit based, etc.)
- Partner performance evaluation and support program (mentoring, training)

The ratio between the "real" partners, i.e. the equity partners, and other professionals is usually 1:3.5 in large law firms – this does not include non-legal professionals such as tax consultants and patent attorneys. A large law firm is defined as one with 50 or more professionals. The top law firms with the highest revenues usually have more than 100 professionals: Freshfields Bruckhaus Deringer (500 professionals), CMS Hasche Sigl (560 professionals).

Example distribution: 96 Associates, 7 Of Counsel, 82 Salary Partner, 9 Senior Salary Partner, 46 Partner

Note:

Counsel and salary partners are essentially on an equal footing. In this case, the title of partner serves more as a "label" to the outside world without any real decision-making authority internally. Due to the variable bonus, the remuneration of a salary partner can even be lower than that of a counsel.

Caution: The Level Salary Partner serves either as an alternative to partnership (end station) or as a formal intermediate step to partnership (pass-through station):

- In the first case, more emphasis is placed on sales;
- In the second case, the first management and leadership tasks already arise here.

Conservative law firms tend to rely on “up or out”. What are the arguments?
- The will to entrepreneurship is inherent in excellent lawyers.
- Salary partners do not deliver sufficient performance for the partnership; they are not taken seriously within the firm.
- The salary partner status takes into account the phenomenon that there are too many lawyers with good degrees (“specialist idiots“).

Today, it is often the next generation that decides against “up or out”. Why?
- Because partnership with the additional tasks in management and leadership does not seem very attractive with regard to work-life balance, or
- the question of whether one shares the values and culture of the firm and would like to stand for them as a partner is answered openly and honestly with a NO (as an employee, distancing is possible).
- Partnership is designed for the long term, which no longer fits into the concept of flexible life stages (hence high turnover in the first five years of a law firm’s career).

Example use of Salary Partner status:
- Salary Partner as intermediate stop: Beiten Burkhardt
- Salary Partner as final stop: Hengeler Mueller
- No Salary Partner: Herbert Smith Freehills

Remuneration[24]:
- Junior associates up to three years of professional experience: annual salary at €50,000–140,000
  Commitment to further training, network building, integration into the firm and the teams
- Senior associates up to five years of professional experience: annual salary at €120,000–170,000
  Works on his positioning: specialist lawyer, doctorate, LL.M.; participates in events for the firm and supports the firm brand
- Counsel with five years of experience or more: annual salary at €150,000–250,000
  Establishes himself as an expert (lawyer brand), specialist and management responsibility, stands for the law firm brand, own client base

24 By the way, you can check your own market value online at the recruitment agency Legalhead: https://legalhead.de/blog/karriere-in-der-grosskanzlei/.

- Salary Partner from six years of professional experience: annual salary at €100,000–130,000 plus < €50,000 bonus
  Like Counsel – but is the "face" of the firm as a "fake" partner
- Senior Salary Partner: annual salary at €130,000–180,000 plus < €100,000 bonus
- Salary Partners, as highly qualified technical experts, are primarily responsible for strong sales, employee salary plus variable (based on sales or billable hours); external appearance as partner often without distinction; have voting rights but no decision-making rights; do not have to buy out shares in the firm; administrative and management duties
- Managing/Senior Partner: annual income at €250,000–500,000
  As above
- Equity Partner: annual income at €350,000–500,000[25]
  Salary depends on turnover; has certain additional tasks of law firm management; has decision-making rights on all issues: owns shares of the law firm as founder or as partial purchaser

The annual adjustment rate is 5–10 %. The weekly working time is 50–80 hours plus events and business trips.

Partnership compensation systems vary widely and are often hybrid. As a rule, they are perceived as outdated and family discriminatory. Recent figures show that with 43 %, however, an above-average number of young female lawyers start out in commercial law firms (overall, the proportion of women in the legal profession in Germany is 35 %, with 49 % graduates; in rural regions, female lawyers are hardly represented; in the eastern German states, the proportion of women is particularly high, in some cases 38 %). Nevertheless, the proportion of women in the higher career levels in corporate law firms, such as counsels, is only 31 % and among equity partners only 11 %, which indicates that the systems there are outdated and hostile to families. This is roughly in line with the figures from the USA. The only countries with a lower percentage of women in the legal profession are Switzerland (29 %) and Austria (22 %)[26]. The most common is the merit-based method, followed by the lockstep method. The two extreme solutions "eat what you kill" (non-genuine partnership) and "all for one – one for all" (everything in one pot and distributed in equal parts – genuine partnership) are the least common.

25 According to the portal www.finanz.at,this can be up to € 700,000 even in Austria.

26 Kilian, Geschlechtsspezifischer Wandel in der Anwaltschaft, Anwaltsblatt from 30.01.2020; brand.eins/thema 2021, Die Branche in Zahlen, p. 79.

Executive Summary of the 2015 Partner Compensation Study (Schoen and Company[27]):

1. One third of the systems are older than 15 years.
2. One third of the partners are dissatisfied and find the system unfair.
3. A total of 61 % of the partners see a need for adaptation.
4. 42 % of all systems are based purely on one type, the others are mixed systems.
5. In lockstep systems, performance is negatively affected; in merit-based systems, partner appointment is negatively affected.
6. Merit-based systems will increase strongly in the future.
7. More complex systems that take many influencing factors into account are desired.
8. In particular, marketing, acquisition performance and management tasks should be taken more into account.
9. The highest profit margins are achieved with Eat What You Kill systems based on team performance and with some Lockstep systems.

Remember:
In addition, it will be important in the future to what extent soft factors, such as climate neutrality, diversity, social commitment, mentoring and knowledge transfer, and the advancement of women are included in monetary terms in these remuneration systems and partnership agreements. Only then will these factors really play a relevant role in law firms and a change in values and culture take place.

In times when more and more partners are breaking free from this tight corset and taking their own new paths, modern partnerships are in demand[28]. On the one hand, to take away the crisis potential for the partnership from the departure of a partner and, on the other hand, to keep these partners in the partnerships with modern concepts.

The status of partner in large law firms is now being critically observed with regard to the “independence of the lawyer as an organ of the administration of justice”: Can the individual lawyer still represent the interests of the client freely, objectively and independently within the meaning of § 43a BRAO in strongly commercialized partnership structures[29]? The BVerfG establishes as a guiding principle the “independent, discreet lawyer who is only committed to the interests of his own client” who, however, “also bears economic responsibility as a freelance entrepre-

27 http://www.schoen-company.com/files/redaktion/pdf/schoen__company_-_studie_gewinnverteilungssysteme_in_kanzleien.pdf.
28 See the story of Dr. Naber and Neuwerk aka Freshfields on the CLP blog.
29 Hartung in “Berufsbild des Anwalts: Großkanzleien, Geld und Werte”, p. 3 LTO from 10.1. 2018.

neur"[30]. In this respect, the legal sector also has its own individual balancing act to master on its way to entrepreneurship.

A special form of cooperation can have the status of "counsel" or "off-counsel", where one partner cannot yet or no longer wants to fully contribute to the partnership. The reasons are as varied as life itself. Here, it is necessary to make and implement special agreements that ensure a balanced partnership relationship for all involved[31]. But whether this alternative form of collaboration will develop into a real competitor to the pyramid system – as some think – remains to be seen[32].

2. Managing Partner and Management Team

If law firms have a certain size, a special management team is required.

As a rule, this applies to firms of 50 or more attorneys, which includes a good 75 law firms in Germany[33]. The top 5 even have to manage up to 700 lawyers per firm, who generate a good 20 % of the total revenue of the entire industry[34].

Managing Partner

Law firms are usually not established with a management board and a management system, but evolve towards it:

- Single law firm
- Office partnership
- Classic partnership: No management support, no release for management tasks
- Functional partnership: Individual partners are functionally responsible for core areas; no release for management tasks, individual support staff (usually: accounting, HR, IT, marketing)
- Management team: Management team has own decision-making authority; release of partners for management tasks (usually initially with time budget), professional support staff
- Management Board (supra pares): Managing partner and executive team preside over the partner group and make some decisions independently; management is compensated separately; large professional support departments; the firm begins to evolve into a business

30 BVerfG from 3.6.2003 and 12.12.2006 to § 1 BORA.
31 Heussen, "Anwaltsunternehmen führen", p. 123 et seq.
32 Hartung in Schieblon, Kanzleimanagement in der Praxis", p. 105.
33 Heussen, Anwaltsunternehmen führen", p. 322.
34 Schieblon, "Kanzleimanagement in der Praxis", p. 1.

- External management: C-level functions are staffed with external experts (usually with business background) who do not perform client work; all major divisions and functions are established; the (large) firm has become a business enterprise

At what size are which structures and tasks necessary and do non-legal areas such as management develop proportionally to the growth of the law firm?

For a better understanding, I compare a law firm with 50 professionals and one with 150 professionals below[35] and show the proportion of support staff in each case in relation to the size of the firm:

Finance/Accounting:	22% / 16%
Office Management:	19% / 9%
IT:	15% / 28%
Personnel:	10% / 16%
Other:	10% / 2%
Marketing:	9% / 8%
Controlling:	6% / 6%
PR:	6% / 3%
Business Development:	4% / 11%

One can see that as law firms grow in size, they standardize and automate their processes to handle the growth: However, the proportion of IT support staff has only doubled as the size of the firm has tripled. By contrast, the proportion in the administration-intensive areas of accounting and office management has fallen sharply, and the "other" area has also "cleaned up". Personnel and business development are in greater demand – in the case of the latter, the share has even tripled in proportion to the growth of the firm.

Depending on the partnership agreement, managing partners are given special rights by majority resolution for a certain period of time, which at best allow them to make not only day-to-day but also, to a certain extent, strategic decisions regarding the direction of the firm. In this context, a management team is often at their side.

In contrast to other industries, this "managing director" in the legal industry will in most cases be a lawyer, who should, however, also have a certain understanding of business administration. Why? On the one hand, the managing partner should have an idea of the business of a law firm, and on the other hand, he should be at eye level with the partners in order to be taken seriously by them.

35 The figures are taken from a 2015 study by Schön und Company.

It is not astonishing that this position has not yet been explored by female lawyers[36]. However, there is no rule without an exception: In the business law firm PHH, which was established in Vienna 20 years ago, not only a change of generations was initiated, but also history was made. Senior Partner Stefan Prochaska handed over the management to Rainer Kaspar and Julia Fritz, who have since been leading the firm very successfully towards the future. After all, the position and tasks of the Managing Partner and his team do not make him a "favorite colleague" or a "colleague of the month". He should have a certain insensitivity to pain and stubbornness[37] and not be dependent on a steady career in this law firm over many years. Similar to interim managers, they are "for the rough stuff". His job is to tidy up, speak plainly, put things in order, structure things, ask uncomfortable questions and insist on compliance with rules and agreements. Heads roll here – in some cases his own[38]. You have to want it that way; you have to be able to endure it. Above all, however, you should be aware that this leaves its mark on your own personality[39].

In this respect, from a certain size onwards, it can also be advantageous if, as the owner of a law firm, you no longer solely hold these tasks, but can delegate them to a certain extent.

Since managing partners often operate in very lonely positions in their own firms, an exchange with management partners from other firms can be quite valuable. The Professional Management Network (PMN) is an exchange network for management and business service professionals in law firms, such as management partners, financial management, human resources, marketing and business development, which also offers training and has been presenting the PMN Management Awards since 2009[40].

3. Performance management and compensation system

The primary system for performance motivation in law firms is still the compensation system[41].

36 For example, Schieblon has for years only gathered men as managing partners of large German law firms as authors in her book "Kanzleimanagement in der Praxis".
37 As well as humor and life experience says Heussen in "Anwaltsunternehmen führen", p. 235.
38 For more on the complexity and difficulties of these tasks, see Rizor in Schieblon, "Kanzleimanagement in der Praxis", p. 76 et seq.
39 Especially since supervision for "mental hygiene" has not yet been established here.
40 Schieblon, "Kanzleimanagement in der Praxis", XV.
41 All the more so as long as becoming a partner depends on such "advance contributions".

In addition to the classic lone wolf models of "share equality[42]" and "lockstep[43]", however, team models such as the "contribution system[44]" or "distribution according to teams[45]" are becoming increasingly common. The reason for this is the strong specialization of lawyers and the incomparability of mandates from different areas of law[46].

All these remuneration systems require correct data collection and evaluation. In addition to these "hard" factors, so-called "soft" factors can also be evaluated, such as when and how the fee note was created and paid[47]. Which remuneration system is the right one for a particular law firm can be based on the client structure, but even more so on the quality of the partnership and the firm's values. Thus, the less performance-oriented systems presuppose much more mutual trust[48].

Is this still up to date today?

On the one hand, the employed lawyer is, of course, also an entrepreneur to a certain extent. He should therefore be aware of the market and target group as well as his resources of knowledge, time and manpower, in other words act in an economically oriented manner.

After all, his legal advice should be neither a purely voluntary commitment nor a hobby. And remuneration is the only measure of this.

On the other hand, it is important to meet the challenges of the industry with innovation and holistic services. However, especially in the period of development and testing, these cannot be integrated into the current compensation systems. As a result, innovation does not take place. In addition, streamlined, well-structured processes can reduce costs thanks to legal tech and thus generate added value, without their implementation being particularly remunerated.

It is therefore important to create incentives for developing sustainable solutions, at least with mixed forms of remuneration.

---

42 Equal profit shares for each partner.
43 Point system that defines entry, period of affiliation and plateau as score.
44 Oriented to who fetched the mandate, who handled it, and who served the client.
45 Oriented around which team did what.
46 Seisler in Schieblon, "Kanzleimanagement in der Praxis", p. 81 et seq.
47 Seisler in Schieblon, "Kanzleimanagement in der Praxis", p. 88 et seq.
48 Ibid.

What did you get out of the chapter?

You now know what is important in good law firm leadership, are familiar with different leadership styles and the difference between them and law firm management, and can assess the important role that partner and compensation systems play in this context.

II. Human Resources Management

Why should you read this chapter?
You will learn how to find and retain good employees.

Overview
1. **Legals, Paralegals and Legal Tech**
2. **Personnel development and team building**
- Segmentation
- Specialization
- Diversity

1. Legals, Paralegals and Legal Tech

Employees are a law firm's greatest asset. This is true for lawyers as well as for paralegals, assistants and technical staff. It's a people business.

Finding those employees who are committed and sustainable for the firm is not easy. This has to do with loyalty, but also with investment and trust. Losing a long-term employee to the competition means that the investment in training or familiarization does not pay off. In the worst case, you might even lose clients.

So law firms would do well to invest in junior staff in good time and develop systems to ensure that they stay. For decades, this was realized through in-house training. Law firms and lawyers were and are therefore also trainers[1].
The Vocational Training Act (BBiG) regulates the rights and obligations of the training relationship.

It is also important to take a strategic approach to personnel management, to plan for the long term and to make provisions. It is true that peak times can also be covered by part-time staff, lawyers on demand or interim staff. However, this is no substitute for a well-functioning and coordinated law firm team. A prerequisite for this is that you, as the law firm owner, know exactly what you need the individual employees for: Competence, job and task descriptions are therefore the basis of a smooth office organization[2], which also requires coordinated work processes. Regu-

1 Fendt, "Der Rechtsanwalt als Ausbilder", p. 9 et seq.
2 Philipp, "Die erfolgreiche Kanzleigründung", p. 118 et seq.

lar employee meetings, further training and team measures support the development of your strongest resource.

For years, the personnel cost ratio has been significantly higher than the comparative figures for other industries and, at around 34 % of revenue, is still relatively high[3] for most law firms. As shown above, a ratio of about 25 % would be adequate. The same applies to training costs. The consequence is not only savings through increased efficiency but also higher pressure on employees and reduction of training. The latter in particular have decreased significantly in recent years, especially when one considers that the industry with lawyers has tripled in that time[4].

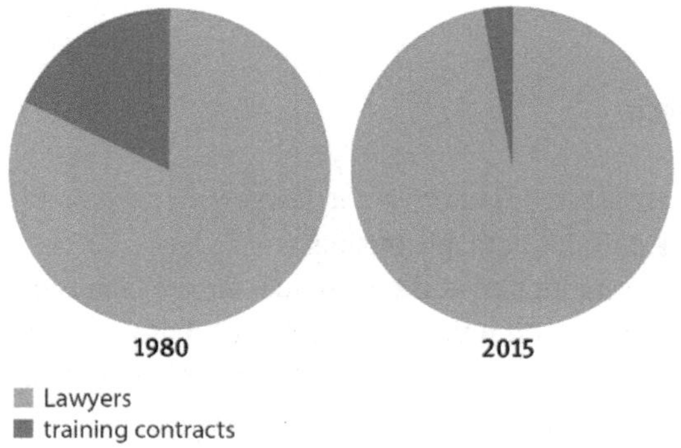

Relationship between lawyers and ReNo trainings[5], © Dr. Geertje Tutschka

The introduction of the beA is being used by most law firms as an opportunity to review, modernize and expand their work processes and the law firm software that supports them. This often leads to the streamlining of processes, reduction of duplications, and unnecessary work steps. Personnel services are saved.

But what is good for the firm, employees view critically. Every software change is viewed with suspicion, even sabotaged. Legal tech is scary. Employees fear for their jobs.

A clear concept of the law firm owner, when and for what purpose legal tech tools are used and when and for what purpose employees, how free capacities of

3 Branchenbericht der Sparkassen 2020, p. 2.

4 This is certainly due in part to the reorganization that took place in the wake of German reunification.

5 Kilian, Forschungsbericht "Rechtsanwälte und Ihre Mitarbeiter" Soldan Institut.

employees are handled and what they are now used for, would in many cases significantly relax the situation and make many things easier.

Career

It can sometimes be difficult for newcomers to the profession to decide between a smaller law firm, a boutique law firm or even a commercial law firm. Taking over a law firm right at the start of their career is usually out of the question, but self-employment is also becoming more attractive with increasing digitization.

Commercial law firms have a lot to offer: For ambitious lawyers, working on the really big cases is the highest level of professional fulfillment. Having important clients and working for a firm with an exceptional reputation fills every passionate lawyer with pride and satisfaction. Not to mention the thrill of a case with significant economic and real-world implications. In large law firms, exciting mandates often await attorneys. In addition, interesting acquaintances can be made while working in a large and international network of clients. Those who know how to network skillfully can lay the foundation for future professional opportunities.

Once your foot is in the door, there are also promising career opportunities in business, for example as an in-house lawyer. A career in business away from working as a lawyer is also not out of the question. In Austria, in particular, trainee attorneys are very much attracted to the business world after passing the bar exam (after five years of practical training in a law firm). This is where female lawyers in particular are drawn, who want to leave the conservative, male-dominated, family-hostile and work intensive world of the lawyer quickly.

Today, commercial law firms entice their clients with internal and external training programs, for which considerable financial resources are spent in order to further develop their own experts. It is well known that lawyers who have worked in corporate law firms have enjoyed an outstanding education and are among the best of the best. Afterwards, all doors are open to them in terms of career. In addition, the offices spread around the world offer people who like to travel the opportunity to get to know other cultures and legal systems during business trips for international mandates and longer stays abroad.

In addition, the opportunity is offered to obtain a doctorate or an LL.M. degree: With the doctorate, the doctoral candidate works his or her way into a special legal subject and thereby acquires special knowledge in it. The doctorate makes the candidate a specialist and thus attractive for law firms of all kinds. The Master of Laws (LL.M.) is a postgraduate study of 2–5 semesters to become a business lawyer. It is true that this can also be completed as a correspondence course, e.g. at the Distance Learning University of Hagen – also on the subject of law firm management (formerly lawyer law). Most, however, use the LL.M. as an opportunity for a stay abroad and acquire this additional qualification, for example, in English-speaking countries – often combined with a station in one of the law firm's foreign offices. In addition to improving language skills, the focus here is on getting to know a foreign legal system. Major international law firms in particular regard this as an important additional qualification. But even without an LL.M., negotiation skills in English are indispensable for working in a large law firm. A lack of English skills is an absolute exclusion criterion. Additional language skills are of course welcome. Stays abroad are also highly valued, as insights into and an understanding of foreign countries and cultures are of particular importance at internationally oriented large law firms.

Commercial law firms train highly specialized lawyers: Anyone who would like to become an expert in a specific field is often at the right address at large law firms. So you will not find a generalist there. Nor will you look after a client on your own from the beginning to the end. Here, you are part of a large team and deal with very specific sub-processes within many different projects. The interpersonal level between lawyer and client is therefore much more impersonal than, for example, in a boutique or medium-sized law firm. The representatives of the company act with the team of the large law firm and not the lawyer with a private person.

Commercial law firms also have a high workload: Between 60 and 80 hours are considered normal and unfinished tasks are often taken home over the weekend. Lawyers are also required to perform excellently during this time. The high demands of important clients result in tremendous pressure to perform. What is an exciting and thrilling incentive for some ends in stress for others. The frequent business trips can also affect the mind and health in the form of jet lag. In this respect, the high starting salaries of €50,000–150,000 per year are put into perspective by cuts in the quality of life and possible health impairments.

The complex hierarchy structure often makes career paths seem structured, but also very lengthy and uncertain. In medium-sized and boutique law firms, the path to partner is much shorter and the competition is smaller. This is especially relevant for young female attorneys who have their family break ahead of them or are in the middle of it. Very few law firm systems make it possible to fulfill the business plans for becoming a partner on a part-time basis or as a mere assistant. Also, it is often uncertain how long a family break will last and whether one would ever want to return to the usual 60–80 hour work week with a young family. It is also a fact that these are still traditional male systems that clearly favor young male lawyers: While female graduates usually have the better degrees, after three years they are at a clear disadvantage compared to their colleagues – even without family leave: partners intuitively prefer to compose their teams of young male colleagues, hand them different mandates, more responsibility and let them gain more experience – which in turn gives them an uncatchable advantage when it comes to promotion. Kerstin Knopp, Partner at Clifford Chance, therefore reports on the firm's internal

"Inclusion and Diversity" network, which seeks to provide more support for young female lawyers[6].

Overall, vacant positions at large law firms are highly sought after among lawyers. Commercial law firms are therefore in the comfortable position of being able to select the right talent among the best specialists. The requirements that large law firms place on the qualifications of their lawyers are correspondingly high: as a rule, a double honors degree is required. This is communicated as "above-average academic performance", which in reality means at least 9.00 points in the first and second state examinations. It is clear that there are also exceptions among the accepted applicants. Even without a double honors exam, one has a chance at the popular positions. Especially the LL.M. and professional experience through relevant part-time jobs are popular means to increase the prospects for the dream job.

It is not at all uncommon for renowned major law firms to express interest in candidates without a double degree. Those who can convince with their curriculum vitae and qualifications and finally shine at the interview with an authentic and competent appearance, can most likely look forward to one of the most sought-after positions among lawyers.

As a rule, the application process in commercial law firms follows structured patterns. While the recruitment of associates and counsels is carried out by HR, the responsible partner and the line manager in one or two interviews, the admission to the partnership takes place over a period of four to twelve weeks:

1. Initial meeting with one founding partner and questions
2. Second meeting with other founding partners and questions
3. Third meeting after sending the partnership agreement and meeting with all founding partners
4. Finalization of the partnership agreement and admission to the partnership

However, because the supply of young lawyers has been increasing only slowly for almost ten years, the labor market in the legal environment is increasingly turning into an employee market, which means that even young lawyers without an honors degree have opportunities to join a large law firm.

The pandemic brought movement into the market with staff turnover. Staff reductions were offset by many new hires. The general economic crisis was mitigated with funding when needed. Reductions in partner retirements and salary freezes consolidated law firm budgets. It is true that 40 % report having made no new hires. However, this contrasts with 50 % who hired and received 50 % more applications. Hiring interviews took place online far more often than not, two-thirds. However,

6 *Kerstin Knopp*, Top-Anwältin Kerstin Knopp im Interview, Business Insider from 23.12. 2020.

there was often a lack of valuable training time. As a rule, however, 80 % of legal positions are filled within three to five months.

Most used industry job markets (93 %), career websites (92 %), and trainee hiring (91 %) for this purpose, as well as career events (9 %)[7].

After initial difficulties, the industry has largely embraced the home office and digitization and has calmed down. Nevertheless: For many, working remotely remains an integral (part of) working life – hardly anyone wants to return to the old rut of endless office hours: 46 % now regularly have the option for home office, 28 % even to a predominant extent[8].

The pandemic also had a lasting impact on training positions: Almost one-third of law firms completely abandoned training programs as a result. Overall, training budgets were cut by a third.

Experts therefore see the greatest challenge in finding suitable applicants in the next few years. 69 %[9] consider visibility as an employer brand to be critical to success, followed by improving employee retention and building a talent pool.

2. Personnel development and team building

Law firm development is personnel development.

Most of my clients think of personnel development in terms of job interviews and terminations, as well as training and development, and thus in terms of quantity rather than quality in personnel development.

Classically, personnel concepts thus contain[10]:
- the job descriptions
- the salary structure
- the training measures

However, this does not do justice to very important aspects.

7 Das Legal Recruiting Playbook, LTO 08/2020.

8 *Christian Dülpers*, Ergebnisse der Arbeitgeber-Umfrage: So reagiert der juristische Arbeits-markt auf die Corona Krise, LTO from 26.6.2020; *Marion Proft*, Corona trifft Fachkräftemangel in Kanzleien, Legal Profession vom 29.7.2020; Jutta Rump, Personalpolitik in der Corona-Krise, Studienbericht from 9.4.2020; Konrad Fischer, Geht nach Hause, Wirtschaftswoche from 22.5. 2020.

9 brand.eins/thema 2021, Die Branche in Zahlen, p. 79.

10 Pothe in "Kanzleimanagement in der Praxis", p. 164.

Remember:
The development of a coherent personnel concept is the key to future, sustainable success.

Team

Team development measures such as training, coaching, team building and assessments aim to program the team for optimal performance – without friction losses due to disputes, boycotts and trench warfare.

The first question is, of course, are you a law firm team – or just a collection of people who happen to work together on a daily basis?

This constellation does indeed remind us of our case study 1, in which the small teams do not cooperate with each other as a large whole. Team development measures could provide valuable support here. i

---

A team is a collection of people with at least one common goal, as well as common values, who are together in a particular system.

Remember:
A team is therefore more than the sum of its members.

This does not include the manager. In team coaching or team building, the coach supports the achievement of the common goal by accompanying the development of the team in a creative and reflective process, using dynamics and relationships within the team.

A group, in contrast, is a collection of people with at least one thing in common. Group coaching usually means that the coach supports learning and promotes the individual learning outcome.

Remember:
A group is the sum of its members.

The leader is responsible for the performance of individual or multiple people or entire teams. In leadership coaching, the coach helps the manager to work on his or her leadership skills and style and to fulfill his or her responsibilities.

The manager's own attitude should express philanthropy, appreciation and respect for the sovereignty of the employee, i.e. a certain humility towards the life decisions of others. The manager should work on this continuously, become aware of his or her own imprints, values and moral concepts, and reflect on his or her own behavior. The goal is an open, respectful, inquisitive, empathetic and neutral (not objective) attitude toward fellow human beings.

Based on the principle that a person is a social being and dependent on his or her counterpart, he or she should recognize and develop him or herself. For this purpose, the supervisor provides him or her with a professional, structured and protected framework.

When I and my team are called into law firms to accompany, moderate and structure partner meetings, the reason is often not that – as stated in the assignment – strategic input is needed. Usually, in these cases, months of unproductive, exhausting and grueling partner meetings have preceded and the situation may have already escalated.

Behind closed doors I am told: "Perhaps the gentlemen can at least behave like adults in the presence of a lady.

Here, it is primarily a matter of consolidating the relationship and trust level of the partnership in order to be able to work at all on the substantive level.

And this is a peculiarity of the industry in terms of organizational development: most law firms are led by management teams.

1. Unlike in organizations, this level lacks controlling and balancing hierarchies and the "division of responsibility" practiced since the 19th century, i.e. the division of responsibility into sub-areas/responsibilities. The partners are more or less equal and even in the case of different shares or partner levels, ego (upper) trumps partner level (lower). In the absence of responsibilities and division of responsibilities, everyone feels responsible for everything and no one for anything.
2. Unlike in organizations, these partners are also more or less the best employees, in other words, working lawyers. To make matters worse, profitability and success as a working lawyer determine whether one becomes a partner and thus moves up into the management team. In this way, the skills and competencies required for the leadership role are left to chance[11]. Nor is the management team assembled from suitable types and characters with regard to the firm's strategic goal. On the contrary, the firm is made to fit the existing partners.

11 Somewhat cushioned by internal training measures and the "partner check".

Dysfunctional leadership teams are therefore the cause of 90 % of the firm's problems.

This is not to say that lawyers are not good leaders per se, or that they cannot very successfully navigate their small team through the day-to-day work of a lawyer. But in order to lead together in the partner round, you need more, or rather: something else. Specifically, it also requires togetherness, a partner team.

And it takes the ability to skillfully switch between these different roles and leadership styles.

Now the fact is that very few management teams see this as the real problem, or at least a common problem. After all, you yourself are good at what you do and everything is going well. Who needs couples therapy? So it must be the others.

As always, I start with an analysis of the situation – because every firm is different, of course. Confidential one-on-one interviews, personality profiles of the partners[12] and a team assessment[13] can effectively assist in diagnosis. The image of the individualized firm-leadership team pyramid with several levels in the colors green (everything is cuddly, we all love each other), yellow (I don't have to see them every day) and red (how am I going to get out of here), which the assessment creates, has so far convinced every round of partners to say: Okay, we have a problem.

This is the first step towards forming a team out of this group of partners. Only then can the development of the firm actually begin.

After all, you wouldn't recommend building a house or bringing a child into the world to a couple who can't really get along with each other.

The strong competition in the legal industry has increased the internal performance pressure on law firm teams enormously. At the same time, well-trained and committed employees are sought after by many law firms, so that they definitely have the choice of which firm they want to go to or switch to. This makes the in-house training of junior staff more risky, because there is a danger of losing them to the competition.

Legal tech makes the training of junior staff more expensive. The standardization of processes associated with legal tech in turn means that employees are more easily replaceable. What is often overlooked when investing in the technical future of the law firm or legal department is that it is first and foremost about the employees, the people in the teams, who face enormous challenges, changes and uncertainties in

12 The Strength Finder can help you quickly. If you need a little more, you can also use the MBTI or, even better, the Hogan.

13 I like to work here with Lencioni's "5 Dysfunktionen eines Teams" and the Table Group's assessment.

this area and are left alone to deal with them. Without picking up the teams and bringing them along, any investment in legal tech is doomed to failure.

Accompanying such a process professionally, especially when it involves far-reaching changes, means dealing responsibly with one's most important resource – the firm's team.

I am generally bought in with my team as a personnel development measure. In the coaching sessions, we learn about the enormous pressure to perform that has often built up since the school career and has become an everyday companion. We learn of the frustration and resignation of promising talents in the face of encrusted structures and power relationships, we learn of existential fears of failure, overwhelming double burdens and heartbreaking loneliness. The legal profession could be a very fulfilling one, because it can help people in need in a meaningful and sustainable way. Unfortunately, the day-to-day reality for lawyers is different. With all the challenges and opportunities in the profession, we must be careful not to crush lawyers.

In the coaching sessions we can achieve small improvements by addressing time management, mindfulness, work-live balance. However, we are much more effective when we are hired with foresight FOR HR development measures: we then start evaluating the status quo of the HR concept based on the firm's strategy with the partner team as well as possible HR support teams, usually accompanied by feedback rounds of the different relevant levels including personal interviews. The result of our audit can be a positive recognition of valuable work and a confirmation that the firm is on the right track. As a rule, however, we are not called in without reason and our audit reveals the firm's untapped potential or weaknesses and risks. In a next step, the firm can decide whether we should accompany the creation of an updated concept with know-how, the moderation of partner meetings, team coaching and the development of internal budget planning, communication and implementation steps (the classic personnel concept comprises about 25 pages – today, however, with appropriate software, it is also possible digitally and inclusively). Only then will it be decided to what extent we will additionally take on individual modules such as coaching hour budgets, whether in-house resources can be built up for this in the long term, or whether other external providers are suitable for this. Supporting HR managers in this way from the outset means acting strategically and thoughtfully; not just reacting to overload, staff shortages, poor kununu ratings and recruitment worries. In the long term, this not only eliminates collateral damage, spares nerves and relationships, but also saves real money, because the right measures in the right places have a leverage effect for successful personnel management and contribute to the strategic goals of the firm. Don't get me wrong: Soft skill trainings and career coaching "off the shelf" have their justification next to the professional training, if they are well-trained and certified trainers and coaches who know the legal industry. The mistake is to confuse these continuing education kits with strategic personnel development. Given the increasing demands on lawyers and law firms to prove their raison d'être in a highly complex and technologized world (organizational developers call it VUCA), there will have to be a focus on creating smart HR concepts and closely linking them to the strategic development of the law firm: Personnel development becomes a matter for the boss[14].

The challenges of the industry (digitalization, competition and changes in the professional image) therefore also have a direct impact on law firm structures. Strategically sensible personnel development must meet the challenges of the industry and find the right solution for your law firm. In this context, it makes no difference whether the development of junior lawyers or non-lawyer employees is concerned.

But who takes care of the important topic of **personnel development** in law firms?

Usually, law firms do not have their own human resources department until they reach a certain number of employees or turnover. Until then, the respective partners are responsible for hiring additional attorneys or the department heads are responsible for hiring young attorneys and non-legal employees. Law firm culture, positioning and strategic orientation play as little role in this as employer branding and personnel development programs: you can no longer do the work alone, so you need support – preferably a cheap copy of yourself. Thus, a very homogeneous personnel structure has been established in law firms over decades. As a result, the services and service providers they offer are so homogeneous that they are interchangeable – replaceable by colleagues or by technology. One-dimensional world views prevent innovation. Leadership is confused with management. An attempt is made to generate more quality with quantity.

Increased demands regarding the professional qualifications of junior lawyers, such as above-average exam grades and additional qualifications such as specialist lawyer degrees, LL.M. and doctorate, are an attempt to reflect specialization. Market segmentation is feigned by focusing on special target groups[15].

Today, personnel development programs cover three areas in particular, in addition to specialist training

---

14 Today's VUCA world: volatility, uncertainty, complexity, ambiguity – requires special strategy and leadership. Similar to architecture, such conditions need clearly defined goals, flexible structures, agility, lightness and speed. Steel-and-concrete skyscrapers and complex factory sites made of baked brick – of which some law firm structures are indeed metaphorically reminiscent – are not made for storms, quakes and tidal wave Heussen, "Anwaltsunternehmen führen", p. 213.

15 Heussen, "Anwaltsunternehmen führen", p. 213.

- Mentoring on the way to partnership[16]
- Coaching for personal development[17]
- Coaching for returning to work after family leave (promotion of women)

In my experience, these areas are often mapped internally by ambitious HR managers or partners. In mentoring, a partner is assigned to young associates as a mentor. This is usually the partner and thus the supervisor of their own business unit. As a mentor, he can pass on his own experience on his way to becoming a partner in this firm. However, reflective guidance of the young associate on his individual path is not provided. There is no training or at least no uniform idea of what mentoring is.

In coaching, mostly in-house HR staff become active. The goal is individualized career counseling, which should also cover internal disputes and stress strategies. It is overlooked here that in-house coaching only makes sense from a certain company size[18], which allows sufficient distance between the coachee and the internal coach. Even then, internal coaching can only be used for certain delimited topics and report structures[19], if a corresponding quality management of individual coaching is implemented at the same time, such as supervision, special confidentiality, combination with external coaches etc.[20].

Some law firms can afford a pool of external coaches from which employees can choose based on an annual budget. Others rely on cooperation with intermediaries such as BetterCoach or Coachimo. The personnel programs offered to female attorneys after family leave to facilitate their return to work tend not to be used by the employees. On the one hand, female lawyers do not want to be seen as particularly "worthy" of support compared to their colleagues. On the other hand, these programs regularly do not go beyond platitudes and the placement of general posi-

16 *Dr. Geertje Tutschka*, "Der Blick über den Tellerrand" in Unternehmensjurist 05/2018.
17 *Dr. Geertje Tutschka* Article series "Coaching in der Rechtsabteilung" in Unternehmensjurist 02/2021; Dr. Geertje Tutschka "Coaching ist das was der juristischen Fachexpertise fehlt" in Coaching-Magazin 01/2019; Dr. Geertje Tutschka, "Coaching oder nicht" in PE Managerseminare from 06/2018.
18 In business, regularly from several 1,000 employees, whereby the structure and reporting of the company, the qualification of the internal coach as well as the scope of the internal coach pool also play an important role (Dr. Tutschka in an interview on the brochure (Dr. Tutschka im Interview zur Bro-schüre "Qualitätsmanagement im Einzelcoaching" in "Managerseminare – Sonderheft Coaching" 05/2018).
19 See also the "Global Consumer Awareness Study" ICF 2017.
20 Dr. Tutschka, "Qualitätsmanagement im Einzelcoaching", p. 5.

tions[21]. Young fathers are not usually addressed. Here, too, family breaks are highly personal and individual matters. According to today's understanding, they are also no longer a purely female issue. Individual professional support from outside and the creation of family-friendly structures, such as care contingents in thedaycare next door, flexible working hours and home office possibilities, part-time models as well as alternative ways to partnership beyond turnover would be models that actually meet the needs of young lawyers. Traditionally, however, law firms still only offer the option of a doctorate or a second degree while working. Linklaters is already breaking new ground here: with "YourLink", individual working time quotas can be agreed without having to sink into meaninglessness with the negatively associated part-time status[22].

In reality, however, the challenges facing the industry can only be met in their entirety:

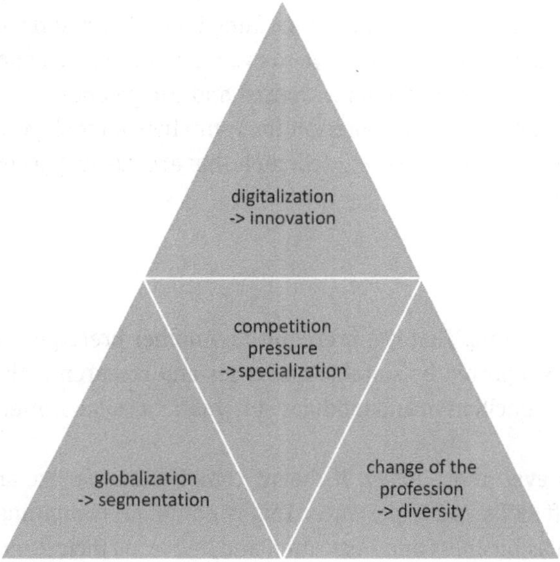

Sensible responses to the challenges of the legal industry, © Dr. Geertje Tutschka

21 Initiatives to change this state of affairs, to create awareness and to break up structures already exist: such as "Breaking.Through" for role models by Nadja Harraschain in Frankfurt or comprehensive law firm childcare by attorney Kosa in Vienna (both presented with articles in the blog at CLP).

22 A very detailed and up-to-date overview can be found in the annual e-fellows "Perspektiven für Juristen" ("Perspectives for Lawyers"), in which 20 of the largest law firms are presented in 2021 alone with regard to their strategic orientation, values and culture, personnel profile and personnel development measures, in the book from p. 174, 247 et seq. Dr. Tutschka, "Verlässliche Arbeitszeiten trotz Großkanzlei" of 9.2.2018 in the CLP blog.

Segmentation:
It is also and especially important for personnel development to implement the values and culture of your law firm as well as the strategic orientation that has been developed. In the vast majority of law firms, however, this does not happen[23].

What good is it then if a law firm describes itself as innovative, modern and open in order to strategically align itself with start ups and young technologies that regularly organize members of Generation Y and Millennials in a flat hierarchy – if its own law firm team of homogeneous people in their mid-forties is strictly hierarchically organized and authoritarian? It is obvious that not only the lawyer but also the paralegals must like the target group of the law firm with all its peculiarities. But do you have to live the values of your target group yourself? The answer is yes. Counter question: Do you like to have your business explained to you by someone who is full of prejudices against lawyers and paralegals and has no idea about your industry? I have been advising law firms in Germany, Austria and Switzerland with my company for ten years now: the most important thing I have learned from this is that you can only provide advice if you see eye-to-eye with your clients and have relevant industry experience. That has to do with trust and competence.

And that is exactly what your team must represent for your clients: Employees who not only know and like the peculiarities of your clientele, but are ideally part of the target group and live its values.

Specialization:
Professional qualification is one thing. That is a prerequisite. Another prerequisite is that specialization today is supported by suitable databases and research tools, specialized software for data reconciliation and modular systems, and collaboration with experts.

But specialization means even more today. It means combining a particular combination of education, soft skills and experience. This is not about combining two standard educations such as business administration and law or medicine and law in order to position oneself as a business lawyer or medical lawyer. It's about more. It is about cultivating and professionalizing your special qualities and talents. So if you are a particularly good negotiator, you should consider further communication training or perhaps even mediation training. If you are a team player, perhaps intercultural training makes sense. If you are a strategist and a born leader, leadership training makes sense.

23 There is not even a written concept.

Diversity:
Teams that bring together a wide range of different life experiences are more innovative and can respond to challenges with flexible solution strategies. Different life experiences can result from different cultural backgrounds, different life phases, or gender perspectives[24]. Taking the diverse challenges of the legal industry seriously therefore also means being able to actually grasp the complexity of the situation with diverse decision-making teams[25].

It is striking that female lawyers have so far not caught up with men in the top earning professions, in management positions, or in law firms and partnerships. In fact, the gap to men's incomes is greatest in the legal professions. So should there also be a women's quota for law firms in the future?

	Germany	Austria	Belgium	Netherlands
Lawyers	164.000	5.800	17.800	17.500
Share of women appprox.	33 %	20 %	42 %	43 %
Inhabitants per lawyer approx.	500	1.500	600	1.000

Diversity in the Legal Profession 2019, © Dr. Geertje Tutschka

It is good that the number of female lawyers admitted to the bar has risen from 33 percent to 49 percent in recent years. According to a 2013 study by the German Bar Association, the number of female law students is already close to 60 percent. It is also good that the working group of female lawyers in the DAV has already pushed through a quota of women for speakers at the German Lawyers' Academy in recent years. So it is all the better that initiatives such as PANDA Law are now also providing targeted support for up-and-coming female executives in the legal profession[26].

24 Hasebrook, "Lebensphasen- und Kompetenzmanagement", p. 12 et seq.
25 Dr. Hohenstatt on the ALICE initiative, "Diversity in deutschen Kanzleien" from 18.11.2016 in the CLP Blog.
26 Dr. Tutschka, "We are PANDA. Und was machen Sie?", from 6.10.2017 in CLP Blog.

"Gender diversity is not a nice-to-have for law firms. It is a must-have: a mandate criterion, a key competence of the future, and proof of good law firm management. How can you credibly stand up for the law if you don't live and breathe equal opportunities in your own firm? All sides benefit when women and men have the same development opportunities."

Katharina Miller, President European Women Lawyers Association in Madrid and on the advisory board for PANDA Women Leadership Contest & Network, as well as, Isabelle Hoyer, CEO PANDA Women Leadership Contest & Network

Mixed decision-making teams, in which women no longer naturally take on the issues of personnel and event organization, areas of law that are no longer plowed exclusively by male or female colleagues, and networks in which male colleagues exchange ideas with female colleagues are leading to a new understanding within the legal profession.

Does this have an impact on hierarchies within law firms? Yes.

Can this change the culture of dispute? Absolutely.

Anyone who still only thinks about the "gender shift" and the change in the legal profession in terms of the compatibility of career and family, home office and work-life balance fails to realize that the next generation of lawyers will demand this as a whole. Just as gender equality in society is always about gender diversity, the difference between the sexes must also remain tangible in the legal system. So that our legal system stays in touch with social reality and reflects it.

In the legal profession, there is another important aspect: It has long been known that women and men communicate differently. And it is also known that lawyers are human beings, but above all men and women. Ultimately, however, the traditional role models of argumentative behavior and authority are still consciously or unconsciously haunting people's minds. A disputatious female lawyer can be perceived as a "bitch" or a "man-woman" – her colleague, on the other hand, as a "combative winner"[27].

27 Dr. Tutschka, "Jurist oder Juristin – (k)ein Unterschied", from 8.3.2015 in the CLP Blog.

Implications for practice:
the chance to harmonize the masculine and feminine principles.

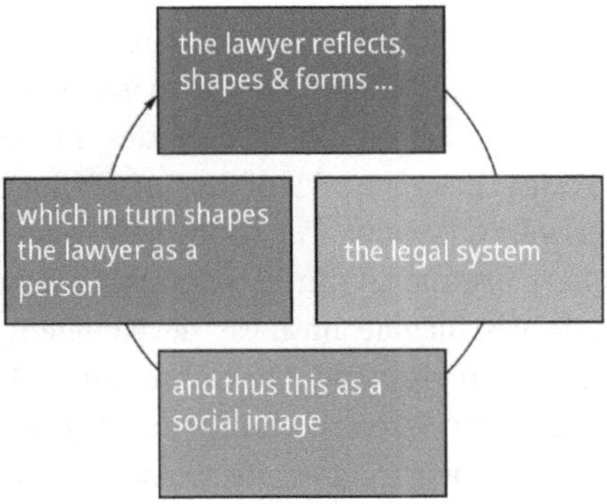

Diversity in the Legal Profession, © Dr. Geertje Tutschka

"Lawyers are society's professional problem solvers." Rennard Strickland & Frank T. Read

Then the legal profession should also reflect society. And that society is made up half of men and half of women[28].

Companies today deliberately use either a male or a female lawyer in difficult negotiation situations, depending on the situation. Clients either want to be represented by only a man or only by a woman in their divorce. Is it all in the head? More than almost any other profession, the legal profession demands typical male and female communication patterns[29].

Human resources development for law firms must therefore not only be value-based and aligned with their strategic direction, but also provide diversity, segmentation and specialization in order to be fit for the future.

A task that should not be underestimated is ultimately to form a team from the employees built up in this way. The law firms that are already investing in team development are the large firms. And not because they have the necessary money for it, but rather because they can afford the people with the economic and strategic vision: These people consider the development and investment in the team essential. In small and medium-sized law firms, team development works more "naturally":

28 Diversity par excellence, such as origin, age, culture, etc., is a key factor.
29 Dr. Tutschka, "Frauenquote für Anwaltskanzleien", from 8.11.2015 in the Blog JurCoach.

you set the rules and then leave the team to its own devices. Something will certainly develop there, too, but the question is: what?

Do you know the law firms where everyone gets along well with each other, is on a first-name basis and is even friends with each other in private? As soon as you enter the office, you feel exhilarated. There is joking and laughter, and people meet in the kitchen for a pleasant chat over homemade cakes. Even the piles of files on the floor are not disturbing. Whoever has the time answers the phone. The young new colleague can wait with his inquiry. And then there are the law firms that meet every Thursday afternoon for a team meeting. Topics include business development, training and development programs, and strategic positioning. Areas of responsibility are not described there by one's own desk. There are such things as office-defined workflows, priorities and control systems. Efficiency and effectiveness as far as the eye can see. Everyone gives their best and focuses on the work. Being a lawyer is not a child's birthday party. Passion, friendships and "humanizing" should be elsewhere. So do you have to choose between a super team and the professional efficiency of a well-oiled machine? Do you even need a team feeling when everything is running smoothly?

Remember:
Higher than personnel costs are only the costs of having to replace good personnel with good ones.

But how do you know how good or bad your team is and how it actually works? I like to recommend to my clients to figure this out in the context of a team event. The team event must fit the team culture and be tailored to the needs and topics. Otherwise, you will have had an afternoon of fun together at best – but you will not have achieved any teamwork.

In team sports, it's a matter of constantly working with professionals to remain or become a team. One that is greater than the sum of all the individual players. What does it cost to replace a well-trained and ingrained employee – even more so if you lose her to the competition? What does it cost not to have made an attractive offer to a promising young lawyer on how he can spend more time with his young daughter in the future – especially when many clients felt they were in good or even better hands with him? Today, we can no longer afford to give away talent and potential or to leave it unused. They must be discovered, promoted and retained in the long term. A team can do all that. A good team can do even more: it multiplies the talents that have been bound in this way.

"Those who work alone add; those who work with others multiply." (Nossrat Peseschkian).

A law firm is a business. It's about numbers, about economic success. And about people. The products of a law firm are ultimately produced by people: from knowledge and skills, life experience and empathy. Employees are both a resource and a capital. And the products shape people's lives. When was the last time you invested in your team?

What does this mean for our three case studies?

While **case study 1** with growing pains is about a leadership issue, **law firm number 2** with the "wrong clients" faces the task of recruiting the right human resources. Lawyer on demand or project lawyers can help in the short term and to bridge the gap.

In the long term, a coordinated personnel concept will be needed here, which has built up the right staff in the right numbers at the right time and has united them into a well-coordinated team. Firm number 1 would be well advised to look at its own internal structure and create meaningful and efficient ways of making uniform decisions quickly. Whether this already requires management depends on the size of the firm. At the moment, at least in terms of numbers, it seems more likely to be a firm with about 50 professionals (see Schön's study) or a large firm with a cost problem due to poor management.

And **law firm number 3** with the recruitment problem? The change in values and culture must not only be initiated by the management level, but must also begin there if the future of the firm is to be taken seriously. The personnel management and the well thought-out programs had already achieved results – but these could not bring lasting success[30]. Sometimes a reconsideration of the partnership agreement, including the existing partner structures and the remuneration and credit rating system, can also be helpful at this point. Sometimes a reconsideration of the partnership agreement, including the existing partner structures and the remuneration and credit rating system, can also be helpful at this point. In this case, the change for the partners is about facts and figures and, above all, about their own

30 In recent years, I have seen numerous committed initiatives by junior staff at the lower career levels initiate good and very good projects, e.g. on the topic of "how can we retain junior staff", some of which were even commissioned and initially supported by management or the partners, only to fail in the end when it came to implementation and sustainable implementation, either intentionally or unintentionally, and then disappear into a drawer because the foundations were not meant to be shaken. This in turn caused even greater frustration among the junior staff, as it now seemed like a "stalling, pointless occupation" with the result that they left the firm even more quickly and also told others about it.

and not only about values and attitude – which will then (hopefully) follow. After all, the partnership agreement and the partner structures are supported by the established and outdated value system and cement it at the same time. This interaction can be cleverly exploited.

What did you get out of the chapter?
You know the personnel structure of a successful law firm and how to establish it.

F. Law firm marketing and acquisition

Marketing for law firms has always been a very diffuse topic with industry-specific peculiarities, characteristics and rules of the game – for marketing agencies this has always been a great challenge.

Covid-19 with its lockdowns and the economic crisis has increased competitive pressure in the industry and fueled digitization. This has not been without impact on law firm marketing.

'Before 2020, marketing was a more casual topic in most law firms. It was largely left to itself. There was hardly any connection to the firm's strategy. The management did not see themselves as responsible: After all, they had been successfully relying on their professional network for decades, had cultivated their client structure and had internalized the classic, historically grown assumption that marketing was nothing for the serious lawyer business. Yes, it was understood that the website was the digital representation of the law firm and that a corresponding investment was required for this. But rarely was the actual potential of these glossy pages used specifically for strategic marketing and sales.

After all, law firm marketing was further discovered in the battle for high potentials. Thus, law firm websites suddenly received innovative additional modules for employer branding or people even invested in separate units with close links to social media.

For employer branding alone, law firm marketing was used strategically and professionally.

This seemed to be a promising investment for the future and, after all, it taught us quite a bit about general law firm marketing.

But from March 2020, everything was different: the lockdown and economic crisis led some law firms to lay off staff in batches in order to save on personnel costs. Others froze all budgets for staff development, networks and marketing. The entire industry, from individual to large law firms, was preoccupied with the conversion of business operations to home office, the development of office hygiene concepts and the rapidly changing mandate topics or even the mandate structure.

Employer branding virtually no longer existed: companies said goodbye or tried to retain their people with all their might. Virtual job interviews and virtual onboarding had not yet been invented.

As a consulting agency specializing in law firms, we were able to directly capture this shift in marketing across the entire industry:

By the first quarter of 2020

- 1/3 of our consulting business still comprised pure marketing topics from strategic positioning to websites, with a tendency towards major contracts in the sense of comprehensive and fundamental strategic concepts for positioning,

https://doi.org/10.1515/9783111058160-006

marketing and communication for both law firm founders and existing law firms,
- 1/3 related to supporting, organizing and holding network meetings and event formats for marketing and sales and
- 1/3 dealt with private inquiries from lawyers about personal branding, i.e. the acquisition of an expert status for specialized lawyers, jurists, etc.

In the second and third quarters, all this had stopped; it was all about survival in day-to-day business.

But with the pressure of everyday life, "old trouble spots" and weak points in the law firms clearly came to light.

Poor management now became unbearable, cumbersome processes were no longer acceptable, overwork, underpayment and lack of training – if at the beginning of the crisis every employee was still happy to have a job, now many were ready to leave and make higher demands.

Only a few law firms used the second half of the year to ask themselves fundamental strategic questions after the Covid 19 experience, to actively address internal process and leadership issues and to realign their online presence accordingly, and to boldly and consciously position themselves in digital branding activities such as podcasts and life discussion rounds and as crisis spokespersons for politics and administration, or to score points with unusual formats such as online wine tastings and to expand these.

Recruiting and hiring suddenly worked online. Employer branding was back.

The job market had dramatically gained momentum and speed. Also, qualifications and experience in online formats, personal reach in social media and professional networks, and podcast talent were suddenly in demand.

In our perception, it was mainly small and medium-sized law firms that acted courageously, flexibly and agilely, even though investments in initial trials with modern formats were hotly debated in the partner rounds and met with a lot of opposition.

Today, 15 months after the first lockdown, the winners of the pandemic are clearly those law firms that have

1. comprehensively and fundamentally reorganized their law firm strategy,
2. developed a coordinated marketing and acquisition concept, and
3. courageously tried out new and modern digital formats outside their comfort zone.

Did this only apply to law firms? Yes and no: On the one hand, Covid-19 with its lockdown, economic crisis and digitalization push certainly fundamentally changed marketing and sales in every industry. Screen times increased dramatically: More was consumed, communicated and offered digitally than ever before. It was not without reason that Amazon and Zoom achieved record figures, that all networks presented "dream figures" or were completely relaunched, such as Clubhouse. Work and teaching were forcibly digitized. And although screen fatigue increased:

User behavior changed permanently toward the digital and toward valuable or at least entertaining content.

The special features that had always existed for marketing in the legal industry could now no longer be used as an excuse for deficits.

Also, the situation of law firms, having to perform virtually 200 % in Corona crisis mode, has made it clear that you can no longer afford unused potential in marketing[1].

Remember:
Law firms that still do the same marketing today as they did before 2020 and do not have a strategic marketing concept will irretrievably lose crucial market share and will soon no longer be relevant.

---

1 *Dr. Tutschka,* Wie Covid-19 das Kanzleimarketing für immer veränderte, Haufe.Recht from 23.7.2021.

I. Marketing and communication

Why should you read this chapter?
Marketing and acquisition are at the heart of your firm, the heart of your entrepreneurial activity, and therefore a matter for the boss. You will learn the complexities of marketing, understand the subtle differences in branding and have fun directly implementing one or two marketing tips.

Overview

1. Brand development and personal branding
- Law firm brand
- Product brand
- Brand ambassador
- Lawyer brand
- Corporate influencer
- Personality types
- Expert status and authenticity post Corona

2. Communication concept
- Client communication
- Law firm field
- Website
- Social media
- Summary

3. Sustainable client retention
- Newsletters and circulars
- Blog
- Youtube and podcast
- Messenger
- Press articles and co.
- informative downloads
- Non-fiction and technical books

4. Reputation
5. Business Networking
6. Cooperation partner
7. Employer Branding

The ban on advertising for lawyers was lifted in 1996; just in time to kiss the industry awake with the boom in opportunities that digitization, new technologies and social media brought.

But what is marketing anyway? "Marketing" is an iridescent term. Marketing is understood as a business discipline, a universal science that draws on the insights of numerous disciplines, and the art of establishing and maintaining relationships with clients. Marketing is also defined as an art that does not consist of "thinking up a tricky way to get rid of what you create[1]. Marketing is the art of creating real value for the customer. It is the art of taking care of customers in a way that makes them feel better." All these descriptions have something in common despite their different statements. Marketing theory deals with a complex subject.

From the outset, it is important to dispel a widespread prejudice: marketing should not be equated with "advertising" in the conventional sense. Marketing is far more extensive. Advertising in the conventional sense, such as advertisements in newspapers or classic TV commercials, which readers who are not from the Netflix generation may remember, is only a secondary and subordinate component of marketing, and a smaller one at that. Marketing is still a young but very important component of business administration. To put it in somewhat simplified terms, marketing theory deals with the marketing of goods, services and commodities. The business scientists themselves have not yet agreed on what the valid definition for the term "marketing" should be.

A common definition is: Marketing means planning, coordination and control of all company activities aimed at the current and potential markets. The company's goals in the overall economic process of supplying goods are to be realized through the lasting satisfaction of customer needs. Marketing is thus nothing else than the sum of all market-related activities of a lawyer. However, like any activity, marketing should not be carried out spontaneously, but in a planned and organized manner.

Unfortunately, dealing with marketing issues is still not a mandatory part of the professional profile of most lawyers – whether as a lawyer or as a law firm owner. This may be due to the fact that marketing is considered to be part of business administration and thus foreign to the profession. The shyness about marketing may also stem from the false equation of advertising and marketing. For a long time, advertising for a lawyer's services was erroneously considered to be completely forbidden because it did not seem appropriate for the lawyer, as an organ of the administration of justice, to advertise[2]. This is, of course, nonsense and to be seen as

---

1 My favorite definition.

2 Branchenbericht der Sparkassen 2020, p. 23.

a "purely protective claim" – to stay in the context of the industry – not to have to deal with it or to hide one's own inability in this area. In addition, services marketing follows different rules than pure product marketing. However, legal advice has only recently been understood as a service.

But admittedly, the lawyer does not sell a car repair or a cheap haircut, where the aim is to stand out from the competition. Legal advice, representation and support of the client is not just any service. Successful lawyer marketing must take into account that the use and the selection of a lawyer is to the highest degree a matter of trust. Because the service of a lawyer is hardly visible, not tangible and in its quality only in rare cases controllable by a client, the trust in the quality of the lawyer and his work plays such an important role. Both the acquisition of trust, which works through substitute indicators, and the lasting preservation of this trust place very special demands on the lawyer in marketing his services. Finally, law firms are put at a considerable disadvantage in their distribution policy compared to other service providers by the fact that they are not allowed to choose their clients in every case. According to §§ 48 to 49a BRAO, every lawyer is obliged to accept mandates that he may not even want. He can only refuse such mandates for good cause. Thus, a lawyer may under certain circumstances even be forced to take on litigation representation that does not fit into the marketing mix of his law firm at all.

But what makes good marketing?

Good marketing follows an overall concept in which all marketing instruments that promise success and are relevant to the target group and market are finely tuned to each other and interlock. The overall concept serves to achieve the firm's goals, which are pursued with the strategic orientation of the firm and the firm's strategy. Law firm marketing without a marketing strategy is worthless and sometimes even harmful!

If law firm marketing is to bring in business and increase revenue, it should be done primarily in those business areas that are of interest to the firm and in which the firm has expertise and the necessary resources. Otherwise, marketing was a bad investment. Law firms that continue to conduct law firm marketing without a marketing strategy or not in line with their own law firm strategy will no longer be able to afford it. However, it is no longer possible to do without law firm marketing altogether in view of the current development of the industry. Communication and marketing have become too intertwined. Law firms that think they can do without marketing today will no longer exist tomorrow.

Law firm marketing should include both the law firm as a whole and the personalities behind it: Law firm marketing must therefore place the lawyer personalities, the faces of the law firm, at the center of marketing, bring them closer to the target audience, make them more tangible and human.

At the same time, law firm marketing today must not only be available for client acquisition, but also for the recruitment of high potentials (keyword: employer branding). With the right marketing, you can attract the attention of future lawyers and professionals – those who fit you, your team and your firm's strategy. Last but not least, top performers often bring top mandates with them. This also increases business and turnover. Only in this way can your law firm marketing unfold its full potential: The only thing more expensive than unstrategic law firm branding is no marketing at all[3].

Your marketing should therefore
1. be in line with your firm's values, positioning and strategy and
2. should present both your firm and your lawyer's personalities
3. to the two different target groups of clients and future employees.

Clients can be further differentiated based on whether they are current or future/ potential clients.

Why is an entire chapter devoted to this topic once again here?

Many colleagues are not yet aware of the complexity of marketing, the importance of branding, sales and acquisition. It is therefore either completely ignored or outsourced by purchasing external service providers who are then supposed to deal with this topic "for the law firm". The same applies if marketing experts are integrated into the firm or if an employee within the firm is given responsibility for marketing[4]. In most cases, what is meant is "instead of the law firm owner". However, the marketing strategy, the marketing concept and the branding are a matter for the boss, since they represent the direct "external" counterpart to the more "internal" process of developing the firm's values and culture and its positioning. Expertise and know-how can therefore only be bought in as a second (supplementary) step. After all, you also no longer have your clothes laid out by your mother in the morning[5]!

---

3 Dr. Tutschka, "Kanzleimarketing kompakt" p. 25.

4 For example, Deloitte has been so successful in establishing and expanding its in-house marketing department that it now operates externally as a marketing agency.

5 Please answer YES.

Remember:
I would therefore like to clear up five illusions about law firm branding at this point. Please internalize them:
1. Marketing is something you must do as a law firm owner and as a lawyer
2. You cannot completely outsource marketing to employees or service providers.
3. There is no universal law firm marketing concept
4. There is no eternally valid law firm marketing concept for your law firm
5. Marketing is an accompanying process, not a project. It will never be completed.

Lastly, a word about external service providers in law firm marketing. Various agencies specializing in the legal sector have now established themselves, knowing on the one hand about the special features of regulation and the job description and on the other hand about the special relationship of trust between lawyer and client. This was and is certainly a very good starting position, if you do not want to have to explain these things to a random agency that is just around the corner or in town. Also, these specialized agencies can of course draw from their experience with other law firms and often know much faster and better what works well and what does not:

"Try and error" is fine, but it's better if it's not just at your expense.

Pia Löffler, a lawyer herself and owner of Anwaltstexte.com puts it in a nutshell:

"Law firm marketing as marketing for the service "legal advice" holds some challenges, but they are worth facing.

First of all, not all law firms are the same. As banal as it may sound, the strategy and size of a law firm play a decisive role in determining which marketing channels and measures suit the firm. A family law firm in a small town has completely different marketing requirements than an established business law firm in Berlin. Search engine marketing can be very efficient in the first case and completely unnecessary in the second. This must be recognized and consistently implemented in an individual marketing concept – offline as well as online.

In addition, compared to other services, legal advice is a complex service that often requires explanation. Addressing target groups or clients in marketing communication in a way that is appropriate and thus understandable is therefore enormously important for successful law firm marketing.

What are the concrete implications of this? When it comes to support in law firm marketing, in-depth content knowledge is necessary, as well as knowledge about the client needs of the individual target group. Because it is only possible to create and disseminate credible content if it is correctly prepared for the target group and communicated via suitable marketing channels (print, website, social media, etc.). This creates a sense of trust, even before a mandate arises. And this is necessary, because legal advice is not only a complex service, but also one based on trust.

Last but not least, legal advice is a "product" without comparability of prices in the market. This also has an impact on its marketing. The consultant personality must be the focus alongside the consultant competence, and this is precisely what will become even more important in the future. This is because the online-based sale of standardized consulting products at a fixed price, e.g. via lawyer portals, will increasingly create nationwide competition in parts of the market. It is precisely this competition that will make it even more important in the future to use effective law firm marketing to unerringly communicate the consultant's personality in order to stand out from the competition – whether in a small, medium-sized or large law firm."

Pia Löffler, lawyer/business lawyer at the University of Bayreuth and owner of Anwalttexte.com (Anwalts.marketing agency)

So accept marketing and communication as an essential building block of your firm's strategy and business, which can neither be handled exclusively by experts and specialists outside your firm, nor can it be neglected completely. Learn to love marketing. Experienced experts are there to filter out and use the right marketing approach and the right tools for you and your law firm from the abundance of possibilities.

But here too, the journey is the destination. Marketing is a process that constantly accompanies you.

This applies both to the founding of a law firm and to its management. A founding process requires a different marketing concept than a law firm that has been established on the market for years. The support of a business reorientation can and must also be carried out with marketing.

"To successfully manage a modern law firm today and in the future, the integration of law firm marketing and legal tech is becoming increasingly important. This is true at every stage of the law firm lifecycle – and especially in the start-up phase."

Markus Weins, Managing Director FFI-Verlag GmbH

Do not be under the illusion that this "project" will eventually be completed. And this process will also be a lot of "try and error," undergoing realignments and adjustments. There is no one true law firm marketing for all, nor is there your forever law firm marketing strategy. Some things simply have to be tried out in order to be able to assess their effort and effect.

This is not the only reason why marketing is also subject to **controlling**. On the one hand, it is a matter of keeping an eye on the budget and costs. On the other hand, however, it is much more about filtering out the really effective marketing instruments[6], in order to increase effectiveness and efficiency. At this point, you will be

6 This is again reminiscent of the Pareto principle (80:20).

familiar with one or the other. However, I would like to break it down again specifically to marketing.

The essential elements of controlling in marketing are also planning, information, control and steering measures. Here, too, controlling is a cycle-like process that permits results-oriented management of the individual measures. Without controlling, the success of marketing activities is left to chance.

The controlling cycle begins with the definition of **marketing objectives**. Once the objectives have been set, the key performance indicators required to achieve the objectives must be defined and marketing activities determined. The planning phase also includes setting the time frame until the goals are to be achieved. It must be clarified with which material, monetary and personnel expenditure the measures are operated (budget). Finally, it is essential to determine who is to carry out which activities themselves or be responsible for their execution.

All employees of the law firm involved in marketing measures must be informed about the marketing objectives as well as the nature and scope of the subtasks assigned to them in each case. Conversely, the person responsible for marketing controlling must be continuously informed about the progress made and any problems that may arise. Depending on the size of the firm, a formalized reporting system is not necessarily required. Short agreements can suffice. It is important that the controller not only collects and checks the information, but also evaluates it.

Thus, on the one hand, it must be checked whether and to what extent the target has been achieved by comparing the situation aimed at for this point in time, and the actually existing situation, and, on the other hand, the deviations found must be analyzed. The deviation of the actual situation from the target may, on the one hand, result from the fact that the firm has not taken the appropriate measures to achieve the target. It is also possible that the measures taken were suitable, but were not pursued with the necessary intensity, that the quality was not right, or simply that the timing was not right. Finally, the result of the analysis may also be that the goal was not chosen correctly or no longer appears to be correct from today's perspective.

Practical example: A law firm in Austria had set itself the goal of holding two workshops for trainee lawyers over the course of a year to prepare candidates for the oral bar exam. In Austria, future attorneys complete a five-year trainee program at the law firm instead of the German legal clerkship, which ends with the bar exam. On the one hand, the firm wanted to offer added value to its own trainees so that they would graduate with a good result and create a good image for the firm. However, the seminar was also and above all intended to be part of the employer branding and to draw the attention of external trainee lawyers to the law firm. An initial analysis showed that this offer was very well received, especially by many external candidates. Current and popular legal topics were selected in order to be of interest to as many participants as possible. The seminar itself was enthusiastically received by the participants. However, a more detailed analysis revealed that many participants were not suitable as future lawyers for the firm because they specialized in other areas of law. In this case, I worked with the firm to develop a much more differentiated marketing strategy for the subsequent seminars, which was intended to target the "right" participants. In return, however, the first seminar was very well evaluated for the second strategy.

A wealth of information is therefore required to determine the reason for the deviation from the target. In many cases, this information, which is necessary for controlling, is not collected in a targeted manner, let alone evaluated consistently.

Admittedly, it is not always easy to obtain the necessary information. Time and again, it can be observed that lawyers get enthusiastic about new ideas, set about implementing them with great zeal – and leave it at that. Surprisingly often, the results of "great measures" are not checked. The evaluation of marketing results is regularly postponed in favor of the completion of "urgent" tasks. The only remedy is to consistently adhere to fixed deadlines for the evaluation of marketing measures, even in a closed meeting with all responsible persons if necessary. In principle, however, a monthly jour fixe should be established at which the lawyers and employees entrusted with marketing tasks deal exclusively with the evaluation and control of marketing measures. On the other hand, when planning short-term marketing measures, such as the organization of a lecture or a direct mailing, the date should already be determined at which the project result is evaluated. One thing is certain: marketing costs not only money but also time and effort, which cannot be charged to the client. The lawyer who wants to do marketing properly must take the necessary time for it.

To establish marketing controlling in a law firm, it is also necessary to pick up the employees. They must be informed not only about the marketing strategy, but also about individual measures and their objectives. If marketing is not a priority for the firm's owner or partners, it will not be for the employees either. The same applies to controlling. And this is especially true for the effectiveness of marketing: A marketing measure will always be seen as half-hearted. Not only will it be less effective, but in the worst case it will even damage the firm's image.

1. Brand development and personal branding

The desire to stand out from the crowd, to stand out, to appear particularly interesting in the eyes of consumers, to be distinctive, is neither new nor reserved solely for producers and sellers of goods. Lawyers who want to maintain, consolidate or establish their position on the legal market must also strive for recognition, if possible a unique position.

An established brand does not replace, but supports persuasion and proof of quality. Successful brands, no matter what product or service they stand for, have a few things in common. Brand names are short, memorable and easy to remember. Brands convey an attitude towards life and, under certain circumstances, create an image that goes far beyond the actual benefit of the product or service. In extreme cases, those who do not use products of a certain brand can become outsiders.

When it comes to branding, a fundamental distinction must be made between the law firm brand and the lawyer brand. The law firm brand is the corporate brand. The lawyer himself can additionally be regarded as an expert in a particular field of law and, at best, even build up his own personal brand. This is also referred to as a "corporate influencer".

The two are mixed when it comes to a solo attorney. The lawyer's personal brand should then be in the foreground: People hire people. The authenticity and trust of the brand in the case of an individual lawyer is therefore based on the person. In partnerships, on the other hand, the firm's brand is in the foreground; the partners and lawyers do not necessarily have to build their own lawyer brands if it is not explicitly expected as part of becoming a partner. As a rule, however, individual distinctive attorney personalities will "stand for the law firm brand" over time, so that there is an interlocking effect here as well. Law firm brands can additionally be supported by so-called brand ambassadors. These are employees who identify strongly with the law firm brand, carry it to the outside world, promote it or recommend it.

- **Law firm brand**

Lawyers in Germany only began to discover a brand as an important component of communication policy about fifteen years ago. English and American law firms have taught us that the name of each partner does not have to appear in the firm's name. Two, or even better, only one name is sufficient. Whereas in the past it was customary to write the names of all the lawyers working in a law firm on the sign attached to the outside of the office, today this is no longer possible at all, at least for the very large law firms. In view of the large number of attorneys employed, the law firm sign would have to extend over several floors in order to list the names of all attorneys.

The owners and partners of law firms see this development with one laughing and one crying eye. As much as it may bother some people not to find their name on the firm's signboard and printed matter on a daily basis, they will be reassured that the services of all the lawyers employed are primarily attributed to the firm, which is the only one that appears to the outside world, and no longer to the individual lawyer. There is no longer any need to fear that expertise will be attributed to only one particular lawyer and that the attributed expertise may move to another office together with the lawyer in question. For those who want to be served by "International Lawyers", it does not matter whether the lawyer Müller or the lawyer Meier does the work, as long as it is just any employee of "International Lawyers". This is the hope of many lawyers. However, building a service brand is much more difficult than building a product brand. The lawyer's service is shaped to a considerable extent by the trust a client places in "his" lawyer. This trust is personal. It is very difficult to transfer to a brand. Legal advice is a "people business". It is therefore necessary to distinguish between the brand of the lawyer and that of the law firm. At the same time, these are by no means to be considered detached from each other. Of course, the heart of law firm marketing is "marketing the lawyers"[7]. It would therefore be wrong to focus only on marketing for the law firm or only that of the lawyers[8]. Personal branding for each individual lawyer is therefore an indispensable part of the profession today: both from the point of view of the law firm and from the point of view of the individual in each case[9].

In most law firms, the development of the firm's brand is left to external specialists without giving them any further input regarding the lawyers or the firm's products. Thus, the most professional marketing can fizzle out to an empty shell. At the same time, almost every lawyer, especially of the new generations, finds themselves in social media in some way, professionally and/or privately; often even intermingled, having joined as a student/scholar and at some point still using the same account as a lawyer. However, this can be fatal for the brand of the law firm, on which it then falls back on.

But what is involved in **building a brand**?

1. an image that corresponds to the firm's positioning and values (e.g. logo)
2. a uniform overall image (of the individual attorneys and of the firm's communication)
3. Consistency and sustainability in the market.

---

7 Even if some prefer to put their clients and mandates first.

8 Dr. Geertje Tutschka "In drei Schritten zu Ihrem Kanzlei-Marketingplan" in Huffington Post from 18.11.2015.

9 Schulz, "Erfolg braucht Dein Gesicht", p. 62 et seq.

The brand should also associate the law firm, its business area and positioning with its special assets and its special style of work, so that the mention of the brand immediately evokes the association with these special assets in the minds of market participants.

In terms of content, then, branding takes place:
- the market-known name
- of the specificity of the service
- of your personality

The **recognizability** of a law firm is promoted by a uniform and constant external appearance. This includes a logo, a uniform web presence, a defined letterhead, business cards and other printed matter. A law firm logo must be eye-catching, but not obtrusive. The simpler the better. My recommendation: completely dispense with all the classic/traditional symbols of the industry (Justitia, scales, paragraph, pen with paper, books, etc.). After all, you don't want to distinguish yourself from the master hairdresser with the logo, but from your colleagues (who may, however, all use the same symbols). The names of the most important partners or founding partners – written out or abbreviated – is also provided for by professional law. However, it is much more important to develop a unifying concept with brand theme, color and images. I can recommend, for example, the sports motif of the Viennese law firm Fellner-Wratzfeld und Partner (www.fwp.at), which is not only coordinated with the firm's values but is also reflected in the pictures of the lawyers and the brochures.

When it comes to the **color concept**, the colors black, gray and blue still dominate the industry, as these stand for seriousness, competence, trust and conservative understatement. Green is gaining ground as an alternative, as are all combinations of traditional shades with bright colors[10]. Whether you adjust the color concept to your personal preferences or success colors or even try Fengshui and other things is a matter of taste. It is important that you, as the owner of the law firm, personally find yourself reflected in the color concept, because after all, you should enjoy presenting your law firm to the outside world in this way.

If you are on the market with a large workforce with a name like Schönherr[11], your branding essentially consists of adapting the existing corporate identity of Schönherr nationally and setting up the same structures and systems internally. It is es-

---

10 Kocourek, "Rot in der Anwaltskanzlei" auf Kanzleimarketing.de from 7.2.2018.
11 Schönherr is among the top 10 in Austria and Southeastern Europe.

sential that you do not differentiate yourself from the brand in other countries and can guarantee consistent quality.

- **Product brand**

If, on the other hand, you want to position yourself as someone who comes to the market with a modern, promising and legal tech based idea, such as "Flight Right", then it is primarily a matter of putting this idea and the advantages of automated and uniform processing of these legal cases in the foreground of your branding.

As stated above, the decision will have to be made whether a spin-off would not be better for this idea. This may not only make sense due to liability issues, corporate form and investment, but also with regard to the professional marketing restrictions for lawyers and law firms. The competition in this market will generally consist of tech companies from outside the industry that do not have such restrictions. So it's only fair to be able to compete on equal footing here. On the other hand, these tech companies are still restricted from offering legal advice.

In the vast majority of cases, however, it will be a matter of identifying your "Unique Selling Point" based on your personal attributes, experience and skills.

Branding your firm then consists of putting your person and personality front and center[12]. The advantage is that you know yourself best. The disadvantage is that you are not interchangeable[13].

Remember:
You don't have to become a marketing expert yourself. Let professionals support you and invest in the best[14].

- **Brand ambassador**

Brand Ambassadors are also referred to as Job Ambassadors or "Employee Advocacy". These are employees who act as advocates for their law firm and its topics, products, services, or also as an employer on their personal social media profiles such as Facebook, Instagram, LinkedIn, but also offline, such as at neighborhood barbecues, at the soccer club, or at parents' night out.

12 Ilona Cosack, "Praxishandbuch Anwaltsmarketing", p. 13 et seq.

13 Branchenbericht der Sparkasse, p. 24.

14 The annual Law Firm Marketing Directory sorts the best by their specialty: such as CLP for strategic positioning (Law Firm Marketing Directory 2022).

They share, like and comment on the content of their law firm and the lawyers they like and even defend them when they are criticized.

---

i Marketing with brand ambassadors works through quantity: Therefore, many brand ambassadors with a large reach should be active as often as possible.

Ideally, these ambassadors should
- either receive credit for their working hours or additional compensation/ bonuses and appreciation, but they should also
- be linked to and included in the current marketing strategy and the goals pursued, the firm's corporate branding, and the most important tips and (legal) pitfalls via workshops and seminars.
- A central coordinator of the posts and the corresponding information to the brand ambassadors increases the effectiveness enormously.

Brand ambassadors are the perfect fit when it comes to giving the law firm brand reach to the general public with a simple message – either with a theme or as employer branding for recruiting.

Remember:
Brand ambassadors are a variety of trained employees who maintain their own private profiles on social media and are willing to use them to support the law firm brand.

- **Lawyer's brand**

Personal branding or also "human branding" refers to a person brand, i.e. the lawyer brand in our industry. Only lawyers who define themselves as a "person brand" will be able to generate and maintain the necessary attention in the future. It has therefore long since become a must not only for politicians and speakers but also for lawyers, CEOs, executives, freelancers, scientists as well as employees in companies – in short, for everyone who wants to make a relevant contribution to society. In the meantime, it has become a super-trend. If you want to be noticed, you have to use storytelling to build your own brand via social media. The necessary attention builds opinion leadership; the follower count testifies to expert status. If you can't be found online, you have nothing to say. For a long time, this did not apply to law firms organized in partnerships: the law firm brand was the focus and people did not like it when someone became more visible than the law firm.

This has changed:
Particularly in large law firms, but increasingly also in medium-sized law firms and boutique firms, it is important for lawyers to build up an expert status that is only attached to their person. Today, law firm partnerships and attorney careers in the same law firm are no longer for eternity. The personal brand is understood as an "asset" that increases the market value similar to soccer players. It will be one of the few things you can legitimately take with you when you leave the firm. And it will play a decisive role in the new start, whether in the next employment, in the next partnership or in self-employment.

On the other hand, law firms have understood that "it's a peoples business" also applies to marketing: law firm brands are no longer as cool as they once were. Companies have their lawyers select the next law firm for the major contract – and they choose the specialized colleague they can trust rather than a brand. That is why it is increasingly demanded for a successful career path through the partner structures that you not only pay into the law firm brand as a brand ambassador, but also consistently build on your own expert status and the lawyer brand the higher you climb the career ladder.

- **Corporate Influencer**

In contrast to brand ambassadors, corporate influencers are concerned with their own specialist expertise for a rather small but particularly influential audience of the law firm for which they represent their specialist topics. In doing so, they are closer to their subject-specific content than to the brand, sometimes even on the side of the legal industry in general and not just on the law firm side. They produce their own, very individual content, discuss with experts in forums and LinkedIn groups, can be found at industry events, host their own podcasts or maintain channels on YouTube, TikTok, Instagram, etc. They can also be found at industry seminars or at general continuing education forums, but then with their specific topic. Publications, whether regularly in trade magazines, in specialist forums or even by book, are standard repertoire. This commitment is an official part of their job and they usually have dedicated resources for it[15].

Excellent corporate influencers not only act as ambassadors for the firm to the outside world. Internally, too, they often play a key role in shaping their employer's

15 Daniel Hanke, Die Corporate Influencer Formel: Expertise + Engagement + Einfluss, LinkedIn from 9.6.2020.

ambitious change initiatives. If you want to make a big difference, it's much easier if you perceive them as someone who stands for something, who has influence, who makes a difference, and who is known for it[16].

An influencer brand personality can be recognized by four points:

- The personality brand **authentically** corresponds **to the value system** of this person.
  They want to make a contribution to society and have a purpose.
- This human brand is associated with an image with **recognition factor**.
  It has a distinctive accessory, a saying, a motto or a quirk. For example, Angela Merkel's motto, or trademark, was the rhombus, ex-Daimler CEO Dieter Zetsche's was the mustache, and Ulrich Wickert's closing sentence on the news was "I wish you a restful night!"
- She captivates her audience with **storytelling**.
  Figures, data, and facts don't entice anyone to listen: Too long-winded, too boring, too uninspired. But if you tell a story in an engaging and inspiring way, people listen to you and like to follow you.
- The personality brand is **constant and consistent.**
  Regular, interlinked activities that build on one another have a stringent effect and mutually reinforce one another. Online and offline activities should be intertwined. The person virtually disappears behind the brand.

In general, a distinction is made between sought-after influencers according to reach: in the at least mid-6-digit range, we are dealing with the so-called mega-influencers, who are compared to pop stars or movie stars. Macro-influencers are in the just under 6-digit range – still as much as the reach of TV shows. Micro-influencers, on the other hand, are in the 4–5 digit range depending on the niche, but stand out as specialists in their industry/niche and achieve an extremely high "engagement rate." This made micro-influencers a sought-after marketing partner for certain products and services post Corona. In the legal sector, we are mostly dealing with micro-influencers. I count myself as one of them with a reach in the mid 5 figures as well. That's not for everyone.

- **Personality types**

So what personality type should influencers have?

16 *Oxana Zeitler*, Lead the Future, Shape your Brand, Haufe 2019.

Extroverts are outward-looking, they appreciate new experiences and need activity. They are attracted by attractive goals and the thrill of the unknown. Optimism and carefree attitude are their trademarks. They seek variety and take life lightly. Their disposition makes for a pioneering spirit, which often makes them appear charismatic and makes it easy for them to quickly win over a large following. On the other hand, they also stand for incalculable risk-taking and sometimes for chaos. Patience is not their strong point; they also appear flighty, restless and unreliable. They have a high need to communicate and sometimes express their unfinished ideas too hastily.

Introverts are inward-looking. They appreciate calmness and predictability, think things through carefully and play out the possible variants in detail. They are reliable, persistent and thorough and think and act very independently of others. They are therefore less dependent on the direct response of other people – such as likes. It is much more important for them to feel secure in an environment. Many Nobel Prize winners are introverts, as they are usually persistent in a cause to which they are committed. On the other hand, they tend to be cautious and hesitant, tend to worry and are sometimes plagued by doubts. Unfortunately, out of a need for harmony, they often prefer to keep their mouths shut. Thus, they cannot always show how valuable they really are. Public applause is rather embarrassing for them. This is not necessarily an advantage in the fast-paced world of social media.

However, because they argue in a well-founded manner and thus appear very credible, their gentler way of influencing is nevertheless very efficient in many cases[17].

Every person has introverted and extroverted characteristics. Those in whom both parts are roughly equal, we call ambivert or **centros**. In most cases, however, one side or the other is (much) more pronounced. Many believe that extroverts are better suited as influencers. But, as we have just seen, this is only partly true.

Few tax consultants and lawyers are born to be rock stars, and very few want to be in the spotlight. Personal external presentation therefore takes place at most during the pitch and the acquisition for the law firm. And that is almost too much for most colleagues. But what happens when the next career step comes up, e.g. the question of partnership is raised or another law firm beckons with better conditions? And what happens when founding one's own law firm seems to be the next logical step and one has to convince both old and new clients of one's own expert status without a large law firm in the background?

---

17 *Anne M. Schüller*, Querdenker verzweifelt gesucht, Gabal 2020, p. 15 (a title that post Corona seems less than fortunately chosen).

In these situations, among others, one's own expert potential is directly put into the balance for one's own market value.

- **Expert status and authenticity post Corona**

Whether one perceives oneself as an expert or one is objectively really THE specialist who knows much more about a topic than all the others, is in fact initially of secondary importance.

But how do you build **expert status**?

This is where personal branding helps. It is no longer a secret in the consulting industry that success needs a face. What this means is that real, authentic people are best suited to being booked in the trust-based consulting business – again and again. People are relationship animals. They need to be able to feel their counterpart and want to be addressed emotionally with stories. Not being able to be exchanged is the secret of every consultant. This is also reflected in his positioning, marketing and personal branding. Today, professors use this insight just as much as politicians and CEOs. Nothing lasts forever – especially not a well-paid position. So it's good to take precautions so that your name has market value even without a specific position. It is true that for a few, the development of a certain expert status through publications and lectures has always been part of the business. The same goes for building up a network and taking on honorary positions. However, very few of them proceeded strategically, at best intuitively and spontaneously.

A start for most is to create a profile in the professional networks Xing and/or LinkedIn. With updating and maintenance, however, it becomes tedious for most. On the other hand, considerations about positioning and strategic development, the definition of the target group, the selection of suitable measures and content as well as the decision in which groups they show themselves and why and how, or whether they should even found their own group, do not take place.

At the same time, these profiles and the network attached to them are directly worthwhile for one's own expert value and that for free or for relatively little money. It is no coincidence that these profiles today offer many features that can give a profile recognition value, e.g. individualized headers. Recruiters and head hunters scour these profiles daily for high potentials. HR managers, colleagues and supervisors regularly check the profiles before appointments. And last but not least, the good old application folder is no longer just replaced by the online application, but also by the link to the LinkedIn profile. Advancing digitalization makes it possible to access this information at any time and from anywhere – which is a natural part of the job market for the new generation. The profiles on Xing and LinkedIn are integrated into the overall strategy for building up one's own expert status. A publication plan, well thought-out networking, a personal website as a business card on the Internet, the targeted use of social media such as Facebook, Twitter, Instagram, YouTube and Co. as well as the feedback to the law firm's website are just as important components. In addition to the actual profile, interaction with "fellow users" should not be underestimated, because this often allows values, thought and communication patterns to be read much more authentically. This is what Gen Z call the "vibe" of a person and means a little more than the conservative term "charisma". This is of interest to potential clients, but also to potential employees or partners. Statements on current political topics should therefore only be published in a filtered form.

It is remarkable that the demand for professional support in the establishment process is explicitly and quite naturally demanded by younger professionals. And this is before the step from employment to partner/law firm owner takes place, in order to prepare this, as it were.

Remember:
No marketing is better than bad marketing.

"I can recommend anyone who is thinking about creating an Instagram profile to do so. Especially in a professional context, the aspects of acquisition and networking are enormously important. I often receive inquiries directly via Instagram, or clients tell me that they discovered me on Instagram. Many of the clients also follow me. Through the insights into the day-to-day work of the law firm, they know what our processes are like. The networking aspect is also huge on Instagram. I've often found appointment representatives through a simple post in my Story, or I've been given a tip by colleagues. And I have also discovered or found my two networks @mastermind.law and @femalelawyership through it. I have to admit that the Instagram profile involves work: I write all the texts myself, create the graphics myself (including research) and always have to provide a suitable photo. I often take the photos with my iPhone and the self-timer when my husband is not around. In order to get all this under one hat, I usually create a rough content plan for the week. Of course, I can't always stick to it meticulously, but I can use it as a guide. There are also other examples: Colleagues who really only use Instagram to show their everyday life as a lawyer. That's okay, too. Everyone should show as much as they like. Give it a try. And while you're there, leave a like."

Self-employed lawyer Alisia Gianna Liebeton, Heinsberg. Instagram profile: @rechtsanwaeltin-liebeton, 1,617 followers

---

Remember:
There are many good lawyers. Some are better known than others. Only a few are in demand as experts in their field or even famous. The strategic development of an expert status as a lawyer or attorney is not part of the standard repertoire of law firm marketing. And that is a good thing.
Personal branding is not for everyone.

After all, personal branding is not about "making a noise" with marketing tools. Personal branding is more than that: It starts with the personality and gets to the core values of the lawyer personality. That is where **authenticity** is to be found. It is a matter of (re)discovering this and using its powerful energy.

On the other hand, it's about skill, knowledge, experience and expertise. This unique combination needs to be turned into a personal brand. A lawyer brand, if you will.

Remember:
An attorney brand is a statement that is visible.

"The focus of personal branding is not on the 'what' as in classic product marketing, but on the 'who'. After all, it's called PERSONAL Branding. It's about the person behind the brand and his or her personality. In today's world, products and services are interchangeable – the range on the market is almost limitless. It's the person who makes the difference and it's exactly this person who is made accessible and authentically presented to the outside world through personal branding. The core of our work is personal branding and thus ultimately the human being – it is about empowering entrepreneurs. It is the combination of marketing, sales and entrepreneurship that makes it possible to become a personal brand. It is far more than classic marketing, which aims to squeeze products into a shape that suits the target group; it is about bringing people to the forefront. In principle, personal branding can be used in all industries and for all people. Nevertheless, there are different conditions under which someone decides to use personal branding for himself. For example, people have the possibility to use personal branding specifically when looking for a job. Or, as an employee, to strategically position oneself internally and differentiate oneself from colleagues. It also offers the chance to build up a unique closeness to customers, business partners, suppliers, etc. and thus a resilient bond. Companies that do not use their own name as an independent brand have the opportunity through personal branding to consciously and purposefully shape their personal impact both internally and externally. Entrepreneurs and self-employed persons, whose own name is the brand, are always in focus. By means of personal branding this succeeds more authentically and creates a lasting customer loyalty.

Lawyers are said to be aloof, matter-of-fact, and paragraphenic. I believe that personal branding offers great advantages when it comes to building trust on a human, emotional level. Clients who come to see a lawyer have an emotional pressure issue. However, they are usually only approached on a factual level and in a very matter-of-fact manner. Personal branding offers the chance to appear close and empathetic and thus to pick up the client emotionally. With CLP, we are able to bundle different competencies in cooperation, which have an overall added value for every law firm in this country.

People buy from people. If we understood that it is not just any service or thing that is bought, the view of the customer would change and with it the experience and the behavior toward the customer. It needs, in my opinion, the basic attitude of 'people buy from people'."

Personal Brand Specialist Ben Schulz[18]

---

18 More about Ben Schulz in the CLP interviews and in his book "Das große Personal Branding Handbuch", Campus 2019. With him and his full service agency Ben Schulz und Partner we at CLP

Not everyone likes that: those who would like to be and those who stand for other core values. And you yourself are always the worst critic anyway.

But they don't have to please everyone either. One of the most common misconceptions about personal branding is that it involves creating a slick, artificial figure that has to cater to the mainstream. That's not the point at all. A striking, approachable lawyer personality or an outspoken charismatic lawyer is much better received.

Youtube star Solmecke, Insta-influencer Carmen Thornton, or singing TV lawyer Dominik Herzog are bound to come to most people's minds now. Personal brands and lawyer brands from the front row. But these are giants, the unicorns of the industry, if you will.

"It all started eleven years ago. I shot my first video with a webcam. It was about Ed Hardy warnings. At that time, the fashion label sent warnings to eBay sellers if it turned out that Ed Hardy clothing brought from Turkey was counterfeit. For me it was already a challenge at that time to manage the YouTube website properly. Therefore, I had not worried about the look of the video and the technology. A friend of mine just shook her head over this first YouTube video. She worked at Stern TV and was used to much better quality. This led me to put YouTube aside for a year, but then I started with better equipment and above all good lighting exactly ten years ago. I now have two lawyers who are exclusively responsible for our publications and especially the YouTube channel. Every Wednesday is an editorial conference. New topics are presented there. We find the topics in legal journals, in tweets by well-known colleagues or in the traditional media. Most of the time, they are topics that interest a broad audience. Usually, the topics do not lead directly to business for us. The spectrum we select is far too broad for that. I take the following approach: YouTube is content marketing. Content marketing is 90 % entertainment and 10 % sales. This means that most videos are intended to entertain people with legal topics and only a few videos are aimed at giving people an understanding of our legal services. So far, this is working out very successfully. The bad news up front is that my audience is 92 % men and only 8 % women. We have not yet been able to clarify the background to this. Even such topics as the liability of the hairdresser in the case of faulty hair coloring have curiously appealed to more men than women.

However, it is pleasing that our core audience is between 25 and 38 years old. That's a very nice target group; among them are quite a few startups who then turn to us first when they have a legal question. However, each platform has its own audience: we reach even older people through our Facebook presences, on Instagram we can appeal more to women, and we reach a very young audience with our latest presence on the TikTok platform. Our Instagram channel recht2go, which we run together with the makers of Stern TV, is currently very successful. There, we explain everyday legal issues for one minute every day. That goes down well with people. Ultimately, everyone has to ask themselves what exactly they understand by the profession of a lawyer.

During your studies, you learn how to work through legal issues. However, it is all too often forgotten that you can only work through what is on the table. The decisive question for me right from the start of my career as a lawyer was: How do you get clients? In this respect, I see acquisition quite clearly as part of my job. And of course, acquisition can only be successful if you approach it with passion. You can be passionate when you enjoy things, and I really enjoy YouTube. By now, we have put together a larger team that is responsible for the firm's publication. But YouTube is only one component. Two lawyers write the texts, others create the

---

have accompanied many a personal branding, many a job application process and political career and also the implementation of the law firm marketing strategy.

thumbnails, You Tube specialists upload the videos and I now shoot the videos completely on my own in the self-driving studio.

Two years ago I finally realized what I had been dreaming of for a long time: A studio of my own, set up so that videos don't need to be edited after shooting. I cut the different camera perspectives in real time with my feet during the shoot.

It's a bit like playing the piano; you have to learn it once and then it works automatically. For us, it has meant that we have also been able to react to daily topics in real time and are thus rewarded with a high position by the YouTube algorithm.

Colleagues who want to get into marketing may not necessarily want to start with YouTube. As always in life, persistence pays off, of course, but with YouTube it can take up to a year to amass an acceptable number of fans. It's quicker to set up a blog or join Twitter first. A Facebook community is also relatively easy to set up, and Instagram is just as easy if you have an affinity for beautiful photos. And then, of course, don't be intimidated if growth is very slow at the beginning. For example, it took me seven years to get my first 100,000 fans on YouTube; three years later I'm now at 600,000 fans. When you cross certain thresholds, social networks tend to help you and you grow faster, too."

Attorney at Law Christian Solmecke, Law Firm Wilde, Beuger, Solmecke, Cologne
Christian Solmecke can be found on almost all social media channels, but is particularly at home on YouTube. His videos are regularly viewed by over 600,000 subscribers.[19]

"With my presence on social media, and especially Instagram, I want to show young women in particular that being a lawyer is an exciting and multifaceted profession that is also compatible with families. I started writing an online column in WOMAN magazine almost three years ago. I wanted to make these columns better known and therefore urgently needed an online presence.

The choice of Instagram, on the other hand, was rather random. I became aware of Instagram through friends and didn't understand the platform's usefulness at all at first. The purpose of Facebook was clear to me, because with Facebook you could stay in touch with acquaintances, but to follow strangers via Instagram I found strange. But then I noticed that in Austria it is hardly used professionally in the more conservative industries, whereas in the USA, for example, it is widespread.

Initially, I posted my media-related posts and columns on family law, but since Instagram is a visual medium, that only worked moderately, as visual posts with characters get demoted in visibility. Things went far better when I started posting my day-to-day work, office, and office outfits. I regularly post my work day with court dates and meetings, but also my personal day with children's birthdays, private invitations and vacations. However, the focus remains on my columns and the legal problems and socio-political issues behind them. In addition, I regularly try to answer personal inquiries from my followers and to connect women with each other. My follower structure consists mainly of women and especially many female students."[20]

---

19 (The many profiles can be found listed with the CLP interviews).

20 Carmen Thornton is an independent lawyer in Vienna. Her law firm specializes in separation and divorce as well as custody and maintenance proceedings. She regularly writes columns on family law and socio-political topics in the daily newspaper Der Standard and the magazine WOMAN. She is married and has two children. She is one of the first lawyers in Austria to be represented on social media to make the profession of law more attractive among aspiring female lawyers. She received the JUSTITIA AWARD in 2020, the award in the Promoting the Best Awards in the category

Self-employed lawyer Carmen Thornton, Vienna Instagram profile: @carmenthorntonlaw, 17,600 followers

---

"I use my YouTube channels primarily for entertainingly motivating the next generation of lawyers (over 16,000 subscribers) and for imparting legal tips. Currently, I am exclusively on YouTube and Spotify for colleagues, junior lawyers, but also audiences from outside the field who like to be inspired. I may also be back on a real stage at some point, law firm and Corona permitting. I think that's the difference between pale and interchangeable paralegals and real lawyer personalities, whether from a large or individual law firm: those who have understood that you have to follow your inner voice (and listen to it in the first place) have a different charisma than those who do things they think they have to do because the outside world might expect them to."

Attorney at Law Dominik Herzog, SILVENSTEIN, Munich
(You will find the numerous interviews of Dominik Herzog listed with the CLP interviews).[21]

Is personal branding also something for the employment law nerd or the ever-ready criminal lawyer?

The strategic development of such a brand makes sense for individual lawyers and in many cases replaces law firm marketing. In recent years, however, lawyers from large law firms and boutique law firms in particular have discovered this topic for themselves: After all, an expert in his field does not want to reap his laurels exclusively for the brand of the law firm according to its compliance policy. He wants to be visible himself and also decide to some extent for himself and independently how he strategically builds up and expands his expert status. After all, the expert status and the clientele he has built up with it are the only things he has left if the law firm does not last forever.

But how has the buildup of expert status changed with the **pandemic**?

Point 1: Online is the new offline

As described in the previous article, the lockdowns catapulted people into the online world. Whereas previously a large part of the marketing budget was spent on business network events, conferences and trade shows, re-presentative ads in trade magazines and well-placed, paid articles, it suddenly no longer made sense to spend thousands of euros on face-to-face events and print media.

Best Female Lawyer 2020 and was among the top 3 in the Legal category of the DIGITAL FEMALE LEADER AWARD. Read more about Carmen Thornton in the CLP interviews on 11/19/2020.

21 More from Dominik Herzog and his Law songs at CLP interviews 10/23/2020.

Some things were simply copied and transferred to online. However, it quickly became clear that online formats follow a different logic and that online target groups have different needs.

Social and business networks have benefited from this: Twitter, Instagram, LinkedIn, for example, have seen rapid growth and now compete on an equal footing with traditional broadcast media. And: They are people-related – no longer subject-or topic-related. That's a difference that works for you if you want to stand as an expert on a particular topic.

"Social media has opened up the legal profession like never before. When I was 18 and considering a career as a lawyer, the profession felt closed and difficult to access. Now, students can see how lawyers go about their professional lives online, interact with them, and make initial professional connections. More broadly, the public has an appetite to learn more about a profession that – in the UK at least – can be quite unusual. The wigs and clothes we wear are old-fashioned, and it is often assumed the profession is too. We hope to demystify this and explain the profession so a wider range of students will consider joining us."

Self-employed lawyer Joanna Hardy-Susskind, London Twitter profile: Joanna@Hardy-Susskind, 44,205 followers[22]

Daily and trade journals and magazines have also grown significantly with their online versions since 2020. They have expanded their online event offerings in particular, for which they are looking for experts.

New formats have also been added:

Clubhouse[23], for example, was launched in Germany as an exclusive Apple Network for live discussions in the New Year's days of 2021, following its launch in the USA in 2020. LinkedIn took off with stories and livestreams and saw massive growth in LinkedIn video tutorials. Reels and IGTV as video snippets on Instagram are the new mega boosters.

But the podcast and continuing education markets also grew.

With the new online options, the offerings became increasingly low-threshold: a small online tutorial, a mini-webinar series, a how-to comic – and the whole thing available 24/7 on a training platform.

---

22 Joanna Hardy is a criminal defense attorney living in London. She is award-winning. Her fight against sexual jokes about female lawyers by her colleagues went viral in 2019: In several tweets on Twitter, she had appealed to her male colleagues to stop making jokes about breasts and skirts in court. Hardy has about 34,000 followers on Twitter. Her goal was to stop the flight of women from the legal profession. Read the full interview at CLP Interviews 10/27/2020.

23 *Dr. Tutschka*, Clubhouse – der neue heiße Scheiß in der social media Welt, CLP-Blog from 22.1.2021.

Point 2: Personnel is the new professional

Whereas before Corona it was rather advanced to have a few short videos with technical articles on the law firm website in addition to the technical articles and publications, today these seem old-fashioned and dusty. Live and approachable is what the audience wants. Clubhouse with its live discussions was therefore soon discovered in Germany not only by celebrities and politicians, but also by lawyers, who distinguished themselves in the discussion rounds and even set up their own regular formats. A different and new facet was shown by lawyers who got involved and did so publicly to set an example: For example, in the lockdowns, as an expert on the ever-changing rules for business from an employer's perspective. The Kliemt law firm was a prime example here.

Others joined Lawyers4Future, a subgroup of Fridays4Future that politically advocates for active climate protection in Germany. Lawyers4Future – founded months before Corona – experienced a rush of new members last year[24].

"Pulse of Europe" was also founded by lawyers: Frankfurt attorneys Sabine and Daniel Röder provided the impetus in 2016.

And as a lawyer, why not take responsibility for the contents of the largest knowledge database as a Wikipedian? After all, Wikipedia, a non-profit project for the creation of a free Internet encyclopedia, is now part of the mass media. Since 2018, Lukas Metzger, a lawyer, has headed the honorary board of the Wikimedia Deutschland association, which, among other things, employs 160 people to look after the software behind Wikipedia.

Punkt 3: new content for new customers

On the one hand, this involves "edutainment" – the entertaining (and comprehensible) communication of the basics – and, on the other hand, "coachsulting" (also known as legal coaching for lawyers) – client-centered counseling that focuses not on specialist knowledge but on humility before the life decisions of others. The online magazine "Legal Layman"[25] stands for this, as do "Herr_Jurist" and "Frau Rechtsanwältin" on Instagram and "Herr Anwalt" on TikTok.

"Legal Layman" is a legal magazine for non-lawyers, in which we aim to explain current topics and complex matters from the legal field in a simple and understandable way. So here, too, the aim is to design and communicate legal requirements and backgrounds in such a way that everyone can understand them. I therefore

---

24 With CLP – Consulting for Legal Professionals, we support Lawyer4Future in strategic development, positioning and leadership.

25 Business lawyer Anna Murk addresses non-lawyers with "Legal Layman" on legal topics.

do not see my professional activity as separate from "Legal Layman", but rather as a perfect symbiosis. We already mentioned it at the beginning.

"What I usually do in companies, I can now also do within the population. I'm creating appropriate access to legal knowledge for those who don't have a legal education background – after all, laws are not only made for lawyers, but for everyone. The magazine is aimed at interested non-lawyers. By non-lawyers, we mean not only consumers, but also entrepreneurs. We want to address those who are not satisfied with the information in the usual mass media, but who would not buy a legal journal at the same time. In terms of content, we also place a lot of emphasis on innovation and a 'breath of fresh air' in the magazine."

Wirtschaftsjuristin Anna Murk[26], founder of Legal Layman

"Legal advice is becoming more and more complicated, and at the same time digitization has simplified a lot of things – it just hasn't become more human. That's why we think this innovative approach by CLP is great and are pleased that the focus is finally being placed on the lawyer as a human being.

A big thank you for this great compliment to the team around Anna Murk at Legal Layman[27].

"I started using social media (especially Instagram) three years ago, when my son was 15 years old. On the one hand, I wanted to fulfill my educational mission and see what there was to see and do on this platform, and on the other hand, I wanted to stay competitive with him, of course. After a short time, I noticed that I meet an incredible number of interesting people there, with whom a personal, friendly exchange is also possible. We have now set up a special group of lawyers (Mastermind Law), in which regular personal meetings take place outside of social media, everyone takes turns giving a lecture to colleagues from their specialist area, and spontaneous exchanges from other areas of law are always possible if you are stuck with a particular problem in a file. That's great! Social media is not work for me, but pleasure and therapy at the same time. I sit in the kitchen at 6 o'clock in the morning with the first coffee and write about the cases that concern and move me the most at the moment and where I feel an injustice that could have been solved or prevented better with minimal knowledge. Sometimes, however, I get so upset about something I've experienced that I immediately feel the need to share it with as many people as possible so they don't make that mistake. This then can't wait and has to be written down immediately, which often amuses my family. After that, the normal lawyer's life begins for me: Family, office, court, clients. However, I regularly take the time in the evenings to respond to followers' questions and answer them, or to discuss certain topics with Instagram friends, or to tell each other private things and event tips, or to motivate each other. My followers – like my clients – are almost equally

26 Business lawyer Anna Murk offers seminars, management consulting and external compliance management using the Legal Design Thinking method and designs legal tech tools for non-lawyers. For them, theoretical requirements must be designed and communicated in such a way that they actually reach them, can be understood by them, and can be put into practice. The Legal Layman team also includes Justin Völkel, Business Lawyer and Legal Engineer, Lina Krawietz, Co-Founder of "This is Legal Design" and Dr. Benedikt Quarch, M. A., Co-Founder and Managing Director of "RightNow Group". Read more from Anna Murk in the CLP interviews of 11/19/2020.
27 Legal Layman, 03/2021, p. 17.

male and female, with women being much more communicative and courageous to get in touch. They range from 13 to 70 years old, which makes me particularly happy, since legal topics are obviously interesting for all age groups and preventive knowledge is especially important for young women. The other day, a young mother wrote to me that she had actually been looking for a mothers' group on Instagram because she had just had a baby, but had now realized that she enjoyed my page much more and had learned much more important things there. This makes me happy and strengthens me in the knowledge that this part of my work is important. There are many smart and interesting people from almost all professions, also many colleagues, law students, fashion lovers, but also, for example, a professional musician from New York. I am especially proud of a whole group of female pastors who are friends with each other, who also enrich my life with a completely different way of thinking and living, and provide completely new insights. However, it should not be concealed that some men also want to abuse social networks as a contact exchange. Fortunately, you can already tell from the salutation what follows, so you don't even open these messages. I find my followers consistently great. Some become conversation partners or good acquaintances, some become clients. If you're not engaged as a lawyer, you're definitely in the wrong profession. How can I represent people's interests well (even in court) if I don't get involved and don't burn for it? It's completely unthinkable. We have a certain obligation to the state, to the law, and, of course, to people. This obligation does not end when the file cover is closed or the office door closes. This always applies, even in the private sphere. In addition, we are privileged by our education alone with a bonus of knowledge in a field that is not always easily accessible and understandable for laypersons. That is essential and obligatory. And it is also a pleasure. Furthermore, it is now also important for lawyers to be visible in social media channels. It is not for nothing that even renowned large law firms are starting to maintain channels or blogs. Both social commitment and commitment to one's own cause are a must today. Contrary to many assumptions, my blog is a completely self-made thing and is not accompanied by a professional or an agency. It's just my cell phone, my morning coffee and me. This also explains the occasional typos because I don't have my glasses on yet in the morning. My son takes the best photos and supports me to that extent. But since that is no longer at the top of the priority list of an 18-year-old, I have to be friendly and am somewhat at his mercy. In general, however, I find the support of fellow Instagram followers very pleasant, with whom I can discuss victories, new thoughts and projects, or even exchange occasional defeats."

Self-employed lawyer Anna Maria Göbel
Instagram profile: frau.rechtsanwalt, 48,800 followers[28]

"The media can help us build a larger base of support, and it can accelerate certain things. I am part of the #metoo movement. When I gave an interview about it in a Belgian legal magazine and suggested that there should be a permanent confidential advisor on sexual assault in the legal profession at the bar associations on a regular basis, the Antwerp bar association was the first to support me. We must assume that many people are directly affected, but that there is also much resistance to disclosure and change. However, every woman should be aware and know that she is not alone. Small comments, for example, about the clothes she wears, the way she smiles, the use of her voice, activities outside of work hours, and more, can have major consequences on a career as a lawyer – but they shouldn't. An important point to remember is that not everyone is ready to change these things, and some are even in denial about them to this day. Change just doesn't happen

28 Read the full interview in the CLP Interviews, 11/19/2020.

all of a sudden. It will take many years, but eventually we will get there. I just hope we get there faster than in 300 years, as they say. That's what I want to do my part for."

Self-employed lawyer Nele Somers, ARTES Antwerp (Belgium). Instagram profile: Nele.Somers, 22,300 followers

---

To return to the question posed at the beginning:

Personal branding is definitely something for the employment law nerd, for example, following companies through lockdowns on LinkedIn with livestreams and regular updates.

And there's definitely something to be said for the criminal lawyer who shows up close and authentic on Instagram on her way to the most important trial of her client's life, like Dr. Arabella Poth on Instagram[29].

There are many more very individual examples of how the last fifteen months have set the course for (or against) a lawyer brand for many lawyers. Both are a personal decision of the individual. It only remains for me to show where a lot is currently happening and what works for colleagues.

So personal branding remains an exciting topic for the legal industry: And it has only just begun[30].

In our three case studies, the marketing challenges are as follows:

In **case study 1**, it is to be expected that when these small teams merged, a uniform law firm brand was formed. Usually, this is often even the reason for the merger: marketing is perceived as a burden and is supposed to be as resource-efficient and optimized as possible – preferably by an external agency. These then often do their best to implement what they have learned. In most cases, however, this does not include the specifics of the lawyer's professional law on the subject of marketing and sales. Therefore, they are kept on a short leash by the law firms; communication between law firm and agency takes place only to a limited extent. Thus, neither creativity nor authenticity and spontaneity can develop. But marketing thrives on situational humor, punctual insiders and attractive liveliness. Filling the uniform law firm brand with joint activity, and doing so in a strategically clever and centrally coordinated manner, will be one of the challenges of this law firm on its way to becoming a large law firm.

---

29 Dr. Arabella Poth (Instagram profile @arabella_poth), a criminal lawyer in Dortmund and already mentioned in the topic of founding a law firm with her book on the tax issues of founding a law firm, is definitely considered an influencer with 17,800 followers.

30 Dr. Tutschka, Verändertes Personal Branding – Was Anwälte in und nach der Pandemie zu Experten macht, Haufe.Recht from 23.7.2021.

Case study 2 faces the decision of realignment: Marketing is an essential part of the positioning adjustment. A sensitive and logical marketing strategy can accompany the existing mandates without creating irritation in the market and destroying the existing brand. As explained above, the decision will have to be made as to whether a spin-off would not be better for this idea. This may not only make sense due to liability issues, corporate form and investment, but also with regard to professional marketing restrictions for lawyers and law firms. The competition in this market will generally consist of tech companies outside the industry that do not have such restrictions. So it's only fair to be able to compete on a level playing field here. On the other hand, these tech companies are still prevented from offering legal advice.

At first glance, **case study 3** does not have a marketing problem; as shown above, it should first work on modernizing its own values and culture. Nevertheless, it is a misconception to think that in this situation marketing, e.g., in the sense of employer branding, is the last thing that is acute and necessary. In fact, even those who leave the firm are perceived as indirect brand ambassadors. Even if they do not actively mention the firm online and offline in their social environment, their immediate environment usually knows about the firm's problems. Here it is important to actively counteract and to do so immediately. Otherwise, a massive loss of reputation or damage to the law firm brand in terms of employer branding is to be feared, which is difficult to repair.

There are plenty of examples of this:

During the first 2020 Covid 19 lockdown, some major law firms relied on precautionary staff reductions, laying off research assistants, student assistants, and associates in droves. The social media shitstorm was unprecedented.

A post Corona example can be found on Instagram: Under @IchbinRefa, a paralegal posts bitter things like this from her day-to-day work at the law firm on an almost daily basis:

- "Morning Routine – work or crime?"
- "The good lawyer, the unicorn of every law firm – does not exists"
- "O is for OMG, I will never a para legal."

She has not yet announced herself or her firm. But the growing number of followers, likes and comments under her posts shows that she is not alone in her views and experiences. It is only a matter of time before the law firm becomes blackmailable in terms of law firm branding and employer branding.

2. Communication concept

Law firm marketing and communication should be conceptually holistically thought through and prepared.

The communication and marketing concept essentially consists of the following points:
1. Target definition including key figures and indicators based on the firm's strategy
2. Target-group-defined and specific measures that are interrelated and complement each other
3. Financial budget and time schedule
4. Clarify responsibility
5. Purchase of expertise
6. Evaluation, adjustment or realignment if necessary

The definition of goals is based on the law firm strategy, which includes the concrete economic goals on the one hand and the values lived in the law firm and the law firm culture on the other hand.

---

i Important impulses for professional values and ethics are provided by the professional code of conduct for lawyers!

In addition, it should communicate your unique selling proposition and your special field of law to the outside world and focus on you as a personality.

Here we are again in the area of personal branding. For individual and small law firms, there is a very important feature to consider in relation to freelancers and consultants from other industries: It is true that a charismatic and authentic personality of the lawyer scores points here as well. Unlike, for example, experts from the speaker scene, success coaches or management consultants brands, the marketing concept here must be structured thematically rather than person centered. The legal profession still takes a critical view of advertising that presents and focuses on the lawyer as a person. The lawyer's personality must therefore ALWAYS be presented first and foremost with the expert topic. This is a subtle but important difference, which only a few marketing agencies have understood AND are able to implement – it means breaking out of the standardized paths within the agency. For every single marketing tool, from the color to the logo design, the visual language to the texts[31].

Remember:
The larger the firm, the more impersonal the communication concept will (have to) be.

At the same time, it should include both direct (e.g. newsletter, client circular) and indirect customer approach (flyers, articles) as well as online (e.g. website, blog) and offline communication (e.g. Christmas card), but above all the channels in which your target clientele is usually found.

- **Client communication**

Once a marketing strategy has been developed that is aligned with the strategic direction of the law firm, the next step is to plan and implement appropriate marketing measures to achieve the firm's goals. Unfortunately, most law firms still resort to the wrong measures: According to a study by Soldan, for example, law firms prefer to use precisely those classic branding tools of which they are least convinced[32] or which are, in fact, the least suitable. In addition, the branding measures taken suffer from the fact that they are not supported by an overall concept or are only implemented half-heartedly or the lawyers and law firm owners are not fully behind them. Thus, even very effective and targeted marketing instruments can fizzle out[33].

In addition to direct, personal contact with potential clients, three main instruments can be used for advertising purposes: advertisements, direct mailing and the Internet.

"A proper lawyer is only in the newspaper twice in his life: with his birth announcement and with his death announcement". – Twenty years ago, this was the exact answer you could hear in the corridors of a large German law firm when asked whether an interview should be given to Manager Magazin. Those days are over.

Lawyers advertise their services in daily newspapers, trade journals and occasionally business magazines. The number of advertisements in which readers are

31 The law firm marketing directory lists appropriately trained agencies. At CLP, we have been working for years with the large full-service agency Ben Schulz und Partner, which we have trained in several pilot projects on the various marketing tools (photo, video, book, website, press, etc.).
32 Dr. Kilian in "Wirksamkeit anwaltlicher Marketingmaßnahmen", p. 29, 32, Soldan-Study 2011.
33 Busmann, "Chefsache Mandantenakquisition", p. 220, De Gruyter 2016.

directly asked for a mandate is comparatively small. In most cases, lawyers advertise in print media to promote their firm's image, which is more of a public relations activity. The law firm is to be made known. Also the job advertisements in the NJW, which sometimes mainly describe the advantages of the advertising law firm but the expectations of the applicant only in very brief words, serve not to fill a vacancy but to present the law firm itself much more often than one might think. Another advertising medium is addressed advertising letters, which can be sent not only to clients who have already been served, but also to potential clients. With direct mailing, it is important to generate a response from the addressee. Only a reaction of the addressee enables the creation of a mandate. Direct mailings are possible by letter post as well as by e-mail. Direct mailings from lawyers are still unusual. The advertising lawyer must expect that direct mailings will have a rather alienating effect on his potential clients. Another form of direct mailings are client circulars and newsletters. These primarily serve the purpose of client loyalty and image promotion[34]. Only in rare cases, for example, when a report is made about a current change in the law resulting in a need for advice, can this form of direct mailing be aimed directly at a mandate or recommendation. Caution is advised when cold acquisition is combined with direct mailing: Advertising letters, whether by mail or email, sent to an abundance of potential customers whose addresses simply come from the telephone directory or have been purchased, is prohibited and can result in severe fines in addition to warnings.

Marketing theory traditionally distinguishes between four instruments of operational marketing. These instruments concern the product, the way in which the product is brought to the customer, the price and other conditions which are demanded in return for the product, as well as communication, which uses both information elements and influencing elements to enable the sale of the service offered. The customer/client is at the center of a successful marketing concept: the client with his needs, preferences, problems and other characteristics.

As with the question of the right product strategy and positioning of the firm, the needs of the client also play a central role in marketing:

34 But beware: After the introduction of the GDPR in May 2018, you should not only have adapted your website accordingly, but also adjusted your communication (double opt-in) and data management as well as the corresponding cookie settings.

Traditional marketing

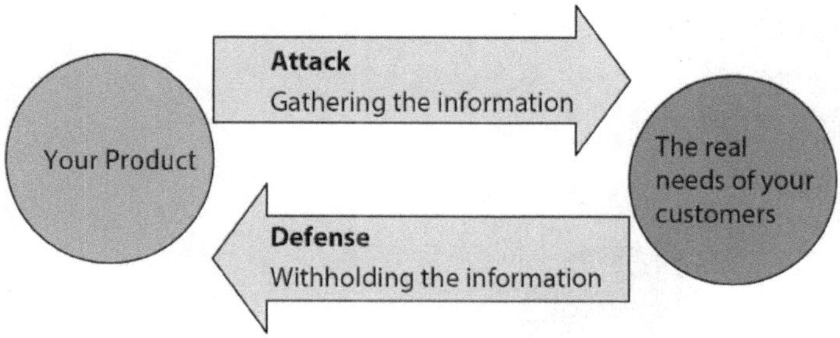

Traditional marketing1, © Dr. Geertje Tutschka

Traditional marketing

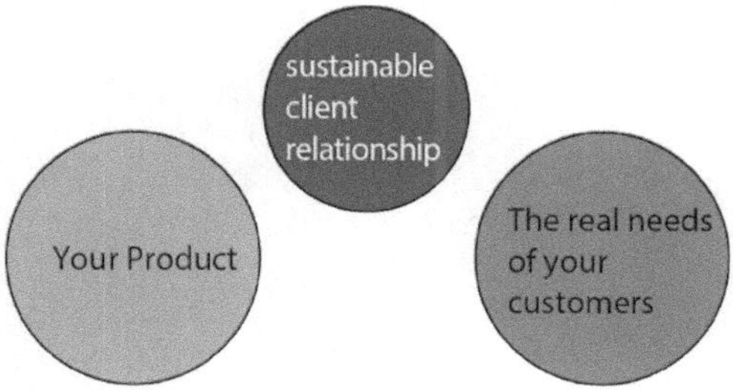

Traditional marketing2, © Dr. Geertje Tutschka

Target group oriented marketing

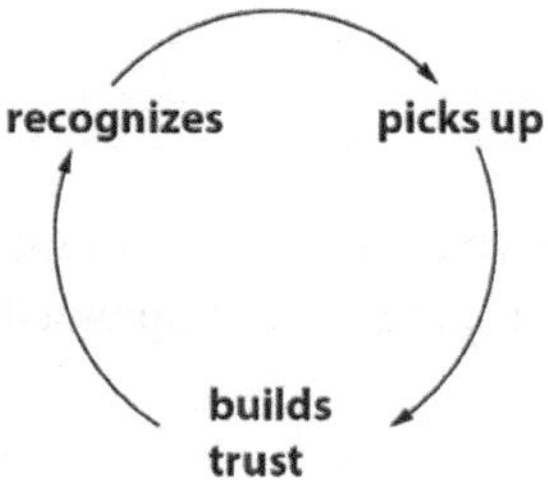

Traditional marketing3, © Dr. Geertje Tutschka

Target group oriented marketing

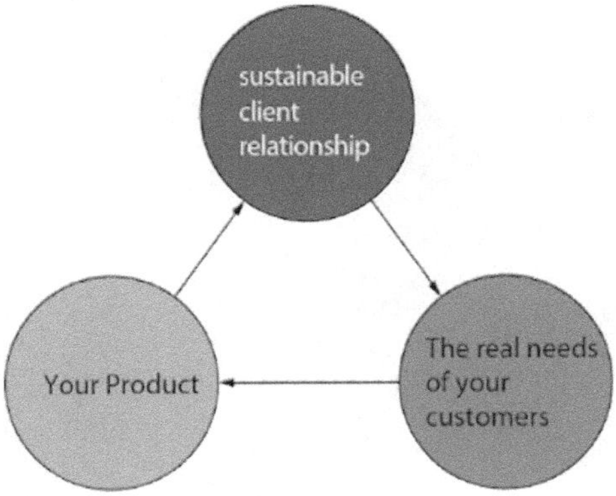

Traditional marketing4, © Dr. Geertje Tutschka

Creating an individual solution

Traditional marketing5, © Dr. Geertje Tutschka

So, your marketing needs to be directly aligned with how your product serves the needs of your clients while working to build a sustainable client relationship based on trust[35].

– Law firm environment

The starting point of your law firm marketing strategy offline is your law firm premises.

35 Which marketing strategy is suitable at which point in time has already been discussed in the context of crisis management.

It goes without saying that your law firm as well as attorneys and employees are also visually adapted to the target group.

If, for example, the lawyers see themselves as specialists in corporate law, possibly as those who want to work predominantly for large corporations, then the office equipment and also the external appearance of the lawyers must do justice to this claim. In our latitudes, someone who wears a polo shirt and Bermuda shorts may be a brilliant lawyer, but he or she will not be perceived as a specialist in stock corporation law. So this always depends on the target clientele of the law firm. If you have families with children among your clients, you should have a play corner in the office. Those who specialize in advising women should place much more emphasis on typical female communication and appropriate design in their communication concept. But beware of clichés: not all women automatically like the color "pink" and like flowers.

However, this is only the case if you also want to sell your personal legal advice within the framework of your law firm[36]. However, if the concept is to offer standardized flat-rate services, for example, the focus of your marketing and communication strategy will be to emphasize the transparency and predictability of flat-rate legal advice.

– **Website**

This is somewhat more differentiated when it comes to the website, i.e. your online web presence when it comes to various websites.

A professional looking website can be obtained today for very little money. From a monthly fee of about €10 both the registration of your domain, that is your "www.address" as well as your website provider including various designs and options such as newsletter and blog as well as linking to social networks is possible. All this can be created quickly and easily by yourself on a Sunday afternoon, without the need to involve specialists. The question of whether a self-made modular website is professional enough for a law firm is open to debate. But you can also simply decide for yourself whether it is the right thing to do. A website is not for eternity. It is immediately offline ("invisible") or online again in a completely new design. In any case, most people fearfully assume that the whole world, and even more so colleagues and clients, will immediately start browsing the website as soon as it goes online. I can reassure you – or disappoint you, as the case may be – this is not the case. Your website will not have a single visitor unless you draw attention to it.

36 Dr. David Hoeflmayr, "Kanzleimarketing", p. 81 et seq.

Think of it this way: Your website is your virtual representative premises, i.e. "your law firm". However, this office is located somewhere in no man's land without roads and public traffic. It's up to you to build roads and paths, maybe even create an additional incentive[37].

---

i The fact is that these **self-made websites** today are only actually recognizable as such by professionals. However, have the advantage of being flexible and easy to adapt to your needs. Especially those who plead for a website from a professional have never really dealt in depth with the self-made creation. All in all, this discussion is more political than constructive. The look and content of these pages can definitely be described as quite good.

The advantage of the **professional websites** is not – as most people think – that you save the time for creating your own. Of course, the look and content should be flawless from the professional. And, certainly you get an individual solution only after a certain investment. Professionals also work with modular systems just like self-made websites. But a disadvantage can be that the professional has not been sufficiently prepared and informed and he has simply done his work to the best of his knowledge and belief. Such pages then seem like the eulogy of the substitute priest – somehow strangely inappropriate. So even if you hire a professional agency, you should always and absolutely plan enough time for the cooperation and the briefing. Good agencies work with clients to develop a value-based branding (including logo, colors, image concept and keywords). Combined with a professionally defined and optimally developed page in terms of SEO, keywords and meta-tags, this page can soon be your most important acquisition tool[38].

When calling in professionals, the price range is of course open to the top. With an investment starting at € 5.000 you can at least expect a solid "one pager" – if you add

---

37 Back in the day, resourceful country innkeepers came up with the idea of building a church and a rectory next to the inn – the business model has proved successful, the Landgasthof Gmachl in Elixhausen near Salzburg was opened in 1334 and is now one of the oldest family-run hotels in Austria. We were very happy to hold our regular face-to-face seminars here until the pandemic. Not quite as old are the oldest law firms, such as the family-run firm of Dr. Wolff in Salzburg (Austria) from 1919 or Dr. Eick in Hamm (Germany) from 1909 – the latter, no longer family-run for a long time, was one of my first professional stations as a young lawyer. Dr. Wolff represents the Austrian lawyers as President of the Austrian Bar Association ÖRAK. After more than 100 years at the Wolff law firm and as President of the ÖRAK, he knows the challenges of a successful law firm history better than anyone else, and I am particularly proud that he was willing to write the foreword to this 2nd edition.

38 Pia Löffler, "Praxishandbuch Onlinemarketing für Rechtsanwälte", p. 30.

SEO optimized text revisions, an extensive professional photo shoot as well as certain "additional tools" like newsletter subscription, a blog or download area etc., you will be closer to € 7.000–8.000 (development time from 2 weeks). If it is about setting up a multi-page site with extensive additional tools, it moves towards € 10,000–12,000 with at least 6 weeks development time.

All this of course not from the start, but at this point

- the law firm positioning and strategy
- the marketing and communication concept
- he preliminary work on colour, layout, logo are already settled in terms of price with up to € 3,000–5,000 (for a law firm with up to 3 partners).

In addition to the running costs for the domain and hosting, you should also plan for "maintenance costs" and a complete "make over" every 2–3 years. "Nothing is as old as yesterday's newspaper" – this also applies to websites.

---

i

Practical tips for the creation of a website or for the commissioning of appropriate specialists are provided by various Internet forums, but also the **practical manual "Onlinemarketing für Rechtsanwälte" (online marketing for lawyers) by Pia Löffler.** Useful tips on SEO and SEM optimization, on AdWords as well as on lawyer search services and the inclusion of social media complete this edition. It also includes legal information on data protection and the imprint, as well as on the copyright of texts, photos and videos.

As a lawyer, pay particular attention to all legal requirements such as imprint, image rights and data protection etc.[39]. Some colleagues seem to get a lot of fun or a business model out of meticulously checking their colleagues' websites for inadequacies and legal missteps, in order to then send them expensive warnings[40].

One can assume that you are not necessarily primarily concerned with the honor of the profession. You should be. So do your homework!

In this context, it is particularly important that you feel comfortable with your website, that it radiates what you and your law firm represent and that you feel reflected in it. "It's a people business" should definitely be reflected in the website. Experience has shown that small and medium-sized law firms succeed quite well in this: the lawyers and also the law firm team are in the foreground. Justice, judge's hammer, paragraphs, scales of justice and especially the paper pages with pen are finally a thing of the past. Also avoid so-called paid "stock photos" of "consulting situations" and "human body parts" (e.g. shaking hands with each other). Visitors to

---

39 Ibid.

40 This is especially true now that the immense penalties for GDPR violations have come into effect.

your website are looking for you, the lawyer. That means you should be in the photos, too – confidently, calmly, and happily embodying your values. This is hard work; but it is worth it. Totally forbidden is to use the last family photos or ask a friend with a good camera/the nice wedding photographer to take a few snapshots. Pictures are worth a thousand words. There's a lot of it. Make sure they are the right ones. Personal branding means you and your employees need to show up. So a professional photo shoot with a photographer who specializes in personal brands and has been briefed on the firm's values and target group is a must (approx. € 500).

The homepage of a law firm is a particularly important figurehead. In many respects, the homepage of the law firm resembles a law firm brochure. Compared to the law firm brochure, however, it has the advantage that it cannot be thrown into the wastepaper basket as soon as the lawyer has left the office of the target client. But with the website it is the same as with the office premises and the marketing as a whole: it is also part of the accompanying process from the foundation of the law firm over the entire time. The website will never be fully completed as a "project", just as your office premises will always need improvement, renovation and modernization.

Therefore, make absolutely sure that your Internet presence works as soon as it is indicated. It is frustrating for clients and other interested parties to dial the Internet address of a law firm indicated on the letterhead or business card only to find that this Internet presence is still under construction.

Finally, something about the structure:

Again, there are no universal rules for the **structure and scope of a lawyer's homepage**. However, every law firm's Internet presence should contain at least a few basic elements:

The entry page should at least list the **name** of the law firm and an overview of the content of the website (menu navigation), as well as the logo, if available.

On a subpage, the lawyers should provide information about their **areas of work**. In doing so, they do not need to adhere to the categories of main areas of activity and main areas of interest, which are not very informative for laypersons anyway. It also makes little sense to list as many areas of law as possible in which the law firm supposedly works. Clients are not interested in areas of law. They are interested in the solution of their problems. A sub-page should provide information about the firm's style of work, its target audience, and other activities of the firm that may be worth knowing for prospective clients, such as pro bono work on behalf of a non-profit organization. Attorneys can inform visitors about the firm's goals. Furthermore, they should point out the special benefits they offer to their clients ("need-satisfiers" and "problem-solvers").

Clients want to know who they are dealing with. A **short portrait of the professional career** of the lawyers working in a law firm, information about their special fields of work and special qualifications (academic degrees, double studies, specialist attorney designations) are common. A second and third picture of the lawyer in question should not be missing. Unlike in the past, today's law firm personnel are also pictured with a photo and their area of responsibility, which suggests an appreciative, employee-centered law firm culture. One step further is the idea of placing a second portrait photo behind each one, depicting a "still life" with symbols for the interests and hobbies of the person in question. You can see this for example at www.indigo-headhunters.com.Please note that you leave nothing to chance here. Just as with direct contact, everyone can tell immediately from subtle signs whether the appearance is professional and confident or "homespun". This starts with the photos, which not only a photographer should have made, but also one specialized in this kind of image photos, which must work in the Internet. A wedding photographer, artist or passport photo specialist will bring a different focus. The same applies to the text, the logo and the image colors. Here, too, there are now not only specialists, but especially those who have specialized in the particularities of the legal industry. Do not save at the wrong end. Consider that the investment in a good expert is cheaper in the end than the repeated attempts of amateurs. After all, you want to present yourself and your firm in a professional manner. So you should work with professionals. Incidentally, in my work I experience time and again that working with a professional coach to develop the firm's brand[41] (color, logo, USP) significantly shortens and simplifies the subsequent implementation process. Other images on the firm's website should be integrated coherently and not be so-called "stock photos" that are not very meaningful. the visual language, style and color must fit into an overall concept.

So-called 3D visualizations are new. These are short videos in endless loops. This should only be integrated by an agency, since these need certain technical devices, so that the page does not load too slowly.

The extent to which the site is offered in multiple languages is up to you, but should soon be taken care of with the constantly improving automatic website translations.

Employer Branding: Website category Career

Employer branding must be aligned with firm values and firm vision: nothing is more damaging to business than building the "wrong" high potentials into partner candidates – for senior partners, for clients, and for next-generation high potentials.

It can't hurt to familiarize yourself with the "needs" and the language of the "next generation: Topics such as sustainability, sense-making, opportunities for

41 And I don't mean "brainstorming" with the IT specialist, but professional coaching.

further development, social engagement, diverstity, climate compatibility, health and "well beeing" are among the "must haves". The same applies to the possibility of applying with one's LinkedIn profile. Listing and good ratings on the relevant job platforms are also part of it.

Remember:
Young lawyers today can choose their employers. And they do.

Personal development programs with various training courses on soft skills, individual coaching and mentoring for network building should therefore be communicated just as much as the cooperation with the company's daycare center, the wholefood organic caterer and the climate-friendly shirt dry cleaner next door.

Brief presentation of the firm

In addition, a short presentation of the firm and your area of specialization cannot hurt. This "pitch" can be put on the site in writing or as a video. A "call-to-action" button should also not be missing[42], that is, the clear request to get in touch with the law firm immediately regarding certain topics. Process transparency helps the customer to assess when he can expect what. And thus paves the way for customer satisfaction.

Customer communication: Newsletter

Another useful aspect of your website is that you can use it to integrate clients and customers into a communication process, e.g. with the option of ordering a newsletter. This not only binds active clients in the long term, but also attracts interested potential clients.

Attorney's fee on the website?

In particular, potential clients are interested in the amount of the attorney's fee to be expected. The information that the law firm calculates its fees according to the RVG does not help interested parties. In this case, it is better if the law firm offers calculation examples on its homepage or provides a fee calculator. However, one must be able to use the fee calculator. A client does not need to know that the settle-

---

42 Branchenbericht der Sparkassen 2020,, p. 17.

ment fee is calculated at a rate of 1.5 for out-of-court proceedings, but at a rate of 1.0 for court proceedings. It is a matter of taste whether the law firm discloses its hourly rates on its homepage. At the very least, lawyers should inform visitors to their website about the mode they use to calculate their fees, from which point on it costs money and that a free initial consultation is a given.

Contacting the law firm

A subpage should be reserved for the data required to contact the law firm, such as the address, telephone number and (still) fax number as well as the e-mail address. This also includes the other information required under § 5 TMG. A printable sketch of how to get there, possibly a route planner, and the possibility of giving feedback to the law firm directly by e-mail round off the content of the contact data sheet.

---

i

Finally, the homepage of a law firm must be able to be set up quickly and opened at least with the usual Internet browsers. Not every Internet user has fast Internet access. A lawyer who adds too many technical bells and whistles to his website, causing excessive loading times, should not be surprised if Internet users do not visit this web address a second time.

SEO and SEA

The law firm website should be optimized for SEO and SEA regardless of whether it was created by yourself, with building block system or by professionals.

SEO is search engine optimization. SEA is search engine advertising (online ads).

SEO is about making your website attractive to Google. For the older generation of readers: This can be compared to getting your "store" into the Yellow Pages. What does this mean? Google jumps as a programmed intelligence on certain "indicators" like certain search terms, access numbers and updates of a web page. It basically follows the logic that if a page is updated by the provider again and again and at the same time contains "relevant" search terms for the user (e.g. consumers search for "specialist for short-time work" very often), then it must be especially "important" at the moment. I call this "cat logic", because the home office cat also always purrs and lays down exactly on what my attention is currently focused on: be it the keyboard of the laptop, the newspaper or the building law file in five folders. Google likes it when these keywords are found in headlines, in the text and on the subpages.

SEA is about online advertisements, i.e. either the so-called ads that appear in the 1st–3rd place when a search term is entered on Google or appear in the "social media" on the sidebar and header bar as banner ads.

The important thing here is that you fine-tune these succinct ads precisely
1. to the target group (language, color, link)
2. to the product (pitch)
3. to the link (landing page or website)

Since SEA measures ALWAYS cost money, a lot of money can be "sunk" not only with an inaccurate and unprofessional ad placement, but also with a budget that is too tight. Even with a "Pay for click" Ad campaign it needs a certain base amount, in order to lead the investment to success[43]. And the ads should not be placed for too short a time: the ad algorithm learns to land more and more accurate hits. That needs approx. 2 weeks per Ad, often longer. So an ad campaign should be set up either for the long term for several months or better a year for the law firm in general, for individual offers at least over 3–6 months with a budget of at least €50 a day, so about €1,500 a month plus the ad agency's costs of about €4,000 setup and about €1,500 a month for monitoring the ads.

What else?
Optimization of the site for mobile devices should be a given. Also the business entry as well as the entry in Google (Google.maps or Google my business) and possibly other search engines, to be found on the one hand but also to get reviews and Google stars for a better ranking. Backlinks from other sites also contribute to this. The connection to the social media profiles (and back from them) and maybe even a small news ticker of a profile creates movement on the page.

– **Social Media**
Your website needs "movement" and "traffic" to avoid cobwebs on the web. You can achieve this through the social media and appropriate linking to or from the page with the appropriate icons to the social media presence[44].

For me, a social media presence is not a communication tool like a newsletter or a podcast, but a web presence: for the law firm and/ or for the lawyer and additionally for certain lobby and interest groups and events.

It is therefore more comparable to the website (for law firm and/or lawyer).

43 Pia Löffler, "Mandanten dringend gesucht –so klappt kurzfristige Akquise", Beck-Shop-Forum from 22.2.2021.
44 Löffler in "Praxishandbuch Onlinemarketing für Rechtsanwälte", p. 55, TeleLex.

The options for social media channels are now many and varied. Facebook is probably still somehow part of it for some small law firms.

However, in my opinion, it actually has no positive effect on acquisition and thus means time and money badly invested. I cannot imagine any area of law for which the client would want to find his lawyer on Facebook. It may be worthwhile for certain events, interest groups or even LIVE circuits in isolated cases. Maybe even for certain paid advertisements, since Facebook still has the best algorithm, the most users and yet the best price-performance ratio. However, it is important to know that Facebook is perceived as unserious in a business context, which is not only due to data protection regulations. And the user audience of 50+ from the socially weaker classes to the middle class is rather manageable for law firms.

Xing and LinkedIn as purely professional networks can pay off, but only if the lawyer profiles are prepared professionally and in line with the brand and show a reference to the law firm. On the other hand, separate law firm profiles are of secondary importance on these professional networks, although they should definitely be present for the purpose of linking. Xing, however, is currently losing massively in importance – although it was firmly established in the German-speaking community in recent years. Functions are often only available in the paid versions, recruiting, analysis tools and hashtags are only available in rudimentary form. Attempts such as the Top Coach seal with the special Xing Coaches platform or the Xing Freelancer platform have failed. At most, Xing is still relevant for certain topic groups or events – but even then, not particularly so.

LinkedIn is therefore becoming increasingly interesting, especially the lawyer's profile and certain subject groups. Usually more important than the implied resume is the tool for articles and blog posts, the skills and endorsements, the publishing and feature section of one's own profile and the two target groups contacts and followers. Recruiting and sales are supported by effective search engines on LinkedIn in the professional profiles. In most cases, the mobile app is less practical, but with emojis and stories, as opposed to posts, it allows for a faster response and now, in some cases, even features that are only available in the app. The PC version, on the other hand, offers everything that a modern network has to be able to do today, with the display of short presentations, live video broadcasts, polls, etc.

Remember:
The personal LinkedIn profile is increasingly becoming the defining web presence of the legal professional for personal branding.

Whether a small website is also necessary is (almost) a matter of taste. The fact that social media is fast-moving and the morning post is already old in the afternoon, as well as the fact that all contacts/followers, testimonials, groups, etc. are on the network's servers and can be shut down overnight or even just one's own profile can be blocked or hacked, makes me recommend a personal website in the end if you are serious about building your reputation. Of course, this does not apply to individual lawyers.

Twitter plays a role in the German-speaking world, at least in the business and political context, if it is a personal profile. The example of Donald Trump shows that this network/news service also functions exclusively via people, not via institutions and companies.

So, if you're a law firm that tweets with the help of a "professional," you're outing yourself as a social media neanderthal who still hasn't understood the principle. And believe me, your supposed "Twitter professional" will be the last person to tell you about it. It's easy when the Twitter profile is linked to the LinkedIn account and to that extent is usually operated in parallel. As a rule, I do not recommend the automation tools such as Buffer for so-called cross postings, since the benefit is relativized by the high error rate in my opinion.

Instagram is also increasingly being discovered by the legal profession: Originally launched as a "picture platform," small video sequences, so-called reels or IGTV, are now part of the standard repertoire here as well. Numerous examples have been shown above.

TikTok – which evolved from musical.ly for the target group of 8- to 14-year-olds and was originally known for short playback upper-body dance interludes – has become the main communication tool to be taken seriously by Generation Z, today's 20-year-olds. Some forward-thinking lawyers have successfully discovered the platform as a playground for potential clients, as shown, for example, by the lively interludes of "Herr Anwalt" (Mr. Lawyer).

Remember:
On all these channels, the principle applies that whoever uses them actually wants to network and exchange ideas there on an almost daily basis.

This also means that the focus here is not primarily on self-presentation, marketing and acquisition, but on meaningful, positive factual contributions. It is true that these business network sites are now much more personal – private posts about lunch, the cat or the weekend are also allowed. However, the professional exchange is in the foreground and the giving should clearly outweigh the receiving. This also requires investing time every day and having fun. Because no one likes "negative vibes" here, and the same goes for anemic posts drafted weeks in advance without any reference to the events of the day.

A sensitive topic is who you let into your network and who you follow yourself: Only really familiar faces or also exciting colleagues or experts to broaden your horizons? I recommend the latter: every network thrives on inspiring exchange. The approach of only wanting to network with people you know comes from an offline world before digitalization and in any case before Corona. So, take heart and ask to be contacted with a nice message.

Especially after the pandemic, a lot has changed in terms of social media in (large) law firms: According to the latest studies, even marketing and business development teams are now allowed and expected to tweet, post, and link[45].

For English and American law firms, CRM (Customer Relationship Management) has clearly gained in importance, i.e. structured client communication using analysis tools. Budgets have also increased significantly: In the UK, before the pandemic, only seven percent of law firms spent more than 30 percent of their marketing budget on digital marketing. For the period after Covid-19, 87 percent of all law firms expect to invest a significantly larger portion of their marketing budgets in digital marketing and new technologies over the next three to five years. This is also in line with the statement of over 90 percent of the law firms surveyed that digital capabilities will be more in demand after the pandemic[46].

Dominic Krohne, Head of BD at Squire Patton Boggs, also assumes that the additional tasks resulting from the shift to digital will continue after the pandemic. "The original people's business, including business initiation, as we know it, is currently experiencing a break, of course. We are benefiting from the pre-pandemic network, but we also see opportunities in the current situation, since clients and business contacts are also located in the home office and this results in an exchange via telephone calls or video conferences, which is sometimes more personal and private than in non-Corona times. So the focus has not changed, but the ways of communi-

---

45 *Barbara Helten/Adrian Raub*, Kanzleimarketing in der Pandemie – dem Wandel angepasst, lto from 18.3.2021.

46 Ibid.

cating are different and more creative. Covid-19 has also shown that it makes sense to have digital natives and millennials on the BD team."

Allen & Overy and Morrison Foerster, for example, are not only relying on digital natives. The two law firms have set up their own video and audio studios where live discussions can take place – hybrid events, with people present in the studio and viewers at home.

Ulrich Horstschäfer, Head of Marketing and Business Development at Allen & Overy, reports that the firm has already had 350 attendees with this new format. "If we had done this as an event in the office, maybe 35 would have come," Horstschäfer says. It's a sensible investment, since it makes sense to use such a studio for pitches, rehearsals and much more, even after the pandemic is over.

Susanne Krüger, Director of Business Development and Corporate Communications at Greenberg Traurig, also reports that her firm has seen higher attendance at digital events compared to analog. Another positive, she says, is that they can redistribute content later via social media. But she goes on to explain, "where there are opportunities, there are often challenges, for example, in acquiring new business. While we were able to acquire many new clients last year, some came through our global partnership. However, live conferences, events and industry meetings are sorely lacking as a means of personal networking and establishing contacts. So, I see a big opportunity in sophisticated testing strategies for events while vaccination rates are still not high enough."

There is hardly a law firm that has downsized its business development and marketing teams in the pandemic. Because work is there, it's just shifted. "Our events team is fully engaged with virtual events. We accompany our lawyers in web seminars, create exciting formats, support the entire online process from invitation management to moderation and follow-up. That was a huge change. We had to learn a lot of new things. How do you make purely digital products interesting and entertaining?" says Christoph Tillmanns, Director Marketing at Clifford Chance. "Great feedback" for the effort has come from clients and attorneys, he says. He believes that from now on, all marketing will be about linking virtual with analog formats and channels[47].

However, almost everyone agrees that it will no longer be possible to make up for long-winded events with fine appetizers and champagne. "Content is king," says Ulrich Horstschäfer. "We have to get away from long, drawn-out campaigns that are endlessly coordinated in advance, and move toward faster and more spontaneous formats."

47 Ibid.

"The work of the marketing and business development teams has become more demanding overall, and the topics change much more quickly than before the pandemic," says Janine Weller-Beunings of Beiten Burkhardt. So now the idea and impulse generators are in demand, who pick up on or anticipate current trends. Changes in politics, society, technology, the economy – the work of business development teams is becoming much more demanding.

"Globally active law firms need BD managers who understand complex economic and technical issues and can identify opportunities from these – the job description, but also standard market remuneration, will certainly become even more attractive under these changing conditions," says Ulrich Horstschäfer[48].

Since our three example law firms will only come back to us at the end of the chapter with their respective challenges in the area of marketing and communication, I would like to report at this point from my personal experience with Internet presences and social media. To be quite honest, I don't think much of supposed "theory experts" when it comes to this topic. Whether, since when and how successfully someone deals with it and has the necessary experience as an expert can be seen directly in the analysis tool of the website he is in charge of (visitor frequency or its growth, dwell time on the page, Google ranking, etc.) as well as in the well-sorted contacts and followers as well as their testimonials – ideally on exactly these channels, i.e. Google reviews and references on Facebook or LinkedIn. However, beware: Cheating may have taken place here, as "artificial" followers can be bought for new accounts, which either turn out to be fake profiles or have been paid for with cents somewhere in the world. These contacts and followers do not interact, i.e. they do not like, do not write comments that fit the content and do not reshare. So when you see profiles with high follower counts and look at the individual posts that then have little or only single-digit interactions, you know what I mean. I advise our clients against this as well as against supposed "networks" in which people follow each other on the snowball principle in order to quickly increase the number of followers. If you really want to use social media to build your brand and network, please don't mix such dummies into your audience out of impatience. Your real audience will notice, feel fooled and say goodbye.

CLP – Consulting for Legal Professionals (www.consultingforlegals. com) – is an extensive, multi-page web presence with numerous features (newsletter, keyword cloud, download area, interactive, directly shareable news posts for social media, and multiple domains including the non-public CLP Academy learning platform).

In contrast, you will find my personal page at www.geertje-tutschka.com as a so-called one pager, i.e. a single page on which all information about my person can

48 Ibid.

be read by folding it down. The small web presence of our law firm (www.kanzlei-Tutschka.de/at)focuses mainly on the balancing act between Germany and Austria as well as our special fields of contract law and legal mediation.

With 20,000 visitors a year by now, the CLP site has become well established after about three years, consisting of a healthy mix of new and existing customers and solid dwell times. My personal site, with just under 6,000 visitors annually, is a lively destination for those who know me as an expert in the industry, which is all the more remarkable considering that the site is not advertised anywhere. Both sites have grown in popularity since the spring of 2020 when the pandemic began. In contrast, the law firm website serves only as a "business card" on the web with the necessary information to make contact. Acquisition does not take place through this page – nor should it. If you take a close look at the law firm website, you will notice that it hardly differs noticeably from other law firm websites. So, are most of the pages not built for acquisition on the net?

Both CLP and the CLP Academy maintain company profiles on LinkedIn, Xing, Instagram, and Facebook; on LinkedIn and Xing, we also maintain the JurBiz interest group from our alumni and client network. In addition, I am personally represented on all relevant social media channels: The focus, however, is on LinkedIn, as this is where by far the largest part of my German- and English-speaking global target group of lawyers and coaches can be found.

The company profiles in the professional networks with a total of just under 1,000 contacts are growing slowly but steadily. More interesting, with an engagement rate (reactions from my followers in relation to their number) of around 3 %, are my personal profiles, which are now approaching 40 K in total. That may not make me a mega-influencer yet, but it does make me a micro-influencer, because in relation to the relatively small target group of the industry, this is already so remarkable that there are only a handful of experts with a similar reach in the industry worldwide. It should also be noted that I started using these networks back in 2012 and was already the "most viewed LinkedIn Profile" in 2012 (top 10 % out of 200 million LinkedIn members) and the "Best Xing Networker" in 2016 (top 5 % out of 10 million Xing members). I "socialize" daily with 10,000 contacts and nearly 11,000 followers on LinkedIn alone, with another 10,000 on Xing and Facebook. Twitter and Instagram, the most recent profiles, are each just scraping the 500 mark. Some of the reels are doing exceptionally well, with an average of 2,500 views, sometimes just under 5,000. The average interaction rate varies between the different platforms, but the peaks are in the upper two to three digits. About once a month, one of my posts goes viral, which means that it reaches an extremely high reach and interaction rate above 1,000 and is usually pushed by the now numerous multipliers in my network. Since my strength lies in writing and this also continues to harmonize with the preferences of my target group, I do not (yet) use the latest tools with videos and live circuits, although these often bring enormously improved rankings to the profiles as new search engine darlings. Usually, it can only get better as a LinkedIn Top Voice or LinkedIn Trainer.

In the meantime, I am (also) invited as a speaker to be able to use my well-sorted reach for the events, such as by a Dutch network of female lawyers to their annual congress in London. But more importantly, I can also support the marketing and outreach of our law firm and lawyer clients by consciously interacting with their profiles that we have developed and thus introducing them to my network in a targeted way – which usually initiates a rocket launch of our clients' social media presence.

All in all, I'm an avid social media junkie and pull about every other job from these networks, even though I take a multi-week detox break at least once a year, which I would also strongly recommend to everyone here because of the addictive potential.

Finally, a word about the mandatory program:
You should visit the analytics tool as often as your profile page, and both should be evaluated and optimized regularly. Also, hashtags (and tagging – linking – from other profiles) and their regular evaluation and analysis ensure that the time you spend here is more valuable and not lost with each passing day. If at all possible, you should also check the composition of your contacts (do you correspond to your target group?), whether multipliers and A-contacts (high potentials) are included, and whether, what and how often your activities have resulted in opportunities, benefits and mandates.

For yourself, but in case of doubt also for your law firm and employees, there should not only be guidelines and compliance rules, but also so called How-To trainings with Cook Books and Corporate Influencer Programs[49].

And of course, as a lawyer, you should not only have a well-written imprint along with a privacy policy, but also know exactly when and how to declare your posts as advertising:

According to the guidelines of the media institutions[50], there are labeling obligations for advertising in social media offerings such as Xing, LinkedIn, Instagram, Twitter, Facebook, YouTube, TikTok and other online media such as blogs and podcasts. This is based on the advertising rules of the Media State Treaty (MStV) and the

---

49 *Dr. Pascal Schneider,* Führungskräfte bei Social Media – Karrierekiller oder Booster, ZUJ 06/2020, p. 61.

50 Guidelines of the Media Authorities, 06/2021: The guidelines also contain a labeling matrix.

Telemedia Act (TMG), which serve to protect users from being misled and make commercial content transparent. Different labeling requirements apply to video and audio offerings than to image/text offerings, so a distinction must be made between the two:

Labeling requirements may follow from the following regulations:
- Video and audio offers: § 8 and § 10 MStV apply accordingly via § 74 sentence 1 MStV
- Image/text offers: § 22 para. 1 MStV, § 6 para. 1 sentence 1 TMG
- Requirements under youth media protection law from § 6 Interstate Treaty on the Protection of Minors in the Media.

Special features may arise in the case of
- Sweepstakes, from
- imprint requirements
- data protection guidelines as well as
- BRAO

The mention or presentation of products, brands, services, companies, regions, events, travel, etc. on the basis of an advertising agreement or cooperation is always advertising, especially if a service in return is provided in the form of a benefit of some kind.

In the case of videos (at least YouTube videos, IGTV content, on-demand videos in media libraries) as well as podcasts and similar audio content, the advertising regulations for broadcasting apply. Therefore, the correct labeling of advertising content depends on the manner and intensity in which advertising is inserted into the contribution. For example, if a product is mentioned or shown only in passing in a segment, a label at the beginning of the segment with "contains product placement," "supported by <product name>" or "contains paid advertising" is sufficient. This labeling is only required for products received free of charge if the value of the product (or the sum of the products of a brand) exceeds 100 euros. Advertising, not product placement, is present if the product of the corresponding sequence is in the foreground and the positive highlighting is the core of the sequence, even if this only makes up a small proportion of the time compared to the rest of the video. Also the fading in of discount codes, discount tactics or purchase possibilities in the video leads to the fact that no product placement is given, but the video and/or the appropriate sequence is to be judged as advertisement. If, on the other hand, the video focuses on the product, the company or the brand, i.e. if the advertising character dominates the content (main role), the video is an overall advertising contribution. This is therefore to be marked in the video with a continuous insertion of "Advertising" or similar (e.g. "Advertising video"). The lettering must be sufficiently large, clearly visible without being overlaid by other image elements, and in a color that can be easily perceived. In the case of audio content such as podcasts, the labeling is carried out in advance by means of a corresponding acoustic notice. It is also possible to use a suitable jingle (specific sequence of tones or a sound) that is only used to announce the advertising.

If advertising content is inserted in the style of an "advertising block" in the editorial contribution, this part of the video must be clearly announced by a lettering/graphic with the word "advertising" for a sufficiently long time or by an announcement. Alternatively, the corresponding advertising sequence can be permanently marked with the insertion "Advertisement". In the case of podcasts, this announcement can also be made by means of an acoustic hint or jingle. The continuation of the editorial part of the contribution must also be made clear by an announcement or jingle if this is not already clear from the design of the transition.

If a program is supported by a sponsor, this must be indicated at the beginning in reasonable brevity. The reference may only be image-promoting for the sponsor but may not aim at the sale of products by appealing for purchases. If, on the other hand, products and their purchase options are presented or discount codes are announced, this is not a sponsor's reference, but rather an advertising section preceding the broadcast, which must be labeled as advertising accordingly.

If posts in social media or blogs (static image/text posts, individual short videos such as Instagram Stories or TikTok clips) contain advertising, this must be clearly marked. Users must be able to recognize at first glance that a post is advertising. Therefore, the advertising label must appear at the beginning of a post and on each story slide. In the case of blog articles containing advertising, this must also be indicated at the beginning of the text, i.e. above or immediately below the headline. If it is a purely image-based article without text, a clearly visible graphic reference is required in the image. An indistinct, small or transparent marking is not sufficient in each case.

In addition to the "advertising" or "advertisement" designation, the designation may also be preceded by the words "paid advertising partnership". The advertising contribution itself is subject to labeling.

If there is neither cooperation with a company nor a corresponding commercial incentive from a third party, the mention and presentation of products, etc., which have been purchased at the usual market conditions or are shown for purely editorial reasons, does not generally constitute advertising. This refers in particular to the presentation of products with advantages and disadvantages, but also to a positive product presentation for personal motivation without advertising intent. Also, the linking by so-called tagging of acquaintances, places or other accounts as editorial indication and without advertising co-operation does not need an advertising marking. However, advertising intent can be assumed if the product or service is advertised in such a way that, when viewed objectively, the impression is created that sales and sales are to be promoted. Indications for this can be, for example: Excessively positive portrayal, invitation to purchase, advertising language, always talking about the same products/services/brands, lack of reason for publication, naming of prices and sources of supply, combination with affiliate links. If an advertising article is linked, it must already be recognizable in the teaser (article overview) that the linked article is advertising. Otherwise, users will not be able to recognize that they are being taken to a text with advertising content when they select a (supposedly) editorial article[51].

Remember:
If the linking or naming of brands is done solely for information purposes, the state media authorities are of the opinion that no advertising label is required. This also applies to references to own publications, events or products that have a clearly recognizable connection with the person's own person or a professional activity.

Finally, we would like to point out the Telecommunications Telemedia Data Protection Act, which came into force on December 1, 2021.

Profiles on social networks are subject to post-mortem privacy protection in Germany. The relatives therefore have the right to prohibit any manipulation by the heirs. The heirs exercise the post-mortem right of personality on behalf of the decedent and can prevent violations by seeking injunctive relief in court. Facebook, like Instagram, offers the option of an estate contact. This contact, specified by the account holder, can take care of the account after the death of the Facebook account holder. Unfortunately, this useful function is not available in Germany.

Apart from the possibility of a memorial state, relatives can request the deletion of the account with Facebook by filling out an appropriate form and providing proof (this is also the case, for example, with Xing and most others). Facebook, like all other platform providers, has so far ruled out handing over account access data. Since 12/2021, the digital estate can only be protected by a corresponding testamentary disposition. By the way, the digital estate can include not only profiles on social networks and chats in messenger services, but also PayPal assets, bitcoins, e-books and contracts with network services, streaming services, e-mail or online gaming services. Anyone who keeps their passwords secret during their lifetime is just as much at the mercy of their heirs after their death as the chat partners. Service providers are obliged to grant heirs access to user accounts even without knowledge of login data. If you want to prevent this, you must include a corresponding provision

---

51 Ibid.

in your will so that you can take your communications in social networks with you to the grave. Irrespective of social media, please also use lawyer search services such as www.Anwalt.deor www.advocado.deand platforms such as the member platform of the German Lawyers' Association at Deutsche Anwaltauskunft – the legal portal of the German Lawyers' Association (www.anwaltauskunft.de) – or networks such aswww.insolvenzanwalt24.de.

– **Summary**

Back to our three case studies:

The **first firm** with the growth problems does not really have a marketing and acquisition problem – even if experience shows that there is always something to optimize in this area. However, it would be appropriate to take a longer look at the market positioning and the external appearance of the small teams: keyword market confusion through contradictory messages.

At **law firm number 2**, this is already different: the market confusion has already occurred here or is imminent. A basic strategic decision has to be made as to which clients will make up the core business in the future – and for which corresponding infrastructure and resources will be built up. Once this decision has been made, it is imperative that a finely tuned marketing and communications concept accompanies the implementation of the decision as quickly as possible – and that it is coordinated with the target group of old and new clients, the internal and external employer branding, as well as networks and cooperation partners of the law firm.

The **firm with the gender and generation shift** has a tangible culture and value change ahead of it. It won't happen overnight. And above all, it won't work painlessly, without resistance and setbacks. The focus is on internal communication, especially in the first half of the process. In this phase, it is important to take employees along with you, to celebrate even small successes, to reduce the external impact to a minimum, and initially to meticulously rid yourself of everything that represents the old days. Once the first successes have been achieved and certain new routines have been established, this change process can be carefully translated into an intelligent and sensitive new marketing and communications concept.

3. Sustainable client retention

An **elegant communication and information policy** is necessary for sustainable client loyalty.

Thus, with legally prepared information on the home page, you can not only position yourself in the search engines, but also attract the attention of general Internet users. A success criterion for the Internet presence that should not be underestimated is its easy findability through entries in Internet directories and search engines.

– Newsletter and circulars

The availability of a newsletter is also recommended. Such a newsletter can be used to provide factual information about upcoming dates, lectures or new lawyers, i.e. to communicate with customers. Another question to be distinguished from this is whether to send out circulars on new legal regulations or decisions. I recommend that law firms do not mix the two and use one as an "excuse" for the other. Last but not least, for legal reasons alone – and not just from a marketing point of view – a clean description is essential for new subscribers. As, by the way, is the "unsubscribe" button and a clean unsubscribe process, in addition to the perfect imprint.

– Blog

In addition to these two communication channels for clients, a BLOG with entertaining, narrative articles can also be considered.

A block is the feature section of your website: a topic that fits your expertise is presented in an entertaining and well-researched way. Mind you: a blog is not a review of a judgment! You get the attention of potential clients or existing customers because your text is good! No matter how relevant it is.

Here, the vast majority of law firms make the mistake of using the blog for mere reporting on mandates and trials or – even worse – as a platform for their personal feuds with judges and colleagues. Such contributions will only harm the author.

– Youtube and Podcast

Furthermore, more and more lawyers and law firms are discovering youtube/ Vimeo and podcast. The providers for video formats are diverse. From "drawn explanatory videos" to short teaser films on a specific topic to image films – it is important that the videos are not only professionally recorded, but also professionally edited, set up (with logo, jingle, credits, still image and optimized search engine definition) and professionally placed and advertised.

Podcasts, for example, as audio-only formats, can regularly summarize the most important information for your target audience on specific topics in less than five minutes. A podcast is quite different from your law firm marketing video, which you should be created by a team of specialists. Podcasts can be created professionally with numerous providers such as Periscope, Anchor, etc. and uploaded to Spotify or Apple – or to your own website.

A modern alternative to video and audio today are LIVE – streams, such as possible on LinkedIn and Facebook or also Instagram and Snapchat or TikTok. They primarily serve to provide short experts with live input and thus build up attention. The situation is similar with Clubhouse, the new live app for Apple users, which invites users to live discussions with experts in various forums (as already described in detail above).

---

i The most important thing: under no circumstances should these videos be longer than five minutes. Unthinkable for many lawyers, which is why they tend to avoid this effective medium.

The successful newcomer podcasts "Awesome Lawyers", "Das Rechtsgespräch"[52], "The First Year"[53] and "Du bist. Laute(r) Impulse für Deinen Kanzleialltag"[54] as well as the Podcast of the LTO "Irgendwas mit Recht" for trainees[55] are examples of how the target group of these offers is newly composed: From legally interested parties (potential clients), professional newcomers (potential new employees) and law firm employees (potential multipliers). Even the Federal Ministry of Justice[56], the BRAK[57] and the DAV[58] have been represented with podcasts since Corona. Also recommended are the FAZ podcast "Einspruch" and "Recht, Justiz und Politik", "Die Rechtsbelehrung", the "Fußnote – zwei Juristen drei Meinungen", "Jura und die Welt da draußen", "Jura to go", "JuraCast", "iudicum – the podcast by and with law students," "BeYourBestLawStudent," "The Last Word," "The Judicial Reporters," "The

52 Attorney Cord Brügmann is also a historian. In his podcast, you will find topics on the rule of law, the legal market and its regulation, as well as the perspective of the law-seeking public.

53 Attorney Dr. Arne Fischer presents "The First Year", an interesting overview of the topics of the first professional year as a lawyer. You can hear Dr. Tutschka on the topic of "Kanzleigründung als Berufsstarter" (Starting a Law Firm as a Career Starter) in this podcast in Episode 19. Unfortunately, Arne has temporarily discontinued the podcast due to time constraints in 2021.

54 Sina Töpfer offers with "You are. Laute(r) Impulse für deinen Kanzlei-Alltag" (You are. Loud impulses for your everyday life at the law firm), a variety of insights into everyday life at the law firm from the perspective of the lawyers. Unfortunately, Sina has discontinued the podcast due to time constraints in 2021.

55 LTO's podcast "Irgendwas mit Recht" at https://www.lto-karriere.de/podcast?

56 BMJ's podcast "Recht so", at https://www.bmjv.de/DE/Themen/Rechtso/Rechtso _node.html

57 BRAK's podcast "(R)echt Interessant", at https://brak.de/service/podcast/.

58 DAV's podcast "zuRechtgehört!", at https://anwaltverein.de/de/der-dav/eber-uns/geschichte/150 JahreDAV/podcast.

State of the Nation," the constitutional blog "Corona Constitutional," and the two "True Crime" series."

"The podcast 'You are. Laute(r) Impulse für Deinen Kanzlei-Alltag' was born in the idea in 2019. I am a big fan of this medium and draw the bulk of my information and inspiration from it. It's an answer for me to spend my time doing something meaningful when I can't read a book right now because I'm sitting in the car or spending time waiting. And I'm not busy staring at my phone all the time because I don't have to take in anything visual to get information. The process behind it was pretty tough. The short version is: I take away so much from the recruiting processes in terms of topics that I have discussed every now and then with my network or in my circle of friends. However, I have noticed that this is not enough to actively shape the changes that we are all already feeling as a result of digitalization, the shortage of skilled workers, the climate crisis, and so on. The approach behind this is education and making things visible, along the lines of: 'Have you ever thought of this in this context?'"

Legal specialist Sina Töpfer, podcast operator[59]

And this is precisely where the change lies: personal branding, the development of a lawyer's brand, must now always serve all these target groups. Not simultaneously, but holistically.

- **Messenger services**

WhatsApp, Threma, WeChat, SnapChat &Co can certainly be used in addition, if this corresponds to the image of the law firm and the lawyers – and the target group – and is easy for them. For a Chinese target group, "WeChat" can therefore play a role, for example. A knack for the effectiveness of photos, images and posts and their placement as well as the "unwritten rules" of these networks (e.g., time and frequency of posts, whether and when repetitions are necessary, likes and follows of others, live chats and hangouts, image editing, etc.) is a must.

- **Press professional articles and co.**

The presentation is rounded off with regular contributions and articles in corresponding print and online media on the special field. You should base your selection on where and what your target group reads or which platforms offer your target group a certain added value and not primarily on which ones you read yourself. For example, advice series for families and mothers with children are suitable for fa-

59 You can find the podcast at CLP at https://www.consultingforlegals.com/aktuelles/tag/podcast/.

mily lawyers, or medical forums for medical lawyers, while business magazines are suitable for business lawyers.

- **informative Downloads**

In general, when developing your sustainable law firm communication and marketing strategy, you should think about which products you would like to offer free of charge here as added value for your customers in the long term.

Checklists and instructional sketches or even studies and white papers on a special topic are, in our experience, very welcome by potential clients. They can be easily offered as downloads on your website, just like general draft contracts.

These are easy and unproblematic to create with free tools and apps. Even an appealing eBook cover is easy and fast to create nowadays. Powerpoint presentations or special products like small magazines and reports are easy to create with tools like Canva or Prexi and to put online with a tool like Issue.

- **Non-fiction and technical book**

In addition to articles and podcasts and videos, the publication of expert non-fiction books or specialist books should also be considered, which can also be very variable in terms of size, form and edition and can range from e-books of just a few pages to self-published small non-fiction books and publishing books.

With this part of the marketing concept, you build on the reputation of the law firm through the personal branding of the individual lawyers. In my experience, this is taken for granted by small to medium-sized law firms, but often neglected by large firms. The dilemma here is that the lawyers become interchangeable as soon as they are faceless without their own profile and are lost in the mass of lawyers in the firm. At the partner level, this may not necessarily apply to the name givers and founders. However, if well-known specialists with international expertise are under contract without being featured on such websites, valuable potential for law firm marketing is wasted. Here it is important that the personal branding for the expert is carried out separately – possibly with their own personal website. The aim of the websites of such large law firms is completely different from that of smaller and medium-sized firms. It is not used for acquisition, just as these law firms do not live from walk-in customers. It is merely their "location" on the web: just like the local location, it is supposed to radiate status, prestige and size.

At the same time, it is also strongly recommended that individual lawyers work on their personal branding and reputation building at an early stage and build up their own website with a domain (a so-called "one-pager" is sufficient for this).

4. Reputation

And that brings us to the topic of reputation.

Advertising, publicity, image cultivation, marketing, public relations – there is a lively confusion in the use of these terms. Marketing is a generic term. This generic term refers to all activities that a market participant carries out with a view to the market. Advertising is only a small part of marketing. The word advertisement has an unpleasant connotation. Jurisprudence (still) qualifies inadmissible advertising as "advertising and market-shouting". Wrongly so, because advertising is nothing more than self-promotion. And that is exactly what a lawyer must do in order to win new clients and retain existing ones.

The **public relations work** of a law firm serves to increase the reputation of the law firm among clients, potential clients, intermediaries and other market participants. It is intended to increase the level of awareness of the law firm and the esteem in which it is held by others, and thus to build and maintain a certain "image" of a law firm, to establish it as a brand.

Law firms and lawyers must therefore promote themselves and their service portfolio. And self-praise is quite permissible, as long as it does not become unobjective. However, crude self-praise is hardly suitable to increase the fame and reputation of the individual lawyer or his law firm. It is better to demonstrate to the public the lawyer's commitment and working methods in areas other than file processing.

The author of a commentary or a specialist book not only increases his level of awareness through publication, but at the same time, with his book, he has an **advertising medium** in his hand which he can hand over to his clients in order to convince them of his competence. The co-author or even editor of a handbook identifies himself as a specialist in the eyes of the public. Contributions in legal journals do not only impress colleagues. The client, to whom a special print is sent with the author's kind recommendation, quite naturally assumes that the publication proves the outstanding professional competence of his lawyer. Also, generally understandable publications to legal topics in industry sheets or the notices of the local Chambers of Industry and Commerce do not miss their effect. Often not the article, but the name of the lawyer is read. With the number of publications, the level of awareness and reputation of the lawyer increases. In order to achieve the desired effect, however, it must not remain with one publication. Continuity is important. It is also true for public relations that constant dripping wears away the stone. When you are quoted by colleagues for the first time, you know that you have reached the next level of reputation.

One possibility for continuous **reputation** building is certainly to use press services and agencies for relationship work with journalists. Hardly any lawyer is capable of formulating a press release that is suitable for arousing the interest of a journalist. Lawyers must abandon the idea that they can instrumentalize journalists for their own purposes. A journalist will only report on a topic and possibly mention the name of the law firm in his report if the topic is of interest to him and his audience. Apart from a magazine specializing in this, the media are regularly not interested in whether Partner X or Associate Y has left one law firm and joined the other. However, a fundamental, sometimes even a bizarre decision of a court on an issue of interest to the public can be newsworthy. In this context, the local press often does not differentiate between a decision of the Federal Supreme Court and a decision of the local district court. The news that the Federal Court of Justice has ruled on the validity of marriage contracts can be just as interesting for journalists as the news that the local labor court has ruled in favor of the works council in a dispute with a well-known company. You should not underestimate: Media work is relationship work. If a journalist has repeatedly received interesting information from a lawyer that he can use for his work, then he will possibly ask this lawyer for background information when he has to work on a legal topic and possibly also quote or even interview the lawyer as his informant in his article. Selective contacts with journalists are regularly of no use. The key to successful media relations is continuity.

Reputation also feeds on the profiles of the professional networks Xing and LinkedIn. If the profile is not only professional but also brand-effective, it should definitely also be used to build up the company's own reputation.

Reputation is generated here on the one hand by building up a meaningful network. Both quantity and quality are important here. 23 contacts can only be argued if the profile is not older than 6 months (the profile start can be found in the profile). A specialist and expert should have a "network" of several thousand contacts if he is not directly at the beginning of his career or a change. The network must consist of relevant contacts, i.e. experts of the same level and higher in your field, A-clients and multipliers as well as well-known "celebrities" of your business field. 250 contacts with key account managers, assistants, old school friends and profile corpses are not only of little use, but also damage your reputation if these are your only contacts. In 2,500 contacts, however, these disappear. Reputation can also be built in these networks through posts and comments in relevant groups and postings of others on your topic. You should also consider posting specific events (on Xing Event) or articles (on LinkedIn). Another option is to get recommendations and endorsements from customers and colleagues (LinkedIn), and to add to your profile not only your website, but also documents as pdf, videos and awards and honors. Positions in honorary positions are playing an increasingly important role, which not only indicate additional competencies such as experience in leading volunteer teams, but also show honorary service and special social and/or societal cJust like a badly set up and neglected profile in professional networks, other "careless" remarks and bad representations can also damage your reputation. Therefore, just as you build your reputation, you should also pay attention to protecting it. Damaged reputation can have more serious, lasting consequences than no reputation at all. Press representatives in the courtroom who spontaneously hold the microphone in your face with a desire for sensation, quick statements to journalists and industry representatives by telephone or even private irregularities[60] can quickly turn into an uncontrollable “shitstorm”.

Sometimes, mandates or entire areas of law and target groups also bring an increased risk potential with them. You have to deal with this and be able to handle it. Ignoring it is not very helpful, as these issues then develop a dynamic of their own. Experts such as Martin Wohlrabe from Consilium provide the necessary know-how for dealing with such situations:

“Lawyers fight primarily within the courtroom. However, they must not lose sight of the public. What to watch out for, so that in the end it's not a case of: successful operation, patient deceased.

While the strict rule of law applies in the courtroom, the world outside looks different. Here, the public judges according to morality and justice. This is a dangerous mixture when those affected fight to win a legal dispute and in the end find that they have won the case but lost the publicity. So that this does not happen, it is especially important for lawyers to include the public impact in their considerations. In the case of an attack, it is a matter of supporting one's own claims in the media; in the case of a defense, it is primarily a matter of protecting one's reputation. It is always necessary to look: How could the legal dispute develop in the media? When do you use publicity and how do you use it? Equally important: How do you keep a case out of the press without immediately using the cudgels of media law? The method of choice is often background interviews. These are confidential conversations with journalists. They help the journalists to classify the facts of the case. Only when an overall picture emerges can they report in a differentiated manner. And when it comes to reputation protection, this is the key to success. The top priority in litigation PR is to support the lawyer's strategy – in other words, it's not about building a PR parallel universe alongside the actual case.

The goal of attack mandates is to conduct PR in all relevant markets of the opposing party in the interest of one's own client. The opposite party is to be made to believe that a prolonged public discussion of the disputed facts tends to be more damaging than the legal dispute. The situation is different with defense mandates: The goal here is to protect one's reputation or even to pay as little of the demanded sum as possible for once. Lawyers quickly tend toward the “no-comment” strategy. Apart from individual cases, this is a fatal decision. Because in this way, those affected give up their own power of interpretation. The result: uncommented negative reports spread quickly (especially online). In addition, this behavior usually leads to unnecessary mistrust among journalists and, in the worst case, to defiant reactions.

Lawyer Martin Wohlrabe is managing director of CONSILIUM Rechtskommunikation GmbH. The PR consultant holds a lectureship in strategic legal communication at the University of Freiburg. His company organizes the annual Legal Communication Summit.

---

60 As well as the unreflected publishing of your unpopular private opinion on explosive topics such as abortion etc. on Facebook and Co. (Politics and religion should be treated with caution, not only as table talk).

On the other hand, **lectures and seminars** (also online as webinars) held or led by a lawyer himself are reputation-enhancing. On the one hand, they have the opportunity to convince their audience that they have specialist knowledge and can convey it in a generally understandable and practical manner. On the other hand, the lawyer usually has to deal with an interested audience. A law firm can organize its own seminars to which not only clients but also other persons whom the law firm would like to win as clients are invited. A "client seminar" does not always have to deal with antitrust law, corporate law or the latest changes in tax law and be intended only for entrepreneurs as clients. General law firms can also hold such seminars, information events or "open days". A law firm that mainly deals with residential tenancy law can achieve a high level of response with an invitation to an "information evening for residential tenants" if it also succeeds in publishing this invitation in the local press. Lectures and seminars automatically lead to questions from the event participants and a subsequent discussion. In a round of talks, any "fear of contact" with lawyers is easier to overcome. Seminars and lectures do not always have to be organized and advertised by the company itself. Cooperation with non-colleagues is also possible, as are series of events organized by municipalities, offices, institutions, or even continuing education programs such as those offered by the German Lawyers' Academy.

Finally, there are rankings, awards and distinctions. Rankings and "Top 100 – Seals[61]" may be viewed critically and in a differentiated manner. But they certainly enhance reputation. Especially since they are often supported by major media and thus generate a certain marketing reach.

The situation is quite different, however, for earned certificates, titles and awards for lawyers and law firms. These classically include the doctorate and the LL.M., but also a specialist attorney title or the training certificate for mediator, legal coach or legal project manager can be evaluated in this way. The same applies to the further training certificate of the BRAK "Quality through Training".

In the meantime, a diverse award culture has established itself, which annually selects the "best" in very different categories with different objectives. I would just like to mention as examples the JUVE Awards (e.g. "Law Firm of the Year") and the azur Awards (e.g. "Training and Education"), the "Innovation Award" of STP or the "PMN Management Awards" or the "Women in Law Award" as well as the "Legal Awards" and the "Global Law Experts Awards". The German Lawyers' Association

61 Due to dubious quality criteria or the combination with monetary license fees for the use of the logos.

and the Association of Women Lawyers also award special prizes and distinctions for dedicated professionals, such as the "Maria Otto Prize".
Especially in recent years, this area has evolved from a relatively conservative corner to fresh formats and target groups:

First and foremost, of course, the legal tech sector was looking for new incentives, as it was denied the classic awards. In addition to the American Legal Technology Award and the British Legal Technology Award, the Leaders in Legal Tech Award and the European Women of Legal Tech Award as well as the Woman of Legal Tech Award were created.

Especially the highlighting and honoring of deserving women lawyers can be found in other fields worldwide: The Justitia Award for women lawyers, the Women in Law Award for women lawyers, and the Marie Elisabeth Lüders Award for women lawyers and economists.

Dr. Alix Frank-Thomasser, Viennese lawyer and chairwoman of Women in Law, on the Justitia Award:

"In 2020, the association "Women in Law"[62] together with the law book publisher MANZ offered the award JUSTITIA for outstanding women in law with the award ceremony in the ceremonial hall of the Palace of Justice in Vienna. Among the first prize winners was Brigitte Bierlein, who was the first (interim) Federal Chancellor of the Republic of Austria. We address female lawyers and their male allies from all legal professional groups and specializations of the legal professions as well as students, professionally active and also already retired female and male lawyers in Austria and Europe. Our cooperation partners are also located outside Europe, such as WOZA, Women in Law South Africa. We want this international exchange of ideas, because we believe that we can learn from each other and therefore achieve a lot together. We also deliberately want to exchange ideas with academia and practitioners. I think it is very important to build a bridge between theoretical discussion and practical implementation in everyday work. Only with sound background knowledge and an understanding of causes and effects can we, as an association, seriously and sustainably bring about a change in thinking and achieve change."

Dr. Alix Frank-Thomasser, Vienna, Women in Law and Justitia Awards.

But awards aimed at employer branding are also becoming increasingly popular:

From my own experience, I can say that further training or personnel development programs receive an enormous boost both internally and externally when they receive an award from an independent jury of experts. Since 2017, for example, I have been responsible for presenting the Prism Award of the world's largest professional association for coaches, the International Coaching Federation, in Germany. In addition to Volkswagen, adidas, SAP and vodafone, the award winners in-

62 Mehr dazu bei den Netzwerken.

clude CMS Legal Services with its Partner Peak Performance Program (PPPP). As a solid coaching component, embedded in a well-structured and evaluated further training system, it is aimed primarily at the top performers, the so-called rainmakers of the law firm, in order to strengthen their personalities and their ties to each other and to the large law firm. This effectively counteracts staff turnover, especially in times of major upheaval – for example, due to digitalization. Above all, however, the firm's PPPP is intended to usher in sustainable and future-proof change, with the involvement of all stakeholders, and to establish a coaching culture in an industry that is only just discovering its effectiveness:

"For lawyers, coaching can be beneficial in many ways. Whether it is to support one's own career prospects, when moving from an associate role to a partnership in a law firm, but also for seasoned partners and executives up to GCs who work with large teams and want to increase their effectiveness. A (side) effect can also be that the experience as a coaching client awakens the desire to complete coaching training oneself in order to pass on what has been learned or to change or expand one's own leadership style in the direction of coaching. Finally, I also believe that the change of perspective learned in coaching enables lawyers to more easily put themselves in each other's shoes in negotiation situations, ask the right questions, and thus achieve a better negotiation outcome for all parties. In our company, one of the world's largest law firms, we use coaching on an international level specifically for the development of our partners. In particular, we want to support partners who lead teams and perform leadership functions within the organization with offers for self-reflection, for example with regard to their leadership style, and in this context also with coaching. The offer is very much appreciated, and for me it is always wonderful to see how great impact can be achieved with relatively small interventions. We work with re-nowned business coaches who receive tremendous appreciation and excellent feedback from our program participants."[63]

Ulrike Staats, Head of Global HR, Learning and Development, CMS

"The 'Stonewall Top 100' index, a ranking that assesses companies in terms of LGBT equality, is very popular in the UK. Almost all companies want to be in the top 100 and go to great lengths to meet the many criteria that Stonewall sets. This creates the right awareness. It's no longer about having 'no problem' with LGBT+, it's about proving that you are positively committed to diversity. Variety and diversity are really in the self-interest of companies. Mixed teams, in terms of gender distribution, origin, sexual orientation and also disability, create a more collegial atmosphere. Those who can openly be themselves are more efficient. By the way: Good employees and managers are becoming increasingly scarce – why should successful companies close themselves off from such a large and creative group as the LGBT+?"

Dr. Klaus-Stefan Hohenstatt, Partner in the law firm Freshfields Bruckhaus Deringer in Hamburg

---

63 Press release in Unternehmensjurist 02/2019, p. 68.

Certificates that require certain auditing results also continue to have an impact and have a positive influence on reputation. In recent years, these included ISO certifications that attest to particularly efficient and modern processes. Currently, sustainability and environmental seals, such as the Ecological Footprint, are the most important.

But also, online ranking evaluations – from Google to Amazon to employer platforms – play an increasingly important role and should no longer be left to chance. Reputation is built up through the trust of current clients, who in turn generate a certain amount of trust from potential new clients through direct recommendations or modern online evaluations: this can be done in special portals for experts or employers, but also on lawyer search services or in Google (Maps). With asterisks, similar to Amazon, certain services are rated anonymously or with names, with or without text, which in turn can lead to a certain ranking for the search engine within the portal. This pays directly for the findability (keyword SEO) or can be shown as a "seal of trust" on the law firm's website (e.g. "ProvenExpert"). Of course, there are also various formats on an international level.

In the end, you have the choice in which area you would like to particularly distinguish yourself and be measured.

5. Business Networking

Competitive pressure and competition have increased dramatically in our profession in recent years. One would like to think that lawyer networks have become obsolete because everyone is next to himself. The opposite is the case:

The pooling of human, material and communicative resources (e.g. rooms, technology, finances, contacts, competencies) expands the scope of action for each individual and enables new and larger joint (network) offers and services (events, publications, public campaigns, services), through which the individual participants can also experience greater satisfaction and recognition. Confirmed by the major BRAO reform coming into force in August 2022, interdisciplinary networks and cooperations will also become increasingly interesting for lawyers and are likely to become an absolute must in the future.
The expansion of professional and personal experience horizons can also bring new opportunities for professional development. Each network operates according to its own rules and has a specific focus.

Finally, a network can also support each other, create a sense of belonging, a sense of home and identity, or simply be fun. Casually creating new ideas, pursuing common goals, meeting in a pleasant atmosphere and getting to know new ideas and new people: this "feel-good factor", the emotional ties are enormously important for the willingness to get involved in a network and to stay involved[64].

There are exactly three categories of people. Those who simply approach their fellow human beings offline and online with an open mind and curiosity. They are communicative, extroverted, have a sense of humor and compassion. These people not only find it easy, they love to "network", they need the exchange with others. They "network" as it were in passing. However, there is no benefit for any of the people involved – at best a few entertaining moments. The opposite is true of people to whom small talk is anathema. These are rather quiet and introverted. These are the shy ones and thinkers. "Networking" for them is a chore, often uptight and wooden. Usually both sides are grateful when it's "over." Added value? Zero.

And then there are the people who want to achieve something with "networking," for whom networking is simply a method of achieving their goal. With the goal in mind, it plays a subordinate role for them whether they are communicative or not. The success of an entrepreneur is not primarily determined by whether he is a superstar on stage (Steve Jobs) or not (Bill Gates).

So, keep your goal in mind and use **networking as a "means to an end"**. Think carefully about who you contact, how and when.

Your networking should be:

1. Be strategically
2. target group defined and
3. scheduled

What opportunities are there for lawyers and legal professionals in the German-speaking world to network? Of course, there are the professional associations (such as the DAV), the moderated lunch meeting or even the informal monthly get-together with colleagues.

But even beyond that, there are many opportunities to network with colleagues:

1. Training

   Training programs bring participants together and close mutual support often develops even after the training has been completed ("buddy program").
2. online networks

   With little time and money you can use the online possibilities for networking: Xing groups such as JurBiz, but also posts and exchanges in blogs offer uncomplicated, regular exchanges with other lawyers and legal professionals.

---

64 Dr. Tutschka, "Drei Gründe, warum Netzwerken für Juristen so wichtig ist" in CLP's Blog from 22.2.1015.

3. Congresses, conferences and trade fairs
   The most important annual congress of our professional group is certainly the German Lawyers' Day every year in early summer with the accompanying trade fair, Advotec, and the evening program. But there are also Lawyers' Days on a regional level. Or with our Austrian colleagues every year in September. In addition, LegalTech conferences and trade fairs such as the "Future Congress" or Legal ®Evolution, symposia such as the STP conference in Bensberg, the Traffic Law Day and many others, and not forgetting the Lawyers' Day every two years in September are good opportunities to meet colleagues and exchange ideas. In most cases, groups are soon formed that meet on a regular basis for various events.
4. Balls
   Of course, there are also the social events where lawyers and attorneys meet, such as the annual Lawyers' Ball at the Hofburg in Vienna, the DAV receptions or the gala and award events.

This list is certainly not exhaustive. And it also refers exclusively to purely industry events for lawyers and attorneys. In addition, there are certainly many other industry events where lawyers are present, but not exclusively together. Also, everyone should find out what suits them best, because what works for one person may be anything but satisfactory for another.

---

i But be careful. You should also approach business networking strategically and purposefully. After all, not every meeting is networking.

A meeting only becomes networking when you
1. have tailored it in advance to your needs and goals,
2. go to the meeting with a specific agenda and then follow it there, and
3. do a dedicated follow up afterwards.

Independent of this offline network, the online network is becoming increasingly important. In the offline network, appointments at specific times and places ensure that all relevant people can communicate with each other.

The online network is different. The online world knows no opening hours. It doesn't even know the term 24/7 – because that's part of its DNA. Nor is it limited to just one place: it is here and everywhere at the same time. Yes, they still exist: the colleagues who run their law firm without the Internet and are never "online" as a lawyer.

But what exactly is your online network?

Your online network is your "lists". Which lists? Well, the contacts sorted by the different categories. These can be for example your managers, your cooperation partners but also your colleagues. You can also specify them further. For example, you can distinguish between family law mandates and criminal law mandates, between regular clients and one-time clients, and between these clients and "interested parties" and "potential clients". It is important to define and sort your contacts. You can see how easy it is to get started, because everyone has contacts in some form or another.

---

i

Before you get started now, you should sit back for a moment and define what you want to achieve with your network. Only then will you be able to make the right choice from the abundance of possibilities among the contacts and from the variety of ways to get in touch with them.

This is especially important in online networking, because the online possibilities offer you an inexhaustible variety around the clock. This makes it all the more important for you to be clever in selecting the most promising ones. You can't try out everything[65]. Because the online world is networked, opportunities can multiply or turn into disasters. A satisfied contact, a satisfied customer can increase your market value enormously in a fraction of a second with a single mouse click – across national borders – or scare away a large proportion of your potential new customers forever[66].

Networking and "works on the net" are just not the same thing[67].

How exactly do online and offline networks mesh?
How often do you exchange business cards in everyday life and in a professional context? Back in the office, you should both write an individual follow-up by e-mail and network with the interview partner on Xing or LinkedIn. It is often easier to stay in touch in networks, to present your own competencies, and to follow the further development and activities of the person you are talking to.

The importance of business networking is summarized by my colleague Dr. Schunder-Hartung as organizer of the network meetings AHA-Kanzleireihen:

"Why lawyers need to network: The legal profession is under pressure as never before – and for the first time in its history, as a professional group. Legal tech is on the rise, and the more algorithms will be able to map even complex if-then subsumptions, the more it will get down to brass tacks. At the same time, § 5 RDG has opened the door to service providers from other industries who actually sell banking products or insurance or repair accident cars, but are allowed to provide their clients with the associated legal advice at the same time. Clients,

65 Dr. Tutschka, "Fünf Erfolgstipps für Netzwerken im Internet" im Blog bei CLP vom 14.10.2016.
66 Dr. Tutschka, "Die drei größten Fehler beim Online-Netzwerken" in CLP's blog from 9.6.2016.
67 Pardon the little pun :-).

on the other hand, are more demanding than ever, especially in the areas of business law that used to be the most lucrative. In the financial crisis, they learned to work in-house, now they are "pitching and paneling". And instead of working harder, young lawyers are increasingly focusing on the work-life balance that is so notorious among the older generation.

Anyone who claims to be ideally positioned as a law firm in this situation has one thing above all: self-confidence and/or a very offensive marketing strategy. For everyone else, the main thing is to look specifically for what is still viable and what is not. Normality strategies are particularly in demand in this situation! These, however, cannot be found in the exchange with colleagues of one's own firm, not even in the specialized working groups: In one case, lawyers are stewing in their own juices, in the other case they are exchanging ideas with people who (can) only represent a partial level of their firms. Instead, what is needed is an honest look over the fence at all the neighboring properties. How can this be done? Through (a) continuous, (b) confidential exchange on (c) the most diverse topics (c) at eye level. Networking, in the best sense of the word."

Dr. Anette Schunder Hartung is the owner of aHa Strategische Kanzleientwicklung. She is a lawyer, Business Coach IHK and has been working exclusively in the legal market and related professions for over 20 years. In Frankfurt, Munich and in the Rhineland, she currently runs a total of seven regular aHA Kanzleireihen network meetings, some of them specifically on future topics.

Networks often address specific target groups within the industry. For example, there are offers for graduates and career starters as well as for women or on certain specialist topics.

The network often pursues very specific goals, such as professional exchange, mutual business relations, recruiting and job search, exchange on the latest developments and products in the legal market, the awarding of scholarships, the compensation of disadvantages or even meaningful social or societal change. With CLP, we are involved in almost all of these formats from the very beginning of concept development and market launch, providing support in the form of event modules and prizes, or accompanying top management in strategy development.

In addition to a large number of working groups on the respective specialist lawyer topics, the professional association Deutscher Anwaltverein also offers the FORUM Junge Anwaltschaft (Young Lawyers Forum), the AG Anwältinnen (Women Lawyers Working Group), the AG Kanzleimanagement (Law Firm Management Working Group) or the transnational networks of the foreign associations or, since recently, online intervision groups[68]. But there are also spontaneous, project-related associations such as the Master Mind Law group on Instagram for regular collegial exchange beyond large institutions. In addition, quasi-networks are often initiated by large law firms or service providers and product developers in the industry[69].

---

68 I myself currently chair the DAV Auslandverein Österreich, the network of German and Austrian lawyers.

69 Like WoltersKluwer, for example.

Liquid Legal Institute's mission is to be an innovation network for the legal industry[70].

The Netzwerk multikultureller JuristInnen e.V. (NMKJ) (Network of Multicultural Lawyers) is a place of encounter, exchange and career advancement for lawyers who perceive themselves as multicultural. They see their diversity as an enrichment and additional qualification.

The Afro German Academic Network (ADAN e.V.), which also counts numerous poc lawyers among its ranks, should be mentioned specifically for people of color (poc).

In the USA, the importance of networking has long been recognized: Especially for LGBTI lawyers for professional success and the enforcement of LGBTI rights:

The Lavender Law Conference & Career Fair is the largest event for LGBTI lawyers with over 400 visitors, 167 law firms and other legal organizations. This is where people learn from each other, exchange ideas and "network". Since 2015, there has also been such a platform in Germany: With ten companies and 50 visitors, ALICE 2015 had its kick-off as a small career fair. Now the concept has been intensively refined to make the event more attractive and interactive. The program: Under the slogan "Finding Unicorns – Connecting LGBTI Lawyers", the ALICE Juristensummit 2016 in Cologne will feature a diverse program and offer even more space for networking, continuing education, political discussions and joint activities.

Large law firms are taking on these issues because "certifications" hold the promise of employer branding:

"Lawyers are generally freedom-loving and liberal people. In the meantime, one can assume an LGBT-friendly and open-minded climate, at least among the internationally active law firms. The progress is not to be overlooked. Some of our clients at Freshfields have very large and active LGBT+ networks, first and foremost the banks and insurance companies, but increasingly also industrial companies. In Germany, it is not yet as common for service providers to have to account for their attitude to diversity as is often the case in the UK and the US. At Freshfields, however, we are already noticing that our strong commitment to LGBT+ is viewed very positively by the majority of clients.

Halo' is the LGBT network at Freshfields with around 100 members. 'Halo' means 'halo' and alludes to our firm logo – the Archangel Gabriel from the Freshfields family crest. We meet regularly to plan joint activities, support the firm in its diversity endeavors, support recruitment for Freshfields – and simply as a social platform where we feel comfortable. In addition, we have an even larger network of supporters – Friends of LGBT+ – who we call 'Halo Champions' at Freshfields. These are over 130 lawyers and business services worldwide who support us in our activities and ensure that openness and diversity is lived by the entire firm."

Dr. Klaus-Stefan Hohenstatt, Partner in the law firm Freshfields Bruckhaus Deringer in Hamburg

---

70 *Kai Jakob* a.o.., Liquid Legal: Towards a Common Legal Platform, Law for Professionals.

However, diversity can also be lived in cross-sector networks:

For example, I would like to mention the Women in Law Initiative, the PANDA Lab LAW for women starting their careers, where CLP holds the famous career speed coaching sessions, as well as the Role Model Initiative of Breaking. Through[71] and have given the initiators a chance to speak:

"I remember feeling that it was not always easy for me to exist and be perceived as a woman in a male-dominated business world and in my profession in the 1980s. There is a lot to tell from the professional 'sewing box', funny, unpleasant, but also very nice situations. As a very consistent woman, I have always achieved what I really wanted. When I look at our profession today, I am saddened by the fact that more than half of us are graduates of law schools, and more than half of us are still preparing for the legal profession, but at the end of the day, women make up a maximum of 20 % of the lawyers in Austria. This is not an isolated case in the legal profession. In many other legal professions in Austria, but also internationally, the picture is quite similar. In the course of my international activities, I have become acquainted with many different women's fates in industry, commerce, politics and, of course, in the legal profession. What was initially an exchange of ideas has become, and continues to become, more structured networking with the goal of promoting women's careers in the legal profession. In spring 2018, I received an international award for being a woman in law. That was ultimately the final trigger to become really active. The basis for this was our firm's longstanding work in anti-discrimination law and the impressive work and cooperation with a very wise fellow lawyer and former president of the Law Society in London, Christina Blacklaws. Together with my professional partner Professor Mag. Franz J. Heidinger, we launched the nationally and internationally oriented initiative Women in Law, Vienna in spring 2018, in line with our initiative, only together will gender find the right approach to successful diversity in business. The association organized and held a first international conference in 2019. The second international conference planned for 2020 was postponed to September 2021 for 'Corona' reasons. In cooperation with the University of Vienna, it was nevertheless possible to hold the first course Women in Law – Frauen im Recht in the elective courses Gender Legal Studies and Legal English in the summer semester 2020."

Dr. Alix Frank-Thomasser, Women in Law Initiative, Vienna

"During my several years of working in a commercial law firm, I experienced how a trainee lawyer who had been employed for a few weeks reported on his experiences at the regular soccer match in a loose group across departments and hierarchies, to which he had been invited by several lawyers. Of course, no one had thought of inviting women to the regular meetings; many did not even know of the existence of these regular meetings. I do not necessarily assume that there was any malicious intent behind this selective invitation practice, and I do not think it even had to have happened consciously. But the example vividly illustrates how much easier it can be for men to establish connections with colleagues from other departments and across hierarchical levels that are often denied to women.

It is therefore all the more important for women to seek and obtain access to networks. This starts by attending events that interest you or by joining a network. We want to encourage female lawyers not to give up a possible career too quickly. Of course, it is a highly individual decision how one wants to shape one's professional career. But we see time and again that women, due to a lack of role models, have the impression that

71 https://www.breakingthrough.de/portraet-geertje-tutschka.

they 'can't make it' and therefore give up a career earlier than necessary. In addition, doubts simply take away valuable energy that could be invested sensibly in other things. By pointing out role models in personal interviews on career and women's issues, through our advice and our events, we want to create inspiration and thus release new energies that can encourage women in their careers. breaking.through is generally aimed at female lawyers interested in careers, regardless of their stage in life. Our events are attended by female lawyers in training, practitioners from various professions with several years of professional experience, but also by professors and presidents of universities. There are also always women lawyers who have already completed or almost completed their professional lives and are interested in whether the younger generations are still dealing with the same issues. This diversity shows us that we are addressing topics that are burning under the nails of numerous female lawyers. But men who are interested in the same issues are always welcome to join us."

Dr. Nadja Harraschain, Frankfurt, founder of the legal role model platform "Breaking.Through"

"We are PANDA has existed in Germany since 2013 and was originally developed as a cross-sector event for women leaders. Today, three to five PANDA events take place each year – the main event with 200 participants remains open to all industries and types of companies, as well as additional industry-specific specials. In addition, a Women Leadership Community has been developed with currently about 800 participants. Since 2015, PANDA has also been available specifically for women in the legal industry. The premiere in 2015 was already a complete success. There are so many highly qualified female lawyers that it can't be long before the leadership ranks in law firms are largely made up of women...' Dr. Ulrike Binder is a partner at Mayer Brown LLP. This makes her an exception, because although more than half of law graduates are female, the proportion of female law firm partners is less than 10 %. The legal industry is considered conservative and resistant to change. At an average of 42 %, the salary gap between men and women in legal services is even significantly larger than the 23 % average for the industry nationwide. And so the opening quote goes even further: '... One might think. But professional quality alone does not lead upward. It is also important to show oneself, to be courageous and to use chances. For that, you need sponsors, role models and opportunities.'

Promoters, role models, opportunities – that's exactly what the initiators of PANDA want to offer women. PANDA is an initiative and community for more women in leadership. Women in leadership and management trainee roles find a platform here to specifically expand their networks, exchange experiences and strengthen each other through constructive feedback. They are actively brought together with companies that offer opportunities or are explicitly looking for women leaders. The PANDA Lab LAW is a format that reflects the facets of a leadership career: Learning from others, developing oneself, working in a team, asserting oneself, discussing relevant topics together and, at the end, networking among the participants and discussions with the partner law firms present. Offers such as the CV check and speed coaching make the participants fit for a steep career."

Isabelle Hoyer, Initiator PANDA

But I would also like to mention Legal (R)evolution, Europe's largest event platform with online and offline formats, which brings together lawyers from all over the world to discuss the latest trends in the legal market and supports CLP with the CoachingLounge, Lawyer4Future, and career networks such as clavisto, talentrocket, or e-fellows[72], which award interesting scholarships[73].

"When a lawyer tells me he is not interested in using new digital technologies such as contract automation, knowledge management and e-discovery, I ask him: What are you personally doing to remain competitive in the future? The legal consulting industry, unlike comparable industries, has managed to get by without significant change for the last 50 years, so the digitization of the legal market is still in its infancy. So the objections stem from the familiar argument 'we've always done it that way'. The crucial question, however, is: 'Quo vadis, Advocatus? Already today, computer algorithms are checking claims and notices, for example checking certain claims of airline passengers or checking a Hartz IV notice, i.e. they are applying the law. Extensive expansion of algorithm-based application of law is to be expected in the future. The digitization of law has accelerated rapidly and will fundamentally change the order and structures of the legal market. This circumstance is reinforced by the tendency of European legislators and jurisprudence to dismantle barriers to professional practice. Favoured by investments in legal innovation, completely new market participants will enter the legal market in the coming years and decades.This is to be understood as a great opportunity for the legal profession, since lawyers still have it in their own hands to play an important role in the legal market of the future by exploiting the potential of newer and more efficient digital technology. Lawyers and other specialists in the legal market will only find adequate answers to these developments if they start to develop a better understanding of digital techniques now. This was exactly the motivation to organize an annual congress fair on legal innovation and legal technology."

Jochen Brandhoff, Initiator of the Legal (R)evolution, Frankfurt

---

"e-fellows.net is a career network and recruiting service provider. We attract very good students via scholarships and put them in contact with interesting employers. What I love about e-fellows.net is that we create a win-win-win situation. Our scholarship holders receive attractive benefits and support in starting their careers, the companies find absolute high potentials with us, and of course we ourselves also benefit from the exchange. We currently support around 34,000 scholarship holders, who are among the top 10 percent of students in Germany and around the world. Our focus is clearly on high potentials who not only have excellent grades, but also demonstrate their suitability for joining top companies through internships and stays abroad. Around a quarter of our scholarship holders are economists and lawyers, followed by medical graduates and students from the STEM subjects.

With over 7,000 law graduates, we probably have the largest pool of 9-point junior lawyers in Germany. Our three partner firms Freshfields Bruckhaus Deringer, Hengeler Mueller and Clifford Chance also belong to

---

72 e-fellows.net, Perspektiven für Juristen, 2021.

73 My tip: If you want to stay up to date on the latest formats, event dates, and application deadlines in the industry, subscribe to CLP's monthly newsletter. In addition, special partner offers and scholarships are offered several times a year to CLP clients and newsletter subscribers. The CLP blog also features interviews with all the industry specialists featured in the book.

the absolute top class in the legal market and have been with us for almost 20 years now. Our fellows can get to know other law firms at events. Perspektive Wirtschaftskanzlei at Montabaur Castle is considered by many HR professionals as well as graduates to be the top event in Germany. LL.M. Day is an important student recruiting tool for numerous international law schools, including several Ivy League universities – and a great fortune for information-hungry students: Where else can you meet ten of the top 20 U. S. law schools in one afternoon? You can network as early as your undergraduate years! If you put out feelers early on through internships and recruiting events, you'll have the best shot at starting a career."

Dr. Michael Koch, Product, Account and Marketing Manager at e-fellows.net, Munich

6. Cooperation partner

Networking and cooperating can and should go hand-in-hand.

Cooperating instead of competing with colleagues can create a win-win situation: Writing a large textbook like this is not everyone's cup of tea; it's a major project and unattractive for most colleagues because they simply don't have the time. But why not, as in this case, use the functioning network for cooperation and let it have its say? Or, as in Ms. Schieblon's book "Kanzleimanagement in der Praxis", use the PMN network of management partners to create a joint work of these colleagues?

But it can also pay off to cooperate with providers in other areas who also generate added value for your target group. This does not have to be the classic car dealership or the car repair shop or the insurance broker as a partner. It can be more creative: for example, establish yourself as a speaker or keynote speaker for car dealership events or use the opportunities at family services to establish yourself as a contact for legal issues[74].

Finally, at this point, a word about cooperation within the law firm: In addition to the perennial question of how a lawyer can best serve his clients, he must also address the ways in which he can promote the achievement of the firm's goals and how he can best support his colleagues. This is not just a question of personal honor or even the "pecking order" in a law firm. This duty of cooperation applies to every lawyer in the firm. Older lawyers, who guard particularly successful draft contracts like the holy grail and are careful to let their special knowledge trickle down to younger colleagues, fail to realize that such behavior is in stark contrast to the service mentality that is indispensable for the success of a law firm. Their duty is not only to put their knowledge and experience at the service of their clients. It is also

74 Busmann, "Chefsache Mandatenakquisition", p. 405.

their duty to allow younger colleagues to partake of it for the good of the firm. A law firm will only be able to retain good young lawyers in the long run if it also promotes them. Those who try to "keep young lawyers stupid" are irresponsibly damaging their firm.

Any measure – whether networking, cooperation or recommendation – will only be successful if the lawyer succeeds in demonstrating to the potential client the benefits of the mandate and, in particular, the special advantage that the mandate of this particular lawyer and no other offers the client. In practice, an emotionally based emphasis (unique advertising proposition) may be more successful than a factually based emphasis of the special features of a law firm and its range of services (unique selling proposition).

7. Employer Branding

- **Employer Branding**

A word on employer branding, i.e. the positioning and strategic orientation of your law firm with the aim of attracting highly qualified employees and junior lawyers to your specialty and your team.

The top employers among young junior lawyers are:[75]

1. Federal Foreign Office
2. Freshfields Bruckhaus Deringer
3. European Commission
4. Federal Criminal Police Office
5. Audi
6. BMW

Today, future high potentials are still measured by whether they have passed one or two predicate examinations, i.e. whether they have passed the first and/or second state law examinations with the grade "fully satisfactory", "good" or "very good".

75 FAZ No. 206 from 3.9.2016, p. C1.

Grades in the 2nd state law examination

Grades in the 2nd State Law Examination[76], © Dr. Geertje Tutschka

After all, just under 1,700 trainee lawyers complete their training with such a distinction each year, but the demand for good graduates is much higher. The market for these future top lawyers is therefore fiercely competitive.

Commercial law firms primarily entice their clients with high starting salaries. Today, an honours graduate can expect up to €120,000 per year at more than forty law firms. Ten years ago, only three law firms were prepared to pay such a sum[77]. Other firms must therefore find ways to attract these highly qualified young professionals. Special training programs – such as the possibility of an in-service doctorate, communication and performance training, and trainee programs with postings abroad[78] – must be supplemented by marketing (employer branding) tailored to these future employees.

Employer branding takes place at the intersection of positioning, recruiting, team building and marketing.

Those who rely exclusively on internal training of junior staff fail to realize that the cost factor for this is many times higher today than it was a few years ago. Another factor that is often underestimated is the fact that today's competitive market forces law firms to be able to access top performance with pinpoint accuracy and within the shortest possible time. As a rule, however, many years of training cannot be completed with such precision. It is essential, however, that the internally trained em-

76 Soldan Institut, Press release from 28.1.2016.

77 Branchenbericht der Sparkassen 2020, p. 18.

78 *Dr. Tutschka* USA Expat Quick Guide, p. 5.

ployee does not bring along mandates or valuable impulses and a view from the outside on well-worn routines and processes.

Instead, climbing the career ladder internally often faces even more headwinds, which is why a coach disproportionately often needs to be called in for support in these situations.

When recruiting high potentials, on the other hand, people like to focus solely on job descriptions and salaries. But top performers and high potentials, i.e. your reliable and committed employees of tomorrow, want to be wooed today. They want to know what your firm stands for and which projects it supports. What the working atmosphere is like and how the firm takes care of its employees' health. What training programs your firm offers and how it supports employees in difficult situations, through coaches, trainers and mentors. Some law firms are therefore currently discovering various event formats beyond assessment centers for themselves in order to present themselves as an attractive employer – for example, at free workshops with a joint evening program and in an informal atmosphere.

Talentrocket, a platform specializing in recruiting for lawyers, sums it up:

"Personnel development is one of the fundamental areas of law firm development. In order to be successful in personnel development, it is important to pursue the right personnel marketing strategy. This does not depend on the budget, but rather on a planned, coherent approach. In this regard, many new opportunities have emerged for law firms in the online sector in recent years. In particular, a law firm should pay attention to three points in order to recruit new employees as efficiently as possible:

1. *First of all, it is important to understand your own law firm as a brand. A strong brand automatically attracts interested personnel and makes it easier to stand out and differentiate from other law firms. In particular, each unit should find out what its unique selling proposition is and communicate this online.*
2. *This only works with a well thought-out online presence. This should have its own career section and thus not only address potential clients, but also pick up and convince the interested candidate. A law firm should show its own face as best as possible in its online presence and give the candidate an overview of what it has to offer as an employer.*
3. *last but not least, it is essential that you write modern job advertisements and place them appropriately".*

Sebastian von Glahn, Managing Director of TalentRocket GmbH, the leading career platform for lawyers in Germany

---

TalentRocket works with over 125 law firms and reaches over 150,000 lawyers a month.

A "Careers" section is now common practice. However, this should not be limited to advertising open positions, but should be used for a strong presence in the course of employer branding. This includes promotion and career programs as well as an image and employee brochure for download.

Employer branding must be aligned with the firm's values and vision: Nothing is more damaging to business than building "false" high potentials into partner candidates – for the senior partners, for the clients and for the high potentials of the next generation.

It can't hurt to familiarize yourself with the needs and language of the next generation: Topics such as sustainability, sense-making, social engagement, diversity, climate compatibility, health and wellbeing are among the must haves[79].

Personal development programs with various training courses on soft skills, individual coaching and mentoring for network building should therefore be communicated in the same way as cooperation with the company's daycare center, the wholefood organic caterer and the climate-friendly shirt dry cleaner next door.

Our CLP mentoring program, for example, has been in high demand in recent months, even though most law firms already have a variety of mentoring programs (e.g., for newcomers, but also for becoming a partner). In our experience, however, these programs are sometimes not advertised at all, are structurally weak, provide little material to accompany the process, and the people involved are largely left to fend for themselves.

We assist in developing and establishing a successful program, with a short additional training for the future mentors and in process management. A well-designed mentoring program is gold for the network and knowledge transfer of any law firm. If done half-heartedly, however, it can be ineffective to the point of damaging the business, and only cost everyone involved time and nerves.

What did you get out of the chapter?
From now on, you make marketing and acquisition a matter for the boss and can implement the first marketing tips directly.

What are you focusing on in marketing and what will be your next step in market Sales and acquisition can be lurid and pushy or elegant anding today?

79 *Dr. Tutschka* u. a., Kanzleimarketing kompakt – wie Sie Mandanten finden und binden, Deutscher Anwaltverlag.

II. Sales and acquisition

Why should you read this chapter?
Sales and acquisition can be lurid and pushy or elegant and stylish. In this chapter, you will learn what makes the difference.

Overview

1. **Finding and retaining the right clients**
2. **Holistic services**
3. **Selling know-how and expertise**
4. **Transferring knowledge**
5. **Commitment to the profession and society**

"Nothing is harder than selling yourself" – perhaps for this reason, many lawyers shy away from an advertising method common in other industries, direct advertising by visiting a potential client. Of course, it is more advantageous to have a point of contact for a lawyer's interview with a potential client, such as an initial meeting at a previous cultural event. But "cold calling" is also possible and permitted. The lawyer should just not be afraid of getting turned down. The success rate of cold-calling attempts is relatively small, even among rainmakers. But there is a success rate.

Cold calling is not only frowned upon, but also only permitted under very narrow conditions.

A more elegant form is to present yourself in top form on "arranged" occasions. The decisive factor here is the convincing "pitch". It is true that the lawyer is prohibited from soliciting for the award of a mandate in an individual case, § 43b BRAO. However, the lawyer may solicit a specific client. Lawyers may directly approach their desired candidates for a new client relationship, introduce themselves to the potential clients and ask them to grant them a mandate or at least recommend them to others.

Only the solicitation of an already specified mandate is prohibited. The potential client is to be protected from intrusive lawyers. Sometimes the client does not even need this protection. In the case of a beauty contest[1], the mandate to be granted is already described in very concrete terms. The client does not want protection from intrusive lawyers. Rather, it is the client himself who invites several

1 Busmann in Chefsache Mandantenakquisition", p. 39.

lawyers to compete for the granting of this particular mandate. For this reason, I consider beauty contests to be compatible with § 43b BRAO.

The possibilities are therefore manifold. However, recommendation is still the supreme discipline and is considered one of the best advertising methods used by lawyers. Strictly speaking, recommendation is not an actual advertising tool. The lawyer has at best indirect, but not direct influence on this advertising method.

1. Finding and retaining the right clients

This is not just about optimally **rounding off the marketing and communication process** so that mere prospects (such as readers of the firm's newsletter) become clients and remain clients in the long term. It is about finding the right clients and keeping them. Sales and acquisition go hand in hand with marketing and communication and build on each other.

If your positioning and strategic direction is clear and your marketing and communications strategy is aligned with it, it can only target the right clients for your specialization and resources.

Why is this important?

On the one hand, you can naturally serve these clients very well. This increases the potential for referrals and supports your expert status. I would also like to remind you of the Pareto principle. Only the right clients will have the potential to generate 80 percent turnover. On the other hand, you are also in a much better position to work cost-consciously, optimize processes and improve your overall quality. The fact that there may be a sudden increase in these mandates from time to time, which exceed your capacities, is intentional. After all, you want to grow. Peak times can, of course, be absorbed with temporary solutions (this was reported on in the context of business development).

Attracting the wrong clients or serving them in the long term can have fatal consequences. They block resources and force ineffective processes. You have to work your way through unfamiliar areas of law and create a high liability risk. It can even lead to these mandates becoming important financial building blocks in your business plan, so that sooner or later you will even have to consider adjusting your positioning and strategic orientation accordingly. A feeling of foreign control and "hostile takeover" will set in.

So even at the end of your acquisition chain, you should align yourself with the needs of your ideal target group and also draw the consequences: If in doubt, refuse a mandate or refer it to a colleague, no matter how lucrative it may be.

So, as a reminder, here are the questions you should ask yourself in order to become the "need-satisfier" of your target audience:

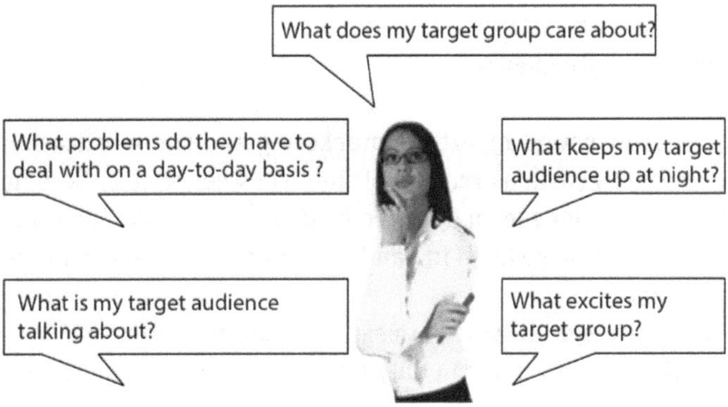

Needs analysis questions, © Dr. Geertje Tutschka

To sum up – and at the risk of repeating myself – I'll let Johanna Busmann, author of "Chefsache Mandantenakquisition", have her say. For this book, she has summarized her personal instant acquisition tips for newcomers to the legal market:

A, B and C clients!
Not every client is of equal "value". Even if you initially find this remark "politically incorrect": You cannot avoid dividing up your clients:

- *A-clients bring high "organic reference potential "(pastors, tax consultants, doctors, hairdressers, members in the tennis club etc.), fit into your (future) orientation, bring high sales, are suppliers of your actual goals or introduce you to a completely new client group. Sometimes they introduce you to an area of law that is new to you, which you spend nights familiarizing yourself with – and later fall in love with!*
- *B-clients are "the masses" – for the bread and butter business. Especially important at the beginning of the firm and in the transition phase of a concentration on only one client group. Focus little by little!*
- *C-clients do not belong in your client file. They have mini dispute values, needs in the "wrong" area of law", behave inadequately. Delegate away!"*

Johanna Busmann, author of "Chefsache Mandantenakquisition" and owner of www.anwalts-akquise.de in Hamburg.

2. Holistic services

Holistic services are characterized by comprehensively picking up the client in the reality of his or her life. Families, for example, may have a specific range of needs as a target group. However, this does not always have to be served with legal advice.

Information evenings, office processes tailored to families (opening hours, play corner, etc.), and suitable offers from cooperation partners can help clients feel that they are in good hands and that they have been taken care of.

The needs-based cultivation of these existing client contacts can not only develop them into long-term client relationships, but also turn them into so-called A-clients[2]. Accompanying services can also be offered with so-called "cross selling"[3].

Finally, a **well-briefed assistant** on the phone and reception of the law firm is also part of the job. In most cases, this assistant is caught between the dilemma of clients wanting to speak to the lawyer, but the lawyer not wanting to speak to the client. Certain structures and routines help the assistant to elegantly satisfy the client and, if necessary, even extend the mandate. Remember that the assistant is your communication channel to your clients. An appropriately professional assistant can increase your sales and acquisition enormously[4].

3. Sale of know-how and expertise

For certain mandates it will be necessary to deliver a so-called **pitch**.

This so-called "beauty contest"[5] requires the presentation of a specific law firm service in competition with other law firms. In addition to the substantive arguments, the presentation and performance of the presenting attorneys is of primary importance. There are many specialists, for example for the professional preparation of presentations or voice and performance trainers, who can provide support in this regard. In the end, your own experience will also play a certain role. You will get better with every pitch!

"A good pitch is characterized by various factors. The self-promotion of one's own firm plays the least important role – how many offices and lawyers worldwide, that's simply not important and we've usually read up on that beforehand. I could well do without the pitch document!"

---

2 Constanze Eich, Networking und Akquise für Rechtsanwälte, p. 32 et seq.

3 Johanna Busmann, Chefsache Mandanten Akquisition, p. 60.

4 Dr. Geertje Tutschka, "Wie aus Ihrem Kanzleiteam eine Mannschaft wird" in NJW 24/2016.

5 Johanna Busmann, Chefsache, Mandantenakquisitition, p. 39,

Less glossy brochures, more real knowledge about companies, topics and business models. In return, listening carefully is essential. The lawyers still talk a lot in the pitch meetings and ask few questions. But this is immensely important in order to better understand where external help is needed, the corporate lawyers interviewed wonder. "I often observe that lawyers don't take the time to change their perspective," says the head of the legal department of a global technology company. This is indispensable for good advice and is usually given far too little time[6].

In addition, one should not only think carefully about the composition of the diverse team, but also prepare this team in terms of content as well as practice the presentation in the team. "We conduct role plays before larger pitches to simulate the situation. However, we only know afterwards whether it will actually suit the counterpart in the real pitch," says Dr. Thomas Lappe, practice group leader for corporate at the law firm K&L Gates.

Nevertheless, rehearsals are still far from being institutionalized in many law firms. Yet there is a consensus that a well-organized role play with a neutral observer and precise evaluation is always worthwhile – even if it only serves to strengthen the team spirit[7].

"I am very surprised that the appearance of many law firms in 2021 is still strikingly outdated," says the lawyer of a large German corporation. "Quite often, for example, there are no female lawyers in the teams – even if the firm knows that the mandate is composed in a balanced way on the part of the legal department or is mainly handled by a female lawyer. The composition of the pitch teams, the poor working atmosphere among each other, but also the lack of diversity is often breathtaking!"

This and other criticism are voiced when you ask in-house lawyers about their experiences with law firms. Rarely is it a matter of professional weakness; almost always, the focus is on interpersonal issues. Why is that? Companies cultivate their culture, employees are used to intercultural training and, of course, teamwork, and diversity is emphasized[8].

"I have no problem at all with the pitch being associates or senior associates who don't have thirty years of professional experience under their belt. I would like to meet those at the pitch meeting who I can then call on a short distance if I have questions. The fact that several partners usually come to the pitch meeting instead rather annoys me," continues the head of the legal department of a large German project development company.

---

6 Barbara Helten, "Tipps für den erfolgreichen Pitch" in LTO from 25.5.2021.

7 Ibid.

8 Ibid.

Even the cross selling that is universally desired in law firms sometimes misses the point, says the legal department head. She understands that law firms have many good experts. However, she does not usually need them in her very specific area of law. What's more, in-house lawyers like to ask questions about the pitch documents that the firm brings or sends. For example, about the selected photos, which often showed the company's facilities. Sometimes it turns out that the lawyers didn't know which assets were involved.

"It's good if the lawyer has thought about what my department is currently concerned about and makes me offers on how he can help me. A discussion about this helps me much more than reciting his reference mandates. These may be impressive – but they have nothing to do with me or my work," says the head of the legal department[9].

A pitch is subject to a certain structure. As a rule, it should last twenty minutes. You should use this time to convince the customer of your merits. This will not work with "Power Point battles" or "Bull Shit Bingo".

You should concentrate on convincing a (non-)lawyer in a short time
- of your competence,
- of the return on investment in the case of the proof of confidence of the mandate, as well as
- of your person within the shortest possible time.

A pitch usually follows the following structure:
1. Introduce yourself, your firm, and your solution (5 min.)
2. Explain why your solution is so ingenious, what your budget is for it, and why this budget is worth the investment (10 min.)
3. Make an offer (2 min.)
4. Conclude your pitch with a surprising idea, a compelling argument, an overall social reference that captures your audience and makes you memorable (3 min.)

While at the beginning and at the end it is mainly about so-called "framing", i.e. the presentation of your competence and the urgency of the solution of the legal problem, point 2 and point 3 are about the perfect presentation of the key facts, the legal question brought to the point, as well as the presentation of an elegant, individual solution. It is also important here to pay attention to the respective strengths and weaknesses within the presentation team and to precisely define responsibil-

9 Ibid.

ities and speaking slots in advance. A team presentation also has the advantage of being able to react flexibly to the counterpart.

If you have chosen an area of law in which pitches are regularly required, you should definitely invest in professional pitching and train your team accordingly[10]. And finally: after the pitch is before the pitch. "After the pitch, we are self-critical and question what we could have done better. Here, too, there is always the risk that this step is missed due to time constraints. But that's the only way we can learn. It is particularly important to me to find out the reasons when we fail to win a mandate. I am not afraid to ask directly," says Dr. Peter Schorling, Managing Partner at Greenberg Traurig Germany.

Inquiries are still far from being the rule at all law firms. The corporate lawyers surveyed found that far too few lawyers still ask about the reasons for rejection.

Even though they are available to give the reasons and do not rule out working with them at a later date. However, if hardly anyone asks, they cannot give any tips for improvement.

So, there are many possibilities for law firms to optimize their self-presentation and to stand out from the crowd. For example, a friendly follow-up e-mail thanking the client for the interesting discussion after the appointment is very helpful[11]. Know how and expertise are not only "sold" in pitching, but also in all **reputation-enhancing marketing tools**, e.g. publications, lectures, seminars. Here, too, you should orient yourself on the essential points of pitching in order to actually achieve a mandate.

But lawyer marketing doesn't just start at the office door. Lawyers must also **market themselves and their services within the firm**. This applies to the founding partner as well as to the youngest associate. Many young lawyers do not realize that their advancement in a law firm also depends on how they market their own performance internally. Those who are not committed to the concerns of the entire firm, who are not prepared to develop their own initiative and, for example, to work out the concept for a small seminar on their own initiative, who are not interested in which cases their colleagues in the firm are currently working on and how they can possibly support them, should not be surprised if all they find on their desk are "old hats" and "uninteresting cases". Young lawyers often have the impression that their partners do not let them "get to the real stuff". Sometimes they are (unfortunately) right. But young lawyers can counteract this. Nobody forbids a young law-

10 Oren Klaff, Pitch Anything, p. 97.
11 Ibid.

yer to look for a special field, a niche in which he excels. For example, a young lawyer may want to revise the firm's somewhat dusty website and improve both the content and perhaps the layout. The young lawyer can also try to expand the firm's product range. LegalTech products in particular offer new opportunities here. He will check whether there is an area of law that fits the strategic orientation of the law firm, in which the firm has not yet offered any services or perhaps only rudimentary ones. If he finds such an area, then he can continue his education in this area and, through his specialization, benefit not only himself, but also his law firm. In a proper law firm, the better is always the enemy of the good.

If the junior lawyer makes his proposal at the right moment – not when the two senior partners have been brooding over a complicated project for twelve hours without interruption – then he will probably be successful with his proposal. The foundation for trusting him with more has been laid. In addition, he has proven that, in the interests of the firm, he can think outside the box when it comes to the files he has been assigned to work on.

Internal law firm marketing is not limited to the lawyers alone. Lawyers must also constantly "sell" their firm and its goals to other members of the firm. The employees of the law firm do not only have to know about the strategy and marketing goals. They must also stand behind them. People would much rather be part of a successful team than a bunch of losers. Employees are proud to work at xyz. They identify themselves with the company, the firm they work for, and are accordingly more committed to their company. They will be far more likely to tell their acquaintances and friends about their successes at the re-nowned law firm xyz. Successes of the law firm must therefore not only be communicated externally, but also internally. A law firm should share its successes with all of its employees, regardless of whether they involve winning a lawsuit, being awarded a particularly interesting mandate, or winning a marketing prize. If a lawyer is interviewed on television or if his essay appears in the NJW, then all employees of the law firm should know this. Besides, nothing spreads as fast as "rumors" and "bad news". If you have neglected to provide your employees with "success stories" and "talking points", they will still talk about the law firm. At worst, they will complain about their ignorant boss and how much they are being exploited. So, prevent this in good time. Finally, part of marketing within the firm is always dealing fairly with all employees. Overtime and extra work occur more frequently in the secretariat of a law firm than in other companies. Every lawyer should show his employees that he appreciates their overtime commitment. Showing appreciation to employees does not always mean giving them a raise. Even little things count. Passing on a compliment from a client, a bouquet of flowers on a birthday or a remark that the only bright spot in the chaotic contract negotiations was the perfectly prepared documentation of all relevant documents by one's own secretary show that a lawyer thinks of his employees and thanks them for their commitment[12].

4. Knowledge transfer

One link between selling expertise and know-how and volunteering is knowledge transfer.

On the one hand, this should also be done internally by passing on experience and "products" to the next generations. It is recommended that this be approached strategically and in a structured manner, especially in the key qualifications of the members of the law firm, within the framework of the development and expansion of knowledge. This can be done through internal databases, regular meetings for the joint development of current case law, etc., but also through targeted day-to-day management and personnel development. This category also includes internal mentoring programs, in which experienced partners accompany young associates on their way to partnership.

By imparting knowledge outside the law firm, attorneys can distinguish themselves as committed experts, for example, in the context of promoting young talent at universities and repetitoriums or in professional training for colleagues or non-lawyers.

Here, too, new, innovative products from the LegalTech sector can provide support and playfully pave the way to the next mandate. My recommendation is therefore to meet regularly with interested colleagues for "design thinking" in order to think about new ways and product ideas for knowledge transfer (with or without technology).

Dr. Jochen Brandhoff, founder of the Legal ®Evolution sums it up:

"Applying law well – that's no longer enough. Today, a lawyer has to be innovative, think in terms of business processes and use technology to be competitive."

Dr. Jochen Brandhoff
Founder of the LEGAL ®EVOLUTION and Managing Director of European LegalTech Expo GmbH, Frankfurt

12 Dr. Tutschka in "Kanzleimarketing kompakt", p. 34.

5. Commitment to the profession and society

For most, commitment to the profession and society is not a natural part of their job description.

Even though lawyers are welcome members and officials in associations, organizations and self-governments, they tend to see this as a chore and/or at best a leisure activity.

However, associations offer good acquisition opportunities. A lawyer will hardly find a sports club, a political party or the regional industrial club in which at least one other lawyer is not already a member – not infrequently: board member. Here, too, the motto applies: competition stimulates business. By actively participating in an association, a lawyer can very quickly give the other members an impression of his common sense, his willingness to serve and occasionally also his professional competence. Not every association is equally suitable for every lawyer as acquisition terrain or stage for self-promotion. Only those who are interested in the association's activities and who have a genuine interest in the subject matter of the association's activities will be able to conduct successful public relations work for their law firm and themselves in this association. For the lawyer who has preferred law to a possible career as a professional soccer player, an association activity in the field of sports or the promotion of the local soccer club will be more suitable than membership in the small animal breeders' association. The lawyer whose professional goal is to provide legal assistance and support to socially disadvantaged individuals may not feel comfortable in the business club. Anyone who does not think much of "club formality" should not pursue it either.

Membership in professional associations, such as the local lawyers' association, is also part of this. I myself am also involved in the Lawyers' Association, the Association of Women Lawyers and the Austrian Bar Association (ÖRAK), but for years I have been particularly involved in the international professional association for coaches (International Coaching Federation – ICF). Working as an association lawyer would never have been an option for me, as I would like to play a creative and leading role in the coaching profession and help develop the potential of coaching internationally. As a delegate in the Round Table of German-speaking Coaching Associations (RTC), I can help shape the legal definition of coaching and the profession of coach throughout Germany and Europe. A very exciting task.

Therefore, every lawyer should think carefully about which kind of association participation suits him personally (leadership, consulting or mere membership). The young lawyer striving for an international orientation will be interested in a membership in AIJA. Contacts with young entrepreneurs and the next generation of managers can be made with the Wirtschaftsjunioren Deutschland e.V. (Junior Chamber of Commerce Germany). Membership in a political party has opened up a career for many a lawyer, albeit not always as a lawyer, but as a professional politician. The services provided by the lawyer are not only honorary, but often also "pro bono", i.e. free of payment (not free of charge). A pro bono activity may consist of drafting articles of association for a non-profit association, organizing the general meeting of members, arranging for the registration of the association in the register of associations and issuing the certificate of tax exemption for the association. Pro bono work should be done with the same commitment and quality as professional legal advice. After all, you want to be perceived as a professional and not as a dilettante. Only then will they have the desired publicity effect. These unpaid services generally serve a good purpose, i.e. they are provided in the interest of a non-profit institution that cannot afford qualified legal advice for financial reasons, or in the interest of another good cause. A person who works for a good cause not only promotes the common good. He also gains the goodwill and recognition of his fellow human beings. This requires that the pro bono activity of the firm be publicized.

In the end, however, voluntary work is always more than a pure marketing investment: You are doing it first and foremost for yourself, for your firm, your employees, colleagues and clients. For you personally, it is meaningful and satisfying. To everyone else, you are proving that you have done your homework and that you have achieved a certain level of success as a lawyer and law firm owner: You remember Maslow's pyramid of needs – honorary work is considered the supreme discipline.

III. Fee discussion

Most lawyers are still reluctant to talk about fees during the initiation phase of a case. Yet this is a natural and important part of the relationship of trust between lawyer and client.

The situation is familiar: The client is sitting in a meeting with the lawyer for the first time. He has presented all his documents and information and the lawyer has developed an initial proposal for a solution. Before the client gives the corresponding power of attorney, he asks about the fee. The lawyer gulps and sheepishly leafs through the documents. Generally, he has a capable assistant who properly prepares the fee invoices. He himself is only roughly informed. In order not to give himself away, he remains vague in his information. Fortunately, at the beginning of the mandate, in most cases it is not foreseeable which concrete actions are necessary until success and would thus be billable. After all, a lot can happen during this time, which often covers a period of several months or years. Thus, when quantifying his fee, the lawyer tends to rely on his feeling, which is fed by experience in billing comparable cases, and throws a lump sum value into the conversation. If the client now asks more precisely how this value is made up, the lawyer can only make a general reference to the fact that the value of the subject matter of the dispute is decisive and that there is a legal basis for the settlement.

It is clear even to a sales layman that this is not a sales pitch that encourages the client to close the deal immediately.
This is due to the following errors:
1. Lack of detailed knowledge on the part of the lawyer with regard to the law on fees and his cost structure
2. Legal constraints in the billing of fees
3. Lack of creativity on the part of the lawyer in the design of his fee calculations
4. Private prejudices and prejudices under professional law to relate legal services and payment directly to each other.

These reservations and prejudices of the lawyer are immediately transferred to the client who is willing to invest and make him suddenly doubt whether to assign the mandate.

What prevents you from addressing the fee openly and directly?

In addition to ignorance and half-knowledge, it is often one's own beliefs on the subject of money. Sentences like these are common:
- Money is not something to talk about
- A bird in the hand is better than a pigeon on the rooftop
- Money doesn't stink

- Money is something to have
- Sellers are dishonest

Get to the bottom of your own beliefs! Write down your own beliefs that come to mind on the subject of making money, winning goals and selling, and also write down key points on how you personally feel about these topics. Now write down how you think you are perceived by others. In a next step you should ask family and friends, perhaps even co-workers in the office, how they perceive you in dealing with money, in selling or in the acquisition of mandates. In most cases, there are already some revealing aha moments here.

If you would like to delve deeper into this topic or if your personal assessment and the perception of others differ too much, I recommend that you hire a coach or consultant at this point, who will professionally filter out and work with you in a relatively short period of time on exactly those sticking points that prevent you from conducting successful sales conversations and block you from fully developing as an entrepreneur. At this point, I would urge you to be attentive and responsible in dealing with this issue. In my consulting practice with lawyers and law firms, I repeatedly encounter situations where success strategies fail because of personal blocks and paradigms of the law firm owner on this topic.

IV. Law firm marketing post Corona

Law firm marketing should be simple and direct, playfully light with a touch of humor and self-irony. Difficult enough – but what is the law firm marketing of tomorrow still allowed to do? Data protection, labeling requirements and the obligation to use "clean language" place high demands on advertising slogans.

The pandemic has changed a lot. Political movements like Black Lives Matter, LGBTQ+ and Fridays For Future have changed a lot. Equal Pay Day, the salary disclosure law, and the women's quota are changing when it comes to equality. Species extinctions and floods are changing. Refugee movements and Brexit are changing. Where is the lightness in all this?

One rule of etiquette recommends not speaking about politics and religion in the social arena. Does that also apply to law firm branding?

Law firm marketing post Corona – here are the ten future-relevant factors in law firm marketing, the ten must-haves of post Corona law firm marketing:

1. the long road of client acquisition

Marketing has one goal: to attract new customers. Therefore, marketing is determined by the behavior and needs of potential clients. They expect legal content to be easy to understand, simple and direct, up-to-date and available free of charge. They choose the lawyer they trust based on the criteria of expertise and charisma. They expect lawyers to be approachable and to show themselves personally. They would also like to see the lawyer of their choice publish or podcast on relevant topics. In technical jargon, this is called multiple touch points. If a legal problem actually arises, they expect uncomplicated, modern and time-saving processes. Until then, everything – including your law firm marketing – takes place online.

And: Your marketing should promise exactly what you can deliver – no more and no less.

2. human rights and diversity

Law firm marketing must not only sensitively address current issues, but also reveal a point of view. Nobody likes general statements. Not taking a stand means – with all due neutrality – unintentionally taking a stand after all.

3. Environment, climate and sustainability

The same applies to environmental issues. In law firm marketing in particular, the additional question is: How climate-neutral is my marketing? By having its welcome folders for new members made of plastic and filling them with a flood of print flyers that no one reads, the German Bar Association, for example, is positioning itself on this issue – whether consciously or unconsciously. So do it better.

4. Social Business and Social Change
Marketing means facing up to the big questions of our time. It follows that no company can avoid asking itself whether and how it is involved on its own doorstep, in its own community, or in the bigger picture – true to the motto "Do good and talk about it. Whether it's social projects, charity and fundraising, support for the district school, cycling across the Alps for the kilometer sponsor or something else entirely: that's what your clients want to know.

5. Local Offline and Global Online
Marketing will have to be able to do anything and everything everywhere: Offline and online, local and global. This will require a significant upgrade of global online marketing in most law firms. Translation programs are getting better and better, and soon it won't matter what language they read, speak and listen in – because content will be simultaneously translated into every language in the world.

This expands your options – take advantage of them.

At the same time, maintaining local relationships will become increasingly important. People need human contact outside the online world. Establishing this contact professionally and building a trusting relationship that offers more than just retrievable expert knowledge will be one of the most important challenges for the raison d'être of lawyers.

6. Authenticity
In times of permanent sensory overload, no one needs glossy, uniform marketing anymore. Marketing must tell stories about real people, needs a close and sensitive photographic and visual language, and should at the same time fit in with the values and visions of the firm.

Just be authentic.

7. Strategy
Only strategic marketing is marketing.

Hiring professionals to do law firm marketing but not giving them a law firm strategy or a marketing strategy is a waste of money.

Therefore, marketing is a matter for the boss. After all, it should convey the face of the firm and your personality to the outside world.

8. Cooperations and multipliers
The good thing is: No one is alone. You should get out of the habit of thinking first and foremost about competition. That is wasted energy. Instead, if you think about strategic partnerships, networks and multipliers among colleagues, everyone will succeed together and with each other.

Valuing the people around you, showing gratitude and acting sustainably is the most important marketing tool.

9. Office staff and employees
Law firm staff and associates are often underestimated. They not only build up their "own" client base. Often, the lawyer is not even aware of how much clients are actually more attached to the associate than to him or herself. This becomes obvious when the employee leaves. Law firm marketing must therefore also have an internal effect: The employees, the law firm team are one of the most important target groups.

10. Personal branding and law firm positioning
Today, law firm marketing must be able to do many things. One of the most important tasks, however, is the sensible coordination between personal branding of the individual experts and the development of the law firm brand as such. This requires a lot of commitment and budget, but in the long term, both factors will reinforce each other.

Using the available resources strategically and sensibly here will be a challenge.

All in all: Marketing is becoming more and more a matter for the boss and thus requires a higher time budget than a financial budget[1].

What did you get out of the chapter?
Sales and acquisition have lost their terror. You conduct fee discussions confidently and naturally.

What are you particularly good at with a new client? What will you do differently with the next mandate and why?

And last but not least, I would like to invite you to choose three marketing and sales measures (ideally in the short and long term) for our three sample law firms (keywords: Growing pains, wrong clients, gender and generational shift) that could make a difference at the firms. (Tip: Read through the specific situation of all the sample law firms at the beginning of the book). Feel free to write me your suggestions, I will respond no matter what. You will find me. Wherever you are looking. So much for marketing.

1 *Dr. Tutschka* Kanzleimarketing post Corona – die neuen "Must Haves", in: Haufe.Recht 08/ 2021.

G. Back to the future

Why should you read this chapter?
Today, a law firm is no longer founded primarily for eternity or at least for old-age provision. You will learn what is important in the event of a case and where the "exit door" is.

Overview
I. Routine work: Firm vision and strategy
II. Observe, orient, invest
III. Back to square one

Germany's leading visionary of the future, Sven Gabor Janszky of "2b AHEAD", has determined in his trend study on **customer behavior** in 2020:

"Today, tomorrow's customers are just 17 years old. In 2020, people will be communicating at the same time via cell phone, game console, ICQ, studiVZ, and listening to MP3s in the background, and maybe the TV will also be on. People will meet their communities and decide whether brands are relevant or not. The networking of the consumer has shifted the balance of power. Consumers trust their elective relatives more than ever. They interact and communicate with other people. The way to the customer is therefore increasingly no longer through advertising media – but through his relationships. Product differentiation takes place primarily in immaterial dimensions – not in technical details and price. The consumer's needs are social and emotional: recognition, belonging, trust, orientation. The most important future innovations will take place in the service sector. Specialist knowledge, as with doctors and lawyers, will become less important," he explicitly warns.

Experts identified the three most important issues in today's **workplace** as:

1. Security: more in the psychological sense than in the actual (emotional and communication management)
2. Clarity: in structures, goals and tasks (reliable relationships)
3. Significance: of one's own work, of corporate values

This Google study from 2016 did refer to the company's own employees – and you could say that this is not meaningful for the legal sector, for German-speaking law firms – that lawyers are different. Perhaps. But the paralegal teams in law firms are not, in our experience. What is definitely comparable, however, are the teams in the business world – in other words, the clients.

Security, clarity and significance: What comes into focus here is the **human factor**. The human being with his fears and needs: his charisma and personality, his talents

https://doi.org/10.1515/9783111058160-007

and abilities, his empathy and his capacity for and need for community, communication and relationship. Simply everything that makes him unmistakable; what distinguishes him from every reproducing, effective machine.

Does this mean that yesterday's law firm is tomorrow's law firm? The shirt-sleeved field, forest and meadow lawyer as a lone fighter with charisma, charm and typewriter as the winner? There is no question that the "human factor" is part of the equation; for better or for worse.

Legal information will be available to anyone, anytime, anywhere, free of charge. A meeting with the lawyer in a few days? Much too long. Today, new mandates tumble onto the breakfast table via Messenger on Instagram. Law firms will adapt to customer/ client behavior and react just as flexibly, online and around the clock, at least with automated processes. Client acquisition will take a back seat, while maintaining sustainable client relationships will have to become the focus.

Law firms need to develop a **service culture**. And a "**human identity**". Only then can their services be distinguished and serve the needs of clients and employees[1].

Continuing education and attorney specializations? Exchangeable! Can the lawyer really hold his own against the knowledge competition from the online forums? And what exactly distinguishes the specialist lawyer for traffic law from the colleague around the corner, also a specialist lawyer for traffic law? What makes us as lawyers unmistakable and will bind our clients to us will be our personality.

Acquisition through law firm marketing and development of law firm brands? This can be an embellishment. But at the end of the day, we can only convince in person. A crisp slogan or a corporate identity in dark blue will not be able to convey the emotional recognition and affiliation to the clients or give trust and orientation.

The forecast for the lawyer market sounds like the "good old days" to me: when the client came to the lawyer because he was always able to help, was a really great guy, and really got those one or two projects going in the city.

1 Dr. Geertje Tutschka, "Die Kanzlei des 21. Jahrhunderts" in HERO 02/2018.

I. Routine work: law firm vision and strategy

As a lawyer, you can't prepare your firm for everything[1].

What you can do, however, is to be open and curious:

- Watch trends,
- follow innovations,
- listen to your kids.

And to work on yourself and your firm continuously[2].

That means using regular strategy meetings to adapt to changes in the market in general and your target group in particular. It also means continuously working on your firm's values and culture. And not keeping this to yourself afterwards but communicating it to those it primarily affects: your employees and clients.

---

i

My recommendation:
Focus yourself! Find your own personal challenge!
Formulate it loud and clear. Choose your own personal way to face this challenge! And no matter how often this path leads you astray, you stumble or have to take detours: if it is your path, then keep your eye on your goal until the day comes when you have reached your goal.

Founding and managing a law firm is first and foremost law firm development. And your personal development. Consciously, purposefully and professionally. It is growth, but not at any price.

At this point, it may be interesting for you to hear that there are certain automatisms, patterns and structures in every development process – similar to the change process mentioned above. Knowing and understanding these patterns and structures helps you to keep an overview and to remain calm when, as in the case of child rearing, everything gets out of hand in the hectic daily routine. The so-called Spiral Dynamics of Beck and Cowan – based on the model of Clare Graves – clarify these connections and growth movements of complex systems such as organizations, companies, societies, but also of teams, cultures and families. As a law firm consultant, I see time and again how law firms fail to introduce modern processes or women's advancement programs, to take on new partners or to merge large law firms, even though this would represent an important added value and capable people have thought about it for a long time beforehand. However, they have neglected

---

1 The original text from the 1st edition of 2018 has a different reading in the 2nd edition of 2021 and makes one think mainly of economic crises and the pandemic.

2 Instead of working around the clock **in** your law office, as Gerber points out in "The E-Myth Attorney," p. 57.

Spiral Dynamics – innovations can only be implemented successfully and sustainably if the measures are adapted to the respective development stage of the law firm, team and leadership. At the same time, this model can also be used to forecast the development of specific business models, industries or even the future of your law firm[3].

Routine work

Especially in the two pandemic years 2020 and 2021, the legal market has changed permanently in one place or another – whether because of or in spite of Covid-19 is irrelevant for the time being.

In the meantime, these developments can be viewed with (relative) foresight, study results can be presented and the first lessons are learned.

For example, the short-circuited reactions of senior management during the pandemic[4] described above took place not only in large law firms, but in every industry worldwide. After evaluating the data, the leading Hogan Leadership Assessment was able to determine that many organizations had homogeneous management floors and therefore only a very limited response to crisis situations was possible: Only very few acted confidently and in a leading role even in the crisis. Most of them withdrew, shied away from decisions or behaved aggressively toward employees.

The MBTI (Meyer-Briggs Type Indicator) had already determined in 2012 that 85 % of managers and executives tend toward so-called hard leadership because they embody the types of commander (ETHG) and inspector (IPHG)[5]. The organizations were dependent on such leaders in their value and hierarchy system for strategic development and therefore hired them preferentially. A few years later, these leaders had left their "typical" footprint in the system and cemented it. Patriarchal and conservative leadership structures played to their advantage. It is important to understand that it was not "the men" per se who kept these structures alive, but primarily business enterprises that preferred this particular type of leadership for years.

Hogan therefore strongly recommended – similar to a crisis plan for the pandemic – to prepare for crisis situations with a heterogeneous, diverse leadership team.

3 Unfortunately, there is still no book explicitly on Spiral Dynamics in the legal industry. For general information on the model, however, see Beck/Cowan, "Spiral Dynamics" or Krumm, "9 Levels of Value Systems".

4 This refers to the dismissal of academic staff at Taylor Wessing in March 2020.

5 Ashridge Study about MBTI from 2012.

This requires change management know-how, which can be acquired from external experts or acquired by oneself. Syndicates seem to be lengths ahead of the legal profession in this respect[6].

But the law firm market has also changed. For most of them, business is still going well. 44 % and 46 %, respectively, stated that they had not experienced any losses in revenue or declines in mandates[7]. 55 % have no larger outstanding accounts than before. And the number of incoming mandates has also stabilized since the summer of 2020 (46 %). Although court dates via video link have increased by approx. 35 %, 40 % of proceedings are still delayed.

However, law firm ratings are on the decline[8]. Cooperations and strategic networking with colleagues need to be reconsidered in view of the de-bureaucratized representation regulations according to §§ 53,54 BRAO since August 2021.

Nevertheless: "The legal profession is in the middle of the crisis – even if not as dramatic as before". This is the conclusion of the third survey of the German Federal Bar Association (BRAK) on the effects of the Corona crisis on the German legal profession, in which more than 6,500 professionals participated between 05/2021 and 06/2021.

However, almost 53 % of all respondents had experienced a drop in sales overall. According to BRAK, the large proportion of those who believe that they will not be able to overcome the crisis economically remains "worrying". From one tenth of the respondents in the fall, the proportion of those affected decreased only minimally to just under 9 %.

Lawyers working in administrative law (47.3 %), tax law (56 %), medical law (48.5 %) or commercial law (around 59 %) are doing particularly well, i.e. without any loss of revenue. Other lawyers, on the other hand, seem to be particularly at risk: 12.2 % of all social lawyers, 15.9 % of road traffic lawyers, 11.4 % of criminal lawyers and just under 12 % of insolvency lawyers fear that they will not be able to recover from the crisis. With their areas of law, they are well above the average of around 9 %.

Partners in law firms with more than 20 lawyers are only worried about their livelihood in 2 % of all cases, while individual lawyers are worried about their livelihood in 11.8 % of all cases. Schleswig-Holstein is in a particularly good position when viewed by state. Here only 6.4 % worry about their future. It looks worse in Rhine-

---

6 Sind Syndizi die besseren Changemaker? diruj 6/2020, p. 12.

7 Survey on the impact of the Corona crisis on the German legal profession, BRAK, 15.6.2021, p. 6.

8 Branchenbericht der Sparkassen 2020,

land-Palatinate (12,2 %) and "worrying", according to the BRAK, is the situation in Thuringia: There around 22 % feared for their future.

Many lawyers are dissatisfied with the progress of digitization in the judiciary due to corona; the proportion of video hearings is still extremely low: almost 74 % of respondents stated that they had not participated in any such hearings at all. 19 % reported a share of video hearings of 5–15 %. Not even 2 % of the lawyers could report more than 50 % of video hearings.

In the third Corona survey, the lawyers' assessment of the technical equipment of the courts was asked for the first time: Almost 60 % stated that they felt that the equipment had remained the same during the pandemic. Only 15 % had the impression that the courts' equipment had improved and that significantly more video hearings had therefore been held. 26 % said that although the equipment had improved, there had not been more video hearings.

BRAK President, attorney and notary Dr. Ulrich Wessels expressed his disappointment in this context: "Particularly in view of the Pact for the Rule of Law and the demands of BRAK, this is more than regrettable, as a rapid digital upgrade of the courts could have helped to avoid procedural delays and thus at least a temporary standstill in the administration of justice. Improvements are urgently needed here!" The pandemic also continues to have an impact on the duration of court proceedings: Around 41 % of all respondents stated that there had been delays in proceedings of more than eight weeks on average. The legal fields of criminal law, social law, tenancy law and family law, among others, are particularly affected. In medical law, as many as 48.17 % of respondents are currently having to contend with particularly long delays, and more than 51 % of respondents in administrative law stated the same.

Looking at the federal states, Thuringia also occupies an inglorious top position here with 62.5 %. However, an above-average number of delays of more than eight weeks were also reported by just under 49 % of respondents for Berlin and 46.5 % for Brandenburg.

Because numerous attorneys had contacted the Chamber this year with questions about vaccination prioritization, BRAK now- for the first time- also asked a question about vaccination – at a time when prioritization had not yet been lifted, as has been the case nationwide since June.

According to the survey, problems with getting an appointment for vaccination as a lawyer were particularly prevalent in Thuringia (16 %), North Rhine-Westphalia (20.3 %) and Saxony-Anhalt (16.67 %). In other federal states, however, the vaccination of the legal profession was progressing particularly well, as the BRAK survey revealed: at the time of the survey, almost 53 % in Saxony, 38.8 % in Baden-Württemberg, 35.41 % in Bavaria and around 33 % in Schleswig-Holstein had already received the second vaccination[9]. The immunization process in Austria was similar: Depending on the country, almost all Austrian lawyers could receive a second vaccination in late summer 2021 – if they wanted to.

The global pandemic was a catalyst for immediate change in response to the crisis and also a time machine that accelerated the shift in the legal market toward digitalization.

Monitoring this market and adjusting the strategy accordingly will become even more important in the future.

9 *Hasso Suliak,* Anwaltschaft noch immer mitten in der Krise, LTO from 23.6.2021.

II. Observe, Orient, Invest

Observing the industry and your target audience, looking at competitors and effective solutions from other industries to invest in the right places will be the basis of your law firm development.

The following trends are emerging:

- There will be fewer, but larger law firms, and more cooperation between the smaller ones[1]
- Quality management is becoming increasingly systematic and thus also technology-based
- the client structure becomes decisive for the future

Specialization on the one hand and holistic client processing on the other are pushing lawyers into cooperation with colleagues and other service providers. At the same time, this optimizes processes, conserves resources and reduces costs. Less than half of young lawyers do not want to run their own law firm in the future but prefer to focus on their legal work[2].

For you as a law firm owner, this means that your leadership and management tasks will increase and you will need professional support for these issues. It also means that the two most valuable resources for your firm's development are your employees and your firm's IT (legal tech):

Take the needs of **young lawyers** seriously and align your law firm and employer branding accordingly. Do not draw conclusions from yourself. Do not invest in the training of future partners with partner programs, but in comprehensive specialization and personal development of your high potentials. Match the development and specialization of non-lawyer employees to the know-how and structure of your junior lawyers and not to that of the partners. Your employees and your law firm team are your most valuable development potential.

The deployment and development of custom-fit **law firm IT** will re-sort internal law firm structures and processes. These investments will simultaneously free up resources and save costs. The essential aspect, however, is that you can not only increase the quality of your consulting products, but also deliver them time and

---

1 The lone wolf will disappear, according to the current Sparkasse 2020 Branchen Bericht (industry report) and the 2013 Prognos study on the future of the legal profession for the German market and Lexis-Nexis WhitePaper "Die Digitalisierung der Rechtsbranche", p. 58 of 11/2017 for the Austrian market.

2 LexisNexis WhitePaper "Die Digitalisierung der Rechtsbranche", p. 57 from 11/2017.

again – and even know exactly which measures can be used to increase quality even further on the basis of numerically accurate evaluations.

In addition, you should also use legal tech for innovation and product development[3]. Because behind legal tech are often not young tech-savvy non-lawyers but established law firms: e-recht24.de, flightright.de, perconex.de and janolaw were all co-founded by law firms[4]. In most cases, this is a matter of "standardization" and "packaging" through to "commoditization" and "industrialization" of (then formerly) legal services. These services will (have to) disappear from the portfolio of legal advice provided by lawyers[5] – at least that is what 89.4 % of law firm partners in the USA predict[6].

So-called robot lawyers with KI would be used by clients in the following order of priority, according to a survey: For

1. Compensation claims
2. Rental and housing law service
3. Contract drafting and review
4. Criminal law

It was striking that

- the lawyers ranked the clients' answers completely differently[7],
- men always preferred standardized technology products much more than women (34 % to 24 %) and
- significantly fewer were not interested in robot lawyers at all (16 %) than assumed by the lawyers (5 %)[8].

Blockchain technologies, smart contracts and intelligent search are the future wild cards among Legal Tech product.[9]

3 Branchenbericht der Sparkassen 2017, p. 22.

4 LexisNexis WhitePaper "Die Digitalisierung der Rechtsbranche", p. 57 from 11/2017.

5 Law Firms in Transition Survey, n=356, Altmann Weil.

6 LexisNexis WhitePaper "Die Digitalisierung der Rechtsbranche", p. 7 from 11/2017.

7 Both in rank and in motivations (98 % of lawyers thought because of the price advantage technology would be preferred, actually only 73 % did).

8 According to the LexisNexis survey by Online Marktforschungs GmbH 04/2017.

9 LexisNexis WhitePaper "Die Digitalisierung der Rechtsbranche", p. 38, 57 from 11/2017.

III. Back to square one

The legal industry is in the midst of the biggest upheaval in decades:

- the so-called "Gender and Generation Shift – Millennials and families are confidently making entirely new demands on the workplace; women lawyers are claiming the same and just as many decision-making positions for the same pay in the industry; corporate mandates require diversity
- digitization and global networking – The day-to-day work (processes and structures) of lawyers and legal professionals is undergoing a fundamental restructuring, and not just since the beA.
- Competition and disruptive innovation – Legal tech and new business models are pushing into the legal market from the outside and exacerbating the competitive situation, which is already becoming increasingly intense.

These topics ("legal tech", "beA" and "gender equality") are still being touted as "hot topics" on all conference programs, media and networks in the industry. But are they really?

Although the so-called "Future Study of the DAV" already stated in 2013 that "the future of the legal profession is female", the column of the NJW was still titled "The female lawyer problem" three years later in April 2016. Although the German Lawyers' Day DAT 2016 of the German Lawyers' Association with its working group on law firm management already focused on "Digitalization and Legal Tech", the DAT 2017 was also held under the motto "Innovation and Legal Tech", thus promising "particularly forward-looking topics that will move the legal market even more in the future". Similarly, the so-called Lawyers' Future Congress (Soldan/ Wolters Kluwer), which has been dealing exclusively with legal tech and digitalization since 2016 – and, incidentally, relied almost exclusively on the gentlemen of the profession. So none of these topics are really new.

The topics of the industry are presented and discussed in an ever-changing format in the hope of being able to show alternative courses of action. Of course, it is our task to legally shape digitization. Of course, as a strong partner of small and medium-sized businesses, we must accompany them in their digitalization. However, if we lawyers and law firms are serious about the new service culture and want to finally see ourselves as a business factor, then we must, above all, also express more than just "legal concerns" on our own behalf regarding the international discussion on the topic of digitization. We should fill terms like "legal innovation" and "start up LEGAL" with life, ideas and projects. Think tanks, scrum and agile teams, interdisciplinary conferences and round tables can provide impetus here. Above all, however, it should be on the weekly agenda of every single law firm.

It is a pity that these topics have so far received so little attention at lawyers' conferences, at AdvoTec, which accompanies the German Lawyers' Day, or even at working group meetings of the DAV. We are only concerned with the implementation of the so-called e-Justice Act, instead of actively approaching companies and innovators and seizing opportunities. Digitization will happen. With or without us. We can retreat to the role of "worrier" and continue to block the beA or confidently participate in building new markets and opportunities[1]. Each of us has the choice; the choice to be a part of it[2].

But one more thing in conclusion:
We should not lose ourselves personally in the process.
Our individual resources, our private needs and desires are not only drivers and motivators, but at the same time also gauges and boundaries. Just as we should not work in business fields that contradict our personal values (keyword: tobacco industry or weapons lobby), we should also not constantly ignore our need for sleep, regeneration, exercise, family and intimate relationships.

We are human beings. We only live once and this lifetime is finite.

If you manage that your law firm is aligned with you and your needs, corresponds to your values and serves satisfied clients for many years with a motivated team – you have achieved everything. And you should start anew and not pass on the firm to someone else.

Why?
Nothing is as difficult as maintaining the status quo. It's no coincidence that the saying "When it's at its best, that's when you should leave" comes to mind. Only then can you give the firm "wings". If you miss this moment, you will soon perceive the constant further development as a hamster wheel or at some point simply close your law firm. Development is growth. You are not building the "law firm of eternity".

So, if you take away just one insight at the end of this read, it's this:

Have the courage for new beginnings!
Make mistakes. Learn from them. Do it better.

If you don't see any development potential in your law firm – for whatever reason: Give it up!

Do not ride a dead horse.

1 Dr. Tutschka, "Change is not in our DNA" in JurCoach's Blog from 25.3.2016.
2 Theiss, "Digitalisierung – wir brauchen keine Rechtsanwälte mehr" on trend.at 2016.

Bring the next generation into the firm so that new ideas, values or perspectives bring a breath of fresh air. Restructure it completely to the point of reorganization.

Or have the courage to close them!

It doesn't always have to be insolvency that brings things to a close.

---

i A person needs to "reinvent" himself every 5–7 years to live his identity, to be authentic and satisfied. Your firm should be just as alive: allow it to be!

And allow yourself to.
You are a lawyer and entrepreneur (even without a law firm).
Make decisions as a grown up!
You define success!

Start again from the beginning ... and sometimes you don't even need a closing point for the beginning:

"Running the Summer Academy in Zakynthos is both a profession and a vocation for me. It has been a deeply fulfilling activity for me for almost three decades, satisfying my need to build places where people can develop their potential and engage with art, body and soul. The project landed on my lawyer's desk in 1991 as a disdainful act – with considerable legal and economic problems. When these had been solved to some extent in the following season, the operator at the time decided, to my surprise, to give up the location. Since I had invested a lot of heart and soul in the matter in all these years (there was never any fee), I spontaneously decided to keep the disheveled but charming academy alive.

An exciting adventure with a very uncertain outcome began, especially since I was neither a tourism expert nor the director of an art school. Also, as a young lawyer working on his career, I had just three weeks to take care of the business on site, which had been running for several months. The rest consisted of almost daily phone calls with the organizational management working in Greece. Somehow we got through the summer and planning for the next one began.

These days, despite the Corona virus and Medicane "Janos", we have already put the 28th successful SOAK season on the beach parquet. I think that especially the skills acquired in the legal profession, for example negotiating skills and analytical-strategic thinking, helped me a lot in realizing my goals."

Dr. Wolfgang Löhnert has been working as a lawyer in Vienna since 1989. He was a partner in a law firm for seven years and founded his own law firm in 1998, where he works primarily in the areas of architectural and construction contract law, copyright law and tourism law[3]. The SOAK is an insider tip in the Austrian tourism scene, which offers a fixed home not only for the participants but also as a holistic creative project for the local people as well as the artists and creative people from Germany and Austria.

---

3 Read the full interview on the CLP blog.

What did you get out of the chapter?
It is always good to know where the "exit door" is and what exactly the so-called "worst case scenario" looks like. Even if you end up deciding to do things differently or things turn out differently than you think. You are prepared.

The best for last

Founding of the law firm: Is it even worth it today? Shouldn't everyone be advised to study something else or at least not to work in their own law firm? Should one become an entrepreneur in an industry that imposes many limitations and regulations on itself in terms of entrepreneurship and is facing a profound change, perhaps even facing extinction?

Law Firm Management: a term that has only become established in connection with law firms in recent years and has so far "happened" rather incidentally. And which today must move from the pure administration and optimization of a law firm to strategic law firm development.

The consulting business is dying[4]. One of the greatest achievements of the 20th century is that the knowledge monopoly of individual experts has become largely obsolete: thanks to the Internet and digitization, anyone can now access information anywhere at any time and free of charge. So anyone who still relies on the sale of knowledge today is a dinosaur.

The same applies to processes that can be automated:
- Online divorces already exist in the Netherlands and account for 5 % of all divorces there,
- Canada provides a low-cost platform for simple civil disputes to relieve the burden on the judiciary and as a low-cost legal arrangement
- UK plans an online court for claims under £25,000

Austria's public authorities, notaries and judiciary are pioneers in digitization, which started already 30 years ago over there. Today, 74 % use this online service and a total of 10 % of government services are handled digitally – more than any-

4 Terpitz, "Das Geschäftsmodell der Strategen wackelt", in the Handelsblatt from 7.11.2010. e-fellows, "Perspektiven für Unternehmensberater" 2021.

where else in Europe[5]. With the "Justice 3.0" in 2016, the Austrian courts are to become paperless by 2020[6].

Firm Leadership: However, this also creates the opportunity for the human factor to come more to the foreground in the future. As a result, universities, publishers[7] nd even consultants will have to rethink and redesign their business concepts.

And that's not all: legal tech, diversity, millennials, and digitization are dissolving traditional industry structures and redistributing established power relationships. The strongly conservative professional profile with the shamefully low proportion of female lawyers in positions of power and leadership[8] and the largest gender pay gap of all industries[9] will not be able to withstand this pressure. It is simply not sustainable. You can see this, for example, in the sharp drop in membership of the only professional association, the German Bar Association (DAV), of ten percent last year[10] in Germany[11]. But you can also see this from the fact that the even more conservative Austrian legal sector (here, due to professional and social structures, only every second female lawyer even makes it into the legal profession[12] despite a tripling of the number of lawyers) will lose 86 % of its law firms in the next few years[13].

Law firm marketing: This structural change in the legal industry frightens many. It is not WHAT (the information) that will be important in the future, but HOW (the advice). Instead of advice, clients will demand mediation, support and even management. And the personal, trusting relationship, which is not interchangeable, will become more and more important. Coaching will find its way into consulting and teaching, where it will professionalize individual learning and guidance. Instead of

5 For comparison: in Germany, only 45 % use this service, BRZ Direkt 01/2016, BRZ Read_It03/2016.

6 LexisNexis WhitePaper "Die Digitalisierung der Rechtsbranche", p. 36 of 11/2017.

7 So also LexisNexis on the ARD magazine in the WhitePaper "Die Digitalisierung der Rechtsbranche", p. 58 of 11/2017.

8 Dr. Tutschka in "Justitia, wie haben ein Problem: ein Anwältinnenproblem", JuraBlogs from 24.4.2016.

9 Dr. Tutschka in "Female Leadership im Legal Sector", djbz 03/17, p. 137; Koch, "Anwältinnen im internationalen Vergleich, Anwaltsblatt 05/2017.

10 Dr. Tutschka in the Interview "Es gab ganz entscheidende Entwicklungen", Wirtschaft und Weiterbildung 07-08/17, p. 54 er seq.

11 In Austria, the professional association plays only a subordinate role, if at all, due to the dedicated and expanded chambers.

12 Despite 55 % female law school graduates, the rate of female attorneys has stagnated at less than 30 % for years.

13 LexisNexis WhitePaper "Die Digitalisierung der Rechtsbranche", p. 58 of 11/2017.

legal advice, there will be legal coaching. What has long been the super tool of management consultants for entrenched or difficult consulting and implementation processes will finally be discovered by legal advisors as well. With the appropriate training, attorneys and lawyers will finally have methods and tools at their disposal to really find the best solution for their clients[14].

Individual industries are already showing the way: no family counseling service, no management consulting firm works without coaching today. It is part of the standard repertoire of holistic professional consulting services. It is not uncommon for the client to simply not be ready to recognize or implement certain necessary steps at the beginning or even in the middle of the journey. The client alone decides when coaching is used, for what purpose and within what framework[15]. The only important thing on the part of the coach and consultant is that coaching be as professional as the consulting itself, that is, with solid training and a recognized certification[16] as well as profound experience.

Just as you expect in other service areas – such as tourism – the same high level in all areas of a four-star hotel – in the kitchen as well as in the room and in the service. So if someone asks me today whether I am a consultant-coach, a coaching consultant, just a consultant or a coach, my answer is: It depends. And it depends solely on the customer, what he needs and what he wants. I am a service-oriented service provider and can offer my clients added value by expanding my competencies. So, depending on the need, consulting or coaching[17].

Futurologists attest that everything that requires original human, emotional and social skills – such as empathy, individuality, intuition, trust and the ability to relate – has bright prospects in a future that will be characterized by digitalization, automation and standards. Other methods such as mediation, therapy, training, mentoring can also reflect this, but unlike these, coaching focuses on the personal future of the coachee. Coaching is a very young method compared to consulting, teaching and therapy. For a long time it was a component of psychology, which itself only established itself as an independent, recognized science at the beginning of the 19th cen-

---

14 I offer this "Legal Coaching" training with CLP (Consulting and Coaching for legal professionals) in Germany, Austria and Switzerland.

15 Buhse, "So sieht die Beratung der Zukunft aus" in Wirtschaftswoche from 23.6.2016.

16 Similar to specialist attorney training in Germany with a combination of training (theory), evaluated practical experience and ongoing quality management (annual continuing education obligation).

17 *Dr. Tutschka* in "Coaching vs. Beratung – eine Frage der Perspektive" in Xing Coaches Magazin 06/2017.

tury. Over the last fifty years, coaching has been continuously developed, standardized and defined as a method and profession largely thanks to professional associations, so that it is now ready to unfold its full potential.

In this regard, **coaching** can work in three directions for the consulting industry:
1. as a special method it completes the consultant portfolio (keyword: Legal Coaching)
2. in combination with supervision it can support consultants to better cope with emotionally stressful aspects of their work (keyword: psychohygiene) and
3. coaching can better support an industry in transition than consulting, which has to find its own way (keyword: consultant advisors)

I, too, invest in a coach time and again – be it before important decisions or challenges or during upcoming changes. With my coach, I specifically discussed why I do certain things and not others.

This means that I am very aware at all times of WHY I do things, commit myself to things or give up initiatives, where exactly I want to go, what moves me forward and what does not. I rarely have the feeling of being "in the wrong movie".

Because there are exactly two ways to fail:
1. we leave everything as it is and stick to what we are good at, or
2. we chase after every new idea, every innovation.

---

i The fact is: What has helped you to be successful and meet the needs of your customers in the last five years will not let you grow any further. Only those who are prepared to grow are fit for the future.[18]

And not just quantitatively, but qualitatively:
- Those who are willing to adapt to changing conditions;
- ready to say goodbye to things;
- willing to change perspective.

So what is needed today – for tomorrow?

What is needed is the change of systems, such as the system of education of tomorrow's lawyers, the system of specialist attorneyships, the system of care for future lawyers or the system of partnership appointments.

How are systems changed? Systems crash at the changed conditions of the market and the industry. Or they are changed from within in a forward-looking and tar-

18 *Dr. Tutschka*, "The Future of the Legal Profession", im Blog JurCoach from 24.2.2017.

geted manner: by changing the underlying strategy, adapting the management, the necessary cultural change.

What it takes for the legal industry:

1. *Diversity (instead of gender and generation shift).*
   The world is becoming more transparent and at the same time ethically more complex; diversity does not result from a balanced gender ratio thanks to women's quota, but from religious, biographical, cultural, perspectival, human and ethnic differences. Ever heard of "Third Culture Kids", of "Synaesthesia"? The world is colorful. So are we.

2. *Cultural and structural change (instead of digitalization and global networking)*
   "Soft skills," IT skills[19], personal maturity and reflectiveness, charisma, communication skills (asking questions, listening, and turning off personal filters/ego management), change and crisis management are in demand. The law exams are to be seen as a general starting point for the actually decisive, differentiating specializations (post graduate talent development). Traditional professional training and specializations are only quality assurance of the initial training. Business know-how, the development of soft skills, personality development and communication training differentiate and prevent interchangeability[20].

3. *Cooperation (instead of competition and disruptive innovation)*
   With team events and incentives, you invest in your strongest potential. Networks and cooperations accompany you and your team through emotional white water, on business summit tours and into unknown business terrain.

Time to define new goals. Time to ask new questions.

What has gotten us this far, focusing on the challenges of our industry, will not get us into the future. We need to broaden our focus and ask questions:

How can we help our clients and their customers and/or their families with legal advice as a trustworthy partner and companion?

In this case, our core competence is not legal advice, but the establishment of a trusting partnership and the competent support of our clients.

And then it is somehow true:
Yesterday's law firm will be tomorrow's law firm.

---

19 LexisNexis WhitePaper "Die Digitalisierung der Rechtsbranche", p. 13 from 11/2017.
20 Susskind, "The Future of the Legal Profession", p. 157.

Because the “lawyer for any situation” has always been able to do that.

Many a prediction will not come true, or not in the same way. But investing in ourselves and our personal development today will pay off either way: even if we end up just being happy as lawyers.

In this sense – back to the future.

Author and contributors

Author

Dr. Geertje Tutschka, MCC has been a lawyer in Germany, Austria and the USA for over twenty years and accompanies law firms in difficult change processes and during reorientation.

Born in Saxony-Anhalt in 1970, she was initially prevented from studying her chosen field of study in the GDR for political reasons. She had been involved in the political culture movement for years and was under surveillance by the state security. As a result, she first went to the theater working as a professional cello musician. After reunification, she completed her studies and legal clerkship at the University of Bielefeld and the Regional Court of Bielefeld/OLG Hamm in the shortest possible time. With both state exams she was among the best 30 % of her year, so that her student loan was subsequently converted into a scholarship.

Since her career goal from the beginning was to become a lawyer in her own firm, she worked in law firms during her studies in order to gain as much practical experience as possible, but above all experience in law firm management and leadership, strategic orientation, acquisition and marketing. After years as a salaried lawyer in various law firms and legal departments, she took a four-year family break, during which she had her three children, completed her doctorate in contract law and set up her own law firm. When her husband was sent to the USA as a corporate lawyer during the automotive crisis, she moved her law firm to Detroit, USA and specialized in assignment law. In addition, she was trained and certified as an intercultural trainer and professional ICF business coach. She was already involved in organizational development, leadership and strategy as President of the PA International School and the First International Round Table. Together with a team of authors, she published the "USA Expat Quick Guide" and the novel "Fern der Heimat so nah" ("Home far away from home"), which supported Detroit's street children with its proceeds and was shortlisted for the Indie Award at the Leipzig Book Fair in 2013.

Since her return to Europe, she lives and works as a consultant, coach and trainer in Salzburg and Munich. With "CLP – Consulting for legal professionals" she founded a consulting company for law firm and career development, specialized in lawyers and law firms. She specializes in leadership and strategy and has developed the methods "LEAD. Learn. Create. Care." and the "5 steps to success".

Since 2016, as Director of Training at the CLP Academy, she has been training lawyers and legal professionals in legal coaching, a method she developed that is based on the international quality standards of an accredited training by the International Coaching Federation for conflict coaches and crisis managers and in-

https://doi.org/10.1515/9783111058160-008

creases the communication skills and performance of lawyers, thus meaningfully supplementing their training. The training is accredited as ACTP, so called Level 2 with the highest possible international accreditation level as a professional coaching training, making the Legal Coach degree one of the most commercially valuable coaching degrees in the world, and forward-looking.

She herself represented the world's strongest association of professional coaches for Germany as Chair of the Board of ICF from 2016–2019 and developed it into the top 10 associations worldwide (for which she and her team were awarded the international Chapter Recognition Award as well as the Gift of Coaching Award), and was a member of the Global Leaders Forum and delegate in the Round Table of German-speaking Coaching Associations (RTC). Today, she prepares future board teams for their responsible leadership role as a member of the ICF Germany Election Commission and is responsible for awarding the ICF Germany Coaching Prism Award to organizations, which in the past has gone to coaching programs of Volkswagen AG, adidas, Vodafone, SAP as well as to CMS Tax Legal for the Partner Peak Performance Program.

Since 2020, she has been President of the German Lawyers' Association Abroad (DAV) Austria, which she developed into one of the largest DAV Abroad associations within one year as the 12th Abroad association with the aim of promoting exchange and cooperation between German and Austrian professionals.

She regularly writes for professional magazines in Germany and abroad such as NJW, Legal Business World, Anwaltsblatt, Östereichisches Anwaltsblatt, anwalt aktuell, LTO, LinkedIn Pulse, Xing Magazin, NJW, Haufe, Soldan, Beck, Managerseminare, CoachingMagazin, Wirtschaft und Weiterbildung, Training Aktuell and other professional magazines. As a sought-after keynote speaker on the topic of "Leadership and Strategy", she has been one of the top international speakers in the industry for years. Today, with a 5-digit follower count from the international legal industry alone, she is one of the top influencers in this field. She received the "Women in Law Award" for the development of the internationally recognized certificate training in legal coaching.

She is a speaker of the DAV and the ÖRAK, mentor of the AG Anwältinnen and the Juristinnenbund, and has meanwhile published numerous non-fiction and specialist books on the topics of law firm management, marketing and development.

She is also responsible for the study materials "Strategic Orientation and Marketing for Law Firms" and "Zeitmanagement in der Anwaltskanzlei" (Time Management in Law Firms) for the Distance Learning University of Hagen. She is involved in the voluntary promotion of young lawyers, e.g. at Panda Law and MentorMe, as well as in climate and species protection.

Dr. Tutschka lives right on the German-Austrian border with her husband and their three young adults, as well as various animals. As a synesthete, she plays several instruments, paints intense acrylic paintings, writes novels and poetry, is passionate about cooking and enjoys Salzburg's culture. On weekends you can find her alone with her dog in the Alps, in winter with the sled dogs and in summer on one of the long-distance hiking trails.

Contributors

Many thanks to the numerous colleagues who have contributed to this book:

Dr. Petra Arends-Paltzer, Lawyer and Mentor
Founder Davos Digital Forum, Switzerland

Theresia Bohl,
Business mediator and law firm manager (tb-kama), Hamburg

Dr. Jochen Brandhoff, Attorney at Law
Founder and Managing Director of LEGAL®EVOLUTION, Frankfurt

Dr. Iris Brokamp, lawyer and business and management coach
Owner of LegalFit, Breme

Johanna Busmann,
Owner of anwalts-akquise.de, Hamburg

Dr. Arndt Eversberg, Attorney at Law
Member of the Board of ROLAND ProzessFinanz AG, Cologne

Christiane Eymers, lawyer, mediator and coach
specialist lawyer for labor law, specialist lawyer for family law, in-house lawyer in the legal department of ADEXA-Die Apothekengewerkschaft, Hamburg

Dr. Alix Frank-Thomasser, Attorney at Law
Founder of Women in Law and the Justitia Awards, Alix Frank Rechtsanwälte, Vienna

Elisabeth Gawrych, lawyer and legal coach
Lawyer on Demand, winner of PANDA Law 2015

Sebastian von Glahn
Managing Director of TalentRocket GmbH, Munich

Anna-Maria Göbel, lawyer and influencer
Frau.Rechtsanwalt, law firm in Hagen

Dr. Burkard Göpfert, LL.M., Attorney at Law
specialist in labor law, partner KLIEMT Rechtsanwälte, Munich

Dr. Nadja Harraschain, then trainee lawyer
Winner Panda Law, Founder Breaking.Through, Frankfurt

Joanna Hardy, attorney at law
Red Lion Chambers, London, UK

Markus Hartung, lawyer and mediator
Chairman of the Professional Law Committee of the German Bar Association, Berlin

Anke Haug, Attorney at Law
Managing Director of Anwaltsseminare und Fortbildung GmbH, Renningen, Germany

Dr. Dominik Herzog, Attorney at Law/Singer/Influencer
Partner SYLVENSTEIN Rechtsanwälte, Munich

Prof. Dr. Klaus-Stefan Hohenstatt, Attorney at Law
then Partner Freshfields Bruckhaus Deringer LLP, Hamburg

Jennifer Hülskötter, Hülskötter and Partner
Part of the management of Hülskötter & Partner and successor of the company founder Gerhard Hülskötter (law firm software advoware)

Dr. Michael Koch,
Product, Account and Marketing Manager at e-fellows.net, Munich

Lina Krawietz, lawyer, design thinking expert
Managing Director This is Legal Design, Co-Editor-in-Chief REthinking Law, Advisor Lawyers Magazine, Berlin

Dr. Christina-Maria Leeb, Lawfluencer
Professor LL.M. Legal Tech, University of Regensburg

Pia Löffler, Attorney at Law / Business Lawyer,
Owner of anwaltstexte, Munich

Dr. Wolfgang Löhnert, Attorney at Law
Managing Director of SOAK, law firm in Vienna

Christof Kleinmann, Attorney at Law
Specialist in Employment Law, Managing Partner Graf von Westphalen, Frankfurt

Katharina Miller & Isabelle Hoyer
Advisory Board & CEO PANDA Women Leadership Contest & Network, Mering

Julia Müller, Lawyer and Coach
Legal Recruiting for Clients and Candidates, Frankfurt

Anna Murk, Business Lawyer
Founder Legal Laymann

Dr. Sebastain Naber, Attorney at Law
NEUWERK, Hamburg

Jörg Overbeck, Attorney at Law
COO Oppenhoff und Partner, Cologne

Dr. Daniel Röder, lawyer and conflict coach
Kanzlei GREENFORT, Frankfurt

Dr. Andreas R.J. Schnee-Gronauer, lawyer and graduate economist
Der Unternehmeranwalt, Schüttorf

Dr. Julia Schönbohm, LL.M.
Partner Linklaters, Frankfurt

Dr. Anette Schunder Hartung, Attorney at Law
Owner of aHa Strategische Kanzleientwicklung, Frankfurt

Sonja Ewerdt-Schlaak, M.M., Mediator and Supervisor
Judge at the District Court of Leipzig

Anika Seidenfaden, lawyer and coach
Formerly Corporate Legal Councel Xing, Hamburg

Sarah Settele, Attorney at Law
Owner of Rechtsanwaltskanzlei Settele Krumbach (Swabia)

Christian Solmecke, LL.M., Attorney at Law, Influencer
Kanzlei WBS, legal tech entrepreneur, Iurratio, Juridicus

Dr. Nele Somers, Lawyer and Influencer
Owner of Kanzlei ARTES, Antwerp, Belgium

Ulrike Staats, lawyer and coach
Prism Award 2018, Senior Manager of Global HR/L&D at CMS Legal Services, Frankfurt, Germany

Carmen Thornton, lawyer, influencer
Justitia Award 2020, Kanzlei Thornton-Law, Vienna

Sina Töpfer, legal specialist, mediator and coach
Recruiting Sina Töpfer, podcaster, Hamburg

Markus Weins
Managing director of FFi Verlag GmbH and owner of Kanzleimarketing.de, Hürth

Christina Wenz, fully qualified lawyer and mediator
Praxis Mediation-Wenz, Kaiserslautern

Stefan Winheller, Attorney at Law, LL.M. Tax (USA), Specialist Attorney for Tax Law
Managing Director WINHELLER Rechtsanwaltsgesellschaft mbH, Frankfurt a.M.

Martin Wohlrabe, Attorney at Law
Managing Director of CONSILIUM Rechtskommunikation GmbH, Berlin

Some were even willing to do an in-depth interview.
You can find the interviews here:
www.consultingforlegals.com/aktuelles/tag/interviews/

References

ABA Profile of the Legal Profession 2021.
Astrid Auer-Reinsdorff/Andrea Brandenburg, Multimedia und Urheberrecht, 2003.
Edward Beck/Christopher Cowen, Spiral Dynamics, 2011.
Marc R. Benioff, Enterprises in Germany in 2030, Deloitte.
Kenneth Blanchard, Führungsstile, situatives Führen, 2016.
Sabine Bode, Kriegsenkel: Die Erben der vergessenen Generation, 2017.
Claudia Bonacker, Kanzleigründung und Kanzleistrategie, Haufe vom 20.1.2014.
CLP-Interviews, https://www.consultingforlegals.com/aktuelles/tag/interviews/
André Boße, New Work, Nachhaltigkeit, Purpose – Consulting in der Post-Corona-Zeit, Karriereführer vom 1.7.2021.
Prof. Ursula Bredel (Professorin und Expertin für Orthographiedidaktik) in "Es ist gut für's Gehirn, mit der Hand zu schreiben", Die Welt vom 15.1.2015.
Studie "Dafür nehmen wir uns einen Anwalt – Erwartungshaltung von Unternehmen an moderne Anwälte im Konfliktmanagement", Bucerius Law School (CLP) in Zusammenarbeit mit Taylor Wessing.
New Directions in Legal Services, ARK Group, Bucerius (CLP).
Marcus Buckingham, Entdecken Sie Ihre Stärken jetzt! Frankfurt/New York 2014.
Johanna Busmann, Chefsache Mandantenakquisition, Berlin 2016.
Dr. Nicola Byok, Partnerinnen-Barometer 2015.
Campus, Business Model Generation; Business Model YOU; *Ash Maurya*, Scaling Lean,http://www.startplatz.de/business-model-buecher/
Ilona Cosack, Praxishandbuch Anwaltsmarketing, NWB Verlag 2013.
Ilona Cosack, Die Wahl der passenden Kanzleisoftware, ffi Verlag 2020.
DATEV, Effiziente Anwaltsorganisation, 2. Auflage, TeleLex, Nürnberg 2014.
DAV, Ratgeber für junge Rechtsanwälte und Rechtsanwältinnen, 13. Auflage, Berlin 2013.
Zach Davis, Zeitmanagement für Rechtsanwälte, TeleLex, Nürnberg 2014.
Jochen Dieselhorst/Lars Schreiber, Die Rechtslage zum E-Mail-Spamming in Deutschland, Computer und Recht (CR) 2004, S. 680 ff.
Sind Syndizi die besseren Changemaker? diruj 6/2020, S. 12.
Thomas Degen/Ulrich Emmert in Elektronischer Rechtsverkehr, Verlag C.H. Beck, 2. Auflage, 2021.
Brigitte Dennerlein/Achim Ludwig Otto in Wirksame Führungstechniken in Stuerberater- und Rechtsanwaltskanzleien, Erich Schmidt Verlag, 2021.
Hubertus Drinkuth, Der Nachhaltigkeitsberater im Interview, Karriereführer vom 1.7.2021.
Christian Dülpers, Ergebnisse der Arbeitgeber-Umfrage: So reagiert der juristische Arbeitsmarkt auf die Corona Krise, LTO vom 26.6.2020.
Dietmar Dworschak, Integrated Dispute Management, Anwalt aktuell 01/2021. E-fellows.net, Perspektiven für Juristen, 2021.
Constanze Eich, Networking und Akquise für Rechtsanwälte, C.H. Beck 2016.
Constanze Eich, Leadership für Rechtsanwälte, Verlag C.H. Beck 2021.
Stefan Ernst, Wireless LAN und das Strafrecht, CR 2003, S. 898 ff.
Michael Felser/Hans-Willi Philipp, Die erfolgreiche Kanzleigründung, Köln 1997.
Andrea Fendt, Der Rechtsanwalt als Ausbilder, TeleLex, Nürnberg 2014.
Eberhard Fedke, Wirtschaftsunternehmen Anwalts- und Notarkanzlei, Köln 1993.
Dr. Konstantin Filbinger, Was bedeutet Legal Tech für deutsche Anwälte und Kanzleien, Haufe vom 12.7.2018.
Konrad Fischer, Geht nach Hause, Wirtschaftswoche vom 22.5.2020.

https://doi.org/10.1515/9783111058160-009

Foitzik, Projektmanagement in Kanzleien, Kanzleimarketing.de vom 21.2.2018.
Alix Frank-Thomasser, Advokaten 1938, 2. Auflage 2021
Future-Law Studie "Die digitale Rechtsabteilung 2035", 2019.
Future-Law Umfrage "Der Anwaltsberuf 2035", 2018.
Future Fit Lawyer, Wolters Kluwer 2019.
Future Ready Lawyer, Wolters Kluwer 2020.
Future Ready Lawyer, Wolters Kluwer 2021.
Ignaz Füsgen, Legal Service Portfolio Management, Legal Revolutionary 24.2.2021.
Carolin Gattermann, Drei Business Bücher, die jeder Gründer lesen sollte, Startplatz vom 11.4.2017.
Wolfgang Gaube/Arno Schubach, Musterhandbuch zur Organisation und Qualitätssicherung in der Anwaltskanzlei, Neuwied 1999.
Karlheinz A. Geißler, Zeit – verweile doch ..., 5. Auflage, Freiburg 2003.
Michael Gerber, The E-Myth Attorney, Wiley & Sons, Inc. New Jersey 2010.
Hans Ferdinand Groß, Sozietäten, Bürogemeinschaften und sonstige Zusammenschlüsse von Freiberuflern, TeleLex, Nürnberg 2015.
Maja Göpel, Unsere Welt neu denken – Eine Einladung, 6. Auflage, Berlin 2020.
Dr. Anja Hall, Warum sollte man in der Großkanzlei nicht alt werden können? Legal Tribune Online vom 29.6.2016.
Daniel Hanke, Die Corporate Influencer Formel: Expertise + Engagement + Einfluss, LinkedIn vom 9.6.2020.
Hartung/Bues/Halbleib, Legal Tech – Die Digitalisierung des Rechtsmarktes, München 2018.
Niko Härting, Anwaltliche Werbung im Internet, AnwBl 2000, S. 343ff.
Niko Härting, IT-Sicherheit in der Anwaltskanzlei, NJW 2005, S. 1248ff.
Wolfgang Hartung/Volker Römermann (Hrsg.), Marketing und Management (Handbuch für Rechtsanwälte), München 1999.
Markus Hartung, Auf ewig Dein, Anwaltsblatt vom 8.1.2021.
Hartung/Bues/Halbleib, Legal Tech – die Digitalisierung des Rechtsmarktes, 2017.
Joachim Hasebrook, Lebensphasen- und Kompetenzmanagement, Springer 2018.
Dirk Heckmann, Rechtspflichten zur Gewährleistung von IT-Sicherheit im Unternehmen – Maßstäbe für IT-Sicherheit, MultiMedia und Recht (MMR) 2006, S. 280ff.
Joachim Heilmann/Claudia Tege, Rechte und Pflichten bei der Kommunikation, Arbeit und Arbeitsrecht (AuA) 2001, S. 52ff.
Matthias Heine, Es ist gut für's Gehirn, mit der Hand zu schreiben", Die Welt vom 15.1.2015.
Barbara Helten/Adrian Raub, Kanzleimarketing in der Pandemie – dem Wandel angepasst, LTO vom 18.3.2021.
Barbara Helten, Tipps für den erfolgreichen Pitch, LTO vom 25.5.2021.
Andreas Hermanutz, Kanzleiorganisation als essentieller Bereich der Digitalisierung, DStR 40/2020.
Benno Heussen, Anwalt und Mandant, Band 6 der Schriftenreihe "Wege zur erfolgreichen Anwaltspraxis", Köln 1999.
Benno Heussen, Akquisition und Mandatsentwicklung, Neuwied, Kriftel 2001.
Benno Heussen, Time-Management für Anwälte, München 2004.
Benno Heussen, Anwaltsunternehmen führen, München 2016.
Dr. David Hoeflmayr, Kanzleimarketing, Erich Schmidt Verlag, 2012.
Stefan Hradil, Zukunftsszenarien für Deutschland, Bundeszentrale für politische Bildung (bpb) vom 31.5.2012.
Michael Hülskötter im advoblog vom 24.7.2018.
Martin Huff/Dr. Henning Löwe (Hrsg.), Textsammlung, Anwaltliches Berufsrecht 2020, Köln 2021.

Matthias Irle, Miteinander statt gegeneinander, brandeins thema 05/2020.

Kai Jakob/Dierk Schindler/Roger Strathausen, Liquid Legal: Towards a Common Legal Platform (Law for Professionals), 2020.

Dennis Janz/Arabella Poth/Thilo Schnelle, Gründung, Erwerb und Veräußerung einer Rechtsanwaltskanzlei, Erich Schmidt Verlag 2020.

JUVE Handbuch 2017.

Kanzleihandbuch für Anwälte: Effiziente Anwaltsorganisation – Ablaufsicherheit durch optimierte Kanzleiprozesse, TeleLex, Nürnberg 2014.

Dr. Matthias Kilian, Wirksamkeit anwaltlicher Marketingmaßnahmen, Soldan-Studie 2011, Deutscher Anwaltverlag.

Dr. Matthias Kilian, Anteile der Arbeitszeit, Anwaltsblatt 01/2018, S. 32.

Prof. Dr. Matthias Kilian/Kerstin Heckmann, Forschungsbericht des Soldan Instituts "Rechtsanwälte und ihre Mitarbeiter" (Band 22), B. A. Deutscher Anwaltverlag.

Rudolf Kissel, Internet für und gegen alle? NJW 2006, S. 801ff.

Oren Klaff, Pitch Anything, McGrall Hill, New York 2011.

Nancy Kline, Time to think, London 1999.

Kerstin Knopp, Top-Anwältin Kerstin Knopp im Interview, Business Insider vom 23.12.2020.

Prof. Dr. Harald Koch, Anwältinnen im internationalen Vergleich, Anwaltsblatt 05/2017.

Robert Koch, Haftung für die Weiterverbreitung von Viren durch E-Mails, NJW 2004, S. 801ff.

Andreas Krämer/Reinhold Mauer/Anton Braun, Erfolgreiche Anwaltswerbung, Band 7 der Schriftenreihe "Wege zur erfolgreichen Anwaltspraxis", Köln 1999.

Rainer Krumm, 9 Levels of a value system, 2014.

Eckard König, Einführung in das systemische Denken und Handeln, 2016.

Florian Körber, Neue Medien und Strafrecht, K & R 2004, S. 20ff. Mitarbeiter-Engagement verstehen, kununu.

Werner Küstenmacher/Tiki/ Lothar Seiwert, Simplify your life, 8. Auflage, Frankfurt a.M., New York 2003.

Lars Kutzner, Die Beschlagnahme von Daten bei Berufsgeheimnisträgern, NJW 2005, S. 2652ff.

Kristina Läsker, Das Ende der alten Welt, brandeins thema 05/2020.

Frederic Laloux, Reinventing Organizations, München 2015.

Trimborn von Landenberg, Erfolgreich starten als Rechtsanwalt, Deutscher Anwaltverlag 2013.

Patrick Lencioni, Die 5 Dysfunktionen eines Teams, 2014.

Leitfaden der Medienanstalten, 06/2021.

Das Legal Recruiting Playbook, LTO 08/2020.

Jan Lies, Feelgood-Management in der Kanzlei, NWB Verlag Herne, 2021.

Jeffrey Liker, The Toyota Way to Service Excellence, 2016.

Janwillem van de Loo, Palandt umbenennen – das Ende der Geschichte? Anwaltsblatt vom 28.7.2021.

Lars Lorber, Menschenkenntnis – Der große Typentest, C.H. Beck, München 2015.

Pia Lorenz, Ist das beA noch zu retten? LTO vom 28.12.2017.

Pia Lorenz, Näher am Business, doch von Legal Tech weit weg, LTO vom 29.4.2020.

Pia Löffler, Mandanten dringend gesucht – so klappt kurzfristige Akquise, Beck-Shop-Forum vom 22.2.2021.

Pia Löffler, Praxishandbuch Onlinemarketing für Rechtsanwälte, TeleLex, Nürnberg 2015. LTO-Redaktion, Bundesregierung beschließt Gesetzesentwürfe, LTO vom 20.1.2021.

Dr. Nicolas Lührig, Gesetz zum Legal Tech Inkasso – Erfolgshonorar auch für die Anwaltschaft, Anwaltsblatt vom 20.1.2021.

Dr. Nicolaus Lührig, Große BRAO-Reform gilt ab 1.8.2022: Mehr Freiheit für die Anwaltschaft, Anwaltsblatt vom 14.7.2021.

Stephen Lundin, Fish, 2003.
Prof. Dr. Bruno Mascello, Risikomanagement im Rechtsmarkt neu gedacht, Anwaltspiegel vom 6.1.2021.
Jochen Mai, Zufriedenheit im Beruf, Karriere-Bibel vom 1.5.2016.
Perry Marshall, 80/20 Sales and Marketing, 2013.
Sophie Martinetz/Sarah Maringele, Quick Guide Legal Tech – Schritt für Schritt zur digitalen Kanzlei und Rechtsabteilung, Wiesbaden 2020.
Reinhold Maurer/Andreas Krämer, Marketingstrategien für Rechtsanwälte, 2. Auflage, München 2001.
Prof. Dr. Cordula Meckenstock, Rechtsmarkt 2021, ZUJ 01/2021.
Andreas Molitor, Die Wächter der Ordnung, brandeins thema 05/2020.
Ingo Müller, Furchtbare Juristen. Die unbewältigte Vergangenheit der deutschen Justiz, Edition Tiamat 2018.
Klaus J. Müller, Anwälte und Sprache, NJW 2003, S. 638.
Marco v. Münchhausen, So zähmen Sie Ihren inneren Schweinehund, Frankfurt a. M., New York 2002.
Dr. Sebastian Naber, Partner vs. Associate, JurCoach-Blog vom 17.6.2016.
Joseph S. Nye, The Means To Success In World Politics, 2004.
Ulrich Noack/Sascha Kremer, Professionelle Online-Dienste für Juristen, NJW 2006, S. 3313 ff.
Sabine Olschner, Jedem Partner sein eigenes Süppchen, LTO vom 16.4.2021.
Viola Palupski in Mitarbeiterführung und Personalarbeit; ein Leitfaden für Steuerberatungs- und Rechtsanwaltskanzleien, Verlag Erich Schmidt, 2021.
Dr. Andrea Panzer-Heemeier/Tobias Neufeld, The next big Thing im Rechtsmarkt: Nachhaltigkeit, Anwaltspiegel vom 6.1.2021.
Verena Pausder, Das neue Land – Wie es weitergeht, 2. Auflage, Hamburg 2020.
Werner Pepels /Brunhilde Steckler (Hrsg.), Anwalts-Marketing, München 2003.
Dirk Ploss/Stefan Kramer, Der erfolgreiche Ausbau der Anwaltskanzlei, Frankfurt a. M. 2002.
Marion Proft, Corona trifft Fachkräftemangel in Kanzleien, Legal Profession vom 29.7.2020.
Prognos AG, Der Rechtsdienstleistungsmarkt 2030, Eine Zukunftsstudie für die deutsche Anwaltschaft, DAV 2013.
Thomas Riehm / Sina Dörr, "Digitalisierung und Zivilverfahren" De Gruyter Berlin 2023.
Rachelle Römermann, Anwaltliches Marketing-Management, Band 10 der Schriftenreihe "Wege zur erfolgreichen Anwaltspraxis", Hannover 2003.
Jutta Rump, Personalpolitik in der Corona-Krise, Studienbericht vom 9.4.2020.
Thomas Sassenberg, Umgang mit IT in der Anwaltskanzlei, AnwBl 2006, S. 196 ff.
Claudia Schieblon, Kanzleimanagement in der Praxis, 3. Auflage 2015, Verlag Springer-Gabler.
Wolfgang Schiefer/Ulrich Hocke, Marketing für Rechtsanwälte, 3. Auflage, Bonn 1999.
Caspar Tobias Schlenk, Der Smartlaw-Gründer startet das nächste Legal Startup, Gründerszene vom 3.4.2016.
Dr. Wolfgang Schade, Überlegungen zu Szenarien der verkehrlichen und ökonomischen Folgen der Corona-Pandemie in Deutschland, Deutsche und Europäische Szenarien für 2013–2015 (M-Five).
Dr. Anke Nordemann-Schiffel/Dr. Julian Klagge, Brexit and Brands – Was Markeninhaber beachten müssen, Anwaltspiegel vom 6.1.2021.
Dr. Pascal Schneider, Führungskräfte bei Social Media – Karrierekiller oder Booster, ZUJ 06/ 2020, S. 61.
Marktstudie "Moderne Führungsstrukturen in Kanzleien" von Schön u.C.
Maurus Schreyvogel, Rechtsmarkt 2021, ZUJ 01/2021.
Anne M. Schüller, Querdenker verzweifelt gesucht, Gabal 2020.
Ben Schulz, Erfolg braucht Dein Gesicht, 2016. *Ben Schulz*, Artgerechte Bodenhaltung, 2017. *Ben Schulz*, Mit Vollgas in den Crash, 2018.
Ben Schulz, Das große Personal-Branding-Handbuch, Campus 2019.

Bärbel Schwertfeger (Psychologin), Sie können alles erreichen, KarriereSpiegel vom 6.12.2013.
Lothar Seiwert, Das neue 1x1 Zeitmanagement, 24. Auflage, München 2002.
Lothar Seiwert, Wenn Du es eilig hast, gehe langsam, 5. Auflage, Frankfurt a. M., New York 2000.
Lothar Seiwert/Hans Buschbell/Dieter Mandelkow, Zeitmanagement für Rechtsanwälte, Landsberg 1992.
Lothar Seiwert/Horst Müller/Anette Labaek-Noeller, 30 Minuten Zeitmanagement für Chaoten, 4. Auflage, Offenbach 2002.
Alexander Sieben, Kanzleistrategie: Mut zum Big Picture / Warum und wozu eine Kanzleistrategie? Haufe vom 18.7.2019.
Alexander Sieben, 5 Gründe, keine Kanzleistrategie zu haben, Sieben&Partner.
Alexander Sieben, Gestärkt aus der Krise, Haufe, Taxulting vom 16.4.2020.
Simon Simek, Start with why, Penguin 2009.
SLM-Redaktion, Digitalkompetenz im Jurastudium, smartlegalmarket vom 7.5.2019. Soldan Institut, Pressemitteilung, 28.1.2016.
Soldan Institut, Statistisches Jahrbuch der Anwaltschaft 2017/2018.
Sparkassen Branchenbericht Rechtsmarkt 2017.
Arne Storm, Alles was Recht ist, brandeins thema 05/2020.
Hasso Suliak, Anwaltschaft noch immer mitten in der Krise, LTO vom 23.6.2021.
Richard Susskind, The End of Lawyers? Rethinking the Nature of Legal Services, Oxford Univesity Press 2008.
Richard Susskind, Tomorrow's Lawyers: An Introduction to Your Future, Oxford University Press 2013.
Daniel Terwesche, Optimale Online-Identität und Internetpräsenz für Steuerberater- und Rechtsanwaltskanzleien, Verlag Erich Schmidt, 2021.
TQM, Qualitätsmanagement in der Anwaltskanzlei, Deutscher Anwaltverein 1997.
Claudia Tödtmann, Die umsatzstärksten Kanzleien in Deutschland, blog.wiwi.de vom 1.10.2020.
Dr. Geertje Tutschka, Kanzleimarketing post Corona – die neuen "Must Haves", Haufe.Recht 08/2021.
Dr. Geertje Tutschka, Wię Covid-19 das Kanzleimarketing für immer veränderte, Haufe.Recht vom 23.7.2021.
Dr. Geertje Tutschka, Kanzleimanagement und Krisenkommunikation in Zeiten der Corona-Pandemie, Haufe.Recht vom 29.4.2020.
Dr. Geertje Tutschka, Coaching oder nicht, PE Managerseminare 06/2018.
Dr. Geertje Tutschka, Coaching ist das, was der juristischen Fachexpertise fehlt, CoachingMagazin 01/2019.
Dr. Geertje Tutschka, Artikelserie "Coaching in der Rechtsabteilung", Unternehmensjurist 02/2021.
Dr. Geertje Tutschka, Der Blick über den Tellerrand, Unternehmensjurist 05/2018.
Dr. Geertje Tutschka, Agile Leadership in a digital World, Legal Revolutionary vom 31.7.2018.
Dr. Geertje Tutschka, Die Kanzlei des 21. Jahrhunderts, HERO 02/2018.
Dr. Geertje Tutschka, Verändertes Personal Branding – Was Anwälte in und nach der Pandemie zu Experten macht, Haufe.Recht vom 23.7.2021.
Dr. Geertje Tutschka, Clubhouse – der neue heiße Scheiß in der social media Welt? CLP-Blog vom 22.1.2021.
Dr. Geertje Tutschka, Kanzleigründung leicht gemacht, MKG 2018.
Dr. Geertje Tutschka u. a., Die Anwaltskanzlei als erfolgreiches Unternehmen, 2019.
Dr. Geertje Tutschka, Was ist Ihnen Ihr Kanzleimarketing wert? Kanzleimarketing.de vom 26.1.2017.
Dr. Geertje Tutschka, Female Leadership in der Legal Branche, S. 138 in djbZ 03/2017.
Dr. Geertje Tutschka, Jurist oder Juristin – (k)ein Unterschied, LTO vom 16.12.2015.
Dr. Geertje Tutschka, The Future of the legal Profession (Teil 1 und 2), Blog JurCoach vom 24.2.2017.
Dr. Geertje Tutschka, Der Rechtsanwalt als Unternehmer, TeleLex, Nürnberg 2016.

Dr. Geertje Tutschka, The Pink Elephant in the room, Blog JurCoach vom 24.5.2017.
Dr. Geertje Tutschka, Kanzleigründung ist Unternehmensgründung, Haufe vom 17.12.2015.
Dr. Geertje Tutschka, Partner vs. Associate, Kanzleijob.de vom 17.6.2016.
Dr. Geertje Tutschka, Warum Ihr Kanzleibusinessplan jetzt zählt, JurCoach vom 6.11.2015.
Dr. Geertje Tutschka, In drei Schritten zu Ihrem Kanzlei-Marketingplan, Huffington Post vom 18.11.2015.
Dr. Geertje Tutschka, Diversity in deutschen Kanzleien, Edition F vom 30.3.2016.
Dr. Geertje Tutschka, Justitia, wir haben ein Problem, JuraBlogs vom 26.4.2016.
Dr. Geertje Tutschka, Spot Awards – der ideale Baustein für die Personalführung, Blog JurCoach vom 20.6.2016.
Dr. Geertje Tutschka, Männer und Frauen in juristischen Berufen, LTO vom 16.11.2015.
Dr. Geertje Tutschka, Warum Gender Diversity in deutschen Kanzleien so wichtig ist, Soldan Insight vom 25.2.2016.
Dr. Geertje Tutschka, Business Coaching für Anwälte, NJW 24/2015.
Dr. Geertje Tutschka, Wie aus Ihrem Kanzleiteam eine Mannschaft wird, NJW 24/2016.
Dr. Geertje Tutschka, Wie die Fußball EM Ihre Kanzlei verändern kann, Blog JurCoach vom 27.6.2016.
Dr. Geertje Tutschka im Interview, Coaching ist keine Beratung, IHK-Magazin für München und berbayern – Wirtschaft, 01/2018, S. 55.
Dr. Geertje Tutschka, Coaching vs. Beratung – eine Frage der Perspektive, Xing-Coaches Magazin 06/2017.
Dr. Geertje Tutschka im Interview, Es gab ganz entscheidende Entwicklungen, Wirtschaft und Weiterbildung 07/2017, S. 54.
Dr. Geertje Tutschka, Der Anwalt als Konflikt- und Krisenmanager, JurCoach-Blog vom 3.10.2017.
Dr. Geertje Tutschka, Female Leadership im Legal Sector, DjbZ 03/2017, S. 137.
Dr. Geertje Tutschka, Frauenquote für Anwaltskanzleien, Blog JurCoach vom 8.11.2015.
Dr. Geertje Tutschka, Der Rechtsanwalt als Unternehmer, TeleLex, Nürnberg 2016.
Dr. Geertje Tutschka, Verlässliche Arbeitszeiten trotz Großkanzlei, Blog JurCoach vom 9.2.2018.
Dr. Geertje Tutschka, Legal Coaching – ein Hybrid. Oder: Was der Rechtsberatung Beine macht. NJW vom 19.7.2018.
Dr. Geertje Tutschka, Weiterbildung für Juristen, CLP-Blog vom 13.12.2020.
Dr. Geertje Tutschka, Legal Coaching – the new fish in the pond, Legal Business World 03/2019.
Dr. Geertje Tutschka, Herausforderungen im Beratungsmandat – geschulte Kommunikation in juristischen Krisensituationen, Haufe vom 25.9.2019.
Dr. Geertje Tutschka, Vom Jurist zum Legal Coach, TalentRocket vom 15.8.2018.
Dr. Geertje Tutschka, Verhandlungsführung 4:0; Mediation vs. (Legal) Coaching, Soldan vom 29.1.2019.
Dr. Geertje Tutschka, Der Anwalt als eierlegende Wollmilchsau – was Mandanten heute zusätzlich zur juristischen Fachexpertise einfordern, CLP-Blog vom 24.2.2019.
Dr. Geertje Tutschka im Interview, Legal Coaching – Juristische Fachexpertise wirkungsvoll mit speziellen Kommunikationstechniken unterstützen, AnwaltSpiegel vom 3.4.2019.
Dr. Geertje Tutschka (Autorenteam), Kanzleimarketing kompakt, Deutscher AnwaltVerlag 2016.
Dr. Geertje Tutschka (Autorenteam), Qualitätsmanagement im Einzelcoaching, ICF 2018.
Dr. Geertje Tutschka/Anja Dittmeier/Birgit Kuschel, USA-Expat Quick Guide, Norderstedt 2018. Umfrage Future Law 2018.
Guido Wagner, Outsourcing – mit Sicherheit, Datenschutz und Datensicherheit (DuD) 2005, S. 130 ff.
Jens Wagner, Legal Tech und Legal Robots – Der Wandel im Rechtswesen durch neue Technologien und Künstliche Intelligenz, 2. Auflage, Wiesbaden 2020.
Christopher Wagner, Die größten Anwaltskanzleien nach Umsatz, Fachmagazin vom 11.11.2020.
Harald Willenbrock, Hausrecht, brandeins thema 05/2020.
Wolters Kluwer, Checkliste Grundlagen des Mandatsmanagements, 2020.

Zukunftsinstitut, White Paper 2021: der Corona-Effekt – vier Zukunftszenarien.
Zukunftsideen für 2040, Laborpraxis Vogel.
Oxana Zeitler, Lead the Future, Shape your Brand, Haufe 2019.

Index

https://doi.org/10.1515/9783111058160-010